The Social Engage
of Social Science

CW00539569

A series in three volumes

Volume I: *The Socio-Psychological Perspective*
Volume II: *The Socio-Technical Perspective*
Volume III: *The Socio-Ecological Perspective*

The Social Engagement of Social Science

A Tavistock Anthology

Edited by Eric Trist and Hugh Murray

Assistant Editor: Beulah Trist

Volume I:
The Socio-Psychological Perspective

'an association in which the free development of each
is the condition of the free development of all'

Free Association Books / London / 1990

First Published in Great Britain in 1990 by
Free Association Books
26 Freegrove Road
London N7 9RQ

Permission is acknowledged to reprint portions and excerpts from published
materials:

H. Bridger, "The Northfield Experiment," *Bulletin of the Menninger Clinic* 10, 3
(1946): 71–76; and W. R. Bion, "The Leaderless Group Project," *Bulletin of the
Menninger Clinic* 10, 3 (1946) 77–81. Copyright 1946 by the Menninger Foundation.

J. D. Sutherland, from *Bion and Group Psychotherapy*, ed. Malcolm Pines. London,
Routledge and Kegan Paul, 1985. Reprinted by permission of Routledge and Kegan
Paul.

Elizabeth Bott (Spillius), "Hospital and Society," *British Journal of Medical
Psychology* 49 (1976): 97–140.

Articles appearing in various issues of *Human Relations*. Volume, issue, and pages
are indicated at the opening of each portion.

Articles and books published by Tavistock Publications. Specific references are
indicated at the opening of each portion.

British Library Cataloguing in Publication Data
The Social engagement of social science : a Tavistock
 anthology.
 Vol. I The socio-psychological perspective.
 1. Social psychology
 I. Trist, Eric II. Murray, Hugh
 302

 ISBN 1–85343–165–6

Printed in Great Britain by
Billing and Sons Ltd, Worcester

These volumes are dedicated to

DR. A.T. MACBETH WILSON

Founder Member and Chairman (1948–1958)
Tavistock Institute of Human Relations

Contents

Preface

The Tavistock Institute of Human Relations, a novel, interdisciplinary, action-oriented research organization, was founded in London in 1946 with the aid of a grant from the Rockefeller Foundation. It was set up for the specific purpose of actively relating the psychological and social sciences to the needs and concerns of society. In sustaining this endeavor for more than forty years, it has won international recognition.

The circumstances of World War II brought together an unusually talented group of psychiatrists, clinical and social psychologists and anthropologists in the setting of the British Army, where they developed a number of radical innovations in social psychiatry and applied social science. They became known as the "Tavistock Group" because the core members had been at the pre-war Tavistock Clinic. Though only some of them continued their involvement with the post-war Tavistock organization, those who did built on the war-time achievements to introduce a number of far-reaching developments in several fields. This style of research related theory and practice in a new mode. In these volumes this style is called "The Social Engagement of Social Science."

The word "engagement" (which echoes French Existentialist usage) has been chosen as the best single word to represent the process by which social scientists endeavor actively to relate themselves in relevant and meaningful ways to society. This overall orientation is reflected in what the editors have called "perspectives," of which there are three: the socio-psychological, the socio-technical and the socio-ecological. These perspectives are explained in the Series Introduction on the Foundation and Development of the Institute. They have evolved from each other in relation to societal change. They are interdependent, yet each has its own focus and is represented in a separate volume.

The Institute's theories and projects have resulted in a considerable number of books, many of which are regarded as classics. A large collection of articles of continuing interest are dispersed through various journals. There is a further collection of little known manuscripts containing some outstanding contributions. These have been available only in document series maintained by the Institute and two or three closely related centers. This body of work by many hands has never been gathered together. The present volumes offer a comprehensive selection of these writings—a Tavistock anthology.

There are now very few people left who were at the Institute at the beginning of this saga. As a founder member and sometime Chairman I felt I should undertake the required compilation. Having been in the United States for more than twenty years, however, I needed a co-editor still on the scene in London. Accordingly, I invited one of my oldest colleagues, Dr. Hugh Murray, to join me.

All the contributions contain innovations in social psychiatry and the social sciences, either in concept or in the nature of the projects undertaken; these have led in many cases to widespread developments in their fields and in some cases to the foundation of entirely new fields. They look backward to show the origin, in the period following World War II, of much in current theory and practice whose historic depth is not widely known or appreciated. They look forward to show the continuing relevance of the material presented to tasks that lie ahead in many areas of the social sciences and, more widely, to the post-industrial social order that is beginning to emerge from the "turbulence" of the present.

In order to allow the inclusion of as many contributions as possible, the Volume and Theme introductions have been kept short. The papers—many of them recent—are primarily by members of the founding generation and their successors over the following two decades, whether they are still at the Institute or have moved elsewhere, as most of them have. Some of the papers are by authors from related centers that developed later. This wide dispersal of people has enabled the original tradition to be enriched by developments in different settings in institutes and university departments in Commonwealth and European countries and in the United States. In this way, new insights have been added to those of the founding body. From its beginnings as simply an organization in London, the Tavistock has become an international network.

More than half the contributions have been remodeled or specially written for these volumes. Many have one or more co-authors, as befits an enterprise characterized by a group orientation. Co-authors have not necessarily been members of the Institute.

The three volumes comprising The Social Engagement of Social Science are dedicated to Dr. A.T. Macbeth Wilson, affectionately known to us all as "Tommy." He was the one senior psychiatrist involved at the beginning who chose to stay with the separately incorporated Institute when the Clinic entered the National Health Service in 1948. He was endowed with what C.Wright Mills called "the sociological imagination." His seminal contributions date from the pre-war period and continued uninterrupted thereafter. Throughout his years as Chairman (1948–58) he carried the main burden when the Institute was struggling to find an independent identity.

Gainesville
Florida
February 1989   *Eric Trist*

Eric Trist and Hugh Murray

Historical Overview
The Foundation and Development of the Tavistock Institute

The Formative Years

The Founding Tradition

Pre-War Antecedents

After the fall of France in 1941, the Royal Air Force, by winning the Battle of Britain, prevented German invasion of the British Isles. The evacuation from the Dunkirk beaches prevented the capture of the core of the regular army, including many of the generals who were later to distinguish themselves. There was, therefore, a chance to fight again but there was no land army of any size to do so. It was thus imperative that Britain build a large land army in a hurry. Attempts to meet this need created immense problems in the utilization of human resources (problems far more severe for the army than for the other services), but no measures tried in the first few months seemed to be effective.

In 1941 a group of psychiatrists at the Tavistock Clinic saw that the right questions were asked in Parliament in order to secure the means to try new measures. As a result they were asked to join the Directorate of Army Psychiatry, and did so as a group.

To understand how such a small group was able to be so influential, we must go back to the period immediately after World War I when there was a growing recognition that neurotic disabilities were not merely transitory phenomena related to the stress of war, but were endemic and pervasive in a modern society. In order to respond to the "felt social need" thus arising, the Tavistock Institute of Medical Psychology (better known as the Tavistock Clinic), the parent body of the post-World War II Institute, was founded in 1920 as a voluntary outpatient clinic to explore the implications for treatment and research.

The founding group comprised many of the key doctors who had been concerned with neurosis in World War I. They included general physicians and neurologists, as well as psychiatrists, and one or two multiply-trained individuals who combined psychology and anthropology with medicine. The group, therefore, showed from the beginning the preparedness to be linked to the social sciences and to general medicine, as well as to psychiatry, which has characterized it ever since.

Interest focussed on the then new "dynamic psychologies" as representing the direction which offered most hope. Because of the uncertain and confused state of knowledge in these fields, tolerance of different viewpoints was part of the undertaking and the Tavistock Clinic functioned as a mediating institution, a clearing-house where the views of several contending parties could be aired. On the one hand were the adherents of Freud, Jung and Adler, who were preoccupied with establishing their own professional societies and advancing their own theories. On the other were a neurologically-oriented general psychiatry, a somatically-oriented general medicine and a surrounding society puzzled, bewildered, intrigued and frightened by the new knowledge of the unconscious and its implications for important areas of life.

Since "authoritarian" government of the medical kind in a pathfinding organization such as the Tavistock Clinic proved dysfunctional, a transition to a collegiate professional democracy took place in the early 1930s, when problems arising from the Depression shook many cherished beliefs and raised new questions concerning the role of social factors in psychological illness. This organizational revolution brought to the front a younger generation of clinicians with a level of ability and a maverick quality that would otherwise have been lost.*

This younger group now began to take on a conceptual direction consonant with the emergent "object relations approach" in psychoanalysis. The object relations approach emphasized relationships rather than instinctual drives and psychic energy.

As Dicks's (1970) history (*Fifty Years of the Tavistock Clinic*) shows, there were great variations in the quality of the services offered by the pre-war Clinic. Among the 80 physicians who contributed six hours a week, many had little or no psychiatric training. Nevertheless, by the beginning of World War II the Tavistock had attained international standing. It had developed links with organizations in the main Commonwealth countries and the United States, and had undertaken systematic research and teaching. It had obtained pe-

*The staff now elected as their Director Jack Rawlings Rees, grouped around whom were Henry Dicks, Ronald Hargreaves, Tommy Wilson and Wilfred Bion, all of whom subsequently made world-wide reputations. They would have left the Tavistock had it not been for the opportunities opened up by the organizational revolution.

ripheral academic standing in London University with six recognized teachers. The outbreak of war, however, prevented this arrangement from being implemented.

WAR-TIME BREAKTHROUGHS

The group who entered the Directorate of Army Psychiatry took a novel approach to the human resource problems facing the army. Rather than remain in base hospitals they went out into the field to find out from commanding officers what they saw as their most pressing problems. They would listen to their troubled military clients as an analyst would to a patient, believing that the "real" problems would surface as trust became established, and that constructive ideas about dealing with them would emerge. The concept thence arose of "command" psychiatry, in which a psychiatrist with a roving commission was attached to each of the five Army Commanders in Home Forces.

A relationship of critical importance was formed between the Clinic's Ronald Hargreaves, as command psychiatrist, and Sir Ronald Adam, the Army Commander in Northern Command. When Adam became Adjutant General, the second highest post in the army, he was able to implement policies that Hargreaves and he had adumbrated. New military institutions had to be created to carry them out. The institution-building process entailed:

- Earning the right to be consulted on emergent problems for which there was no solution in traditional military procedures, e.g., the problem of officer selection.
- Making preliminary studies to identify a path of solution—the investigation of morale in Officer Cadet Training Units.
- Designing a pilot model in collaboration with military personnel which embodied the required remedial measures—the Experimental War Office Selection Board.
- Handing over the developed model to military control with the psychiatric and psychological staff falling back into advisory roles or where possible removing themselves entirely—the War Office Selection Boards (WOSBs) and Civil Resettlement Units (CRUs) for repatriated prisoners of war.
- Disseminating the developed model, securing broad acceptance for it and training large numbers of soldiers to occupy the required roles, e.g., CRUs.

To meet these large-scale tasks the range of disciplines was extended from psychiatry and clinical psychology to social psychology, sociology and anthropology. The members of these various disciplines were held together by participation in common operational tasks in an action frame of reference. To varying extents they began to learn each others' skills. The group became, to use a term that arose after the war in a project concerned with alternative forms of organization in the mining industry, a "composite" work group. (Vol. I, "The Assumption of Ordinariness as a Denial Mechanism")

Undertaking practical tasks that sought to resolve operational crises generated insights that led towards new theory. This process was familiar to those members of the group who were practicing psychiatrists, but it was new to those coming from other disciplines. This led to a generalized concept of professionalism.

The innovations introduced during the war years consisted of a series of "inventions":

- Command psychiatry as a reconnaissance activity leading to the identification of critical problems.
- Social psychiatry as a policy science permitting preventive intervention in large scale problems.
- The co-creation with the military of new institutions to implement these policies.
- The therapeutic community as a new mode of treatment.
- Cultural psychiatry for the analysis of the enemy mentality.

By the end of the war a considerable number of psychiatrists and social scientists had become involved in this comprehensive set of innovative applications of concepts of social psychiatry. They saw in these approaches a significance which did not seem to be limited by the condition of war, and were determined to explore their relevance for the civilian society. Obviously, individual programs could not be transferred without considerable modification; entirely new lines of development would have to be worked out. Nevertheless, a new action-oriented philosophy of relating psychiatry and the social sciences to society had become a reality in practice. This event signified the social engagement of social science.

Post-War Transformation

OPERATION PHOENIX

New questions now arose. Who would be the next pioneers? Who would accept the risks, which were great? Could a setting be found that could nurture the new endeavors? An answer to these questions came about in the following way.

Toward the end of the war the existence of a democratic tradition in the Tavistock Clinic made possible the election by the whole staff (through a postal ballot) of an Interim Planning Committee (IPC) to consider the future of the organization. The election gave power to those who had led the work in the Army.* The IPC began meeting in the autumn of 1945 to work out a re-definition of the Clinic's mission in light of the experiences gained during the war. The IPC was chaired by Wilfred Bion, who used his new findings about groups to clarify issues and reduce conflicts within the planning group itself. Council approved its report by the end of that year.

The IPC made a crucial decision in recognition of an impending political event—the then new Labour Government's intimation that it would in 1948 create a National Health Service. The IPC resolved:

- To build up the Clinic to enter the National Health Service fully equipped with the kind of staff who could be entrusted with the task of discovering the role of out-patient psychiatry, based on a dynamic approach and oriented towards the social sciences, in the as yet unknown setting of a national health service.
- Separately to incorporate the Institute of Human Relations for the study of wider social problems not accepted as in the area of mental health.

This readiness enabled the IPC in 1945 to attract the attention of Alan Gregg, Medical Director of the Rockefeller Foundation, who was touring the various institutions that had been involved in war medicine. He was interested in finding out if there was a group committed to undertaking, under conditions of peace, the kind of social psychiatry that had developed in the army under conditions of war. So began a process that led the Rockefeller Foundation in 1946 to make a grant of untied funds without which the IPC's post-war plan could not have been carried out.

The Rockefeller grant led to the birth of the Tavistock Institute of Human Relations, constituted at first as a division of the Tavistock Clinic. With these funds it became possible to obtain for the then joint organization a nucleus of full-time senior staff who would otherwise have been scattered in universities and hospitals throughout the country and abroad.

---

*The six elected members were J.R. Rees, who was later to found the World Federation of Mental Health; Leonard Browne, who became a prominent Alderman in the London County Council; Henry Dicks, who founded the field of cultural psychiatry; Ronald Hargreaves, who became Deputy Director of the World Health Organization; Mary Luff, who retired after the war; and Tommy Wilson, who became Chairman of the Tavistock Institute. The IPC met twice a week for two or three hours in the evenings. There were rarely any absentees. The group co-opted two people not previously at the Clinic—Jock Sutherland, a psychiatrist, who was to become Director of the post-war Clinic, and Eric Trist, a social psychologist, who was later to succeed Wilson as the Institute's Chairman. Both had played prominent parts in the war-time developments.

A Professional Committee (PC), with Rees in the chair, and a small Technical Executive representing the new permanent staff, chaired by Bion, came into existence in February 1946. These arrangements lasted until the separate incorporation of the Institute in September 1947. The situation required the transformation of a large part-time staff, appropriate for the pre-war Clinic as a voluntary out-patient hospital, into a small nucleus of full-timers, supported by others giving substantial proportions of their time, and committed to the redefined mission of the post-war organization. Decisions were taken as to who should stay, who should leave and who should be added. Criteria included willingness to participate in the redefined social mission and to undergo psychoanalysis if they had not already done so. This critical episode became known as Operation Phoenix.*

As regards the requirement for psychoanalysis, it was felt that object relations theory had proved its relevance during the war in the social as well as the clinical field. It represented the most advanced body of psychological knowledge then available which could provide a common foundation for those who would in various ways be continuing, in the peace, the work begun under war conditions.

Training would be in the hands of the British Psycho-Analytical Society, and social applications in the hands of the Institute. This understanding equilibrated relations between the two bodies. The Society agreed to provide training analysts for acceptable candidates, whether they were going to become full-time analysts, mix psychoanalytic practice with broader endeavors in the health field or use psychoanalytic understanding outside the health area in organizational and social projects. The Society, therefore, recognized the relevance for psychoanalysis of work in the social field, while the Institute affirmed the importance of psychoanalysis for psycho-social studies. In this way some 15 individuals, some in the Clinic and some in the Institute, most of them in mid-life, undertook personal psychoanalysis as part of the enterprise of building the new Tavistock. It was a major "experiment," the outcome of which could not be known for a number of years.

The PC now faced painful tasks. When the decisions stemming from Operation Phoenix began to be implemented, a great deal of guilt developed over the termination of most of the pre-war staff who in one way or another did not meet the criteria for inclusion in the post-war body. An abdication crisis ensued. The PC agreed to stay in power only after a searching self-examination

*In addition to Sutherland and Trist, a number of other outsiders who had played prominent roles in the war-time effort, were brought in at this point. John Bowlby, a child psychiatrist and analyst, was made head of what he came to call the Department for Children and Parents. (The other senior psychiatrists appointed to the Clinic were all from the wider Tavistock group.) Elliott Jaques, a young Canadian psychiatrist and psychologist, was invited to join the Institute and played a prominent role during the five years he stayed.

that enabled them to separate task-oriented factors from the tangle of personal feelings. Tension and confusion developed throughout the entire organization. Bion resigned as Chairman of the Technical Executive and restricted himself to the role of social therapist to an overall staff group that held weekly meetings to work through these matters. Without them the post-war organization could scarcely have survived its conflicts. Our first experiment with group methods was on ourselves.

THE JOINT ORGANIZATION

In preparing to enter the National Health Service (NHS) the Clinic had to develop therapeutic methods that would allow the maintenance of a patient load sufficiently large to satisfy the new authorities that out-patient psycho-therapy could be cost effective. War-time experience suggested that the best prospect would lie in group treatment. Accordingly, the PC asked Bion, considering his special achievements in this field, to pioneer this endeavor. His response was to put up a notice which became celebrated—"You can have group treatment now or wait a year for individual treatment." The groups he started, however, were not only patient groups but groups with industrial managers and with people from the educational world. He was developing a general method reflected in a series of papers in Human Relations (Bion, 1948–51), which put forward entirely new theory. By the time the Clinic entered the NHS most of the psychiatrists were taking groups, though none used precisely Bion's methods.

Meanwhile, in the Department for Children and Parents, Bowlby laid the foundations of family therapy (Vol. I, "The Reduction of Group Tensions in the Family"). Also at this time he began his world famous studies of mother/child separation.

Another major and still continuing enterprise that began during this early period emerged from a crisis in the Family Welfare Association (FWA), which co-ordinated family case work in the London area. The coming of the welfare state rendered unnecessary its task of dispensing material aid to the poor. Its offices were now besieged by clients with social and emotional problems with which its staff were unable to deal. Through Wilson (1949) the Institute was consulted. An attempt to train FWA staff proved unsuccessful. The Institute therefore set up within its own boundary what was called the Family Discussion Bureau (FDB), which later became the Institute for Marital Studies (IMS). This created the first non-medical channel in Britain for professional work with families. In time it was supported by the government through the Home Office.

Michael Balint, one of the senior analysts at the Clinic, introduced a group method of training family welfare workers in which stress was laid on making them aware of their counter-transferences: their projections of their own problems onto their clients. Balint later developed these methods for training large numbers of health professionals, including general physicians (Balint, 1954). This allowed the Clinic to have a multiplier effect which, along with group treatment and the inauguration of family therapy, showed that what had been learnt in the Army about using scarce resources to meet the needs of large scale systems could be applied in the civilian society in entirely new ways.

Hostility to the Institute's work, however, developed in the academic world. The Medical Research Council dismissed the first draft of the WOSB write-up as being of only historical, not scientific, interest. No further funds were granted.

Several strategic moves were nevertheless made to establish the Tavistock's academic claims. There was very little chance at that time of getting much of its work accepted by existing journals. A new journal was needed that would manifest the connection between field theory and object-relations psychoanalysis. With Lewin's group in the U.S., the Research Center for Group Dynamics, now at the University of Michigan, the Institute created a new international journal, *Human Relations,* whose purpose was to further the integration of psychology and the social sciences and relate theory to practice.

In 1947 a publishing company—Tavistock Publications—was founded, which in the longer run succeeded in finding a home in a major publishing house (the Sweet and Maxwell Group) while retaining its own imprint. A joint library was also established with the Clinic that provided the best collection of books and journals then available in London in the psycho- and socio-dynamic fields. This was needed for teaching as well as research purposes. John Rickman, a senior analyst closely associated with the Tavistock, said that there should be no therapy without research and no research without therapy and that the Institute should offer training in all the main areas of its work.

By the time the Institute was separately incorporated there was a staff of eight with Wilson as chairman. Six of the eight had taken part in one or other of the war-time projects. The disciplines included psychology, anthropology, economics, education and mathematics.

Achieving a Working Identity

INDUSTRIAL ACTION RESEARCH

By 1948 the British economy was in serious trouble. The pound had been devalued, productivity was low and there was a scarcity of capital for investment in new technology. The government formed an Industrial Productivity Committee which had a Human Factors Panel. This made grants for research aiming to secure improved productivity through better use of human resources.

The grants were for three years and were administered by the Medical Research Council. The Institute proposed three projects, all of which were accepted. The first focussed on internal relations within a single firm (from the board to the shop floor) with the aim of identifying means of improving cooperation between management and labor and also between levels of management; the second focussed on organizational innovations that could raise productivity; the third pioneered a new form of post-graduate education for field workers in applied social research.

A site for the first project was obtained in the London factories of a light engineering concern (the Glacier Metal Company) whose managing director had a special interest in the social sciences. The project, headed by Elliott Jaques, led to far-reaching changes in the organization and culture of the firm. A novel role was elaborated that enabled process consultation to take place across areas of conflict. Some radically new concepts were formulated such as the use of social structure as a defense against anxiety (Vol. I, "On the Dynamics of Social Structure"). Jaques's (1951) book, *The Changing Culture of a Factory,* was the first major publication of the Institute after it became independent. While it was an immense success in the literature, being reprinted many times, no requests were received to continue this kind of work. As Jaques said at the time, the answer from the field was silence.

A component of the second project, under Eric Trist, led to the discovery of self-regulating work groups in a coal mine—the first intimation that a new paradigm of work might be emerging along the lines indicated by the Institute's work with groups. It opened up the study of "socio-technical systems" which has become world-wide.

The training program for the six industrial fellows was for two years and experience based. All participated in a common project (the Glacier Project) while each took part in another Institute project. To gain direct experience of unconscious factors in group life each was placed in a therapy group. To gain experience of managing their own group life they met regularly with a staff member in attendance. Each had a personal tutor. After the first year they returned to their industries to see what new perceptions they had gained and reported on them to a meeting of Institute staff. They also attended regular staff seminars at which all projects were discussed. This was the first opportunity which the Institute had to apply its methods in training. It was, however, too experience based to receive favor at that time.

CONSULTANCY DEVELOPMENTS

With the ending of the government's Human Factors Panel, no further research funds were available from British sources. Though Rockefeller help continued, the Institute had to develop its work in the consultancy field and prove that it could pay its way by directly meeting client needs while at the same time furthering social science objectives.

Further work in the socio-technical field was arrested in the coal industry, but unexpected circumstances yielded an opportunity in India to work collaboratively with the Calico Mills, a subsidiary of Sarabhai Industries, in Ahmedabad. In view of his experience of the tropics, the MC selected A.K. Rice to go to India as the project officer. He proposed that a group of workers should take charge of a group of looms. The idea was taken up spontaneously by the workers in the automatic loom shed who secured management permission to try out a scheme of their own creation. This led to developments that continued for 25 years showing that the socio-technical concept was applicable in the culture of a very different kind of society.

Unilever had established a working relationship with the Institute immediately after the war. It was now expanding. It needed to recruit and train a large number of high caliber managers. The Chairman, Lord Heyworth, had been interested in the WOSBs and approached the Institute for assistance. The result was the joint development of the Unilever Companies' Management Development Scheme based on a modification of WOSB methods. This led to a still continuing collaborative relationship, with many ramifications, of which Harold Bridger has been the architect.

With the profusion of new products in the 1950s, advertising agencies and the marketing departments of firms were under pressure to develop new methods for increasing sales. Motivation research had made its appearance but was narrowly conceived. One or two trial projects gave rise to a new concept which brought together Lewinian and psychoanalytic thinking—the pleasure foods region. This consisted of products of little or no nutritional value that were consumed, often in excess, because of their power to afford oral satisfactions which reduced anxiety and relieved stress.

Early studies by Menzies and Trist (1989) concerned ice cream and confectionery. Later studies by Emery (Emery et al., 1968) and Ackoff and Emery (1972) concerned smoking and drinking. The smoking study identified the affect of distress, as formulated by Silvan Tomkins (1962), as a continuing negative state (as distinct from acute anxiety and depression) which required repeated relief such as smoking affords. The drinking study produced a new social theory of drinking behavior that distinguished between social, "reparative" and indulgent drinking, only the last leading to alcoholism.

As regards the consultancy style that developed, the method was adopted of having two Institute staff attend the early meetings. This was both to obtain binocular vision and to show that the relationship was with an organization and not simply with an individual. With only one person, the dangers of transference and counter-transference would have been greater. A project officer was appointed. After the opening stage the second staff member remained largely outside the project so that a more objective appreciation could be made. Other staff were added as required by project assignments.

The funding crisis had proved a blessing in disguise. The Institute had now proved to itself that it could earn a substantial part of its living from private industry. Though it still needed support from foundations and government funding agencies, it was no longer completely dependent on them. It needed these funds to add a research dimension to projects that clients could not be expected to pay for and to cover the costs of writing up the results.

Towards an Optimum Balance

In 1954 the Institute succeeded once more in obtaining research funds. A four-year grant enabled the socio-technical studies in the coal industry to be resumed through the government's Department of Scientific and Industrial Research (DSIR) which administered counterpart US/UK funds that were part of the Marshall Plan. The Nuffield Foundation supported the research component of the family studies program, while the Home Office supported the operational part.

The most difficult funds to obtain were untied funds such as had been provided by the Rockefeller Foundation. As no further grants of this kind were available, a development charge was added to all consultancy projects so that a special reserve could be built up to tide staff over between projects and to enable them to be taken out of the field to write up work that had already been done. It was felt that 15 percent of the Institute's income should be from untied funds. A much larger proportion—35 percent—should be sought from foundations or government for specific long-range projects of a primarily research character, though the research would largely be action research. Experience in the consultancy field had now shown that long-range projects with serious social science outcome could be obtained of a kind too unconventional to be supported by foundations or governments. These could account for another 30 percent of income. Experience had also shown the value of short-range projects which could lead into new areas. The remaining 20 percent of income could best be generated by projects of this kind.

Another dimension concerned the sectors of society in which the projects would take place. The aim was to have work going on in more than one sector, though the larger proportion would be in industry. By 1961 there were nine industrial projects and six in other sectors.

Separately categorized were projects related to the Clinic which was regarded solely as a treatment institution by the NHS. As originally intended, however, it was developing large research and training programs. These were financed by foundation grants, especially from the U.S., and were administered by the Institute through what was called the Research and Training Committee (RTC). Some of the Institute's own activities came into this area. The RTC succeeded in resolving conflicts as to which projects should be put forward for funding.

Among such Institute activities was a program to develop new projective tests and to train people in their use. This led during the 1970s to the creation of the British Society for Projective Psychology through which a large number of clinical psychologists have been trained. New Tavistock tests which were widely adopted included Phillipson's Object Relations Technique. His book with R.D. Laing (Laing et al., 1966), *Interpersonal Perception,* opened up fresh ground. A leading part in these developments was played by Theodora Alcock (1963), recognized world-wide as a Rorschach expert, who was kept on by the Institute when she reached the retiring age in the NHS. This path of development represents a pioneer effort that would not otherwise have taken place.

Of crucial importance was the duration of projects. Action research projects concerned with change tend to be long-range as they unfold in unpredictable ways. Projects lasting more than three years were regarded as being in the long-range category, those between 18 months and three years were considered medium-range, and those lasting six to 18 months short-range. A balance was needed between these types of duration. In addition, it was found advantageous to keep going a few very brief exploratory assignments as these sometimes opened up new areas and led to innovative developments which could not be foreseen.

In the industrial sector, socio-technical studies continued in the coal industry and then in industries with advanced technologies, both funded through DSIR. There was also a program of research on labor turnover, absence and sickness (Hill and Trist, 1955: Vol. I, "Temporary Withdrawal from Work"). Under conditions of full employment there was widespread concern about these phenomena. New theory and a new practical approach emerged.

Towards the end of the 1950s problems of quite a new kind began to be brought to the Institute. They arose from changes taking place in the wider contextual environment and led to what has been called the socio-ecological perspective. These problems and the theories and methods to deal with them are encompassed in Volume III. The opportunities to build up this perspective came initially from exploratory projects with Bristol Siddeley Engines, the National Farmers' Union and a Unilever subsidiary in the food industry, all of which were facing major changes in their contextual environments. (These changes were not understood.)

As regards other social sectors, the work in family studies produced a major book by Elizabeth Bott (1957) entitled *Family and Social Networks* (Vol. I, "Conjugal Roles and Social Networks"). This put the concept of network, as distinct from that of group, firmly on the social science map and generated a whole new literature. The Prison Commissioners asked the Tavistock to test the value of a scheme for greatly increasing time spent in "association," which had been successfully tried out in the Norwich local prison. A systematic action research study was carried out of its adaptation in Bristol. The prison officers' union, the inmates, and the staff immediately reporting to the Governor were all involved. This study, which broke new theoretical ground, was carried out by Emery (Vol. I, "Freedom and Justice Within Walls"). Also during this time Dicks completed studies of the Russian national character at the Harvard Center for Russian Studies (Vol. I, "Notes on the Russian National Character"). They were a sequel to his work on the German national character during World War II to which he returned in *Licensed Mass Murder* (Dicks, 1972). These studies established a firm empirical base on which cultural psychology using psychoanalytic findings could develop.

Another development during this period was the creation, in collaboration with the University of Leicester, of a U.K. equivalent to the form of sensitivity training pioneered by the National Training Laboratories for Group Development in the United States. This is still continuing. An overall review of it is given by Miller in Vol. I, "Experiential Learning in Groups (I/II)." Two other models were developed (Bridger, Vol. I, "Courses and Working Conferences . . ."; Higgin and Hjelholt, Vol. I, "The Psycho-Dynamics of an Inter-Group Experience"), the idea being to experiment with alternative forms. These are also still evolving.

A basic pattern could now be discerned in the projects of the Institute:

- They were all responses to macro- or meta-problems emerging in the society with which the Institute, in Sommerhoff's (1950) terms, became directively correlated.
- Access to organizations struggling with meta-problems was initially obtained through networks of individuals who had come to know about the Institute's work during World War II. As time went on the initiating individuals became people with whom the Institute had made contact in the post-war period.
- There was not yet a wide appreciation of these emergent meta-problems so that the connections through which the Institute could become directively correlated with them were scarce and fragile. To discover the role of networks in this situation was new learning.
- The projects were carried out by interdisciplinary teams with the project officer having a second staff member as his consultant. Later on these

teams became joint with internal groups in the client organization. Project reviews took place not so much in Institute seminars as in joint meetings with these internal groups.

- Though seminal projects might begin from short-term relations, those with the most significance as regards the advance of basic social scientific knowledge depended on very long relationships being maintained with client organizations or other sponsoring agencies. Change processes take time. They unfold in interactions between the system and its environment in complex ways which are not predictable. One is able to understand the course of a social process only so far as it has manifested itself and then only so far as one is able to stay with it.

- Clients actively collaborated with the Institute. The projects were joint enterprises of action research and social learning. No results were published without the agreement of all parties.

- Great stress was laid on "working through" difficulties and conflicts by analogy with the psychoanalytic method. Not that interpretations of a psychoanalytic kind were directly made. Jaques called the process "social analysis." No standardized procedures, however, were established. Suitable interpretative languages had to evolve in different projects and some of the methods introduced were manufactured more by the clients than by the Institute.

- The aim was to build social science capabilities into organizations that they could then develop by and for themselves.

- Some of the innovations were ahead of their time, often by a number of years. There was little recognition of their significance and no short-term diffusion of the practices involved.

- New theory was as apt to be generated by research paid for by client organizations as by work paid for by research-funding agencies. One of the functions of the latter was to fund work in which organizations would be willing to collaborate operationally, but for the scientific analysis of which they were not yet willing to pay. There were, of course, other projects which could only be initiated if research funds were available.

- The aim was eventually to secure publication at a fully scientific level, but this had sometimes to be delayed for several years and sometimes never emerged at all. Those concerned were often understandably unwilling for work to be made public that described internal processes of a sensitive kind or led to changes the outcome of which could not be assessed for a long time.

This pattern established the Institute's working identity. It expresses what is meant by the social engagement of social science. It treated all projects as opportunities for organizational and personal learning, both for the client and for itself. Though this basic pattern has since undergone much elaboration and improvement, its fundamental character has remained the same.

The Sequel

Division into Two Groups

Before describing how this division came about, it will be convenient to outline the Institute's structure and mode of functioning. It is an independent, not-for-profit organization based on an Association of five hundred members—well-wishers in key positions in the medical and academic worlds and also in industry and other social sectors. To obtain such a support base became possible only after prolonged effort. At this time, at its annual meeting, the Association elected a small working Council that met with the Management Committee (MC) every quarter. Members of the MC were nominated by the staff and approved by the Council so that it could operate with a double sanction. The MC proposed its own chairman but the Council had to confirm the appointment. The MC met weekly to guide all aspects of the Institute's affairs as a group.

The permanent staff were of four grades—consultants, principal project officers, project officers and assistant project officers. When the Institute was separately incorporated in 1947 there were eight staff members, in 1961 there were 22. A pension scheme had been negotiated by the Secretary after persisting difficulties. This gave a much needed addition to security which, during the formative years, had been exceedingly low. There were a number of people on temporary assignment and many overseas visitors, especially from the United States, who usually stayed a year. Administration was in the hands of a professional secretary, Sidney Gray, who had voting rights as a member of the MC.

The MC met with the consultants quarterly and once every year with the whole staff for a period of two days. There were fortnightly seminars to discuss project and theoretical matters. The Council insisted that members of MC be of professorial status. Salary scales had to be approved by the whole staff and were in line with those of the universities, the Scientific Civil Service and the National Health Service. This system had functioned well; relations in working groups had been good. A strong collegiate culture had persisted from the war and was strengthened by the Institute having to contend with a largely hostile environment.

In 1958 Wilson had left to take up the position of strategic adviser to Unilever world-wide. This was the first time a social scientist (other than an economist) had been asked to fill a strategic position at this level in industry. For ten years a balanced relationship had existed between Wilson and Trist, as chairman and deputy chairman. Wilson was a man of daring seminal insights. He had immense prestige in both the medical and non-medical worlds and an exceedingly wide range of contacts. He was adept at negotiations with govern- ment and foundations, and opened up diverse channels which led to new projects. Trist had complementary capacities in formulating concepts, project design and research methodology and in acting as mentor to the growing body of younger staff who required rapid development. This partnership, however, was no longer an organizational necessity; there was now a well-developed staff, several of whom were active in finding and maintaining projects and in coming forward with new ideas and methods.

The Institute had become over-busy with its growing project portfolio. The quarterly meetings with the consultants and the annual retreats were not kept up. The place that had so strongly affirmed the need to pay attention to the process side of organizational life had been neglecting its own. With the departure of Wilson, the MC should have asked for a radical reappraisal of the whole situation; but the requisite meetings with the consultants and with the staff as a whole were never called. It was assumed that the status quo would continue and that Trist would become chairman with indefinite tenure. It was as though a quasi-dynastic myth had inadvertently crept in to a supposedly democratic process.

The staff was now beyond the limits of the small face-to-face group it had been in 1948. There was a far greater range of interests, capabilities and projects and the problem of managing the Institute as a single unit grew correspondingly greater.

Conflicts, latent for some time, came to a head while Trist was in California on sabbatical. Rice, as Acting Chairman, proposed that the Institute should divide into three self-accounting project groups. This division was resisted by many of the senior staff who wished to preserve the unity of the whole. The differences were partly personal, partly professional, but there was also dis- agreement over the direction in which the Institute should best develop in the increasingly turbulent environment and how it should be shaped to meet the new challenges. On Trist's return an attempt was made to resolve the differ- ences but in the end two groups were formed, the larger around Trist (the Human Resources Centre) and the smaller (the Centre for Applied Social Research) around Rice.

Though not ideal, the partition provided a "good enough" solution, to use Winnicott's (1965) term. Each group proceeded to work productively on its own lines.

The Matrix

The expansion of the Clinic and Institute during the 1950s led to the need for more space. The Ministry of Health offered to build new premises in the Swiss Cottage district of Hampstead on the other side of Regent's Park from the existing set of buildings and the question arose as to whether the Ministry would agree to the inclusion of activities of the Institute that were not health related. The Minister at first said, "No." Sir Hugh Beaver, the then Chairman of the Council, had become convinced of the need to keep the Clinic and Institute together and persuaded the Ministry to allow all activities to be included so that the overall unity could be preserved.

The 1960s were now beginning. Many changes and developments had taken place. How far was the original definition of mission, made 15 years ago, still applicable? How far was the requirement of psychoanalysis for all still relevant? How to find a formulation that would no longer make the Institute appear as a para-medical organization but would express the broader idea of the social engagement of social science. Emery came up with the notion that everything it did—clinical and non-clinical—was at a more general level concerned with improving what he called "the important practical affairs of man." He prepared a document along these lines which was accepted by the Council.

The Institute continued to administer the Clinic's research and training activities, which had grown into a large enterprise. Bowlby had molded them into what he called the School of Family Psychiatry and Community Mental Health. An attempt was made to get the School affiliated to one of the London medical schools but the Tavistock was still too marginal and too identified with psychoanalysis to be countenanced.

Another development which began at about this time led to the setting up of an Institute for Operational Research. A growing number of management and decision scientists had become concerned that the capture of operational research (OR) by academic departments focussed on mathematical model-making was leading OR away from its original mission of dealing with real-world problems. They were interested in establishing a connection with the social sciences. Russell Ackoff of the University of Pennsylvania, a leading authority on OR, who was in England on sabbatical during 1962–63, suggested setting up an institute for operational research in the Tavistock orbit in conjunction with the British Operational Research Society. This suggestion came to fruition. Ackoff also found a British colleague, Neil Jessop, a mathematical statistician with social science interests, who was willing to give up a senior post in industry to head up the new enterprise.

There had been a large-scale development of OR in Britain in industry but nothing had been done in the public sector, outside defense. If it were to enter the policy field where problems were often ill-defined, ambiguous and interest-group-driven, OR had to find new concepts and methods to which the social sciences could contribute. OR people had found that their recommendations were only too often left on the shelf. They needed to involve the various stakeholders far more than had been their custom, to admit the limits of rationality, to pay attention to unconscious factors in organizational life and to acquire process skills in dealing with them. The OR people had considerable experience in dealing with large-scale problems at the multi-organizational level which the Institute was just beginning to enter and for which it lacked concepts and methodologies. On both sides there was a need to establish common ground and to find an organizational setting in which this could be explored. The status of an independent unit within the Tavistock orbit provided the required conditions. The new unit became known as the Institute for Operational Research (IOR).

The Family Discussion Bureau had also developed into a large undertaking of national standing. It needed a suitable identity to pursue its mission of setting up a non-medical but professional channel for dealing with marital difficulties. The title of the Institute for Marital Studies was proposed and accepted. It became an autonomous unit within the Tavistock orbit (Vol. I, "Non-Medical Marital Therapy").

There were now five units: those deriving from the original Management Committee—the Human Resources Centre (HRC) and the Centre for Applied Social Research (CASR); the School of Family Psychiatry and Community Mental Health; the Institute for Marital Studies; and the Institute for Operational Research. The Institute had become what Stringer (1967) called a multi-organization, a federation of interacting units with the same overall mission of furthering the social engagement of social science. Emery suggested that it had acquired the character of a social matrix—a nourishing and facilitating environment for all components. This matrix form of organization had the merit of showing to the external world that the overall mission could be pursued in different but nevertheless related ways.

The mutation required a new organizational structure. While each unit worked out its own form of internal governance the overall organization was steered by a Joint Committee of the Council and Staff, chaired by Sir Hugh Beaver with Trist as staff convener.

The broader formulation of mission and the greater variety of activities and people made it no longer possible or desirable that all staff should undergo psychoanalysis. This had been falling into disuse since 1958 and became a matter of individual choice. Awareness of psychoanalytic concepts and their relevance in the social field had become more widely accepted. They were absorbed "by osmosis." Moreover, one or two people with strongly Jungian views regarding archetypes and the collective unconscious were now on the staff. It was also found that capacity to work with groups and the process side of organizational life was to a considerable extent a personal endowment. Some of the best practitioners were "naturals." Nevertheless, a number of people continued to enter analysis and several became analysts.

The matrix worked well for several years. Major new projects were undertaken and a number of influential books produced. The HRC, for example, embarked on what became known as the Norwegian Industrial Democracy Project (Thorsrud and Emery, 1964; Emery and Thorsrud, 1969; 1977) and the Shell Management Philosophy Project (Hill, 1971). The CASR was instrumental in setting up an activity in the United States based on the Tavistock/Leicester Group Relations Training Conferences and Rice (1965) published a general account of this field. Miller and Rice (1967) published their now classic book *Systems of Organizations*. The IOR broke new ground with a project in which they worked collaboratively with the HRC on urban planning. It was jointly carried out with the city of Coventry with the support of the Nuffield Foundation (Friend and Jessop, 1969). The Institute for Marital Studies, having published a book, *Marriage: Studies in Emotional Conflict and Growth* (Pincus, 1960), which stated its theories and procedures, secured a multiplier effect by training case workers from a large number of organizations and extending its influence into continental Europe.

There were unanticipated developments. Several key people left the HRC. At the end of 1966, Trist was appointed to a professorship at the University of California (Los Angeles). Emery returned to Australia in 1969 as a Senior Fellow in the Research School of the Social Sciences at the Australian National University. In 1971 van Beinum went back to Holland to develop a new Department of Continuing Management Education at Erasmus University and in 1974 Higgin left to set up a similar department at the University of Loughborough. Pollock became a full-time analyst. Growing out of his work with Unilever, Bridger instituted a unit of his own—a network organization for career counselling. These individuals had all been at the Institute either from the beginning or for a great number of years. Though the moves all made sense and led to the appearance of new nodes in an emerging international network, they severely reduced the capacity of the HRC. The CASR was greatly impeded by the unexpected death of A.K. Rice at the height of his powers.

The IOR also suffered the death of its first leader, Neil Jessop, but the type of social-science-linked OR that he was developing created such a demand that the unit underwent extraordinary growth. It established offices in Coventry and Edinburgh in addition to the London base; at its peak it had 20 professional staff, more than all the other units taken together. Three books—*Communications in the Building Industry* (Higgin and Jessop, 1963), *Local Government and Strategic Choice* (Friend and Jessop, 1969) and *Public Planning: The*

Inter-Corporate Dimension (Friend, Power and Yewlett, 1974)—established its academic reputation. The theory and practice of reticulist planning which it introduced are now taught in planning schools throughout the world.

In the mid-1970s, the International Monetary Fund intervened dramatically in the British economy. Public spending was cut by four-and-a-half billion pounds sterling. This meant that the funds for the large IOR programs with government departments were instantly cut and reductions in staff took place. The larger parts of HRC and IOR merged to form a unit subsequently known as the Centre for Organizational and Operational Research (COOR). In the early 1980s even more drastic measures became necessary; all the working groups became one unit in which the members were on individual contract. There were no reserves to tide people over between projects.

It seemed that the Institute might go under but this did not happen. None of those left wanted the organization to die. They had the tenacity to keep it going and have been rewarded by seeing it re-expand and enter new areas of activity in which a younger generation has the task of proving itself. The 1987 annual report showed a staff of 20.

During the financial crisis the IMS could no longer accept the risk of remaining within the Institute. A new host organization was available in the Tavistock Institute of Medical Psychology, kept in existence for just such a need. IMS's sponsors preferred this arrangement with its even closer connections with the Clinic.

Recently, the Clinic has acquired university status by becoming affiliated with Brunel University in north-west London. There is no teaching hospital at Brunel. There is, however, an inter-disciplinary Department of Social Science founded by Elliott Jaques, one of the Tavistock founder members. New opportunities, therefore, open up. The search for university status by the Clinic and the School of Family Psychiatry and Community Mental Health has ended in a novel way that by-passed the medical school connection. This development was without precedent in Britain.

The International Network

With the establishment of the matrix there began to emerge an international network of Tavistock-like centers. These came into existence through the efforts of pioneering individuals who had spent some time at the Tavistock or through the migration of Tavistock staff to these new settings. The growth of such a network was inherent in much that had been going on for several years, but events in the 1970s and early 1980s prompted its actualization. Some of the projects were (and are) joint undertakings between people at the Tavistock and people in the other centers. A number of new endeavors have been large in scale and have emerged in the socio-ecological perspective. They have needed more resources than the Institute alone could supply. They have often been international in scope and it has been necessary for them to be mediated by organizations in the countries primarily concerned.

Work in these different settings has had a far-reaching effect on the concepts and methods employed. It is rarely the case that a single setting can carry forward a major innovative task for more than a limited period of time. The variety created by multiple settings sooner or later becomes a necessary factor in maintaining social innovation.

The following tables summarize what has emerged. Table 1 briefly describes the centers or nodes and the principal initiating individuals. The entries are by country in the order in which they commenced operation. Table 2 shows how far the movement was from the Tavistock to the node or in the other direction. Visits were often for several months or a year. Some key individuals migrated permanently or for several years, playing major institution-building roles.

The network in its present state of evolution may be characterized as follows:

- All nodes express the philosophy of the social engagement of social science. The engagement is with meta-problems that are generic and field determined rather than with issue-specific single problems.
- The work is future oriented and concerned with the transition to the post industrial social order and the paradigm shift which this entails.
- Since they are concerned with bringing about basic change, the activities undertaken encounter opposition. This makes it hard for the various nodes to acquire the resources they need.
- This situation creates severe stress which in turn generates internal strain in both organizations and individuals.
- The nodes have been developed by pioneering individuals who gather groups around them and connect with similar individuals in one or more of the other nodes.
- Though most of the nodes have existed for a considerable number of years they are, nevertheless, temporary systems. Unless they can engage with the next round of critical problems they have no further useful function.
- The nodes wax and wane, go out of existence or trigger new developments elsewhere.
- A number of them are no longer linked with the London organization.
- Apart from the London center, the most densely connected are the Work Research Institute, Oslo; the Centre for Continuing Education, Canberra; the University of Pennsylvania group and the Faculty of Environmental Studies, York University, Toronto.

TABLE I   International Network: Description of Nodes*

Node	Initiating individuals	Description
United Kingdom		
Scottish Institute of Human Relations	Jock Sutherland	When Sutherland returned to his native Edinburgh in the late 1960s, on retiring as Director of the Tavistock Clinic, he set up this independent center to deal with the range of activities covered by the School of Family Psychiatry and Community Mental Health.
Centre for Family and Environmental Research	Robert and Rhona Rapoport	This center was set up in London in the early 1970s when the Rapoports (both anthropologists and the latter also a psycho-analyst) moved their work on dual career families and related concerns with the family/work interface outside the Tavistock to establish an independent identity.
Department of Continuing Management Education, Loughborough University	Gurth Higgin	In 1974 Higgin was appointed to a new chair in this field and developed the first department of its kind in a British university with a new type of graduate diploma and strong links with industry in the region. There has been an emphasis on participatory methods.
Organisation for Promoting Understanding in Society (OPUS)	Eric Miller	This was set up in 1975 by Sir Charles Goodeve, the dean of British OR and a member of the Tavistock Council. It has an educational function, through which citizens can be helped to use their own "authority" more effectively. It seeks to investigate whether psycho-analytical understanding can be applied to society as a field of study in its own right.
Foundation for Adaptation in Changing Environments	Tony Ambrose Harold Bridger	This small Foundation concerned with projects in the socio-ecological field was set up in the early 1980s by Ambrose, originally a developmental psychologist, at the Tavistock's Department for Children and Parents. It has the form of a network organization, being without permanent staff. Originally at Minster Lovell, a village near Oxford, it has now moved to Geneva as so much of its work has become connected with the World Health Organization.

TABLE I   *Continued*

Node	Initiating individuals	Description
Europe Work Research Institute, Oslo, Norway	Einar Thorsrud Fred Emery David Herbst Eric Trist	This has become one of the principal institutions world-wide for the development of the socio-technical and socio-ecological perspectives. Thorsrud, its Director from 1962 until his untimely death in 1985, had been a frequent visitor at the Tavistock. Emery—and to some extent Trist—played a major role in its development during the 1960s. Herbst, also from the Tavistock, became a permanent staff member.
School of Business Administration, Erasmus University, Holland	Hans van Beinum	In 1971 van Beinum returned to Holland to set up a department of post-experience management education at Erasmus University. It has influenced the development of the socio-technical and socio-ecological fields in Europe.
Institute for Transitional Dynamics, Lucerne, Switzerland	Harold Bridger	This small but promising institute, set up by Bridger in the 1980s, focusses on organizational transitions. It is a network organization without permanent staff.
Australia Centre for Continuing Education, Australian National University	Fred and Merrelyn Emery	When Emery returned to Australia in 1969 as a Senior Fellow at the Research School for the Social Sciences at the Australian National University, he became associated with this center which is on the boundary between the academic and practical worlds. It has become a southern Tavistock in all three perspectives, being responsible for many of the key conceptual and methodological developments.
Canada Action Learning Group, Faculty of Environmental Studies, York University, Toronto	Eric Trist	In 1978 Trist joined the Faculty of Environmental Studies with which his relations had been growing for several years. The purpose was further to develop the socio-ecological perspective, especially in Third World projects, and to foster socio-technical projects throughout Can-

TABLE I   *Continued*

Node	Initiating individuals	Description
		ada. Search conferences have been introduced and teaching begun in futures studies. The center functions as a Canadian Tavistock.
Ontario Quality of Working Life Centre	Hans van Beinum	Towards the end of the 1970s the widespread interest in quality of working life (QWL) in Canada caused the Ontario government to set up a center for advancing this field, supported by employers and unions. Van Beinum resigned from his chair in Holland to become its executive director. Changes in the industrial and political climate in Canada have just recently prompted the Ontario government to close the Centre despite its considerable success.
India		
BM Institute, Ahmedabad	Kamalini Sarabhai Jock Sutherland	Kamalini Sarabhai, the wife of Gautam Sarabhai, head of Sarabhai Industries, one of the largest industrial concerns in India, came to the Tavistock for training in child development. On returning to India she and her husband set up what is called the BM Institute, very much along the lines of the Tavistock Clinic School of Family Psychiatry and Community Mental Health.
National Labour Institute and Punjab Institute for Public Administration	Nitish De Fred Emery	An unusual Indian social scientist, the late Nitish De, pioneered the socio-ecological and socio-technical approaches in the sub-continent. He had to move from one center to another because of political difficulties. He maintained strong relations with the Australian node.
United States		
Wright Institute, Berkeley, California	Nevitt Sanford Eric Trist	Sanford, a principal author of *The Authoritarian Personality* (1950), spent a sabbatical at the Tavistock in the early 1950s. Prevented by constraints at both Berkeley and Stanford from integrating

TABLE I   *Continued*

Node	Initiating individuals	Description
		social and clinical psychology, he set up, during the 1960s, an independent organization modelled on the Tavistock. It has functioned as a U.S. Tavistock (West). Since Sanford's retirement, however, it has been principally concerned with training clinical psychologists.
A. K. Rice Institute	Margaret Rioch A. K. Rice	In 1964 Margaret Rioch from the Washington School of Psychiatry, with which the Tavistock had close connections, set up an American version of the Leicester Conference with the assistance of A. K. Rice. On his unexpected death in 1969 she named the American organization the A. K. Rice Institute. It has since developed chapters throughout the United States.
Center for Quality of Working Life, University of California, Los Angeles	Louis Davis Eric Trist	Davis, an engineer turned social scientist, had introduced the socio-technical study of job design in the United States. In 1965/66 he spent a sabbatical at the Tavistock. The next year Trist joined him at UCLA and together they developed the first graduate socio-technical program in a university at both the master's and doctoral levels.
Department of Social Systems Sciences, Wharton School, University of Pennsylvania	Russell Ackoff Eric Trist	Wishing to set up a new Department of Social Systems Sciences, Ackoff persuaded Trist, then at UCLA, to join him in 1969. A very large and successful Ph.D. program developed, beginning a U.S. Tavistock (East). However, many Wharton faculty have not been friendly towards a systems approach and recently the University has phased out the academic program. One of the two associated research centers has been absorbed into the Wharton Center for Applied Research. The other, with Ackoff, has become linked to the Union Graduate School, where doctoral and master's programs are about to begin again.

*In order of establishment

TABLE 2   International Networks: Interconnections and Perspectives

Node	People establishing			Perspectives of work*		
	Visitor to Tavistock	Visitor from Tavistock	Migration from Tavistock	sP	sT	sE
Centre for Family and Environmental Research			*	*		*
Scottish Institute of Human Relations			*	*		
Department of Continuing Management Education, Loughborough University			*	*	*	*
Organisation for Promoting Understanding in Society (OPUS)		*				*
Foundation for Adaptation in Changing Environments		*	*	*		*
Work Research Institute, Oslo, Norway	*	*	*		*	*
School of Business Administration, Erasmus University, Holland		*	*		*	*
Institute for Transitional Dynamics, Lucerne, Switzerland			*	*		*
Centre for Continuing Education, Australian National University			*	*	*	*
Action Learning Group, Faculty of Environmental Studies, York University, Toronto			*	*	*	*
Ontario Quality of Working Life Centre			*		*	
BM Institute, Ahmedabad	*	*		*		
National Labour Institute and Punjab Institute for Public Administration		*			*	*
Wright Institute, Berkeley, California	*	*		*		*
A. K. Rice Institute, Washington, D.C.	*	*		*		
Center for Quality of Working Life, University of California, Los Angeles	*		*		*	
Department of Social Systems Sciences, Wharton School, University of Pennsylvania	*	*	*	*	*	*

*The codes, sP, sT and sE, indicate in which of the three perspectives (socio-psychological, socio-technical, socio-ecological) work has been carried out in the new settings.

- Several centers have added new ideas beyond the scope of the original organization. This is particularly true of the four mentioned above in which very substantial advances have been, and are being, made both conceptually and in the type of projects undertaken. As these concern the socio-ecological perspective their exposition is reserved for Volume III.

It is postulated that networks of this kind will play an increasingly important role in the future development of fields concerned with the social engagement of social science.

General Outcomes

Type C Organizations

The experience of building the Tavistock seemed to be relevant to a number of organizations in one country or another that were engaged in pathfinding endeavors. The Institute, in fact, had become a member of a new class of organizations whose importance was increasing as the turbulent environment became more salient. In addition to university centers engaged in basic research, and consulting groups, whether inside or outside operating organizations, engaged in applied research, there is a third type of research organization whose mission is distinct from either and which requires a different kind of distinctive competence.

There has been a good deal of confusion about what this third type does—"problem-oriented research" has been a common label—and denigration of its worth. The Institute has had to work out its properties in order more fully to understand itself and to gain general recognition for the kind of work it undertakes (Trist, 1970).

The three types of organization, shown in Table 3, have distinctive patterns and may be described as follows:

Type A Centers of basic research associated with major teaching facilities, located within universities as autonomous departments undertaking both undergraduate and graduate teaching. Here, research problems are determined by the needs of theory and method, and express a research/teaching mix.

Type B Centers of professional social science activity that undertake work on immediate practical problems, located within user organizations or in external consulting groups. User organizations require a means of identifying areas of social science knowledge relevant to their interests and need

TABLE 3   Characteristics of Main Types of Research Organization

	University departments	User organizations	Special institutes
Source of problem	Needs of theory and method	Specific client needs	General "field" needs (meta-problems)
Level of problem	Abstract	Concrete	Generic
Activity mix	Research/teaching	Research/service	Research/action
Disciplinary mix	Single	Multiple	Interrelated
Overall pattern	Type A	Type B	Type C

social science professionals in continuous contact with administrators. In such centers research problems are determined by client needs. They express a research/service mix.

Type C Centers of applied research associated with advanced research training. They may be regarded as a resultant of Types A and B and supply the necessary link between them. They may be located either on the boundaries of universities or outside them as independent institutes. They are problem-centered and inter-disciplinary, but focus on generic rather than specific problems. They accept professional as well as scientific responsibility for the projects they undertake, and contribute both to the improvement of practice and to theoretical development. Their work expresses a research/action mix.

These three types of institution form an interdependent system. One type cannot be fully effective without the others since the feedback of each into the others is critical for the balanced development of the whole. The boundaries of A and B can easily extend into C, and those of C into either A or B.

The Institute is a Type C organization. It has had continually to face the dilemmas and conflicts of needing to be an innovative research body at the leading edge and an operational body to a considerable extent paying its own way. This has been a condition of preserving its independence. To accomplish both of these aims simultaneously constitutes a paradox fundamental to the existence of such bodies.

Type C institutes are not organized around disciplines but around generic problems (meta-problems or problématiques), which are field determined. They need the capacity to respond to emergent issues and to move rapidly into new areas. Sub-units need to be free to move in and out. So do staff.

The experience of fashioning the Institute showed that Type C organizational cultures need to be based on group creativeness. This contradicts the tradition of academic individualism. A group culture is inherent in projects that depend on collaboration for the achievement of inter-disciplinary endeavors. What gets done is more important than who does it. This affects questions of reward and recognition. A very strong tradition of group values had been inherited from the war-time Tavistock group. Appropriate ways had to be found of reaffirming them. These have not always been successful.

A difficult question arises regarding financial stability. The funding pattern described in the discussion of optimum balance is an ideal which the Institute succeeded in approximating only at certain times. Two organizations with which it has compared itself—the Institute for Social Research at the University of Michigan and the Work Research Institute in Oslo—have been able to achieve financial stability in ways unavailable to the Tavistock. In the first, the University allowed the Institute to retain overheads which would otherwise have gone to the University itself and staff to hold part-time faculty appointments which were not at risk. In Oslo, the Norwegian government provided for a certain number of senior appointments and assisted with overheads. The Tavistock has never attained such conditions. A priority for any Type C institute is continually to search for appropriate means of securing financial stability.

A structural necessity is to allow a very high degree of autonomy to subsystems and to tolerate wide differences of viewpoint. This creates the need for a democratic system of governance such as that constituted by the pre-war Tavistock organizational revolution that laid the basis for future developments. The form of organizational democracy that grew up after the war had become eroded when the division into two groups occurred.

This failure points to the need for a Type C institute to maintain the process side of its organizational life. In the rapidly changing conditions of a turbulent environment fresh appreciations have to be made frequently and staff conflicts worked through. If the organization is to remain an open system in its environment it has to maintain an open system within itself.

This concept of the Institute's basic organizational character was strengthened when it became a member of an international network. Beyond a certain stage innovative Type C organizations need such a network. They cannot go it alone.

Innovative organizations that come into existence in response to critical problems in their societies can usefully continue only so far as they remain capable of addressing further problems of this kind. Some of the organizations in the Tavistock network have already gone out of existence, but new ones have emerged. The London organization has survived several crises, but is still, after 40 years, a transitional organization. Though its member organizations may change, it is much less likely that the network itself will go out of existence. The evolution of the Tavistock enterprise has now reached a higher system level—that of the network. Yet in time, many of the nodes are likely to become more closely linked with other networks than the original set and to be absorbed in the more general stream of the social sciences.

Three Research Perspectives

As the matrix became established it became evident that most of the Institute's activities could be subsumed under three perspectives, called in these volumes the socio-psychological, the socio-technical and the socio-ecological perspectives. These emerged from each other in relation to changes taking place in the wider societal environment. One could not have been forecast from the others. Though interdependent, each has its own focus. Many of the more complex projects require all three perspectives.

The original perspective, which grew out of World War II, is called the socio-psychological rather than the psycho-social, as, in Institute projects, the psychological forces are directed towards the social field, whereas in the Clinic it is the other way around. The source concepts for this perspective are: the object relations approach, field theory, the personality-culture approach and systems theory, especially in its open system form. The Institute's contribution has been to bring them together in a new configuration, which it has made operational.

Experience during World War II had shown that psychoanalytic object relations theory could unify the psychological and social fields in a way that no other could. This was the reason for making psychoanalytic training an essential ingredient of the capabilities required to fulfill the post-war mission of the Institute. It soon led to entirely new concepts: those of Bion (1961) concerning basic unconscious assumptions in group life, which he linked to Melanie Klein's (1948) views on the paranoid-schizoid and depressive positions; and Jaques's (1953) theory on the use of social structure as a defense against anxiety.

Field theory appealed to several of the Tavistock psychiatrists who were impressed with Lewin's emphasis on the here-and-now, the Galilean as opposed to the Aristotelian philosophy of science and the theory of joint causation expressed in the formula $B = f(P,E)$. His work on group decision making and on the dynamics of social change, particularly as put forward in his two posthumous papers for the first issue of *Human Relations* (1947), were found to be most cogent. His dictum that the best way to understand a system is to change it gave prime importance to action research.

In 1933 Trist had attended Sapir's seminar, given to his graduate students at Yale, on the impact of culture on personality, the theme of his epoch-making international seminar the previous year. To link personality and culture was foreign to the structural approach in British social anthropology. While learning from the structural approach, Trist (Vol. I, "Culture as a Psycho-Social Process") was led to a concept of culture as a psycho-social process which could mediate between purely sociological and purely psychological frames of reference, a combination of which was needed in action research.

While on sabbatical at the Institute from Australia in 1951, Emery alerted his colleagues to the significance for social science of Von Bertalanffy's (1950) notion of open systems. This provided a new way of considering individuals, groups and organizations in relation to their environments and foreshadowed the importance later to be attached to Sommerhoff's (1950, 1969) theory of directive correlation. As time went on the theoretical underpinnings of projects became an amalgam of these four conceptual traditions. The socio-psychological perspective (represented in Volume I) enables work at all system levels, from micro- to macro-, to be covered within a single framework.

The socio-technical perspective (represented in Volume II), was entirely novel. It originated in the early mining studies (Trist and Bamforth, 1951). Numerous projects have shown that the prevailing pattern of top-down bureaucracy is beginning to give way to an emergent non-linear paradigm. The new paradigm is based on discovering the best match between the social and technical systems of an organization, since called the principle of joint optimization (Emery, 1959). The notion of one narrowly skilled man doing one fractionated task was replaced by that of the multi-skilled work group that could exchange assignments in a whole task system. This led to the further formulation by Emery (1967) of the second design principle, the redundancy of functions, as contrasted with the redundancy of parts.

Efforts to bring about changes in this new direction have encountered resistances of profound cultural and psychological depth. These can be more readily understood when their basis in unconscious processes is recognized, for they disturb socially structured psychological defenses in management and worker alike, and threaten established identities. The loss of the familiar, even if beset with "bad" attributes, often entails mourning. The possibly "good" may threaten because it is untried. Change strategies have to allow for the fact that working through such difficulties takes time. Moreover, intensive socio-technical change threatens existing power systems and requires a redistribution of power.

The main developments as regards operational projects took place in the 1960s and 1970s and are still continuing. Until well into that latter decade the socio-technical field developed largely in terms of projects carried out by members of the Tavistock in a number of countries.

The importance of self-regulating organizations has become much greater in the context of the increasing levels of interdependence, complexity and uncertainty that characterize societies at the present time. Beyond certain thresholds the center/periphery model (Schon, 1970) no longer holds. There come into being far more complex interactive webs of relationship that cannot be handled in this way. These changes in the wider environment prompted the creation of the socio-ecological perspective (represented in Volume III).

The coming of the new information technologies and the signs of a transition to a post-industrial society pose new problems related to emergent values such as co-operation and nurturance. Competition and dominance are becoming dysfunctional as the main drivers of post-industrial society. The value dilemmas created are reflected in the conflicts experienced by client organizations and in higher levels of stress for the individual. A first attempt to conceptualize the new "problématique" was made by Emery and Trist (1965) in a paper entitled "The Causal Texture of Organizational Environments" (Vol. III). This introduces a new theory of environmental types which arranges environments in terms of their increasing complexity. The contemporary environment is said to be taking on the character of a "turbulent field" in which the amount of disorder is increasing. In the limit is a "vortical" state in which adaptation would be impossible.

Turbulence cannot be managed by top-down hierarchies of the kind exhibited in bureaucratic forms of organization. These are variety-reducing, so that there is not enough internal variety to manage the increase in external variety (Ashby, 1960). Needed are organizational forms that are variety-increasing. These are inherently participative and require a substantial degree of democratization in organizational life.

No organization, however large, can go it alone in a turbulent environment. Dissimilar organizations become directively correlated. They need to become linked in networks. A new focus of the Institute's work has been, therefore, the development of collaborative modes of intervention for the reduction of turbulence and the building of inter-organizational networks that can address "meta-problems" at the "domain" level. Projects of this kind have led it into the field of futures studies—"the future in the context of the present" (Emery and Trist, 1972/73) and "ideal-seeking" systems (Emery, 1976). New process methodologies such as the "search conference" have been introduced (Emery and Emery, 1978) to solve multi-party conflicts, to improve social coherence and to envision more desirable futures.

The socio-ecological approach is linked to the socio-technical because of the critical importance of self-regulating organizations for turbulence reduction. It is further linked to the socio-psychological approach because of the need to reduce stress and prevent regression. Primitive levels of behavior can only too easily appear in face of higher levels of uncertainty. This is one of the greatest dangers facing the world as the present century draws to its close.

These three perspectives, all arising from field experience, would appear to have general significance for work concerned with the social engagement of social science.

References

Ackoff, R.L. and F.E. Emery. 1972. *On Purposeful Systems*. Chicago: Aldine-Atherton.

Adorno, T.W., E. Frenkel-Brunswick, D.J. Levinson and N. Sanford (Editors). 1950. *The Authoritarian Personality*. New York: Harper and Row.

Alcock, T. 1963. *The Rorschach in Practice*. London: Tavistock Publications.

Ashby, W.R. 1960. *Design for a Brain*. London: Chapman & Hall.

Balint, M. 1954. "Training General Practitioners in Psychotherapy." *British Medical Journal*, I:115–20.

Bion, W.R. 1948–50. "Experiences in Groups." *Human Relations*, 1:314–20, 487–96; 2:13–22, 295–303; 3:3–14, 395–402; 4:221–27.

———. 1961. *Experiences in Groups and Other Papers*. London: Tavistock Publications; New York: Basic Books.

Bott, E. 1957. *Family and Social Network* (2nd edition, 1971). London: Tavistock Publications.

Dicks, H.V. 1970. *Fifty Years of the Tavistock Clinic*. London: Routledge and Kegan Paul.

———. 1972. *Licensed Mass Murder*. New York: Basic Books.

Emery, F. 1959. *Characteristics of Socio-Technical Systems*. London: Tavistock Institute Document 527.

———. 1967. "The Next Thirty Years: Concepts, Methods and Anticipations." *Human Relations*, 20:199–237.

———. 1976. *Futures We Are In*. Leiden: Martinus Nijhoff.

Emery, M. and F. Emery. 1978. "Searching: For New Directions, In New Ways . . . For New Times." In *Management Handbook for Public Administrators*, edited by J.W. Sutherland. New York and London: Van Nostrand Reinhold.

Emery, F.E., E.L. Hilgendorf and B.L. Irving. 1968. *The Psychological Dynamics of Smoking*. London: Tobacco Research Council.

Emery, F. and E. Thorsrud. 1969. *Form and Content in Industrial Democracy*. London: Tavistock Publications.

———. 1977. *Democracy at Work*. Leiden: Martinus Nijhoff.

Emery, F.E. and E.L. Trist. 1965. "The Causal Texture of Organizational Environments." *Human Relations*, 18:21–32.

———. 1972/73. *Towards a Social Ecology*. London/New York: Plenum Press.

Friend, J.K. and W.N. Jessop. 1969. *Local Government and Strategic Choice*. London: Tavistock Publications.

Friend, J.K., J.M. Power and C.J.L. Yewlett. 1974. *Public Planning: The Inter-Corporate Dimension*. London: Tavistock Publications.

Higgin, G.W. and W.N. Jessop. 1963. *Communications in the Building Industry*. London: Tavistock Publications.

Hill, J.M. and E.L. Trist. 1955. "Changes in Accidents and Other Absences with Length of Service." *Human Relations*, 8:121–152.

Hill, P. 1971. *Towards a New Philosophy of Management*. London: Gower Press.

Jaques, E. 1951. *The Changing Culture of a Factory*. London: Tavistock Publications. Reissued 1987, New York: Garland.

———. 1953. "On the Dynamics of Social Structure." *Human Relations*, 6:3–24.

Klein, M. 1948. *Contributions to Psycho-Analysis 1921–1945*. London: Hogarth Press.

Laing, R.D., H. Phillipson and A. Lee. 1966. *Interpersonal Perception: A Theory and a Method of Research*. London: Tavistock Publications.

Lewin, K. 1947. "Frontiers in Group Dynamics." *Human Relations*, I:5–41, 143–53.

Menzies Lyth, I. and E. Trist. 1989. In I. Menzies Lyth, *The Dynamics of the Social*. London: Free Association Books.

Miller, E. and A.K. Rice. 1967. *Systems of Organization: Task and Sentient Systems and Their Boundary Control*. London: Tavistock Publications.

Pincus, L. (Editor) 1960. *Marriage: Studies in Emotional Conflict and Growth*. London: Methuen.

Rice, A.K. 1965. *Learning for Leadership*. London: Tavistock Publications.

Schon, D. 1970. *Beyond the Stable State*. New York: Basic Books.

Sommerhoff, 1950. *Analytical Biology*. Oxford: Oxford University Press.

———. 1969. "The Abstract Characteristics of Living Systems." In *Systems Thinking*, edited by F.Emery. Harmondsworth: Penguin Books.

Stringer, J. 1967. "Operational Research for Multi-Organizations." *Operational Research Quarterly*, 18:105–20.

Thorsrud, E. and F. Emery. 1964. *Industrielt Demokrati*. Oslo: Oslo University Press.

Tomkins, S. 1962. *Affect, Imagery, Consciousness*. New York: Springer.

Trist, E.L. 1970. "The Organization and Financing of Social Research." In *UNESCO. Main Trends of Research in the Social and Human Sciences. Part I: Social Sciences*. Paris: Mouton.

Trist, E.L. and K.W. Bamforth. 1951. "Some Social and Psychological Consequences of the Longwall Method of Coal-getting." *Human Relations*, 4:3–38.

Von Bertalanffy, L. 1950. "The Theory of Open Systems in Physics and Biology." *Science*, 3:22–29.

Wilson, A.T.M. 1949. "Some Reflections and Suggestions on the Prevention and Treatment of Marital Problems." *Human Relations*, 2:233–52.

Winnicott, D.W. 1965. *The Maturational Process and the Facilitating Environment*. London: Hogarth.

Volume I

The Socio-Psychological Perspective

Introduction

The contributions selected to represent the socio-psychological perspective of The Social Engagement of Social Science are arranged in five "families" which form the Themes of this Volume. They show the variety of work included in each Theme and its underlying coherence.

The first Theme, *A New Social Psychiatry: A World War II Legacy*, is the foundation on which the concept of The Social Engagement of Social Science has been built. The second, *Varieties of Group Process*, describes experience with the primary group, which was one of the first two fields with which the post-war Institute became pre-occupied. The other was the family—hence the Theme of *New Paths in Family Studies*. Somewhat later, work under the fourth Theme, *The Dynamics of Organizational Change*, became salient. From this background projects emerged related to the fifth Theme, *The Unconscious in Culture and Society*.

The range of social phenomena thus presented, is from micro to macro: the primary group; the family; organizations; the larger society. Different system levels are represented.

As explained in the Historical Overview, the source concepts which gave rise to the socio-psychological perspective are psychoanalytic object relations theory, Lewinian field theory, the personality-culture approach and the theory of open systems. These have been drawn on to guide action-oriented projects of considerable scope and duration. The experience of these projects has led to further conceptual developments. Usually more than one, sometimes all four, of the source concepts have been drawn on in order to obtain a better understanding of what was taking place or what had to be designed.

Though it would be preposterous to suggest that everybody did everything, most staff members moved with some facility from one domain of inquiry to another and from one system level to another. An ideal was to keep alive in one's experience the reality of the person, the group, the organization and the wider society, so that one could sense their interconnections. It was also thought desirable to maintain contact with projects in more than one social sector—not, for example, to spend all one's time in industrial projects.

Because most of the projects were conducted in an action-oriented frame of reference, multiple aspects of the situation came into play. This compelled an holistic approach. Experiential holism reinforced cognitive holism. New perceptions arose from this reinforcement.

A generalist capacity was needed as a background for specific competence. What one lacked oneself could be supplied by a colleague, since projects were carried out by teams. But communication in such circumstances fails without the common background of a shared perspective such as that provided by the source concepts.

The aim was to maintain a variety of experience, however much at a given time a staff member was focussing on a particular level or domain. Experiential learning provided a basis for conceptual advance.

A New Social Psychiatry:
A World War II Legacy

The papers under this Theme give accounts of three projects arising at different phases of the war that defined the nature of the new social psychiatry. Each led to innovations in practice and advances in theory. They all involved the building of new special purpose military institutions.

The Transformation of Selection Procedures. This is an overview of the War Office Selection Boards which constituted a major innovation. The solution to a crisis in officer selection that developed in 1941 was to build a residential institution in which groups of candidates were assessed by a group of judges— military and technical (psychiatrists and psychologists). The process through which this evolved as a collaborative undertaking between the military and technical teams is described by Murray as an exemplar of creating this type of relationship.

The candidates had come to compete for the privilege of going on to officer training. They were faced, however, with situations in which they had to cooperate. How they handled this dilemma was the key question in the "here-and-now" real-life situation they were in. The leaderless group method introduced by Bion (1946) showed that when formal structure was removed a group spontaneously developed structures of its own. A therapeutic element was built into assessment procedures which became a learning experience for all concerned.

As the war went on a large variety of selection projects was undertaken and far-reaching attempts were made to test the reliability and validity of the procedures. The follow-up in theaters of war was designed in a way that secured the full participation of commanding officers.

Murray gives the first overview to be published of this far-reaching multi-faceted enterprise and its implications for the future.

The Discovery of the Therapeutic Community. At the height of the war all available manpower was needed. Too many soldiers were being invalided out because of psychological illness. An attempt to reduce this outflow was made by Bion and Rickman (1943) at Northfield Military Hospital where they introduced for the first time the notion of a therapeutic community—a completely novel idea. In countervailing the conventional bureaucratic and authoritarian medical model this innovation produced so much anxiety in the staff that it was stopped. Later it was reintroduced in a form developed by Harold Bridger, and elaborated still further by S.H. Foulkes (1946) who exercised a major influence on post-war developments. Bridger's overview, which evaluates the contributions of all the main actors, is the only such account to be published.

The experience of being at Northfield was an intense one for staff and patients alike. The therapeutic results were beyond expectations. Many of those involved felt they had been introduced into a world where far more was possible in human relationships than they had previously thought. They came to believe that the creativeness and cooperation released might, if replicated on a wide enough scale, provide a means of bringing into existence a more reparative society.

Transitional Communities and Social Reconnection. The beliefs that arose from Northfield were strengthened by experiences with the second therapeutic community which was designed for the civil resettlement of repatriated prisoners of war. Twenty of these units were brought into existence with some 200 repatriates in residence in each at any one time. This whole scheme was conceived by Wilson (1946). Follow-up showed it to be profoundly successful. It was not under medical auspices but run by regimental personnel with a handful of psychiatric and psychological advisers. It brought forward a new general concept—the function of transitional communities in establishing the "social reconnection" of those who, for a variety of reasons, may find themselves outside or alienated from the main society.

After agreements had been reached at ministerial level to use the experience gained in a number of post-war applications their implementation was prevented because of political interventions based on complete misunderstanding. Fortunately, the form of therapeutic community developed in parallel by Maxwell Jones (1968), which had medical protection, survived. In the mental hospital world therapeutic communities gained ground but reached certain limits not present in other settings. It is a tragedy that the war-time transmedical versions did not spread; but the obstacles at that time were all but insuperable.

These war-time innovations need reassessment as regards their usefulness for addressing current problems and Bridger is testing out their relevance to AIDS and the drug problem in the United States and Italy. They have continuing potential as arenas for promoting personal growth and group cooperation in many settings. Their participative and democratic aspects have value for institution-building for the future.

A New Social Psychiatry   43

References

Bion, W.R. 1946. "The Leaderless Group Project." *Bulletin of the Menninger Clinic*, 10:77–81.

Bion, W.R. and J. Rickman. 1943. "Intra-Group Tensions in Therapy." *Lancet*, 2:678–81.

Foulkes, S.H. 1946. "On Group Analysis." *International Journal of Psycho-Analysis*, 27:46–51.

Jones, M. 1968. *Social Psychiatry in Practice*. London: Penguin Books.

Wilson, A.T.M. 1946. "The Serviceman Comes Home." *Pilot Papers*, 1:9–28.

Hugh Murray

The Transformation of Selection Procedures

The War Office Selection Boards*

The Presenting Problem and the Initial Response

Towards the end of 1941, the impending rapid expansion of the British Army required a large number of officers. The ensuing crisis in officer selection was of sufficient magnitude for a major innovation in assessment procedures to emerge—the War Office Selection Boards. These boards enabled the army to officer itself when traditional methods were failing and when there was doubt as to whether a sufficient reserve of officer material existed among the other ranks. The process of collaboration between experts and administrators, which the boards exemplified, became a model for many other joint undertakings. The methodological revolution consisted in replacing a military judge using a short interview by an inter-disciplinary group of selectors who assessed groups of candidates over two-and-a-half days. The extent of the participation achieved among all those concerned made the Boards profoundly acceptable to the wartime army.

Failure rates at Officer Cadet Training Units (OCTUs) had risen to over 20 percent in many courses and to over 30 percent in some. Not only did these failures represent a great deal of effort wasted on unproductive training (courses were of three months), they created undue stress in the training units. Next, there were insufficient numbers of good applicants. This lack was complex in its origins; letters of complaint received by the War Office indicated that there was a reluctance to apply for a commission. Furthermore, the return to their units of a noticeable number of failures reinforced this reluctance.

At this time candidates for commissions went before a Command Interview Board (CIB) consisting of a permanent president and two commanding officers (COs) as ad hoc members. These boards conducted a short interview with each

*A new paper based on original documents and unpublished papers, drafted by B.S. Morris, J.D. Sutherland and E.L. Trist, held in the archives of the Tavistock Institute.

candidate, usually some 20 minutes, and decisions were made on the impressions gained, together with the information contained in a brief report from the man's CO. Many candidates felt that they could not do themselves justice in such short interviews. The presidents felt equally dissatisfied. Reports from units were also proving less helpful than had been hoped. COs had not yet had experience of men under sufficiently varied conditions and the course of the war had been such that relatively few candidates had had the critical test of battle. Potential officers were being drawn from an ever-widening range of social classes so that presidents no longer had those signposts to leadership qualities with which they were familiar in young men from the public (USA = private) schools. The uncertainty felt about such short interviews was increased by pressure to find all possible candidates rather than to take only those who were obviously good.

BACKGROUND TO THE CHANGE

Early in 1940 a psychiatrist was posted to each of the Army Commands and soon afterwards other psychiatrists were added to assist the Command psychiatrists. Many of the breakdowns they encountered were obviously precipitated by factors in the military environment as well as by limitations in the individual. The psychiatrists began to occupy a therapeutic role in relation to their employing institution, the army, as well as to individual patients within it by making suggestions for the prevention of psychiatric illness from social causes (Sutherland and Fitzpatrick, 1945). One of the most important causes of difficulty in adjustment was unsuitable employment in the army itself. A new Directorate for the Selection of Personnel was established which, working in close collaboration with the Directorate for Army Psychiatry, prepared a scheme which radically altered the recruiting arrangements of the army and entailed the building of a new social system—the General Service Corps—into which men were now taken for a short period before being sent to a specific arm of the service. During this induction period they were given several psychological tests and a short interview which enabled Personnel Selection Officers to make recommendations for each man's training in keeping with his abilities and, as far as possible, his preferences (Vernon and Parry, 1949). The psychometric under-pinning of this scheme was in sharp contrast to the methods then used for the selection of officer cadets.

In creating practical schemes for handling various manpower questions, it became the rule that the schemes had to be jointly planned by the army officer and the "expert," each contributing from his own special experience and knowledge (Rees, 1945). The social-therapeutic role of the psychiatrists, both in diagnosing problems from the human side of the military environment and in fostering the development of specially adapted military institutions to meet them, paved the way for the early experiments and for some of the most characteristic features of the selection boards.

PRELIMINARY EXPERIMENTS

Experiments by army psychiatrists with both officers and officer-cadets pointed to ways of providing the CIBs with more evidence than they were accustomed to have. An experiment by Bowlby was stimulated by comments on the unsuitability of many officers recently commissioned: the numbers of unsuitable officer-cadets were intolerably high, they lacked the ability to master the technical training or the degree of leadership required for an armored regiment, or both. Since psychological tests and interviews had proved useful in identifying other-rank recruits likely to prove failures, the new inquiry aimed to discover whether an intelligence test and an interview by a psychiatrist could accurately predict the technical ability and officer-like qualities of cadets at OCTU.

A critical experiment with serving officers (Wittkower and Rodger, 1941) arose out of a Command psychiatrist's work with problem officers and the interest of his Army Commander in the methods of officer selection used in the German army. An initial experiment was set up at a school for company commanders whose commandant and staff had, during an intensive five-week course, formed a thorough-going opinion of the students' all-around capabilities as officers, their technical proficiency and their human qualities. They could give ratings of their students with which the opinions of the psychiatrist could be compared.

The investigation included written and laboratory tests and an interview. In order to compare opinions, the commandant and the psychiatrists each made a brief evaluation of the student's personality, together with a judgment on his suitability as a combatant officer. Both sides read their reports and then rated the results of the comparison according to the degree of agreement. Of the 48 comparisons, 26 (55 percent) were in essential agreement, 12 (25 percent) in substantial agreement and 10 (20 percent) in essential disagreement. Nine-tenths of these disagreements were due to underlying personality deviations which had escaped the attention of the commandant, in some cases the psychological abnormality being very severe.

The program, with the addition of a psychologist to administer intelligence tests, was repeated with another course of officers at the company commanders' school. The results reduced the 20 percent disagreement by half. The improvement appeared to be due not only to the psychiatrists incorporating the results of the intelligence tests into their reports, but also to the mutual education of the psychiatrists and the commandant. The psychiatrists learned more of the variety of talents which could successfully be used in officer roles, while the commandant became aware of the possible psychological significance of certain aspects of a man's performance during the course. It was recognized that some differences of opinion would be inevitable because of the limitations of the methods used by each judge—the one using interviews, supported by written and laboratory tests, and the other observing men in a variety of practical training activities.

The assessment of these officers, while presenting many difficulties, was nevertheless an easier task than the assessment of younger men who did not have occupational or military records as evidence of their potentialities. The investigations were therefore repeated with several groups of cadets at an OCTU. A similar degree of overall essential and substantial agreement, 80 to 90 percent, was found between the reports of the training staff and the psychiatrists. The relationship between training outcome and performance in the field was, of course, unknown.

So long as the categories of substantial and essential agreement were combined, the level of agreement was higher than might have been expected. But if the category of substantial agreement was added to that of essential disagreement, a more negative picture emerged. It was concluded that an opinion based simply on interview and intelligence tests would not be sufficient for making reliable judgments on the substantial proportion of candidates likely to be near the threshold of acceptance—and boards were under pressure to accept as many of these as they could, with safety, pass. From the nature of the discrepancies between the judgments of the psychiatrist and the OCTU staff, it appeared that practical tests would be a valuable addition to an interview, as a man could then be seen in action. If a way could be found of combining the resources and methods of military personnel and the opinions of psychiatric and psychological specialists, rather than of using one as a criterion for validating the other, a type of selection procedure might be instituted which would be reliable in assessing officer candidates and acceptable to military opinion.

INITIAL WORKING PRINCIPLES

From the preliminary experiments six general principles emerged for an improved selection procedure:

- The responsibility for selection must belong, and manifestly so, to the employing institution, i.e., the army. If selection were to be delegated to the "expert," insuperable difficulties would follow regarding the acceptance of new methods by both officers and men.

- The introduction of scientific procedures could best be effected by grafting them onto the existing Command Interview Boards. To do this entailed creating a new social institution, for the original board would be transformed in character. The president of the new board would retain responsibility for selection, but with evidence provided by other examiners. His experience of the army was essential. He should carry a rank—full Colonel—which would strengthen his position in relation to the COs of units from which candidates would be drawn.
- Data from interviews needed to be supplemented by observation of the individual in action. The president should have a junior regimental officer with experience of battle conditions, to be known as a Military Testing Officer (MTO), who would conduct a number of practical tests based on common tasks of an officer's role.
- The psychological contributions to the board's evidence should be of two kinds. First, evidence about each candidate submitted by a psychiatrist and a psychologist. As full an interview as possible should be preserved. In addition to tests which had been proved worthwhile, such as tests of intelligence, ways of estimating qualities of personality should be developed.
- Candidates should live in a hostel with the MTO for a period of three days—the time estimated to process an intake of, say, 30 candidates.
- Working out a practical testing procedure required further experimentation. An experimental board should, therefore, be established with a president, an MTO, two psychiatrists and a psychologist.

The proposals were well received. The creation of a new type of military unit for the selection of officers which would introduce scientific methods in the context of a residential procedure was acceptable to the presidents of the Command Interview Boards.

The Work of the Experimental Selection Board

The experimental selection board* assembled early in January 1942 to begin working out an operational procedure on the principles agreed. Whatever aspects of a candidate might need special attention in the light of job analyses—which were carried out by officers with recent battle experience—the

---

*W.R. Bion, J.D. Sutherland (psychiatrists) and E.L. Trist (psychologist) became the nuclear technical group which, in conjunction with Colonel J.V. Delahaye (President) and Captain W.N. Gray (MTO), worked up and tested out a reproducible model. Three psychological assistants (sergeant testers—later commissioned) supported this group.

"whole man" had to be taken into account. Many kinds of men made good officers. Few personal qualities were specific to the job. Almost all an individual's attributes could contribute to his effectiveness and could affect the attitudes of his men and of his fellow officers towards him. It would be his competence to fill the main roles of the officer's job that would matter rather than his particular method of carrying them out. Preconceptions about officer qualities or types of potential officers had to be overcome. Judges needed an extensive knowledge of officer roles and then had to assess how candidates could use their resources to fill them.

Three main demands of the officer's job needed assessment: quality of social relations with superiors, equals and subordinates; competence in practical situations; stamina over long periods and under stress. The president and the psychiatrist had their own distinctive method of assessment (the interview) already available but suitable testing methods for the MTO and the psychologist would have to be created.

QUASI REAL-LIFE SITUATIONS

The first military tests were decided by the background, training and battle experience which the MTO brought to his task. As a regimental officer he judged men on the basis of their performance in actual situations and roles. Therefore his intuitions and discriminations were likely to be most effective with tests which enabled him to relate what he observed directly to his field of experience. The most suitable tests were, therefore, quasi real-life situations in which the essentials of various officer roles and problems were imitated. The situations had to be such that they depended as little as possible on special military knowledge and amount of military training.

The tests were of two types: command situations and practical individual situations. Command situations consisted of asking each candidate to play the role of officer in simple military situations using the other candidates as his men. Such situations typically required the officer to deal with his men at the same time as solving concrete problems created by things. Two different kinds of situations were used, one with the candidate in independent command in an outdoor practical situation; the other focussing on his administrative and man-management roles.

The practical individual situations were designed to bring out certain qualities thought to be related to the capacity to endure stress. They consisted of physical obstacles arranged in a series or "course" with specially constructed apparatus. Athletic prowess was largely irrelevant. The candidate had to assess his own resources in relation to each obstacle. What was looked for was his judgment in overcoming them, as well as his stamina.

PSYCHOLOGICAL TESTS

The best arrangement was for the psychiatrist to provide an integrated technical report that combined clinical assessment with the more objective measures which psychological tests could give. Four types of test were chosen: questionnaires, intelligence tests, projective tests of personality and individual tests of a laboratory type based on those used in the German army (Ansbacher, 1941). The latter were subsequently dropped as being redundant or impractical. The first two were group-administered written tests and the third soon became so. The function of the two questionnaires was to have recorded, for the convenience of both interviewers, the main features of the candidate's scholastic, occupational and military history and, for the psychiatrist and psychologist, more personal information about family history and health.

In choosing and developing intelligence tests, the following factors had to be taken into account: the capacity to reason with both verbal and non-verbal material (the influence of different educational opportunities being reduced to a minimum); flexibility—the test items were arranged so that each problem would be approached afresh; the maximum discrimination should occur among the top 30 percent of the army population. Candidates were separated into those clearly acceptable, those of borderline acceptability and those unacceptable. Individual confirmatory tests (Semeonoff and Trist, 1958) were given to three categories of candidate: those whose educational or occupational record was out of keeping with the test results; those showing unusual discrepancies between performances on the three tests; and candidates of borderline ability who did well in interview or on the MTO tests.

The projective method creates conditions for the total personality—its conscious and unconscious forces and their organization—to reveal itself in a spontaneous way. Certain projective tests were identified for further work because of their ease of group application and assessment. Three were eventually chosen: a modified Word Association Test, a short series of Thematic Apperception Test pictures and a written Self-Description. These were all given in group form after the questionnaires and intelligence tests.

The purpose of the Word Association Test was to explore spontaneous attitudes towards the officer's job. Words were chosen because of the likelihood of their being linked with such attitudes, including the anxieties aroused (Sutherland and Fitzpatrick, 1945). The Thematic Apperception Test (Murray et al., 1938) was expected to throw light on unconscious conflicts revolving around officer/men relations, those in authority and those who might be enemies. The Self-Description (Wittkower and Rodger, 1941) illuminated the candidate's insight into his strengths and weaknesses and how he handled hostile or favorable attitudes to himself.

The written responses to the projective tests had to be interpreted in a clinical manner and thus gave scope for large subjective influences. Nevertheless, it was soon proved that psychological assistants who had a fairly advanced psychological training in their university courses before the war could be trained to interpret the material along psycho-dynamic lines with a reasonable degree of consistency. This was a crucial finding, because the few experienced psychologists available were required for much-needed research and development. Furthermore, the projective tests were not intended to be used as independent measures but to provide leads to personality features requiring clinical assessment in psychiatric interview. Their limited scientific status was signified by calling them personality pointers. The pointers helped to identify early in the program those candidates on whom the psychiatrist's assessment would be particularly valuable. They threw light on assets and liabilities in a way that enabled interview time to be used most effectively. To produce the personality pointers for each candidate from the four hours of written tests took, on average, half an hour.

ADAPTING TO INCREASED DEMANDS

Candidates were given the status of cadets and shared a mess with the MTOs. There was little difficulty throughout the three days in maintaining an informal atmosphere consistent with the basic features of army discipline and custom. Badges of rank were replaced by identification numbers on arm-bands which, while convenient to board staff, indicated to all that judgments would be made on what the candidate was, not who he was.

The president with the two local COs formed the board proper, while the psychiatrist, psychologist and MTO played the part of expert advisers. The president interviewed all the candidates himself and the two visiting officers usually conducted a joint interview. The two psychiatrists each interviewed half the candidates, and the MTO and the psychologist used the tests described. At the final board meeting the independent interview judgments were placed alongside the data from the specialist advisers and a new composite judgment was made.

While this form of board was appropriate for working out test methods, it was not optimum for operational use. Accordingly, a deputy president and an extra MTO were added and the staff soon divided into two boards, each with its own team of president, MTO and psychiatrist. The psychologist and two psychological assistants worked with both psychiatrists. Each team could handle 16 candidates in three days so that a board with two teams could see 64 men a week.

A system of reporting, analytical only to the point of separating facts, interpretations and gradings, emerged. Though not ideal, it facilitated communication between military and specialist members, while allowing freer exploration of preconceptions and conflicting beliefs about "officer quality." Differences of opinion were not always resolvable. The difficulty of collating independent reports for the first time at the final conference was one of the main reasons which led to the abandonment of having completely independent roles for the judges.

The experimental board had only just begun to get a program under way when it emerged that 15 to 20 boards would have to be established within the next six months, each with a throughput of 80 to 100 candidates a week. The application of the new methods would not be possible unless the necessary staff could be secured and trained, and the testing program modified to meet such urgent and large-scale needs. To occupy the military roles—president, deputy president and MTOs—suitable officers could be found and trained; but filling the technical roles posed a problem. The psychiatrists' interviews would constitute the main bottleneck. Fortunately, the increasing skill of psychological assistants in making personality pointers enabled the psychiatrist to obtain a sufficient preview of the candidate's personality to distribute his interview time more economically, considerably increase the number of candidates he could see in a day and still feel a reasonable degree of confidence in his judgment.

With a staff of president, deputy president, two psychiatrists, assisted by two (later three) psychological assistants, the interview load could be carried. As regards the practical tests, the MTOs were increased to four. A trial program capable of extension to new boards with intakes of 40 was organized as follows: the psychological tests were confined to the first (half) day; on the next two days the president and deputy president each interviewed 20 candidates, being provided with the intelligence results and notes on the biographical questionnaire; the two psychiatrists each interviewed 20 candidates with the aid of the pointers. All four interviewers prepared reports by the end of the second day for the final board meeting next morning. The MTOs' tests proceeded as before, all candidates carrying out individually prescribed physical tests and taking part in both indoor and outdoor command situations.

This program was accepted by the army authorities and the decision was taken in April 1942 to convert existing CIBs to the new style and to add a number of new boards.

Operational Development and Expansion

The boards were brought under direct War Office control in order that officer selection could develop as a centrally co-ordinated activity. They were named War Office Selection Boards (OCTUs)—WOSBs for short. Simultaneously, the composition of the boards was altered. The psychiatrists and the MTOs were not members of the board but acted as advisers to a board which retained the composition of CIBs. Visiting members were dispensed with. Nonetheless, their presence had been valuable. They saw what was being attempted and took back to their units first-hand impressions of the work being done.

The changeover from old to new took place rapidly, staff being trained at the experimental board (renamed No. 1 WOSB) and at one of the earliest of the new boards to be established. There were 15 new boards at work by September 1942. There were not enough psychiatrists to have two per board. Commissioned psychologists were appointed, who interviewed the less problematic candidates so that only one psychiatrist became necessary.

The staff of the experimental board had a continuing concern with the inadequate nature of the tests used by the MTOs and with the feelings of the president and psychiatrist that their judgment would be improved if they themselves could see something of the candidates in action. Conversely, the MTOs needed to know something of the inner man so that their cross-sectional view could be better interpreted. The unsatisfactory system of bringing independent reports together for the first time at the final conference required revision.

THE LEADERLESS GROUP METHOD

The general difficulty with the MTOs' tests was that they had little or no coherent conceptual framework governing their content and sequence. The method of leaderless groups in which a group was left to its own devices in coping with a situation with which the MTO had confronted it, or which it set for itself, was conceived by W.R. Bion (Bion, 1946; Trist, 1985). Formal leadership was removed and leadership patterns were left to emerge through a series of group situations, beginning with the least structured and proceeding to more structured events. The aim of the leaderless group tests was to reproduce those aspects of an officer's job principally concerned with his approach to, and his relations with, others.

While other methods and interviews informed the testing officers to some extent about the quality of the candidate's social relations, the leaderless group method forced the candidate to reveal this quality directly in the here-and-now. The method made use of the candidate's anxiety to do well for himself, to further his own hopes and aspirations. In individual tests his desire to do better than other candidates presented no problem, but when he was put through tests as a member of a group without a leader, a problem was introduced. The anxiety to look after his own interests remained, but the MTO's instruction called into activity not individuals, but a group formed by those individuals. Moreover, no indication was given as to whether judgment would be on the performance of individuals or the performance of the group. The conflict for each individual candidate was that he could demonstrate his abilities only through the medium of others. This being true of everyone in the group, a common purpose was created, namely, to act towards one another so that each would have an opportunity to display himself.

There were two problems set by the leaderless group method—the real or social problem, i.e., to reconcile group purpose with individual aspirations, and the quasi-real or presented problem. Candidates direct their attention to the quasi-real problem which conceals the real problem, so that the latter is only vaguely sensed. The more that candidates accepted the quasi-real problem, the more could the MTO identify what was spontaneous in their behavior and through this get an indication of their cohesive and destructive tendencies. It was not the artificial test, but the real-life situation that the observers had to watch—the way in which a man's capacity for personal relationships stand up under the strain of his own and other men's fear of failure and desire for personal success (Bion, 1946).

The leaderless group tasks were set in a series intended to parallel phases in the formation of a group faced with a common task. These phases would overlap, but to separate them made observation easier. Groups of eight candidates were found to be best, though groups of 10 were manageable. The interplay of personalities was freer and more illuminating when the groups could be made as homogeneous as possible in regard to age, rank, arm, and length of service. A basic series of tests lasting about two-and-a-half hours was evolved to represent four phases:

Exploration. The phase of preliminary contact in which members of the group sized each other up and began to know each other, represented in mutual introductions in which each candidate took about three minutes to give personal particulars of himself. This led on to a free group discussion in which the group had to choose a subject which would make for a good argument and then discuss it, 30 minutes being allowed in all.

Competition. In this phase the group members were competing for dominance and the group got some experience of its members in leadership roles. This was represented in spontaneous situations in which several military problems were presented in quick succession, the MTO using the immediate outdoor surroundings as material. The situations were not complex enough to call for action by the group as a whole. It was up to each individual to declare his preferred method of participation (or non-participation).

Co-operation. Each individual had to learn that only by pooling of resources and setting aside self-centered attitudes and motives could a goal be reached. This was represented in the progressive group task which con-

sisted of a practical problem. Characteristically the group had to carry a
heavy and awkward load over a series of obstacles of increasing difficulty, in a military setting with an air of urgency. The group had to
cooperate to produce an acceptable plan and build an organization around
the most effective leadership it could produce. The group had to sustain
its activity over a period of time—30 to 45 minutes—to reach an objective.

Discipline. The individual had to identify himself with the group's decisions
and subordinate himself to a pattern of organization in which he had to
accept the role assigned to him. This was represented in the group game,
usually, between two groups, carrying a heavy object, competing against
each other for 20 to 30 minutes around an obstacle course.

THE OBSERVER TEAM

The leaderless group tests dealt with the general qualities of social relations
which concerned all members of the board. There was an advantage, therefore,
in their being observed by the full team of selectors—the president or deputy
president, psychiatrist and psychologist as well as the MTO. When a group of
observers watched the basic series it was almost impossible for them not to
discuss what they had seen and thus difficult to maintain strict independence.
With shared observations, differences in opinion were aired early on and this
was formalized in a "query conference" at the end of the basic series. Each
judge noted those candidates on whom his specialist attention would need to be
centered.

"The leaderless group method changed the entire character of the WOSB.
The board became a learning community which improved collective capacity
through the sharing of common here-and-now experiences of the candidates
instead of conducting acrimonious and unresolvable debates on independently
based judgments" (Trist, 1985). The creation of the observer team enhanced
the value of the special contribution which each member would make in the
final board conference. It greatly improved the basis for the collaboration of the
three types of judge, both in their feelings about each other's role and in their
common task. The shared observations indicated to each member his prejudices and biases. The comparisons of judgments on the same data did much to
keep standards similar amongst observers in the same team.

With candidates who failed there was a strong desire among board members
to advise them and to secure conditions in which they could develop or use
their assets to the best advantage of the army and themselves. Thus letters to
COs would explain the board's opinion and ask them to give these candidates

such facilities for gaining leadership experience as were available. A special training center was set up for immature candidates. Transfers to more appropriate jobs were suggested in the case of men of high ability who would never acquire the personal qualities needed in an officer. It appeared to be virtually impossible to sustain selection procedures without extending some form of guidance to those who failed. For general satisfaction a selection procedure had to be a two-way process in which the observer team got a lot out of the candidates and the latter, in turn, got something from the observer team.

As the number of WOSBs increased it was decided to set up near London a headquarters called the Research and Training Centre (RTC). It was desirable for the original group of psychiatrists and psychologists to be geographically close to the War Office where they could give help on policy questions affecting the WOSBs as a whole. Unhappily, the way the RTC was set up prevented the development of more refined assessment methods for the ordinary work of the boards. For example, it could not also function as an ordinary working WOSB and so directly encounter the emergent problems in regular selection. Access to neighboring boards could not provide suitable conditions for further development as the pressure of work was too great. The professional group at RTC became increasingly absorbed in planning follow-up and allied investigations. They had to devote a very large part of their time to an increasing range of selection problems to which the start of the WOSBs had given rise.

Attitude to the New WOSBs

Within a remarkably short period the new methods gained the almost unanimous approval of the other ranks. The opinion of candidates was sought by asking them to give, anonymously, their frank comments on the whole program. This was done after the testing was completed and while the board was sitting so that nothing said would be "used in evidence against them." These spontaneous comments showed a remarkable support for what the board was trying to achieve. Ninety-eight percent approved whole-heartedly of the new procedure.

Despite the fact that many COs were in sympathy with the aims of the board, there was, not unexpectedly, skepticism and hostility. This was minimized only when more officers could visit a board for a whole intake and go through the work with the president. Apart from negative attitudes of a more personal origin, resistance to the new methods could have been predicted because the role of COs in the selection task had not been clearly worked out— and certainly not with them. They were, in fact, being asked to accept a change introduced from above and one which was not in response to a need that they were experiencing directly at this stage of the war. The attitudes of the COs to the new methods was basic to their participation in the larger task of the production of officers.

The Crisis of Candidate Supply

The staff of the experimental selection board became aware that the task was not only to improve the quality of officer cadets by suitable selection methods but also to ensure that every soldier with officer potential should come to a board and that all men who reached minimum standards of suitability should be identified. It had been quite widely felt that a large number of good candidates were not available through COs discouraging them, directly or indirectly, from leaving their units. Many COs feared that if they gave up some of their best men they would seriously weaken their units as a fighting force. The staff of the experimental board could not directly remedy this situation, but they could ascertain to what extent it might be true.

The other armed services and the war industries were all being provided with leaders at the expense of the army. Compared with the first world war, the ratio of officers to other ranks was nearly doubled so that, from sources already creamed to some extent, far more officers had to be found. Indeed, anxiety was expressed as to whether the army could provide its own officers.

In the first four months of the experimental board the supply of candidates in the country as a whole was barely one-third of what was needed and in the catchment area of the board itself it was even less. A survey was made of the sources of candidates in a command area with the startling result that their numbers were absurdly small from the majority of units. Over two-thirds of the 700 independent units (Lieutenant Colonel or Major commands) provided no candidates in a 15-week period and 14 percent only one candidate, the proportion of units then decreasing as the number of candidates increased. The accepted, though tacit, convention was not to put candidates forward. Further analysis showed that the nearer a unit was to going overseas to take up a role in combat, the smaller the number of candidates it produced; the larger the unit, the smaller the proportion of candidates; and, the more candidates a unit sent to a selection board, the higher the proportion accepted (A.T.M., Wilson, 1951). Furthermore, units producing most officers usually had internal institutions to discover such candidates.

THE REGIMENTAL NOMINATION EXPERIMENT

Bion suggested that the knowledge the men had of each other should be used in finding candidates. If a CO was interested the men in the entire unit could be asked to give the names of those of their fellows whom they thought highly of and whom they would trust to lead them into action. Trist recognized this proposal as a use of sociometric principles (Moreno, 1934) and worked out a method of carrying it out, which became known as Regimental Nomination. It was based on the notion that whole battalions or equivalent units of good reputation should be awarded the privilege by the Army Commander of pre-selecting their WOSB candidates in such a way that they came forward in the name of the regiment. To secure this, officers, NCOs and men had all actively to participate. The suggested method would be additional to the usual one by which men became WOSB candidates exclusively by CO recommendation. Any NCO or man nominated by the new method would have the right to refuse his nomination. A necessary condition of success would be the complete co-operation of the CO, who would take the lead in launching the experiment in his unit. The nomination procedure would be simple and, in the long term, self-administered within the unit itself. All nominations would be made independently and without prior discussion under conditions approximating those of psychological group testing. Particularly for fully trained units which had been in existence for some time, the aim was to provide the army with a more efficient social technique of bringing its potential officers to the surface.

Sanction for a crucial experiment was sought and given at the highest level and thereafter at each level in the hierarchy down to the units invited to participate in the scheme. In these the CO invited his unit, as a regimental whole, to share with him the responsibility for nominating candidates. Each of the four units selected by the Army Commander had a good military reputa-tion. They were varied in their military function and in their state of readiness for action, and were representative of the general position regarding candidate supply. The nominating groups in each unit were of company size—between 100 and 200 men. There were 11 such groups among the four units selected for the experiment. A nominating group was seated indoors and split into pla-toons, or equivalent units, of 20 to 30 men. In the presence of representatives of the Army Commander and the WOSB organization, the CO explained the invitation of the former, the need for more officers, the nature of WOSBs, and the Regimental Nomination scheme. "To get our regimental candidates we are all going to vote: yourselves, your NCOs and your officers. We want to know if you can put up people so good that they do better than people who are put up in any other way. Choose good ones. You may have to fight under them. . . ." Under conditions of secrecy, each person was invited to write down the names of any individuals, first in his own platoon, and next from the rest of the company, whom he regarded as potential officers. He need nominate no one if he thought no one was suitable.

Two types of nominative information were available: how the individual was perceived as a potential officer from the viewpoints of different ranks in the whole company—privates, junior NCOs, senior NCOs and officers; how he was regarded by those closest to him in military life (all ranks in his platoon) and also by those at a greater distance (members of other platoons in the company). This gave six nominative criteria. All who received an appreciable measure of support on any three or more were identified and discussed at a unit conference at which the CO gave his opinion and his grading of officer potential. He then published throughout the unit the names of all those who had received this appreciable spread of support and invited them to go forward to a WOSB. Special arrangements were made to ensure that the examining WOSB could not identify candidates who came to it as a result of the regimental nomination procedure.

The percentage of the 114 regimental nomination candidates from the four selected units who passed WOSBs (54 percent) was not significantly different from those who came through the usual channels (56 percent). The pass rate was clearly related to the number of nominative criteria satisfied by the candidates as shown in Table 1. The supply of candidates from the four units through regimental nomination represented 6.8 percent of the unit strength compared with 0.1 percent per month through the usual procedures. In round figures, that is equivalent to 10 candidates from an average company nominating group of 150 men compared with two men per year. There was thus strong support for the view that the difficulty in the supply of candidates was not, as often stated, due to a lack of suitable material, but to the "in-group" mentality in field force units, which increased as preparedness to go overseas increased. Giving up some of its best men in the larger interest of the army was not popular in such units. A method of releasing this supply had been demonstrated which increased regimental pride. Together with the discovery of an unsuspected amount of officer material, it offset the COs' anxiety over being stripped of their best men. In any case, the training of key other-rank replacements would not take as long as that of officers.

Careful planning was required to show how selective, low profile implementation might best be possible, as well as further work on how to identify and approach suitable units. But, as the success of the experiment became known, the whole of a famous division and the whole of a technical corps asked for regimental nomination. Even though there was no selection of officers, only nomination of candidates and no change in the rights of COs, a complex situation developed at the highest level (Trist, 1985). The technical staff did not effectively represent to higher authority the dangers of implementing regimental nomination without further development. This led to a premature and widespread disclosure of the scheme, disputes about matters of protocol and an ensuing meeting of the full Army Council. The military members of the Army Council, who favored the adoption of regimental nomination in the interests of the army, were in a minority of four to six to political

TABLE 1   Regimental Nomination Candidates

Nominative criteria satisfied	6	5	4	3
WOSB pass rate (percent)	77	54	35	23

and civil administrative interests, who thought the scheme possibly subversive ("Soviets in the British Army"). Further reference to regimental nomination was banned. To make the best of this situation a scheme, known as Exercise By-Pass, was developed in the Directorate of Selection of Personnel. To get as many candidates as possible to WOSB before they went to field force units, unit boards were set up in Corps Training Centres. Officer members of these boards could consult NCOs informally. However, the extension of the WOSB system at home and overseas, in itself, largely solved the problem of supply. The fear that the army could no longer officer itself was not expressed again.

Evaluation and Its Problems

The establishment of WOSBs had immediate effects. There was a rapid increase in the supply of candidates, the average number rising from 2,000 during the first quarter of 1942 to over 6,000 in October of that year. In the three years in which the WOSBs operated, from mid-1942 to mid-1945, over 125,000 candidates were assessed in the United Kingdom of whom nearly 60,000 were accepted. During most of this period there were also many boards at work in the Middle East, Italy, and in North Africa, where of 12,700 candidates, 5,600 were accepted. A board working in the British Liberation Armies in Europe (1944–45) saw 1,500 candidates and accepted 900. Another group of boards in India selected a large number of officers, both British and Indian.

A marked change took place as the war progressed in the predominant type of candidate appearing before the boards. The candidates accepted in the United Kingdom were younger, had less service, but a higher standard of education. To deal with such changes there had to be modifications in technique, particularly in the content and conduct of the MTO's tests. It was one of the virtues of the WOSB methods that these could easily be effected.

DIFFICULTIES WITH THE EARLIER FOLLOW-UPS

Nevertheless, the need to bring boards rapidly into operation had unfortunate effects for the subsequent validation studies (Morris, 1949). The new boards had started before there was an agreed series of military tests. Boards developed their own idiom and to some extent their own techniques (Garforth, 1945; Harris, 1949). The difficulties over common standards between board members were greatly reduced by the introduction of the observer team, but wide differences between boards were known to exist. A common grading system was not introduced until some months after most boards had begun working and staff did not receive any common training in its use. Boards passed about the same percentage of candidates, but one would be less prone than another to award the higher gradings. The task of a board was not to discriminate at the top of the grading scale, but to find every possible officer. A high percentage of gradings, therefore, occurred in the area of marginal acceptances. In these circumstances it would have been desirable to use some form of profile assessment but it was not found possible to bring one into common use until late in the war. Apart from data collected by the psychologists, the only WOSB assessment available for follow-up purposes was the final grading on suitability.

After hostilities ceased in Europe a carefully designed experiment was conducted using the best and most experienced staff available, who were given an initial period of common training in reporting, and who adopted a standard personality profile. Two independent parallel boards, mutually incommunicado, simultaneously observed the same candidates doing the same tests. The average inter-correlation of the final grades of the two boards was 0.80; of the two presidents 0.65; psychiatrists 0.65; the MTOs 0.86 and the two psychologists in observer roles 0.87. The average inter-correlations showing the level of agreement between the different members—presidents, psychiatrists and MTOs—were 0.60. These figures, obtained under optimum conditions, show a satisfactory degree of reliability for work of this kind (Morris, 1949).

In making the comparison of gradings at boards with ratings of success after OCTU and after a campaign, the main problem was how to get the CO to give a reliable and valid report. Little previous work had been done on how to assess success in such a complex role as that of a junior officer and the problem proved to be in obtaining discrimination. A detailed report was obtained on each cadet or officer to be followed-up. The earlier follow-up studies included a questionnaire check list, a pen-picture, ratings and rankings and a discussion between the reporting officer and a follow-up interviewer to clear up ambiguities or disagreements.

The following results show how difficult it was to evaluate the work of the WOSBs. The first follow-up carried out soon after they had been started showed that the new boards, although passing the same proportion of candidates as the old, found significantly more above average and significantly fewer below average cadets as judged at the conclusion of OCTU training. In contrast to these findings, a follow-up conducted after the campaigns in North Africa and Italy showed officers selected by the old and new methods did not differ according to ratings given by their COs. The samples covered the earliest period of WOSB operation when the boards were learning their job. Nevertheless, the result did not "make sense." Was the method faulty?

CREATING AN OPERATIONAL FRAME OF REFERENCE

In these first field follow-ups the academically conventional approach to assessment failed to match the real-life conditions under which COs had to make judgments. A CO thought about his officers in two groups: those on whom he could rely and those on whom he could not rely. These latter had become problem officers whom he might have to remove from his unit. He regarded them as "unsatisfactory" and the rest as "satisfactory" about whom he did not have to bother. Among the satisfactory were a handful who might be promoted or sent on special assignments. These operational distinctions became the basis for an anthropologically derived rating scale. In the field follow-up after the liberation of France, the MTOs conducting the procedure (under Bowlby) asked each CO to rate all his officers so that the War Office could know directly the opinions of commanding officers in the field. This made every sense to them. They co-operated whole-heartedly. They never knew which officers in their units belonged to the follow-up sample.

With officers reported on after the liberation of France, the correlations between WOSB opinion and CO ratings were positive, though rather low. These correlations became higher when the youngest age groups were separately considered, i.e. board judgments were better on the younger candidates. Nearly all of these would have passed through new Boards—which had become more experienced and presumably more efficient as the war went on. On the other hand, the correlations between gradings given at OCTUs and CO ratings were negligible. Such complexities in evaluation were not unique to the WOSB scheme (OSS Assessment Staff, 1948).

As the war progressed more officers appeared in the field in reinforcement roles—a role more difficult than that of being an officer in a unit with which one had gone abroad. Of particular interest was the finding that the quality of reinforcements to units after battle was maintained, whereas in the first world war it deteriorated.

Overall, the important thing to the Army higher authorities was that only 12 percent of officers were unsatisfactory—unable to do their job. The COs were pleased to be able to say this. The War Office was delighted and inclined to leave the development of more precise follow-up methods to the future.

Later Developments

NEW TASKS FOR THE BOARDS

The impact on the army of a machinery which could investigate the individual in a way helpful both to him and to the army was not long in being felt at the boards. Within a few months of their being established, a wide range of assessment tasks was brought to them, each of which had to be carefully reviewed by the senior staff at RTC to ascertain what was involved. The particular kind of help requested varied from merely giving advice to working out a new procedure which was then executed by one or more WOSBs. A parallel scheme was evolved for selecting officer cadets for the women's auxiliary service; another to select officers for permanent commissions in the Regular Army. From time to time boards were used, or set up, to assess officers for various types of work such as paratroops, psychological warfare, the civil administration of occupied territories and special operations—the equivalent of the OSS in the U.S. (Morgan, 1955). A few boards were used to advise on suitable employment or disposal of officers with adverse reports and officers who had had psychiatric breakdowns. Towards the end of the war several boards were adapted, and a few specially created, to advise on the employment of both officers and NCOs who became surplus to establishment with the changing course of the war, and to give guidance to returned officer prisoners of war.

A nation-wide review of all engineers was undertaken on behalf of the Ministry of Labour, screening 130,000 registrants of whom 31,500 were interviewed and 12,500 accepted for a pool from which candidates for technical commissions in the services were drawn. A specially difficult task was the selection of 17-year-old schoolboy applicants for short university courses in science subjects (2,200 candidates, 1,170 accepted) and candidates for engineering cadetships in the army or navy (980 candidates, 620 accepted). Owing to the youth and under-developed characters of the applicants, the assessment of their potential officer quality presented an unusually difficult problem. Accordingly, a longer and more detailed procedure was required, because an order of merit had to be produced regardless of the particular board they happened to attend. Successful candidates had to be batched according to their knowledge and ability and sent to the appropriate university which was supplied with a report on each candidate's competence and educational background.

In the course of these additional tasks, the research staff were sometimes able to develop, as experiments of opportunity, such new assessment tools as real-object performance tests to explore the interests and motivation of candidates for engineering cadetships. Opportunity was at last on hand to develop profile methods of assessment and to facilitate a common standard of decision-making at ordinary WOSBs. Most of these new tasks were necessarily undertaken before any evaluation became available of the methods used for the work the WOSBs had originally been set up to do. Had the WOSBs not, in general, satisfied the expectations and needs of the army, the candidates themselves and the civilian community, it is improbable that they would have become involved in such a wide array of problems and tasks.

THE WIDER IMPACT

The Royal Navy, the Royal Marines, the Royal Air Force, the National Fire Service and several of the Dominion and Allied armies later adopted the new methods in whole or in part. Many organizations with similar selection problems closely followed the work of the boards. Experimental procedures were tried out for those within the central government sector. The Civil Service modelled part of its reconstruction and post-war selection procedure for administrative trainees on WOSB procedures (Wilson, N.A.B., 1948; Davies, 1969). A number of industrial firms subsequently began to use similar methods in recruiting trainees for various grades of management (Bridger and Isdell-Carpenter, 1947; Munro Fraser, 1947; Rice, 1961). More than 40 years later multiple assessment methods, albeit different, but traceable to war-time methods used in WOSBs, continue in use for the appraisal of individual potential (Anstey, 1977; Dulewicz and Fletcher, 1982). Assessment centers have gained widespread acceptance throughout the world and constitute one of the most extensive, if expensive, practices for attracting, and evaluating the qualifications of, scarce human resources.

The readiness with which the methods of the WOSBs were elsewhere adopted indicated the disparate and widespread need for advances to be made in the field of personality assessment. The specialist staff concerned with their development were surprised that visitors wanted to take over the new methods with little, if any, preliminary critical inquiry regarding their appropriateness for selection tasks other than finding potential officers. Both the constitution of the boards and the nature of their methods played a part in creating this enthusiastic attitude at a time when scientific tests of their value were still not yet to hand. Their constitution seemed specially attractive because some of the resources of the psychological sciences were incorporated into the board, yet responsibility for decisions concerning selection remained vested, and manifestly so, in the senior representative of the employing authority. The other members of the board acted as advisers who provided special evidence. All members, however, were integral parts of the whole; the contributions of each had to be fully discussed with the others—in a group. Hence there was a high degree of sharing among members of each others' special knowledge and experience. There were many reasons for the wide appeal of this particular way of integrating the wisdom of institutional representatives who recognized intuitively the kinds of person their institution could successfully employ, with the skills of experts who contributed a more general understanding of human personality.

The mutually educative and mutually supportive nature of the roles of regimental and expert members was reflected in the high morale of all board teams, sustained over long periods of time, often under intense work pressures. The other main source of attraction was that the methods used brought out the personality of the candidate in a direct way. Observers saw him respond to a variety of simple practical situations in which he had to deal with people and things spontaneously. In such situations the behavior of the candidate seemed often to speak for itself. Aspects were seen which would never have been revealed in interview. Interviews, however, were necessary to add a historical perspective to a contemporary one.

The choice of officers in any army is a markedly conservative process. It was a very considerable event for an army in the middle of a war to take such radical steps as to introduce psychiatrists and psychological tests into a procedure for choosing its officers and to allow a novel type of military institution to be created for this purpose. Collaboration between expert and administrator and its maintenance on a constructive basis is one of the pressing problems in large organizations. WOSB experience has yielded a wealth of insights and findings relevant to all those who must address these problems.

References

Ansbacher, H.L. 1941. "German Military Psychology." *Psychological Bulletin*, 38:370–92.

Anstey, E. 1977. "A 30-year Follow-Up of the CSSB Procedure with Lessons for the Future." *Journal of Occupational Psychology*, 50:149–59.

Bion, W.R. 1946. "The Leaderless Group Project." *Bulletin of the Menninger Clinic*, 10:77–81.

Bridger, H. and R. Isdell-Carpenter. 1947. "Selection of Management Trainees." *Industrial Welfare*, 29:177–81.

Davies, J.G.W. 1969. *The Method II System of Selection: Report of the Committee of Enquiry*. London: Her Majesty's Stationery Office.

Dulewicz, V. and C. Fletcher. 1982. "The Relationship between Previous Experience, Intelligence and Background Characteristics of Participants and their Performance in an Assessment Centre." *Journal of Occupational Psychology*, 55:197–207.

Garforth, F.I. de la P. 1945. "War Office Selection Boards (OCTU)." *Journal of Occupational Psychology*, 19:97–108.

Harris, H. 1949. *The Group Approach to Leadership Testing*. London: Routledge and Kegan Paul.

Moreno, J.L. 1934. *Who Shall Survive? A New Approach to the Problem of Human Inter-Relations.* New York: Nervous and Mental Disease Publishing Company.

Morgan, W.J. 1955. *Spies and Saboteurs.* London: Gollancz.

Morris, B.S. 1949. "Officer Selection in the British Army 1942–1945." *Occupational Psychology,* 23:219–34.

Munro Fraser, J. 1947. "New Type Selection Boards in Industry." *Occupational Psychology,* 21:170–78.

Murray, H.A. et al. 1938. *Explorations in Personality.* New York: Oxford University Press.

OSS Assessment Staff. 1948. *Assessment of Men.* New York: Reinhart.

Rees, J.R. 1945. *The Shaping of Psychiatry by War.* London: W.W. Norton.

Rice, A.K. 1961. "Selection for Management." *Secretaries Chronicle,* 37:306–08; 352–54.

Semeonoff, B. and E.L. Trist. 1958. *Diagnostic Performance Tests.* London: Tavistock Publications.

Sutherland, J.D. and G.A. Fitzpatrick. 1945. "Some Approaches to Group Problems in the British Army." *Sociometry,* 8:205–17.

Trist, E.L. 1985. "Working with Bion in the Forties: The Group Decade." In *Bion and Group Psychotherapy,* edited by M. Pines. London: Routledge and Kegan Paul.

Vernon, P.E. and J.B. Parry. 1949. *Personnel Selection in the British Forces.* London: University of London Press.

Wilson, A.T.M. 1951. "Some Aspects of Social Process." *Journal of Social Issues,* Supplement Series No. 5.

Wilson, N.A.B. 1948. "The Work of the Civil Service Selection Board." *Journal of Occupational Psychology,* 22:204–12.

Wittkower, E. and T.F. Rodger. 1941. "Memorandum on an Experiment in Psychological Testing Applied to the Selection of Officers." Unpublished.

Harold Bridger

The Discovery of the Therapeutic Community

The Northfield Experiments*

Introduction

One of the most important achievements of social psychiatry during World War II was the discovery of the therapeutic community. The idea of using all the relationships and activities of a residential psychiatric center to aid the therapeutic task was first put forward by Wilfred Bion in 1940 in what became known as the Wharncliffe Memorandum, a paper to his former analyst, John Rickman, then at the Wharncliffe neurosis center of the war-time Emergency Medical Service (EMS). When he tried to put this idea into practice Rickman got virtually nowhere in face of severe resistance among medical and administrative staff. It entailed a radical change in staff/patient relations which produced a figure/ground reversal in the traditional authoritarian hospital. In order to achieve active patient participation in treatment, power was to be redistributed away from its monopolization by the doctor and shared by other staff and patients in appropriate ways.

An occasion to test the efficacy of the therapeutic community idea arose in the autumn of 1942 at Northfield Military Hospital in Birmingham when psychiatrists were invited to try out new forms of treatment which would enable as many neurotic casualties as possible to be returned to military duties rather than be discharged to civilian life. Rickman, now in the Royal Army Medical Corps, had been posted to this hospital for some weeks when Bion joined him from the War Office Selection Boards (WOSBs).

The therapeutic community created by Bion in the training wing (TW), of which he was in charge, existed only six weeks before it was stopped by the Directorate of Army Psychiatry. The scheme had begun to succeed, enabling a number of alienated individuals to re-engage with the soldier's role. The chaos created, however, was intolerable to the wider hospital staff who clung to the traditional medical model. This brief project became known as the First Northfield Experiment.

*A new paper presenting the first comprehensive account of these developments.

A year or so later, after discussion between Bion and Ronald Hargreaves (the anchor man throughout the war in the Directorate of Army Psychiatry), the scheme was revived in a new form. It was decided to put the TW under non-medical direction. Having had relevant experience in the WOSB organization, I was chosen as the officer in charge. Thus came into being the Second Northfield Experiment which for the first time embodied the therapeutic community idea in a whole organization. The success of the scheme had a profound effect on the civil resettlement units for repatriated prisoners of war, which followed on from it, and on many post-war developments. A new paradigm had been born.

Out of a personal, historical description I will draw some key principles affecting the nature of therapeutic communities as open systems, considered as part of, and interacting with, the wider society. I shall distinguish such principles from those which govern a community endeavoring to operate as a relatively "closed system," that is, one regarded as sufficiently independent to allow most of its problems to be analyzed with reference to its internal structure and without reference to its external environment.

The experience to be revisited was the first attempt at creating a therapeutic community as an open-system by intention and not just by accident. It was conducted during World War II at a critical phase of the war as an integral part of army psychiatry. I shall be reviewing that endeavor with the insights, knowledge and experience of the more than 40 years which have followed that beginning.

The country-at-war emphasized an environment which, at one level, could not be denied by the professional staff and patients of a hospital. Yet returning people to health in that setting posed considerable problems and difficult decisions for both staff and patients. All were military personnel with the professional staff in various therapeutic roles. The issues arising were not dealt with explicitly but appeared in stressful and rationalized forms, as when decisions had to be made concerning the return of men to the armed forces or to civilian life. It is important to consider how far the professional staff member's own purposes, values and approach to treatment were affected by the war-time environment. In the community and organizational life of today such problems and choices may not appear so sharply, but they are just as real and critical.

Northfield I

The Philosophy

While Bion and his colleagues at the WOSBs (Bion, 1946) were coming forward with new ideas about groups, some serious problems were affecting military psychiatric hospitals dealing with breakdowns in battle and in units. The withdrawal of psychiatric casualties back to base and then to hospital seemed to be associated with a growing proportion of patients being returned to civilian life. It was as if "getting one's ticket," as it was called, had replaced the objective of hospital treatment—to enable rehabilitated officers, NCOs and men to return to the army. Even at one of the largest hospitals with 800 beds, Northfield Hospital near Birmingham, where the military medical staff appointed to develop their own treatment methods were highly qualified psychoanalysts and psychiatrists, the TW to which patients were transferred for review before leaving for the army or "civvy street" had no better statistics than the rest.

Bion was appointed to the command of the TW to develop his own approach based not only on the experience gained in WOSBs but on the Wharncliffe Memorandum in which he had adumbrated the idea of a therapeutic community. He undertook a double role as officer commanding the TW and as psychiatrist helping his men to face the working through of issues following their treatment and to make decisions about their immediate future. Returning to the army might include changes of role, unit and conditions of work; returning to civilian life might entail relocation or learning a new job. Either course meant confronting not only the conscious and unconscious attitudes and desires of individuals, but the values and norms that had been established in the TW and hospital as part of the war effort.

Bion has made two public statements about the First Northfield Experiment, one with Rickman (1943) and one (1946) in an issue of the *Bulletin of the Menninger Clinic* devoted to Northfield. The following extract from the latter sets out his objectives, his approach and his views on the meaning of his success/failure:

> An observer with combatant experience could not help being struck by the great gulf that yawned between the life led by patients in a psychiatric hospital, even when supposed to be ready for discharge, and the military life from which their breakdown had released them. Time and again treatment appears to be, in the broadest sense, sedative; sedative for doctors and patients alike. Occupational therapy meant helping keep the patients occupied—usually on a kindergarten level. Some patients had individual interviews; a few, usually the more spectacular, were dosed with hypnotics. Sometimes a critic might be forgiven for wondering whether these were intended to enable the doctor to go to sleep.
>
> It thus seemed necessary to bring the atmosphere of the psychiatric hospital into closer relationship with the functions it ought to fulfill. Unfortunately for the success of any attempt to do this, psychiatry has already accepted the doubtful analogy of physical maladies and treatments as if they were in fact similar to neurotic disorders. The apparatus of the psychiatric hospital, huge buildings,

doctors, nurses and the rest, together provide a magnificent smoke screen into which therapists and patients alike disappear when it becomes evident that someone may want to know what social function is being fulfilled, in the economy of a nation at war, by this aggregate of individuals.

It must of course be remembered that in a psychiatric hospital there are collected all those men with whom ordinary military procedures have failed to cope. Briefly, it was essential first to find out what was the ailment afflicting the community, as opposed to the individuals composing it, and next to give the community a common aim. In general all psychiatric hospitals have the same ailment and the same common aim—to escape from the batterings of neurotic disorder. Unfortunately the attempt to get this relief is nearly always by futile means—retreat. Without realizing it, doctors and patients alike are running away from the complaint.

The first thing then was to teach the community (in this case the TW) to seek a different method of release. The flight from neurotic disorder had to be stopped; as in a regiment, morale had to be raised to a point where the real enemy could be faced. The establishment of morale is of course hardly a prerequisite of treatment; it is treatment, or a part of it. The first thing was for the officer in charge not to be afraid of making a stand himself; the next to rally about him those patients who were not already too far gone to be steadied. To this end discussions were carried out with small groups. In these the same freedom was allowed as is permitted in any form of free association; it was not abused. These small groups were similar in organization and appearance to the leaderless group tests, known as group discussions, which had already been used, though for a different purpose, in the WOSBs.

As soon as a sufficient number of patients had in this way been persuaded to face their enemy instead of running away from it, a daily meeting of half-an-hour was arranged for the whole TW consisting of between 100 and 200 men. These meetings were ostensibly concerned only with the organization of the activities of the wing. The wing by now had been split up into a series of voluntary groups whose objects varied from learning dancing to studying the regulations governing army pay. In fact the problems of organization, of course, hinged on the problems of personal relationship. Lost tools in the handicraft section, defective cinema apparatus, permission to use the local swimming baths, the finding of a football pitch, all these matters came back to the same thing, the manipulation and harmonization of personal relationships. As a result almost immediately these big meetings as well as the small ones spontaneously became a study of the intra-group tensions and this study was established as the main task of the whole group and all smaller groups within it.

As a result the group began to think, and a deputation voiced the thought, that 80% of the members of the TW were "skrim-shankers," "work-shys," malingerers and the rest, and ought to be punished. A month before the TW had complained indignantly that inmates of a psychiatric hospital were regarded by the rest of the community as just these things. It was disconcerting, but a revelation of what psychiatry could mean, when the psychiatrist refused to accept this wholesale diagnosis and simple proposal of punishment as the appropriate form of therapy, as a sound solution of a problem which has troubled society since its commencement. The therapeutic occupation had to be hard thinking and not the abreaction of moral indignation. Within a month of the start of this metier these patients began to bear at least a recognizable resemblance to soldiers.

Throughout the whole experiment certain basic principles were observed. In order of their importance they are set down here even though it involves repetition:

- The objective of the wing was the study of its own internal tensions, in a real life situation, with a view to laying bare the influence of neurotic behavior in producing frustration, waste of energy, and unhappiness in a group.
- No problem was tackled until its nature and extent had become clear at least to the greater part of the group.
- The remedy for any problem thus classified was only applied when the remedy itself had been scrutinized and understood by the group.
- Study of the problem of intra-group tensions never ceased—the day consisted of 24 hours.
- It was more important that the method should be grasped, and its rationale, than that some solution of a problem of the wing should be achieved for all time. It was not our object to produce an ideal training wing. It was our object to send men out with at least some understanding of the nature of intra-group tensions and, if possible, with some idea of how to set about harmonizing them.
- As in all group activities the study had to commend itself to the majority of the group as worth while and for this reason it had to be the study of a real life situation.

One of the difficulties facing a psychiatrist who is treating combatant soldiers is his feeling of guilt that he is trying to bring them to a state of mind in which they will have to face dangers, not excluding loss of life, that he himself is not called upon to face. A rare event, but one that does occur, is when an officer is called upon to stop a retreat which should not be taking place. His prominence at such a time will certainly mean that he will be shot at by the enemy; in extreme cases he may even be shot at by his own side. Outside Nazi Germany psychiatrists are not likely to be shot for doing their job, though of course they can be removed from their posts. Any psychiatrist who attempts to make groups study their own tensions, as a therapeutic occupation, is in today's conditions stopping a retreat and may as a result be shot at. But he will lose some of his feeling of guilt.

In conclusion it must be remembered that the study of intra-group tensions is a group job. Therefore, so long as the group survives, the psychiatrist must be prepared to take his own disappearance from the scene in not too tragic a sense. Once the rout is stopped even quite timid people can perform prodigies of valor so that there should be plenty of people to take his place.

Abrupt Termination

Within six weeks Bion had succeeded dramatically in getting the large majority of the men in the TW to re-engage with the soldier's role and to return to military duties. But there was a price. The disorder created on the way so disturbed the rest of the hospital that the experiment was abruptly terminated by War Office order. Patrick de Maré (1985) who was on the psychiatric staff at the time comments as follows:

> Bion saw the large meeting of 100–200 people as the main trunk of the tree which could explore the tensions of the smaller activity groups—once he could persuade them to meet—which he arranged, partly by persuasion through small group meetings of chosen members, and partly by simply issuing an order to parade every day at 12:10 p.m. for announcements and other business of the TW. The result of this radical approach was that it produced a cultural clash with the hospital military authorities. The fear that Rickman's and Bion's approach would lead to anarchy and chaos occasioned War Office officials to pay a lightning visit at night. The chaos in the hospital cinema hall, with newspaper- and condom-strewn floors, resulted in the immediate termination of the project.
>
> I personally helped Rickman and Bion to pack. Clearly, Bion was put out by these events. Rickman, on the other hand, merely exclaimed unrepentantly and unperturbedly: "Pon my soul!" in the high-pitched tone he sometimes adopted in mock surprise.

The notorious indiscipline, slackness and aggressive untidiness of the unit which Bion took over was one form of showing him and the review panel how unsuitable it was for returning any of its members to the army. Main (1983) among others ascribes Bion's premature departure to the inability of the commanding officer and his professional and administrative staff to tolerate the early weeks of chaos. He was only partially correct. Bion was facing the TW and the hospital professional staff with the responsibility for distinguishing between their existence and purpose as a military organization and their individual beliefs that in the majority of cases health entailed a return to civilian life.

The degree of success Bion achieved in that six weeks demonstrates not only the validity of the principles he and Rickman had evolved but says even more for the double professional approach he had employed: he was in uniform, an officer in the organization (i.e., the army) confronting his men with the state of their unit; he was also a professional psychiatrist consulting with these same men in assessing their condition and deciding with them their future in a nation at war.

Lessons

On succeeding Bion to the command of the TW and making my own analysis of the situation, there seemed to me to be critical lessons to be derived from his "sacking." While he had established his own approach, he had not appraised the effect this would have on the very different psychiatric and organizational approaches of his colleagues. In my discussions with him between the time of his leaving and my appointment, it became clear that his philosophy, value system, technical and organizational appreciations were poles apart from those of the other psychiatrists and medical administrators then at Northfield. This is not to say that it was Bion v. the rest. There were differences between the others' approaches too but, in general, they were consistent in their aim of assessing the present and future life needs of the individual regardless of hospital, army or war needs. As one of them said to his patients in a first group session, "I want you to look on me as you would the doctor in a white coat and not as someone in uniform." With this view Rickman and Bion voiced their total disagreement.

Foulkes, who came to Northfield later, began by using the small group setting as a way in which the problems of any one individual could be observed and reflected upon by other patients, so that an interactive group therapeutic process was created. I was able to enlist his full cooperation in working with activity groups where the strength and persistence of the forces operating towards the attainment, distortion or avoidance of group goals demonstrated to him their relevance for treatment in the military setting. He was to say later (Foulkes, 1964): "The changes which went on in both patients and staff were nothing short of revolutionary." His part in subsequent developments has been described by de Maré (1983). These experiences played an important part in forming his approach after the war which led to the establishment of the Institute for Group Analysis (Foulkes, 1964).

The introduction of change processes requires a search for a common understanding of purpose and methods. While only a few of the likely consequences may be predictable, it is important to explore the implications of any steps envisaged. A forum or "mini-scientific society" needs to be set up in which a collegiate climate allows these explorations to take place. What is needed are conditions and circumstances "good enough," to use Winnicott's (1965) term, to effect the transition.

Bion was fully aware in his organizational and professional roles of the central importance of the country at war as a critical environmental force which had implications for the internal worlds and defenses of his men. But he neglected—and was indeed somewhat disparaging of—the more immediate environment of the hospital-as-a-whole and the traditional reactions of the bureaucratic aspects of the military machine.

The commanding officer at that time was, by profession, a psychoanalyst who perceived his task as maintaining co-operation between the professional and administrative functions in the hospital. Bion, in contrast, demanded that the external organization, as the environment of his unit, should tolerate the forces and pressures which his efforts and ideas might release. He expected people to see for themselves that what was happening was a microcosm of the tasks and problems facing military hospitals as a whole. As a Major commanding tanks in the first world war and a psychiatrist in the second, he had shown a vast range of capabilities. But he could expect too much of his immediate environment. In addition, he did not recognize, or perhaps did not accept, that it was his task to take the hospital environment into account just as much as he had taken the army and the country at war so very seriously. Bion, in my view, was not at ease with the group as an open system. He was not at home with the implications of ecological change in groups, institutions and communities (Bridger, 1982).

Northfield II

Orientation

So far as I am aware, the term "therapeutic community" was first coined in connection with this second experiment which I initiated over the period 1944/45. A large number of people contributed to its development, not least the transient population of officers, NCOs and men who learned to take responsibility for their own return to health. In so doing, they found that the *process* of creating and developing the community enabled them to make full use of the resources it made available to them.

Following Bion's departure, Ronald Hargreaves had approached me and discussed the possibility of my taking over command of the TW. I was not a psychiatrist or psychologist but had held a command, was an educationalist and teacher by profession and had extensive experience of the group approaches developed at the WOSBs. My remit was to understand the group and organizational processes that were going on. Although it was not remotely like the field command from which I had come, Northfield was a chance to test out the ideas I had gained in an organization with a very different mission. In one sense I welcomed the opportunity; in another I was quietly terrified, since I had no idea of what a mental hospital was like and felt as if I had suddenly been deskilled.

My posting was to take place only when the last commanding officer had been replaced by a medical CO, professionally a pathologist, but with regular army command experience. In the culture of the army, when trouble in any form arises in a unit leading to the transfer of the central figure in the storm, it is almost invariably accompanied by the transfer of the accountable senior officer. I remember thinking that the hospital staff might also be wondering what was likely to happen when a regular officer and a field officer were replacing the psychiatric specialists who had occupied these roles before. As I discovered later, they had expected a law and order campaign!

In the meantime, I was to acclimatize myself by visiting other military psychiatric hospitals and neurosis centers in the EMS. I also read a book on the "Peckham Experiment" (Pearse and Crocker, 1943) which described an *unintentional* therapeutic community that had grown up in Peckham, South London, in the 1930s. It arose from an attempt by biologists, physiologists and others to monitor a number of health related factors over the long term. The subjects were local families prepared to volunteer, as families, to take part in a program of regular tests. Originally a swimming-pool was the main draw—only family units could join. While fulfilling its part of the bargain in relation to the tests, over time the community developed a life of its own. I was struck by the emphasis laid by the Peckham staff on working with those who are prepared to work with you—rather than on the use of some established form of sampling technique; and on using the swimming-pool, consciously or unconsciously, as a focus for the families who accepted. These families and the development process they set up represented the community as a whole at any one time.

My discussions with Bion encouraged me to build on my own capabilities and not to attempt a follow-on of his experiment in the restricted area of the TW. I decided to work in some dynamic form with the institution-as-a-whole, while also being prepared to consult with those parts of it which showed a readiness to take some responsibility on to themselves for creating an entity which could grow.

In teaching mathematics, that frequently unpopular subject, I had always searched for growing-points on which to build and had used various kinds of institution that could draw on real-life interests and yet have mathematical thinking inherent in them, e.g., a school Stock Exchange. Similarly in my battery command we had overcome the difficulty of getting men to read and digest battery orders by publishing them accompanied by "battery disorders." The latter were a set of cartoons prepared by a talented corporal, which could not be appreciated without reading the orders first. Only later did I come to learn how these transitional systems linked up with Winnicott's (1971) work on transitional objects in psychoanalytic theory and treatment.

Of the many experiences which contributed to my orientation I would like to compare two hospitals which influenced the strategy and practice I eventually formulated. The first, Mill Hill, a neurosis center in the EMS, seemed to me a large hive housing a conglomerate of every type of treatment—physical, psychotherapeutic and psycho-socio-therapeutic, where the patients seemed incidental. In Maxwell Jones's ward everyone was taking part and shared in the various therapeutic tasks—but it was a relatively closed system and centered on Maxwell Jones himself. I was later to compare his approach to that of Joshua Bierer, who also used a dependency closed-system relationship in his ward at Northfield as the setting for his therapeutic work. After the war, of course, Maxwell Jones had much more scope to develop hospital-wide activities of which he has written fully (1968).

The second hospital, Dumfries in Scotland, was not as large but it seemed more like a well-managed workshop or depot. Although not the CO, the person at the center of things was Major Elizabeth Rosenberg, later better known as Elizabeth Zetzel, the psychoanalyst. She encouraged activities in every form, especially those which patients could run with the help of central resources—a hospital newspaper, for example. It was noticeable that care was taken to encourage what one might call the "recovering" patient to draw the newer ones into the various groups—when they were ready for it.

This experience reinforced my choice of the hospital-as-a-whole as the frame of reference for the work to come. I decided to adopt what I called the "double-task" approach, with one task located at the level of the hospital as an institution and the other at the level of those parts which showed leadership in developing relevant creative work. This leadership had to include a readiness to review the way the part was working.

Entry and Joint Planning

I reported to the CO of Northfield with some trepidation, wondering whether my half-formulated ideas would ever take root. Two divisional psychiatrists, Emmanuel Miller and Alfred Torrie, gave me every support in getting the design started, as did Tom Main when he replaced them. The new CO and I had, together, to settle down, to meet the professional staff of the different disciplines and to learn about the hospital as a whole. Foulkes and others invited me to observe their group sessions. I had discussions with nurses, social workers, administrators, occupational therapists and indeed every section of the staff, including building and maintenance engineers. Learning about the various systems and the role of those who operated them, in whatever form or at whatever level, allowed me to appreciate the prevailing, and indeed conflicting, cultures. At this early stage I could not know how they all hung together, but it was important to experience the confusion of a newcomer and gain some sense of what the whole place was about. I learned, for example, that while devolution to wards, in almost every respect, had its advantages, the atmosphere of live and let live was more apparent in some wards than others. Politics within and between the professional and administrative staffs left much to be desired.

While I would assume command of the TW it was agreed that I should also undertake a role involving special responsibility for the hospital-as-a-whole in a social process sense. This role would be that of social therapist thus distinguishing it from my unit command. The respective offices for myself and my two staffs would be distinct and separate. I proposed a drastic reformulation in the hospital layout. Influenced by the Peckham Experiment and recognizing the social gap in ward, professional and administrative relationships, I suggested that, without reducing the number of beds, the ward in the very center of the hospital be cleared and named the "Hospital Club." A meeting of representatives from each ward was held to explain the move. They were asked to discuss equipment and organizing methods. This was the only positive action regarding the club taken by the staff. My social therapy office was, however, close by and so were the offices of staff related to that role.

I explained to all staff groups and departments that I wished to create some identifiable equivalents of the hospital-as-a-whole with its mission and recommended the following steps:

- Staff seminars to explore what was intended by social therapy and what the implications might be.
- Independent professional discussions, e.g., psychiatrists, nurses.
- Ward meetings for exploring the implications of "external effects"—the impact of internal stresses on the wider environment.
- Greater emphasis by all activity supervisors on changing the pattern of relationships with patients from one of prescription to one of watching for initiatives on their part and responding to them.
- To make the hospital club with its deliberate emptiness, but space for potential development, into an arena which represented the patient's own personality and social gaps within his "life space."

When the various steps were agreed, a series of staff discussions was begun and gradually the empty hospital club made its presence felt. It took a little while for the representatives' meeting to be arranged—not because of finding appropriate people but because each ward would be asked to contribute from its recreational armory. Already talk and feelings were beginning to flow within and between wards. The various staffs ranged in their attitudes from highly skeptical to highly interested.

Things did not happen at once. Growth was "horticultural." The activity patterns across the hospital were more tree-like, with branches in all directions, than representing any tidy curriculum or program. Even when a rich array of societal endeavors became established, many would fall into decline, be abandoned or wrecked and then rebuilt, depending on the population and the different needs or states or illness. There was never any chance to say, "Now we have arrived!" In this sense the therapeutic community became far healthier than many business organizations. The individuals comprising the former might be sick, mad or bad; those of the latter might be sane and physically healthy; but institutions are not the same as the sum of the individuals comprising them. We were continually learning and relearning this at Northfield.

Returning to the club, the cumulative awakening of interest led, not to a meeting of ward representatives to reach some mutually agreed business-like arrangement but to a protest meeting which I was summoned to attend. The protest, with full and prepared arguments, was to ask why we were wasting public money and space in wartime—money and space that could be put to so many good uses! I agreed and suggested that we work out what could best be done with the resources of the club and how, since they were ours to do with as we wished, we could use them for the war effort quite directly.

Without giving a blow-by-blow account it is difficult to convey the tremendous energy and directive ability that can be generated when it becomes possible to find a transitional setting through which insights from therapy can be allied with social purpose and satisfaction. One of the most critical boundaries crossed was when the ebb and flow of social change led towards serious patient/community efforts on the part of those "recovering." They began to share responsibility for those entering the admission ward and to care for those who might benefit from the empathy and the experience of those who had been through it. The growth of the hospital newspaper, the external schools' repair teams and many other activities not only facilitated the interaction between outer society and inner struggles but were themselves workshops for self-review of the forces and emotions affecting the life and work of the groups.

The Community After Eight Months

After eight months I was able to make an overall assessment of the position reached. The large majority of men coming into Northfield say "I am browned off with everybody and everything," "I am fed up with the Army," "I seem to have lost confidence in myself," "I hate being pitied." Let us trace the progress of one such man. He enters the admission ward in the company of a few others. They are met by the nurse and a group of patients whose "selected activity" is to act as receptionists and guides. After the allotment of beds, they are joined by the ward psychiatrist. Each man is handed a program for his first three days and a copy of a magazine produced by the patients called "Introducing you to Northfield." He is requested to read it, discuss it and ask questions. The receptionist group then splits up to take the newcomers on a tour of the hospital, so that the contents of the magazine come alive.

They visit the hospital club—run entirely by patients who have selected this as their activity. They see patients working on the newspaper in their own offices; the band practicing for dances and socials; men painting scenery and arranging lights for stage shows; gardens and gardeners; a tennis court in use; the sports facilities; building construction and the selected activities yard, where painting, sculpture, handicrafts of all kinds, carpentry and radio construction are taking place. They see and enter the ever-open doors of contact officers, welfare workers, etc., who are there to help them at any time.

They see all these activities as contributing to a total pattern. They hear from patients that these are part of treatment. They see and hear that in the selected activities yard, while each patient is making something for his wife, child or himself, there is an overall project in which individuals and small groups are providing toys, accessories and fixtures for child guidance clinics and nursery schools. They learn that one can graduate to become a member of a small group which has its own circuit of nursery schools to maintain: mending toys, redecorating playrooms and occasionally helping the nurses bathe the babies!

"But," a man may say, "I'm not interested in any of this. I'm interested in engineering, farming, poultry-keeping, plumbing. . . ." His guide tells him that when he meets his psychiatrist and the activities officer he can arrange to conduct his activity at the Austin Motor Company, the Avoncroft Agricultural College or elsewhere, trying himself out and taking part in the life of these organizations.

The man returns to the admission ward with a sense of security in his surroundings. He then has a short individual interview with the senior psychiatrist and an initial interview with his own psychiatrist during which his activity is jointly selected (it can be changed later). Should it need special arrangements, the patient is passed on to a social therapy officer who makes the man a partner in achieving his particular objective. Many men select an activity as a test for the psychiatrist and social therapist; or they may use it to test themselves in a real or fantasy role. Particularly is this true of the returned prisoner of war who wishes to have a farm or a cottage in the country, or to help to look after horses.

Whereas eight months ago the new patient would say that he did not want to do anything while in the hospital, and the older patient would describe the limited range of activities as jobs to occupy the time between interviews, each now accepts the activity, selected by himself in conference with his psychiatrist, as a recognized part of his treatment. The term "occupational therapy" which had contributed to the earlier conception is no longer used. The extensive range of options and the principle of joint selection gives the man every opportunity to satisfy needs or test out fantasies. The soldier not infrequently says, "I have always wanted to try my hand at . . . but I don't suppose you can do anything about that." Now he can experiment and test himself out.

That he is a real partner in achieving the opportunity is vital. This does not mean that all new patients immediately settle down to following their activities with enthusiasm. If a man wanders off for walks on his own or with a friend this is information for the psychiatrist, the nurse and the social therapy staff—and the men with whom he is working. The patient is not checked in the military sense; this can be left to the social and therapeutic forces at work. He will find his place and activity in a little while, even if he changes the latter several times.

For the rest of his stay in the admission ward the man spends a portion of his time being re-kitted, completing questionnaires and taking psychological tests. In the intervals and in the evenings he revisits one or more of the places he has found attractive. The notice-board in his ward tells him what is "on." His host-patient may also invite him to join a party going to a dance, theater or a social run by members of local firms, clubs or societies, where he can meet men and women who are themselves having fun, and not just giving him a good time. In some cases these are the first steps in an England which he may have left three, four or five years ago. The decision is at all times left to him.

On the afternoon of the third day he is introduced to his treatment ward, which is in the charge of his psychiatrist and nurse. The ward-workers' group (whose selected activity is to look after all domestic affairs in the ward) will "put him wise" to everything going on. He realizes that he will be a member of the ward for the rest of his stay in the hospital, and he can now embark on a secure but flexible program involving not only the life in his ward and his selected activity, but also the social opportunities inside and outside the hospital.

Every day his psychiatrist sees him during the morning round. Each week the commanding officer makes his inspection and is ready to hear requests and complaints. In addition, the ward holds its own weekly meeting attended by the psychiatrist and nurse. The men elect their own chairman who, together with two other elected representatives, attends a full meeting of ward committees each Friday. These meetings, on "constituency" and "House of Commons" levels, are extremely useful conductors by means of which domestic and hospital tensions can be transmitted and resolved. Matters affecting the ward are dealt with by the constituency; matters bearing on hospital affairs are referred to the House of Commons. The latter meeting is attended by the commanding officer and the senior officer of the social therapy staff, who act as links with all hospital departments, any member of which has a standing invitation to attend.

Despite a constantly changing patient population, committee meeting minutes make it possible to trace the trends of a society developing in almost direct proportion to a growing sense of achievement and responsibility. At the beginning there was a collection of individuals, most of whom were self-appointed ward representatives, airing personal grievances and grumbles. Now the meeting of ward committees is a constitutional body conscious of its value and responsible to the hospital community as a whole.

Its work is not bound by the confines of the hospital. The links between Northfield and the city are becoming more numerous and more clearly defined, with plans being made for a total hospital project related to building an extension to the Crippled Children's Hospital in Birmingham. The growing contacts opened up by selected activities, sports and parties have brought large industrial concerns well within the hospital's consciousness, with the result that its psychological as well as geographical field has widened to an extent that tests both ward and overall committee meetings to the full.

In the frame of reference set up by the social life of the ward and hospital communities each psychiatrist has the opportunity of treating his patients, individually and in groups. He can see how the cohesive and disruptive social forces act on members of his ward. His observation of the patients' behavior has proved its value in treatment.

So far little has been said of other functional groups within the hospital. They each have their role not only in maintaining hospital services but in contributing to the total community. The women's auxiliary services take a full share in the social life of the hospital. It may be said that the social therapy staff is the whole staff together with the whole of the neighboring population. Unless this is so, treatment becomes restricted and may even be sterile. The treatment—one may call it an education in sincerity and tolerance—which the patients give to all related groups is no less important!

Although it is not possible here to trace in detail either the phenotypical picture of development or the process of "Lewinfiltration" (our term for describing the growth dynamics of a community) some conception of its progress may be gained by considering the field existing just prior to the beginning of the experiment. Entertainment, recreation, education and occupational therapy had been additional responsibilities for three different psychiatrists. Rehabilitation, which dealt only with patients in the last two or three weeks of their stay in the hospital, consisted mainly of para-military training and was in the hands of a para-military staff.

I have said little so far about the staff groups but they too developed many different directions of interest and inquiry. Previously, the nurses all worked according to the principles governing hospitals dealing with physical illnesses, despite the fact that there was only one medical ward. Now, there emerged the problem of discovering the role of the nurse in a therapeutic community where only a few patients were in the ward all day, let alone in bed! Their patients were out in Birmingham schools; repairing toys in a department store to raise cash for charity or hospital activities; in the car factory opposite the hospital; in the club, etc.; and in many additional types of treatment sessions with psychiatrists. There was only one way—for the nurse to learn a different role—to be with the patients where *they* were.

The force-field of therapeutic functions had changed. The therapeutic task now involved far greater inter-disciplinary practice. Hospital and environmental endeavors involved collaboration between professional therapeutic staff and social practitioners from a variety of functions. A few months before the boundaries between them had been distinct and their tasks separate.

The Doctor in the Therapeutic Community

When Tom Main arrived, the psychiatric scene developed still further. He was the first to spell out explicitly the changed role of the psychiatrist in the therapeutic community (Main, 1946):

> These are not small requirements and they have demanded a review of our attitudes as psychiatrists towards our own status and responsibilities. The anarchical rights of the doctor in the traditional hospital society have to be exchanged for the more sincere role of member in a real community, responsible not only to himself and his superiors, but to the community as a whole, privileged and restricted only insofar as the community allows or demands. He no longer owns "his" patients. They are given up to the community which is to treat them, and which owns them and him. Patients are no longer his captive children, obedient in nursery-like activities, but have sincere adult roles to play, and are free to reach for responsibilities and opinions concerning the community of which they are a part. They, as well as he, must be free to discuss a rationale of daily hospital life, to identify and analyze the problems, formulate the conditions and forge the enthusiasms of group life.

> . . . he does not seek ex cathedra status. Indeed he must refuse any platform offered to him, and abrogate his usual right to pass judgment on inter-group claims or problems. The psychiatrist has to tolerate disorder and tension up to the point when it is plain that the community itself must tackle these as problems of group life.

> . . . It must be pointed out that the medical man, educated to play a grandiose role among the sick, finds it difficult to renounce his power and shoulder social responsibilities in a hospital and to grant sincerely to his patients independence and adulthood. But it is no easier for the rest of the staff. It is difficult to live in a field undergoing internal stress without wanting to trade upon authority and crush the spontaneity which gives rise to the stress, to demand dependence and to impose law and order from above. Such measures, however, do not solve the problem of neurosis in social life, but are a means of evading the issue.

The extent to which the therapeutic community idea had taken root among key psychiatric staff may be further illustrated by the following remarks of S.H. Foulkes (1946) concerning his relations with myself:

> Co-operation between us was perfect and there was not a single question of principle or detail in which we did not see eye to eye. Thus the relationship of the therapeutic group in the narrower sense towards the hospital changed, the smaller unit becoming more definitely oriented towards the larger community of the hospital. Neither of them is workable, or even thinkable, without the other. It never occurred to us to ask how much one or the other of them contributed to the therapeutic result, so fully did we look upon it as an integrated whole. Apart from this, the psychiatrist was (or should have been) operative in all the different groups in which his patients were engaged. To look upon this experiment otherwise is to misunderstand its basic ideas as well as that of the psycho-therapeutic group itself.

The Hospital at the War's End

When hostilities ended in Europe Foulkes took over my role of social therapist as the principal means of mobilizing the hospital behind its new mission of rehabilitation for civilian life. He writes (Foulkes, 1946):

> The war was now over, Bridger had left, the staff was depleted by demobilization. The hospital policy had changed semi-officially to one of rehabilitation for civil life. Everything was affected. The old division between khaki and blue had changed its meaning completely. A certain note of apathy had descended upon both staff and patients. The hospital life had become stale and incoherent, the activity side somewhat departmental and institutionalized. What was to be done? I had the good luck, on my own request, to be transferred to the activity department. It became quite clear that levers had to be used to bring about an effect on the hospital spirit as a whole. The situation suggested the remedy. Groups had to be formed whose task was directly related to the hospital itself and who, from their function, were forced into contact and co-operation with others.
>
> . . . I founded one group called the Co-ordination Group who with new-found enthusiasm soon became a most active factor in the life of the hospital. Their influence was felt within a week or two throughout the hospital, from the CO to the last patient, orderly or office girl. New life blossomed from the ruins, brains trusts and quizzes between psychiatrists and patients, and similar events resulted, producing once more healthy and positive contact and co-operation.

He adds some general reflections on working with groups in the therapeutic community which merit being more widely known:

It will be seen that in the development described, the following shifts of emphasis emerged:

- From individual centred to leaving the lead to the group.
- From leader centred to group centred.
- From talking to acting and doing.
- From the still artificial setting of a group session to selected activities and to groups in life function.
- From content centred to behaviour in action.
- From the controlled and directed to the spontaneous.
- From the past to the present situation.

. . . The narrowest point of view will see in it merely a time saver perhaps, or a kind of substitute for other more individual forms of psychotherapy. Possibly it will concede that it might have special advantages, have its own indications, say, for instance, for the treatment of social difficulties. A wider view will see in it a new method of therapy, investigation, information and education. The widest view will look upon group therapy as an expression of a new attitude towards the study and improvement of human inter-relations in our time. It may see in it an instrument, perhaps the first adequate one, for a practicable approach to the key problem of our time: the strained relationship between the individual and the community. In this way its range is as far and as wide as these relationships go. Treatment of psychoneuroses, psychoses, crime, etc., rehabilitation problems, industrial management, education, in short, every aspect of life in communities, large and small. Perhaps someone taking this broad view will see in it the answer in the spirit of a democratic community to the mass and group handling of Totalitarian regimes.

Conclusions

The question of the renunciation of power and the sharing of responsibility with an interdisciplinary team had been at the bottom of the trouble stirred up by Northfield I. This issue is still with us, as Maxwell Jones's (1968) persistent struggles for forty years have demonstrated, especially when patients as well as staff are allowed a voice.

Several studies of substantial, as distinct from marginal, innovation (Chevalier and Burns, 1979) have shown that the first entry of a radically new model is usually arrested but that the learning acquired permits an extensive development when, after a delay, the environmental situation has become favorable for a second entry. The seed planted at Northfield I did not fall by the wayside. In another two years it flowered not only in Northfield II but in several forms in relation to the concluding phases of the war. As Bion observed in *Psychiatry in a Time of Crisis* (1948), a chain reaction had been started. Foulkes (1964) has traced further developments in the post-war period.

For innovative initiatives to persist in any of its parts sanction is needed from the highest levels of the organization. The whole in which the parts are embedded can then begin to change in a consonant direction. High level sanction is especially necessary when the initiatives are of a kind which create a discontinuity with what has gone before and are the harbingers of a paradigm shift.

As happens not infrequently, discoveries made within the protection of a therapeutic setting later find numerous applications in the wider society—until they become seen as general. Winnicott (1971) has talked of maturation and the facilitating environment regarding the child. Northfield showed that an unusually facilitating environment can lead to unusual maturation in adults. Approaches and methods first learnt in a specialized psychiatric setting may be adapted to bring into being degrees of commitment and levels of performance unreachable by conventional bureaucratic organizations in industry and other social sectors. The individual can grow through the life-enhancing experiences now provided which he himself, by his own participation, has helped to bring into existence. Most people doing organizational change projects, which have become such a vast enterprise since World War II, have little knowledge of where, how or under what circumstances the seminal work was done.

Northfield I was undertaken at the height of the war when the military outcome was still in doubt. There was a deep necessity for the work group concerned with the reality situation (W in Bion's sense) and his basic assumption fight (baF) to be constructively fused (Bion, 1961). What Bion and Rickman did reflected this situation and was congruent with it. Northfield II was undertaken when the military outcome was no longer in doubt. In this situation a need began to suffuse the society to restore those who had become "casualties" in any form through their part in the war effort. The therapeutic community that now came into existence as Northfield II created a reparative society. The profound healing effect of the need to make reparation had been explicitly stated by Melanie Klein (Klein and Riviere, 1937). Northfield II exemplified this effect at the social level and demonstrated the connection between personal and social healing.

Northfield II also created a democratic society. This showed that there was a link between participation and the release of creative forces. This link suggests also that democratic and reparative processes are connected at a deep psychological level. They mutually reinforce each other. These connections are still little appreciated and need to be taken into account in institution-building for the future.

Despite their promise, the war and immediate post-war developments of therapeutic communities reached a limit unexpected by their pioneers. They pose a persisting threat to authoritarian institutions and the prevailing bureaucratic culture. The resistances encountered by Bion and Rickman in one hospital-as-a-whole, though worked through in Northfield II, reappeared in society-as-a-whole. In the course of the 40 years that have elapsed since these experiments manifested that there was a new way, only small progress has been made towards establishing a more democratic and more reparative social order. In making further progress towards this goal the experiences they yielded and the models they built provide a rich ground on which new efforts may be based.

References

Bion, W.R. 1946. "The Leaderless Group Project." *Bulletin of the Menninger Clinic*, 10:77–81.
———. 1948. "Psychiatry in a Time of Crisis." *British Journal of Medical Psychology*, 21:81–89.
———. 1961. *Experiences in Groups and Other Papers*. London: Tavistock Publications; New York: Basic Books.
Bion, W.R. and J. Rickman. 1943. "Intra-group Tensions in Therapy: Their Study as the Task of the Group." *Lancet*, 2:678–81.
Bridger, H. 1980. "The Kinds of 'Organizational Development' Required for Working at the Level of the Whole Organization Considered as an Open System." In *Organization Development in Europe, Vol. 1A: Concepts*, edited by K. Trebesch. Berne: Paul Haupt Verlag.
———. 1982. "The Implications of Ecological Change on Groups, Institutions and Communities, with Particular Reference to Membership, Leadership and Consultative Roles." In *The Individual and the Group*, edited by M. Pines and L. Rafaelsen. New York: Plenum.
Chevalier, M. and T. Burns. 1979. "The Policy Field." In *Management Handbook for Public Administrators*, edited by J.W. Sutherland. Englewood Cliffs, N.J.: Nostrand Reinholt.
de Maré, P.B. 1983. "Michael Foulkes and the Northfield Experiment." In *The Evolution of Group Analysis*, edited by M. Pines. London: Routledge and Kegan Paul.
———. 1985. "Major Bion." In *Bion and Group Psychotherapy*, edited by M. Pines. London: Routledge and Kegan Paul.
Foulkes, S.H. 1946. "On Group Analysis." *International Journal of Psycho-Analysis*, 27:1–6.
———. 1964. *Therapeutic Group Analysis*. London: Allen & Unwin.
Jones, M. 1968. *Social Psychiatry in Practice*. London: Penguin Books.
Klein, M. and J. Riviere. 1937. *Love, Hate and Reparation*. London: Hogarth Press.
Main, T.F. 1946. "The Hospital as a Therapeutic Institution." *Bulletin of the Menninger Clinic*, 10:66–70.
———. 1983. "The Concept of the Therapeutic Community: Variations and Vicissitudes." In *The Evolution of Group Analysis*, edited by M. Pines. London: Routledge and Kegan Paul.
Pearse, I.H. and L.H. Crocker. 1943. *The Peckham Experiment*. London: Allen & Unwin.
Winnicott, D.W. 1965. *The Maturational Process and the Facilitating Environment*. London: Hogarth Press.
———. 1971. *Playing and Reality*. London: Penguin Books.

A.T.M. Wilson, Eric Trist and Adam Curle

Transitional Communities and Social Reconnection
The Civil Resettlement of British Prisoners of War*

The Prisoner of War Experience and the Problem of Repatriation

THE BACKGROUND OF THE SCHEME

In the early years of World War II the need of repatriated British Prisoners of War (PsOW) for assistance in readjusting was not urgently manifest, but, as more men returned after escape or were repatriated on medical grounds, the rate of sickness and disciplinary offenses caused anxiety. Officially, PsOW were regarded both as "casualties" and as men awaiting trial by court of inquiry to re-establish their military rights. Though this attitude was largely historical and was weakened by experience of returned men, ambivalence, shown by simultaneous idealizing and scapegoating, remained.

Through the Army the POW returned to his own society. It was the Army that possessed special understanding of his difficulties, just as it had been responsible for his troubles. Among institutions in his home society it was of the Army that he was most suspicious, yet it was on the Army that he was most dependent. Despite a certain opposition to differential treatment, among both military and civilian groups, and also among PsOW themselves (many of whom were determined to deny the existence of their difficulties), it was decided at Cabinet level that the repatriate needed not only special training to

---

*No comprehensive account of the Civil Resettlement Scheme developed in the British Army during 1945–1946 had been available prior to the publication in G.E. Swanson, T.E. Newcomb and E.L. Hartley (Editors), *Readings in Social Psychology*, 1952, of this paper prepared by the second author from existing manuscripts.

refit him for military duty, but that the Army should itself undertake the first steps toward re-equipping him for civilian life.

This policy sanctioned the development of a scheme based on technical studies. At the beginning of 1945 a pilot Civil Resettlement Unit (CRU) was formed. By the end of that year (PsOW having been repatriated from all theaters of war), there were twenty CRUs operating in different parts of the United Kingdom, each capable of dealing with some 240 men at any one time. These units acted as bridges between the Army and civilian life. They were designed as *transitional communities* to permit change of attitudes which retarded reassumption by the repatriate of a fully participant role in civilian life.

THE NATURE OF DESOCIALIZATION

Unsettlement on repatriation could not be understood solely as a disturbance in the repatriate himself. His family was also affected. On the larger social scale this was reflected in the relations generally between those returning from the services and those who had remained in civilian life. Resettlement was a two-way process, calling for emotional readjustment by all members of the re-formed family and the wider community.

From this wider point of view unsettlement may be regarded as a process of *desocialization*. Desocialization can be defined only in relation to a general concept of society, since it appears differentially related to various components in the total social order, such as *social structure, social roles, social relationships* and *culture*.

SOCIAL STRUCTURE

This term covers social forms (economic, kinship, governmental, etc.) which together act as a more or less stable and organized framework within which the basic needs of the individual may be met. Structure is external to the individual—something felt as "out there." The effects of structural breakdown on the individual cannot, however, be traced without additional concepts, for considerable structural breakdown may often be survived with little desocialization, while desocialization may occur apart from structural breakdown.

SOCIAL ROLES

Structure by itself gives no information on the position taken up by the individual within it. A number of such positions are possible, referred to as social roles. While structure is there, it is up to the individual himself whether he takes an available role. Through failure to take roles he goes out of the social framework in certain directions. *Failure to take roles* may be proposed as one criterion of desocialization.

SOCIAL RELATIONSHIPS

Once roles are taken, social relationships begin to be made. Their course, however, is not determined by the roles which are a condition of their beginning. The structure of his society may initially determine whether or not an individual may take a certain role, but other factors enter with respect to his ability to handle and make good the widening and changing series of relationships, variously personalized and intimate, in which he is involved if his participation and satisfaction are to continue. *Failure to sustain social relationships* provides a second criterion of desocialization.

CULTURE

Culture represents the means, however imperfect, at the disposal of the individual for handling his relationships. On it he depends for making his way among, and with, other members and groups belonging to his society. The central thesis of this paper is that *it is the internal assimilation of culture that is primarily disturbed in the process of desocialization.* This gives the third criterion to which the other two may be related.

An inquiry into desocialization, therefore, implies an assessment of the level at which an individual possesses internal assimilation of his culture. So far as he has reached a state of cultural dispossession, the breaking of relationships and the refusal of roles have serious consequences, for he now lacks the resources to make the restorations necessary and the resilience to resume abandoned activities. The process will now be traced which induced desocialization in repatriated PsOW, despite the degree of structural equilibrium in post-war Britain.

THE COURSE OF DESOCIALIZATION IN THE REPATRIATE AND HIS FAMILY

At first, while serving in his home country, the soldier carried over into the Army a good deal of his former civilian being. Nevertheless, it was a common observation by servicemen that they soon found it difficult to take an effective part in their family affairs.

When the soldier was drafted overseas he had to make a second adjustment.

As he neared the combat zone, the in-group solidarity of his unit insulated him from his old life. Whether or not a man had traumatic battle experiences, emotional disturbances were commonly associated with capture. The feeling of guilt over "allowing" oneself to be taken and of rejection from the fact that the Army had "allowed" it made capture a painful experience. Life in a POW camp entailed a third adjustment—to the condition of being rendered useless, though something of the soldier's role could be maintained by engaging in a morale battle with the prison authorities. Men learned to lead a double life of surface compliance and concealed activity.

On return, after a period of leave, most repatriates spent some months in the Army before release. This had a protective effect and the full impact of desocialization was only felt when they re-entered civilian life. On demobilization men found themselves lost and out of place, separated by a gulf of experience impossible to share and by a sense of guilt related in part, and however irrationally, to the fact of having left home. When a husband or father goes away, he takes not only himself but those activities that have become part and parcel of everyday life. In his family, readjustment takes place toward the altered situation. When the absent member returns, a disequilibrium is caused comparable with that created by his departure. Outside the family, his associates had similar difficulty in accepting the repatriate into the milieu they had established without him. Such experiences led many men to feel that their rejection had been callously prepared.

Often, however, the gain in maturity was very great. One difficulty of many was how to use their maturity in a society they felt they had outgrown. The consequent isolation was as painful as the isolation of captivity.

Stress tended to pile up between the second and fourth months. If this period could be weathered, a man was set toward resocialization. If it went badly, satisfactory adjustment often posed formidable problems. The policy of the CRU was to reach men at a point when they had begun to feel the force of their difficulties—and so be willing to seek help—but before they were overtaken by the crisis of their desocialization.

THE SEARCH FOR SANCTION OF POW EXPERIENCE

After the initial shock of capture many men regressed to quasi-psychotic states, but the majority gradually became aware of the existence and power of various supranational organizations governed by the Geneva Convention on PsOW, and the International Red Cross. They also learned the extent to which their survival as individuals depended on their success as a group in keeping some kind of society alive in their midst. The European prison camp situation may be summarized as follows:

- Separation of officers and other ranks (noncommissioned officers and privates) under the Geneva Convention created the need for an alternative leadership from below. This centered in an elected "man of confidence" who represented the group to the Protecting Power.
- The removal of material weapons meant that alternative weapons had to be forged with cultural resources, since the fight had to go on and the degree of capture held as low as possible.
- The two points above had effects which reinforced each other so that a strong democratic culture developed with the double function of preserving the group and waging war.
- The prison camp emerged as a society of "creative casualties" in whom a deep revaluation and skilled utilization of certain components in their culture had occurred; but in whom, because of the severity of the trauma and the limitations of the situation, a partial mastery of their experience was alone possible.
- The democratic society of prison camps was largely self-sanctioning. It recognized no societal "parent," except the para-medical maternal authority of the Geneva Convention and the International Red Cross.

The repatriate was in a state which led him to search for consistent sanction for the values of his prison-camp experience in the culture of the controlling societal authorities of his home society. If he did not find such sanction there remained such painful reactions as:

- Regression once more to the isolated existence of early captivity. A man would live as a passive prisoner of his own society. Men were found who had not left their houses for weeks.
- Renewal of his cultural war in a particularly embittered form—against his own society, now regarded as the enemy. He would tend to align himself with malcontent minorities.
- Alternatively, he might seek revenge by taking up a role based on unrecognized identification with his late captors, whom he would outdo in authoritarianism (and even brutality).
- He could attempt to escape from his problem by emigration.
- He might be forced to accept the role of a psychiatric casualty.

All these reactions must be thought of as techniques of living, not so much mutually exclusive as coexisting or alternating in any individual man. The first four are based on aggression. It is only in the last that there remains any conviction of success in the search for sanction from the home society. But the repatriate was an unlikely person to declare himself as a psychiatric patient. Yet his own illness remained a fact whose denial whether by himself or others had serious consequences. Early follow-up studies showed that only a minority of repatriation states were self-adjusting. A special scheme was necessary but had to be built up in a wider para-medical setting.

The Character of the Transitional Community

PRINCIPLES AND POLICY

To meet the situation described it was necessary to secure acceptance of the principle that participation cannot be imposed. Military authority had either to take no action or to sanction the development of a permissive community within the Army. This meant offering a voluntary scheme and reversing a number of rules and regulations.

By conferring the right to volunteer for a CRU the Army gave evidence of its willingness to accept the negative feelings of the repatriate (who could reject the offer), and also of its evaluation of his worth and its trust in him (by risking a considerable investment in a scheme which only a few might utilize). By abrogating its authority over him it recognized its responsibility toward him. The method of gaining his trust was to take *informed social action*.

To volunteer implied for the repatriate the acceptance of a role which opened up relationships in a community whose culture was fashioned in terms of his own values and whose existence was itself proof of their compatibility with the home society. His shattered sense of security, mistrust, and need for consistency made him a "connoisseur in sincerity" and adept at looking for snags. He could accept only a community where acceptance of his values was consistent.

The production of this self-consistent participant community did not in the first place depend on action taken within the Civil Resettlement organization, but on decisions made—and maintained—by the controlling War Office branches of all sections of the Army, and also by civil ministries and organizations, both industrial and social. It was from widespread discussions on implementing these decisions that the intergroup relations between the repatriate and the home community were clarified.

THE DEVELOPMENT OF THE SCHEME

It was postulated that if the scheme was planned with the participation of repatriates no difficulty would arise in obtaining volunteers. Over-all, 40,000 to 50,000 men attended CRUs. Contact with as many more was made latterly, on a day basis, through the Extension Scheme.

A survey of the regional distribution of the homes of PsOW permitted the scheme to develop so that men could attend a CRU in their own part of the country, units being located on the boundaries of industrial areas to provide contact with social and industrial life. The staff had to bear the stress of an unfamiliar para-military and para-medical community and were specially selected. In training, they received, first, opportunities of contact with repatriates, then group discussions on repatriation problems and finally a brief apprenticeship at a working unit. The pilot unit was administered under medical and social-science auspices. In working units, administrative control reverted to regimental authorities advised by psychiatrists and psychologists. New units budded off from old.

The initial task of a new CRU was to make contact with the Ministry of Labour, through which groups of guests representing various industries and trades were invited to the empty unit, an explanation of the scheme made and suggestions received as to how repatriates could make informal contact with those on the job. A developed CRU was in touch with 200 to 400 firms and social institutions willing to allow visits by repatriates.

The Staff and Organization of a CRU

The officer staff consisted of a commanding officer, second-in-command and nine officers for casework—four "syndicate" officers and five specialists. A syndicate was a man's living group and each syndicate officer was parent to 60 men—four sections of 15 from successive weekly intakes of 60 to the whole CRU. This staggered intake allowed each syndicate to contain old as well as new members.

Specialists ran "practices." All attendances were voluntary. With a monthly turnover of over 200, units with a disproportionate load of disabled required two medical officers. Two units had a resident psychiatrist; in others he was part time. A vocational officer and sergeants helped men to evaluate, on a reality basis, long-cherished vocational plans and fantasies. A Ministry of Labour officer facilitated practical openings. The technical officer provided, through workshops, an opportunity to rebuild confidence. The women social workers—known as Civil Liaison Officers—were psychiatric social workers. Matrimonial problems made up two thirds of social case work in returned service people and were abundant at CRUs.

Clerical and domestic arrangements were standard for a static military establishment, but the scale of accommodation was that provided for the ATS (the women's branch of the Army). It included, for the whole unit, beds and sheets as opposed to boards and blankets. The proportion of permanent staff was high—the seriousness of resettlement was indicated by allowing repatriates to be fully occupied in learning about civil life. One hundred of the other rank staff (NCOs and privates) of 140 were women (ATS) who enabled the CRU to develop the mores of a mixed community.

Men with experience of starvation placed a high value on food and the conditions of eating. Meals were served at pleasantly arranged tables by ATS, midday dinner being taken in a common dining room by all ranks and by repatriates and staff alike. This event symbolized CRU "democracy," while common sharing in the scale of accommodation eliminated trouble between repatriates and other rank staff and assisted them to discover a common identity as potential civilians.

THE RESETTLEMENT PROGRAM

Length of stay averaged four to five weeks. Except for terminal interviews, a man was not ordered to see anyone. He passed through four phases: learning about and testing out the unit; establishing himself within it; orienting himself to the surrounding industrial and social community; making and reality-testing personal plans. These phases may be summarized as neutralization of the suspicion of authority; return to a less regressed social attitude with role-taking in the safety of the unit and assimilation of its culture; a more general movement toward a reconnected relationship with the home society; the structuring of personal goals. The program was sequenced accordingly—reception phase, settling-in phase, orientation phase, planning phase—and the balance of spontaneity and control altered to throw the repatriate more and more onto himself. The gradient was steep so that the anxieties aroused could be dealt with during the program month that made up the standard CRU course. In content, scope, sequence and duration this standard was intended to act as an over-all interpretation of the nature and dimensions of the resettlement task and to indicate a norm in terms of which men could gauge their progress. (Provision was made for lengthening stay up to three months.)

Special care was necessary over the reception phase (Thursday afternoon to Saturday midday). The socialized adult usually belongs to a family group, a work group and an informal group of leisure-time friends. It was postulated that if repatriates could be inducted—as rapidly as possible—into prototypes of these three groups, *on a basis of personal choice*, they would be securely positioned in the unit.

On the first day the unit took little initiative while giving the repatriate full scope to find out about it. After an arrival meal, men were conducted to a dormitory to choose their beds, then left free to hear what those already there thought. On the second day the unit took more initiative. After an introductory talk by the commanding officer, the 60 new arrivals were taken around the unit in informal groups, briefly introduced to key resettlement staff, then invited to redivide themselves, for syndicate allocation, into four sections of 15. A man at once experienced the value of his syndicate in a group discussion with his syndicate officer, with whom he also had a personal interview. During the afternoon he attended a first workshop session. By the evening he had usually found friends. On the Saturday morning he selected civilian clothes, which he wore home, weekends being spent at home to avoid damage to new social roots in the home environment and to keep alive questions related to future planning.

During their first full week (apart from a visit to an employment exchange and to one factory) men were occupied inside the unit, attending workshops and informational discussions. They took part in a social life which included dances, attended by civilians, particularly girls from the neighborhood, who did much to diminish exaggerated fears of women. By the second week they were visiting factories, shops, training centers and social organizations in small self-chosen groups. During the third and fourth weeks assignments became more individual. Men undertook job rehearsals, spending several days acquiring the feel of a job—without the burden of responsibility. Personal problems were discussed with the specialist staff, vocational anxieties usually being brought out before those concerned with family relations. Many of these latter anxieties first appeared in the guise of job problems. As CRUs matured they passed generally from being employment dominant to becoming family dominant, and wives and families were more fully brought into activities and discussions.

THE INTERACTION OF ACTIVITIES AND DISCUSSION

The many-sided activities and the frequent contact with civil life stimulated the need to talk, while the syndicate and other groups provided the occasion. In this way the activities of individuals led to a therapeutic discussion of their significance, and the process of acting out or testing out plans was linked to that of evaluating and assimilating their significance—the process of working through. The raised insight and changed feelings led to further activity—but at a higher social level, e.g., group projects through which the repatriates attempted to express altruistic needs often freed up as they resolved individual problems. A kind of circulation came into existence—from action to understanding and back again to action—which gathered in spontaneity and extent as the community matured.

This circulation made it easier than might be expected to impart CRU technique to a wide variety of people. Social sharing and diffusion of insights are implicit in any group technique, for different kinds of people come into the group. Group techniques represent a change in the means of production of insight, establishing an exchange that permits circulation in an open and public, as distinct from a closed and professional, market. The simpler discussions of the syndicate officer and the more sophisticated discussions of the vocational officer or social worker were events in the same series to which the group session of the psychiatrist belonged. The power of the series was raised as various specialists learned to work together as a team (which had its own discussions).

REDUCING THE "FEAR OF FREEDOM"

Central were difficulties over authority. The development of a morale-based self-discipline was the basic prescription of treatment. Absence of formal discipline caused severe anxiety both to PsOW and to unit staff. Of special importance were the interviews and discussions through which this fear of freedom was reduced.

Some weeks after the first CRU opened, a group of 15 men refused to cooperate, using the CRU as an easy-going hotel. Two or three were flagrantly antisocial and in trouble with the civilian population and the police. All exhibited psychosomatic symptoms and depressive trends. The administrative staff had come to the end of their tether; expulsion was their only solution. The presence of the psychiatrist also created anxiety. In consequence, he and his patients were isolated in a consulting room in a remote part of the building. The remainder of the community felt that they had rid themselves of a doubly dangerous group, and that the delinquents could be conveniently removed by the psychiatrist, via a hospital or, if they refused treatment, by his taking the responsibility of recommending termination of their stay.

For the CRU so to rid itself of its troubles would have been fatal. The first duty of the psychiatrist was toward the staff, his first efforts to impress them with the necessity to keep these disturbing elements within the CRU. Manipulation of the neurotic "attack" on the community was outside the scope of the executive. His second function was to tackle and, if possible, to canalize the neurotic force. This was undertaken by group discussions.

The topic thrown up in these discussions was the failure of the unit to provide discipline; without the discipline of authority there could be no punishment, and without punishment nobody knew where he was. Could they go on behaving in the way they were doing? If they did, would not authority take action? Authority in the person of the psychiatrist assured them that, so far as the CRU was concerned, no action would be taken; but that outside bodies, such as the War Office or the civil authorities, were less inclined to such tolerance, and their behavior might so seriously reflect on the scheme as to bring it to a close. Also there were 385 other people in the CRU who would assert their authority should they be affected adversely. They were up against not the authority of the executive but the wishes of the CRU as a group. A general meeting would be held and a vote taken on their conduct. This approach proved effective. After one memorable and stormy meeting in which this whole situation was made quite clear there was silence. Then, one by one, each gave an assurance that no further trouble would be experienced.

Needless to say, what was going on between the psychiatrist and the neurotic group was being closely watched by the rest of the CRU. The outcome was to decide the future pattern of unit government. Should the neurotic triumph, chaos would result with subsequent dissolution of the resettlement unit; if the neurotic was expelled, authoritarianism would supplant the democratic atmosphere essential to the scheme. The recognition by the neurotic element of the effect they were producing on the rest solved the immediate problem. Their altered attitude became reflected in the unit as a whole, which was now not only tolerant of the "bad boys" but also took up a rather protective attitude, removing them from public places if drunk and so shielding them and the unit from the outside world.

Practically no further difficulty was experienced in disciplinary matters after this showdown; nor did one arise later with similar intensity at any other CRU subsequently opened. The solution of this single psychiatric event influenced the growth of the whole scheme. The psychiatrist emerged from his confinement into the general life of the community. The increasing rate of the demand for his help was shown by the following figures: during the first month about 5 percent repatriates were seen, all referred through a medical or other officer; whereas in the third and fourth months some 60 percent were spontaneously seeking advice.

A Follow-Up Appraisal

METHOD

In one area, chosen in accordance with carefully determined criteria, comparable samples of 50 repatriated PsOW who had, and 100 who had not, been to CRUs were studied in relation to a control group of 40 families from the same area. These represented the civilian norm at the socio-economic levels at which the repatriated groups were settling down some months after demobilization.

The investigator saw most men several times in different settings: (1) *Alone*. Covering at least an hour, often much longer. (2) *At work*. The managements of several factories provided facilities for men to be seen in working hours, a type of contact most effective when it combined a private interview with the man with a subsequent more general discussion involving management, staff, fellow workers and others. (3) *With his family.* These contacts frequently took place over a cup of tea, and were invaluable in demonstrating the whole family situation, including the wife's reactions to the husband's condition. (4) *In group discussion.* The investigator often had other discussions in addition to those listed above. These were sometimes arranged but sometimes grew spontaneously out of meetings in the home or the works. Family members, fellow workers, other PsOW and neighbors took part.

The role adopted by the investigator was that of a supplementary extension officer of the CRU organization—that is, an officer concerned with aftercare, and with extending CRU facilities to non-volunteers, or to men who had canceled their applications. His initial approach—that he had come to see if there was anything he could do—quickly dispelled the apprehension of men or their wives at meeting an officer who obviously knew something about them. This view was supported by the greater difficulty experienced in establishing relations with the control group.

Actual elicitation of information was through observation and discussion, rather than through direct questioning. With the CRU samples, one stage was an explanation of the purpose of follow-up, which involved a modification of the investigator's role as initially described. This was important for two reasons. First, in his follow-up role, he moved out of the part of a counselor who might raise dependency hopes which could not be fulfilled. Second, there was a therapeutic gain in giving men, through the assistance they provided by their information, a chance to participate still further in an experiment which had helped them.

All men were seen at approximately the same juncture of their lives as reestablished civilians.

The Development of Criteria for Norms of Social Participation

Sherif (1936) writes of social norms as follows: "Social norms arise from actual life situations as a consequence of the contact of people with one another. . . . But once formed, they tend to persist. Many times they outlive their usefulness." In the samples under discussion norms had rather neutral prestige value and were described as "all right"; "just ordinary"; "nothing special"; "quite respectable."

Besides the norms, certain forms of deviant behavior were observed. In the first, roles are rejected: the husband deserts his wife; or the worker leaves his job and makes no effort to get a new one. In terms of the norm, this behavior lacks prestige. The man concerned is judged as either "sick" or "wicked."

A second type of deviation occurs when a man accepts the roles, but cannot use the culture to manage the relationship: he gives his wife housekeeping money, but never goes out with her or helps her in the home; he works, but without loyalty or friendliness to employers and fellow workers. Such a role has great persistence, but behavior of this kind is inadequate to any emergency in which flexibility is required. Sometimes judgments about these men are more harsh than about those in the first category, since an element of pity often enters into references to a man whose domestic or social life is completely disintegrating.

A third type of deviation was *positively* assessed and appears to represent congruence of individual development with the realities of social situations. In this third deviation the patterns are the good husband and neighbor; the man who has a certain capacity for leadership; the men who are loyal employees, but prepared to take positive action if their principles are outraged. In such people the approach to situations is flexible, and less governed by stereotypes. This type of deviance, above the norm, appears to represent the cultural aspiration level of the norm itself.

In the norm, certain features of behavior imply anxiety, typified by the erection of barriers which restrict the mobility of human relationships. Many of these barriers take the form of culture stereotypes: that men do not push the pram, that they do not take their wives to football matches. But there is no derogatory evaluation of those who do.

If the norm and the three deviations are scaled by standards of social participation, they occur in the following ascending order: first deviation (roles rejected); second deviation (roles accepted, inability to use culture); norm; third deviation (behavior at cultural aspiration level of norm). These findings are consistent with the concept of desocialization. There follows an analysis of behavior which illustrates the application of this scale. The sequence of these illustrations corresponds with the arrangement of the different regions of the life space of the individual. These are ordered to radiate out from family relationships through neighborhood and work groups to the more abstract relationships with authority.

For convenience, the two infranorm deviants, the norm and the supranorm deviant are named grades on a four-point scale, and appear in the later tabulations as *Grade* 1 (first infranorm deviant); *Grade* 2 (second infranorm deviant); *Grade* 3 (norm); and *Grade* 4 (supranorm deviant). In some of the statistical tables these grades are used as scores and treated as equal class intervals.

FINDINGS

1. The first step was to determine whether the criteria of social participation could be regarded as valid indications of the degree of resettlement. Two other criteria were available. The first may be called a psychiatric criterion—con-

cerned with the presence or absence of signs of unsettlement (apathy, restlessness, hostility, extreme dependence, etc.) generally acknowledged in CRU practice. It was a direct over-all assessment by the investigator, unrelated to specific patterns of overt behavior in specific roles or relationships. The second was an over-all opinion of relatives, neighbors, friends, and employers, questioned to assess the local reputation of each man. Both the "psychiatric" and the reputational ratings of "settled"—"unsettled," and "all right"—"not all right," were compared with the social participation ratings. There was a definitely significant relation between both ratings and all fifteen criteria.

2. The mean score of an individual in his performance over all his social relationship criteria may be regarded as indicative of his position on a degree of resettlement continuum. Comparison of the more settled (mean criteria score 3 or above) with the less settled (mean criteria score below 3) shows a significant relationship between degree of settlement and CRU attendance ($p \leq .01$). Similar calculations using the psychiatric and reputational ratings also show a definitely significant relationship ($p \leq .01$ in both cases).

3. The CRU and non-CRU samples were now compared on each of the social criteria. On all fifteen, incidence of below norm scores was greater in the non-CRU group, seven of the differences being of definite, and three of borderline significance ($p \leq .05$). As regards scores above the norm, on six criteria the CRU was superior to the control group. The trend was in the same direction elsewhere. In relation to the norm, Table 3 (a) represents the pattern of negative deviance, (b) the pattern of positive deviance. Only to a limited extent are the directions of significant gain those of significant loss. The negative pattern points to a state of desocialization in which, though a man still exists in the framework of society, he lives only in his home. The positive pattern indicates that resocialization was associated with supranormative use of the culture in the bridge regions, with corresponding improvements in husband-wife relations and a more responsible attitude at work. The relation of Table 3 (a) to Table 3 (b) points to a main fact: the overcoming of negative deviance entailed the appearance of positive deviance—that is, the therapy of desocialization did not consist merely in the restatement of the norm, but in some degree the actualization of supranormative potentialities—the pattern of resocialization was not that of desocialization in reverse.

4. In respect to individual performance (as opposed to total scores with regard to each criterion), Table 4 (a) shows that there is a significantly larger number of low scores in the non-CRU sample ($p < .01$ for t on group means). In Table 4 (b) there is a significantly higher proportion of norm scores ($p \leq .01$) in the control group.

In Table 4 (c) the poverty of supranorm behavior in both the control group and the non-CRU group are shown. In fact, there is a significantly greater

TABLE I   Fifteen Criteria of Social Participation

General definition	Norm (Grade 3)	Supranorm (Grade 4)	Infranorm (Grade 2)	Infranorm (Grade 1)
1. *Husband-wife, domestic work.* Rigidity of role-differentiation, amount and character of husband's contribution in all relationships between husband and wife in the sphere of domestic economy.	Husband helps about the house; may help with the dishes, though it depends on whim or special need; is responsible for business affairs, often making major decisions such as changing one's address—i.e., getting a new house or apartment and making decision to move to same. Decorating and carpentry are his, but he refuses to help with tasks like bedmaking.	Greater cooperation, interchange of jobs wherever desirable. Combining of forces is characteristic, e.g., the investigator would find a couple together decorating a room.	Practically no common roles. The slightest encroachment on the man's role causes domestic upheaval.	Complete failure to accept husband responsibilities, without misconduct on wife's part: separation, desertion or extreme domestic violence.
2. *Husband-wife, leisure pursuits.* Degree of participation between husband and wife in activities beyond those of breadwinning and household management, both inside and outside the home.	Husband dutifully spends at least five evenings at home with wife, but does not cooperate in leisure activity, though a weekly visit together to the cinema is a ritual.	Considerable sharing of interests, both within and outside the home. If one partner does not actively engage in the concerns of the other, he will encourage them.	The husband frequently goes out without his wife, though not for anything in particular. Scorn for the interests of the other, but sometimes subordination to the wife's, the husband tagging along.	Never together. Ignoring or sabotaging each other's activities.
3. *Father-child, play and encouragement.* Nurturant relationship of father with children with respect to	Man does something with or for his children most evenings after work, especially the young ones, up to ages 5–7. After that	Constructive interest as well as affection. Readiness to help children, even in the face of their	Children ignored, irritation shown. Relief when they go out to play. Much time sometimes	Absence of, or withdrawal from, relations with children, or a consistently hostile attitude

play, school, hobbies, achievements, ambitions, etc.; his degree of concern with and approval of these various activities.	little time spent on those who do not follow some paternal preconceived idea.	own disapproval. They are brought into most family activities.	spent, offset by uncertainty of mood. Emulation demanded. The slightest lapse brings discord.	toward them. Neglect, or persecution. Unprovoked violence may be shown and/or children allowed to run wild.
4. *Father-child, authority and discipline.* Methods and consistency of the discipline imposed by father on his children; extent to which he accepts responsibility as representative of authority.	Father has a clear idea of what he wants his children to be like (rather like himself but with a better education). Threats and shouts employed more than beating, but every few days outburst accompanied by indiscriminate cuffs, for little reason apart from accumulated irritation.	Tries to see the children's point of view, slow to punish, but has some standard, relatively unconcerned with his own personal whims and prestige, which he enforces, usually by reprimand, with a fair degree of consistency.	Fixed ideas about upbringing, uninfluenced by experience of his children. Otherwise little consistency, the same action being punished one day and laughed at the next. A common punishment is locking children up.	
5. *Ritual in the home.* Interactions between the individual—whether married or not—and other members of his household, which affect his own status and privileges; extent to which prestige has become a function of maintaining personal idiosyncrasies and stereotypes as rituals in the household group.	Has three or four fads to which the whole family must conform. If not, a noisy row, which does not last long. Male prestige is carefully guarded by both husband and wife, even if the latter is dominant.	Lack of ceremony, coupled with toleration of unusual behavior. Likes and dislikes, the expression of which is tempered by the exigencies of the moment, replace rigid rituals of propriety. No high value set on prestige.	Dependence on things being "just so." The slightest deviation produces a domestic crisis. Prestige at a premium which increases with the decline of effectively exercised authority. In a minority of cases the man will accept almost any treatment.	Idiosyncrasies are divorced from any relationship with the everyday domestic round.

TABLE I Continued

General definition	Norm (Grade 3)	Supranorm (Grade 4)	Infranorm (Grade 2)	Infranorm (Grade 1)
6. *Quarreling in the home.* The ways in which hostilities are expressed and dealt with in the household group: frequency and duration of quarrels, degree of their violence, extent of their repercussions, methods used to adjust differences of opinion and restore situations.	"Words with the wife" every week or two about some matter, tacitly accepted as a harmless, but long-standing difference of opinion. He gets over it by going to the pub, the garden, or keeping quiet. These rows spread through the household, but blow over in a couple of hours without need for reconciliation.	Quarrels, sulks or glooms replaced by acrimonious discussion of differences, so that rows are not only nipped in the bud, but subjects which have been a chronic cause of argument become settled once and for all. Such real rows as occur are usually excusable, concerning, for example, neglectful conduct toward children.	Quarrels more frequent, often last overnight. They are made up over-emotionally, or smoulder only to blaze up again; upset most other relationships of the individual concerned. The husband may leave the house for days, or refuse to speak to his wife. Children and other members of the family usually implicated.	No restraint over quarreling. Quarrels of indefinite duration and may be so violent that the home is left.
7. *Staying home and going out.* Balance of time spent in and out of the house, degree of purposiveness in outside activities as compared with inside activities, extent to which other members of the household are taken along, or those outside are brought back, i.e., degree of interconnection between home relationships and other regions of social contacts—	One or two nights a week spent in a public house or club, with occasional outings for such purposes as tax-payers' meetings. Considerable reliance on home patterns; most men put out if compelled to spend more time than usual away from home. Time away usually spent in some form of "male" activity. Few people invited in.	More going about, usually with wife, who is inducted into many more types of social contact. A variety of people come in. More entertaining.	Either more time spent away, especially at places where the wife could also come (with overspending or drunkenness), or refusal to go out, especially to places where old acquaintances might be met. When the wife goes out, the man will stay indoors however unpleasant the circumstances.	Going off for spells alone, periods of desertion lasting anything over two days. Alternatively the man never moves out of the house for weeks or even months, though nonparticipant and alone in the home.

the unmarried naturally away more. Cf. time spent in organized group activities, Criterion 14.

8. *Parents and relatives.* Relationships of married men with their parents and in-laws, and of unmarried men living away from home, with their parents. Degree of active participation outside the home, with various members of the home family group, and type of interaction existing with other close relatives (married brothers and sisters, aunts, etc.) living in the vicinity.	(*a*) For unmarried men living away from home, and married men. Periodical duty visits, often arranged, not spontaneous. Fairly strong sense of responsibility manifested by material assistance in times of stress. Relationships to some extent joking relationships, badinage covering up mutual emotional shyness. Visits by relatives not encouraged, save on special occasions, such as birthdays. (*b*) For unmarried men living with parents, as for Criterion 7.	(*a*) Greater inclusion of parents, etc., in various activities; a good deal of coming and going between the various homes. This is two-way, invitations are not needed. (*b*) As for Criterion 7.	(*a*) Lack of visits. In a few cases dependence on relatives, especially the mother. Continual visits to parents' home without wife, but no participatory activity linking the two homes. (*b*) As for Criterion 7.	(*a*) Complete break with parental family. More rarely, abandonment of marital family in favor of a permanent return to the parental roof. (*b*) As for Criterion 7.
9. *Neighbors and neighborhood.* Relationships established by geographical propinquity; extent to which a man tolerates and makes constructive use of the fact that his household inevitably exists in a context of other households.	On "dropping-in" terms with at least three immediate neighbors, says "good morning," to most people living on the same street, but not intimate with many. Emphasis is on keeping the neighbors out, rather than on letting them in.	Positive friendships with neighbors—shared activities of various types. Neighbors not afraid of these people. Several times neighbors—and not even immediate neighbors—looked in while the investigator was there, to borrow something or to arrange a project.	Greater seclusion. Goes out over the garden fence to avoid meeting acquaintances in the street, drops old friends among neighbors and does not accompany his wife when visiting, easier to associate with strangers. His pub is outside his district.	No contact with neighbors, even of merely a formal character, through withdrawal or hostility.

TABLE I Continued

General definition	Norm (Grade 3)	Supranorm (Grade 4)	Infranorm (Grade 2)	Infranorm (Grade 1)
10. *Workmates and unions.* Relationships with fellow workers, taken as those with whom the individual enters into nearness through his economic role; includes men working on the same task, fellow union members, etc. The quality of the relationship is shown by the degree of participation both in work and outside that area.	Lack of hostility to workmates at the bench, intimate relationships with one or two, who visit each other's houses, occasionally go on communal family excursions. In at least one works activity outside his job, but, apart from his intimates, does not like meeting mates out of hours—work and home do not mix. Rarely attends his trade-union branch.	Friendships not exclusive, but include, in a more casual way, many fellow workers known through various activities. Friendship with one group does not entail hostility to another. In many works activities, and usually attends his trade-union branch.	Hostility to groups of fellow workers pronounced; work relationships confined strictly to work hours. Passive lack of cooperation at the bench. Practically no participation in works activities, most often no trade-union membership.	Unemployment if the whole economic role is rejected, otherwise complete lack of communication inside as well as outside working hours, whether this isolation is self-sought or the result of rejection by mates.
11. *Employers and management.* The relationship of the employee to the employer in terms of his behavior at work and his attitude toward it; degree of independence and loyalty in direct relationships with authority in the economic role.	Relations usually quite good, and very infrequent changes of employment; but a good deal of grumbling, little sense of obligation to employer, who is expected to provide various amenities without being entitled to extra service.	Increased wages, positions of greater responsibility than prewar. Employer given credit for good things done, but actively fought for injustices. Absenteeism, indiscipline not used as weapons of opposition; group mechanisms invoked.	In some absenteeism, minor indiscipline, forfeiture of pay, drop in wages; in others anxious efforts to work well. Dissatisfaction confined to morose withdrawal. In a few cases, dependence on employer; the man in and out of personnel manager's office.	Unemployment, or gross indiscipline of a type inevitably leading to dismissal, e.g., chronic absenteeism.

12. *Wider personal contacts.* Ability to establish personal relationships with members of social groups to which the individual has not previously been joined by any common role or relationship; ease or difficulty of crossing barriers of class, caste, education, race, etc.	Friendships, save of a polite and formal kind, not common. Any depth of association going beyond conventional small talk invokes embarrassment and aloofness. Once contact established, difficulties of communication eased, though every difference of background is, as it arises, a disturbing factor.	Far more fluidity between groups, visiting terms easily established. Group differentiation, as judged by income, work, education, etc., almost ceases to exist, or at least to be a barrier. Personality factors rather than class or caste the main determinants in friendships.	Hostility and suspicion against anyone in the larger outgroups. An almost paranoid fear, manifested by avoidance and complete uncommunicativeness toward any intruder in his narrowed circle.	Inability to enter into any type of relationship with anyone outside the individual's ingroup.
13. *Women outside the family.* Intersex relationships, primarily of a sexual, or potentially sexual, nature; degrees of their avoidance or pursuit, emotional investment, inclusion-exclusion from other activities and social networks of the individual, for both the married and unmarried positions.	(a) Married men. Occasional flirtations emasculated by facetiousness. Efforts to make wife party to these. Public joking about them. Relations with other women—mainly the wife's friends—somewhat formal. (b) Unmarried men. Marriage as ultimate end in view. Casual affairs, but all the time developing ideas of what he wants wife to be like. Casual girl friends not brought home; discussion of them taboo; girl's home not visited.	(a) Intimate with women without danger to marital relationships of either party. Women friends of his own, and also independent relationships with his wife's friends. (b) Girl friends, temporary or permanent, brought into all activities. Homes mutually visited. Some intimacy with her family, going out with her brothers and sisters. Often more than one girl at a time; though they know this, he remains on straight terms with all.	(a) Avoids women more than men, or else attempts to establish relationships on a purely sexual basis. Often goes to places where there are women (dances, etc.), but seldom plucks up enough courage to speak to them, except as they are going out, when semijocular advances may be made. (b) As for (a).	(a) Sexual offenses, or complete refusal to enter into any relationships (often combined with impotence). (b) As for (a).

TABLE I Continued

General definition	Norm (Grade 3)	Supranorm (Grade 4)	Infranorm (Grade 2)	Infranorm (Grade 1)
14. *Organized group activities.* Relationships which occur through the medium of some organized social activity—clubs, political parties, etc., in which membership of interest is voluntary; nature of interest involved; its degree of seriousness and narrow-wideness; quality of group tie, and the roles and responsibilities carried by the individual in the organizations to which he belongs.	Few group activities of an intellectual or political nature, but likes to know what is going on, especially in the realm of sport, without taking much active part. Embarrassed, confused, or irritated by any attempt to penetrate below the surface. Prides himself on some special skill or knowledge of the hobby type, such as horticulture, or pigeon breeding, around which relationships may be built.	Has interests leading to some sort of active, responsible membership of social organizations. Is obviously open to new ideas, especially in their practical application. Whatever his level of interest and intelligence, is looking for, or has found, a social means of expressing himself in action.	Lack of interest in political or other matters, or overexcitement uncompensated by any positive attitudes toward social issues, i.e. violent opinions are not transformed into social action. Activity is disorganized and destroys the possibility of constructive participation in social organizations.	Serious restriction of the interest field amounting to complete mental apathy; or violent hostility, unrelated to group action or to the needs of his own situation.
15. *Impersonal authorities.* The individual's behavior and attitude toward the city council, the government, U.N., etc.; degree of feeling, if microscopic to macrosocial, an active, contributor to social events; quality of social projection on to "gods" and "powers that be," who represent to the individual his sense of being in a total society which he cannot control.	Expects things to be done for him by a power vaguely described as "they." Criticizes "them" a good deal, particularizing them as some special party or organization, but not prepared to act unless his personal interests are drastically impinged on. This occurs, not when affects as a citizen, but as a particular category of person—a tax-payer, a car owner, etc. Lukewarm about all political parties on all levels; if he does play a part in public affairs it is a protesting one.	Does not feel servile toward, or dominated by, "them." Sees himself as a small component of the forces which control him and is alive to his own share in the business. Active at election times, tax-payers' meetings, locality clubs, etc., with a realistic approach.	Impotent rebellion or submission, sometimes alternating. The rebel belongs to no organized body of opposition. This noisy helplessness allied to apathetic helplessness, equally common a feeling that "someone" must be concerned and will eventually act; in the meantime dice are loaded against him, activity on his own part futile.	Complete absence of any personal attitude to authority except, in some cases, an undifferentiated hostility which may lead to antisocial activity—even the lonely sabotage of crime.

TABLE 2   Distribution of Degree of Settlement Between CRU and Non-CRU Attenders (%)

	More settled	Less settled	Sample size
CRU sample	74	26	50
Non-CRU sample	36	64	100

TABLE 3   Comparison of CRU, Non-CRU and Control Groups on Social Criteria

Criterion of social participation	(a) Frequency of scores below the norm Non-CRU/CRU	(b) Frequency of scores above the norm CRU/control group
1.	Borderline significance	Significant
2.	—	Significant
3.	—	—
4.	—	—
5.	—	—
6.	Significant	—
7.	Significant	—
8.	Borderline significance	Significant
9.	Significant	Significant
10.	Significant	Significant
11.	—	Significant
12.	Borderline significance	—
13.	Significant	—
14.	Significant	—
15.	Significant	—
Totals	7 Significant criteria (3 borderline cases)	6 Significant criteria

proportion of supranorm behavior in the non-CRU as compared with the control group—this may be accounted for by a small proportion of the non-CRU sample who have been able to make a very good adjustment through social utilization of their supranorm potentialities. Most important, there is a significant difference between the CRU sample and the control group (and the non-CRU group) in the proportion of these scores ($p \leq .01$). More than half the CRU cases score five or more times in Grade 4. This general superiority of the CRU sample occurs in spite of the existence of individual cases in which treatment has been inefficacious, and in spite of a higher degree of current stress in the sample.

TABLE 4   Comparison of CRU, Non-CRU and Control Groups on Social Criteria

(a) Distribution of individuals scoring below the norm (1 and 2) in each group on varying numbers of criteria (number of critera above norm)

Individuals in	0–4	5–9	10–15	Total
Control group	38	2	—	40
CRU sample	40	9	1	50
Non-CRU sample	45	40	15	100

(b) Distribution of individuals scoring at the norm (3) in each group (number of criteria at norm)

Individuals in	0–4	5–9	10–15	Total
Control group	—	8	32	40
CRU sample	7	33	10	50
Non-CRU sample	16	58	26	100

(c) Distribution of individuals scoring above the norm (4) in each group (number of criteria above norm)

Individuals in	0–4	5–9	10–15	Total
Control group	35	5	—	40
CRU sample	21	26	3	50
Non-CRU sample	77	20	3	100

CONCLUSIONS

1. In view of the equivalence of the samples, the significantly higher proportion of well-adjusted men among those who had attended a CRU emphasizes the worth of the CRU as a therapeutic community.

2. The extent of social integration among those rated as settled cannot be attributed entirely to CRU experience of approximately one month's duration. Traumatic experience, where circumstances of personality and social setting are propitious, may lead to improved social participation. This suggestion is supported by the supranorm social participation of settled men, in the non-CRU group. The proportion of settled men, was, however, significantly higher in the CRU group. The CRU may, therefore, be regarded as an agency through which the potentially educative experiences of POW life may be released from tensions and anxieties which otherwise inhibit their assimilation and application in civil life.

3. The fact that the settled men appear to be able to manipulate their basic social relationships better than the civilian control sample, raises several

points. Normality is not optimum adjustment and is certainly not synonymous with the most free and unanxious interaction within a given social framework. Whatever their origin, the atomistic tendencies of modern life have greatly reduced the size of the functional family. Outside an individual's immediate family, parental or marital, most relationships of an affective nature into which he enters have no socially organized pattern. This lack of dependable support seems to be one of the major foci of anxiety in Western society. It is conducive to withdrawal and it is such a withdrawal that the pattern of negative deviance exhibits.

4. In a sense the CRU replaces the larger organized family group by providing a series of safe and stable relationships between the immediate family and the wider society. Not only recovery but supranormative quality in these bridge regions characterizes the pattern of positive deviance. It is to be noted that a better level of both husband/wife and worker/employer relations appear in the context of this pattern. When a man has left the CRU, the sense of security seems to persist; the potentialities of relationships are effectively discovered to be congruous with the framework of society.

5. What we have called desocialization cannot be confined to those who have had specific experiences of separation, but is a general social phenomenon. It is a kind of affective dislocation from the exigencies of social interaction which has become highly organized on a cultural basis. To focus attention on gross desocialization such as characterized extreme POW unsettlement would be misleading. Unsettlement which is unspectacular—since it is far more widespread and less easily identified—is in the long run a greater menace than that which leads to broken marriages and crime. The results point to the presence of a certain desocialization in the norm itself. This is a problem that would appear to provide a focal point of study for social scientists.

Reference

Sherif, M. 1936. *Psychology of Social Norms*. New York and London: Harper and Brothers.

Varieties of Group Process

The field of group dynamics was founded out of war-time experience where the competence and cohesion of face-to-face groups of various kinds became of critical importance. The reality of the group as exhibiting a level of behavior over and above that of its individual members became the focus of research inquiry on both sides of the Atlantic. Not surprisingly, the initial emphasis of the Institute's work was on group processes. While group therapy was undertaken in the Clinic, trials were made of various ways in which the dynamics of groups could be studied in real-life situations in education, industry and the social professions.

Bion Revisited: Group Dynamics and Group Psychotherapy. Much use was made of Bion's ideas as put forward in his early *Human Relations* papers (1948–51). This body of work introduced entirely new theory. He postulated two distinct levels of activity in group life: the first concerned with what the group had to do in the real-life situation—*W* for the work group; the second with unconscious activity which all too often interfered with the first. These ideas, which he was greatly to elaborate, have been and are immensely influential, if still controversial. They are evaluated in Sutherland's contribution to this Theme in which he also relates object relations theory to more recent psychoanalytic concepts of the self. These have to be taken into account in analyzing group behavior.

An Educational Model for Group Dynamics. The paper by Herbert and Trist is an analysis of an attempt to bring into existence an educational model for group dynamics, as distinct from a clinical or action model. It weaves together some of Bion's ideas with Dewey's concept of the project method. The research describes how a group of teachers interested in improving their understanding of human relations in school undertook a study of their own relations and went through a number of phases at the end of which they made a book-length report of their experience to the profession. The paper shows how topics they brought to the group were related to the here-and-now dynamic of its relation with the consultant. It contains a verbatim account of a critical session—the only such account in the literature. It analyses the phenomenon of an absent leader and offers new theory on the basis of charisma. Structural factors in subgroup organization, hitherto unobserved, are identified.

Experiential Learning in Groups I: The Development of the Leicester Model. This is a form of group relations training, a British version of the Human Relations Laboratories initiated by NTL at Bethel, Maine and inspired by Lewin. The British version began in 1957 and continues at the present time. It is heavily influenced by Bion's ideas and by psychoanalytic thinking on matters such as projection and group transference in the here-and-now. The conferences are residential under social island conditions.

A novel feature is that they include events at three system levels: the primary group, the inter-group and the large group representing the entire membership of the conference. Outside sessions, staff contact with participants is held to a minimum. Interpretative comment is process-centered at the level of the group. Participants come from a great variety of organizations, but predominantly from the helping and social professions. The aim is to make them more aware not only of their own relations with others but with the new factors that come into play at the inter-group and large group levels. In his first paper, Eric Miller makes an overview of this whole development. The model has been taken up in many countries, especially in the United States.

Experiential Learning in Groups II: Recent Developments in Dissemination and Application. In this paper Miller describes new methodologies that have only lately been introduced, such as how to make a society an intelligible field of study through direct experience.

The Psycho-Dynamics of an Inter-Group Experience. The dynamics of inter-group as distinct from intra-group phenomena had remained an unexplored field until Harold Bridger introduced an inter-group event into an early Leicester conference. A research study was made of its first trial, a shortened version of which is included under this Theme. Spontaneously and unconsciously, the conference membership partitioned themselves into three groups to carry out the over-all task to be accomplished (designing the program for two days in the second week). One group absorbed the depression, another the conflict, leaving a third to work out creative proposals. The findings of this project on complementary group roles in an unconscious division of labor constitute a major contribution to group theory.

Courses and Working Conferences as Transitional Learning Institutions. The Institute made it a point to explore other approaches and Bridger developed what he has called the task-oriented model of group development. This model is concerned with the roles and relationships of the participants in organizations, and personal change as a by-product of this. The aim is to improve role performance and organizational understanding through a transitional learning institution.

As well as being purpose-oriented, organizations have also to be learning and self-reviewing entities. His model is designed to make participants aware of both these aspects, which he calls the "double task." This notion of the double task needs to be built into organizational culture; special events and procedures are necessary to develop competence in handling it. This competence has become essential now that organizations are facing higher levels of complexity, interdependence and uncertainty. The method has been tried extensively in large organizations as well as in external workshops in a number of countries, including the United States.

Action Research in Minisocieties. In the 1960s and 1970s fault lines appeared in Western societies disclosing a number of severely alienated minorities and categories of individuals. Gunnar Hjelholt, a Danish social psychologist with whom the Institute maintained a close association, developed a model of group relations training to address this issue. He called his model the "minisociety." In it, members of different and opposing sub-cultures are gathered together in a temporary society to learn about each other from the confrontation of their differences. Gurth Higgin describes an early encounter of this kind in which he took part. Hjelholt gives the rationale of the method which has spread quite widely in Scandinavia and several other European countries.

Task and Sentient Systems and Their Boundary Controls. There has been much interest in the subject of group boundaries and where they should best be drawn. In Systems of Organization (1967) Miller and Rice made a distinction between the task group that comprises the individuals employed in an activity system and the sentient group to which individuals are prepared to commit themselves and on which they depend for emotional support. The boundaries of these two types of groups may be the same or different. When they are the same there are advantages of cohesion but dangers of closure. When they are different there is the advantage of openness but the danger of too little cohesion. The trade off between the pros and cons of these two conditions is a major factor that needs consideration in organizational design. This concept has opened up new horizons.

Individual, Group and Inter-Group Processes. Projects which entailed bringing together individual, group and inter-group processes posed the problem of creating a formal framework which could include them all. In this paper Rice shows how systems theory can be used toward this end and offers a mathematical notation to represent the various transactions involved.

The developments described all occurred in the group field during the first 20 post-war years. The more complex and interdependent environments that have since come into existence pose problems of active as opposed to passive adaptation (Emery and Trist, 1972/1973). These problems require approaches to group processes which involve the socio-ecological perspective and are described in Volume III. They include the "search conference" (Emery and Emery, 1978), "idealized design" (Ackoff, 1974) and "network therapy" as developed by Laing (Laing et al., 1965).

References

Ackoff, R.L. 1974. *Redesigning the Future*. New York: Wiley.

Bion, W.R. 1948–1951. "Experiences in Groups." *Human Relations*, 1:314–20, 487–96; 2:13–22, 295–303; 3:3–14, 395–402; 4:221–27.

Emery, M. and F. Emery. 1978. "Searching: For New Directions, In New Ways . . . For New Times." In *Management Handbook for Public Administrators*, edited by J.W. Sutherland. New York: Van Nostrand Reinhold.

Emery, F.E. and E.L. Trist. 1973. *Towards a Social Ecology*. London and New York: Plenum Press.

Laing, R.D., D. Cooper and A. Esterson. 1965. "Results of Family-oriented Therapy with Hospitalised Schizophrenics." *British Medical Journal*, 2:1462–65.

Miller, E.J. and A.K. Rice. 1967. *Systems of Organization: Task and Sentient Groups and their Boundary Control*. London: Tavistock Publications.

J.D. Sutherland

Bion Revisited
Group Dynamics and Group Psychotherapy*

Bion's First Statement

Bion's account of his experiences with groups falls into two parts. The first contains the description of his method of work, the phenomena he noted following its use and the tentative theories he evolved to understand them. While he regards his views as an extension of Freud's (1922), his whole thinking has a quite distinctive character. Like Freud, he refers frequently to very different entities by the word group, e.g., to organizations, or institutions such as the church and the army, and to such ill-defined groupings as "the aristocracy." His theories, however, stem from his observations in his "laboratory," the small group, and it is against the background of this "pure culture" that we have to appraise them.

In *Experiences in Groups* (Bion, 1961), he refers to two groups, each with a different task as perceived by the members at the start. In one, composed of "non-patients," the accepted aim was to study group behavior. In the other, the members were patients seeking help from a medical clinic. After an interview, the psychiatrist explained to each prospective patient that an understanding of his conflicts in personal relationships could help in the amelioration of his symptoms. Such understanding was facilitated by meeting in a group in which relationships could be studied as they developed. To Bion, the use of his approach, i.e. one in which the sole activity of the leader or therapist is to make interpretations of the phenomena in the group as these develop, made any difference between the two groups irrelevant. The different expectations of members in the opening phase, however, are reflected in the groups. In fact his main references are to the therapeutic groups in which a strictly group-centered stance is stressed.

We readily recognize that the development of his method was in itself a major achievement. With a remarkable courage from his convictions, he

*A shortened version of the original in M. Pines (Editor), *Bion and Group Psychotherapy*. London: Routledge and Kegan Paul, 1985.

showed that a psychoanalytic approach permitted the exposure of unrecognized, irrational and powerful relationships that were specific to the group situation. Bion was explicit on the highly subjective nature of his method, especially in its use of counter-transference feelings and in the detection of processes of projective identification wherein the therapist picks up the feelings of the members through what he senses they are projecting into him. As in psychoanalysis, the observer learns to attend to two levels of mental activity: the manifest conscious and the latent subconscious and unconscious. It is its subjectivity that arouses so much antipathy in those who consider that scientific research into human relationships can rest only on behavioral data. Nevertheless, that he had described something that illuminated the depths of group phenomena was clear from the remarkably rapid and widespread interest in his observations. There was little doubt that his work had made a profound stir in the new field of group dynamics. Nearly four decades later it continues to be as evocative as it was at the start—and a short scan of the history of theoretical views in psychology and the social sciences during the century readily shows that to be a quite unusual distinction.

To sustain the efforts of any group around its task requires in the first place a readiness to co-operate, which, for Bion, is a sophisticated product from years of experience and training. Next, the mental activity required to further the task must be of a particular kind, because judgments about the nature and origin of actual phenomena and actions designed to overcome difficulties presented by them have to be tested against constant interaction with reality. In short, as opposed to any magical solutions, it must involve rational thinking with consequent learning and development, i.e., ego-activity. It is this capacity to sustain task-focussed activity that the unorganized group greatly alters through the persistent interference from competing mental activities associated, in Bion's view, with powerful emotional drives. These conflicting forces at first seemed to have little in common except to oppose the task by creating a group that would satisfy the emotional needs of members as these become prominent. This state of the group Bion termed the "group mentality," and the way in which it might express itself, e.g., to find another leader, he described as the "group culture." These concepts, however, he soon found did not clarify sufficiently what his further experience perceived, namely, patterns of behavior that gripped the group into a relatively specific group mentality in opposition to the work activity. Bion named these patterns "basic assumptions" (*ba*s) of which he identified *ba*D (dependence), *ba*F (fight/flight) and *ba*P (pairing). In the *dependent group*, the basic assumption is that one person is there to provide security by gratifying the group's longings through magic. After an initial period of relief, individuals tend to react against the assumption because of the infantile demandingness and greed it engenders. Nevertheless, when he confronted the group with the dependence assumption taking over, Bion noted that a hostile response to any intervention by him frequently revealed more than a resentment against his refusal to provide the magical pabulum. A longing for a more permanent and comprehensive support was to be seen in the raising of religious themes, with the group feeling that its "religion," in which the therapist is a phantasied deity, was being taken from it. *Fight and flight* appeared as reactions to what the group wanted to avoid, namely, the work activity (*W*) that forced it to confront the need to develop by giving up primitive magical ideas. The ineffectiveness of these solutions led at times to a different activity, for which Bion postulated the assumption of *pairing*. Pairing occurred repeatedly in his groups in the form of two members, irrespective of sex, getting into a discussion. To his surprise, this was listened to attentively, with no sign of impatience from members whose own problems usually pressed them to seek the center of attention for themselves. There seemed to be a shared unconscious phantasy that sex was the aim, with reproduction as a means of meeting a powerful need to preserve the group as a group.

As mentioned, the group dominated by an assumption evolves an appropriate culture to express it, e.g., the dependent group establishes a leader who is felt to be helpful in supplying what it wants. Moreover, the assumptions can be strong enough for members to be controlled by them to the extent of their thinking and behavior becoming almost totally unrealistic in relation to the work task. The group is then for each member an undifferentiated whole into which he or she is pressed inexorably to conform and in which each has lost independent individuality. The individual experiences this loss as disturbing, and so the group is in more or less constant change from the interaction of the basic assumptions, the group culture and the individual struggling to hold on to his or her individuality.

Basic assumptions originate within the individual as powerful emotions associated with a specific cluster of ideas which compel the individual to behave accordingly and also to be attracted to those imbued with the same feeling with an immediacy that struck Bion as more analogous to tropisms than to purposive behavior. These bonds Bion termed "valency" because of the chemical-like nature of the attraction.

As primal motivating forces, the basic assumptions supply a fundamental thrust to all activity, yet the drive towards interaction with the real environment remains the more powerful dynamic in the long run, for, without that adaptive urge, survival would not be possible. The difficulties of reality interactions, however, are great. The physical environment may present insoluble problems; but it is the social factors that become prominent in their effects on the capacities of the individual when work demands co-operation with all the give and take that entails. The frustrations in sustaining work activity are thus perpetually liable to induce the regressed behavior of the assumptions. The more the individual becomes identified with a basic assumption, the more does he or she get a sense of security and vitality from fusion with the group, along with the pull back to the shared illusory hopes of magical omnipotent achievement inherent in the phantasies of the assumption. From all these sources there is derived what Bion described as a hatred of learning, a profound resistance to staying in the struggle with the reality task until some action gives the experience of mastery of at least a part of it, i.e., until development of new inner resources occurs.

The appeal of each assumption rests in the associated emotion which gets a characteristic quality from the specific phantasies and ideas it involves. The assumptions do not conflict with each other. Instead, they change from one to another and conflict occurs only between them and the work group. When one *ba* is combined with work activity, however, the other *ba*s are suppressed. A further observation Bion made was the way in which the *ba* group could change to its "dual." Thus the dependent group under the frustrations of the leader's failure to gratify its longings could reverse roles so that the group treated the leader as the one in need of help. In this connection, he also noted the tendency of the dependent group when left to its own devices to choose as leader the most disturbed member, as if it could best depend on someone of its own kind, as dependent as itself—the familiar genius, madman or fanatic.

The interrelations of the *ba*s, plus the tenacity and exclusiveness with which the emotions and ideas are bound together in each *ba*, led Bion to what he felt was a theoretical impasse which no available psychological explanation could illumine. He therefore postulated a metapsychological notion that transcends experience in the form of a proto-mental system in which the prototype of each *ba* exists "as a whole in which no part can be separated from the rest." The emotion in each individual that starts the *ba* progresses to the psychological manifestations that can be identified.

The physical and the mental are undifferentiated in the basic levels of this system, a feature which led to his suggestion that certain illnesses, e.g., those in which a substantial psychosomatic component has long been recognized, might well be diseases of certain conditions in groups. To test such ideas needed much larger populations than the small group could provide, but he hoped it might be done in order to establish the basic assumptions as clinical entities.

Bion's concluding observations become increasingly concerned with aspects of group dynamics in general, e.g., the oscillations in attitudes to the leader as leader of the assumption group or of the work group, or splits in the group. On the relationship of the individual to the group, he agrees with Freud that a group instinct is not primitive and that the individual's groupishness originates in his or her upbringing within the family. Bion adds to these, however, from his observations the view that, while the group adds nothing to the individual, certain aspects of individual psychology cannot be explained except by reference to the matrix of the group as the only situation that evokes them. The individual loses his or her distinctiveness when in a basic assumption group, i.e., one in which individuality is swamped by the group valencies. When it has to deal with realities, such a group has to change, or perish.

Earlier I noted that most of Bion's references were to his therapeutic groups and he states how he believes their aim is furthered. His first and most emphatic view is that any help individuals may get from the group situation towards understanding themselves more fully rests on the extent to which they can recognize themselves as torn between the pull of the basic groups and membership of the work group which represents ego functioning. For this reason, any interventions from the therapist directed to the psychopathology of the individual must be avoided because they are destructive of the experience of the basic group. By adhering strictly to his standpoint, he concluded that individuals do become less oppressed by basic group activity within themselves. In other words, what he asserts is that by showing the group the ways in which it avoids its task through regressing to dependency, fight/flight or pairing, it can become more work oriented and so further the development by learning of all members.

Much of the subsequent criticism of Bion's approach as a psychotherapeutic method arises, I believe, from a failure to keep his aims clear and especially to avoid the confusion which the use of the word therapeutic, and especially psychotherapeutic, has engendered. To those seeking to use the group situation in a psychotherapeutic way, i.e., to cope with the enormous diversity of neurotic behavior and its unique configuration in every individual, work has to be based on our understanding of psychopathology. The group processes must therefore be directly relatable to the latter. Bion's approach in fact originated in the problem of neurosis as a social one, i.e., how does the large organization cope with the failures of its members to comply with its work task. The opening sentences in his book make plain that, for him, "group therapy" can mean the therapy of individuals in groups, in which case neurosis is the problem of the individual, but that in the treatment of the group it has to be a problem of the group.

His conception of group therapy may then be put as follows: the individual contains within his or her innate endowment certain potential patterns which are released in the unorganized group. This unorganized group is not a special kind of group identifiable by its external features, but a state of mind that can overtake any group. Once elicited, these patterns or basic assumptions bond the individuals together to give security by preserving the group as a unity and by seeking a course of action for it governed largely by magical phantasies. These patterns remove the individuals' distinctiveness, i.e., their overall modes of dealing with their own purposes as fashioned by their learning from the experience of reality. Because these modes—ego functioning—are always present in some measure, a conflict between ego and absorption in any basic assumption behavior is never absent. Such group-determined behavior is a serious limitation to the individuals in any group when faced with an unfamiliar task. They tend to feel in an unorganized state, so their capacity to tackle the task realistically becomes quite unreliable. (The commonest remarks after intensive exposure to the unorganized group situation at Group Relations Conferences run on the Tavistock model are those describing feelings of being "de-skilled.") To have developed a method whereby these group dynamics can be experienced in adequate depth, and to have shown some of the requirements in the leader for the application of this method, is an extremely valuable contribution to the whole study of group dynamics. His findings can assist those responsible for groups coping with tasks to note when their effectiveness is impaired by *ba* behavior, and this kind of experience features prominently in many management training schemes.

It is a quite separate issue, however, to appraise the value of the principles underlying Bion's work in relation to the use of groups for analytical psychotherapy. The distinction between the study of group dynamics and group therapy has become a clear one in the courses developed by A.K. Rice and his associates, as was seen in the staff attitude to any individual who got into serious personal difficulties during a conference. The staff arranged to get the help needed, but it would not confuse its own role by attempting to provide psychiatric help itself. The strict use of Bion's approach has never been widely adopted by analytical psychotherapists, not even in the Tavistock Clinic. Many have, however, made more systematic use of the group situation in their interpretations than have most other therapists, in the sense of trying to base these strictly on the here-and-now dynamics in the group situation as a whole.

Although we can agree on a separation of these two tasks, we are left with many unsolved questions that affect our understanding of both. To state that the individual's groupishness is an inherent property in his or her makeup as a social animal has not really carried forward our understanding of its nature and origin. Are the phenomena of the basic assumptions as specific to the group situation as he asserts? There is no question that, when activated by them, individuals can show a remarkable capacity to abandon their distinctiveness. The group gives a prominence to these responses by intensifying them, yet they do not appear to be different from the primitive relationships that can be seen in individual treatment, especially in light of our further knowledge of the earliest stages of the development of the person.

One feature of Bion's thought that I believe is unrecognized by him is his underlying adherence to concepts of energy as in the classical psychoanalytic theories of Freud. Thus basic assumptions originate as emotions which are viewed as sources of energy, and Bion is then puzzled by the specific clusters of phantasies around them. Phantasies are of imagined relationships and, if we take emotions to be the affective coloring accompanying any relationship, their specific quality is determined by the specifics of the relationships. The dependence and pairing assumptions are much more complex in this respect than the others. They can be readily seen as the prototypes of human relationships, e.g. as infantile dependence in which the self and the object are not differentiated, becoming the more differentiated clinging or attachment to a differentiated object in *ba* pairing. Fight and flight are the basic responses of all animals to situations that evoke pain or the threat of danger. Bion seems to sense the problem of the individual and the group as needing a good deal of further clarification, and the choice he made for his next step was to turn his microscope, to use his own metaphor, back to the earliest stages of individual development. This move leads to a major amplification in his understanding of the dynamics of all groups.

Re-View of the First Statement

In his re-view of the dynamics of the group, Bion "hopes to show that in his contact with the complexities of life in a group the adult resorts, in what may be a massive regression, to mechanisms described by Melanie Klein as typical of the earliest phases of mental life." This task of "establishing contact with the emotional life of the group . . . would appear to be as formidable to the adult as the relationship with the breast appears to be to the infant, and the failure to meet the demands of this task is revealed in his regression." The two main features of this regression are, first, a belief that the group exists as an entity which is endowed with characteristics by each individual. Distinct individuals become lost and the group is treated as if it were another person. Second is the change within the individual that accompanies his or her regressed perception of the group. For this change Bion quotes Freud's description of the loss of the individual's distinctiveness, with the addition that the individual's struggle to retain it varies with the state of the group. Organization helps to maintain work group activity, and indeed that is its aim.

In the work group, individuals remain individuals and co-operate, whereas in the basic assumption group they are swept spontaneously by the "valency" of identification, the primitive gregarious quality in the personality, into the undifferentiated unity of the *ba* group in which inner realities overwhelm the relationship with the real task.

Although starting his re-view with the regression in groups as their most striking feature, he emphasizes again the fundamental dynamic of the work group, which also has its combination of emotions and ideas. Especially important is the idea that development and the validity of learning by experience is the impetus in the individual to possess the autonomy of his own mental

life. It is as if there was a recognition "of the painful and often fatal consequences of having to act without an adequate grasp of reality." Despite the
dominant influence of the basic assumptions over it at times, work activity is
what takes precedence eventually—as it must. Freud, following Le Bon,
believed the intellectual ability of the group was reduced, but Bion disagrees.
His experience is that, even when basic assumptions are active, the group
shows high-level intellectual work in the assimilation of interpretations. Although this work goes on in a segregated part of the mind with little overt
indication, its presence has to be assumed from the way in which interpretations, ostensibly ignored, are nevertheless worked upon between sessions with
subsequent reports from individuals of how they had been thinking of them,
though they meant nothing at the time they were made. It is only in activity of
the work group that words are used normally, i.e., with their symbolic significance. The basic assumption groups, by contrast, use language as a mode of
action and are thereby deprived of the flexibility of thought that development
requires.

Bion considerably amplifies what he now discerns in the *ba*s. This development is related to his much greater familiarity with primitive mental processes
and their detection by an increased responsiveness to projective identification
as described by Melanie Klein (1940). He believes this method, which requires
a psychoanalytically trained observer, is the only one that can detect the
important subjective processes. Conclusions based on its use have to be
appraised by the effect of interventions and by the experience of many observers over time.

In the dependent group, he adds to the expectation of treatment from the
therapist, a much more primitive phantasy of being literally fed by him. At a
less primitive level he again stresses the presence of a projected deity who is
clung to with tenacious possessiveness. The sexual phantasies which characterized the pairing group, with the possible implication of reproduction as preserving the group, are now taken to be the result of a degree of rationalization.
Nevertheless, Oedipal sexual phantasies are present much of the time in all of
the assumptions. They are not, however, of Freud's classical type, but of the
much more primitive nature described by Klein (1932). According to her, the
phantasies of very young children show, as the self is emerging in relation to its
objects, themes of the parents mutually incorporating parts of each other.
Hungry sadistic urges abound that the child attributes to one or both figures by
its identification with them. The child can then experience a psychotic or
disintegrative degree of anxiety from the fear of being the object of retaliatory
attacks. It then splits off the part of its self involved in the relationship and
attempts to get rid of it by projective identification. These primitive Oedipal
relationships, according to Bion, are distributed in various ways among (i) the

individual, (ii) the group felt as one fragmented individual with (iii) a hidden figure, the leader, used here by detaching him from his role as leader of the work group. A further addition to the Oedipal figures, one ignored in the classical formulation, is the sphinx—a role carried by the therapist and the work group. The curiosity of the individual about the group and the therapist evokes the dread associated with the infant's phantasied intrusions to get at and to devour what is inside the mother and what goes on in the phantasied primal scene.

The anxieties inherent in the primitive phantasies, sexual and other, are instinctively responded to by an attempt to find "allies," figures with whom the feeling of a close contact can bring reassurance. Bion accordingly suggests this need as a powerful stimulus to the creation of the pairing group. Another factor in its establishment and maintenance, also operative with no regard to the sex of the pair, is the feeling of hope, not a phantasy of a future event, but a "feeling of hope itself." This feeling he takes to be the opposite of all the strong negative feelings of hatred, destructiveness and despair and it is sustained by the idea of finding a saviour, a Messiah essentially, an idea that must never be realized.

The fight/flight groups are, as would be expected, much less associated with complex phantasied relationships, since they have the relatively simple aim of getting rid of the threat of danger when no other assumption or activity seems appropriate. On this group Bion (1961) makes, almost as an aside, what I find to be a remarkable statement: "The fight/flight group expresses a sense of incapacity for understanding *and the love without which understanding cannot exist*" (my italics). I do not think its full implications are taken up by Bion in regard to the emergence of any of the assumptions and to the role of the leader, topics to which I shall return.

Recognition of their more specific contents leads Bion to reconsider the status of his notions about the basic assumptions. There was no doubt they were helpful in ordering the chaotic manifestations in the group, but, in view of the primitive phantasies related to them, they now appeared as derivatives of these more fundamental processes. All the assumptions drive the group to find a leader, yet none of them is felt to establish a satisfactory state in the group. There is consequently perpetual instability with changes from one assumption to another with all those remaining opposed to learning and development. For all these manifestations, and for their very existence, Bion could find no explanation. The exposure of primitive phantasies and the anxieties they induce now made it clear that the basic assumptions were derivatives whose function is to defend the group against these anxieties becoming too intense. As defenses, however, they are all inadequate because of their segregation from any reality-testing. For Bion, the dynamics of the group could now be adequately experienced and understood only by the working out of these primitive primal scene phantasies as the factors underlying the basic assumptions and their complex inter-relationships.

Bion always kept Freud's views on groups in mind, and so he now looked at where he stood in relation to them. Leaving aside the references made to complex social organizations such as the church and the army, he re-asserts his agreement with Freud in rejecting the need to postulate a herd instinct. For him the individual is a group animal by nature, yet at war with the group and with those forces in him that determine his groupishness. The latter is in no way created by the group; it is merely activated and exposed by it. The impact of the group on the individual's distinctiveness springs from the state of mind in the group, i.e., the degree to which its lack of organization and structure fails to keep work activity, a contact with reality, the dominant activity. In the organized group the bond between members is one of co-operation, whereas in an unorganized state the bonds become the valencies of the basic assumption states. Bion sees McDougall's (1920) criteria for the organized group as the conditions that suppress the basic assumption trends in the members by keeping them related to reality.

The bonding from valency is a more primitive process than that from libido, which Bion takes to operate only in the pairing group. Freud's view of the bond to the leader as almost entirely an introjection of him by the ego (Bion does not mention Freud's ego-ideal as a separate structure) is again only part of the relationship to a leader. For Bion, Freud does not recognize the much more potentially dangerous bonding that arises in the assumption groups. Here the individual does not introject a leader who carries power for him through his contact with external reality. The leader in the basic assumption exhibits features that appeal to the assumption state in the members, who therefore projectively identify with him. This leader is thus as much a part of the assumption state as the members and just as divorced from external reality, so that he leads as often to disaster as not. Freud's view of the leader as the ego-ideal led him to see panic in military groups as following the loss of the leader. Bion thinks this account is not right, for panic arises when the situation might as readily give rise to rage as fear. Intense fight/flight behavior may resemble panic, but for Bion the group can well be still related to the leader on such occasions. Panic occurs when a situation arises completely outwith the purposes of the group and its associated organization.

Freud saw in the group the kind of relationships present in the family when the individual has developed to the stage of the traditional Oedipus complex, i.e., its emotional features were neurotic in character with the main sources of anxiety being the fears of loss of love or of being castrated. Bion saw them as deriving from much earlier phases in which the fears are of disintegration, i.e., loss of the self or madness. His belief that the only feasible therapeutic help in the group lies in the individual experiencing its primitive emotions and attitudes to him is again maintained.

Much as Bion has contributed, we are left with what seem to be the crucial questions about groups unanswered. What does the individual's groupishness rest on? We have Freud's libidinal bonds supplemented by valencies from primitive projective identifications with a great deal about "mechanisms," all manifested as the individual's distinctiveness is removed. This regressed state, moreover, can come and go with a high degree of lability. For Bion, this distinctiveness is placed in opposition to the groupishness conceived as the expression of emotions with which the individual has to be at war. Freud, on the other hand, sees the conflict as between the id and the culture of the individual's society internalized in his or her own super-ego and ego-ideal. Adult or mature groupishness, if we might put it that way, rests for Bion on co-operation, the sophisticated product of years of training. It is like an activity imposed on the freedom of the individual to be "doing his own thing" and accepted more or less reluctantly. How can such an achievement vanish within a few minutes in the unorganized situation of Bion's groups? Both Freud and Bion from their psychoanalytic studies have emphasized that individual and group psychology constitute the same field of study. If we accept that position we are a long way from understanding it. The intimate inter-relatedness of the individual with his social field strongly suggests that we are dealing with the individual as a highly open system maintained in his organization by appropriate input from a social field itself structured to provide this input. The phenomena seem to require the organization concept of open systems, which neither Freud nor Bion had.

Though stressing the highly tentative and limited status of his study of groups, Freud has reached conclusions of great significance. He has made it clear that what happens in any group is a particular instance of the relationship between the individual's inner world and his social world. Thus he has answered his questions about the group by expanding an answer to the unstated question of what is an individual. He had to advance the theory of the ego and its relationships by showing that a sub-system within the ego, the ego-ideal, entered into relationships that differed in character from those of the ego. Moreover, the most striking feature from his conclusions is the open and rapid dynamic transactions that can occur in the group whereby the individual, sensing his own inability and that of the other members to act effectively, can promptly alter the boundary of his self to internalize the leader as a part of it and so to surrender his previous distinctiveness in favor of a less mature organization of his self. Viewed in terms of Freud's metapsychology, and the meta-science available to him, with the dynamics of the person based upon the redistribution of psychic energies, the phenomena could not be adequately conceptualized. We are clearly confronted again with problems of the organization of the individual as a highly open system in an environment which reacts with him in a correspondingly open way. Individual and environment are structured by, and within, each other.

Recent Psychoanalytic Conceptions of the Individual and Social Relatedness

Clinical work and child observation studies of the last few decades have shown that the personality acquires the capacity to make effective relations with others only when there has been early experience of being treated as a person by the mother, and later the father, with stimulating encouraging interactions conveyed with joy. The satisfaction of physical needs has to be supplemented by a social input that meets the need to become a person. There appears to be from an early stage an overall Gestalt that gives to the potential self a feeling of things being right or not. Bodily sensations and the affects accompanying many specific behavioral systems all contribute to the affective tone in the self, yet a general malaise, even to the point of death, can follow from a failure in being personalized by appropriate mothering. Child studies show the dramatic results under certain conditions of deprivation, e.g., when a consistent maternal relationship is absent (see Spitz, 1965). Clinical findings from the more seriously distorted personalities emphasize lifelong feelings of never having been valued for themselves as with cold or indifferent mothers or, more frequently, with mothers experienced as imposing preconceptions that denied powerful urges to develop autonomously (see Lichtenstein, 1977). The self-system is thus structured by the internalization of the relationship between mother and child, undifferentiated at the start then progressively separated throughout the long period of human dependence.

Early structuring of the personality is inevitably dominated by the physical closeness in which the mother's attitudes are communicated through innumerable signals in her whole handling of, and responses to, her child. The emotional experiences are gradually cohered by consistent reliable mothering into a primary or central self. This integration is a labile process with threats to it producing at times intense anxiety and aggression. Negative feelings from the inevitable frustrations are separated from this primary self, but with ordinary care these divisions are diminished so that a sufficiently coherent, resilient self becomes the dominant mediator in relating to the environment. The primary self remains the visible self, the one adapted to the mother. Should the latter have failed to facilitate development sufficiently well, this primary self acquires distortions of its capacity to relate, and when negative experiences have been strong enough, substantial divisions within the structure of the self-system are formed. These sub-selves embody frustrated needs, especially for unmet recognition as a valued person, and the aggressive reactions to the frustrating mother linked with fears of her retaliation. The self-systems each retain a self-pole and an object-pole, with an imago of the kind of parent desired or feared and hated. The primary self relates to the outer world and so learns from its expanding experience. The sub-selves, while remaining highly dynamic as portions of the original self, have to find covert outlets—the processes described in the whole of psychopathology—because their aims have to be hidden from the feared parental attacks.

Defenses or control measures are evolved by the central self in keeping with its reality pressures and incorporated into its patterning. When the urges cannot be managed in this way they constitute a secret self in conflict with the central one. Stabilizing factors such as family and work, or selected social groups, all assist in their control, though the precarious balance shows when the functioning of the central reality-related self is altered as by drugs or by changes in the social environment. The central self ordinarily copes with such changes but removal of security-pinnings from it rapidly leads to the emergence of sub-system dominance.

When the imagos constituting the object-poles in the inner relationships are facilitative, the impact of infantile sexuality is worked through without undue trouble. Marked divisions in the self make for serious difficulties because the new urges to closeness are dealt with in their terms, e.g., hostile imagos evoke anxieties about rejection and retaliation and so lead to the fusion of aggression and sexuality in sadistic and perverse expression in which the object becomes in varying measure de-personalized.

The essential change in this way of conceiving the person is from one based on theories of psychic energies to one dealing with the organization of experience of relationships in an open system interacting with the social environment. Because of the incomplete differentiation of self and object, relations in the primary self are characterized by identifications and urges to have omnipotent magical control with regressive clinging to objects for security against the threat of "going to bits." With growing appreciation of reality and differentiation of self and others, the primary self is progressively superseded by a strengthened definition of the self through satisfactions from talents and skills. Attachment to others changes to relationships based on shared activities. Goals and purposes become organized, and values add to the integration of the self. The personality acquires its characteristic configuration, i.e., its identity (see Erikson, 1959), and, in keeping with the uniquely evolved patterns from its specific experience, the individual requires constant affirmation from the social milieu. The constant need for this "pyschosocial metabolism" in maintaining a normal degree of effective integrated functioning is readily exposed when sections of the environment are removed, quite apart from any interference with the biologically rooted sexual and procreational needs. Populations dis-

placed from their usual cultural setting show widespread indications of disorganization as in the rise of illnesses of all kinds, not only psychiatric. Again,
when individuals lose a feeling of personal significance in their work, similar
stress manifestations occur (see Trist and Bamforth, 1951). These deprivations
disorganize the most developed adaptive functioning of the social self, and
lead to the increased dominance of the primary self with its insecurities and
more primitive compulsive relations. Such regressive disorganization is almost
universal. With individuals whose sub-systems are a constant threat, the loss of
their usual sources of relative security confronts them with the extra danger of
their secret selves being exposed.

The origin and nature of the individual's groupishness is thus no problem.
From the very start he cannot survive without his needs for social relatedness
being met.

There is no phase in the life-cycle in which man can live apart from his
groups. Bion's statement that the individual is at war "with himself for being a
group animal and with those aspects of his personality that constitute his
groupishness" therefore has to be examined.

Group Dynamics and Group Psychotherapy

GROUP DYNAMICS

From the view of the individual I have sketched, the important questions about
groups are those devoted to the conditions that take away the factors in social
environment that ordinarily keep his self-system in its normal integration. Bion
stated that the basic assumptions are states of mind the individuals in the group
get into. He then described these states and what seemed to constitute them.
What he uncovered was the emergence of the primary mechanisms of relatedness, those of the developing infant to the breast/mother, and it is the intense
anxieties associated with these mechanisms that drive the group into the
assumptions. The individual's state of mind in them, however, remains a more
developed organization than would pertain exclusively to their earliest phase.
In the latter, differentiation of external objects hardly exists, whereas in the
assumptions there are intense needs to relate to a leader and to each other. The
phase in development that appears to be activated here is that of separation-
individuation (Mahler et al., 1975). As described earlier, this phase extends
over several years, and a range in the depth of regression is to be expected. The
dominant characteristic of this early self is its primal instinctive type of
relationship, the precursors of the maturer ones in which the external reality of
others is appreciated. The more the developmental elaborations around the

earliest structures are put out of action the more primitive the levels that are exposed. *Ba* dependence can be interpreted as the re-emergence of this stage in which the need for closeness gives to identifications a considerable urgency and immediacy; and the phantasy clusters around them represent the ways in which this is evoked, e.g., by being fed or protected or held in parental security. Fight/flight responses similarly show this level of identification to provide security. As Bion described, the urgency of the identifications can make the whole group an undifferentiated object within which the greatest security is to be found. Pairing is clearly a more developed state in which more precise definition of the self is sought in the relationship with one other. At the deepest levels it can activate the mother-child pair, in which case the attraction affirms the existence of the self. As he puts it, an ally against the dread of isolation in face of mounting anxiety is then provided. The fact that the rest of the group preserves it by giving the pair their rapt attention suggests that for them it has become their security, either from the primitive relationship or by this combined with the parental sexual couple, by identification with the pair.

Regression to these stages represents the removal of the influence of later structuring and an inability to recover it. The awareness of the group remains in its regressed form because the group is there and so restrains further disintegration which would be tantamount to psychotic states, an eventuality that the early structuring of the self also resists desperately. The problems of group dynamics thus become those of how the normal affirmations of the self system are removed. The situations of groups in this respect are of almost infinite variety. Thus when Bion said that certain illnesses might originate as diseases of the group, he thought specific illnesses might prove to be linked to specific states of the group. So far this has not been established, though there is much evidence now to show that disruptions of some areas of normal relatedness, as in groups displaced from their familiar environment, lead to increased illness of all kinds, physical and psychological. In view of this complexity of factors, it is best for present purposes to consider Bion's groups only. Here the most prominent stem from the task. Although there may have been some nominal description such as "to study group processes," none of the members has any clear notion of what that task involves. There is therefore immediately a considerable loss for the self of its ego anchorage in reality. Important also is the realization that the task, in whatever form it emerges, will involve members in some exposure of their private and even hidden self. This factor I believe to be important in the group dynamics group, although much more so in the therapeutic one. Since the origin of the secret self was its unacceptability, there is a great deal of anxious suspicion among members, alleviated only as each member demonstrates his participation in the task by the freedom with which he expresses some of his feelings about the situation. Likewise the intense curiosity about the leader derives from wondering how he is going to help them with the task at its reality level and from the fears of what he will read into their minds and how persecutory or rejecting he will then be.

What characterized Bion's method of work is his waiting for developments to occur spontaneously no matter what the pressures on him "to help." There is no doubt his stance exposed the regressed basic states with, at times, considerable intensity and persistence. For him it is imperative that members should experience the primitive nature and power of these states, and to have contact with these layers of their personality contributes a great self-integration in that the boundaries of their self-understanding are thereby extended. By focusing exclusively on the group, however, one notes only those features in the shared assumption states. Such recognition is essential, but to learn more about how they are brought into being is as important.

Freud had noted early in his experience how individuals will only with the greatest reluctance give up a source of gratification. The group's hatred of learning has this quality for Bion when he confronts them with clinging to assumption behavior instead of learning to cope with reality. In emphasizing this reaction we have, however, to balance it with the impetus to develop, the impetus which in the work group Bion notes as eventually overcoming the irrational resistances to it. We may then ask if Bion fosters an exaggerated degree of basic assumption behavior by not giving help sooner. This is a question not easily answered. I referred earlier to his almost incidental remark on love as a necessity for understanding, i.e., in this context, some fostering assistance. Bion was an extremely caring person and so one is left wondering whether he was in part fascinated by the basic assumption behavior to the neglect of how much help from the leader the egos of the members required to be re-asserted for the learning task.

The assumption made about the leader's role is that the group will by itself progressively learn to tackle the reality of the task through the leader pointing out what it is doing. Since, however, much of the overt behavior is determined by the need to avoid unrecognized feelings, these must require more explicit interpretation than Bion gives. Interpretations would seem to need more of a "because" clause—an attempt to identify what it is that is feared. Without this "help" the work group cannot function effectively. A group met to study its dynamics is, like any other task group, a socio-technical system and here, as elsewhere, the technical job has to come into the sphere of the ego's resources for mastering and using it. The specific complexity of this situation is that undoing the depersonalizing of the members because of their lost ego-involvement is itself the aim of the technology. A degree of understanding does go on much of the time, but it has to be asked whether it is optimal; when once in the grip of the basic assumptions it is all the more difficult to get back to normal ego-functioning. It thus seems that, as in analytical psychotherapy, a simultaneous relationship with the members' egos and the regressed state has to be kept alive.

Bion referred to the struggle of the individual against his groupishness. We can put this in another way. The groupishness he describes is clearly that of the regressed separation-individuation stage from which the individual has developed to inhabit his adult distinctive identity. This new development, however, has its own needs for group relatedness, namely, in groups in which his identity is affirmed and enriched by the extent of the ego's reality involvement in them.

The situation created in Bion's groups takes away the anchorage of the adult self-identity and it has to be asked whether the resentment of groupishness is because of this loss. The self-identity requires identification by others of its ordinary status plus the engagement with the task in a meaningful way. The organization of the group has to match the nature of the work, and if the latter presents a puzzle the group does not see how to cope with, then the leader has the task of dealing with the tendency of the group members to regress as well as enabling them to see that their belief that they have no resources is not entirely founded in reality. The experience of the latter, i.e., of regaining ego-function, brings back the work capacity.

Group Psychotherapy

As Bion mentions at the start of his book, this term is itself ambiguous as to whether it means therapy of the group conceived as an entity and so concerned with facilitating the group in overcoming barriers from its internal conflicts to its effectiveness as a work group or whether its purpose is therapy of the individuals comprising it. In practice, the latter purpose would be more accurately described as analytical psychotherapy in groups.

When Bion says that his method of work cannot be called psychoanalysis he means that the fundamental principles of psychoanalysis do not apply to it. There is here a source of widespread differences of view even amongst analysts. Both the classical and Kleinian analysts believe that a comprehensive exploration of unconscious processes is possible only in the traditional setting with the analyst preserving a somewhat distant stance in the interests of objectivity, maintaining a certain intensity in the conduct of the process, usually five times per week, and avoiding any other activity than the analytic one, e.g., no reassurances of any kind nor advice; offering understanding of the unconscious solely by interpretation. The value of this approach is not in question. What is, however, is the common assumption that other less intensive and rigorous approaches are relatively poor substitutes and, in short, "not analysis." Analytical psychotherapy on a less intensive pattern than the standard psychoanalytical one has in recent years altered this view; it is widely practiced by analysts themselves with the conviction that it can be of considerable help for the individual. Many unconscious factors in the personality can be exposed and their disturbing effects ameliorated in a range of patient-therapist settings. The critical factors are not so much the latter as the therapist's understanding of the unconscious and the extent to which he focuses on that.

The psychotherapeutic factor in Bion's method—again to be recalled as directed towards group dynamics—can be considered if we take one of his examples, the events in a group occasioned by a woman talking about a fear of choking in restaurants or, on a recent occasion, of her embarrassment during a meal in the presence of an attractive woman (Bion, 1961:182). About half of the group responded by saying they did not feel like that, and the others were indifferent. Bion notes that in analysis such a statement would have evoked various possible interpretations, none of which he felt could be regarded as appropriate to the group. What he did point out to the members was that the woman's difficulty was also theirs, although in repudiating it they made themselves superior to her. Moreover, in doing so they made it difficult for any member to admit any problem because they would then be made to feel more inferior and worthless. From an analytic point of view he appreciates that the woman got no help and is left in discomfort because in fact group treatment is the wrong treatment. He then adds that her manner of speaking suggested that she felt there was a single object, the group, that had been split into pieces (the individual members) by her eating; and that being the recipient of the members' projective identifications was her fault and so reinforced her guilt which, in turn, made it difficult for her to grasp how the actions of the others had affected her. For the other members, they have not only rid themselves of the woman's troubles as part of their own, but they have also got rid of any responsibility for her by splitting off their caring parts into the therapist. The result of this process is akin to a "loss of individual distinctiveness" through the basic assumption state of dependence. The group dynamics are clear; the psychotherapeutic effect is not only nil, it is negative.

The question is why Bion could not have made an interpretation along the lines he indicated in this reflection about the situation, at least to the extent of conveying the woman's hunger (perhaps felt as greed) as destructive to the group, with the latter attacking her, as they did these feelings in themselves. Also, by treating each other's problems in this way they were perpetuating the feeling that there was no help to be had from the group, only from the therapist. The precise interpretation is not so important as long as enough of the underlying dynamics of the total situation are articulated. By focusing exclusively on the group as a whole, certain awareness of group attitudes is made possible. Has that been as helpful as it might have been for the development of each individual? Kleinian analysts frequently use the term "the correct interpretation." It is doubtful if such an achievement is ever possible, especially in the group situation, so that a degree of metaphoric latitude helps to catch some of the wide range of processes going on in each individual. Psychotherapuetic change is a developmental process requiring considerable time, and Bion mentioned, as evidence of intellectual work going on in spite of its covert nature, the fact that patients came back to his comments in later sessions. In other words, reflection on what is happening in the group with delayed assimilation is a necessary part of the individual's "work" activity. The therapist's task, I believe, is to further this by giving individuals as much awareness of all sides of their responses in the group situation, including especially the apparent reasons for abandoning their "distinctiveness" when faced with their own intolerance toward their unconscious processes. In my own experience with groups over thirty years, I have never ceased to be impressed by the importance that members attach to their group meetings, even though only once per week. It is common after only a few months for them to remark that what goes on in the session plays a prominent part in how they feel for the rest of that week. By commenting along the lines I believe Bion could have done in the light of what he described, he would have avoided in some measure in at least some of the members the depressing feelings of the badness of the group as almost inevitable.

In regard to pairing, he again warns against concentrating on the possible unconscious contents of the pair interaction. Here too, however, it is not at all difficult to comment on the group's interest in this interaction and in what this interest might consist. I have frequently heard reports in groups that certain sessions with marked pairing on which interpretive comments were made, were recalled vividly for long periods as having been particularly helpful.

Bion likened the problem of the individual coming to terms with the emotional life of the group as closely akin to that of the infant in its first relationship, viz., with the breast/mother. In his later analytic work he spelled out the nature of the infant's task in overcoming frustration, i.e., when instead of the expected breast there was a "no breast" situation. For this achievement he took the mother's role as a "container" to be crucial. This is perhaps an inadequate term for the active contribution of the mother in making her comforting and encouraging presence felt. It could readily be said that, for the group therapist, Bion advocates a role of considerable withholding.

The importance of Bion's strictures can be granted. The essential aspect in all these issues is whether or not enough of the total dynamics in the group are being brought to notice when an individual is being referred to. Basic assumption behavior occurs in groups, whether the task is explicitly therapy or not. But when the aim is therapy, the individuals need to understand much more of themselves than the tendency to regress to the primal self of their separation-individuation stage of development. I have stressed that the paramount consideration is much more our understanding than using an assumed correct technique. Understanding the unconscious is notoriously subject to individual bias. Increasingly over recent years my bias has been a much greater focus on the state of the self that underlies the particular expression of the unconscious motives. To revert to the example just quoted, one may ask whether Bion's reluctance to use the individual in the group situation is influenced by the Kleinian view of greed as stemming from a high degree of oral sadism. Melanie Klein retained the view that aggressive phantasies were mainly the product of the death instinct. If one takes the view that the most profound aggression arises from the universally desperate struggle to maintain the self— a view that Freud took—then the greed of Bion's patient might well be seen as a primitive expression of her attempt to get possession of the object she needs to maintain a security in her self. In this case the social relevance of her symptoms, and hence their importance for the group, is different from what it would be had her greed been taken as a problem of excessive oral sadism.

The need to cope with anxieties over the self can be seen in another of the examples he quotes (Bion, 1961:144). The members discuss a suggestion to use Christian names. Three are for it as a good idea that would make things more friendly. Of the other three, one doesn't want her name to be known because she dislikes it, another suggests pseudonyms and the third keeps out of it. I do not want to make unjustified use of the example, especially as Bion mentions only certain aspects of the episode to make his point. What he takes up is the way the group seems to regard friendliness or pleasant emotions in the group as a means of cure, as a contribution to their work group. Perhaps more immediately relevant to the work group are the anxieties about whether or not the selves of the three dissidents will be secure if they begin to be looked at by the others.

The disadvantages of groups as a therapeutic medium are well known. They do, however, have several advantages. The sharing of humiliations, shame and guilt is a different experience for many when they receive sympathetic understanding from other members. Also, whereas the projective identification of self-objects from the segregated systems has to be done mainly one at a time with the therapeutic pair, the projection of several around members of the group is active much of the time and their recognition can be used by all.

The individual in psychotherapy has to learn about his or her split-off relationships. This task can become a life-long one for any individual. Therapy, as in other learning, has to give enough capacity to carry on the work. Psychotherapy in groups has to make much more of a contribution to this capacity than can be done through confining attention solely to the group dynamics equated with the basic assumptions.

Bion, like so many creative thinkers, confined his study of the work of others to relatively few. Perhaps he felt, like Winnicott who once said to me, "I did not pay close attention to Fairbairn as I was too absorbed in my own pregnancies at the time." I never heard Bion discuss Foulkes, and I do not think he knew much about his work because he had left groups by the time Foulkes was publishing his accounts of it. He was not given to disparaging the work of others if it differed from his own; for him, experience would eventually find its survival value. Foulkes was convinced the total group interactions had to be used in therapy, and I believe that Bion, had he done more group therapeutic work, would have accepted that position though he would have insisted on what might be loosely put as more rigor and more depth, more attention to the primitive relationships.

None of Bion's Tavistock colleagues engaged in group therapy, in contrast with those concerned with group dynamics, adhered to his view about the sole use of the latter in their work. Ezriel's formulation (1950) of using a common tension in the group once it could be identified as coming from the wish for a specific relationship with the therapist, and adding to its exposure by showing how each individual dealt with it, was considered to be more appropriate. Revisiting both led me to conclude that Ezriel's views could not account for the group dynamics in general, and I believe our understanding of the individual should be such as to account for both. It has seemed to me for some years that a theory of the organization of the self is the emerging task for psychoanalysis and so I used my own rather rough and ready gropings in this direction. Analytic group psychotherapy has usually been considered by its users as a valuable therapeutic medium in spite of the negative findings of Malan and his colleagues (Malan, 1976). Perhaps we expose here the inadequacies in our concepts of the nature of psychotherapy as well as our means of assessing change. Because of my interest in the self as an independent variable in the therapeutic task, Gill and I (1970) carried out an exploratory trial using spontaneous sentences as an indication of conflicts within the self system. Significant changes in patients after eighteen months of treatment were found, so Malan's criteria seem to have referred to different processes.

For me Bion has always been the *preux chevalier* making his doughty forays into the confused tangles of psychoanalytic thought and the complexities of human relationships. His power to look at phenomena with fresh challenges remains a permanent questioning legacy.

References

Bion, W.R. 1961. *Experiences in Groups and Other Papers*. London: Tavistock Publications; New York: Basic Books.

Erikson, E.H. 1959. *Identity and the Life Cycle*. New York and London: Norton.

Ezriel, H. 1950. "A Psycho-Analytic Approach to Group Treatment." *British Journal of Medical Psychology*, 23:59–74.

Freud, S. 1922. *Group Psychology*, Standard Edition, Vol.18. London: Hogarth Press.
Jantsch, E. and C.H. Waddington (Editors). 1976. *Evolution and Consciousness*. Reading, Mass.: Addison-Wesley.
Klein, M. 1932. *The Psycho-Analysis of Children*. London: Hogarth Press.
———. 1940. "Mourning and Its Relation to Manic-Depressive States." In *Contributions to Psycho-Analysis 1921–1945*. London: Hogarth Press, 1948.
Lichtenstein, H. 1977. *The Dilemma of Human Identity*. New York: Aronson.
McDougall, W. 1920. *The Group Mind* (2nd edition). London: Cambridge University Press.
Mahler, M.S., F. Pine and A. Bergman (Editors). 1975. *The Psychological Birth of the Human Infant: Symbiosis and Individuation*. New York: Basic Books.
Malan, D. 1976. "A Follow-up Study of Group Psychotherapy." *Archives of General Psychiatry*, 33:1303–15.
Spitz, R.A. 1965. *The First Year of Life*. New York: International University Press.
Sutherland, J.D. and H.S. Gill. 1970. *Language and Psychodynamic Appraisal*. London: Karnac Books.
Trist, E.L. and K.W. Bamforth. 1951. "Some Social and Psychological Consequences of the Longwall Method of Coal Getting." *Human Relations*, 4:3–38.

Eléonore Herbert and Eric Trist

An Educational Model for Group Dynamics

The Phenomenon of an Absent Leader*

The Conception of the Project

THE THEORETICAL AND METHODOLOGICAL FRAMEWORK

The project from which this paper selects an episode for detailed report represents one of the lines of growth stemming from a program of exploratory studies in the dynamics of small groups inaugurated during 1946–1948 at the Tavistock Clinic and Institute of Human Relations by W.R. Bion. He (Bion, 1961) distinguishes between two levels of group activity: that of the "sophisticated" or "work" group (W), which involves learning and development and is concerned with specific tasks that must be met and undertaken in social reality; and that of the basic assumptions (ba) dependence, fight/flight and pairing, which are unlearned, primitive emotional response systems existing as cohesive patterns that alternate. The basic group organization may be in conflict with the sophisticated or W organization and is often unrecognized by members of the group, whose level of performance may be severely impaired in consequence. The aim of this program was to explore the use of a common method of interpretative group discussion in groups of different kinds: patient groups, student groups and staff groups. Though the method was derived from the *method* of psychoanalysis, recourse was not necessarily had to psychoanalytic concepts in making interpretations. Psychoanalytic concepts had been elaborated in the study of the individual in the two-person, inter-personal, as distinct from the multi-person, group situation. As the aim was now to explore what emerged at the level of the group, interpretation faced a new task: that of assisting a group (as contrasted with an individual) in extending its recognition of what was going on in the group situation as a whole, helping in achieving its work task (W) more effectively and more completely than would otherwise be

*A shortened and rewritten version of the original—*Human Relations*, 6:215–48, 1953.

the case. In making comments on the group's behavior, however, the member of the group in the role of social consultant or therapist could be said to proceed in accordance with psychoanalytic method in that he relied for his information principally on the relation of the group to himself in the immediate here-and-now situation.

The problems and types of stress that arose in these different kinds of group had differences as well as similarities. These differences led to more specialized models of the general method. Among those working with patient groups, there was a tendency to relate interpretation to a more directly psychoanalytic frame of reference by emphasizing the way in which each individual, as a personality, dealt with the "common group tension." This is the line of development that characterized the work of Ezriel (1950) and also of Sutherland (1985). It represents a more specifically clinical model.

By contrast, the development of what may be termed an action research model may be seen in such work of the Tavistock Institute as the Glacier Project as described by Jaques (1951) in *The Changing Culture of a Factory*. Under industrial field conditions he found that the most worthwhile discussions with the social consultant took place not so much in special meetings of an unstructured type outside the action situation as through his presence during the actual proceedings of various executive and consultative groups. Interpretation required to be related to a more sociological frame of reference and to be concerned with the ways in which roles and relationships in the particular social systems in which the groups existed were being used for unrecognized ends.

It remains to consider the experience yielded by the student type of group, in which the group met for educational purposes, usually under conditions of a seminar that gave maximum scope for free, as opposed to set, discussion. This technique may be regarded as initiating the search for a *training* or *educational* model of the method. Considerable difficulty was experienced with this type of group during the period of exploratory studies. The groups consisted of "students" of problems in human relations (industrial executives, social scientists, or practical workers in educational and community activities), prepared to examine their own experiences in a group as a method of gaining direct access to, and so increasing their understanding of, the dynamics of socio-psychological phenomena. These groups, however, tended to develop in one of two directions: when a good deal of interpretation was given the group tended to transform itself into a patient group and ask for treatment; when interpretation was restricted, the group tended merely to discuss the topic as a topic, and very little progress could be made in showing its relationship to the group. As the result of repeated experiences of this kind, student groups were discontinued, students being asked either to face taking the patient role and join a therapy group or to limit themselves to attendance at the workshop type of event. It was not concluded, however, from these experiences that the original idea—that the student group might constitute a distinctive field of study—was necessarily invalid; rather that a suitable form had not yet been found.

The essential feature of the patient group in the treatment situation is that its task is directly and exclusively the study of its own internal tensions and relations. Its activities, so far as these concern the topics that it discusses, are regarded as meaningful only if they provide material which allows the underlying relations to be exhibited. A work group, however, in the action situation has a defined line (direction) of activity which is predetermined by its position in the social system to which it belongs. Its task is to pursue this line of activity. Its problem is that its relations may severely disturb its performance. In first approximation, the clinical and action research models can be described in terms of the different ways in which group relations and group activities are related to the task of the group. The search for an appropriate educational model depends on finding a type of task which requires a relationship between group activities and group relations distinct from that in either treatment-centered or action-centered groups.

The structure of the type of situation required may be regarded as a function of the degree of determinacy of the line of the group's activity. If the action situation is such that this is predetermined by the position of the group in a social system and the treatment situation such that it must be kept indeterminate by the therapist, the training situation may be described as that in which the group goes through the process of determining its own line of activity. In this sense, work with training groups may be related to the frame of reference of the project method in education as developed by John Dewey just as that with patient and action research groups may be related to psychoanalytic and sociological frames of reference. The relevance of the project method is that it is concerned with finding and carrying out types of concrete activity through which immediate experience may form itself into more general understanding.

If the task of the group is to find and undertake a definite project within a general field, it follows that the group will expect to meet on the assumption that its sessions will be limited—though indeterminate—in number. This assumption has a selective effect on the type of material which the group is likely to produce and therefore on the depth and scope of interpretation. If the loyalty of the social therapist is to the W of the group, he must take up whatever is impeding the group in meeting this W, however deep. On the other hand, since the task is limited, he need not take "everything" up; nor, indeed, will everything come up. Moreover, the group will have different phases—that in which the project is found, that in which it is carried out and that in which it is evaluated. The relationship of the consultant to the group changes in consequence. In the discovery phase it is more like that of a group therapist; in the execution phase like that of a contributor; while in the third phase group and consultant can act as collaborators in evaluating what has been done—from complementary viewpoints. The implicit existence from the beginning of such a progression means that a force is acting throughout the entire situation towards establishing the independence of the group from the consultant. This safeguards it against the development of too great a dependence, which would otherwise tend to be unresolvable except under patient conditions. Since the aim is to relate experience in the group to some particular field of outside experience, members should be drawn from a common field, e.g., teachers, nurses, supervisors, works managers. There must be common needs and common problems. The degree of heterogeneity within the common field that will be most beneficial will vary widely according to circumstances.

Treatment and action groups are brought together by a need to solve concrete problems causing immediate tension—personal problems of patients or practical problems of institutions. A somewhat different pressure provides the incentive that convenes training groups, where the felt need is to learn rather than to resolve. Experience of social situations in the past has created in their members a need to learn more about group phenomena and processes for application to social situations in the future. Such learning must be general as well as particular for the "transfer-effect" to be realized. A need for such learning may be regarded as authentic and reality-based (as distinct from simply an intellectual attempt to avoid facing awkward experience more personally) so far as it derives from the roles and responsibilities which members carry outside the group. While the presence of intellectualism as a defense is to be expected in such groups (and will usually be deployed with both ingenuity and strength) this does not negate the reality of the need for intellectual and theoretical, as well as emotional and practical, understanding of group phenomena among those on whom professional or executive responsibility devolves for dealing with many kinds of group problems in community and industrial life. Training groups composed of such individuals require to develop both types of understanding, and in work with such groups teaching is important as well as interpretation.

To increase general understanding of group phenomena may be regarded as the sophisticated task of training groups. It would be a fallacy, however, to suppose that this could be achieved apart from direct experience of the emotional reality of these phenomena. A way must be found through the activity which the group itself undertakes of relating interpretation to teaching. It is the scope that it affords for establishing this relationship that recommends the project method as a supplementary approach to the general method of interpretative group discussion in the training situation. For it is through the project method that the fullest use may be made of the opportunities for more general teaching afforded by the occasions when the interpretation of direct, concrete experience has created emotionally favorable conditions in the immediate situation. The field study to be outlined below, from which one meeting is selected for detailed report, represents an explicit attempt to erect a model of a practical training technique on these premises and to test out its usefulness with a group of practicing teachers presenting a serious professional need for increased understanding of group phenomena in relation to their own work at school.

THE CHARACTER OF THE MODEL

The project consisted of a working seminar on "Human Relations in School" attended by a group of practicing teachers. It took place under the auspices of a School of Education. No special attempt was made to select the members, who registered in the ordinary way. The meetings of the group were conducted by the first author, the second acting as a research consultant with respect to planning and the analysis of the material.

The original group of 19 was drawn from all types of school. Between the ages of 11 and 12 years all children took a national examination as a result of which the brighter ones went on to grammar schools (the equivalent of high schools) which prepared them for university entrance, while the less bright followed a less exacting curriculum in what were known as secondary modern schools, where they stayed until the school-leaving age of 16.

Two positive factors, one professional and the other psychological, affected all members and made for homogeneity: all were teachers and all were concerned in varying degrees about their relations with their pupils. Thus they all belonged to a large and dispersed professional group, i.e., teachers, and to a smaller attitudinal group, i.e., the category of teachers who attach importance to psychology and the study of personality as a means of achieving good pupil-teacher relations. This last factor constituted the overt motive that brought them together to discuss their problems.

There was also a third factor—the group contained no avowed authoritarian. All members, however, taught within the British educational system in which some degree of authoritarian discipline is traditional. To this tradition they had to conform, at least to some extent, in their classroom practice. They could, therefore, be described as an anti-authoritarian minority within the educational system of their society.

Though the project was planned as a three-phase program, the question of there being a second or third phase was not taken up with the group until a point had been reached, towards the end of the preceding phase, when the problem of the group's future became acute. It was then worked through until an agreed solution was reached.

The first, or *discovery,* phase consisted of 10 weekly meetings of one-and-a-half or two hours duration. The group worked out its own program of topics, on one of which a short paper was presented each week by a particular member. Discussion then proceeded in a free manner. A near-verbatim record was kept, of which another member prepared a summary for circulation at the beginning of the next meeting.

The first author, as the consultant working with the group in the face-to-face situation, had two related roles: *interpretative*—to help the group to see its task in terms of its own behavior; *educational*—to help it to relate its own group experience to the common outside work field. Since the object of increasing the insight of group members into group phenomena was to improve their work as teachers, the two roles had a common relationship to the *W* that constituted the group task. For this reason it was felt that no inherent contradiction between them need be expected.

The first role was dominant during the first phase, when a considerable "battle" took place between consultant and group over its insistent demand for intellectual teaching. But during the second, or *execution,* phase, when the group settled down to the examination of a single basic problem over a further series of 10 meetings and had also learned to accept the examination of what was going on in itself as a regular part of its task, there were many more teaching opportunities. Nevertheless, there was often strong, though decreasing, resistance to accepting the consultant as a *contributor* as well as a *social therapist* and the problem was not fully worked through by the end of the phase. The group's difficulty was in giving up the consultant as a therapist.

The third, or *evaluation,* phase was brought into existence by the feeling that arose in the group that they must find some way of reporting back their group experiences to other teachers, and the question was broached of their writing up their own version of these experiences for communication to an educational audience. At this point a special meeting was held at which the head of the department concerned and the second author were present as well as the first author. This was the meeting at which the group had to give up the first author as a member of the group, which from now on was to meet alone. The object of the special meeting was to help the group, by an actual demonstration, to perceive the first author as a member of a technical group and to show them that if they must now lose her as a member of their own group they could still have a relationship with her as a member of this technical group whose support both she and they would need for the next phase of the task.

The outcome of this meeting was that the group decided to undertake the assignment of writing up an account of its experiences for publication to the profession, accepting full responsibility for making its own executive arrangements and the necessary internal role allocations. All this it proceeded to do, with an efficiency and a speed which provides another instance of the reward to be reaped, when it comes to executive action, of preliminary working through.

The group was now able to accept the first author as a *collaborator* with a complementary task, the second decision of the meeting being that she should prepare a parallel account of the group's development as she had perceived it from her position as their consultant. Meanwhile the head of the department undertook to preface both accounts with a critique of the project as an exercise in post-graduate teacher training. The task of the second author was to collaborate with the first in the technical appraisal of the material from the point of view of a research organization concerned with the development and application of group methods in working institutions.

In the subsequent scrutiny of the total material it appeared that certain group phenomena observed during the project might be of general interest, particularly the institution by the group of an absent leader in opposition to the *legitimate* leader during the ninth meeting of the first phase. Accordingly, this episode has been abstracted and in what follows an account of it is presented from a group dynamics rather than an educational viewpoint, which will be that emphasized in the account of the project as a whole to be published elsewhere by the first author and the members of the group.

The Ninth Meeting

Note: The first session of the course was taken up with dealing with the group's reactions to the consultant's refusal to give formal lectures. This produced a format in which each member was to prepare a paper on an agreed topic for discussion by the group. Themes covered were: the difficult child; handicapped children; pilfering; improved discipline; the "crush" in girls' schools. The topic for each session arose out of the experience of discussing that for the current session. In every case the theme was found to have a parallel in the relation of the consultant to the group in the here-and-now. These parallelisms were interpreted and opened up the dynamics of the situation. A paper on truancy, prepared by a headmistress, was postponed by the group three times— the topic was specially threatening—but was finally given in the last but one session, now to be reported. The first author speaks throughout in the first person in her interpretative role.

SUB-GROUP ROLE-TAKING

The ninth meeting opened with a message from the member who was to have spoken on truancy. She sent a letter in which she stated that pressure of work would prevent her from attending this meeting and the next—the last two of the session. As she had previously said that, in the event of the group meetings being continued the following term, she would not be able to attend, her letter was a final leave-taking. She had, however, sent her paper, which the bearer of the message had consented to read.

It seemed indeed as if truancy was not only to be discussed but enacted. Seven members in all absented themselves on this occasion, the largest number since the first session. Of these, only one, who had sent a note of apology, was to return. The headmistresses' sub-group had completely disappeared. The largest element among the remaining twelve members was the grammar school assistants' group. There were six of them, one man and five women, who made up half the attendance. The others were divided as follows: two junior school masters, one master from an all-age school, one mistress from a school for handicapped children and two secondary modern school masters. Their common characteristic was that none belonged to a grammar school. To take another sub-division, the group fell into two halves according to sex: there were six men and six women. Furthermore, there was a distinct group of persistently silent members. The total group was also divided into two halves in this respect: six silent members listened throughout the evening to six speakers.

The various groups did not coincide but the resulting set-up presented a considerable advantage: every member could at any time rely on the support of another five who had something in common with him or her. (Six people had grammar school experience, six lacked it; to talk was to belong to a group of six speakers; to be silent was to belong to a group of six silent members.) See Table 1, note that italic letters designate women.

Lest it should appear—as is often thought in committees and debating societies—that only the speaking members play a part in discussion, it should be emphasized that the silent members were very much part of the group and, on the present occasion, were destined to play a crucial role. If, for a moment, one supposes the silent members to have been absent—i.e., to have joined the absentees' sub-group—the importance of their presence soon appears. In this particular case the speaking members formed one-third of the original group. If two-thirds had been absent those remaining would have represented a very much mutilated, and therefore threatened, minority. The silent members held the balance. By choosing to be present they helped to perpetuate the life of the group. Their passive attitude put them in the position of an audience and the future of the group depended on their being persuaded by the speaking members to continue to attend.

The absentees' sub-group also constituted a force that exerted a considerable effect on the proceedings. Absentees have once belonged to a group and have contributed to making it what it is. Conversely, the group has contributed to making them what they are. On this occasion their participation was evident, since the paper to be discussed embodied the views of one of them and, indeed,

TABLE 1   Equal Sub-Groups in the Ninth Meeting

Women	Men	Grammar schools	Non-grammar schools	Speakers	Silent members
A, B, C, D, E, F	G, H, I, J, K, L	A, C, D, E, F, G	B, H, I, J, K, L	A, B, C, E, G, K	D, F, H, I, J, L

was about absenteeism. The absentee sub-group was also six strong. The original number of members had been 19—an odd number—which left 7 absentees; but the position of the absent speaker was equivocal. She could not be said to be *absent* since she introduced the topic of discussion; nor *silent* since the words were hers; nor could she be described as *speaking*, since she was not present in person. Thus, on the one hand, she did not belong fully to any of the three sub-groups; on the other, she belonged to them all, for she partook of some of the qualities of each.

My position, as consultant, was similar to hers for I could not be said to belong fully to any of the sub-groups either. I was not *absent* since I was there in person; nor *speaking* since I had refused to lead the discussions or indeed to make any personal contributions unless they were called for by members' remarks; nor *silent* since I summed up the arguments and formulated problems raised by members. Conversely, both she and I were ubiquitous since we belonged intermittently to various sub-groups. By this means the members in each sub-group were kept at six, for she and I cancelled each other out.

The recurrence of the number six was not due to chance. Officially, six members constituted the smallest number for whom a course could be held. The group knew that, in the preceding term, a course of lectures on psycho-analysis had been stopped after the second meeting because only five members had registered for it. Throughout the twenty sessions of the seminar, whenever the numbers present approached this threshold the group became anxious lest it should be officially stopped. Thus the threat to the continuation of the group was actual, but this was not always realized. The appearance of anxiety was the sign of it. Anxiety had been noted each time the topic of truancy was raised and had led to repeated postponement of its discussion. On this occasion, when a third of the group had "played truant," the threat had become greater and more imminent. But it did not come from the absentee members alone, though they appeared to be responsible for it. In order to keep the group alive, the speaking members had to be victorious over the negative attitude present in *themselves* towards the W that constituted the group task. All the sub-groups had to contend with ambivalence in this regard. The speakers, in so far as they were dissatisfied with the pattern imposed on the group, would wish to absent

TABLE 2   The Situation at the Beginning of the
Ninth Meeting

Speakers	Silent members	Absentees
A	D	M
B	F	N
C	H	O
E	I	P
G	J	Q
K	L	R
(PL)		(AL)

PL = present leader
AL = absent leader

themselves from it, but the wish to continue was stronger and made them choose to stay in the group and fight for it. The absentees had enough positive feeling to shrink from remaining in the group and overtly attacking it: their belongingness led them to compromise by choosing *flight* rather than *fight* to express their dissatisfaction. In the six silent members the balance of positive and negative feelings made the fight and flight reactions of equal strength, so that they were prevented from taking any action: they did not absent themselves, neither did they fight for the survival of the group.

Throughout this meeting the speakers made use of the absentees' sub-group as a reference group (Newcomb, 1952) into which they projected their negative feelings. They cast the absent speaker, as a reference individual, in the role of spokesman of the absentees, an *absent leader* (*AL*). To her they gave their allegiance whenever they wished to express their criticism of me, the *present leader* (*PL*), and take flight from the group task. At this point, however, they were confronted both by their need to continue with their task and to have my help in enabling them to do so; fear of my loss and of retaliation on my part made them swing back to me. *AL* and *PL* never appeared in the same sub-group (see *Table* 2).

INDIVIDUAL ROLES

The speaking members had unwittingly arrayed their forces in such a way that each assumed a role which he kept throughout the session. The discussion would be started indirectly by a passage of arms between two of them (*A* and *G*), who continued the fight started at the eighth meeting between the men's and women's sub-groups. Very soon a third, K, would intervene, as if to remind them that they should sink their differences, since something of greater moment—the continued existence of the group—was at stake. K's role was that of *PL*'s "champion," his efforts always being aimed at rallying the group under her leadership. His interventions followed a similar pattern throughout: he would indicate explicitly or implicitly that there was no cause for disagreement within the present group, would sum up the arguments, and thus open the way for a new departure. The fourth, *C*, consistently played the role of mediator between the absentees and the present members. She took the role of *AL*'s champion in opposition to K whenever the absentees were excluded. The other two, *B* and *E*, acted as supporters of the speakers' group, and it was one of them who formulated the topic for the next meeting, which was to focus the work of the group during the subsequent phase of its existence.

IDENTIFICATION OF THE SPEAKERS' GROUP WITH THE "LIKED CHILDREN"

Before the paper was read the record of the eighth meeting was circulated. It gave rise to a brief discussion in which all six members spoke who were to discuss the paper later. The report of the preceding week's discussion on homosexuality was the immediate cause. The young master, G, who had raised the topic at the end of the previous meeting to repeat that "it did not exist between masters and boys" returned to the charge. "It had gone unchallenged," he said, "the group had shifted away from it." *C* agreed that the discussion had proceeded rather irrelevantly. K disagreed, "the point had been thoroughly discussed."

But still, in complete disregard of the evening's task, and of K's reminder, *A* and *G* continued the feud about homosexuality in men and women teachers. To G's reiterated assertion that men teachers were guiltless of it *A* retorted that "it did not make much difference whether homosexuality existed between boys and masters or only between boy and boy; the crush of boy for boy and girl for girl proved the homosexual content." The exchange became more and more rapid and the enjoyment of the two protagonists more evident. The more G denied the homosexual attitude of men teachers the more *A* refused to be convinced and airily reaffirmed her own contradictory belief. It became apparent that the excitement roused by this discussion was of a flirtatious kind, which, in view of the topic—homosexuality—might at first seem strange. But if people are preoccupied with heterosexual feelings they often find it easier to talk about homo- rather heterosexuality, for the social taboo on the former makes its expression in reality impossible, and the discussion safely theoretical, whereas heterosexual feelings may lead to actual relations which cannot be admitted in public. It is notable that *A* meets G's denial of his homosexuality not by denying her own but by maintaining that "there is no difference between his feelings and hers."

Curiously enough she disregards the available "tu quoque" reply, for a teacher-boy relationship, which was described in the seventh session, was not unlike a two-way crush. No one thought of it. The men attacked and the women pleaded guilty. This collusion in accepting a statement contrary to evidence shows how carefully the whole group will push aside any facts that do not serve its immediate unconscious needs even though they might justify the behavior of some individual member on the *sophisticated* level. If the men's sub-group had recognized their homosexual tendencies they would by this admission have suggested that they could not have a heterosexual relation with me. But the women's case was different: a love relationship with me could only be a homosexual one. Thus it was from the same *group* motive that one sub-group declared its immunity from a condemned form of behavior and the other accepted the accusation of it.

By a kind of pun on the word homosexual it is made to mean "we are both sexual *in the same way*," i.e., "we are both offering our love to you." Since *A* could feel sure that *G* would not go back on his denial—which incidentally was also an offer to her as a woman—and run the risk of my misunderstanding him, she could safely afford to push him further and further. It was this that gave the impression of sparring, of a kind of Beatrice and Benedick dialogue in which the protagonists paired under the cover of spirited attacks that ill disguised their underlying friendliness and the similarity of their feelings.

For a while the group took pleasure in this dialogue. *A* and *G*, both members of the speakers' sub-group, appeared to be acting as its *spokesmen* in making me a love-offer, since it put them all in the role of liked children (the crush had been described as a two-way situation, and if they loved *me* I must love *them*). Gradually, however, the rest of the speakers' sub-group became uneasy. The "Beatrice and Benedick" pair monopolized the conversation to such an extent that everyone else was relegated to the silent members sub-group, so losing "liked children" status (Table 3).

The verbal duel had had its use as a temporary resurrection of the main defense of the eighth meeting, but if it went on it would disrupt the speakers' group by reducing it to two members. More than two-thirds of the whole group would be put out of action. The remaining speakers, having been driven into the silent sub-group, might from there eventually join the absentees. In addition it made contact with me impossible. All this roused K in his champion role, making him call Beatrice and Benedick to order; the real battle for the survival of the group must be joined, "we have an urgent task to which we must return." They accepted the reproof and settled down to listen to the paper on truancy.

TABLE 3   The Situation Produced by the
"Beatrice and Benedick" Episode

Speakers	Silent members	Absentees
A	D	M
G	F	N
	H	O
	I	P
	J	Q
	L	R
	B	
	C	
	E	
	K	
PL		AL

THE ABSENT LEADER'S PAPER (CASES OF TRUANCY)

The paper was read by C. By accepting to pass on the words of the absent headmistress she established herself in the role of AL's champion.

AL's account of a series of actual cases of girls who had run away from school was preceded by two introductory remarks. First, AL had been struck by the derivation of the word "truant" from a Celtic word that means "wretched." Next, she reported that a headmistress of a boarding school, whom she had asked what her worst experience had been as a headmistress, had replied, "*the disappearance of a girl.*" Her own personal experience of this had concerned a girl—Susan—who had been evacuated from a bombed city and was in need of help, the immediate cause of her running away having been a *row with an impatient young mistress* (but there were no details of her later history). She went on to quote further instances of truancy that had come to her knowledge.

Marjorie (12 yrs.) had played truant from school. She had intercepted letters of enquiry, was buying her meals out and spent her time playing with paper dolls. Her home was poor, her parents went to work early and meals were inadequate. She had run away before when evacuated to another town and had been given lifts on lorries (trucks).

Jean ($12\frac{1}{2}$ yrs.) had been holding up letters to her home. She had played truant when the district in which she lived had been bombed and while her father, of whom she was very fond, was in the army. She truanted again when her father went to Italy. She lived in a world of fantasy and had written love letters to another girl as though the letters came from a man in the R.A.F. Jean said she heard voices telling her not to go to school. She had spent days tramping the streets with a few pennies for chips, buns or a meat pie.

Joyce (13 yrs.) sent a letter purporting to account for her absence and explaining that she was caring for a sick dog. On enquiry this was found to be untrue. Her parents had separated. She had become "boy mad." Letters written by her to a boy had been found by the boy's mother, who threatened to show them to the police.

Mary (15 yrs.) forged her mother's signature on a letter of excuse after playing truant. The mother thought that the girl's interest in politics—she was a member of a Young Conservative group—had some connection with her delinquency. In this instance emotional instability was associated with intelligence of a high order and the child, the speaker said, suffered agony of mind accordingly. (It is also to be noted that she sought security "upwards" in the more traditional groups of her society.)

Finally, all the five girls cited were stated to be in need of medical help. Mary and Joyce had been referred to Child Guidance Clinics and had done well, especially the former. Jean's parents would not allow her to attend for treatment. Nothing was said about the other two.

COMMENTS ON THE MATERIAL PROVIDED BY THE ABSENT LEADER

The picture given by *AL* was a sinister one. All the cases described concerned girls who had fled from school into a world in which they found themselves at war with society. All had become delinquent offenders—truancy being punishable by law—but in addition were mentally ill and needed medical help. Marjorie was backward; Jean had hallucinations; Joyce was said to be boy-mad; Mary suffered from "emotional instability." Such, then, were the dangers to be feared, about which *AL* warned the present members of the group. It is to be noted that for the first time in the history of the group school was described as a "bad" (hated) place from which people run away. Instead of learning they had become ill and wretched. And the etymological discovery which gave the true meaning of the word truant as wretched emphasized the "badness" of school. Thus Susan, the first truant, ran away after "a row with an impatient young mistress."

The aggressive content of the truant's behavior may be supported by further etymological investigation of the meaning of truancy as wretchedness, which provides a clue as to the origin of the wretchedness, for it appears that the word originally means "outcast, an exile." It has the same root as the word "wroec," to drive, and the word "wreak," to punish, to revenge. The truant is wretched, because he has been *driven* into exile, where as a disliked victim and scapegoat, he is loaded with the wickedness of the rest of the school. The person in authority who has thus driven him out must fear the consequences of his treatment. The disappearance of a girl ("the worst misfortune that could befall a head mistress") appears as a punishment and a danger since a victim is always a potential seeker after revenge. If truancy were merely the expression of wretchedness it would be difficult to understand why it should be regarded as delinquent, but seen as an attack on the school—provoked by this wretchedness—its delinquent nature becomes apparent, especially as it carries the projection of the school's own delinquency.

The truant, on his or her side, is constantly in danger of what is now seen as retaliation on the part of the school (into which, of course, will be projected the aggressiveness belonging to his or her own original "forcing" behavior). Every one of the girls described had to guard herself against persecution. Susan's absence was discovered by a mistress who gave the alarm; Marjorie when questioned said she had a cold and carefully intercepted letters addressed to her parents by the Head of the school; Jean had done the same; Joyce had sent a letter explaining that she was caring for a sick dog and Mary forged her mother's signature. They all lived in fear of being "caught" by the school they had harmed by their behavior. They feel persecuted; when they are judged, they are usually found "guilty but insane" and put in the hands of the psychiatrist. One of the truants mentioned (Mary) had done well under treatment. We are told that she had intelligence of a high order and that "*with her co-operation* the Child Guidance Clinic had put her on the road to recovery." Nevertheless, even her high intelligence had not saved her from the "wretchedness" which had caused her to play truant. Jean, the girl who "heard voices" and obviously was in need of medical help, was not allowed by her parents to attend the Child Guidance Clinic.

THE GROUP'S INTERPRETATION OF THE ABSENT LEADER'S PAPER

AL's paper was instantaneously interpreted by *C* in her champion role as an indictment of *PL* (as the bad parent). "The bad influence of the parents," she said, "is obvious in all the cases of truancy described." The same had been said at the preceding meeting about bad cases of crushes. Since I had been increasingly attributed the parental role in one or other of its forms, the comment constitutes a call to desert me as a false and unreliable leader, as the truants had deserted their parents. The reaction of the speakers' group was to answer this call, and, vigorously supporting *C*'s thesis, to align themselves during the next phase of the discussion with the absentees' group, making *AL* their leader and leaving me, *PL*, isolated (Table 4).

As the discussion went on I received blame not only as a parent but also in the other roles attributed to me. *AL* had said that, not content with making their children wretched, some parents also refused the help of the psychiatrist. If we interpret the word "of" as giving the phrase the meaning "*the help that the*

TABLE 4   Blaming PL in Answer to C's Comment

Speakers	Silent members	Absentees
	Silent members' sub-group	Absentees' sub-group
		Speakers' sub-group
PL		AL

psychiatrist can give," it can be seen that this reproach was also leveled at me, since I had refused to teach them psychoanalysis.

What, they asked then, can the *teacher* do when *parents* refuse the help of the *psychiatrist?* This started a disquisition on what I might have done in my original role (the teacher expected to lecture), since I had not helped in the role of parent or of psychiatrist. G having said that bewilderment in lessons is associated with truancy, *A*, his usual friend and adversary, took him up, saying that she failed to see why children should stay away from *school* because they were unhappy *at home.* This apparent contradiction of G's condemnation of parents was in fact a way of reinforcing the attack on me in my teacher role. (I was not providing knowledge in the group that would help them with their professional difficulties at school.)

If we compare the situation of school children with that of group members we find a clear parallelism. For if the latter had come to study "human relations" in the group, it appears that they had not been satisfied with their "relations" in the school—their last group experience before they had come to the group, just as for the children the family was the group experience that preceded school. The *group* is to the members what *school* is to the children, the latest stage in their history; whereas *school* is to the members what *home* is to the children, i.e., the last stage but one in their history.

The absentees had failed to find better relations in the group and so had left it. The problem to be faced by those aligning themselves with them was how to avoid the fate of the truanting children who had all become ill and wretched. However, one of these children—Mary—had been saved. Her mother had not understood her but she had, *by her own co-operation,* made a good recovery under *proper treatment.* Here was the model to be followed. Of all the truants described, Mary, who was intelligent and had impersonated her mother as she should have been—a good mother—was the one with whom the group could identify *AL.* By accepting such an identification for themselves they found a way of returning to the dependent position I had refused to countenance, but this time under *AL,* whom they set up as their true (though absent) leader (good mother), in opposition to me, their false (though present) leader (bad mother). Their hostility to me was thus projected into *AL,* who, in the omniscience ascribed to her, could be trusted to make safe use of it on their behalf.

Mary, their immediate model, had, it may be recalled, joined a Young Conservative club which was disliked by her mother. Similarly, I had shown that I disliked the conservative (traditional) pattern of education. With *AL* they could set up a rival group. Did not they, like Mary, know what was best for them? This rival group—their own prescription—would seek to preserve the structure of the school as they had known it, while being progressive (young) enough not to be averse to some reforms under traditional leadership, which would suffice to meet all problems. Was the pain of radical change really necessary? In such a group there would be proper lectures such as *AL*'s paper and a reliable safety net for truanting casualties (proper treatment). In such a group they would make progress through their own cooperation with what they themselves knew to be right. Moreover, this progress would be shared by all so that this rival group of theirs would be a group that would always remain whole and never become extinct. No one would be forced—as I had forced them—to depend on his own direct experience for advancing his understanding. Each would be given what he wanted. Protected from wretchedness, no one need truant from what need not be faced without sufficient guidance. The rival group and the rival leader sought by the speakers was the dependent group and the dependent leader. My refusal to enter into collusion with the recourse to this basic assumption was the cause of the opposition to myself. Since I would not permit the group to be dependent, the only way to secure dependence was to leave the group, i.e., join the absentees. *AL*'s paper was interpreted as giving earnest, as though through a dramatic and magical message, that the required Elysium might be found with her. The fate of this phantasy must now be traced through the subsequent discussion.

THE DISAPPOINTMENT OF EXPECTATIONS (IN SCHOOL AND IN THE GROUP)

K, in his customary constructive role, now proposed that they should investigate "what children want from school which truants failed to find in it." Once more the here-and-now situation inspired the members' suggestions: in enumerating the motives that might make children want to come to school, the members expressed their own motives for attending the group. First, "they want to be with and to compete with children of their own age." The desire to be with other members had repeatedly been expressed and had been manifested in the fear of seeing the group disappear.

Next it was said that they want the attention of a grown-up whom they can have for themselves—an expression in the here-and-now of the group's wish for dependence and a description of the teacher as an adult who specializes in preparing them for adulthood. "They are interested in some project" equally described the task of our discussions, while "they also want to learn" is perhaps an indication that the flight from *W* was not as wholesale as might have appeared. Yet the quest for dependent security reinstated itself in the remark that followed, "they come to school also for the sake of orderliness," which refers to the methodical arrangements of school life with regard to time-tables, rules, discipline, etc. It is a demand for a good external authority, since "order" has this double meaning—an authority of the kind they felt *AL* could give them.

The next remark, "they want to be helped to grow up," led to the statement that A stream children, especially of 15-plus, because they are able to absorb knowledge and accept the standards set by the teacher, feel they are being helped to grow up and keep their confidence in school, but C children are disappointed and feel that school is *preventing* them from growing up. They do not receive the knowledge ("they can't take it") that could make them into adults. Approval, therefore, is withheld. The A's are the good and happy children, the C's the disliked and unhappy truants. The situation was similar in the group though in this case C and A did not refer to degrees of intelligence but to the capacity to conform to the "imposed" standard (of free discussion) and to absorb knowledge through it.

I pointed out that the more inaccessible the standard of the school the more rejected the C adolescent would feel. He would try to live out the more primitive way of being grown up and his phantasies, as in the cases described earlier, would often be of a sexual kind in which he would imagine adult love relationships. An unsuccessful adolescent had no compensation for being kept at school.

These remarks led to a discussion on sex education and of its value as generally understood. The school only gave physiological facts for there was a conspiracy of silence among all adults—parents and teachers—to keep the children ignorant of the psychological aspects. Their own experiences, such as the crush, were not frankly discussed as sexual phenomena, but either ignored or frowned upon. This made clear at last the nature of the knowledge that had unconsciously been asked for during the early sessions. Just as the child wants to be enlightened on sex matters and feels thwarted—prevented from growing up by the silence of the adults—they had felt my refusal of formal intellectual instruction as a method of keeping them away from me and out of the adult world.

REUNION OF THE GROUP UNDER ABSENT LEADER'S LEADERSHIP

Here *C* suggested that perhaps if the teacher gave love first the crush might be forestalled. This statement, expressing as it does the need to forestall the *crush*—not the *truancy* which was the situation under discussion—is a re-

TABLE 5   Unification of the Group with the Absent Leader

Speakers	Absentees
	Absentees' sub-group
	Speakers' sub-group
	Silent members' sub-group
PL	AL

minder that the crush, although a positive feeling, had been established as an undesirable one, a bad one. And it was bad not only because it could lead to truancy if the teacher's response was either *snubbing* or *encouragement,* but in *itself.* It had been presented as an aggressive means of forcing the teacher to give love. None of the speaking members was safe from the accusation of having made such demands. All had tried first to steal love (by pilfering) and then to force it (through the crush). The favored children had stayed in the group, the disliked ones had run away. My encouragement of the former and snubbing of the latter had divided the group, and I was responsible for the present state of affairs. So I stood condemned on all counts, for I had failed to provide a good external and impartial authority, and I had refused to give them learning or to help them to grow up. This completes the meaning of G's cryptic sentence, "What can the teacher do when parents refuse the help of the psychiatrist." I had failed as a parent, as a psychiatrist and as a teacher.

C's remark went unchallenged. The whole group became silent. In this manner C's remark reunited the speaking and the silent sub-groups with the absentees. She now completes her mission as AL's champion (representing the wish to leave the group that was in all of them) and unites the three sub-groups into one whole on the absentees' side, since the whole group now felt rejected by me. I, PL, am now the bereft person. By refusing the love that "would have forestalled the crush and its consequences," I have lost the whole group to AL. It is my turn to be the outcast and exiled individual (Table 5). From another point of view the situation could be described as the completion of the flight (from W) of the membership group to the reference group.

RETURN TO PRESENT LEADER

This desertion of the whole group roused K to act once more as my champion in opposition to C. Because of their identification with AL the group had been unable to face AL as the bereft person. C's intervention had shifted this role on to me but to face me (PL) as the image of the bereft parent (teacher, leader) was

TABLE 6   Unification of the Group with the Present Leader: The situation created when K's remark "love in the classroom" aroused general laughter

Speakers	Absentees
Speakers' sub-group	
Silent members' sub-group	
Absentees' sub-group	
PL	AL

even more painful—and more dangerous, since to damage me might lead to retaliatory behavior on my part in the immediate present, or to my incapacitation. In either case I would be no use to them as a consultant. Their actual membership group would end, whatever might continue in the reference group they had concocted with AL. But since this reference group was an expression of baD no change could be effected or new learning realized through its agency. Permanent capture by AL, as advocated by C, could only result in their being left with the whole problem on their hands that had convened the group in the first place. The intractability of their W by their reference group seemed to have produced a stalemate, when the silence was broken by K, who pulled back the "departed" members towards PL by a suggestion for the next meeting. Referring to a remark of mine to the effect that sex education in school should not be confined to the biology laboratory—for any lesson could provide a useful opportunity—he laughingly suggested that we should discuss "Love in the Classroom." This mock suggestion was received with a great burst of laughter. The laughter was general, infectious and noisy; the silent members joining in, thus breaking their silence for the first time. Amused by their teasing, I too laughed so that I was reinstated in the speaking group, with which, through their participation in the laughter, the silent members were now also identified. My joining in this laughter was felt by the whole group as a triumphal achievement and heightened the manic atmosphere.

K had sent out, as it were, a general call to all members to change sides: let us have "love in the classroom," i.e., in the speaking group under PL as our teacher-leader; if we have this, we can have all that we seek in the reference group without destroying the membership group. Such a course would reunite the whole group as a membership group, though it would isolate AL, the only member who had definitely said she would not return (see Table 6).

However, the remark and the group's reaction contain a disquieting element. If the solution offered had been considered as real it need not have been put in this disguised, humorous form, nor would it have been greeted with such unanimous laughter. The unanimity marks the psychic agreement of the pres-

TABLE 7   The Realization That the Absentees Have Been Excluded from the Group during the Burst of Laughter

Speakers	Absentees
Speakers' sub-group	Absentees' sub-group
Silent members' sub-group	
PL	AL

ent members to deny that the exclusion of *AL* and of any other absentees was a factor of which they must take account. It was as though, through an omnipotent current group decision "to have love in the classroom," they professed not only to be able to restore casualties in group membership that had happened in the past but to prevent their occurrence in the future. It was as if the very loudness of the laughter was intended to cover up the danger inherent in the situation and to deepen the underlying disbelief in the remedy (Table 7). This, in the limit, contained the assertion that there were no negative, hostile, disruptive forces in their midst, at least none that need be taken seriously, only positive, friendly, constructive forces. K's proposal was an invitation to the group to proceed on this hypothesis.

But could the parts of themselves which the absentees represented be disposed of by abolishing the reference group which these parts had created? To deny the reality of the problem represented by the reference group was difficult when there was also an actual absentee group and an imminent threat of further absenteeism in the present group which might easily lead to its failure to survive. What guarantee was there that those aspects of the group which had produced absentees in the past would not go on doing so in the future? Absentees and absenteeism were part of the group's life and process. K's solution was the obverse of *C*'s: obliteration of the reference group and denial of the reality of absenteeism, as compared with obliteration of the membership group and projective identification with the reference group. As much as *C*'s, K's solution was an invocation of the dependent group, for the phantasy of group life which it depicts with *PL* ("love in the classroom") is, if not an Elysium (which one has to go away into), an earthly paradise where all one's needs may be met (by staying put)—perpetually, so it would seem.

The solution could only be presented as a joke, with the usual component of cruelty that such jokes are permitted to contain. Indeed, the remark was dismissed and did not even appear in the record of the meeting, but the underlying anxiety was present in the next statement, to be seriously expressed this time, that school is a *transitional* community in which the child tries out his love relationships. This was more than a mere serious repetition of the earlier joke, for it contained a reminder that the group was not permanent. The fate that had overtaken the absentees might overcome any or all of the members. Excluding a member of any group, even if he is regarded as a traitor, brings guilt—fear of nemesis for the remaining members not only because of the *external* danger presented by the excluded member and his friends but because of the *internal* damage to the individual's feeling of belongingness. To hurt a fellow member is to hurt that part of oneself that is identified with the victim. Even the death of the member turned traitor is no solution, as is clearly seen in political purges. The killed victims, although unable to hurt the group externally, remain a danger. They draw members who had remained faithful and who might even have been instrumental in their death to join them and to become the victims of the next purge. To bring about the death of an external enemy makes for greater unity among the members of the group, but to kill a fellow member is to put oneself in danger from one's own internal need for the survival of the group in face of one's own destructiveness. To the rule that no man acts merely as an individual, but with a group—large or small, faithful or dissenting—members of the present group were no exception. They never made a move alone but always with one or other sub-group.

THE PARTITION OF THE SILENT MEMBERS

During the last part of the meeting, which was devoted to a brief discussion of future policy, it appeared that there was a change from the situation shown in Table 6. This was the ninth session and the last but one for the term. I stated that I was willing to continue for another term. This meant I was not giving up the group. Of the twelve members present nine wished to continue meeting. The nine included all the six who had spoken and three who had been silent. The other three of these said they would not return. Three of the silent members therefore had joined the absentees. With three silent members remaining, the continuing group would be reduced to half its original strength (Table 8), but, as the number was above the minimum officially required, the battle for continuation had been won.

It was finally decided to discuss "School as a Transitional Community" at the next meeting, the last of the session. Truancy had been a defense assuming that the group was permanent. Acceptance of its transitional nature (as of the school) represents a recognition of reality. They could now face the eventual extinction of the group and so were able to decide on their future behavior as members of it.

The knowledge that the group was to resume its activities with a membership reduced to half made it urgent to consider how it could live on as the transitional community it had proved to be. On the reality plane, the recognition that some of the difficulties of the school situation were due to its being

TABLE 8   The Situation at the End of the Ninth Session

Speakers		Absentees	
Speakers' sub-group	6	Absentees' sub-group	6
Half/silent sub-group	3	Half/silent sub-group	3
Total	9	Total	9
	(PL)		(AL)

transitional marked a definite advance in the pursuit of the group task, for whatever solution reached would have to take this transitional nature into account. It was on this theme, which turned out to involve special consideration of the school's (and the teacher's) relations with outside groups in the community, that the group, at its next meeting, decided to focus in its next term's work. Having found its "project" it was able to pass into the second phase of its existence.

Charisma and the Dependent Group

The session selected for detailed report illustrates the effective role played by an absentees' ("bad") group from which the ("good") present group cannot dissociate itself, since it represents part of itself—its own badness—and ultimately its own extinction. Its efforts to survive are constantly thwarted through re-introjection of the "badness" at first projected into the absentees.

At the level of group leadership this process appears in the institution by the group of an *absent leader* in opposition to the *legitimate leader,* the role of the absent leader being to provide leadership for the *basic group* (in the form of *baD*) with which the *work group* (*W*) under the legitimate leader has to contend.

An individual perceived as completely contained in a particular sub-group is not likely to emerge as the leader of his group as a whole. It was shown that, apart from *PL*, *AL* was the only ubiquitous member. She therefore attracted towards herself any forces in the group seeking an alternative leadership to that of *PL*. The attributes of her position, moreover, made her into a figure compounded of seemingly incompatible opposites—absent yet present in her paper, silent yet speaking through another member of the group. These were attributes which made it the easier to endow her with an omnipresent, magical and compelling omnipotence. It is this quality that constitutes her *valency* for the leadership of *baD*. The charismatic power which she developed appears to be directly related to this phantasmagoric hinterland. A question that has remained obscure in Weber's (1947) conception of charismatic leadership is the nature of the sanction on which the authority of such charismatic leaders depends. A suggestion arising from the present study is that the source of this sanction is the basic group.

References

Bion, W.R. 1961. *Experiences in Groups and Other Papers*. London: Tavistock Publications; New York: Basic Books.

Ezriel, H. 1950. "A Psycho-Analytic Approach to Group Treatment." *British Journal of Medical Psychology,* 23:59–74.

Jaques, E. 1951. *The Changing Culture of a Factory*. London: Tavistock Publications.

Newcomb, T.M. 1952. *Social Psychology*. New York: Dryden Press.

Sutherland, J.D. 1985. "Bion Revisited." In *Bion and Group Psychotherapy,* edited by Malcomb Pines. London: Routledge and Kegan Paul.

Weber, M. 1947. *The Theory of Social and Economic Organization*. Translated by A.R. Henderson and T. Parsons. London: William Hodge.

Eric J. Miller

Experiential Learning in Groups I
The Development of the Leicester Model*

Introduction

The Tavistock/Leicester Conference—or, as it is now more often called, the Leicester Conference—is an intensive two-week residential event devoted to experiential learning about group and organizational behavior, with a particular emphasis on the nature of authority and leadership. Its purpose is educational. The conference brings together an international membership of, usually, 50–70 people drawn from a wide range of occupations and professions, in industry and commerce, education, medical and social services, the voluntary sector, etc. The staff group of ten or so is similarly diverse. The conference has been held once and sometimes twice a year since 1957—over 40 altogether. All have been sponsored by what is now the Group Relations Training Programme (GRTP) of the Tavistock Institute of Human Relations (TIHR), sometimes in co-sponsorship with other organizations.

The first seven conferences were jointly sponsored by Leicester University, and almost all have been held at Leicester in one of the University's halls of residence.

The essentials of the approach, including its theoretical underpinnings, were largely established by the mid-1960s. Since then, the "Leicester model" has provided the basis for numerous other conferences, some run by the GRTP and very many more by other institutions, in Britain and a dozen different countries around the world. In most cases these were developed with the active support of the Tavistock Institute. Around the conference work and its applications there has emerged a substantial literature. For a decade or more, the A.K. Rice Institute (AKRI), the principal exponent of the Leicester model in the United States, has been organizing a biennial scientific meeting focussed on the conferences and their ramifications; the First International Symposium, jointly sponsored by GRTP and AKRI, was held at Oxford (July, 1988) on the theme of "applications to social and political issues."

*A requested overview.

History

ORIGINS

The first Leicester Conference was explicitly an experiment and it was meticulously planned and documented. It was reported in *Exploration in Group Relations:* a residential conference held in September 1957 by the University of Leicester and the Tavistock Institute of Human Relations (Trist and Sofer, 1959). The late Professor John Allaway, then Head of the Department of Adult Education in the University of Leicester, was Chairman of the Executive Committee that planned and ran the Conference; Eric Trist was program director.

As Allaway noted in his introduction to the monograph, this was "the first full-scale experiment in Britain with the laboratory method of training in group relations." This was a direct reference to the laboratory method that had developed at Bethel, Maine, since 1947 by the National Training Laboratories (NTL). Based on the T-Group, it was a model of intensive experiential learning that had sprung directly from the work of Kurt Lewin, whose group theories had strongly influenced the early Tavistock group. The Tavistock approach, however, was influenced also by psychoanalysis.

In the late 1950s, experiential learning of the Bethel type was still a novelty in Britain, and psychoanalysts were somewhat suspect. Cosponsorship by a university, especially by a department in the educational field, was seen as important in adding credibility. Allaway had the courage to back the venture on behalf of Leicester University and secured the Vice-Chancellor's support.

The organizing committee successfully approached a wide range of organizations to nominate members for the first conference. Recruitment through an organizational rather than a personal channel was thought to provide a sociological barrier against members becoming covert patients. More than a third of the 45 who enrolled came from industry (many, but by no means all, in personnel and training roles). Others were drawn from universities and other educational institutions; the Home Office (attendance of a prison governor and a deputy governor being the beginning of a long association of the Prison Service with the Leicester Conferences); the probation service; local authorities; and voluntary organizations. Eric Trist, then Chairman of the Management Committee of TIHR, led the staff group of 14.

Twenty-six of the members attended a two day follow-up session six months later. Suffice to say that the evaluation justified mounting a second conference in 1959, followed fairly quickly by a third, fourth and fifth in 1960–61. Leicester University's co-sponsorship extended over the first seven conferences. It ended with the retirement of John Allaway and of his colleague, Professor J.W. Tibble, who had also become actively involved.

DEVELOPMENTS IN DESIGN

In the earliest conference the central event was the small Study Group, consisting of 9–12 members, a staff consultant and a staff observer. Its task was to study its own behavior, as a group, in the here-and-now. The other main events were lectures (social theory sessions) and Application Groups, which were intended between them to help members make sense of their Study Group experience and consider how it might be applied in their external roles. There were also plenary review sessions. This design was broadly similar to that at Bethel, though the equivalent Bethel T-group was larger—up to 20. Also the Leicester consultant's orientation was less person-centered: it addressed the dynamics of the group, and it concentrated on interpretation rather than facilitation. The 1959 Conference saw the experimental introduction of an Inter-Group Event, in which members were asked to divide into groups and negotiate an agreement on how to use vacant slots in the program. Consultants helped to interpret the inter-group dynamics (Higgin and Bridger, 1964).

In 1962, TIHR gave authority to Kenneth Rice to take over leadership of the group relations conferences. The conferences could no longer be subsidized from the Institute's research funds and Rice was willing to try to make them financially viable. He did indeed succeed in making the conferences self-financing, but only because he and other staff colleagues were committed enough to accept nominal remuneration. (And it is still the case, in 1988, that, in order to keep membership fees at a level acceptable to non-commercial organizations, payments to staff remain modest.)

However, Rice's major contribution to the conferences was not economic but technical and conceptual. The period of his direction saw at least four significant developments in design (Rice, 1965). The first was innovation of the Large Group. Its task was the same as for the small Study Group, but it included all the members (sometimes 70 or more) with 2–4 consultants. Secondly, the Inter-Group Event was re-defined as having a single task: the membership was to form itself into groups and to study their interrelatedness in the here-and-now. Thirdly, a second type of inter-group event (later developed into the Institutional Event) was introduced, in which the focus of study was the member/staff relationship within the conference institution as a whole. Finally, as a natural consequence of increasing the emphasis on experiential learning, the lectures were reduced and eventually dropped. Plenary sessions and Application Groups were retained, and there was increasing use of interim Review Groups, to give members opportunities to reflect on their experience.

The "single-task" model introduced by Rice, with its insistence on the study of the here-and-now, had some critics within TIHR. They believed the interpretive stance was too threatening to some members and could inhibit learning rather than encourage it. Accordingly, Harold Bridger, who was centrally involved in the earlier Leicester Conferences and had introduced the inter-group experiment in 1959, developed an alternative conference model, based on a "two-task" design. In this, membership groups are given specific assignments *and* study the dynamics of the groups in tackling them. Bridger continues to organize these conferences through TIHR and in association with other institutions. That model, however, is outside the scope of this chapter. It may be added that externally, particularly in the United States, the term "Tavistock model" was applied indiscriminately to both, which was a source of confusion. More domestically, there was a period when the two models and their two protagonists, Rice and Bridger, were set up as rivals—a rivalry over legitimacy. In retrospect it is plain that they are complementary (see Bridger I, 2, "Courses and Working Conferences as Transitional Learning Institutions").

Despite some subsequent theoretical and technical developments, the Leicester Conference model of today was essentially established by the time Rice died in 1969. Then, as now, a typical day's program in the first week would comprise four one-and-a-half-hour sessions, with a break in the afternoon or evening; Small Study Group (SSG) and Large Study Group (LSG) in the morning; and two sessions of Inter-Group (IG). In the second week, the Institutional Event (IE) would replace the IG, and towards the end there would be Application Group (AG) and Plenary (P) sessions. Some conferences also include the Very Small Study Group (VSSG), of 5–7 members (Gosling, 1981).

Thus the SSG has become only one of several settings for the here-and-now study of relatedness of individual, group and organization. The conference as a whole, comprising both members and staff, is designed as a temporary educational institution, which can be studied experientially as it forms, evolves and comes to an end.

It also became clear during the 1960s that "group relations" was too broad and vague a description of what was being studied. To be sure, it has always been characteristic of the Leicester model that the focus of interpretation has been on the dynamics of the group as a whole, and not on individuals. In the early days (and I speak from painful personal memories) a trainee consultant would feel grateful to identify any group-as-a-whole dynamic at all. With experience, however, although the consultant may still feel lost at times, often there is an evident choice of interpretations that might be made. Rice recognized that the definition of the *primary task* of the conference as a whole and of the events within it was therefore important. In the early 1960s he was defining the primary task of the conference as "to provide those who attend with opportunities to learn about leadership" (Rice, 1965:5). He then worded it more precisely in terms of studying the nature and exercise of authority. Recognition that there are choices in the definition of primary task and, therefore, in the focus of interpretation, enlarged the scope of conference design. Thus the late 1970s saw the introduction of a series of Leicester Conferences with the title "Individual and Organization: the Politics of Relatedness." These alternated with more traditional conferences on the theme of "Authority, Leadership and Organization" which still continue. In these, the primary task is defined as:

> to provide opportunities to study the exercise of authority in the context of interpersonal, inter-group and institutional relations within the Conference Institution.

The primary task of each event is defined in relation to that overall definition.

Nowadays alternate conferences make special provision for members with previous Leicester (or similar) experience: in some sessions they work separately from first-timers; in others, jointly. Other conferences include a Training Group, members of which have usually already taken part in at least two residential conferences. The first such group was introduced in 1963. Initially, this was designed to expand the pool of potential staff. It now has the broader aim of helping people to understand and practice the consultant role in group and organizational settings.

The Interplay of Theory and Method

In the first Leicester Conference in 1957, the Study Group was the only experiential event. Groups met for twelve one-and-a-half-hour periods over the two weeks. They were designed to enable members to explore group processes and their own involvement in them—processes that were held to be inherent in any human group but which were much more visible in the single-task Study Group setting.

Our central theoretical and practical interest was and remains what we later came to term "relatedness": the processes of mutual influence between individual and group, group and group, and group and organization, and, beyond that, the relatedness of organization and community to wider social systems, to society itself. In all these forms of relatedness there is a potential tension. As Bion (1961) had showed, the individual needs groups in order to establish his or her identity, to find meaning in existence, and to express different aspects of the self. Correspondingly, the group needs the individual member for its own collective purposes—both to contribute to the group's task and to participate in the processes through which the group acquires and maintains its own distinctive identity. But this process is one that often threatens individuality.

As with individuals, so with groups in relation to organizations and wider systems. "Group" and "organization," however, are not entities, with an objective reality; they are ideas or constructs that we hold in our minds. A particular group is a construct substantially shared, explicitly or implicitly, by a number of individuals. But—except in the restricted biological sense—"individual" too can similarly be conceived as a construct, a reification. Thus the relatedness, and the associated tension, is more appropriately conceptualized as connecting not two entities, individual and group, but two processes—individuation and incorporation—moving towards, but never reaching, individual autonomy on the one hand and submergence in the group on the other. This theoretical perspective is central to the conceptualization of the Conference model; and obviously the Conferences themselves illuminate the theory.

However, the primary task of the conference is not to contribute to theory but to provide members with opportunities to learn about their own involvement in these dynamics, with a specific focus on learning about the nature of authority and the problems encountered in its exercise. More generally, the aim is to enable "the individual to develop greater maturity in understanding and managing the boundary between his own inner world and the realities of his external environment" (Miller, 1977:44; Miller and Rice, 1967:269)—in other words, to struggle to exercise one's own authority, to manage oneself in role and to become less a captive of group and organizational processes (Lawrence and Miller, 1976; Lawrence, 1979).

CONCEPTUAL FRAMEWORK

I have postulated elsewhere (Miller, 1976a) that in the field of human behavior no conceptual framework is complete without a statement of the role of the observer and his or her relation to the observed. There is an obvious link to subatomic physics, as illuminated by Heisenberg's principle of uncertainty. If within a group I address myself to a person, I confirm that person's identity as an individual; if I shift my focus to the level of the group, the notion of the bounded individual appears as a reification. Similarly, the conceptual framework that underpins Leicester Conferences rests on a definition of role and task in which the staff are not flies on the wall, but are trying to enable the conference members to understand and gain greater control over the situations they are in. We are integrally part of the process, not outside it.

The intellectual inheritance from Lewin lies particularly in his insistence, from the late 1930s onwards, on the importance of studying the "gestalt" properties of groups as wholes.

Bion, in his concurrent development of an approach to group psychotherapy, adopted a similar focus, but brought to it a psychoanalytic orientation. Bion's views are explained in Sutherland (Vol. I, "Bion Revisited"). He postulates that at any given time the behavior of a group can be analyzed at two levels: it is a *sophisticated group* (or *work group*) met to perform an overt task; and it is at the same time a *basic group*, acting on one, and only one, of three covert *basic assumptions* (fight/flight, dependence and pairing), to which its individual members contribute anonymously and in ways of which they are not consciously aware. It is a function of the basic assumption operating at any one time to keep at bay emotions associated with the other two assumptions— primitive emotional states belonging to the "proto-mental system"—that may be inconsistent with the overt task.

Bion's formulation is one element of the psychoanalytic components in the framework. A second is the formulation by Melanie Klein (who profoundly influenced Bion) of processes of infant development and their effects on adult life (Klein, 1959). She identified two developmental phases: the "paranoid-schizoid and the depressive positions" which to some extent persist through life. The manifestation of these processes in group and organizational life, particularly through the defenses of splitting, denial and projective identification, are discussed in Jaques (Vol. I, "On the Dynamics of Social Structure") and Menzies Lyth (Vol. I, "Social Systems as a Defense Against Anxiety").

Psychoanalysis, besides suggesting that explanations for human behavior in groups may be found in primitive and unconscious processes, has also provided a role-model for Tavistock staff working not with individual patients but with groups and organizations. Nearly all the Institute's work in the 1950s and 1960s (and much of it still today) was a form of action research in which the research worker was also a consultant, taking a professional role in relation to the client system; and indeed consultancy was the method through which research data were generated.

Individuals and groups interact in order to find ways of giving meaning to their experience and also to develop mechanisms that can defend them against uncertainty and anxiety (Wilson, 1951; Jaques, 1953; 1955; Menzies, 1960); these defenses, often unrecognized and deeply rooted, are threatened by prospects of change; hence it is an important part of the consultant role to serve as a container during the working through of change. A still more specific derivation from the analyst's role has been the stress laid on examining and using the transference and counter-transference within the professional relationship. That is to say, the way in which the consultant is used and experienced, and also the feelings evoked in him, may offer evidence of underlying and unstated issues and feelings in the client system: that which is repressed by the client may be expressed by the consultant. Again this was a cornerstone of Bion's approach to groups.

Those features of the framework described so far were part of the conceptual input into the earliest Leicester Conferences. The distinctive additional contribution through Rice was the application of a much more fully developed organizational model derived from open systems theory (von Bertlanffy, 1950a, b).

A key connecting concept, derived from Lewin (1935; 1936) and developed in the open systems formulation, is that of *boundary*. The existence and survival of any human system depends upon continuous interchange with its environment, whether of materials, people, information, ideas, values or fantasies. The boundary across which these "commodities" flow in and out both separates any given system from, and links it to, its environment. It marks a discontinuity between the task of that particular system and the tasks of the related systems with which it transacts. Because these relations are never stable and static, and because the behavior and identity of the system are subject to continual renegotiation and redefinition, the system boundary is best conceived not as a line but as a region (Lewin, 1935; 1936). That region is the location of those roles and activities that are concerned with mediating relations between inside and outside. In organizations and groups this is the function of leadership; in individuals it is the ego function. The leadership exercised in this region can protect the internal sub-systems from the disruption of fluctuating and inconsistent demands from outside; but it also has to promote those internal changes that will enable the system to be adaptive, and indeed proactive, in relation to its environment. The health and ultimately the survival of a system therefore depends on an appropriate mix of insulation and permeability in the boundary region (Miller and Rice, 1967).

From the late 1950s onwards, Rice and some of his colleagues (myself included) were using the open system formulation in conjunction with the notion of *primary task* (Rice, 1958; 1963). It was postulated that a purposeful human system at any given time has a primary task, in the sense of the task that it must perform if it is to survive. Boundaries between sets of activities define *task systems,* around which organizational boundaries may potentially be drawn. Finally people—the human resources of the enterprise—carry *roles* through which they contribute the requisite activities to the task of the organization.

It was this conceptual apparatus of open system and primary task that Rice brought to bear on the design of the Leicester Conference in the early 1960s (Rice, 1965). He was very insistent on identifying the primary tasks of the conference as a whole and of the constituent events. Boundary became a critical concept: time boundaries, territorial boundaries and especially role boundaries—between staff and member, between the different roles that might be taken by the same person at different times. Beyond that are the boundaries between person and role, between the inner world of the individual and the external environment.

This notion that the individual too can be conceptualized as an open system developed in the mid-1960s and perhaps took us one small step closer to the ultimate goal of a unified theory of human behavior. Rice explicated this idea in a seminal paper reprinted elsewhere in this volume (Rice, 1969; Vol. I, "Individual, Group and Inter-Group Processes"; Miller, 1976b).

PRACTICE: THE ROLE OF STAFF

Those invited to join the staff at Leicester have been members of at least two residential conferences and probably also a Training Group. They may first have taken a staff role in a shorter conference, perhaps non-residential. Usually each staff group includes at least two—often more—staff from related institutions. These will have had considerable staff experience in other conferences, often including directorship.

In the early conferences it was considered mandatory that study group consultants should be analysts or at least have had an extended analysis. Analysts were the obvious candidates for an approach that involved interpreting the transference of the group as a whole onto the consultant; and they were likely to be more attuned to, and less dismayed by, unconscious processes. Moreover, the organizers were concerned about the possibilities of individual disturbance in the intensive group setting; it seemed prudent to have a clinician in the consultant role.

By the early 1960s, with increasing demand for conferences, it had become clear that insistence on this qualification would severely constrain growth and dissemination. Initial anxieties about the effects on individuals had turned out to be exaggerated, so that clinical experience was not needed. Indeed, it could sometimes draw the consultant's attention towards an individual and away from the group.

The capacity to be in touch with one's own shifting experience in relation to the group—of being pushed and pulled, attacked and ignored—and to reflect that back to the group, preferably with some explanation of why it might be happening, remained, of course, a central criterion: the group process is not something extraneous, merely to be observed and commented upon. But the fundamental qualification for consultancy seemed to be an ability to stick to the task and role. Accordingly, the early training groups included university teachers, managers from industry and prison governors among others.

Leicester Conference Directors have continued to be people with analytic experience, though not necessarily analysts; indeed, for the first twelve years there was a policy that the director role should *not* be taken by a psychiatrist. It was argued that under psychiatric leadership the membership would be more likely to produce "patients" and that the stance of the Conference might tilt away from the educational towards the therapeutic. By 1970, however, the model was firmly enough established to lessen that risk.

The conference director is appointed by the sponsoring institution(s). He or she is initially responsible for conference design and the appointment of staff. By accepting the invitation, staff members are individually confirming the director's authority; but the staff group as a whole, including both consulting and administrative staff, is conceived as collectively the "management." As such, staff have the shared responsibility for providing the boundary conditions—of task definition, territory and time—within which all participants, themselves included, can engage with the primary task of the conference. Hence the authority of the director has to be confirmed by the staff group at their pre-conference meeting, and that authorization has to be kept under review as the conference proceeds. Once the conference has begun, *the staff group has the authority to replace the director*. If there is irreconcilable disagreement between the director and one or more staff members, then one or the other has to resign. Although in practice this has never happened, it has nearly happened; and it is vital in a conference devoted to examining authority that the authority of the director should always remain to some extent problematic.

The director has to be available for the transference of the staff as well as of the membership. This offers evidence of the prevailing dynamic in the conference institution as a whole; and more generally it yields insight into the collusive processes through which, for example, organizational hierarchies are sustained. At the more overt level, the director has responsibility, on behalf of the staff group, for overall boundary management—the external boundary, especially in relation to the hall of residence in which the conference is held; and internally, the boundaries between staff and membership and between subsets of the staff. Management of practical matters on these boundaries is delegated to the conference administrator(s). The director leads the work of staff in public, for example in plenary sessions, and in its own separate meetings. The director also takes a consultant role, usually in the LSG.

Within the staff group there is a defined pattern of delegation to sub-sets of the staff—for example, one with responsibility for the Small Study Group system, consisting of several SSGs, and another for the LSG. The individual consultant is conceived as deriving authority from the sub-set and as being accountable to it. Examination of mutual projections between these sub-sets is an important, and often difficult, task of frequent full staff meetings.

A consultant's interpretation is essentially a working hypothesis about this set of systematic relations, drawing on observations and internal feelings. For example, when in an SSG a silent member is being picked on by others, the consultant may feel and say that the attack is really on him or herself for not contributing what the members want; and further that the attack is displaced because there is anxiety that if it were directed specifically it would be so violent as to destroy the consultant and throw the group into anarchy; and beyond that again, that the small group has to be kept safe because the wider system—the conference at large—is felt to be evil and indiscriminately destructive. Ideally, therefore, the working hypothesis contains a "because clause"—a possible explanation of why this dynamic is occurring. The consultant is not always able to offer such a because clause immediately: two or three intervening observations may be necessary first. Always, however, the consultant is trying to use the experience of being pushed into this role or that in order to work at the task of the group—the study of its own behavior, as a group, in the here-and-now. Comments on individual behavior and dynamics are avoided. "Personality variables," in the words of a typical brochure, "are for private consideration by the individual member." The consultant will, however, appropriately draw attention to processes in which the group is casting an individual member in a role—as fight-leader, clown or non-speaker, for example—to serve its collective needs.

In taking up this interpretive role, the consultant is operating at the boundary of the system, trying to understand what is happening between the parts and the whole, and between the whole and its environment. One hopes that at times members will learn to take up this boundary perspective themselves. It is partly for this reason that the role of observer to the small study groups has been abandoned: it offers the members an alternative and inappropriate role-model, one through which to escape from the work rather than engage with it. Moreover, it distorts, deflects or dilutes the transference onto the consultant, to whom some processes then become less accessible. These factors outweigh the possible advantages of giving the consultant another perspective in post-sessional discussions and also of providing a niche for a trainee. Analogous to the training of psychoanalysts, it now seems more appropriate to provide the novice SSG consultant with supervision after the session. Peer discussions within the sub-set of consultants are a further learning opportunity.

Two other points may be made about consultant behavior in experiential groups which sometimes causes puzzlement. First, the consultant enters and leaves the group territory strictly according to the timetable. This predictability offers a form of security; it defines the time available and leaves the members with their authority to decide how to use it; and it enables the consultant to interpret the way they use it. Second, the contributions of the consultant are always directed as far as possible to the task: thus conventional social rituals, such as "good mornings," which are not task-related, are eschewed.

In the Review and Application Groups, which have a different task, the role of the consultant is correspondingly different: it tends to be less interpretive and more facilitative, and is occasionally even didactic in that the consultant may offer conceptual frameworks to help members understand processes they have experienced. Recognition that change of role is accompanied by change in behavior is itself an enlightenment to some members.

THEORY AND PHENOMENOLOGY

Conference members commonly have the fantasy that they are guinea-pigs being experimented upon by a staff whose primary interest is in research and the advancement of knowledge. Such a fantasy is understandable. There is an abundant social science literature based on therapy and training groups whose members have knowingly or unknowingly been the objects of observation and experimentation, and some of these studies have indeed been illuminating. Moreover, the Tavistock Institute is known to be in the research business. Beyond that, in the conference itself, staff members are aspiring to use a version of the scientific method in the here-and-now: they are putting forward working hypotheses with evidence from their observations and internal feelings, and are inviting members to use their own evidence to verify or falsify the hypotheses. If, as they often do, members find their experiential learning difficult and painful, it is not surprising that they should take the paranoid view that they are victims of staff's experiments.

The fact is that there has been a rigorous adherence to the primary task of "providing opportunities to learn" and an avoidance of muddying this by pursuing a research agenda. During the 1960s, Pierre Turquet, with the participants' permission, recorded study group sessions in two or three advanced training groups. With that exception, he and others who have worked to distill something from their groups have had to rely on making notes between sessions.

Within the conferences, the place of theory is properly problematic. Until the mid-1960s, lecture sessions were an integral part of the conference design. With some early exceptions, the lecturers were staff members who also had consulting roles in the experiential events. Their subjects included theories of individual, group and organization and also the application of theories to practical problems in the lecturers' own experience. According to Rice (1965:35), the lectures were "designed to give intellectual content to the learning taking place in other events of the conference," and "to provide a framework for articulation of the experience of the conference." He went on to say: "The lecture series has, however, an important secondary task: to provide a traditional form of teaching within a learning situation that is using unfamiliar methods."

By the mid-1960s, that secondary task was becoming redundant. A serious consideration was a sense that the theories and concepts were being used defensively. Such formulations as Bion's basic assumptions of dependency, fight/flight and pairing, or Tuckman's stages of group development (forming, storming, norming, performing) (Tuckman, 1965) were tending to be used as labels for an experience—"Ah! Yes! This is 'basic assumption fight' "—as if that were the end of the matter. Labelling is defensive in that it inhibits puzzling over the actual experience, wondering how one got caught up in it, why at this time, and so on. It also simplifies what is invariably a much more complex set of processes: apperception of other elements, which may be more difficult and troublesome, is squeezed out. One further consideration that contributed to abandoning lectures was the fairly frequent experience that members' projections onto the lecturer were carry-overs from a preceding experiential event. Thus concepts are more appropriately introduced in the concluding application phase of the conference, at a point at which they may help members to relate specific experiences to their external roles. Although conference brochures include a reading list, those participants who use it generally find that it is after the conference, when they can reflect on links with their own experience, that they gain most from the written word.

Most staff have also learned to be cautious about carrying too much conceptual baggage into their consultant roles. Gosling, in "A Study of Very Small Groups" (1981) has made this point eloquently. Having directed very many Leicester and other conferences over the past 20 years, I am highly conscious of the pressures, internal and external, towards becoming an "institutionalized" director. The symptom is loss of capacity to be surprised—the sense of having been here before and knowing what to do next. I know, yet repeatedly have to relearn, that this is precisely what the staff and membership want of me: to provide such containment that they too can avoid surprise. Perversely but properly, members seem to learn more from the inexperienced consultant, who is constantly confronted with the unfamiliar and lacks a comforting repertoire of tried and tested responses. Thus I have to work hard to become "inexperienced"—to lower my defenses against recognizing that I have never before been with *these* people in *this* setting at *this* moment. To give a trivial example, I rarely note down emerging ideas: I am aware that yesterday's jottings may structure and blinker what I see today.

Theoretical formulations, if they are to further rather than inhibit experiential learning, probably have to be held at a very general or abstract level. Thus, as we have seen, Bion's identification of three specific basic assumption groups readily leads to labelling. What remains useful, in the context of the conference work, is the notion of basic assumption functioning in groups and, lying behind that, his proposition that the basic assumptions are to be regarded as secondary formations that defend against primitive psychotic anxieties—related, for example, to "an extremely early primal scene worked out on a level of part objects" (Bion, 1961:164). This makes it clearer that to label a basic assumption is simply to label a defense; whereas by shifting our attention back to the underlying level we are at least potentially open to uncovering the primitive phantasies that, at a given moment, the shared defense is being mobilized to repress.

Jaques, drawing on Klein and building on Bion, offered the equivalently useful theory of larger social systems as providing defenses against persecutory and depressive anxiety (Jaques, 1955; Vol. I, "On the Dynamics of Social Structure"); and Menzies (1960; Vol. I, "Social Systems as a Defense Against Anxiety") was then able to identify the more specific anxieties and associated defenses in nursing. It is, of course, by removing the familiar structures and conventions—or, to be more precise, by reducing them to the differentiation of two roles, member and consultant—that the conference setting makes the defenses and underlying anxieties more accessible.

Rice (1969:565–66; Vol. I, "Individual, Group and Inter-Group Processes") offered a similarly useful perspective for the examination of inter-group relations. These, he postulated, are affected by the defenses that a group mobilizes against the underlying anxiety that the transaction will destroy the integrity of its boundary. His additional proposition was that this dynamic is a feature of all relationships, including those between individuals.

In the same paper, Rice drew attention to limitations in Bion's formulation of basic assumptions, in that they describe only "special cases which are most easily observable in small groups because they are large enough to give power to an alternative leadership" (i.e., leadership of a basic assumption group in competition with work group leadership) "and yet not so large as to provide support for more than one kind of powerful alternative leadership at any one time" (p.578).

It is to Turquet (1975) that we are indebted for a further conceptualization of large group processes, again at a level that encourages rather than constrains the exploration of what is happening in a particular group. In the words of its sub-title, his paper is "a study in the phenomenology of the individual's experiences of changing membership in a large group." It draws entirely on his own experience as one of 2–4 consultants in LSGs of 40–80 members at Leicester and allied conferences.

He points out that the consultant is present in a dual capacity, both in a defined role and as a person. This is, of course, also the case with the consultant in the small group. A common question is: Is the consultant part of the group or not? The answer is both: as a person, inescapably yes; in the role of consultant, no. To be caught in one capacity at the expense of the other is to lose the ability to work. But the forces in the large group are more powerful; the role of consultant may be lost for longer periods.

> He too will find himself alone, an isolate; he too will lose his wits, be de-skilled, filled up, threatened with annihilation—to mention but a few of the many common personal experiences provided by the large group . . . As a consultant, I too . . . am involved in a process, a conversion process whose aim is to make me something other . . . The struggle to resist them, to remain a consultant, is great. In the harsh terms of large-group life, it is a case of who will dominate whom . . . (Turquet, 1975:91–2).

Turquet offers a terminology for the various forms of relatedness of the member to the large group, including non-relationship as one form of relatedness. The conference member comes into such a setting as an "I." "I" refers to "the person who has not yet achieved a role status in the large group, or to a person who has momentarily left such a status for whatever reason, possibly in order to search within oneself for a model or a skill; a member in transition" (p.316). Turquet suggests that at this entry stage such a person should be thought of as a "singleton," "not yet part of a group but attempting both to find himself and to make relations with other singletons who are in a similar state" (p.94). Next he considers the position of the singleton who has established a relationship, with other singletons, with the large group as a whole. The term he uses for such a "converted" singleton is "individual member" (IM). It is a move from a non-role to a role. Searching for an equilibrium in the flux of the large group and its characteristic threat of annihilation, the singleton experiences the constant attempts to convert him or her from an IM into a "membership individual" (MI)—a creature of the group. Turquet goes on to identify the transitional state, "as the individual member in his group life moves between the various stages . . . : singleton to IM, IM to MI, or MI back to singleton" (p.96). At these phases there is at least potentially an opportunity for choice, which is the occasion for expression of individuality, of "I-ness." Reassertion of I-ness may involve a sudden upsurge of idiosyncratic behavior. But (Turquet implies) this may expose the person to conversion again into an MI. For the singleton to become and remain an IM requires finding "a boundary or skin which both limits and defines him" (p.96). Externally one needs the presence of others in order to define "me" and "not me"; and internally a sense of boundary between past and present, then and now. Without this, a person is consigned back into the "undifferentiated non-singleton matrix" out of which he or she had developed (p.97). The experience is one of continual disorientation. On the one hand are powerful pressures towards homogenization, towards the lowest common denominator. This, as Anzieu (1971) has indicated, can be a beguiling world, which gets rid of sexual difference and castration anxiety and may feed the phantasy that the group itself is an all-gratifying mother, perhaps the mother of the infant in the womb. But it is also a destroyer of identity. On the other hand, assertion of individuality lays one open to exploitation and to attacks from unknown sources. Or one may be left to fall into an infinite void. So it is a fearful place, the more so because one does not know what is happening to one's projections or from where and in what form they will come back. There is an experience of being fractioned into multiple parts. Moreover,

the introjected vastness of [one's] external world meets a similar internal experience [i.e., of an internal world that is unencompassable and boundless] and by their mutual reinforcement the level of anxiety is raised, requiring a further projection into the outer large group of the now reinforced sense of vastness, only to increase the fantasied percept of the large group as now greater than ever before, not only vast but endless (p.118).

Turquet also explores the large group's potential for violence—an unpredictable, errant violence, never far below the surface—along with the fears that this evokes and examples of the defenses that are mobilized.

Turquet's paper is a powerful contribution, which succeeds in communicating and beginning to conceptualize the struggle between individuation and incorporation, while at the same time conveying the boundlessness of the territory that is available to be explored in the here-and-now. Arising out of the group relations conferences, very many papers have been written, and some offer valuable descriptions and conceptualizations which contribute to social science; but relatively few have the quality of enhancing the conference work itself by lowering the barriers to seeing and hearing what is happening in ourselves and among those around us.

The Role of Participant and the Nature of Learning

There are no specific qualifications for membership. Undeniably, some members find the Conference stressful, and people going through emotional turmoil in their personal lives are probably not in the best state to make use of an intensive educational program; but the decision has to be theirs. Our assumption has to be that, as managers and professionals with responsibility for the well-being of others, they must be capable of making such a decision. Sometimes we receive enquiries from organizations about whether to send a particular manager to the Conference—perhaps someone with relationship difficulties. Our response is that we do not provide treatment for such difficulties— this is an educational, not a remedial institution. We also recommend against *sending* anyone: learning is much more likely if the individual exercises his or her own authority to apply. The fee structure encourages two or more members from the same organization to attend together: experience shows that they are more likely to apply their learning effectively when they go back.

In the conference opening, the director may typically say: "Staff are not here to teach in the conventional sense but to provide opportunities to learn. What you learn and the pace at which you learn are up to you." There is a starting assumption that application to become a member implies some preparedness to engage in the task of the conference. Beyond that, the role of member is not defined. There is no compulsion to attend sessions on time, or at all. Taking up a membership role is left to the individual's authority.

The experience of being a member is nevertheless initially disconcerting. The task of here-and-now study is unfamiliar and elusive; experience in other roles seems of little help; and members feel de-skilled. They see themselves as acting as individuals, yet the consultants persist in interpreting their behavior as a function of the group as a whole (Miller, 1980). Whereas the individual is clear that he or she intended this, or did not intend that, the consultant seems perversely to focus instead on effects and consequences, and from these infers unconscious intentions at the level of the group. So quite basic, taken-for-granted assumptions about one's identity, one's sense of self, are being called into question; the boundary between self and other, which had seemed obvious, suddenly becomes problematic.

By the end of the second day most members have "joined," in the sense of being caught up in the process, and a conference culture has begun to emerge. For example, almost all are strictly observing the time boundaries of sessions, and the consultant role has become less alien. At the end of the first week there is a 36-hour break, during which most members leave Leicester for at least part of the time. "Ordinary life"—life outside the Conference—is often felt to be disorienting, particularly for members going back to their families. They have become much more involved than they had realized. Before the break there is anxiety: will others come back, will the consultant come back? Behind that is the basic question: will *I* come back? Commitment is tested. The second week tests what members thought they had learned in the first: it is a form of application. "I've learned not to get caught like that again"—and then getting caught in just the same way; or carefully avoiding one landmine, only to tread on another. There are also the more positive experiences: for example, learning about group organization and representation from the Inter-Group Event may prove useful in the Institutional Event which begins after the break. Then, as they come to the final sessions of SSG and LSG, and to the closing plenaries, staff and members are working at the processes of ending. This means sorting out some of the projections of the past two weeks and redrawing the boundary around oneself. Application sessions help in this by re-alerting members to their external roles.

These considerations bring me to the nature of learning and what may be learned. Gosling (1981) is properly skeptical of an identifiable "Conference learning." "Group Relations *Training*" is a misnomer. Training implies transmission of skills, acquisition of which should, potentially at least, be measurable. The Conference provides a set of experiences, but also explicitly states that authority for making use of the experiences and learning from them rests firmly with the individual member. Outcomes are therefore idiosyncratic and unpredictable.

Twenty years ago Rice and I devised a complex methodology for evaluation (Rice, 1965). Because of the assumed synergism of the conference process, and also because we were wary of the effects of intermingling research and educational tasks, we deferred any attempt to identify the impact of specific conference events. For the first phase we proposed a before-and-after set of in-depth clinical interviews combined with assessments by colleagues in members' work-settings. It was a costly scheme, and we were never able to secure funding for it. We therefore remain reliant on impressionistic and anecdotal evidence, from past members, from people who know them, and from our own observations.

It seems that three different kinds, or levels, of learning are likely to occur. At the simplest level, members learn to identify and label some of the unfamiliar phenomena that they encounter, but they do so as observers. A second kind, goes beyond observation to insight, though it is also partly conceptual: the experience adds to the ways in which the individual classifies the world and relates to it—particularly involvement in unconscious processes. There is an awareness of phenomena previously unnoticed or dismissed as irrelevant. Members often speak of Conference learning as giving them another perspective on human behavior, including their own, and that is often what they mean. They may, however, be referring to a third kind of learning, which implies not an *additional* perspective but a *different* perspective. There is a correspondence here to the three levels of learning postulated by Bateson (1973). Palmer (1979) draws on Bateson in an important paper on "Learning and the Group Experience." This third level, as he elegantly puts it, "entails discovering a capacity to doubt the validity of perceptions which seem unquestionably true."

These distinctions are important, but difficult to operationalize. "Learning III" implies some degree of personality re-structuring—a systematic change— of a kind which would be fully in line with the aims of the conference; but how likely is this to happen within the two-week span? And how to measure it?

In the absence of systematic research, I offer the following tentative conclusions.

- Level II learning—the additional perspective—is a fairly common and obviously desirable outcome. Although the groundwork for it is laid by the Conference, it becomes established only in the ensuing months— notably when members identify a process that is dynamically similar to one in which they were involved in the conference. Or, at that moment, they may without realizing it respond in a way different from a familiar pre-conference response.
- Learning is reinforced if the member is returning to an organization where others already share that perspective. Menninger (1972; 1985) gives an account of an attempt in one organization to bring about a significant cultural change by encouraging a substantial number—a critical mass— of its professional and administrative staff to attend Leicester Conferences

and others based on a similar model. The second paper follows up the experiment after some ten years. Most participants were strongly positive: they reported both professional and personal benefits. Menninger also assessed the impact on the organization as largely positive, though he identified some difficulties—a point to which I shall return.

- Level II learning is a necessary but not sufficient condition for Level III learning, which may be even more desirable, but is less common and more elusive. It is often, though by no means always, expressed in significant changes in the individual's work and personal life: for example, a career move, a job change, a change of partner. (Such moves, of course, are not in themselves to be taken as positive indicators: they may also be symptoms of avoiding confrontations that a Level III change might require.)

- Statements made by members at the end of the Conference are a poor guide to outcome. Skepticism tends to be a more positive indicator than enthusiasm or euphoria.

Any account of members' experience and learning must also address the issue of casualties. There is a persistent myth that Leicester Conferences produce psychiatric casualties; and I use the term myth advisedly. Certainly, in the course of a conference many individuals feel disturbed at times, and some may exhibit seemingly bizarre behavior—hardly surprising in a setting that is quite unconventional. Since 1965 I have been aware of only two members having been admitted to hospital, very temporarily, as psychiatric patients, during or immediately following a conference, an incidence of some 0.1 percent. Individual disturbance is treated as a product of group projections and is almost invariably alleviated by rigorous interpretation at the group level.

In almost every conference there is a tiny handful of members who are untouched by the experience. Occasionally, a member will leave, saying: "This is not for me." A few go away with indigestible "lumps" of experience, which they cannot process. As indicated earlier, we have no way of identifying such people in advance. If some people are too defended to learn, all we can do is to respect their defenses. Authority remains with the member.

References

Anzieu, D. 1971. "L'Illusion Groupel." *Nouvelle Revue de Psychanalyse,* 4:73–93.

Bateson, G. 1973. *Towards an Ecology of the Mind.* St. Albans: Paladin.

Bion, W.R. 1961. *Experiences in Groups and Other Papers.* London: Tavistock Publications; New York: Basic Books.

Gosling, R. 1981. "A Study of Very Small Groups." In *Do I Dare Disturb the Universe? A Memorial to Dr. Wilfred Bion,* edited by J.S. Grotstein. New York: Aaronson.

Higgin, G. and H. Bridger. 1964. "The Psycho-Dynamics of a Inter-Group Experience." *Human Relations*, 17:391–446.

Jaques, E. 1953. "On the Dynamics of Social Structure." *Human Relations*, 6:3–24.

———. 1955. "Social Systems as a Defence Against a Persecutory and Depressive Anxiety." In *New Directions in Psycho-Analysis*, edited by M. Klein, P. Heimann and R.E. Money-Kyrle. London: Tavistock Publications; New York: Basic Books.

Klein, M. 1959. "Our Adult World and Its Roots in Infancy." *Human Relations*, 12:291–303.

Lawrence, W.G. 1979. "Introductory Essay: Exploring Boundaries"; "A Concept for Today: Managing Oneself in Role." In *Exploring Individual and Organisational Boundaries*, edited by W.G. Lawrence. London: Wiley.

Lawrence, W.G. and E.J. Miller. 1976. "Epilogue." In *Task and Organization*, edited by E.J. Miller. London: Wiley.

Lewin, K. 1935. *A Dynamic Theory of Personality*. New York: McGraw-Hill.

———. 1936. *Principles of Topological Psychology*. New York: McGraw-Hill.

Menninger, R.W. 1972. "The Impact of Group Relations Conferences on Organizational Growth." *International Journal of Group Psychotherapy*, 22:415–32.

———. 1985. "A Retrospective View of a Hospital-wide Group Relations Training Program: Costs, Consequences and Conclusions." *Psychiatric Annals*, 38:323–39.

Menzies, I.E.P. 1960. "A Case-Study in the Functioning of Social Systems as a Defence Against Anxiety: A Report on a Study of the Nursing Service of a General Hospital." *Human Relations*, 13:95–121.

Miller, E.J. 1976a. "Introductory Essay: Role Perspectives and the Understanding of Organizational Behaviour." In *Task and Organization*, edited by E.J. Miller. London: Wiley.

———. 1976b. "The Open-System Approach to Organizational Analysis with Special Reference to the Work of A.K. Rice." In *European Contributions to Organization Theory*, edited by G. Hofstede and M. Sami Kassem. Assen/Amsterdam: Van Gorcum.

———. 1977. "Organisational Development and Industrial Democracy: a Current Case-Study." In *Organizational Development in the UK and USA: A Joint Evaluation*, edited by C. Cooper. London: Macmillan.

———. 1980. "The Politics of Involvement." *Journal of Personality and Social Systems*, 2:37–50.

Miller, E.J. and A.K. Rice. 1967. *Systems of Organization: Tasks and Sentient Groups and Their Boundary Control*. London: Tavistock Publications.

Palmer, B. 1979. "Learning and the Group Experience." In *Exploring Individual and Organisational Boundaries*, edited by W.G. Lawrence. London: Wiley.

Rice, A.K. 1958. *Productivity and Social Organization: The Ahmedabad Experiment*. London: Tavistock Publications. Reissued 1987, New York: Garland.

———. 1963. *The Enterprise and Its Environment*. London: Tavistock Publications.

———. 1965. *Learning for Leadership: Interpersonal and Intergroup Relations*. London: Tavistock Publications.

———. 1969. "Individual, Group and Inter-group Process." *Human Relations*, 22:565–84.

Trist, E.L. and Sofer, C. 1959. *Exploration in Group Relations*. Leicester: Leicester University Press.

Tuckman, B.W. 1965. "Developmental Sequence in Small Groups." *Psychological Bulletin*, 63:384–99.

Turquet, P.M. 1975. "Threats to Identity in the Large Group." In *The Large Group: Therapy and Dynamics*, edited by L. Kreeger. London: Constable.

von Bertalanffy, L. 1950a. "An Outline of General Systems Theory." *British Journal of the Philosophy of Science*, 1:134–65.

——. 1950b. "The Theory of Open Systems in Physics and Biology." *Science* 3:23–29.

Wilson, A.T.M. 1951. "Some Aspects of Social Process." *Journal of Social Issues*, Supplemetary Series No. 5.

Eric J. Miller

Experiential Learning in Groups II
Recent Developments in Dissemination and Application*

Institutional Reproduction

This is a process that began in 1963; and I take this heading from Rice (1965). During the 1960s and early 1970s, the national and international demand for the Leicester model of group relations training was such that there were pressures to devote more and more time to conference work. However, the staff of TIHR who have been involved in the Leicester Conferences over the years have never wanted to be exclusively or even mainly in the business of running training activities. Continuing experience as practitioners has been seen as a necessary condition for effectiveness in conference work. The TIHR response, therefore, was to encourage and help other institutions in Britain and abroad to acquire their own capabilities to sponsor and staff events based on the Leicester approach.

The earliest examples of the 1960s were, in England, the Grubb Institute (formerly Christian Teamwork) and, in the United States, the Washington School of Psychiatry (initially in association with the Yale University School of Medicine). In both cases, the TIHR co-sponsored a series of "Leicester-type" conferences, initially providing the conference director and most staff, until the institutions were equipped with a large enough pool of trained staff to run the events themselves. By this time the staff were by no means exclusively drawn from the Tavistock Institute and Clinic, or from the other initial sponsoring institution, the University of Leicester. Initiation of an Advanced Training Group from 1962 onwards made it possible to develop a broader pool of trained staff from education, industry, the prison and probation services, and so forth, some of whom were then deployed on the new conferences. Reciprocally, staff of the new institutions enlarged the pool that could be drawn upon for Leicester, in a process that still continues.

*A new paper.

Subsequently, there has been similar collaboration in other countries, including France (with the International Foundation for Social Innovation), India (the Indian Institute of Management, Calcutta) and more recently Israel. One interesting feature of the French development is that the conferences were established as bi-lingual from the beginning. Either language is used by members and staff indiscriminately. Although many members and some staff are essentially monolingual, with very limited comprehension of the other language, this does not appear to be a significant handicap to their understanding of the dynamics; and indeed (as I can confirm from my own experience on the staff of a Finnish conference) ignorance of the words may heighten one's attention to the "music." The French conferences attract an international membership.

Meanwhile the American conference institution, which, after Rice died in 1969, was separately incorporated in the following year as the A.K. Rice Institute (AKRI), has not only developed a set of regional affiliates, straddling the country, each of which runs conferences based on the Leicester model, but has itself engaged in a similar institution-building process in Sweden. There, the earlier conferences that used imported staff were in English; then, as the local institution, AGSLO, became self-sufficient, the conference language shifted to Swedish. Conferences have also been run in other countries without (so far) the subsequent development of a viable local institution. Examples include: TIHR and the Grubb Institute in Ireland; the Grubb Institute in Italy, and AKRI in Iceland. In yet other countries, local groups have taken the initiative to develop their own capability to run conferences. Finland and Germany are well established examples. The catchment area of the German institution (MundO) includes Austria and Switzerland. There are recently formed or incipient institutions in Norway, Denmark and Mexico.

All the above identify themselves both as implementing a version of the Leicester model and as drawing directly on the resources and advice either of the GRTP in TIHR or of one of the established sister institutions. In addition there are some institutions, such as the Australian Institute of Social Analysis, which are developing their own distinctive approaches to training, based partly on the Leicester model.

What has occurred in a partly unplanned way is a consensual process of accreditation, initially by TIHR alone and then increasingly through peer relationships among not only TIHR but other institutions. Interchanges of staff have been crucial to this process. There are nevertheless a few bodies, in the United States and elsewhere, which offer events described as using the "Tavistock model," but which in some cases use staff with minimum direct experience of the conferences and which remain outside this informal mechanism of reciprocal quality control.

To come back to the British scene, there have been collaborative relationships with several institutions besides the Grubb Institute, but these have ended with the departure or death of key personnel. Examples include the Bristol University School of Education, Manchester Business School and the Chelmsford Cathedral Center for Research and Training.

Still nearer home, the close collaboration in this work between the Tavistock Clinic and Institute has persisted, even though as institutions they have been separate for 40 years. Jock Sutherland, the first post-war Medical Director of the Clinic, made a major input into the early conferences, from 1957 onwards. (After he retired, he set up the Scottish Institute of Human Relations, which also organized conferences, some in association with TIHR.) His successor in the role (re-designated Chairman of the Professional Committee), Robert Gosling, was actively involved throughout the 1960s and 1970s, until he too retired. The Clinic's own annual non-residential conference, for students and staff, is based on the Leicester model, and this has swollen the numbers of Clinic professionals equipped for conference staff roles. The current Chairman, Anton Obholzer, continues the tradition. Recent Leicester Conferences have been co-sponsored by the Tavistock Clinic Foundation and he has directed two of them.

Adaptation

Within the series of Leicester Conferences themselves various different designs have been developed. New events have been added to the repertoire. If the Very Small Group (VSG) represents the size of many working teams, the Median Group (MG) of 15–30 reflects the problems of many committees and councils in oscillating between the dynamics of the small and large groups. The Praxis Event (PE), introduced by Lawrence (Miller, 1980; Lawrence, 1985), removes a further layer of structure. During it, the administrator manages the outer boundary of the conference, while the director and all other staff relinquish their managerial and consultant roles, thus dissolving the internal member/staff boundary. Left with only a set of individuals and a negotiated primary task (which is basically to study what is happening while it happens), one is confronted with both creative opportunities and self-imposed constraints in using the freedoms.

The set of events used in any one conference may be programmed in different permutations. For example, although the Small Study Group (SSG) has always had an important place, in some designs the Large Study Group (LSG) has been given priority both as the first session every day and in the overall number of sessions. (This tends to produce some differences in the dynamics: typically, more sustained development of myth and metaphor in the LSG and more concern with individualism in the SSG.) However, the study of authority has remained the central focus and task.

Throughout these 30 years, the Leicester Conference has kept its two-week span and been fully residential; but besides this the Leicester model has been translated into various configurations. An extended non-residential course was introduced in the 1960s. It included all the events of the regular conferences but was held on one evening a week over six months. Rice's evaluation was equivocal; but a critical drawback was the impossibility of drawing a boundary around the membership and staff in such a way as to create the equivalent of the conference institution "with properties of its own that would provide opportunities for learning" (Rice, 1965:182). The full-fledged course was replaced by a simple series of, usually, 10 sessions of weekly study groups; these continue, though currently with a shift of focus away from intra-group processes as such on to the relatedness of these processes to outside society.

Collaboration with other institutions led to introduction of shorter forms of the model—usually 5–7 days, though week-end events offer a useful introduction. Even if non-residential these can be sufficiently intensive for the "conference as an institution" to be experienced. In the United States AKRI offered an annual two-week conference for 10 years or so, but recruitment of membership became difficult; so only Leicester has retained the fortnight.

The basic model nevertheless lends itself to exploration of other themes, which have been the focus of many shorter conferences, from a week-end to a week, residential and non-residential. Inter-group week-ends were an early example—though that implied little more than pulling out one event from the Leicester design. In the early 1970s, "men and women" became the theme for a number of conferences, first in the United States (Gould, 1979) and then in Britain. Other themes on which the Group Relations Training Programme (GRTP) has been running shorter conferences have included "creativity and destructiveness," "interdependence and conflict" and "autonomy and conformity." In these the main events have been the LSG and the PE.

In addition, of course, a great variety of training programs for managers and professionals have included experiential events, such as the SSG, along with more conventional teaching methods.

Application

ORGANIZATIONAL INTERVENTIONS

Over the years TIHR has run conferences on the Leicester model for client bodies. One technical difficulty is the strength of the shared organizational boundary around the membership, which becomes a defense against formation of a boundary around the conference institution. The difficulty is somewhat reduced in, for example, a large multi-national company where many members will not know one another, and the purpose of the conference is clearly educational. Much more problematic are requests to run a Leicester-model conference for a set of people who work together—perhaps for all the staff of a clinic or for the managerial or supervisory staff of a department of a company. Implicitly, if not explicitly, the prospective client system is hoping that this will unlock relationship difficulties and catalyze change. In my judgment a conference as an isolated event can be more damaging than constructive; conferences should be undertaken only as part of a longer-term intervention within which the consultant(s) can take continuing professional responsibility to help the client work through the outcomes.

One such Tavistock intervention was with the US Dependents Schools (European Area), which provide education for children of American servicemen posted overseas. In this case senior staff members from all the schools were brought together initially for an intensive five-day experiential event, which included some training on mutual consultation. This was followed by a six-month application phase during which regional groups met regularly to support each other in using the conference experience to analyze and tackle problems in their own schools. Conference consultants were available for some of these sessions. The intervention concluded with another three-day residential conference, which combined some additional experiential sessions with more practical review and forward planning.

Although it was generally seen as a productive experience, this type of in-house intervention carries an inherent tension: who is the client? In the regular Leicester Conference, the client is assumed to be the individual member. Even though the fee may be paid by an employing organization, it is the member who applies, presumptively on his or her own authority, and correspondingly it is for the member, not for the conference sponsors, to manage accountability to the employer.

How to report back is a common issue in Application Groups towards the end of the Conference. In organizational interventions of the kind just described there are two clients: the organization *and* the individual participant. The tension arises from the fact that the Leicester Conference approach is inherently subversive, in that it encourages members to question the nature of authority, and hence the ways in which they manage their role relationships to superiors, colleagues and subordinates in their own organizations. But in an organizational application the organization, through its management, is also a client. Even though we may demand that membership be voluntary, in reality individuals may feel under pressure to attend. Managers wanting to be "equal" to subordinates as participants within the conference will be under pressure to mobilize their external managerial roles. To the extent that they feel that the conference experience is a threat to their external authority, they are liable to be set up by the rest of the membership to lead an attack on the conference staff;

and so the boundary between membership roles and external roles becomes blurred. In such settings, it is a continuing technical problem for consulting staff to work at this inherent ambiguity and tension of the dual clients.

Another example was a seriously under-performing manufacturing company with just under 1,000 employees, which was part of a large international group (Miller, 1977; Khaleelee and Miller, 1985). It operated on two sites: one, near London, included the main factory and the head office; the other, 100 miles away in the Midlands, contained a much smaller plant. This set up was the result of amalgamating two businesses, which had previously been competitors. As so often happens in such mergers, the accountants expected the combined output and market share to equal the sum of the parts—an expectation seldom fulfilled. In this case, what was now the main factory had belonged to a company that the group had purchased, while the Midlands factory was the residue of the group's own former subsidiary that made a similar product. The sales force had been removed from the acquired company. And there had been other disruptive changes.

The intervention began with a diagnostic survey of all employees. It revealed acute splits cutting across each other: between management and workers; between employees from the two previous enterprises; and between departments. Identification with the organization as a whole was notably absent. Boundaries had been fractured and partly disintegrated; employees had fallen back onto their individual boundaries in a culture of survival.

The consultant team—two internal consultants with one from TIHR—postulated that the fragmented boundaries needed to be reconstructed, and designed what came to be called the "People Programme." Its main feature was an extended version of a Leicester Conference for 120 managers, supervisors and specialists, with weekly small study groups, week-end inter-group events and finally weekly large groups—all of which exactly matched the need to work at the boundaries at three levels: the individual in role relationships; the department and other groupings in their inter-group relations; and the organization as a whole in relation to its environment. Meanwhile, consultancy was being provided to the top management group—which in this case was the primary client. A formal system of employee consultation was also set up.

Within a year, significant changes had occurred: the People Programme, instead of being run by the consultants, had been taken over by the participants; the training was being extended to other employees; the large group was still meeting weekly (and continued for three years); task groups arose spontaneously to tackle pressing problems; inter-departmental co-ordination improved; the organization gained a new sense of identity; and manufacturing performance and profits went up dramatically.

The consultants, who had already been providing consultancy on request to various internal groups, including a joint trade union body, then negotiated a new contract. This established them as a quasi-independent Consulting Resource Group (CRG) with its own budget, and made it explicit that the organization as a whole—not management—was the client system. In addition to servicing internal groups, the CRG took on a new task—to try to elucidate the overall dynamics of the organization. This involved experimenting to see whether the methodology of, say, the Large Study Group, could be extended to a group of nearly 1,000, only a tiny proportion of whom could be present with the consultants at any one time. The common link was use of the transference. The CRG, like the group consultant in a Conference, was both outside the organizational boundary and also part of a wider client-consultant system, and hence available for projections from the organization. The technique used was a weekly session—which anyone, manager or worker, was free to attend—in which the CRG members reviewed their experience during the week in consulting to parts of the organization as a basis for formulating working hypotheses about the system as a whole. Evidence included their experience of being pulled in or pushed out, idealized or denigrated, homogenized or split, and so on, as well as observations of the pattern of projections among different groupings within the client system. Members of the organization present at the meetings worked on these hypotheses and added their own preoccupations; and beyond that the consultants used the interpretations directly and indirectly in their work with various groups in the ensuing week. In these ways the voice of CRG was "heard" by a significant proportion of the organization and seemed to have some influence. "The most overt evidence was in the growing number of individuals able to perceive organizational processes in which they were implicated and able also to act on their understanding by taking greater personal authority in their . . . roles" (Khaleelee and Miller, 1985:363–64).

"The operation was a success, but the patient died." What should have been foreseen was that the culture developing in this subsidiary company was increasingly divergent from that of the rest of the group. Exercise of "authority based on competence is always a threat to an organization that defines authority as based on position . . . if it is exercised by a subordinate it is treated by the supervisor as insubordination" (Miller, 1986a:265). At group headquarters gratification over improved performance was submerged by anxiety about subversiveness; key managers were replaced; and the consultants were shown the door.

An Application at the Societal Level

This experiment encouraged a London-based group, in OPUS (an Organization for Promoting Understanding in Society), to try to extend and adapt the methodology to the study of societal dynamics (OPUS, 1980–88; Khaleelee and Miller, 1985; Miller, 1986a).

As long ago as 1950 Bion—himself influenced by Freud's much earlier speculations—had been eager to do this and offered some provocative ideas. These included his well-known proposition that society hives off specialized work-groups to deal on its behalf with basic assumption emotions that would otherwise interfere with the functioning of society as a "work group." His examples were church (dependency), army (fight/flight) and, perhaps less convincingly, aristocracy (pairing) (Bion, 1961). He had identified these phenomena in small groups. The Leicester Conference and other observations have amply confirmed that, although certain kinds of dynamics are characteristic of groups of different sizes (Turquet, 1974), the larger group is always potentially present in the smaller, and at times the larger group phenomena break through. This, as we also found in the manufacturing company, can be used constructively. For example, the Leicester methodology has proved to be a useful tool in identifying organizational cultures: a small set of people from one organization will display often unrecognized dimensions of their shared culture, in particular by mobilizing them as a defense against the primary task of here-and-now study.

Moreover, as Rioch (1979) has noted, conferences based on the Leicester model often mirror current societal phenomena. For example, she noted that the incidence of violent revolt—including, for instance, invasion of staff territory and kidnapping of individual staff—reached its peak in the American conferences in 1968–69; after that, it subsided, and attempts in the memberships to mobilize collective leadership were less successful. Parallel changes had been seen at Leicester. "The myth that the group is a creative matrix [was] progressively submerged by the countervailing myth that groups and institutions are dangerous and destructive." Correspondingly we saw "a withdrawal of commitment to groups, an increasing reluctance (noted also by Rioch) to use the conference setting for experiment and play (in the Winnicott [1971] sense), and a tendency for the individual to put up protective boundaries against group influences or seek security as an isolate or a pair" (Khaleelee and Miller, 1985:368).

Deriving from this experience, OPUS explicitly set out to use the microcosm to reflect the macrocosm of society, and, indeed, to explore whether society could be classed as an intelligible field of study in its own right, distinct from the large group. Turquet had described the dual role of the consultant in the Conference large groups—the consultant and the person—and hence the struggle to hold a boundary position. But in society there is no outside; hence no boundary role is available. OPUS has attempted to supply an institutional boundary within which its own members and others can examine their experience as citizens of society, and the capacity of this boundary to contain the chaotic and violent feelings evoked has been tested almost to destruction. The "observing ego" has been precarious. However, it is confirmed that significant underlying themes can emerge in quite small groups that are given the task of examining their experience in their role as members of society. Larger groups, of 30–40, may unconsciously enact, in vivid and painful ways, important societal processes. A recent example was an OPUS conference on Society and the Inner City, which belatedly realized that it had reproduced, by creating an isolated sub-group, the very phenomena that it was discussing (Miller, 1986b).

Reflections

Why has the Leicester Conference survived for 30 years—a period of considerable cultural change, nationally and internationally? Why has the Leicester model successfully taken root in so many other countries and cultures? China and Japan have not yet been penetrated, but there is evidence from India of effective use of the model with people drawn from poor rural communities. It has been regularly used by SAKTI, a Bangalore-based organization promoting increased roles for women in development. It is not just a preserve of professionals and managers who share a westernized cosmopolitan culture. Obversely, why has the model failed to diffuse more widely and more rapidly? Why are there not many more institutions running many more conferences every year? What has inhibited growth? Such questions are to be puzzled over. Here I offer only a few observations.

First, the model has proved effective in addressing an inherent feature of the human condition—the tension between individuation and incorporation—which, in most 20th-century cultures at least, is a lifelong tension, never fully resolved. The model confronts us with that dilemma and with the precariousness of a notion of individuality and autonomy that we may have taken for granted. It does so, however, within a structure designed to be relatively containing and within a conference culture whose values promote the idea—perhaps the hope—that through seeing how we get involved in unconscious group processes we can become less vulnerable to them and more effectively self-managing. Such discoveries are nearly always painful, in that they upset past assumptions and defenses. The possibility of becoming more self-managing than you actually were is tainted by recognition that you were really much less self-managing than you thought you were. Nonetheless, most people seem to find that the outcome is, on balance, positive.

Second, there is the issue of what they do with the experience and the learning. Part of it, almost inevitably, is personal and private, relating to one's inner world. For some members it may remain so. But that is not the purpose of the conference: the design is intended to promote the application of experience in their roles in that temporary institution to their roles in institutions outside.

Here I may make two comments. First, if it is effective, such application is inherently subversive. It involves calling into question the embedded assumptions and myths that support the status quo and exercising the authority of one's own competence in an organizational culture where formal authority commonly derives from hierarchy and status. If the member is returning to a position at or near the apex of the hierarchy, this is less a problem, though one hopes such a person will have learned enough to prepare for the likely resistances. The less privileged ex-member may have to scale down his or her initial aspirations or risk being extruded. In any case, however, the fact that only the most enlightened organization actively welcomes employees who question the status quo and exercise their own authority is certainly one limitation on expansion of the conferences.

A second comment relates to inappropriate and superficial application, most commonly in the spirit of "do unto others what has just been done unto me." Despite verbal discouragements and repeated assertions that the Conference is designed for a specific educational task and that other tasks require other forms of organization, we cannot prevent members from identifying with the role-models offered by staff and thus seeking to replicate them. This is one of Roy Menninger's reservations in his largely positive account of the experience of encouraging a critical mass of the staff of the Menninger Foundation to attend conferences (Menninger, 1985). I quote extracts from his paper (pp. 296–97):

> Potentially damaging to the therapeutic process was a tendency, during the immediate post-GRC [group relations conference] period to equate "group process" with treatment. The powerful effects of expressing primitive feelings and the instructive experience of group-induced regression led to a natural but mistaken view that such experiences were the essence of therapy . . . , displacing the primary tasks of learning and understanding.

> This perspective seemed to assume that the GRC was a *model of treatment* rather than a *method of education*. Group process is compelling and deeply involving, but it is not psychotherapy nor is it a substitute for a dynamic understanding of the patient . . .

> Coupled with this pattern was a tendency to use group process to "manage" a patient's deviant or pathological behaviour . . . [and] diminished attention to the dynamic roots of the symptom . . .

An additional question that Menninger might have raised is whether the focus on treatment was in part a displacement from confronting more painful or intractable issues in the organization: were patients being mobilized to voice primitive feelings that staff were repressing?

It also has to be said that there is at least one recorded instance of the success in a psychiatric hospital of using a carefully thought out version of the conference model for the reconstitution of newly admitted grossly psychotic patients (Lofgren, 1976). But overall, Menninger's strictures are soundly based. The reality is that the conference itself is an application—an application of a conceptual framework to an educational task. Many of the more significant applications to understanding of organizations, though informed by experience of conferences, essentially draw on that framework. Studies of a school by Richardson (1973) and of a mental health center by Lewinson and Astrachan (1976) are two examples that come to mind. But all too often, as at the Menninger Foundation, members have come back from conferences with the fantasy that to run a group—or, indeed, to run an internal conference—will solve the organization's problems. Misapplications of this kind have obviously made some organizations less than enthusiastic about the model and have been another factor in limiting its diffusion. Some organizations nevertheless become regular customers.

So we have the paradox that Leicester Conferences which are in their aims essentially subversive of the Establishment have themselves become an established institution, and with it run the attendant risk of losing their task.

A major problem is a shift in the motivation of members. An increasing proportion enroll less with the intention of learning than in order to gain a form of accreditation. Some have connections with the institutions that run conferences based on the Leicester model and have already taken part in one or more of these. Leicester experience may be necessary or at least helpful to progression to staff roles in these institutions. Also, there are various professional circles, especially in mental health, where attending (and surviving) a Leicester Conference has almost become a *rite de passage,* or carries some cachet. Beyond these two categories there are others who have been primed by previous members and have an idea in advance of what to expect. The proportion of "naive members," lacking in such external connections and in prior knowledge, has diminished. The cognoscenti, who outnumber them, tend to bring, in addition to their (at best) mixed motivations, some prefabricated defenses: for example, adopting an observing, interpretive role—a pseudo-staff role—as a way of avoiding involvement; using psychological jargon to outface the naive members; trying to set up situations that will defend them against the uncertainties of the member role by demonstrating their competence in their external professional roles. ("Casualties" perform a useful function for mental health professionals.) In practice, after a day or two, as a consequence of the dynamics of the total institution (with the help of interpretation from staff) the overwhelming majority of members find that they become involved—they "join"—almost in spite of themselves. Other difficulties remain. Inexperienced members, feeling excluded by an in-group that has a psychological jargon of its own, may come to believe that what is to be learned from the Conference is a language.

However, the problems of institutionalization are more insidious than that. The model is in constant danger of becoming a movement. A movement is fed by and feeds ritual. There are quite subtle pressures on staff to become priests of the ritual. The director and those staff who have taken part in several successive Leicester conferences find difficulty in putting boundaries around *this* conference. Newer staff, like inexperienced members, may feel pushed into an out-group, with all the uncertainties and anxieties of the rest of staff projected onto them. A new director or associate director will be the object of envious attack—which may be not at all subtle. Institutionalization makes it even more difficult to hold onto the reality that so far as *this* conference is concerned we are all inexperienced and that what we think we know from the past may be more of a hindrance than a help in understanding what is in the present.

References

Bion, W.R. 1961. *Experiences in Groups and Other Papers*. London: Tavistock Publications; New York: Basic Books.

Gould, L.J. 1979. "Men and Women at Work: A Group Relations Conference on Person and Role." In *Exploring Individual and Organisational Boundaries*, edited by W.G. Lawrence. London: Wiley.

Khaleelee, O. and E.J. Miller. 1985. "Beyond the Small Group: Society as an Intelligible Field of Study." In *Bion and Group Psychotherapy*, edited by M. Pines. London: Routledge and Kegan Paul.

Lawrence, W.G. 1985. "Beyond the Frames." In *Bion and Group Psychotherapy*, edited by M. Pines. London: Routledge and Kegan Paul.

Lewinson, D. and B. Astrachan. 1976. "Entry into the Mental Health Centre: A Problem in Organizational Boundary Regulation." In *Task and Organization*, edited by E.J. Miller. London: Wiley.

Lofgren, L.B. 1976. "Organizational Design and Therapeutic Effect." In *Task and Organization*, edited by E.J. Miller. London: Wiley.

Menninger, R.W. 1985. "A Retrospective View of a Hospital-wide Group Relations Training Program: Costs, Consequences and Conclusions." *Psychiatric Annals*, 38:328–39.

Miller, E.J. 1977. "Organisational Development and Industrial Democracy: A Current Case Study." In *Organizational Development in the UK and USA: A Joint Evaluation*, edited by C. Cooper. London: Macmillan.

———. 1980. "The Politics of Involvement." *Journal of Personality and Social Systems*, 2:37–50.

———. 1986a. "Making Room for Individual Autonomy." In *Executive Power*, edited by S. Srivastva and Associates. San Francisco: Jossey-Bass.

———. 1986b. "Society and the Inner City, OPUS Conference Report." *Bulletin No. 22–23, Part II*. London: OPUS.

OPUS, 1980–88. *Bulletins, 1–25*. London: OPUS.

Rice, A.K. 1965. *Learning for Leadership. Interpersonal and Intergroup Relations*. London: Tavistock Publications.

Richardson, E. 1973. *The Teacher, the School and the Task of Management*. London: Heinemann.

Rioch, M. 1979. "The A.K. Rice Group Relations Conferences as a Reflection of Society." In *Exploring Individual and Organisational Boundaries*, edited by W.G. Lawrence. London: Wiley.

Turquet, P.M. 1974. " 'Leadership': The Individual and the Group." In *Analysis of Groups*, edited by G.S. Gibbard, J.J. Hartman and R.D. Mann. San Francisco: Jossey-Bass.

Winnicott, D.W. 1971. *Playing and Reality*. London: Tavistock Publications.

Gurth Higgin and Harold Bridger

The Psycho-Dynamics of an Inter-Group Experience*

Introduction

This paper offers an analysis of processes that occur between groups collaborating on a task of direct relevance to an objective they have in common. Theoretically it is based on the work of Bion (1961) who distinguishes between two levels of group activity: that of the "sophisticated" or "work" group (W), which involves learning and development and addresses specific tasks that must be met and undertaken in social reality; and that of the *basic assumptions*—dependence (baD), fight/flight (baF) and pairing (baP)—which are unlearned, primitive emotional response systems existing as unconscious patterns that alternate with each other. The basic group organization may be in conflict with the sophisticated or W organization, and is often unrecognized by members of the group, whose level of performance may be severely impaired in consequence. A detailed exposition and critique of his views is given by Sutherland (Vol. 1, "Bion Revisited") who also explains such psychoanalytic concepts as projection and introjection, extensive use of which is made in this paper.

The setting of the Inter-Group Exercise, as it was called, was a two-week Tavistock/Leicester Group Relations Training Conference (Trist and Sofer, 1959; Rice, 1965; Miller, Vol. 1, "Experiential Learning in Groups I"). The conference, held in November 1959, was the second such conference. The core experience had been the "study groups." The Inter-Group Exercise was added to investigate inter-group behavior.

The ideal experience for this purpose would be to analyze inter-group processes in real-life situations. This is not possible in a training setting. At the other extreme were case-study/role-playing activities. The Inter-Group Exercise attempted to find an experience somewhere between these two poles. It provided a task that was real within the conference setting, but which lacked the degree of commitment or emotional involvement that a real-life situation

*A shortened version of the original—*Human Relations*, 17:391–446, 1964.

would evoke. It did, however, create something that was more meaningful and powerful than is possible with a case-study procedure, or even with the more exciting "business game" type of event.

The overall task was to decide on a program of special interest sessions to take place in the second week of the conference. Members were to divide themselves into three groups which would work together in a self-chosen fashion to achieve an agreed program. The Exercise was analogous to what goes on in ordinary working groups. There was a concrete decision to be taken that would affect all the participants. They would experience the results of their decisions. The Exercise was developed by Bridger as a result of previous work with Glidewell of the National Training Laboratories at Bethel.

The conference was held at a large hotel in a small spa in the north of England. To qualify for membership an individual had to be currently in a post of responsibility. Twenty-nine members took part: four prison governors, five lecturers in education, five industrial executives; two hospital sister-tutors; six personnel or training managers in industry; seven applied social scientists from European institutions. Members had been asked on their application forms to suggest topics of particular interest to them which might be taken up during the special interest sessions. There were eight full-time staff, two from the University of Leicester and six from the Tavistock Institute.

Eight $1\frac{1}{2}$-hour sessions would be devoted to the Exercise, which was to start on the afternoon of the second day. By this time the members would have experienced two study groups and one theory session. In the first session of the Exercise members would decide on a method of dividing themselves into three groups, X, Y and Z. Division into study groups was excluded, but any other type of division was allowable.

A questionnaire would evaluate the decisions reached by the groups at various points in the Exercise: the willingness of group members to carry out these decisions; and the degree of satisfaction with the way their group had arrived at them. This evaluation instrument was used five times, the results being made known to the groups.

Each group would proceed in its own way and would have attached to it a staff observer. The observers would help the groups achieve their tasks and were free to make group-centered comments. They had a recording role as a secondary function. The staff not directly concerned as observers formed a separate group. The resources of the whole staff were offered for use during the special interest sessions.

For the second and third sessions groups would devise a system of communicating with each other by means of envoys. The envoys would reach agreement on a single consolidated plan for the special interest sessions. In the fourth session, all the groups would evaluate their experience during the planning stages. The fifth, sixth and seventh sessions would be devoted to carrying out the program decided upon. The eighth would evaluate the members' experience.

The Exercise

FORMATION OF THE GROUPS

The Exercise took place in the ballroom of the hotel, a large room 54 ft. × 47 ft. In the center of one of the long sides was a small stage and about 12 feet into the dance floor there were two large pillars about four feet square. The rest was clear.

The first session opened with the conference members seated in an irregular group in front of the stage but on the far side of the two pillars. The staff were along the front of the stage at floor level with the conference director standing in front of them facing the members. In the haphazard seating a group of seven or eight were to the side of one of the pillars. There was no-one outside the other pillar.

The Exercise was opened by the conference director running over the instructions. There were several requests for further clarification. Two new points were introduced. First, although members of the staff were willing to provide whatever help they could, the conference was reminded that there were resources among the members themselves relevant to many of the special interests listed. Secondly, that the first phase of the Exercise—to arrive at a decision about the basis for dividing into the three groups—should take no longer than 15 minutes. The conference director then said that the Exercise should start immediately and that within 15 minutes the members should have decided on what basis they would split up into groups.

What happened in the next minute or so was unexpected and crucial. After a short pause a member asked what the groups X, Y and Z were to do. The director explained this again. Immediately, somebody else asked about the role of the staff during the first part of the Exercise when the three groups were working separately. This, too, was answered. Then came a question as to whether the groups were to deal with content or were to just set a program without content. The director answered that they were asked to do what they themselves considered to be a planning job and to deal with content or not as they thought fit. In finishing, he reminded them that they now had 14 minutes left to decide on a means of forming into groups.

Immediately $Z1$, an industrial member, said that in industry those responsible for making such a decision would have the advice and help of staff. There was anger in his voice. While he was speaking, the small group of people who were to the outside of the pillar stood up and moved their chairs around to join the main body so that they could participate more easily. At the same time the members of staff, except the three who were to operate as the group observers, and the conference director, stood up and moved off to that part of the hall designated for the staff group. These movements precipitated other movements, some members standing up and picking up their chairs. Immediately after $Z1$ had finished, a member said in a loud voice, "Let's do it alphabetically." He was disregarded. The general stir of movement suddenly increased and within seconds one group of people were heading towards one corner of the room while another were heading for the diagonally opposite corner; in the middle some were standing and some sitting. This central group was made up mainly of those who had come around from behind the pillar. The two groups who had moved were in the corners nominated as X and Z and the two observers for these groups moved off to join them. The third observer joined those in the middle of the floor. In this way, within 15 seconds, the division had been made without any conscious decision as to how it should be done.

A minute or so later, the group in the middle of the floor, with their observer, moved over to the vacant corner nominated for Y. In the X corner there were 10 people, in the Y eight and in the Z 11. All groups then filled out the evaluation sheets regarding the group division process.

PLANNING SESSIONS

SESSION ONE

X: X had a rather sharp division of opinion about electing a chairman but did finally elect one. They fell into detailed discussion of the special interest items and developed two noticeable factions. The two factions seemed to be fairly clear what they were falling out about and reached a compromise solution. To achieve this the group took a vote, but they were not content with voting and did not use it again.

The reaction of X to the results of the questionnaire was one of interest; they were particularly struck by the great degree of dissatisfaction reported by Y. It was as a result of this information that they decided to make an offer to Y of repeating the original division exercise. In this action they showed some awareness of the other groups' reaction to the initial break-up, and of their own position.

Y: Y were the last to move to their corner. They gathered there in a noticeably dispirited fashion after an initial burst of indignation and sat around rather at a loss what to do next. There was some desultory discussion and lapses into silence. The group became a little more lively when they got the results of the first questionnaire. These showed that they were noticeably below the level of the others in their satisfactions about the initial division into groups. It was about this time that an envoy arrived from X to report that, while his own group were content with the division, they had noticed the low satisfaction on the part of Y and offered, if Y wished, to join them in repeating the first part of the Exercise. Y's reaction was to perk up a little but to say that, although they were unhappy, they would continue as they were.

The boost in their morale from this incident was not very lasting and after a time they relapsed into fragmentary conversation and periods of silence. After one of these long silences one member produced the outline of a plan for reconciling the special interests of members and for an organization through which the conference might take account of them in the following week's sessions.

The plan was taken up by some but others paid no attention. A division showed itself between those who were active in the planning task and those who were quite silent, out of touch and apparently depressed. The observer reported that several appeared to be quite shocked with the experience they had had in the initial division. Towards the end of the session the group, in a rather casual way, elected a chairman. It was this member ($Y1$) and the member who had originally produced the outline plan ($Y2$) who later became the envoys for Y.

Z: Z became active as soon as they got to their corner and by the time the observer arrived had already elected a chairman and secretary. They spent the first session arguing volubly over the details of the listed special interest topics. Their reaction to the report of the first questionnaire was one of passing interest only. They seemed hardly aware of any significance it might have and continued with their compulsive inspection of the special interests. Various members took on the roles of "sneerer" at the others and at the whole Exercise; of "clown"; and of withdrawn non-participant. There was little member satisfaction. Two distinct factions were apparent but neither was clear what were the differences between them.

The only movement between the groups during the first session was that of the envoy who went from X to Y.

SESSION TWO

X: X had had an extra meeting before this session. It turned out to be of little value. They simply went over the ground they had already covered. When they were given the results from the questionnaire, the chairman noticed that there were two members who had expressed dissatisfaction. He did all he could to get them to declare themselves, which they did not do. X were the first group to send members outside to make contact with other groups. Their first contact was with the staff to ask questions about the resources available for possible special interest sessions. X were also the first to make contact with the other groups, particularly Y, in connection with arranging the envoys' meeting. X, unlike Y and Z, gave their envoys the status only of delegates, not of fully responsible representatives.

While the envoys' meeting was taking place, the remainder of the group discussed their own activities to date and the manner in which they had behaved as a group. They thought of contacting the other two groups during this period and explaining to them the plan that X had made for presentation at this first envoys' meeting.

The group were eager to hear from their envoys—"How have we done?" The envoys' report sharpened their interest in and commitment to their own plan when they heard that other plans had been put up. They decided that theirs was the best and were determined to defend it and have it carried as the plan for the conference as a whole. X showed considerable glee at the news of a split in Z. The chairman of X was eager that they should come to a decision about their reactions to the plans of the other groups but the group decided that they could not discuss this in the time remaining and resolved to have an extra session before the formal session on the following day.

Y: Y's chairman had had an informal meeting with two other members to discuss the planning problem further. This piece of extra work was useful in the development of the planning task but was not approved by the majority, who felt it was a private meeting that should not have been held without the knowledge of the whole group.

The two factions showed themselves again, one being active in the planning task, the other withdrawn. Y made several approaches to the staff group—to obtain information on the course of the Exercise and on the supposed rulings about the nature of staff participation in the special interest sessions. They were also concerned with exploring the roles that the staff might take in the meetings of envoys. The Y envoys were the first to emerge onto the center of the floor for the initial envoys' meeting. While the envoys were away the rest of the group fell into a withdrawn, inactive silence.

The members of the group were eager to have a report from their envoys. They, like X, showed great glee on hearing that there was a split in Z. They also showed considerable delight in what they took to be the good report of useful activity by their two envoys.

Z: At the opening of the session, the chairman of *Z* offered to resign because he thought he was doing the job badly. He was *Z1*, the man who had played a significant part in triggering the original division of the groups. His offer was not accepted. The group then had the report on the questionnaire. Several members declared that the group as a whole had reported rather a lower level of satisfaction than they felt was true. There were some jokes about their all being hypocrites, which faded away into languid and unsystematic activity. *Z* were slow in sending their envoys to the first central meeting. Those of both *X* and *Y* were out on the floor waiting for them and making signs to hurry up. They clearly felt persecuted by these demands. The envoys they did send included the leader of the minority within themselves. They went off with a very unclear brief.

The mood of the remaining group members noticeably relaxed. They became much easier with each other and with their observer. This was the first time they took account of the observer. They showed no interest at all in the envoys' meeting. Nor did they show any interest in their envoys' report when they came back. The minority leader commented that he thought that *Y*'s plan was very much the best.

Apart from the envoys' meeting in the middle of the hall, there had been several contacts by *X* and *Y* with each other and with *Z*, and also with the staff board. Except for sending out their envoys, late and under pressure, *Z* had not initiated any external contacts.

The first envoys' meeting was taken up with the presentation of plans by each set of envoys. Those submitted by *X* and *Y* were fairly comprehensive. That of *Z* was little more than a confused catalogue.

Z let it be known that there was a split within their group. The leader of the *Z* minority, who was one of their envoys, asked the staff member present if members could change groups during the Exercise. Both the other groups drew the conclusion that *Z* was internally riven and was not a serious contender for making a viable plan. *X* and *Y* each decided that the other was the main competitor.

SESSION THREE

X: Between the second and third sessions *X* had another extra session. This proved to be rather more useful than that of the day before. They became absorbed with whether their envoys should be representatives or delegates. They decided that they should be representatives, but without full authority beyond given limits. These limits were never clearly defined. The group asked for, and were granted, the right for their envoys to refer back to them if the central meeting took them outside the brief they had been given. The group had agreed that they could ignore Z. They decided that they could handle Y by means of a compromise that would not undermine the nature of the X plan.

After their envoys left, the remaining members set out rather enthusiastically on a scheme for research on what had gone on within their group during the course of the Exercise. This project did not get very far because the director invited the remaining members of all three groups to come to the center and act as a silent audience to the final envoys' meeting. X were particularly incensed by this because they had become interested in doing their own research. They angrily declared that the director had changed the rules; however, they did join the central envoys' group. In the course of this meeting, one of the X envoys retired with his group to take advice on a point that had come up that was beyond their brief.

Y: Y held an extra meeting the material from which is reported with that from the third official meeting below. The chairman said he had spoken to the chairmen of the other two groups and suggested that there be a staff chairman for the envoys' meeting. The group did not take this point up enthusiastically. The chairman also suggested that the members of Y might have some informal contact with the other two groups to try to win them over to Y's plan.

Y were noticeably pleased with themselves about their plan, which they thought was very much the best. The discussion now took on a political color, the group deciding that they could ignore Z. Their task in carrying through their plan would be to overcome the alternative bid from X.

The term "reparation" was used for the first time in connection with Y's analysis of the relationships of the other two groups to themselves; they ascribed guilt to them for what they had done at the expense of Y in the initial break-up. However, Y were against their chairman's suggestion of pressing their advantage by attempts to convert the other two groups to their point of view. They condemned this as propagandist.

Y_1 continued to explore with the other two groups the possibility of having a staff chairman for the envoys' group. He got sufficient agreement from X for this plan, but could get no sense out of Z. Some of the members of the non-active, rather depressed, section of Z did not know which of the other groups was which.

Z: Z went through an experience of considerable confusion and strife. They had great difficulty in getting a sufficient briefing for their envoys to take to the central meeting, which caused them to be late for it. They experienced as extremely irritating intrusions the attempts of the other groups to hurry them along. Indeed, the outstanding characteristic of this session was Z's feeling of anger towards the other groups and the staff, and their strong sense of being persecuted by them all.

At the final central meeting, the Z envoys had nothing to offer as a direct contribution to the plan for the special interest sessions, although they played an important part in the process of compromise that went on between X and Y. The next step towards putting the plan into force was to be a further meeting of the group envoys, after they had consulted with their groups, for the purpose of nominating a planning committee. The whole of Z, who had overheard this discussion, misunderstood and thought that the next meeting was to be of the planning committee. They therefore sent two members other than their envoys to this meeting. Faced with this situation, the envoys of X and Y accepted, not only these two nominees, but the original Z envoys on the planning committee. In this way, Z provided half of the eight members of the planning committee.

During the second envoys' meeting, the political alignment that had emerged showed itself from the start. The X and Y envoys were very sharply in competition. Both pairs showed confidence and determination to carry the day. The Z envoys played a much more subdued part, siding at one time with X and at another with Y and, towards the end of the meeting, withdrawing altogether and allowing the final X and Y confrontation to take place. The outcome was seen as a victory for Y—certainly in the eyes of the members of Y, whose envoys gained the political advantage over the X envoys who needed to withdraw to seek a further mandate from their group.

The two Y envoys also played their parts well in a complementary way. Y_1, their chairman, was an aggressive and determined speaker. There was going to be an impasse if there was not some show of meeting the compromise that X were offering, with Z support. Y_2, the woman member, took over and, with equal determination but much more gentleness, carried the Y position through the compromise situation with success. The outcome was an amalgam of the X and Y plans. Each group later claimed the major victory for itself—but the sense of success was greater with Y.

The Evaluation Instrument and Its Results

THE INSTRUMENT

The evaluation sheet contained three questions only: how satisfied were you with the decision made by the group; how willing were you to carry out the decision of the group; and how satisfied were you with the way the group worked on the problem. Respondents were asked to put a tick against one point on a five-point scale, varying from high satisfaction through neutral to low. The instrument was used on five occasions:

Evaluation Sheet 1 was given immediately after the division into groups, when each of the three groups went to its respective corner of the ballroom.

The decision referred to was that of the conference as a whole in splitting up into groups.

Evaluation Sheet 2 was completed at the end of the first session when the groups had agreed on an outline of a plan. It referred to this internal group decision.

Evaluation Sheet 3 referred to the work of the central envoy group as reported back to X, Y and Z. It was due to be given at the end of the second session after the first inter-group meeting. There was some confusion about this and, in fact, it was filled out at the beginning of the next conference session some two hours later.

Evaluation Sheet 4 was completed within the groups again, and referred to the revised plans that the groups sent to the final envoys' meeting after they had been informed about the plans of the other groups.

Evaluation Sheet 5 applied to the work of the final envoys' meeting that decided on the overall conference plan.

The recording counted responses to the three questions. The procedure was to arrive at an algebraic sum of all the positive and all the negative responses, ignoring those that fell at the neutral point. To allow comparison between the groups, which were of different sizes, these final figures were put on a base of ten. The ordinates for the "graphs" on which the results were reported were the indices for each of the groups on the five occasions when the evaluation sheets were filled out. A simple scale of +10 to −10 was used for each of the reactions asked about.

Comment

The three groups produced characteristically different graphs (Figure 1). The greatest change over time is shown by Y and the least by X. For the two questions dealing with satisfaction about decisions, with the exception of Y's first reaction, all group responses are at the top end of the positive side of the scale, and all show less variation than do the other judgments.

X: X showed less variation on all questions than did the other groups and an alternating reaction to the same questions as the Exercise developed. They felt slightly less satisfaction about decisions made within their own group than about those made by the inter-group envoy sessions. They began with a high level of expressed willingness to implement, which rose to a maximum following the first inter-group meetings—at which they thought they had done rather well—and tailed off only slightly thereafter.

Y: The Y graphs are the most dramatic. The group's reaction to the initial break-up decision was 100 percent negative. However, by the time they made a

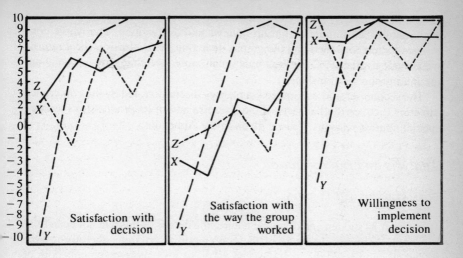

Figure 1. Evaluation sheet results

second report, which had to do with their own internal work as a planning group, their level of satisfaction had changed markedly and took them half way up the positive side of the scale. Thereafter they continued to improve, finding themselves 100 percent on the positive side after their second internal planning session—a level they held to the end of the Exercise. Their unwillingness to implement decisions was never as great as their dissatisfaction with the decisions themselves. Their willingness to implement their own and the inter-group decisions was high and remained high until the end of the Exercise.

Z: The graphs for Z reveal interesting variations. The responses expressing satisfaction with, and willingness to implement, decisions taken in the inter-group arena reached a high level, with corresponding low points for the responses concerning their own decisions. The exception to this zig-zag pattern occurs with their satisfaction about the way the groups worked on problems. Here they showed themselves rather negative to the first break-up decision, neutral about themselves in their first planning session, a little more positive about the first inter-group session, slipping back to dissatisfaction in reflecting on their own second internal planning session, but reaching a maximum of satisfaction regarding the way the final conference decision was taken.

Evaluation Sessions

The first evaluation session started as a plenary for the whole conference, taking the form of a general discussion on the planning sessions. It went on for about 20 minutes. X, Y and Z then met independently with their observers and spent another 20 minutes in group reviews and evaluations. The whole conference then reconvened and the graphs depicting the evaluation sheet returns were made available. There was now much more interchange of views about the inter-group relationships.

The second session was entirely a plenary discussion, led by the conference director. It covered all aspects of the Exercise and of its product for the three special interest sessions. This is given in the Appendix.

Analysis and Interpretation

FORMATION OF THE GROUPS

Because of its sudden and dramatic nature, the details of this had not been fully recorded. As many members of the conference as possible, therefore, were informally contacted the next day and asked to give short statements both of their recollection of the event and of their feelings about it. These were recorded anonymously by a secretary:

X: "Someone said 'come along' and most of the rest got up and moved either to Z or X corners. A group . . . moved towards the middle to take part in a general discussion and found . . . the group formation had already taken place. They became group Y. . . . Z_1 stood up and made a remark—he was the only one who did—that in industry there would be a leader who would select people to form his group. . . . When people rose following (Z_1's) statement . . . I found myself swept into an informal group which settled itself in that corner of the room." "I was feeling pretty sore about the complete organization . . . I did not really want to cooperate and thought we should rebel . . . I wanted to be the leader of a rebellious group . . . I felt a kind of anger."

Y: "Suddenly two groups were formed, leaving a very small number of us who had a very interesting feeling of rejection and of being leftovers, the unwanted . . . It took us, who turned out to be Y, some time to recover our balance. One member of the group was shocked into a state of non-participation. The total development in the group was made by not more than four of its members. . . . All through the time we were trying to develop a proposal we felt quite dissatisfied with ourselves and with the proposal . . . then we sent our delegates to the general meeting and they came back each feeling about seven feet high. The proposals we had made were greatly superior to the proposals made by the other groups."

Z: "We were all left in the center of the room with no one at all taking direction; everyone obviously feeling very lost and rather perplexed . . . there seemed to be a rapid movement towards one corner of the room . . . persons that eventually formed groups X and Z sat down in their respective corners leaving the remainder in the center of the room, who were both amazed and angry . . . they willy-nilly were forced to become the third group. Most people seemed to think that probably a random method of selection for groups was the best way of doing it, although at the time they would have liked a little direction in order to obtain this."

INTERPRETIVE COMMENT

The first session of the Inter-Group Exercise was in the late afternoon of the second day when the members were, as a group, suffused with a basic assumption of dependence (baD). This ba was suddenly confronted at the beginning of the Inter-Group Exercise with an apparent betrayal by the conference leadership that was the object of the dependence. The group were put into a situation in which they had to take a decision for themselves. They were not prepared for this and the basic assumption of flight (baF) immediately took over, frustrating the development of a task-oriented work (W) process.

The group were given two tasks: to take a decision about the principle on which the Inter-Group Exercise groups would be formed—this to take no more than 15 minutes—and the action of actually forming the groups. Faced with this situation, some members were prepared to tackle the first, but the majority were not, and they immediately flew to the second under the dominance of baF.

The minority who resisted this flight into action and stayed in the center of the floor were prepared to undertake the first task. Once the flight had occurred, however, and these eight people experienced their exposure, they too succumbed to flight from the situation in which they had been left.

The quotations given above demonstrate the rebellious anti-organizer fight aspect of this basic assumption. The rationale the members gave for their behavior was, first, that the organizers had been aggressive by giving them a job to do that they considered to be both too difficult and inappropriate; and, second, that it was not possible for such a group to reach a decision in the time given.

GUILT AND REPARATION

The following quotation is from private notes made by the conference director during the course of the first session:

Ask X, Y and Z how they felt about the results. Possible interpretation that X and Y could proceed more actively with the task because of the gesture made by X to

Y. *Y* feel that their troubles and difficulties have been perceived and tackled by *X*, and through this recognition can proceed. *X* have made reparation in terms of their own going off and therefore also proceed with the task. Both, however, have expressed their aggression towards *Z* by having no contact. *X* perceives *Z* as the originator of the selfish act. *Y* will have nothing to do with *Z*. It was *X* (the middle group) that had to make the gesture. It is noticeable that the group that suffered most took no action and said it was prepared to go on working. It would now appear that *Z* is the isolated group. At one point, when, the results were being discussed, all members of *Z* turned round to *Y* with questioning looks and even guilt. To what extent will *Z* now be affected in their work by having to lean over backwards to conciliate the group that they have left? And how far will their program be inappropriately oriented towards providing for the unknown interests of the other members of the conference?

This quotation is given because it was the first appreciation that guilt and reparation were a main theme, conditioning the interactions of the groups throughout the Exercise.

From *Y*'s evaluation comes the following statement: "The actions and attitudes of our small group affected the two other more powerful groups because we accused them of doing something and they felt guilty." From *Z*'s evaluation: "The dislocation in *Y* was almost complete but they have constantly improved and have actually got up to finish level. We saw that we were bobbing up and down."

There is also, of course, the significant move by *X* to *Y* following the distribution of the first evaluation sheet results. From the observer's record it can be seen that this was a move of reparation from *X* to *Y* about whom *X* felt uneasy.

The groups did complete the task of the Inter-Group Exercise; they did not remain suffused by basic assumption processes. There was at work through the course of the Exercise an effective *W* process. From the analysis and interpretation below it will be seen that one of the principal tasks that the conference as a whole had to undertake was to contain the basic assumption forces sufficiently to allow the *W* process to proceed.

STARTING SITUATION

It was a matter of only a very few minutes after the original break-up into groups that their initial differentiation was perceptible to all concerned. *Y* had the painful task of facing each other, all conscious of being the conference rejects. This presented them with a tremendous task in handling their common emotional situation. On top of this, like the other groups, they had their Exercise to perform.

The members of Z were suffused with a feeling of guilt at being principally responsible for the flight from the conference task that had created the painful situation in which Y found themselves. Dominance by guilt as the characteristic of Z was present from the beginning. It had a central effect on all that the group did and was not dispelled until the Exercise was complete.

Between these two emotional climates was X who, like Z, started off with some sense of guilt at what they had done to Y. X, however, chose to perceive Z as the initiators of this move and so were themselves less inhibited by guilt. Their greater freedom from the dominance of guilt allowed X to make a gesture of reparation to Y which enabled them to get on with their contribution to the overall task.

Each group ascribed from early in the Exercise a definite, if not yet clearly defined, identity to the others. From the results of the first evaluation sheet it can be seen that there had also developed a level of common feeling within groups that marked off the members of each as being much more like one another in their reactions than like members of the other groups. As regards satisfaction, all members of Y had reactions that were below the neutral line, all members of Z had neutral reactions and X straddled it. Thus the members of each group had a fairly consistent self-image even at this stage. By the time the first evaluations were returned their identities and their wish to remain together rather than dissolve and start again were strong. This was true even of Y who had had so much pain to contend with. The observers' reports show that competition between groups had already developed as a factor.

DEVELOPMENT OF GROUP CHARACTERISTICS

The first event that took the development of distinctive characteristics a step forward was the reparative approach made by X to Y during the first session. It was a public gesture of reparation that allowed Y to develop sufficient self-confidence to get on with their work. But Y were able to meet both their emotional and task demands only because they effectively divided themselves into those who should be concerned with the group's emotional task and those who, because the emotional task was being carried by others, were free to undertake the group's formal task. This work was done by three or four people, the others were not only silent, but out of touch with what these first members were doing. The silent members were doing the group's emotional work, absorbing pain and shock, thus releasing the others to proceed with W.

The effectiveness of this division of function by Y was such that by the end of the first session and before there had been formal contact with the other groups, they had not only managed to handle their original emotional problem but had made a definite contribution to the task they had been set. This recovery of Y, as the evaluation graph (Figure 1) shows, was a demonstration of the capacity of a group to overcome a forlorn and painful situation. Remarkable though it was, it was possible only because of the roles taken by X and Z, and Y's relationship with them.

One of the factors that determined the membership of Y was a willingness to face the decision-making task given to the whole conference at the beginning of the Exercise and not immediately to fly from this. It would be expected, therefore, that within this group there would be elements of resilience and of ability to hold to a task in face of basic assumption pressures. This proved to be the case, and Y displayed from the beginning a determination to show its potency *vis-à-vis* the task and the other groups.

Y arrived at this position at some cost. The observer recorded the painful few minutes during the first session when the whole group retreated from both its tasks, and members withdrew into silence. Y were not notable for their democratic procedures. Given the emotional/intellectual differentiation of tasks within the group, the democratic process would not necessarily have been appropriate. There were neither emotional nor intellectual group-wide consensuses. All members did not need to be equally involved in the total group life when there was parity of respect for sub-tasks.

Z, on the other hand, achieved practically nothing in terms of the Exercise task during its first session and little more during the second. Members became compulsively active on a mass of detail but added little to the development of the task. There was internal irritation and bad feeling which led to a split into two factions. These, according to the observer's account, failed even to communicate their points of view to each other. Moreover, Z, unlike the other two groups, never felt the need for extra work sessions.

X were again in a middle position. They, too, displayed a certain element of compulsive activity on details but recovered from this. They also suffered some degree of inter-member irritation and the growth of sectional conflict. These were contained and compromises were found. X were thus able to make a satisfactory contribution during the first session. The graphs show that their sense of satisfaction with their internal decisions increased, but not so their willingness to implement them. They slipped back in their general feeling of satisfaction. This reflects that side of the group's task that had to do with containing the remnants of the emotional difficulties originating in the guilt inherited from its part in the initial break-up.

Unlike Y and Z, X did not allow themselves to develop any internal differentiation. At the same time, they did not have a clear and unified voice in their external relationships. They were the only group that did not grant their envoys full representative status. By avoiding sharp internal division and by compromising between conflicting positions, X prevented themselves from developing a defined policy and so were unable to take a clear and definite external stance.

DEVELOPMENT OF POLITICAL POSITIONS

By the end of the first session both X and Y had developed a sufficient sense of self-identity to enable them, during the second session, to initiate external contacts with each other and with the staff group. Their feeling of internal security was such as to allow them to look beyond their own boundaries and to take actions outside themselves appropriate to their developing tasks. It was these two groups who initiated the first meeting of envoys between the groups. Z had made no external contacts at all. They had made very little progress on their internal task. Only pressure from the envoys of X and Y got Z to join the first envoys' meeting.

This meeting was the crucial confrontation at which the political positions of the groups were established. X and Y became the contenders for the role of creator of the plan for the special interest sessions. Z brought little more than marginal contributions. X and Y wrote Z off as a political power.

The development of the second envoys' meeting in the third session was much the same. During the early part X and Y were making a good many external contacts with each other, with the staff group, and with Z, whereas Z, initiating no external contacts, became increasingly persecuted by the attentions of others.

During the first half of the final envoys' meeting the Z envoys teamed up alternatively with X and Y, but for the second half they effectively retired from the discussion, leaving X and Y to final confrontation over the points of conflict in their two plans.

In this political struggle between X and Y, Y emerged as the most potent group. Unlike X, they did not need to withdraw and take counsel. When, after taking counsel, X came back with an acceptance of Y's proposal, this was perceived by Y to be a public acceptance of the greater determination, unity, and effectiveness of Y.

FINISHING SITUATION

The finishing mood of Y was one of considerable satisfaction, almost of glee, at what they as a group had achieved from such an unpromising beginning.

The division of labor between the emotional and the task demands, which was the necessary means whereby Y achieved their success, is illustrated by both the group's and their envoys' reactions when the envoys were away from the group. The envoys were their chairman and the member who was most responsible for the development of their plan. They were the leaders of the W-oriented subgroup within Y. The members left behind were mainly those who had been doing the emotional task of the group. When the envoys were at the center, the group that remained became depressed and worried about what their envoys might be doing. Similarly, the lack of cohesion between their intellectual and emotional life showed itself in a parallel concern on the part of the envoys. During the group's evaluation session both the envoys reported that they were concerned about the group when they were away from it.

During the evaluation session Y became preoccupied with the slight dip to the final position of the graph recording their satisfaction. Their conclusion was that this represented "the group's horror that it was about to die, although the total conference group had achieved its task."

Z's evaluation was much more restrained and introspective. They became interested to interpret the "bumping up and down" of their group reactions at different points through the Exercise. Their conclusion was that "at the end of the negotiations a feeling of satisfaction was the outcome." They decided that their responses to the central envoy meetings showed that the group itself was incapable of doing anything that satisfied it, and that it was only when the overall conference task went forward at the envoys' sessions that any degree of satisfaction could be achieved.

Although the step to an inter-group interpretation was not made by the group, they felt that they "did what was required," even though this could not obviously be seen as a direct contribution to the overall task of the conference. That Z as a whole felt that they had made a useful contribution and were satisfied with the result can be seen from the final positions on the graphs of their expressed satisfaction. At two points they were at the position of maximum satisfaction, and almost so on the third at the end of the Exercise.

X again displayed characteristics of both the other groups in evaluating their experience. They were quite satisfied with themselves although they did not have the euphoria that suffused Y. Their main concern was to learn a little more from the introspection and recollection of why they had done things the way they had. They decided that they had handled their differences rather well. They prided themselves on developing a culture of containment and compromise, which had allowed them to avoid a direct split such as Z had experienced. In arriving at this conclusion the group once again showed their tendency to compromise by finding valuable aspects in the behavior of both their majority and minority groups.

Projection-Introjection Hypothesis

The members of the conference as a whole, divided into three groups in the Exercise, managed to accomplish the overall task. They produced a practical plan for the special interest sessions, and at the same time contained the emotional forces working against this achievement. The principal psycho-dynamic mechanism whereby the work was done was a pattern of projection and introjection of these emotional forces as a division of labor among the groups.

Z was not involved in the (for X cathartic and for Y reparative) activities following the distribution of the first evaluation sheet. From this point Z felt themselves, and were perceived by the others, as the most guilty group. This recognition prevented Z from ever making real contact with the task of the whole. The group became preoccupied with internal struggles, irritation, depression and splitting. Very early they showed themselves as an isolated group. They initiated no outward contact at all. This emotional stance of Z was of value to the other groups. It allowed X to project into Z the remnants of their own guilt. It also allowed Y to project into Z their aggression towards all who had left them stranded. By this means the release that both X and Y had experienced was reinforced. X and Y did the work that resulted in a conference plan for the special interest sessions. They could not have done it had they not had Z doing the emotional work for them, releasing them for the planning work. The group processes that went on within Z can be seen as a replica of the processes on the wider stage. In the evaluation, something of this was seen by the members themselves.

Z had taken on the complementary introjection of the emotional difficulties of the conference as a whole, which the other groups were quite happy to project into them. Z were not unaware of their function in this respect. It was a member of Z who, in the evaluation, would not accept dissatisfaction with the group's contribution to the overall task because "We did what was required." Because of the special emotion-containing role the group were carrying, they were not free to take decisions for themselves or to contribute to those of the whole. As the graphs show, it was only when progress on the common task was made at the inter-group meetings that Z felt any satisfaction. The group seemed to realize that the satisfaction of work done could be achieved only outside itself in the meeting of envoys. It was during group meetings that Z felt any satisfaction. The group seemed to realize that the satisfaction of work done could be achieved only outside itself in the meeting of envoys. It was not the group's function to do this internally: "Contact with external groups made the solution possible." The high level of satisfaction recorded at the end of the Exercise by Z is further evidence of their attitude. It must, indeed, have been a pleasant release for Z to have the task completed so that they could shake off the scapegoat role that they had carried on behalf of the conference as a whole.

Some recognition of the contribution of Z to the task can be seen in the willingness of X and Y to allow Z twice the number of representatives that they each had on the planning committee. X and Y could have insisted that Z should have only the allotted number.

Z's need for the central envoys' meeting to be successful can be seen in the way their envoys behaved. The observer reported that the Z envoys were surprisingly lucid and useful at the envoys' meetings compared with their behavior inside their group. Although the group sent the leader of its minority as well as a spokesman for its majority as envoys, they did not break up the central meeting by carrying their internal split to it. On the contrary, the Z envoys' behavior assisted the work of compromise going on between the other two competing groups. They tended to side with one or the other in the compromise-finding process, and then withdrew for the other two to reach their final settlement, which Z was happy to accept.

Coexistence of Anxieties, Defenses and Work Processes

The Exercise as a whole carried throughout a ground-bass of *baF*. This was shown during the initial break-up and in members' comments about it. It was still present in the final evaluation: "I felt that we had not been given quite enough chance to find our feet before something rather formidable was put upon us. It was asking a bit too much at that early stage in the conference to stand up to this." "Especially when previously we had had two study groups. This was an expression of aggression."

During the Exercise, there were various attempts to make the change back to basic assumption behavior. On several occasions moves were made to involve the staff in making decisions or in taking executive roles for the conference as a whole. Had the staff accepted these implicit invitations, the conference would probably have returned to *baD*. Such a return would have been so deep that the conference would never thereafter have accepted the struggle to achieve its task.

Nevertheless, the conference did have to cope continually with the ground-bass of the fight/flight assumption with which it started and which it never lost. There was, however, genuine emotional learning as a result of the dramatic explosion in the first few seconds of the Exercise. The guilt and aggression left behind had to be dealt with in its various groups if the Conference were to get on with its task. It also had to contain the continuing temptation to flight which it did by creating in Z a part of itself that carried the emotional burden for the whole. Z continued in flight. They remained disturbed and unable to work because of their preoccupation with the guilt that had arisen from the first flight, which they had absorbed on behalf of the whole conference. Because Z were doing this job and having these elements in X and Y projected into them and, in turn, introjecting them, it was possible for the other two groups to be sufficiently free from this basic assumption to get on with the task. In this way, all the groups can be seen to have accepted, and in their different ways acted on, the task-traction of the shared real objective. With any group of ordinary people, once they are convinced that responsibility does rest with themselves, the development of such task-traction is inevitable. Not only is it the way, through reality acceptance, of achieving any degree of positive ego satisfaction, the alternative is an unsatisfying confusion and, in the extreme, universal futility (Fairbairn, 1952).

This process did not completely free the conference from the fight aspect of the basic assumption in operation. The idiom of the working relationship between X and Y was one of sharp competition. Each was fighting the other for the honor of drawing up the conference plan for the special interest sessions.

The three groups took an equal share in the work of the whole conference of which they were all part and for which the task was being done. There were two tasks to carry out. One was the sophisticated task—the planning task; the other was to contain the intruding basic assumption that was interfering with this. This was a fight/flight basic assumption. X and Y were able to handle W, and, through their competitive relationship, the fight side of this basic assumption. Z carried the main emotional burden—containing and manifesting throughout the Exercise the element of flight, by making no real contact with the task, and also by taking on the guilt and aggression of the other two groups.

Basic assumption and W can coexist. In most life situations, which are never free of these processes, the greatest social sophistication is to find a way, as did the conference members on this occasion, of allowing the emotional and the work tasks to be carried on concurrently.

Appendix: The Product

Five members with a staff chairman constituted the Planning Committee which circulated 24 items from the original list of special interests. Members signified their first and second choices. Items were grouped into three sections. A had nine items with which members of staff were willing to help; B four items with which staff had not expressed such a willingness; C 11 items that the staff considered already covered in the program. The returns gave 52 (89 percent) from A, five from B and only one from C.

For X the most popular choice (20 percent) was "Interviewing techniques—especially group techniques," a role-playing session conducted by the staff. For Y (38 percent) "Resistance to change in large organizations," a seminar to be run by a staff member; for Z (27 percent) "How to use the dynamic individual," again a seminar to be run by a staff member. Very close behind (23 percent) was "Problems of verbal communication"—another seminar to be run by a staff member.

The most popular overall was "Resistance to change in large organizations," 22 percent of all preferences. The next was "How to use the dynamic individual," 16 percent of all choices.

Most people had their first choice. Five groups were set up:

- Resistance to change in large organizations (8 members).
- Problems of verbal communication and problems of correlating theoretical and practical training (7 members).
- How to use the dynamic individual (6 members).
- The effects of group work on attitudes (4 members).
- Interviewing techniques—especially group techniques (4 members).

Each group had a staff member allocated to it but was free to decide how to go about its study.

All groups presented material at the third session: one a short dissertation on the results of the work, using their own experience as their case material; three others conducted role-playing sessions—with or without commentary; the fifth, concerned with problems of communication, used a variety of blackboard and tape-recorder techniques and a communication exercise involving the whole membership. In none of these presentations was a staff member invited to participate.

There was no doubt of the involvement of all participants in these sessions. The quality of the final presentations was high. The members had produced a plan which had succeeded in accomplishing the objective set.

References

Bion, W.R. 1961. *Experience in Groups and Other Papers.* London: Tavistock Publications; New York: Basic Books.

Fairbairn, W.R.D. 1952. *Psychoanalytic Studies of the Personality.* London: Tavistock Publications.

Rice, A.K. 1965. *Learning for Leadership: Interpersonal and Intergroup Relations.* London: Tavistock Publications.

Trist, E.L. and C. Sofer. 1959. *Exploration in Group Relations.* Leicester: Leicester University Press.

Harold Bridger

Courses and Working Conferences as Transitional Learning Institutions*

The Background

ORIGINS

The approach to management training and development to be reported in this paper rests on a different premise from the purely group dynamics foundation of the study groups of the Leicester model or the T-group tradition of the National Training Laboratories (NTL) in the U.S. In both of these traditions groups concerned with the internal task of self-study and review are given no external task. My own experience, however, has convinced me that in organizational settings the internal task is best undertaken in conjunction with an external task. I have therefore called my approach the double task model.

In a note on study groups in the review of the first Leicester Conference (Trist and Sofer, 1959) J.D. Sutherland, the then Director of the Tavistock Clinic, who had himself taken a study group, stated

> The special social situation which experience shows most useful for this purpose consists in having a group meet without the "external" task to be done, but with the specific task of examining the kinds of feelings and attitudes that arise spontaneously, these feelings and attitudes being those which each individual brings to any group situation, or which develop within it independently of whatever the external task may be.

In the follow-up of that conference some six months later, it became apparent that most members of the helping, educational and social professions had found study group experience relevant and useful, both personally and professionally. By contrast, most of those concerned with organizational and operational affairs had not found it of value in their back-home situations. Indeed, it created a barrier.

*A new paper.

The account of the follow-up meeting quotes me as drawing "a further parallel with the training work being done by the Tavistock Institute in industry, where there was no attempt to turn groups into study groups." The method was to develop insight during the course of working through existing problems.

In organizational projects as early as 1947, I had introduced the procedure of "suspending the agenda," in executive meetings, when no progress was being made with the task in hand. This allowed the group to review and reflect on the emotional and conflictual elements that were impeding its progress. In the Glacier project, Jaques (1951) gave up using extra-curricular sessions and relied solely on making interpretative comments in the working sessions of executive or union meetings.

My thinking at that time, and indeed since, has been much influenced by my experience, during the war, as a social therapist at Northfield Military Psychiatric Hospital. The activity groups I created influenced material brought into clinical groups in a positive way as regards therapeutic outcome. The two groups became interlocked and were often, with advantage, the same group in different modes. This interconnection expressed the double-task in action.

Shortly after Bion started therapy groups in the Tavistock Clinic in 1945 he gave an extended trial of his method of group-centered interpretation in training groups outside the medical area. One of these consisted of industrial managers, others of people from the educational field. These groups did not fare well. It seemed that a number of the participants were patients in disguise. We thought that it was best to remove this disguise and have the patients admit that they were seeking psychiatric treatment and should therefore be in a therapy group.

In 1946 the Institute held, in Nottingham, under the auspices of the Industrial Welfare Society, an exploratory residential conference using Bion's methods. The participants were fairly high ranking managers from a number of industries. The conference generated such stress that a distinguished member perforated an ulcer. He condemned the conference publicly. This episode had a decidedly chastening effect. Even carefully picked people in industry were not ready for anything of the study or T-group type. Our frontal approach had been a mistake. No more groups outside the medical area were attempted for another ten years, though psychodynamic projects continued and flourished in organizational settings. A seeming exception was a discussion group in the field of teacher training which worked on material provided by the members. This led to their undertaking a project—the production of a report on their proceedings to communicate their group experience to their profession (Herbert and Trist, 1953; Vol. I, "An Educational Model for Group Dynamics").

In 1956 four senior people with NTL backgrounds were invited by the European Productivity Agency to make trials of NTL procedures in European countries. These trials were, on the whole, successful and the Tavistock was approached to work out a design suitable for British conditions. This was how the first Leicester conference originated in 1957—as an experimental endeavor to discover a form of experiential learning acceptable in the U.K.

To make clear that this was not a therapeutic endeavor the Institute created the conference as a joint venture with the Education Department of a University, the link with education being similar to that made by NTL with the National Education Association. Like NTL, again, we had application groups and theory sessions as well as the study groups which were our own version of T-groups. Moreover, participants came through a sociological channel; they were nominated by organizations, though the decision whether or not to come was personal. To make relations with the Leicester community, we introduced external operational tasks in which participants engaged with local organizations (e.g., industrial firms, the police, hospitals and local government) in exploring some specific problem or issue which was of current concern to them. The conference was successful in that no-one came to harm; the patient-in-disguise phenomenon was stopped; the shadow of Nottingham was removed; a relationship with society made.

On behalf of the Institute, I spent the next summer in Bethel to make a thorough study of NTL methods. These summer "labs," as they were called, contained a great variety of activities based on experiential learning which had established itself as an accepted educational innovation. Nevertheless, and despite the overall success of Leicester, I was still disquieted about T-groups and study groups. It seemed to me that the idea of a group of participants with the task of "learning about groups by being a group" meets Bion and Rickman's (1943) conditions for the "study of its own internal tensions" only when the participants are patients prepared to join such a group with the expectation of "getting better." Then the real-life task of the group is for the patients "to get well." It did not seem to me that there was a compelling real task in the non-patient groups that I had experienced. Since this time movements such as the human potential movement emerging from the Esalen Institute, particularly from the influence of Abraham Maslow, have produced groups outside the medical area with a strong commitment to self study, but such groups are therapeutic or quasi-therapeutic in aim.

Bion's original formulation had emphasized the need for the group's situation to be a real-life one, i.e., an action situation. I therefore thought that a suitable real-life situation had to be found for non-medical groups whose members, such as managers, carried out organizational roles. Such a situation might be found if one could discover a way of working with participants in which they could bring into the group problems and concerns arising in their organizational settings. This way of working would entail creating circumstances in which they could recognize and pursue what I have called the double task.

AN ORGANIZATION THEORY BASIS

In his book *Leadership in Administration,* Selznick (1957) distinguishes be-tween concepts of organization and institution:

> The term organization suggests . . . a system of consciously co-ordinated ac-tivities. . . . It refers to a rational instrument engineered to do a job. . . . It has a formal system of rules and objectives. Tasks, powers, procedures are set out according to some officially approved pattern.
>
> An institution, on the other hand, is more nearly a natural product of social needs and pressures—a responsive, adaptive organism.
>
> This does not mean that any given enterprise must be either one or the other. While an extreme case may closely approach either an "ideal" organization or an "ideal" institution, most living associations . . . are complex mixtures of both designed and responsive behavior.

The process of adapting, of projecting and internalizing, of learning and acting, unconsciously as well as consciously, is the institutional characteristic. For convenience and in deference to present day usage of "organization" in both senses, the term organization will, predominantly, be used.

The organization is an open system with regard to its environment and is both "purpose-oriented" and "learning and self-reviewing." The capability of carrying out this double-task at appropriate times and in the course of normal working when relevant, is becoming an essential feature in interdependent multi-disciplinary work forces.

The more rapid change rate has created a situation of far greater complexity, interdependence and uncertainty than organizations have previously encoun-tered. Emery and Trist (1965, 1973) have called this situation the "turbulent environment." More initiative is now required of managers, more innovative capability, more flexibility and more recognition of the need to cooperate. Greater understanding of group life at all levels is needed in order more effectively to manage transitions of one kind or another which are occurring with much greater frequency (Bridger, 1987).

Internal Courses: The Opportunity in Philips Electrical

About this time in the early 1960s the Institute divided into two operating groups, one of which undertook the further development of the Leicester model (Rice, 1965; Miller, Vol. I, "Experiential Learning in Groups I"), while the other, to which I belonged, was interested in the double-task approach. It is scarcely accidental that the opportunity required to pursue this arose in an industrial setting with a company beset with problems of increased uncertainty, complexity and interdependence. The company in question was the British affiliate of Philips, the multi-national electronics firm, in itself a very large organization. To meet the challenge of the new conditions senior management took time out for self-review. As the result of a week's off-site conference they gave priority to Staff Development.

An immediate job was to develop training designs relevant to the new managerial competences (cf. Morgan, 1988). They were called Practice of Management Courses (PMCs) and required attention to process as well as to content. If the attendance was to be secured of the bulk of the most relevant managers for the kind of course contemplated, this could be no longer than a week. The aim was to produce a scheme that would permit extensive use.

Each facet of a pilot course was to be concerned with "managing groups at work"—which entailed **understanding** the dynamics of such groups. Hence the need to appreciate the role of informal systems and other processes affecting groups as operating entities. The **consultative** aspects of management were becoming increasingly significant, whether for more sophisticated and satisfying appraisal methods and career development, or for reaching the most effective outcome with a work force. I came to see the consultative process as a "basic building block" in the development of a group as well as an important element in its own right within any training scheme for organizational effectiveness (Bridger, 1980b).

The Study Group became a Work Group, but with a double task:

- The group had to work on selected issues of importance for group members in their organizational settings and in their roles. It was to manage its own selection of topics and to manage itself. It implicitly posed to itself the problem—and the challenge—of being able to face internal differentiation, thereby enabling leadership and other capabilities to be demonstrated according to the pertinent circumstances.
- The group had to identify the processes operating within it at different times, especially the way the group as a whole, with its particular set of values and norms, was influencing events and modes of working.

An "intergroup" experience (Higgin and Bridger, 1964) could be offered in a variety of forms, but in early models it consisted of an interim review of the course about two-thirds of the way through the week. Each Work Group would review the experience thus far and prepare recommendations for amending the remainder of the proposed program so as to better meet the original or changed expectations of members. In addition, each group was to select an appropriate group member (or two) to represent it at a meeting with the staff representative and jointly make some proposals.

group member (or two) to represent it at a meeting with the staff representative and jointly make some proposals.

"Talk-discussions," which gave a conceptual framework to the experience, were placed at points when they were most likely to be relevant.

The placing and interlocking of these aspects, together with transitions for entry and departure, were carefully thought through to ensure that both the real-life situation and the study of processes were operating for each component as well as for the whole. The course itself was regarded as a process consisting of three phases: pre-course, the residential week and post-course.

The procedure described in what follows represents the mature model which evolved after extensive trials when the demand for a large number of courses had been created. It is based on my joint paper with one of the internal consultants (Low and Bridger, 1979).

PRE-COURSE PHASE

This consists of two operations. In one nominations are submitted from constituent parts of the company of those managers who wish to attend. Invitations are sent by the Management Development Adviser (MDA), setting out the purpose and indicating prior work to be done. In the other, the MDA appoints the course staff and meetings between them are subsequently held two or three weeks before the residential phase.

NOMINATION AND METHOD OF INVITATION

Each participant attends voluntarily. He is free to withdraw at any stage. Invitations are sent on the basis that each participant

- has within the scope of his or her management function sufficient opportunity to influence change in methods of working
- has the motivation to undertake fresh approaches to work and to explore problems without pre-conceptions
- is resilient enough to absorb conflicting pressures and to react with sensitivity.

The description of the course states its purpose as follows:

These courses . . . are designed to enable managers to gain, through participation in group exercises and discussion, a fresh insight into management and to derive general principles and practice from particular experiences. The content emerges from members' interests. No attempt is made to teach hard and fast techniques but rather to encourage learning by participation in joint work, aided by the presentation of theoretical concepts.

The phrasing indicates the duality of task; that through a discussion of management topics which are both valid and real, insight can not only be gained about the content of such issues, but about the processes of group activity.

The nominees are asked to bring, for discussion by heterogeneous work groups of which they will be members, subjects important to them in their roles as managers. In addition, they are asked to formulate a specific problem from their own managerial experience which can be discussed in detail within the homogeneous common interest group of which they will also be members.

STAFF SELECTION AND STAFF MEETINGS

The responsibility for inviting people to take part as staff members in the PMCs rests with the MDA, assisted in this task by the Tavistock Consultant. The increased numbers of courses has obliged the MDA to create a network of staff assistants. The criteria for inclusion are

- a capacity to understand the motivation of people at work in groups
- sensitivity to individual and group behavior
- organizational roles that have credibility in a professional sense
- support from managers to do consultant work, whether with training or with operational groups
- experience as a participant in a PMC

To avoid any feeling that participants are undergoing a selection process for becoming trainee consultants, individuals are encouraged, on later reflection about the course and its impact upon them, to appraise themselves. In this way the initiative can be left with the individual to state whether a consultant role of this type is appealing. The invitation, ultimately, still remains within the prerogative of the MDA, following discussions with the individual.

As group work is a crucial element within the total course design, care is taken in the assignment of individual staff consultants to each group. Unnecessary inhibitions to learning are avoided by ensuring that no staff member has too close a personal or work relationship with any member of his or her group. Although an experienced consultant can work singly with a group of some eight or nine participant managers, it has been found advantageous to have two staff members with each group. Sometimes these are people of equal experience, in which case they work as co-trainers, but more frequently one is a trainee.

Staff meetings are held before the course assembles and have a dual purpose—in content terms, to determine the framework for the week's program; in process terms, to become acquainted with one another, to understand different roles, to recognize overtly the relevance of talent within the staff group and to agree how the work will be shared between staff members.

From the start, the differences are made clear between teaching and administrative roles. Course members will best understand the importance of role clarity in groups if the staff themselves have made a conscious effort to distinguish their own roles.

The Residential Phase

FIRST PLENARY SESSION

At the first plenary session the staff allows time for questions, however trivial these may seem, without creating an undue sense that time is an expandable commodity. The session attempts to be administratively brisk and to explain the rationale of the course design and the roles of the staff. Nevertheless, there is bound to exist, to a certain degree, a sense that participants are the victims of manipulative or even devious stratagems. With the best will in the world, and despite protestations to the contrary, the staff may fail to convince them that such is not their intention.

The course is frequently described as unstructured, not because a basic framework is lacking, but because it starts from the learners' questions, rather than from the teachers' answers. Exploration of problems about managing, about group behavior, begins with discussion between participants, so that their differing or similar experiences may be brought into the open, before any inferences about behavior in general can be drawn.

HOMOGENEOUS COMMON INTEREST GROUPS

The next stage consists of initial brief exchanges between members with a common interest, i.e., homogeneous, group.

These are trios or quartets, consisting of managers with similar roles or functions who can explore their own problems and communicate with each other in a familiar language. No staff member is present at this stage, which immediately follows the introductory plenary meeting, unless a group requests clarification. The group's task is to formulate an agenda relevant to some common interest that each can take with him to his search group. They meet again at later stages for different purposes.

HETEROGENEOUS SEARCH GROUPS*

At the core of the design are heterogeneous groups of 9 managers, which have the task of understanding how content and process are interdependent in achieving group objectives. The first of the heterogeneous group periods takes place once there has been an opportunity to share, in a further plenary meeting, the variety of managerial problems which participants have begun to discuss with each other. They now find themselves members of a group with mixed, perhaps conflicting, interests.

Thus at this stage the design has already established a replica of institutional life. The members belong to one group where they speak a recognized language; to another where they must try to understand the language of others whose ideas and backgrounds are unfamiliar; and to a total organization, represented by a plenary meeting where all participants come together to deal with matters affecting their inter-groups requirements.

ALTERNATION OF CONSULTATION AND SEARCH GROUPS

For the next two days the common interest groups (renamed consultative groups) and the heterogeneous groups (renamed search groups) function alternately. The task of the former is now concerned with learning about the giving and taking of advice between colleagues; the role of the second to undertake free exploration of problems and issues. By reason of this alternation, course members experience, in a temporary system, the conflict of interest that flows from simultaneous membership in distinct groups, and learn to sustain the two-way stretch to which they are subjected. Exactly how these different aspects of the week's course develop will be the function of the staff to observe and interpret in relation to the processes involved in managing groups. The content by means of which such awareness develops is represented by the members' own agendas, brought from their trios and quartets to the search groups.

THEORY SESSION: THE NATURE OF GROUPS

Now that each group has had some experience of handling its own discussions, a plenary period is inserted which takes the form of a theory presentation by a staff member about "The Nature of Groups." Experiences in working groups, however frustrating or uncertain their nature, precede any attempt to draw

*The idea of cognitive search was introduced by Wertheimer (1945) and developed by Fred and Merrelyn Emery (1978) at the social level for the purposes of search conferences.

together more general concepts about groups. The structure is a reflection of the wish to proceed from the known to the unknown. It supports learning by discovery. The expectation is (and experience bears this out) that the participants will relate this talk about groups in general to their own developing perceptions about what is taking place in their own groups.

Thus, about one-third of the way through the course, at the very point where members are feeling that they are lost, that the staff process observations are merely intrusive, unhelpful remarks (not germane to the content discussions), and that confusion is a dominant note, an attempt is made through the plenary presentation to enable them to see their experiences against a fresh set of concepts. There are usually feelings of manipulation, however, as if the course staff have been keeping these revelations up their sleeve.

INTER-GROUP EXCHANGE

Not only does the course aim to provide opportunities to look at small groups, it is also concerned—because management involves such experiences—to examine what happens when groups try to work and communicate with each other. About mid-way through the week, therefore, the search groups have the opportunity to share their experiences to date, by means of an inter-group exchange. Two members from each group describe and discuss with each other their separate views of what has occurred in their respective groups. This is arranged as a "fish-bowl" exercise in which representatives of groups are observed by the colleagues who have chosen them. Members have the chance to evaluate what happens when representatives are faced with conflicting feelings—loyalty to one group yet a desire to understand the attitudes of people from another. The criteria for choice of representatives are also reviewed.

REVIEW AND FIELD FORCE ANALYSIS

Underlying the initial attempts to create this type of course is a belief in the value of "suspending business" for effecting a review of organizational life. Participants have the opportunity to look back at what has been happening, to make proposals about what might happen and to come to jointly agreed decisions about what will best suit the future needs of the course as a total institution. A method for doing this is Field Force Analysis (Lewin, 1951), by use of which managers produce maps of those forces which assist and those which detract from the course objectives. It is a method that course members can use back home. This review affords an occasion to examine, with staff feedback, just how course members are proceeding with this task of managing their own temporary institution. They look at the forces, internal and external, such as competitive pressures and drives, which make up group life. The rational, logical aspects of decision making are seen to be tempered by the irrational. It is at this stage, when awareness of process has been acknowledged, however uncertainly put into words, that the members of each consulting and search group can examine their own group's process and expect to find parallels between them and those in groups in their sponsoring organizations. The group discussions towards the latter part of the week focus on the group's own processes and dynamics. The consultant has opportunities to engage with group members about process, even to make, where appropriate, brief statements about organization theory. Papers brought to the course are best received if introduced when members can gain knowledge from them relative to points arising from the course experience itself.

FINAL STAGES

The final stages of the residential phase prepare members for return to their organizations. So the trios and quartets are reconstituted and meet immediately prior to the brief plenary session with which the course concludes. Members recall their first uncertain, tentative group meetings, and attempt to relate the intervening experience to the pressing tasks they will face beyond the confines of the course. As with a vacation, the descriptions to others not present of an experience not shared is likely to prove frustrating. How to relate again to colleagues who will be incapable of receiving with comprehension and sympathy one's inability to interpret the significance of the week's events?

The ensuing plenary session when participants and staff alike re-convene from their homogeneous groups—for consultants and observers, too, can benefit from a pause to consider jointly the future against the background of the course—is not an occasion for further public review of the groups' process. The need for business now outweighs the need for any suspension of business. On occasions, the staff find themselves giving a lead on content, whilst participants, reversing the usual roles, seem to be more concerned with process.

A practical task is provided by a brief discussion of the interim plans for a follow-up meeting, say, after six months, with the need to make arrangements, to co-ordinate dates, to consult diaries; in fact, to think immediately of that external world to which everyone now must return. Course participants, having shared in a learning experience about membership in, and management of, small groups, are about to take on more familiar roles again. And so they leave the course, as they joined it, as accountants, engineers, production managers, personnel officers and marketing managers.

POST-COURSE PHASE

The objectives in providing an occasion for course members to re-convene some six months later are:

- to evaluate the course's relevance to the roles and functions which people will have taken up again
- to re-appraise one's own performance at work and the feelings about one's career development in the light of the course
- to discover the organizational issues raised, as a result of attempting to relate "group dynamics" to problems at work

The members and staff come back to the same conference center for a period of two-and-a-half days. The temptation for the staff to concentrate on process comments, to the exclusion of any involvement in the content to be examined, has to be resisted. This brief follow-up looks back while still continuing to look forward—what is the relevance of group dynamics to problems at work? Staff and members alike share their experiences. After resuming through work groups—and thereby meeting the need to enjoy a re-union—the course members focus attention on special areas of interest. Case studies of organizational problems are carried out, frequently by new groupings made up of people who now have a new common interest. Whether individuals wish to discuss with others the self-appraisals carried out as arranged before coming to the follow-up session is left to them to decide.

The points raised relate to questions of organizational complexity back at work. Thus the relevance to this complexity—familiar and perhaps inevitable in any large multi-functional enterprise—of the Practice of Management is considered. This leads to work between course members, between members and staff, and between members of different and separate courses, in what may generally be described as "organization development."

The Consultant's Role and Functions

As these courses proceeded, features of the consultant's role emerged which may be regarded as general for all courses and workshops of this kind. I shall now review these.

STAFF CONSULTING ROLES

Staff roles, like course design, are conceived as enabling resources; in addition to the importance of what a staff member does is the way in which it is done. He or she takes different roles at different stages and in different situations: in the early trios and quartets to clarify; in the search group to be an adviser who listens and gives feedback; in seminar activities to reinforce learning; in the small consultative groups to observe and coordinate. By differentiating between these roles from the start the consultant can show the relationship between role clarity and organizational effectiveness.

The point of a consultant's intervention in the early stages is often not perceived, as the group does not yet understand process. It finds difficulty in reconciling the consultant's process comments with its own interests in optimizing task objectives.

The consultant does not refuse to answer relevant questions (i.e., those consistent with the role), but if asked a question about content (e.g., what is your opinion about the influence of trade unions in industry upon the authority of management?) may indicate why, at that moment, the group wishes the consultant to take over their task rather than carry it out themselves.

One way in which a group may cope with uncertainty is to establish a familiar structure, which often means appointing a chairman and perhaps a secretary. There may be opposition, often unvoiced, to these moves. The consultant notes it for future reference when opposition becomes overt—usually in some rationalized form. Intervention is then designed to produce a realization that a particular structure or procedural form is not a general solution to difficulties of operational functioning. The experience can help later to determine when such a structure or procedure should realistically be brought into play. The timing of interventions is crucial, an opportunity for intervening not taken may not recur. Usually, however, the dynamics of the group behavior are repeated, though in another or disguised form.

In the later stages, the consultant has to exercise self-discipline, through recognizing the group's own growth in learning potential, so as not to intervene in the same way throughout, but allow participants to try their hand on process comment whenever they are ready to do so.

THE CONSULTANT'S RELATIONSHIP TO THE GROUP

In the early stages a consultant is liable to be the target for hostile feelings, overt or covert, because a group perceives him or her as having failed to help or lead the group. As time progresses, group members begin to distinguish between manipulating others, being manipulated and feeling that one is being manipulated. The theme of manipulation itself often becomes a means of learning about integrity, and about recognizing when one is either obliged or can choose to conform with certain circumstances. Two forces, often more, are usually involved: the urge to get on with the job in hand and the effort to provoke the consultant into "coming clean."

Later in the process the group is apt to show frustration over failure to achieve goals in content; it may want its own survival as its aim, or be reluctant to "jell" because it would become too "cosy." In various crises such as these, the group's sense of aggravation may be turned on the consultant for failure to help.

The consultant must understand and learn how best to help the group in these circumstances, for instance by suspending business to examine those factors that are determining the group's actions. Concentrating on roles ensures that the consultant is seen to be concerned only with group development and not with judgments about individual behavior. Individuals will be learning about, as well as from, each other and may begin to explore individual aspects, the consultant, however, refers to individuals and their behavior only insofar as it contributes to the group's process task.

One specific phenomenon usually occurs about one-third of the way through the course, and is associated with the underlying wish of the group as to the level of learning with which it will proceed. Critical is the group's discovery that the way forward lies in giving reflection on its own behavior as prominent a place as task achievement. Once this shift, is recognized, the consultant can assume that the group is joining him or her and beginning to show a capacity to share in the second task of looking at process as well as content. Soon afterwards the group sometimes refers to the consultant's having become a "member."

A Consultant Must "Earn the Right to be Trusted"

A consultant may wish to take notes to help remember incidents in the development of the work group. The group is likely to suspect that the notes are for other ulterior purposes, usually because of past association with authority figures displaying judgmental attitudes. No consultant can expect to be trusted as of right, but has to earn trust. Only through consistency of role, and certainly not just through the use of "techniques," will the trust of participants develop. Trust itself will come to be recognized as a process, not a state. Once, however, a "good enough" shared experience has developed, a slip out of role by the consultant may be forgiven (or may even lead to being seen as human after all), but basic discrepancies can have most damaging effects. A consultant (or manager) may grossly underestimate the penetrating and subtle sense of the "music behind the words" which groups use at all times.

Findings Derived from Review of Course Experience

Anyone who feels it desirable to do this type of work places a high value on it. One should, therefore, beware of believing that an experience of learning from the here-and-now will be valued by everybody. The following factors influence attitude:

- Commitment to the course objectives by an individual participant, coupled with a willingness to explore, produce a positive attitude to learning
- An individual who feels he or she has been sent for some vaguely therapeutic purpose will build resistance to what is seen as an intrusive threat
- An individual whose own manager is half-hearted or highly skeptical will tend to deny the value of the experience, whatever he or she may personally feel about the method of learning
- Where a staff member displays, however unconsciously, his or her own uncertainty or anxiety about self, career or competence, this attitude transfers itself to the participants. They will display anxiety and even aggression towards the staff member and the course in general
- If a sponsoring manager's behavior belies his or her words, which may in appearance only support open-ended learning, the subordinate is liable to be guarded in his or her own behavior
- No application of learning from experience is possible in any organizational setting which exclusively rewards conformist "safe" behavior

To take these points into account membership of the course is controlled by the criteria for inclusion set out by the MDA.

Naturally, it is not possible to guarantee that course members will be paragons of influence, resilience and sensitivity. What is essential is that people, with a positive, rather than a negative approach, be encouraged to test themselves out in the temporary system of the course environment provided that they receive "back home" support for their efforts.

Evaluation

In the early courses, participants completed questionnaires on their attitudes and assumptions about management behavior. Questions based on concepts of motivation by such writers as McGregor (1960) and Herzberg (1966) were answered prior to, during and at the conclusion of the course. The purpose was to help participants examine any significant behavioral change deriving from their learning experiences. However, the anxiety of the course staff to prove the relevance of the training was greater than the participants' need to learn. The process of collecting and comparing the data took on an undue emphasis that interfered with the development of course activity, and hindered the consultants in their principal task. Questionnaires are still occasionally used, for example, as a means of introducing a theory session. However, no formal evaluation of the courses is conducted by questionnaire. Currently, however, an attempt is being made to assess their value by means of a survey conducted with all previous participants who have assisted in the preparation of the survey material.

Because of the obvious difficulty, given the number of variables which can affect individual and group behavior in any organization, no attempt to quantify the value of the courses has been made. Significant outcomes, however, are that individuals have been able to evaluate their careers in the light of their course experience. Training managers have been able to respond to the wishes of their organizations to adopt a more open appraisal method. The need to do so arose from conversations about how relevant the learning was to factories, laboratories and commercial offices. A number of management teams, including the executive boards of two subsidiary companies, have asked for assistance from training staff in order to carry out reviews of their group's effectiveness, in the same way that work groups suspend their business in the courses. One factory, where a number of managers have attended the course and whose subordinates have similarly attended off-plant training exercises, has, through its director's initiative, set up project groups comprising people of different disciplines and functions to examine specific problems. Other parts of the company have reviewed the relationship between their objectives and their methods of work through residential conferences. As a result, they have effected their own changes.

Now that many seeds have been sown, the future emphasis in courses in the Practice of Management will be on training the trainers. The recognition of the role which a staff member can take creatively as consultant has brought new demands. It is not the intention to overlay the organization as a whole with courses in behavioral skills, but to increase the possibility of learning from real work groups, whether these be at board room level or on the shop floor.

External Workshops: The Perspective of a Participant

The courses in Philips became woven into the texture of the organization. The model was taken up by several other comparable companies. Then a demand for external courses arose in which people from different organizations could meet together and have the advantage of even greater diversity of experience, though internal preparation and follow-up could not be equivalently intensive. These workshops I have come to call Tavistock Working Conferences (TWCs). Efforts are made to ensure that the firms sending participants are supportive of experiential learning and that the interest of the participant is authentic. Preferably, two people come from any one organization.

For a number of years TWCs have been held at least annually, first in conjunction with Bath University and more recently at the conference center of the Foundation for Adaptation in Changing Environments at Minster Lovell, near Oxford. For many years, also, TWCs have been a feature of the National Training Laboratories' summer program at Bethel, Maine. They have also been held on the European continent. The composition of the membership tends to be highly international.

The best way to give a flavor of what a TWC is like is to reproduce the account of her conference experience by Eleanor Dudar, who participated in the conference held in Toronto in April, 1987. At that time she was Publication Editor of the Quality of Working Life Centre at the Ontario Ministry of Labour. It is always difficult to communicate the essence of any important personal experience verbally or in writing. It is equivalent to demanding that one should communicate the experience of the experience! As Eleanor Dudar so crisply expresses the point, "you have to be there."

The intuitive feel and understanding combined with the high professional competence which she brings to this contribution has met with much gratitude and appreciation by staff and past members who have so far had the opportunity of reading this very sensitive paper. She has captured the "music as well as the words" of the experience and, in the French translation as well as in the English original, it has already been found illuminating and valuable by those who would like to have a better indication of "what would be in it for me."

Ask people who have attended a Tavistock Working Conference (TWC) what went on, what they actually did for a week, what they got out of it, and their answers are likely to be peculiarly nebulous. Something very important took place—they'll agree to that—something at times bewildering, frustrating, positively painful even; something that in retrospect seems to have been of great positive value to their confidence and effectiveness as members of a working group; but also something very hard to put into words. "Well, you see, I guess you really had to be there."

An easier question to answer is why anyone would consider going to a TWC in the first place. Because a TWC offers help in an area where a great many people in business, industry, government, service organizations, unions, you name it, feel that help is needed. Anyone who has ever had to work in and through a group—to get something done in collaboration with six or ten or a dozen other people—knows just how frustrating and at times puzzling an exercise it can be. There are so many ways in which the productive functioning of a group can be sidetracked, highjacked, distracted and derailed by the tangle of human interactions that are woven into the agenda. Sometimes, the problem can seem pretty obvious: he simply can't grasp the issue; she simply refuses to cooperate; those two think they have all the answers; nobody wants to stick his neck out. At other times, it's by no means clear what's going wrong: the conflicts are masked; there is an apparent willingness to work at the task; the inability to reach decisions is distinguished as further discussion. But the collective dysfunction is just as painful and unproductive. Every work group is incapacitated at times, more or less severely, by these demons, and a TWC offers a chance to discover where they lurk, and how they may be exorcised.

So, back to the first question: what actually goes on? Are you dazzled with theoretical insights from high-powered lecturers? Are you given all kinds of quick-fix do's and don'ts for the effective manipulation of your colleagues? Are these pep-talks and personal testimonies and glossy charts on organizational design? No, nothing like that. True, there is some theory along the way; conference staff offer short, pithy talks at strategic intervals—about organizations as open systems, about the need to balance the requirements of an organization's social and technical systems, about the complex nature of work group interaction. The particular issues addressed are shaped by the areas of interest indicated by the conference participants in a pre-registration questionnaire. But a TWC's primary approach to knowing how groups operate is through carefully structured participation—in groups, what else?—Experiential Learning.

What sorts of groups, and what do they do? Several kinds of groups. At the conference I attended, in April 1987 in Toronto, we began conventionally enough with the opportunity to identify with one another as members of particular "entry" groups, categorized initially by type of home organization, then by organizational position and role. In these group settings we were asked to describe the difficulties and opportunities we each faced. Everyone had something to say, and some common themes were quickly identified. In these entry group discussions we had also begun to generate, out of our shared experience, material that would serve as background for the more rigorous group work that we would be getting into. Then, at the end of the opening session, we were assigned to the two different groups that were to absorb so much of our time and thought over the next several days—the "consulting" group and the "search" group.

Dramatically different in function and practice, these two groupings formed the core of the conference experience, the one a highly methodical process with specifically defined roles for each participant, the other a setting of almost unlimited freedom to create and experiment with process itself. Each group met at least twice daily throughout the conference. A consulting group typically consisted of three or four participants, with one member of the conference staff attending each meeting. Its purpose was to permit each participant in turn to work on a real and specifically defined problem from his or her home organization. Members of the consulting group took turns at being consultant, client—the one with the problem—and observer. As consultants we had to learn how to listen, how to question, how to guide our clients to see their problems in a new light; then, as clients, how to widen our perspective on the problems confronting us, to take in the many, often disregarded, so-called external factors that exert such an intangible influence. Often, the shift in perspective gave the client new insight into where the real problem lay. Finally, but just as importantly, as observers we were learning how to see and hear what occurs in the consultative process, and to reflect, "what would I ask at this juncture?" and "how would I respond to that?" This consultative process, an underlying feature of the conference at every turn, became a model for the way an organization can optimize the talents of its people through encouraging participation at all levels. At the end of the week, most participants agreed that the consulting group had been of real benefit in clarifying the group dynamics of the home organization. We would each be returning with a solid, carefully examined, and realistic first step to take in meeting our particular challenges.

But the heart of a Tavistock Working Conference—the most trying and the most rewarding of its experiences—must surely be the search group: seven people, with two conference staff in attendance, thrown together for several hours a day, to encounter in their purest form the turbulence and tribulation that beset a working group. Our task was, first of all, to agree upon a task—to define a collective aim for the seven participants which would contribute towards a better understanding of the issues facing organizations. Much of our time was literally spent in the elusive quest of a consensus on how to spend our time. What issue or issues could we most profitably deal with? How should we deal with them? What kind of outcome should we work towards? Put seven people together in a room— especially seven fairly dynamic individuals from a variety of upper-level positions in large organizations—and tell them to decide on something to do for a week, and you have a recipe for creative turbulence.

But there is more going on here. The other requirement of the search group was that we should periodically suspend operations on The Task (as it quickly became) in order to focus on the workings of the group itself. Like a brain attempting to think about itself thinking, the group was directed to examine its own patterns of interaction. What were the sources and axes of conflict? What was the distribution of roles in the group, between leadership and passivity, concentration and distraction, attempts to dominate and attempts to opt out? How often did the group slip into working as if still addressing The Task, but in reality evading it and allowing all sorts of sidetracking to take place? How many people were being given, or were taking, the chance to pursue their own agenda, at the expense of the collective enterprise? And how far was the group really drawing on the resources of all its members?

However absorbing our own search groups were, group learning did not stop there. Each group at the conference exists in the context of the other groups, and very quickly each begins to wonder how the others manage their time, develop their agendas, do their work. The opportunity for inter-group learning came at mid-week when we were given the task of selecting one of our members to serve as "visitor" to another group. Any method of choosing the visitor—except random selection—was allowed. The process by which we decided upon appropriate selection criteria, and upon which person best met those criteria, sharpened our understanding of how our group typically functioned. Selecting the visitor made it necessary for us to differentiate among ourselves—the activity which, in our experience, groups have the most difficulty doing—in order to choose the best person for the job (a function which, in any setting, has important implications for choosing appropriate leadership).

Selecting the visitor had a second important purpose: it turned our steady inward gaze outward to a consideration of how to relate to the external environment represented by the other group. What was that group like? Did it have any special characteristics which would make one of our members a more suitable visitor than another? What did we want our visitor to look out for and learn about in the other group? Who could we best afford to let go, while still ensuring that the incoming visitor got a worthwhile appreciation of our group?

In the role of visitor, people brought to the eddying turbulence of another group the growing clarity of vision they were developing in their own. Not immediately implicated in the struggle, they could observe with attentive detachment. The presence of the visitor had an effect, in turn, on the group being visited, prompting a degree of self-awareness in the mirror of another's observation. And on returning, the visitors brought with them a modified perspective on the environment of their own groups. Suddenly, there was hardly enough time to explore all of the day's fresh insights into our own and others' behavior. In the evening, we met in plenary session to discuss the dramatically different reactions of each group and each visitor, and to ponder the implications of our learning for similar situations in our home organizations.

The inter-group learning that resulted from selecting and sending a visitor, as well as from being visited, was an exhilarating experience. Relating thus to our immediate external environment further developed our sense of our group as a distinct entity, and increased our confidence in the work we could do together. The two kinds of learning—within the group and between groups—are clearly interactive and mutually reinforcing. A group that has some insight into its own functioning can more readily and coherently respond to the challenges of the external environment, which in turn stimulates the group to a fuller use of its own resources. This phase of the conference was especially exciting, not only because the fruits of our labors within the group were becoming evident, but also because there are so many broad applications of the manifold lessons of inter-group learning.

Because we live in a world of ever-increasing mobility of people, the business of entering and leaving groups effectively is increasingly important, for the group as well as for the individual. It is valuable to be able to go beyond simple stereotyping, to be able to gain a clear understanding of what happens in other groups—to learn how to grasp and respect the differences, but also to discern the underlying similarities common to inter-group functioning. The import of such learnings for an organization is obvious. Put into words, it can even be made to sound dull, clichéd. But the experience itself—which produced in people a new clarity about the self, the workings of the group, and the interactions between groups—is not for a minute dull or clichéd. But to really understand, you really had to be there!

To experience, in a laboratory situation as it were, the dynamics of the complex organism of a work group from inside and outside at the same time— this was the special gift of the conference. We were able, at times, both to feel what was happening in the group, and at the same time to recognize it and, together with the help of the staff members, to identify the pattern at work.

Naming the problem. Such a process bestows a sense of liberation on the participants—we do not need to be trapped so eternally by the knots in which groups entangle themselves. With an enhanced understanding of the ways in which both a group's functioning and the relations between groups may be optimized, we can actually improve a working situation—not just for the sake of the group's effectiveness, but for the well-being and fulfillments of its members considered as whole persons.

I have spoken to several fellow conference participants recently. I was struck by people's enthusiasm for the conference some three months later, and by their readiness to talk about it even while protesting that the experience was hard to communicate. While my sampling didn't elicit reports of world-shaking change, it did reveal, in all but one case, distinctly altered ways of working. One man, after many futile years of attempting to institute a new system of employee communications, has now been given the OK from his senior executive group to develop programs leading to just the kind of system he has desired. Another, an engineer by training who had recently taken a co-ordinator's job in a new manufacturing plant, found the workings of the search group to be an amazing revelation, a marvelous opportunity "to sit there and wonder what it was all about." What seemed to him at the time a privileged sort of learning seems even more so now, as he watches colleagues taking part in a team building exercise conducted within the plant by an external consultant—an exercise espousing some of the same principles of work in groups, but offering almost no opportunity for experiential learning. A chief operating officer of a large government agency felt that the conference gave her a wealth of new resources for managing her organization and for helping her to better understand and respond to her employees' needs. While it was her interest in the management of change that brought her to the conference, one of the most valuable and confirming lessons she took away was the need to live with managed complexity, an ability she thinks essential for senior people in organizations embedded in complicated external environments. The conference lent credence to her intuitive belief that attempts to simplify sometimes in fact constrain and only postpone solutions.

These were just some of the many responses that spoke of gaining a transformed understanding of the processes of work in groups. But one small fantasy has haunted me ever since the conference: what would that work group be like that consisted entirely of Tavistock initiates? Would their combined functioning be a miracle of flexible and efficient cooperation, or would they spend their entire time arguing over what aspect of group process they were actually exhibiting at that moment?

I guess you'd really have to be there.

The Socio-Ecological Setting for Double Task Management

The accelerating rate of change in social, educational, technological, economic and other fields—and, above all, the way these changes interact—has forced communities, organizations and individuals to seek a greater understanding of what is going on within and around them. In learning to cope with the various environments affecting them, all organizations have had to become more open to their environments. In so doing they become more exposed and vulnerable.

Staff specialties of many kinds have been introduced to help regulate open boundaries. There is increasing emphasis on consultation and on collaborative modes that manage both external and internal complexity under conditions of greater interdependence.

Just when the need has become greater for collaboration and interdependence the contradictory tendency to fall back on familiar competencies and structures has asserted itself. This paradox is a more complex issue than just resistance to change. Dealing with it involves acquiring a capability for recognizing and relinquishing valued but outmoded forms of working, while at the same time using insight to face tendencies toward rivalry and envy, which accompany a greater emphasis on interdependence.

In the highly charged environment of today, it is easier to acknowledge such a principle than to act on it. The exploration of options arouses pain, stress or impatience and can result in simplistic rationalizations. This will especially be so when change involves unlearning earlier-held values and ways of thinking and acting. In the process of unlearning those concerned must find within themselves a readiness and capability to understand and work through both conscious and unrecognized attitudes and preconceptions. These are most usefully identified and explored through the experience of examining the ways by which a system is planned, regulated and managed. Working through experiences of this kind has become a sine qua non for those who have to live and work in complex and uncertain environments.

New forms of organizational design do not inevitably result in happier or easier solutions, but rather in a different set of prices and costs, which are often a source of disillusion if their implications are not anticipated. We need to find ways of creating catalytic experiences that provide all concerned with the opportunity to unlearn old approaches and build new ones. Organizations need to develop institutional resources, both personal and organizational, for maintaining and reviewing the new state and for ensuring continuous commitment to it.

Most organizations have been managed in a form whereby the pattern of authority was clear-cut and hierarchical. The environment exercised a much smaller influence: government intervened to a smaller degree; unions had less impact; change was recognizable but less turbulent. Schools maintained their "monastic" walls; hospitals were powers unto themselves as were the professions and universities. Today government intervenes increasingly. Unions, consumers, competitors and suppliers clamor for attention. The technological explosion, and other forms of social, international and economic change impinge on all institutions. Originally, few advisers were required internally.

To help interpret and cope with growing external problems—with all their internal derivatives—far more specialists are now employed. This means that management, both now and for the future, must reconcile institutional needs and environmental forces to a much greater extent than ever before.

This is a tremendous change. Not only does one spend much of one's time and effort considering external affairs, there is the need for continuously re-educating professionals, specialist advisers and managers to ensure the viability of the enterprise.

The model of a relatively closed system is being replaced by a relatively open one (Bridger, 1980a). Subordinates manage their own environment to a greater extent. We have to learn to change from the classic family tree type of organizational structure and authority to a new form of boundary management: the management of external uncertainty and internal interdependence. Continuing this process means that erstwhile subordinates become colleagues whose commitment is required to share the accountable leader's efforts at achieving group objectives. This development can be regarded as an operational definition of participation, which differs from an older pattern of delegating tasks by separating off defined areas of work. Thus the management of complexity and interdependence is more important for today and tomorrow than are the simpler prescriptions for leadership and management on which we have been brought up. The open-system model includes the special feature of a greater network component to fulfill the control and coordination function.

The key organizational areas of competence—such as control and coordination, planning, decision making and action—demand that institutional needs and tasks, and environmental forces and resources, be reconciled to a much greater extent than ever before. What we have called the "accountable authority" has had to develop ways of working that differ from those appropriate for the earlier model. Some of these changes will show a difference in degree, others will be different in kind. For example, giving and taking advice was a **desirable** characteristic of closed-system managing; it is **essential** in open systems. In a closed system, subordinates are more concerned about minding their own shares of the "business"; in open systems they manage their own environment to a much greater extent—throughout the organization—while relinquishing (as do their superiors) relevant control of planning, decisions and actions for levels below them. Thus, the range of organizational forms has widened considerably from an almost exclusive concentration of the classic family tree type of organizational structure to various combinations of the first and second models.

A set of critical changes involved in moving from a relatively closed to a relatively open system is set out in Table 1. These changes are of such magnitude that they constitute a paradigm shift. The internal courses and external workshops described in this paper have been designed to assist organi-

TABLE I   Changes in Roles and Functions

Change from (relatively closed system)	Change toward (relatively open system)
Control and coordination retained in the superior managerial role	Control and coordination retained in superior role for policy, but shared with relevant staff for operational goals
Prescriptive tasks for subordinates with some delegated authority	Decision making and discretion devolved to relevant staff when responsible for the action involved (i.e., executive and consultative mode)
Managing mostly within the confines of the system	Managing at the boundary (i.e., reconciling external and internal resources and forces)
Allocation of jobs to persons and "knowing one's place"	More interdependence in working groups, but more anxiety about one's identity and independence
Managing to eliminate conflict	Managing the conflict by exploring its nature together
Accountability and responsibility located together	Accountability and responsibility may be separate
Single accountability	Multiple accountability
Hierarchial assessment and appraisal (often uncommunicated)	Self-review and assessment plus mutual appraisal of performance and potential
Career and personal development dependent on authority	Mobility of careers and boundary crossing for development, greater responsibility for own development
Power rests with those occupying certain roles and having high status in hierarchy	Power rests with those having control over uncertainty
Finite data and resources utilized toward building a plan	Nonfinite data and resources leading toward a planning process, maintaining a choice of direction in deciding among options
Periodic review and tendency to extrapolate (projection forward)	Control and planning requiring continuous review, prospection as well as projection forward
Risk related to an information gap	Risk related to information overload
Long term/short term based on operational plans (periodic)	Long term/short term based on continuous adaptive planning process
Concentrating on "getting on with the job" and "trouble-shooting" activities	"Suspending business" at relevant times to explore work systems and ways of working
Difficulty with "equality" and "freedom"	Difficulty with "fraternity"

zations in making this shift. They will do so only so far as large numbers of individuals within them make it in themselves.

Training in a form which models the new needs can accelerate the change process. In my view, training of the appropriate kind is an essential requirement for making the transition. For such a purpose it needs first of all to be jointly worked out by all concerned. It then has to be capable of rapid diffusion and ultimately to be carried out without consultants. There is not all the time in the world to get on with this task. It has, in fact, become urgent.

References

Bion, W.R. and J. Rickman. 1943. "Intra-Group Tensions in Therapy." *Lancet*, 2:678–81.

Bridger, H. 1980a. "The Kinds of 'Organizational Development' Required for Working at the Level of the Whole Organization Considered as an Open System." In *Organisation Development in Europe*, Vol. IA, edited by K. Trebesch. Bern, Switzerland: Paul Haupt Verlag.

———. 1980b. "The Relevant Training and Development of People for OD Roles." *Organisation Development in Europe*, Volume:IA, edited by K. Trebesch. Bern, Switzerland: Paul Haupt Verlag.

———. 1987. "Courses and Working Conferences as Transitional Learning Institutions." In *Training, Theory and Practice*, edited by W. Brendan Reddy and C.C. Henderson. Washington, D.C.: NTL Institute/University Associates.

Emery, F.E. and E.L. Trist. 1965. "The Causal Texture of Organizational Environments." *Human Relations*, 18:21–32.

———. 1973. *Towards a Social Ecology*. London and New York: Plenum Press.

Emery, M. and F. Emery. 1978. "Searching: For New Directions, In New Ways . . . For New Times." In *Management Handbook for Public Administrators*, edited by J.W. Sutherland. New York: Van Nostrand Reinhold.

Herbert, E.L. and E.L. Trist. 1953. "The Institution of an Absent Leader by a Students' Discussion Group." *Human Relations*, 6:215–48.

Hertzberg, F. 1966. *Work and the Nature of Man*. New York: World Press.

Higgin, G. and H. Bridger. 1964. "The Psycho-Dynamics of an Inter-Group Experience." *Human Relations*, 17:391–446.

Jaques, E. 1951. *The Changing Culture of a Factory*. London: Tavistock Publications. Reissued 1987, New York: Garland.

Lewin, K. 1951. *Field Theory and Social Science*. New York: Harper.

Low, K.B. and H. Bridger, 1979. "Small Group Work in Relation to Management Development." In *Training in Small Groups*, edited by B. Babington-Smith and B.A. Farrell.

McGregor, D. 1960. *The Human Side of Enterprise*. New York: McGraw-Hill.

Morgan, G. 1988. *Riding the Waves of Change*. San Francisco: Jossey-Bass.

Rice, A.K. 1965. *Learning for Leadership: Interpersonal and Intergroup Relations*. London: Tavistock Publications.

Selznick, P. 1957. *Leadership in Administration*. Evanston, Ill.: Row Peterson.

Trist, E.L. and C. Sofer. 1959. *Exploration in Group Relations*. Leicester: Leicester University Press.

Wertheimer, M. 1945. *Productive Thinking*. Revised edition 1959. New York: Harper.

Gurth Higgin and Gunnar Hjelholt

Action Research in Minisocieties*

In the first part of this paper Higgin describes some aspects of the third minisociety sponsored by Gunnar Hjelholt of Denmark (Hjelholt, 1972). This is followed by an account by Hjelholt of more recent work in the field.

Gurth Higgin

The distinctive quality of the minisociety is that it allows experimental behavior, mutual exploration and confrontation between groups. Since the groups make up a microcosm of society, the themes that engage them and the dynamics that arise between them can throw new light on societal problems. The main theme illustrated here is the confrontation between the demand for personal liberation from the alienation resulting from the conventional demands of society and the opposing fear of chaos and social breakdown.† As this confrontation was acted out, the two groups most directly involved tended to force each other into self-caricature and out of communication with the other and to induce a growing paralysis or disruption in the other groups in the community. A necessary condition for the developments between the two confronting groups was that one of these other groups had to become highly visible in the community as passive sufferers.

Predetermined structure and procedures are kept to a minimum in the minisociety. The purpose of this is to minimize the possibility that what emerges may be determined by instructions, structure or predictions. Similarly, in writing this report I have attempted to let the data create their own understandings. So often in our writing we social scientists give so much attention to explaining and supporting our concepts about human experience that the human beings and the quality of their experiences are barely visible.

In a minisociety about fifty people and half a dozen social scientists get

---

*An extension of the original by Higgin in A. Clark (Editor), *Experimenting with Organizational Life*. New York and London: Plenum, 1975.

†Other minisocieties have explored different themes, such as the generation gap, societal power and the changing roles of men and women.

together—in this case on a peninsula in a lake in southern Sweden—and spend a fortnight living as a community running its own affairs. The community in this minisociety had children as young as four years old, and adults up to sixty. There were senior professional people and unemployed youths, industrial managers and trade unionists. There was a group of nine American students accompanied by one of their tutors. An industrial manager came from England, as did one of the social scientists. Everybody else was Scandinavian, mainly from Denmark. The only thing everyone at the minisociety had in common was that they wanted to be there. Nobody was sent.

Setting it up was very simple. The participants were sorted out beforehand into groups that were as much alike as possible. There were seven groups. One contained the American students; another, people from the helping professions—a doctor, a social agency administrator, a dentist, a personnel manager, the American university tutor, and so on; another was from a clinic/community center in Copenhagen; and there were two mixed groups—housewives, workers, industrial managers, and some complete families who formed two neighborhood groups. The sixth group consisted of the children of the community and the seventh, the sponsoring social scientists.

This mix reflected fairly accurately what the letter of invitation had said. The minisociety would try to

create a society in miniature, where the participants are confronted with other relevant groups from our ordinary society . . . [This situation] gives the possibility for investigating and experimenting with social roles in the small group as well as in the bigger society. We believe that this process of confrontation will make the participants more open to the forces at work in this temporary society and thereby enable them to work constructively with the problems of ordinary society.

This was as near to a statement of "theoretical approach and objective" as Hjelholt and his colleagues wanted to go—after all, if people want to get leave and even some financial support from an organization to go to something like this there has to be a "purpose." Actually, what Hjelholt would have preferred to say was simply, "If you are interested, just bring your interest and curiosity along and let's all see where we get together."

Hjelholt and his colleagues did not want to test theoretical hypotheses. That way we tend to see only things that have to do with our hypotheses and we are likely to miss other things. They thought that it would be much better to let everybody undergo the experience and then try to understand it together. That way everybody knows as much about it as anybody else. There are no special experts, because who knows who can sense most accurately what it all means?

The only rule in the community—accepting it was a condition of coming—

was that everyone would participate in any research activities that were asked for. These activities were ways of getting information about what was happening, with the object of letting everybody know. They were seen as a contribution to the community's efforts to understand what was going on. The research included the gathering of information about where people were living, where they were eating and how many names of people in other groups everybody knew from time to time. It also included pictures that groups drew of themselves and others; lists of words describing other groups and the reactions of these groups to them; and some measurements of people's feelings about interpersonal and intergroup distances at different times. The information was given back to the community as it became available. Some of it caused great interest. Some of it was ignored.

With a community living like this for a couple of weeks with none of the usual community rules applying—apart from the research sessions, everyone was free to do what he liked, when he liked and with whom he liked—all sorts of things, usual and unusual, can happen.

On the Sunday night, the minisociety started. After the groups had spent a little time together they were asked to give themselves names. Of the two neighborhood groups, one called themselves the *Radishes* and the other the *Green Lases and Pjalters* (green rags and tatters), a reference to the *Threepenny Opera*. The children made an acrostic of their names—*Anpekedoch-meka*. They did not pretend it had any meaning or was even easily pronounced. The social scientists were sitting next to the children at this time and hearing what they were doing, did the same. They produced *Hyheph*. They, however, claimed this was an obscure Greek word, the meaning of which they had temporarily forgotten, but would tell the community when they remembered. They never did. The group of helping professionals called themselves the *Association*, the American undergraduates the *Dilemma* and the youth group the *Nine Veiled Hallucinations*. There were, in fact, only eight real people in the latter group at the time; the ninth was a vague but friendly wraith called Thomas (*thom* means empty in Danish).

The Hyhephs had set a timetable for the first three days. Time was allocated for community sessions, for group sessions and for community exploration. Together these sessions filled 40 percent of the time. During this time individuals or groups could do whatever they chose to find out more about the community and its physical surroundings. A Hyheph sat in with each group during their group sessions as a consultant. The Hyhephs did not like this term much, but it was better than leader or trainer. For these three days, Gunnar Hjelholt ran the community sessions; for the whole time he was the community's contact with household staff and outside society.

The Möckelsnäs peninsula is about half a mile across and stretches several miles out into the lake. It is mainly wooded with a few fields. About halfway along it is an old manor house on the lakeside with a couple of dormitories attached to it; the Association, the Dilemma and the Hyhephs were living here. The other groups were in various smaller houses in the woods, the farthest being about a kilometer away. The manor house, which became known as the Main Building, had several public rooms, and at this time everyone was having meals there.

During the community exploration time on the first day, the Association decided to call on the Hallucinations at their house. Nobody was aware of it at the time, but looking back we can see that it was this meeting, sought by the Association and welcomed by the Hallucinations, that started the division between the different life-styles of these two groups. This was to become the pivotal theme for nearly everyone in the community.

At the meeting there was lively, serious, but not very personal discussion about, on the one hand, the need for expressiveness and spontaneity for the individual in the modern world and, on the other, the need for social responsibility, control, and structure. After a time the Hallucinations produced chillums and offered their visitors a puff of marijuana. They explained that this was their house and they would like to show their visitors true hospitality by sharing something that was important to them. They said it was not necessary for their visitors to have it, it was merely an offer. Most of the Association members tried it, but few liked it.

In discussion afterward, the Hallucinations decided that they were aware of both the Association's tolerance of their pot smoking and their suppressed disapproval. This discussion revealed the test-out aspect of the offering. The Hallucinations were saying, "Are you genuinely interested in people so that you will want to know us as we are? Or have you got a block against the things we believe in—drugs, spontaneity, expressiveness—so that you can't see us as people?" A genuine acceptance of others, even those with different habits and beliefs, was for them the most important quality in people. Their test-out of the Association members was typically simple and direct—no tact or diplomacy, no chance for an evasive or equivocal response. Suspicion was both their curse and their shield.

Meanwhile, back in the Main Building, the Association had settled for tolerance with distance, a position they stuck to throughout. Even when things got a bit sharp on the value confrontation front toward the close, the Association, although it became the most powerful group, never picked on the Hallucinations as a group or as individuals. But the two groups never met again.

Nevertheless, during the next week or so, the different styles of these two groups provided the two extremes for a range of beliefs about personal liberation and social responsibility. Exploring these positions, through experience more than through talk, became a preoccupation shared by almost everyone in the community. Other preoccupations were also evident, of course, but to some degree everyone got involved in the liberation question. For some it became all-absorbing. It turned out to be a commonly shared worry, not far below the surface.

If a person or a group has a particular quality that interests other people or other groups, these others can make that person or group show more of that quality, until it becomes their predominant characteristic. The concepts of the role offer and the preemptive role offer capture this process. Part of the process of interaction between individuals, groups and even social classes is an attempt by each party to force the other to choose the role that is desired by the first party. Selective reward and punishment is one means of achieving this. A more powerful technique is selective confirmation or disconfirmation of the reality belief of the other. This process can be most clearly seen when there is a large difference between the parties in respect to power, prestige, experience or education—as between parents and children, group leader and group members, teachers and taught. It can lead to mystification, the result of an other-enforced denial by the weaker party of what experientially he knows is real. Much group process and therapeutic interpretation has this quality, usually justified as an attempt to get the group or the patient to accept "reality." When a more powerful party ruthlessly exploits these processes, the weaker party finds the choice of role effectively preempted (Higgin, 1973).

The Hallucinations and the Association got caught like this. You have to be pretty liberal, or even radical, to come to such a way-out thing as a minisociety. Yet the members of the Association became more and more responsible, reliable and formal as the days went by. Several of them remarked in wonder at how organized and structure-dominated the group and they themselves had become. The same process influenced the Hallucinations. They had not been so completely disconnected from all the formal procedures of the community as they increasingly became at Möckelsnäs. They lived in unworried, easy irresponsibility and open, relaxed contact with all, showing spontaneous jollity and chatter—also equally genuine depression, even despair at times, but this was less public. The message of their behavior was, "What you feel now, you express; tomorrow will look after itself."

These positions were taken by the two groups mainly because the other groups in the community had a rehearsal script for the liberation of man in society. They wanted to experience the evidence about it. They needed to interact both with the liberated and with those who questioned liberation. They wanted to try being liberated, and to find out what the unbelievers did to them when they tried it. They wanted the liberated role of the Hallucinations, so they exaggerated it. They wanted the questioning, responsible role of the Association, so they blew that up, too.

These differences became increasingly clear as the days passed. As a group, the Association were responsible, consistent and rational. The members attended community meetings dutifully, usually with clear, agreed statements about various issues. They had spokesmen to state their position, which was done fluently, with rational argument and often wit. They lived tidily, each in his or her own room, and went punctually to meals and meetings. After a few days they announced they had changed their name. They were to be known henceforth as the *Establishment*. They said that they had thought of this name on the first Sunday night, but were not quite sure enough of themselves to take it. Now, after several days' experience of the community, they felt they could appropriately do so.

The Hallucinations, by contrast, became more communal among themselves, but less active in the formal life of the community. They moved their mattresses from the bedrooms in their house and put them all in one room, in which they all slept. They moved the furniture, except for a very low table, out of one downstairs room and lived almost exclusively in that and the communal sleeping room. They attended community meetings less and less. At the same time, members of the community became increasingly interested in them and their house became an open house for visitors. At any time of the day or night people would drop in. They were always accepted and not so much invited as expected to join in anything that was going on—eating, talking, doing nothing, smoking pot or whatever.

The way the two groups reacted to the community was also quite distinct. Early on, the Association/Establishment decided to do something to fill the need for a community bar. They took over a cellar room in the Main Building and sold cans of beer that they bought wholesale. It was open each night for all comers. The enterprise was efficient and showed a profit which was paid back into community funds. At one point, the Hallucinations thought they would like to do something for the others. They settled on drawing little colored pictures and designs and giving one to everybody. This project started with enthusiasm, but after a few days petered out. They never got more than about halfway through. This was typical of all their activities. They acted only on impulse; they would do what they wanted to do when they were in the mood. Once the mood passed, they dropped it, only to pick it up if the mood returned. They felt no guilt or worry about unfinished jobs. Their position was quite explicit about this. They considered that if you do something from duty it has no value; it is only good if you want to do it, so that there is something of yourself in it.

As time went on, the Hallucinations increasingly presented themselves to the community as the liberated ones. They took less part in the formal life of the community. At times only one of them, or even none, would be present at community meetings. They did not visit any other group, except occasionally as individuals. But they had a lot of informal contact both through their visitors and through dancing, talking and drinking in the Main Building in the evenings. They smoked more pot, now bought with the housekeeping money, and mixed it up with other things. One night one of them had so much of a mixture, including alcohol, which had already been identified as the Establishment drug, that he became ill and had to go to the hospital. This caused real concern in the community. There was considerable relief when he returned none the worse after twenty-four hours.

While the difference between the two groups was increasing—they were beginning to display a caricatured version of their starting positions—the rest of the community was feeling the mounting tension of the silent confrontation. The children's group had broken up quite early. Most had joined their parents, though several had experimented with joining other groups without their parents. The two neighborhood groups were also breaking up. They found they could not agree among themselves. The Green Lases and Pjalters were wandering around the community rather like a band of gypsies. The Radishes had split into two; the new group was a family that called themselves the *Pearl Divers*. Both main groups seemed to find these solutions satisfactory.

It was the Dilemmas who were feeling the most strain. They found they had given themselves an apt name on that first Sunday night. Being university students, but young, lively, and critical and, further, an American group alone among Scandinavians, they found themselves emotionally torn and confused by the developing situation. They were drawn to the Establishment, which represented the university from which they very much wanted to acquire the skills and knowledge education could give them. But they spontaneously identified with the Hallucinations' position; it represented the youthful, expressive, liberated life and rejection of the square world. This tension immobilized them. They stayed together, indeed grew tighter as a group, but found their internal life increasingly stressful and confusing. The community recognized this, and, as with the Establishment and the Hallucinations, used it.

When you want to experiment with an issue as exciting but also as frightening as the liberation/responsibility dilemma, you cannot do it if the usual fears and worries it provokes in you get in the way. So why not get someone else to do the worrying for you while you get on with it? This is where the Dilemmas came in. With the main roles fixed and the action about to begin, the need was felt for a role to absorb the worry and tension, to free others so that they could feel their way into what was happening. The Dilemmas, already feeling something of the tension of the confrontation anyway, were handed this role. They became the *Ophelia* (Higgin and Bridger, 1964).

The community kept the Dilemmas locked in their confusion; they did not want them to break out. It was discovered by many, and especially by the Dilemmas, that being in the Main Building was not a privilege: it was prison.

Privilege was running your own living and eating arrangements in your own way and in your own time on twenty crowns a day. Even the freedom to have an unmade bed or not to clean up your house was felt to be a privilege. Several times the Dilemmas asked for a move from the Main Building; but they never managed it. The Establishment, although less keen on a change, did move as did two of the Hyhephs. By contrast, the Dilemmas were kept against their will in the regimen of the household staff on fifty crowns a day.

Yet everybody liked the Dilemmas. The information collected on the last day showed that the community felt closer to the Dilemmas than to any other group. They were sitting in the middle of the community with the other groups at varying positions and distances around them. Fortunately they sat tight; the center held, though at some cost to its members. It was like calling in the New World to facilitate the rebalancing of the Old.

At the community meeting held on the Wednesday of the second week the Establishment announced they had changed their name again. They were now the *Saints*. This led to some discussion about fantasy in the community, and another reversal of perception seemed to be occurring. Up till then people had believed that the hippie/dropout position of the Hallucinations was a wild, fantastic, if fascinating, way to go on and that the ways of the Establishment represented sober, responsible reality. But now that the Establishment had become the Saints, people began to wonder. After all, to call themselves Saints was a pretty fantastic idea, a bit big-headed too, even a bit mad. People now wondered if the Hallucinations were not closer to reality and if the Saints were not dominated by fantasy. After all, the Hallucinations in their openness and their ups and downs, their gaiety and moroseness, were getting close to what was really going on inside them as individuals and as a group. Their behavior was real. But the structure of roles and rules the Saints lived by was made up of "idea" things, just as fantasies are. And how close was their responsible behavior to what they were really feeling and thinking inside themselves? Some of the Saints wrinkled their brows and wondered about this, but as a group they did not think much of it.

In the community meeting on the last day there was much talk about the events of the minisociety and especially those of the last few days. By this time the community was beginning to recognize one of the main rehearsal scripts it had been working on and the roles that different groups had taken in it. Few people were very sure any more of their definitions of what was real, what was fantasy and what was mad; but they were much more aware of the amount of fantasy about reality that was around. It was felt that the confrontation between the Saints and the Hallucinations was real enough and that it had set off some actual power moves.

The Saints seemed to have seen themselves as Saints and Saviors toward the end. They behaved as if they thought the liberation experimenting had gone far enough. They seemed to feel it was time they exerted themselves to stop the irresponsibility, the self-expressive but undisciplined activities, the uncontrolled and indecisive meetings and the general air of chaos. They would save the community and bring it back to its senses in time for its members to go home to reality. They blamed the Hyhephs for letting things develop as far as they had. The Hyhephs were the initiators of the minisociety and at the beginning had been its establishment that ran things. They had then resigned and let anarchy loose.

From this story of what happened, it would seem as if some people might have gone home, especially the Saints and the Hallucinations, with no more than confirmation of the beliefs they came with. They would not have explored the liberation/responsibility theme, in the sense of getting to know it better and of feeling a little differently about it by getting inside other people's experience of it. But it could be said that everyone participated in the liberation rehearsal script by making different contributions to it. For example, the Dilemmas, like Ophelia, participated by taking the strain so that the action could go on. The Saints contributed by taking the role of devil's advocate; several of the group expressed surprise at the stuffy position they had adopted as they felt their way into opposition and experienced how the liberated reacted to this.

The social distance measurements done on the last day showed that the Dilemmas were the group that the community felt closest to. They were clearly in the middle. Of the six other groups, the Hallucinations considered that there were only two they felt closer to than the Saints; the Saints felt there was no group they were closer to than the Hallucinations. Moreover, the Hallucinations, who had done their job of exemplifying liberation, felt they had moved closer to the community as a whole than any other group.

Gunnar Hjelholt

Since the 1970 conference which Gurth Higgin described, large minisocieties or workshops, lasting from a week to a fortnight, have been set up in Austria, Germany, Sweden and England (Spink, 1974). The largest had 14 different groups and 140 participants and took place in a partly abandoned village. The aim is to provide participants with the opportunity to encounter the other systems which are relevant for them in their social life and which play a role in their identity self-image. At the same time they can explore and experiment with options in this microcosmos of contemporary society. This holds true for the social scientists as well.

Two variations have come out of the ordinary minisociety as some groups came into focus. Gurth Higgin vividly describes the Hallucinations and the Establishment, the one being the "drop-outs" from society, the other the professional group which had to take the stuffy, responsible role.

The Hallucinations came from a Danish Youth Clinic. The movements in the minisociety where they as a group drew toward society continued after the conference. The workshop had had a therapeutic effect; a reconnection with society had taken place. It led the Youth Clinic and other clinics to take a hard look at their treatment philosophy. A few clinics sent groups to subsequent minisocieties. But the Copenhagen one arranged a series of special mini-societies run on the same principles as the original workshop: separate housing for the groups, communal decision-making about time and money, staff obligation of instant feed-back to the temporary community about what was happening.

The one I took part in had eight groups: two current client-groups, two groups of old and young employees (helpers), a group of old alcoholics, a group of students from a kindergarten college, a mixed group of outsiders, and one comprising staff members and guests.

The drama in these therapeutic minisocieties comes from the difficulties the "helpers" have in redefining their role. Helpers seem to need "clients" and do their utmost to keep clients in a dependent, passive state. If not enough other groups are there for the clients to identify with or conceal themselves in, the helpers tend either to drive the clients out of the conference or—if that is not possible—take over some of the symptoms of the clients: excessive drinking, withdrawal from society, etc.

One staff member, a psychiatrist, wrote, "I am sure the mini-society can be a treatment model which one ought to explore further as I see it as being an extension of the therapeutic community and much better in respect of making the traditional personnel redundant."

The other variation of the minisociety has been focussing on groups of "professional experts" and providing them with an opportunity to explore their social identity and contributions to society. How was it that the "Establishment" became so stuffy, a caricature of themselves as individuals, when they acted as a group? And why in contemporary society do professional associations seem to become unions fighting for power and defending status and neglect their function or mission as social systems in society?

Here the example of exploring the role, attitude and relationship of "professionals" inside a 1982 minisociety in Sweden is the best documented (Asplund, 1983). The groupings in five houses in a holiday resort were: economists, psychologists, priests, unskilled laborers on social security—and one "staff" person, a pensioner. In this temporary society it was not surprising that the fight for the souls happened between clergy and economists with an uneasy alliance between clergy and psychologists. The "proletariat" had the passive, suffering role never getting their proper share of the capital, money and time.

To a large extent the three groups fought their battles on their own territories. The common meeting hall, where decisions were supposed to take place and grievances and research findings could be discussed was used only with great reluctance. As soon as possible it was abandoned—the interpretation being that here the power (a fantasy bear) resided which might show the groups that their self-image and their image of others had to be changed.

There have been other variations of the minisociety concept. Since 1976 the Universities of Leyden and Utrecht in Holland have run conferences for their students which are influenced by the minisociety idea as well as the Tavistock-Leicester conferences. Here the staff act in a professional role as facilitators of the learning process and the main purpose seems to be an educational one (Prein, 1983). Other conferences of this sort have been run in France, Belgium and Germany, but here the underlying theoretical work has been that of Max Pages (1973) and George Lapassades (1967) regarding flexible structures and the repressive character of institutions (Hjelholt, 1976a).

Recently (1987/88), the minisociety concept has also been used to prepare a group for living together. Fifty families about to move into a new housing area held a minisociety to see if they could get along and what sort of problems they would encounter. After having occupied their houses for eight months they repeated the experience in order to further improve relations in the neighborhood. Here the participants' ages ranged from the newborn to 80 year old pensioners.

The minisocieties are an attempt to combine the reality of the Northfield Experiment as described by Bridger (1946) with the temporary workshops or conferences based on Bion's (1961) and Lewin's (1951) theories.

The focus is on the relationship between different social systems or roles. The systems are kept together through the necessity of handling capital—money and time—and by each system being defined by the other systems present. The community meetings provide the forum for handling practical and emotional issues in the conference and help participants to understand the ways in which they and their system handle the anxiety of being confronted in practice with its social identity and the other systems they influence.

The role of the staff is different from the usual human relations conferences. It is more in line with the role of staff in the therapeutic community—one of many contributing systems. For many social scientists it is difficult to give up the privilege of being the expert and outside the happenings. Here we are not different from other professional groups. Several staff groups have split or retreated into writing large reports for their university.

The analogy which most often comes to mind is the Shakespearian drama.

Theatrical expression is one of the often used ways of indicating changes and bringing to the attention of the minisociety what is going on. Weddings or burial ceremonies might be held, kings crowned, duels fought. The actors are representatives impersonating the group feeling.

The dramas can take their theme from issues inside the conference— marriage between the youngest member of one group and the oldest member of another—or from society outside. In an Austrian workshop (Hjelholt, 1976b) one group took the name of one of the estates, *Peasants*, and quickly named the other groups *Citizens, Nobility* and *Church*. The workshop, with moves from one group to another, then started to re-enact German-Austrian history from 1530 to 1930. The last 50 years, with their traumatic effect on Austrians, could not be handled, because a good deal of the former "Citizens" left the mini-society before it was over.

The workshop can also be a stage for rehearsals of impending events whose advent is sensed. The small group of students in the 1968 spring minisociety tried out the occupation of a house, locking others out and making overtures to the workers to join them in a revolution. Later in the autumn, the students' revolution with occupation of the University of Copenhagen took place.

The minisociety model plunges the participants, including the social scientists, into the psycho-dynamics of social systems, a field which—with dire consequences for society—has been avoided by most researchers.

From the point of view of action research, the experience of the minisociety highlights the difficulty of the social scientist acting in multiple roles; he is researcher, consultant, and participant. At the least, the other participants have a dual role. They are at the same time exploring their own group relations in a protected environment and attempting to understand how they can be reconciled with broad societal constraints. Drawing all participants into the collaborative tasks of collecting and interpreting data is an attempt to meet these problems. Whatever internal arrangements are arrived at, the minisociety emerges as a useful arena for action research, focused, in this case, on the conflict between the desire for personal liberation and the need for social order.

References

Asplund, C.J., R. Issal, K. Jonnegard, M. Lindqvist, L. Sjoberg and N.G. Storhagen. 1983. *Minisamhallet (The Minisociety).* Reports from University of Vaxsjo, Sweden. Series 1: Economics and Politics, No. 3.

Bion, W.R. 1961. *Experiences in Groups and Other Papers.* London: Tavistock Publications; New York: Basic Books.

Bridger, H. 1946. "The Northfield Experiment." *Bulletin of the Menninger Clinic*, 10:71–76.

Hjelholt, G. 1972. "Group Training in Understanding Society: The Minisociety." *Interpersonal Development*, 3:140–51.

———. 1976a. "Der Schlussel (The Key)." *Gruppendynamik*, 7:18–22.

———. 1976b. "Europe is Different: Boundary and Identity as Key Concepts." In *European Contributions to Organization Theory*, edited by G. Hofstede and M.S. Kassem. Amsterdam: Van Gorcum.

Lapassades, G. 1967. *Groupes, organisations et institutions*. Paris: Gauthier-Villars.

Lewin, K. 1951. *Field Theory and Social Science*. New York: Harper.

Pages, M. 1973. "Das Laboratorium mit Flexiblen Strukturen (Laboratory with Flexible Structures)." *Gruppendynamik*, 4:18–26.

Prein, H. 1983. "Improving the Quality of Life in a Large Training Conference." Paper presented at the Third Organization Development World Congress, Dubrovnik, Yugoslavia.

Spink, P. 1974. *Early Thoughts from the Minisociety*. Paper presented to the British Psychological Society's Conference. London: Tavistock Institute Document 931.

Eric J. Miller and A.K. Rice

Task and Sentient Systems and Their Boundary Controls*

Foreword (by E.J.M.)

What follows is a lightly edited version of the concluding chapters of a book by the late Kenneth Rice and myself, first published in 1967: *Systems of Organization: The Control of Task and Sentient Systems*, pp. 251–69. It extended Rice's previous applications of open system theory to the study of organizations (Rice 1958, 1963).

In this book we defined a *task system* as comprising the "system of activities . . . required to complete the process of transforming an intake into an output . . . plus the human and physical resources required to perform the activities." A *sentient system* or group is one that "demands and receives loyalty from its members." "An effective sentient system relates members of an enterprise to each other and to the enterprise in ways that are relevant to the skills and experience required for task performance"; it also provides its members with some defense against anxiety.

In the body of the book we drew on material from our own action research and consultancy in a range of enterprises in order to explore several themes: transactions across enterprise boundaries (sales, dry-cleaning); disentanglement of coincident task boundaries (family businesses); temporary and transitional task systems (design and construction of a new steel-works, research institutions, airlines); and the elimination of organizational boundaries within enterprises (a computer-controlled production system in a steel-works).

Most concepts and theories of organization had been based on production activities. In the open system framework these are "conversion systems," lying between the "import" and "export" activities of the enterprise. The Tavistock Institute's early applications of the concept of the *socio-technical system* had been in similar settings and there was a strong interest in seeking joint optimization of the social and technical. Rice's experiments in textile

*A reproduction of the two last chapters in *Systems of Organization*. London: Tavistock Publications, 1967.

weaving fell into that category. But many of our examples concerned activity systems, such as sales, which cross the boundaries of the enterprise, and also temporary and transitional systems, such as construction or research, where teams are brought together for a specific task: when that is completed they are disbanded and redeployed in new configurations. These suggested that the primary work-group concept of coincident task- and sentient-group organization is not essential to provide the means through which the individual is affiliated to the enterprise. Obversely, if the individual is exposed to frequent changes in work-group membership, in role, or in organization, then he needs some relatively more secure and enduring affiliation to relate him to the task of the enterprise. He must therefore occupy at least two work-oriented roles—one in a task system and the other in a sentient system. In a research enterprise, for example, sentient needs may be provided by a relatively permanent scientific or professional base, from which the individual is assigned to transient project teams.

Conceptually and practically, therefore, it is necessary to create three forms of organization: to control task performance; to ensure people's commitment to enterprise objectives; and to regulate relations between task and sentient systems. These requirements are inherent in temporary and transitional systems of activity; and the corresponding project-type organization provides the most appropriate basis for a general theory of organization.

That is one major theme running through the book. The second is that such a model requires the precise definition and control of the boundaries of activity systems and of groups. These two themes are taken up again, with other examples, in the concluding chapters.

Task and Sentient Systems

TASKS PRECLUDING COINCIDENCE OF TASK AND SENTIENT BOUNDARIES

If a task system, and hence a task group, straddles an enterprise boundary, it cannot be contained within the organizational boundaries of the enterprise; discrepancy between task and sentient systems is therefore inevitable. More importantly, if managing systems and their accompanying control and service functions are modelled on factory production systems, they tend to give hierarchies that are too simple and too inflexible to fit the complexities of such task performance. The representatives of a sales force and establishments in the dry-cleaning industry illustrated this part of our thesis.

The organization of professional service could also be considered within the same conceptual framework. The characteristic feature of a professional relationship is that it is made between a client (or patient) who wants help and a professional person who gives it, or tries to do so. The activity system through which the help is given has a boundary that encompasses professional and client. On the one side, the client has to rely on the skill, experience and integrity of the professional to do what is necessary; on the other, the professional has to forswear exploitation of the dependent relationship involved. Implicit in the professional-client relationship is the possibility of failure, with corresponding anxieties, conscious or unconscious, that the client's problems may be intractable or the professional's skills inadequate. The more there is at stake, the more intense the confused and ambivalent feelings associated with the dependence are likely to be.

The sentient groups to which professional men and women commit themselves and from which they draw their support are the professional associations and their related learned societies. Membership is a qualification to practice. And the sanction to practice those professions that are concerned with the lives, liberties and property of their clients has, in our society, the force of law. Society, in effect, not only defines the boundaries of the task system and of the sentient system, and separates them, but also, through the sentient system, controls professional conduct in the task system.

Attempts that have been made to devise organizations based on person-centered task systems have also ignored the more general case of the task system that is temporary and transitional. We used building, research and air transport as our examples. The theater provides another. In the theater the task group is the cast and other staff assembled for a play. While the play is running, task group and sentient group are, or should be, coincident; but actors have "the profession" as their superordinate sentient group, to which they can commit themselves whether acting or "resting." Without the profession and the regard in which it is held, both by its members and by the public, it is doubtful if the theater could survive.

NATURAL COINCIDENCE

In the family business, by definition, task and sentient boundaries must coincide. But such a form of organization requires for its effectiveness conditions of stable equilibrium. In conditions of social, economic and technical change, commitment to the one group, the family, can not only distort judgments about task decisions, but can also lead to disruption of sentient-group relationships. In addition, as the group increases in size, it is less able to provide either satisfactory relationships or adequate self-regulation.

The great religious institutions are also examples of enterprises with coincidence of task and sentient boundaries. A church is characterized by its members' collective belief in a deity or system of deities on whom they can depend, and also in some kind of life after death as well. The sentient system of a church, to which its members commit themselves, is therefore unbounded, in that it has no ending. In the spiritual sense there is no export system. Yet many of the tasks undertaken by the church are performed in activity systems that must have a finite life, if only because in human terms death is an end. As religious beliefs change, and scientific knowledge questions more and more of the assumptions on which they are based, a church finds it increasingly difficult to reconcile its bounded practical responsibilities for the living and the unbounded sentient system on which its membership depends.

CONTRIVED COINCIDENCE

One of the earliest attempts deliberately to invent a form of work organization in which task- and sentient-group boundaries coincided was in the textile industry (Rice, 1958). The invention, which accompanied the introduction of automatic looms, was stimulated by the need to counter the human deprivation caused by job breakdown and the concomitant loss of a traditional craft skill. The outcome was the formation of internally led, quasi-autonomous, primary work groups. The results showed greatly increased production, higher quality, reduced costs, and, so far as could be judged from their behavior, much greater satisfaction for the workers.

From this and subsequent experiments and observations we were able to postulate the particular conditions under which such autonomous work groups were likely to be effective:

- The task must be such that those engaged in its parts can experience, as a group, the completion of a whole task.
- There must be a well-defined boundary with a measurable intake/output ratio that can serve as a criterion of performance.
- The group has to be of such a size that it can not only regulate its own activities, but also provide satisfactory personal relationships.
- Neither the range of skills required nor differences of status should be so large as to prevent internal mobility.
- The task/sentient group should not be unique. Disaffected members need the possibility of moving to another similar group. Otherwise the investment in the one group is likely to be so great as to distort values and judgements, and the possibility of expulsion so threatening as to be destructive.

This last condition in particular certainly does not hold in the family business. The commitment of their members that such groups require for their effectiveness is itself a barrier to accommodating change. Even so, there is undoubtedly scope, in industries with relatively stable technologies, for improvements in productivity by creating socio-technical systems in which task and sentient boundaries coincide.

COINCIDENT BOUNDARIES AND CHANGE

The pace of change is, however, becoming faster: for enterprises in industries facing frequent product obsolescence or technological innovation, organization must become a readily dispensable tool.

The case from the steel industry showed that introduction of computers for scheduling and for production and process control had already disrupted not only accepted task-system boundaries but also the associated sentient groups; and, in consequence, had called into question the validity of the location of traditional organizational boundaries and of the associated management roles. Comprehensive data-storage with instantaneous access, the computer programming of routine decision making and the building of simulation models to allow the results of alternative strategies to be compared before they are implemented, can lead only to a greater centralization of power and control. The inherent evolutionary capacity of modern computer technology—the capacity of the computer to learn from experience—will rapidly make redundant much of the specialized experience, particularly in middle management and administration, on which so much decision-making has had to rely in the past. With this redundancy many established career patterns and their associated promotion paths will disappear. New kinds of organization will provide new roles requiring new skills, and attempts to preserve traditional organizations and traditional roles must inevitably lead to inefficiency and social dislocation.

In industry the invention of a new product can give its inventors several years' start over potential competitors. If the market for the product is lucrative, imitations enter the field. As soon as that happens the inventive phase is over. Thereafter, modification and new applications of the product can give a competitive advantage, but the start gained by such innovations rapidly shortens as know-how in manufacturing and application becomes more generally available. If by this time the market for the product has become a mass market, then mass production—which by reason of its heavy investment in specific manufacturing processes is the enemy of invention and innovation—takes over and inhibits further change until the product itself becomes obsolete.

Institutions tend to follow the same pattern. A new institution in a new field starts up with high hopes and little acceptance. If it survives the early indifference to its outputs (or even attempts to crush it), its ideas and methods gradually become acceptable and it becomes respectable. A new institution can command great investment from its members. Their task and sentient groups coincide. They are prepared to work long hours often for little money because of their belief in their cause. In time, other sentient groups exert their pull—family, other jobs, established professions—and members leave; the remainder may struggle on, but, unless new ideas emerge, the institution can easily be submerged and become indistinguishable from its contemporaries.

DIFFERENT KINDS OF SENTIENCE

This brings us to the point that while sentient groups have to have meaning, or else commitment will be inadequate, the sentience may arise in different ways and have different meanings at different times. Sentience is likely to be strongest where task and sentient boundaries coincide and, more particularly, where members share both a common belief in the objective of the group and complementary beliefs about their respective contributions to it. As our work with family businesses demonstrated, beliefs that the contributions of the various members are not merely complementary but indispensable introduce such ambivalent stress into situations that task performance suffers and the sentience itself is correspondingly vulnerable. At the other end of the spectrum, a group in which every member has a similar role, so that all are interchangeable and each individual is all too dispensable, cannot acquire sentience unless it finds supplementary activities through which members can make individual and complementary contributions. Many groups of semi-skilled and unskilled workers fall into this category. The professional body is in yet another category since, although it is largely undifferentiated in terms of the qualifications and the rights and obligations of its members, it is at the same time the powerful sanctioning body that confers on them the right and security to engage in professional relations with their clients. To be effective as sentient groups, the kinds of scientific base that we adumbrated earlier need to have something of this professional quality.

The nature of the sentient requirements is also determined by the nature of the task of the enterprise. An enterprise that carries out a socially reputable task usually has little difficulty in obtaining the commitment of its members; one that is socially questionable will have much more difficulty; and one that is socially objectionable can get commitment only from rebels and deviants. Indeed, antisocial enterprises require elaborate codes of behavior to ensure adherence and, furthermore, have to impose severe penalties for their breach.

In fact, most institutions have had to devise special mechanisms to reinforce commitment. Pension and housing schemes, staff parties, salesmen's rallies, exhibitions, house magazines, are among the more frequently used. But it is notable that welfare activities, sports clubs and profit-sharing schemes have had a very limited success in industry. Even types of co-ownership, in which employees have had equity voting rights, have proved less attractive than their inventors hoped. The sentient group of ownership has been insufficiently professional, usually because the majority of co-owners have not had the experience and skill required to make strategic decisions about relations with the environment.

One widespread mechanism through which highly structured organizations reinforce both their internal differentiation and the commitment of their members is ritual role-reversal. This may be observed, for example, in an Indian temple festival when, on one day in the year, a member of an untouchable caste may be accorded the honor and respect normally reserved for a Brahman. In our own society there is the comparable army tradition that officers serve Christmas dinner to the men. Similarly, during a sale in a large department store, the ordinary selling staff may elect managers from among themselves, and the normal managers become staff. But successful mechanisms like these are not easy to invent.

Some enterprises may seek to mobilize more commitment than is necessary for effective task performance. We have known companies in which the cost of a high turnover of staff has been more than outweighed by the flexibility and new ideas that it infuses into the system. Management's desire to reduce turnover and increase loyalty may sometimes be motivated more by a desire to be loved than by the need to be efficient.

What is important is the relative balance of sentience of groups committed to the status quo and groups committed to change. Efforts by other workers to replicate elsewhere the experimental changes in weaving cited above often foundered through a failure to create initially a strong sentient group committed to experimentation. It was only such a group that could provide the necessary protective boundary within which innovation could be encouraged to take place. However, once the new autonomous groups had established themselves, they acquired their own valency and froze into a new status quo, and the group committed to experimentation disappeared.

To maintain adaptiveness, the greatest sentience must remain vested in a group committed to change. A contribution to the literature on institution-building by Perlmutter (1965) carried the subtitle "The Building of Indispensable Institutions." A major lesson from our own work is that the indispensability of the whole institution may depend on building dispensability into the parts. But the sentience of the overall institutional boundary within which this can happen is not easy to sustain. It is here that personal leadership often has a part to play. During a period of critical changes in particular, a charismatic leader who embodies a belief in the future of the enterprise can be a focus of its sentience and enable members to withdraw sentience from the parts that need to be dispensed with.

Boundary Controls

THE PROTECTIVE FUNCTION OF CONTROL

The need for boundary controls to protect the conversion process from interference from the environment and to adjust both intake and output to environmental demands was demonstrated in our studies of research organizations and of air transport.

In its purest form, boundary control permits only those transactions between the system and its environment that are essential to performance of the primary task. It admits the necessary intakes, releases the outputs, and maintains and replenishes the resources of the task system.

Strict controls are necessary to protect experimental situations, especially those that involve social change. Without protection—diminishing as the experimental changes become more acceptable—interference can lead to "too early crystallization in social and economic dimensions because of anxiety about the disturbance of traditional patterns" (Rice, 1958).

In the same way, conferences and courses that provide opportunities for experiential learning about the human problems of leadership have to impose strict boundary controls both between the conference and its environment and within the conference between its various events, in order to protect both members and staff during a process that can be stressful (Rice, 1965). The boundaries of the conference itself are protected by the exclusion of all visitors and by the refusal to make reports on participants or to publish anything that could be attributed to any individual. Within the conference program the specific task of each event is defined as precisely as possible; staff roles and role-sets are also defined and staff members adhere to them. Time, too, is used as a boundary: events start and stop at the times published. Overspill, at least as far as the staff are concerned, is avoided as much as possible. These controls are reinforced by clear definition of territorial boundaries.

The throughput of a conference or course, like that of any educational institution, is, however, human. No conference management could guarantee to control member behavior. This is not attempted except by example. All rules are made for, and enforced on, staff. In effect, boundary controls are strict, but they are imposed only where they can be effective.

In other settings, one observes all too often controls being imposed not to protect the task system from interference but to protect management against anxiety. Parameters are controlled not because they are relevant but because they are measurable. Their function is to create an illusion of certainty as a means of coping with intolerable uncertainty.

INHERENT AND IMPOSED CONTROLS

The easiest kind of control to maintain is that over a physical throughput when the transformation in the conversion process never leaves the throughput in an unstable condition. Machine shops in engineering provide an obvious example. The process can be stopped at any time to check the accuracy of the work done and to make any necessary adjustments. Materials or part-processed products do not deteriorate or change in form while the inspection is carried out. Mo· difficult and more dangerous are controls over chemical processes or those that involve unstable materials such as molten metal or atomic reactions. In these processes boundary controls can be imposed only at infrequent intervals and monitoring is the only form of regulation possible at other times. More difficult still are controls over a human throughput: the throughput has a will of its own which is often at variance with the controlling agency. Adequate control is possible only when the dependence involved in the process is fully accepted both by the members of the enterprise and by the individuals who comprise the throughput. Otherwise it is necessary to provide members with the support that enables them to tolerate the uncertainties involved.

The nature of the controlling agency can radically affect attitudes towards, and acceptance of, the kinds of control imposed. Where, as in religious institutions, the authority for sanctions is derived from a deity, those who believe cannot question the rightness or the wrongness of decisions based on belief. To be engaged in God's work precludes most human interference. There are other spheres, again, in which control is easier to maintain because it is derived from natural sources rather than from human agency. The managers of enterprises concerned with the sea, with agriculture, mining and the care of the sick have for a long time exploited their own dependence on "acts of God," and hence their inability to take responsibility for what happens, as a means of controlling those employed by them.

In many chemical processes, once chemicals are mixed the process starts and is self-activating: the process itself takes control and so imposed organizational controls can be kept to a minimum. Generally speaking, the greater the number of controls that are implicit in the task or its technology, and the more effective they are, the fewer the managerial controls it is necessary to impose. When neither task nor technology provides effective built-in controls, management must devise regulatory mechanisms to ensure that it can manage. Conversely, the greater the number of automatic processes, the fewer the managerial controls that should be required. It is, of course, true that automation often involves more inflexible activity systems; and, since they must by kept going, additional controls may be needed over intake and output. The total system has to live up to its automated parts. In other words, if appropriate boundary conditions are to be maintained, managerial control at the boundaries may have to be increased. The introduction of automation allows for more integration between the parts of the process and avoids some intermediate stocks and hence the tying up of working capital. But the elimination of intermediate stocks also demands greater sensitivity to market demand, with correspondingly more frequent adjustments throughout the process.

CONTRACTING OUT

The confusion between task and sentient systems and the problem of differentiating their boundaries and of controlling their interrelations are in some measure simplified by greater differentiation between the subsystems of complex enterprises. One large oil refinery, for example, directly employs only the few chemists and engineers that are required for its operating activities and for its technical and financial control functions. All other work—maintenance, transport, and even site security—is contracted out to other enterprises specializing in such services. This is by no means unique. An airline, particularly at stations away from its base, will commonly contract out passenger-handling, catering, and even load-control calculations and some aircraft maintenance activities. And, of course, the majority of industrial companies import parts of their products from manufacturers who have specialized in the required technology. The trend appears to be increasing: firms of professional architects, civil engineers and accountants have existed for a very long time, and agencies that provide temporary secretaries have also been available for many years. It is now possible to make continuing contracts for domestic as well as office cleaning, for canteen catering, long-term car hire, management recruitment, draughtsmanship, babysitting and a host of other services that were formerly the normal activities of the enterprise concerned.

Contracting out intakes and services can relieve management of many of the headaches of control of the relationships between different task and sentient groups within the enterprise. In particular, it simplifies the problem of controlling internal sentient boundaries. Against this, however, management faces greater difficulties when what is contracted out is the essential maintenance activity required to keep the process going, or a vital ingredient of the import-conversion-export process by which the enterprise performs its primary task. Management may well find that it has lost control of its own enterprise by giving too many hostages to other managements. In the building industry, the major problem is to get sufficient commitment to a project group to maintain any kind of control over the activities of its various parts. With strikes and other stoppages one group can hold the total enterprise at ransom, as has been demonstrated only too often in the automobile industry.

Specialization of technology and product in subenterprises or separate enterprises can no doubt increase the efficiency of the parts, but until new forms of organization are invented—with activity system, task group and sentient group adequately differentiated and their interrelations controlled—it is not certain that greater efficiency of the parts will add up to greater efficiency of the whole.

Permeable Boundaries

Strict boundary controls are especially difficult to maintain in those systems that by their nature have to be more open. Hospitals, for example, cannot easily control emergency admissions. In general, those institutions and professions that offer help of any kind, physical or spiritual, frequently find that either their intake or their output is intractable to control. Those who come for help tend to be accepted—however hopeless their case—and once admitted are frequently difficult to export. In a study of disasters Raker, Wallace and Rayner (1956) reported: "The general pattern has been that the nearest hospitals are overwhelmed and the hospitals more remote from the disaster zone receive fewer casualties than their reasonable share." The authors show the value of triage as a control mechanism for the most effective allocation of limited medical resources. More discrimination in admission leads to greater chances of recovery for the majority; but imposition of the controls to achieve this discrimination demands an exercise of judgment and a decision-making process that run counter to all the training of most of those who manage the institution, particularly if it has a moral or religious basis. In consequence from the point of view of society as a whole, far too many resources are often spent on the virtually hopeless, while those who could recover with the minimum of help go helpless.

The introduction of medical services into developing and overcrowded countries can have tragic consequences when food, housing and other services necessary to sustain the resulting increased population are not provided as well. To advocate only "balanced" progress is, however, easy when one is not face-to-face with the suffering that absence of medical care can entail— particularly if medical services are available and others are not. Members of the medical profession cannot just deny the Hippocratic code that has been at least implicit throughout their training. Nevertheless, their failure to control their boundary can result eventually in greater suffering for the very people they save.

DESTRUCTION AND RECONSTITUTION OF BOUNDARIES

Disasters also provide extreme examples of the obliteration of normal boundaries. Floods, hurricanes, earthquakes or nuclear bombs literally annihilate familiar landmarks by which human life is guided. It has been suggested that behavior in disaster can be analyzed in three overlapping phases: impact, recoil and post-traumatic stress (Tyhurst, 1951). The first can last from seconds up to one-and-a-half hours; the second from hours to weeks; and the third for the rest of life. In the period of impact, up to a quarter of those affected remain cool and collected, appreciate what has happened and plan recovery; up to three-quarters are stunned, bewildered, lost and numb; the remainder become hysterical and show other pathological symptoms. In the period of recoil the majority move about aimlessly, seeking shelter without plan or real purpose; they are in a dependent, childlike state in which anyone who takes charge and proposes action is followed. In other words, anyone who can replace the destroyed boundaries can assume control of the new boundaries. If, however, in anticipation of disaster, a new set of landmarks and guideposts is got ready—rescue stations, precise directions about evacuation and so on— and the boundary control functions are manned in advance, casualty rates can be lowered dramatically.

Disasters are fortunately rare, but they serve to emphasize the importance of defined boundaries and of boundary control functions. Any transaction across enterprise boundaries, an essential process for any living system, involves the drawing, temporarily at least, of new boundaries. And the drawing of new boundaries contains the possibility that these will prove stronger than the old. Such a transaction therefore has in it the elements of incipient disaster, in which not only are essential tasks undone, but sentient systems are destroyed as well.

We can learn something more from the examination of disaster. So far as is known, the actual occurrence of mass panic is rare; but the myth of panic in disaster is strong. The myth, and belief in it, is a mechanism by which stress is discharged and control restored. The destruction of boundaries is so stressful that someone has to go to pieces, or has to be believed to do so—someone or some group has to carry the role of panic leader. In more normal situations, religious sects, immigrants, racial groups, delinquents or other socially condemned minorities can threaten, or be perceived to threaten, the integrity of group boundaries. The preservation and protection of adequate sentient boundaries often depend, therefore, on finding or inventing other groups on whom can be projected the feelings and behavior that, if retained within the sentient group, would destroy its sentience.

It is indeed very often the charismatic leader who identifies such out-groups and so mobilizes the commitment of his or her followers. While this is no doubt functional during a period of crisis and individual disorientation, in the longer term it carries dangers of its own. Commitment to the boundary represented by a charismatic leader implies a corresponding withdrawal of commitment to the most important human boundary of all—the individual's own boundary between outside and inside. In Bion's terminology (See Sutherland, I, 2, "Bion Revisited"), charismatic leadership promotes "basic assumption" behavior, and at the level of the "assumption group" the individual in effect surrenders ego function to the group.

Long-term solutions to the problem of maintaining adaptiveness to change cannot therefore depend on manipulative techniques. On the contrary, they must depend on helping the individual to develop greater maturity in controlling the boundary between his or her own inner world and the realities of the external environment.

References

Perlmutter, H.V. 1965. "Towards a Theory of Practice of Social Architecture: The Building of Indispensable Institutions." *Tavistock Pamphlet No.12.* London: Tavistock Publications.

Raker, J.W., A.F.C. Wallace, J.F. Rayner with the collaboration of A.W. Eckert. 1956. "Emergency Medical Care in Disasters." In *Disaster Study No. 6. National Research Council Publication 457.* Washington, D.C.: Committee on Disaster Studies, National Academy of Sciences.

Rice, A.K. 1958. *Productivity and Social Organization: The Ahmedabad Experiment.* London: Tavistock Publications. Reissued 1987, New York: Garland.

———. 1963. *The Enterprise and Its Environment.* London: Tavistock Publications.

———. 1965. *Learning for Leadership: Interpersonal and Intergroup Relations.* London: Tavistock Publications.

Tyhurst, J.S. 1951. "Individual Reactions to Community Disaster." *American Journal of Psychiatry,* 107:764–69.

A.K. Rice

Individual, Group and
Inter-Group Processes*

This paper is an attempt to apply to individual and group behavior a system theory of organization normally used for the analysis of enterprise processes. The use of such a theory will inevitably concentrate on the more mechanistic aspects of human relationships, but I hope that the approach will help to clarify some of the differences and similarities among individual, group and inter-group behavior and throw some light on the nature of authority.

The Individual

The theories of human behavior and of human relationships are in many ways analogous to those of system theory as applied to institutions. Like an institution, an individual may be seen as an open system, existing and capable of existing only through processes of exchange with the environment. Individuals, however, have the capacity to mobilize themselves at different times and simultaneously into many different kinds of activity system, and only some of their activities are relevant to the performance of any particular task.

The personality of the individual is made up of biological inheritance, learned skills and the experiences through which he or she passes, particularly those of early infancy and childhood. A baby is dependent on one person—and gradually assimilates father and any brothers and sisters into his or her patterns of relationships. The growing child includes other members of the extended family and of the family network. The first break with this pattern is usually made when the child goes to school and encounters for the first time an institution to which he or she has to contribute as a member of a wider society. It is the preliminary experience of what, in later years, will be a working environment.

The hopes and fears that govern the individual's expectations of treatment by others, and the beliefs and attitudes on which to base a code of conduct

*A shortened version of the original—*Human Relations*, 22:565–84, 1969.

derive from these relationships and are built into the pattern that becomes one's personality. They form part of the internal world. It contains, besides the skills and capabilities as developed, the primitive inborn impulses and primitive controls over them that derive from the child's earliest relations with authority, together with the modifications and adaptations incorporated in growing up.

In the mature individual, the ego-function mediates the relationships between the external and the internal worlds and thus takes in relation to the individual a "leadership" role and exercises a "management" control function. The mature ego is one that can differentiate between what is real in the outside world and what is projected on to it from "inside," between what should be accepted and incorporated into experience and what should be rejected. In short the mature ego is one that can define the boundary between what is inside and what is outside and can control the transactions between the one and the other. Diagrammatically the individual can be represented at any one time, therefore, as a system of activity. The ego-function is located in the boundary control region, checking and measuring intakes, controlling conversion activities and inspecting outputs. It uses the senses as instruments of the import system; thinking, feeling and other processes to convert the intakes; then action, speech or other means of expression to export the outputs.

The individual is not just a single activity system with an easily defined primary task, but a multi-task system capable of multiple activities. The activities become bounded and controlled task systems when they are directed to the performance of a specific task, to the fulfilling of some specific purpose. The difficulty then is the control of internal boundaries and dealing with activities that are not relevant to task performance. And these controls are the result of the built-in attitudes and beliefs, born of previous experience, which may or may not be relevant to the specific task or system of activities required for its performance.

To take a role requires the carrying out of specific activities and the export of particular outputs. To take a role an individual could be said to set up a task system; and the task system to require the formation of a project team composed of the relevant skill, experience, feelings and attitudes. Different roles demand the exercise of different skills and different outputs. The task of the ego-function is then to ensure that adequate resources are available to form the project team for role performance, to control transactions with the environment so that intakes and outputs are appropriate, and to suppress or otherwise control irrelevant activities. When the role changes the project team has to be disbanded and reformed.

The individual as a multiple task enterprise is shown in simplified form in Figure 1. Task systems I (T_1) and II (T_2) require the individual to take roles 1 and 2 $(R_1$ and $R_2)$. R_1 and R_2 overlap to the extent that they use some, but not all, of the capabilities of the individual. The task systems are related to

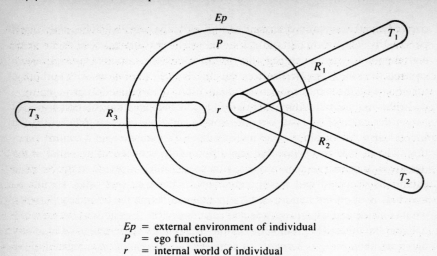

Ep = external environment of individual
P = ego function
r = internal world of individual
T_1, etc. = tasks
R_1, etc. = roles

Figure 1. The role system of the individual

different but neighboring parts of the environment. The management controls required will also therefore be similar, but not necessarily the same. In contrast, task system *III* (T_3) requires the individual to take role 3 (R_3). This requires quite different capabilities, is related to a quite different part of the environment and hence requires a different kind of managerial control. In practice, such complete splits are not usual (except in the schizophrenic), but it is possible to recognize, on the one hand, those individuals who are always the same no matter what the situation is or with whom they are in contact; and, on the other, those who appear to be quite different people in different situations.

More generally we can say the ego-function has to exercise different kinds of authority and different kinds of leadership in different roles and in different situations. Dislike of the role and of the activities or behavior required in it, and the demonstration of the dislike by attempts to change the role or modify the behavior, or the intrusion of feelings or judgments that contradict role requirements, inevitably distort intakes, modify conversion processes and can only result in inappropriate outputs. It is as though the management of a multiple task enterprise were to set up a project team for the solution of a particular problem but not only could not be sure whether the team was working on the right problem but could not even control membership of the team or the resources they used or squandered.

In effect, I wish to suggest that the general conception of a project type organization can be used, however crudely, to represent the individual as a role-taking but sentient being. In the individual, the sentient groups and resource pools of the enterprise become the repositories of the capacities of the individual to fill different roles. The resource pools hold the intellectual power, cognitive and motor skills, experience and other capabilities; the sentient groups the attitudes, beliefs and feelings—the world of objects and part objects—resulting from up-bringing. In effect, because a role demands specific skills and the exercise of specific authority in a particular context it is unlikely to require every personal attribute of a given individual. Some attitudes and some skills will always be unused by any given role. Maintaining a role over a long time leads, therefore, either to the atrophy of unused attributes or to the need to find other means of expressing them.

I recognize, of course, that for human beings the many import-conversion-export processes cannot be so easily defined as the previous paragraphs might suggest, and that "productivity" is seldom a simple measure of the difference between known intakes and known outputs. I hope, however, that this way of thinking about an individual will help to clarify some of the problems of role-taking when we have to consider group and intergroup processes.

The ego-function has therefore to control not only transactions across the individual/environment boundary but also between role and person. When the ego-function fails to locate boundaries precisely and fails to control transactions across those boundaries, confusion is inevitable—confusion in roles and in the authorities exercised in roles. Authority and responsibility appropriate in one role are used inappropriately in other roles. To be continuously confused about the role/person boundaries or completely unable to define and maintain boundaries is to be mentally sick.

The Group

"Individual" has little meaning as a concept except in relationships with others. He or she uses them and vice versa to express views, take action and play roles. The individual is a creature of the group, the group of the individual. Individuals, according to their capacity and experience, carry within themselves the groups of which they have been and are members. Experiences as infant, child, adolescent and adult, within the family, at school and at work, and the cultural setting in which one has been brought up will thus affect, by the way in which they are molded into one's personality, the contemporary and future relationships made in family, work and social life.

A group always meets to do something. In this activity the members of the group co-operate with each other; and their co-operation calls on their knowledge, experience and skill. Because the task for which they have met is real, they have to relate themselves to reality to perform it. The members of the group have, therefore, to take roles and to make role relationships with each other. The work group is now a task system. It may or may not have very much sentience depending on the extent to which its members are committed to each other. Even as a sentient system it may, or may not, support task performance. Controls are then required:

- to regulate transactions of the whole, as a task system, with the environment and of the constituent systems with each other
- to regulate sentient group boundaries
- to regulate relationships between task and sentient groups

But, in the discussion of the individual, I wrote that the role taken by each member of a group is also a task system, and that the management of each of these (the ego-function) has to control the relations between the task and sentient systems of the individual. So long as the role taken by each individual member is supported by that member's own individual sentient system, the task group and sentient group tend to coincide. But individual members may not be aware of all the elements either of their own individual or of total group sentience, even if such exists. To put this another way: task roles are unlikely to use all attributes of every member's personality; the unused portions may or may not support role-, and hence group-task, performance, but neither individual member nor group may be aware of the discrepancies between individual and group sentience or of changes over time.

More importantly, the unused attributes of individuals may themselves have such powerful sentience attached to them that they have to be expressed in some way. That is, an individual, though a member of a task group, may be unable to control those personal attributes that are not relevant to task performance and may seek other outlets for the emotions and feelings that the unused attributes and the inability to control them gives rise to. This represents a breakdown in the management control of the individual so far as role performance is concerned. Group-task leadership may still so be able to control group sentience, as not only to overcome individual discrepancies but also to harness group emotions and feelings in favor of group-task performance. The charismatic leader, for example, can be said to attract to him- or herself as a person the unused sentience of group members and, being concerned with task performance, can thus control any group opposition to that performance. If task leadership cannot either harness group feelings in favor of task performance or contain opposing feelings by personal leadership, then other groups consisting of some or all of the task group members may be formed to express opposing sentience. Such groups may seek and appoint other leaders. If the other group gets support from all other members of the task system, however unaware they may be of this support (since individual management control has broken down), then the other group can become more powerful than the task group.

In the basic assumptions Bion (1961) describes the situation in which the sentience of the roles taken by the members of a group in the task system may or may not be stronger than other possible sentient systems. If the sentient systems of the individual members coalesce, that is, individual members find a common group sentience, then the group can be said to be behaving as if it had made a basic assumption. If the common group sentience is opposed to task performance, that is, the control is not maintained by task leadership, other leaders will be found.

I now feel that Bion's concepts describe special cases which are most easily observable in small groups, because they are large enough to give recognizable power to an alternative leadership, and yet are not so large as to provide support for more than one kind of powerful alternative leadership at any one time. As Bion points out, the capacity for co-operation among the members of a task group is considerable; that is, role sentience in a task group is always likely to be strong. Hence, while the group maintains task definition the strength of the sentience supporting task performance at the reality level makes the life of leadership opposing task performance precarious.

A pair who have met to perform an agreed task can hardly provide alternative leadership and remain a task system. With three, an alternative leader is rapidly manifest and either immediately outnumbered or at once destroys co-operation in task performance, i.e., the three cannot easily remain a task group. (Two is company, three is none.) A quartet can provide some support for alternative leadership by splitting into pairs, but cannot sustain the split for very long without destroying the quartet as a task system. In groups of five and six, the interpersonal transaction systems are still relatively few and task leadership can be quick to recognize alternative leadership, usually before it can manifest powerful opposition to task performance. Above six, the number of interpersonal transactions becomes progressively larger, and hence it may be more difficult to detect their patterning.

In general, the larger the number of members of a group, the more members there are to find an outlet for their non-task related sentience, and hence the more powerful can be its expression, and the more support can an alternative leader obtain. Equally, because of the large number, the more futile and useless can group behavior appear when there is no sentient unanimity among the membership either in support of, or in opposition to, group task performance. In other words, the larger the group the more opportunities members have to divest themselves of their unwanted or irrelevant sentience, by projecting it into so many others.

But the individual is a multiple task enterprise, and his various sentient systems can be in conflict with each other. When he joins a group to perform a group task, he must, by his very joining, to some extent commit himself to take the role assigned to him, and hence to control irrelevant activities and sentience. Mature individuals thus find themselves distressed and guilty when in any attempt to reassert "management control" over their own individual boundaries they recognize, however vaguely, the number of different hostages they have given to so many conflicting sentient groups.

The situation of the group can be roughly approximated symbolically:

Let the members of a group be: $I_1, I_2, I_3, \ldots, I_n$.

Each is capable of taking many roles: $R_1, R_2, R_3, \ldots, R_n$.

Each role, in the way the term is used here, is a task system in itself. It comprises a number of specific activities together with the necessary resources for its performance. The resources should include not only the skills, but also the appropriate attitudes, beliefs, and feelings derived from the individual's sentient groups. But not all individuals are capable of taking all roles, and role performances by different individuals in the same role also differ.

If the role performance is represented by IR, then

$$I_1 R_1 \neq I_2 R_1 \neq I_3 R_1, \ldots \quad \text{and} \quad I_1 R_1 \neq I_1 R_2 \neq I_1 R_3, \ldots$$

Ideally a task system requires only activities and we could then write

$$T = f(R_1 + R_2 + R_3 + \ldots + R_n)$$
$$= f\Sigma (R)$$

But because roles are taken by individuals, we have to write

$$TP \text{ (task performance)} = f(I_1 R_1 + I_2 R_2 + \ldots + I_n R_n)$$
$$= f\Sigma (IR) \tag{1}$$

if we assume R_1 to be taken by I_1, R_2 by I_2, etc. But when an individual takes a specific role not all his or her aptitudes are likely to be used, and performance in any specific role is likely to be reduced by the amount of "energy" devoted to other aptitudes and to other sentience. If we represent these other irrelevant activities and their related sentience by $R°_1, R°_2, \ldots, R°_n$, then any given role performance R_1 by an individual I_1 will have to be written as

$$I_1 R_1 - I_1 (R°_1 + R°_2 + \ldots + R°_n)$$

in which $R°_1, R°_2$, etc. can have zero or positive values so far as they do not affect or oppose $I_1 R_1$. (I assume that all task supporting sentience is included in R_1.) Equation (1) therefore has to be written:

$$TP = f\,[\Sigma\,(IR) - I_1\,(R^\circ_1 + R^\circ_2 + \ldots + R^\circ_n)$$
$$- I_2\,(R^\circ_1 + R^\circ_2 + \ldots + R^\circ_n)$$
$$- \ldots - I_n\,(R^\circ_1 + R^\circ_2 + \ldots + R^\circ_n)]$$
$$= f\,[\Sigma\,(IR) - \Sigma\,(IR^\circ)] \tag{2}$$

Even if $\Sigma\,(IR^\circ) \neq 0$ and has a positive value, it can still be small enough to be controlled, either because of the discrepancy between the many different roles taken by the different Is or because the combinations of different numbers are themselves small. Nevertheless, the sentience invested in the R°s can still produce such disagreements between Is that a sense of futility can grow as Is spend more time and energy trying to find agreement between themselves in roles irrelevant to TP than in R_1, R_2, etc., that are relevant. If overtly or covertly they all agree on a role that is irrelevant to TP (say R°_m) then equation (2) becomes:

$$TP = f\,[\Sigma\,(IR) - R^\circ_m\,\Sigma\,(I)] \tag{3}$$

Writing out equation (3) more fully gives

$$TP = f\,[(I_1\,R_1 + I_2\,R_2 + I_3\,R_3 + \ldots + I_n\,R_n)$$
$$- R^\circ_m\,(I_1 + I_2 + I_3 + \ldots + I_n)] \tag{4}$$

It can be seen that because R°_m is taken by all group members it can become a considerable threat to TP, which requires different members to take different roles. If R°_m is large enough and is a consciously agreed role, there is revolt; if members are unaware both of their agreement and of the role they have agreed upon, they are then behaving as if they have made a basic assumption opposed to task performance.

It can also be seen that the more Is there are the greater the threat of $R^\circ_m\,(I_1 + I_2 + \ldots + I_n)$ but, at the same time, the more difficulty there is likely to be in getting agreement on R°_m. It can also be seen why, with smaller numbers, alternative leadership is difficult to sustain without immediate destruction of task performance. From equation (4), $TP = f\,[(I_1\,R_1 + I_2\,R_2) - R^\circ_m\,(I_1 + I_2)]$ for a pair. If now R°_m has a large value, and is reinforced by $I_1 + I_2$, it will almost certainly give TP a negative value.

Inter-Group Process

I have tried to show that all transactions, even the intra-psychic transactions of the individual, have the characteristics of an inter-group process. As such they involve multiple problems of boundary control of different task systems and different sentient systems and control of relations between task and sentient systems. Each transaction calls into question the integrity of boundaries across which it takes place and the extent to which control over transactions across them can be maintained. Every transaction requires the exercise of authority and calls into question the value of and sanction for that authority.

In the examination of a simple inter-group transaction between two groups in which individuals represent the two groups, account has to be taken, therefore, of a complex pattern of inter-group processes: within the individuals who represent their groups, within the transactional task system, between the groups and their representatives, within the groups and within the environment that includes the two groups. Even a simple inter-group transaction is, therefore, affected by a complex pattern of authorities, many of which are either partially or completely covert. If I now extend the analysis to more than two groups, each with more than one representative, the pattern becomes still more complex. A meeting of pairs of representatives from four groups is illustrated in Figure 2. It will be seen that in the meeting of representatives alone transactions across seventeen different pairs of boundaries have to be controlled: four pairs for each pair of representatives and one pair for the group of representatives as a group.

To understand the nature of the authority of a representative, or of a group of representatives, appointed to carry out a transaction on behalf of a group, involves, therefore, the understanding of multiple and complex boundary controls. In other words, the appointment of a representative or representatives is never just a simple matter of representing a task system to carry out a task-directed transaction with the environment. To put the same thing more colloquially: representatives are invariably chosen not only to carry out the specific transaction, but also to convey the mood of the group about itself and about its representative, and its attitude, not only to the specific part of the environment with which the transaction is intended, but to the rest of it as well. And not all the "messages" are explicit and overt; many, if not most of them, are implicit and covert.

But the representatives have their own intra-psychic processes, and their own intra-psychic groups have had to make inter-group relations with the groups they represent. The same mixture of transactions, overt and covert, have, or should have, taken place before he or she starts the inter-group transaction for which he or she has been appointed. The results of these transactions can seldom endow the representative with personal attributes that he or she did not previously possess, at least latently. The choice of representative(s) therefore offers important data about the group attitude, not only towards its task, but also towards itself and its environment. Further important data can be gathered from the extent to which the representative is given the authority to commit the group, and by his or her status within the group.

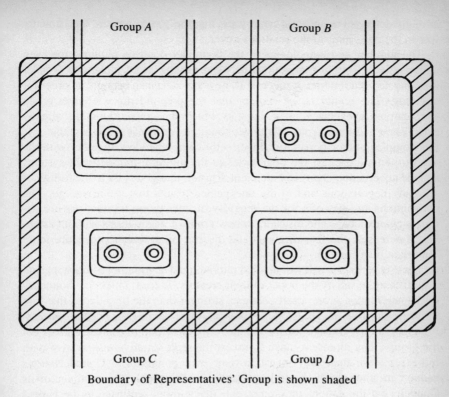

Boundary of Representatives' Group is shown shaded

Figure 2. Meeting of representatives' groups—one pair from each of four groups

Another dimension of complexity has to be mentioned: time. I have spoken about the problems of the control of the representative's own boundaries, of the boundaries between the representative and the group and of the relative strengths of the individual, group and transactional task system boundaries. It is surely rare for them all to be perfectly controlled in the interests of task performance. Even if they are, a transaction takes time, and during the transaction the representative cannot be in continuous communication with the group, not, that is, if he or she is anything more than a relay system. During the transaction the individual, group and task system sentiences may change. Indeed, in any critical negotiation they are almost bound to change, as hopes and fears of the outcome increase and decrease.

The past, during which decisions were made, attitudes formed and resources collected, is always the past; a transaction is the present and, if it is to have any meaning, must determine a future. Individuals, and even groups with strongly defended boundaries can, by staying firmly within them, occasionally live in the past; inter-group relations never.

The number and complexity of the boundary controls required for even comparatively simple transactions between groups might make one wonder how any negotiation is ever successful, how any salesman ever got an order for anything. The reality is, of course, that the preponderance of inter-group transactions takes place in settings in which the conventions are already established and mutual pay-offs understood. Nevertheless, I suggest that it is this complex authority pattern, imperfectly comprehended, together with the need to defend each of the boundaries in the multiple transactional systems against uncertainty, chaos and incipient disaster, that gives rise to the futility of so many negotiations and to the unexpected results that often emerge. The conventions and pay-offs for the majority of inter-group transactions are defenses against chaos and disaster. In new kinds of negotiations without established defenses, the fear of chaos and disaster often makes procedure more important than content.

There is perhaps small wonder that international negotiating institutions find it so difficult to satisfy the hopes of their creators. Indeed, unless the boundary of the negotiating group itself becomes stronger than the boundaries that join the representatives and those they represent, there seems little hope of successful negotiations. But this means that not only the group of representatives but the groups they represent have to invest the representative task system with more sentience than they invest in their own groups. The United Nations cannot, in other words, be fully effective until not only the members of its Council but the nations they represent invest more sentience in the United Nations than they do in their nationalisms.

The Role of Leadership

Finally, I turn to the role of leadership, which can be conceived of as a special case of representation: representation with plenipotentiary powers. Conceptually, it is irrelevant whether the role is taken by an individual or by a group. For convenience, I shall discuss it in terms of an individual leader.

As a member of a task group every individual has to take a role and through it control his or her task transactions with colleagues individually and collectively; the leader as a person also has to control his or her own person/role transactions as well as interpersonal relationships with colleagues. In addition to these, a leader has to control transactions between the group and relevant agencies in the environment in the interests of task performance; without such control task performance is impossible. In this sense, the role taken by the leader and the boundary control function of the group must have much sentience in common. For the leader, at least, sentient group and task group *must* reinforce each other. So far as task performance is unsatisfactory, by reason either of inadequate resources or of opposing group sentience, transactions with the environment are likely to be difficult and the task sentience of the leader weakened if not destroyed.

Using the earlier notation and letting R^L represent the role of leader taken by an individual I, leadership task performance can be written:

$$TP = IR^L - I(R°_1 + R°_2 + R°_3 + \ldots + R°_n)$$
$$= I(R^L - \Sigma R°)$$

For the leader at least, $\Sigma R°$ must be close to zero. What he or she has to provide is an IR model that is task oriented. The model, however, must be a credible one. A leader who puts too much energy into IR^L (with $\Sigma R° = O$) is hardly credible and gives no reinforcement to group members in controlling their own ego boundaries; on the other hand, a leader who puts too much energy into $\Sigma R°$ encourages followers to do the same; their $\Sigma(IR°)$ may only temporarily take the same form as the leader's, with consequent detriment to task performance.

More generally, since transactions with the environment can only be based on adequate task performance, the leader's authority has to be based on sufficient group sentience that is supportive of such performance. It follows that the mobilization of group sentience for any other reason than task performance—for example, personal loyalty, friendship or ideology—always leaves a task group vulnerable. It also follows that any change in the group task, by change either in the environment or in the group, changes not only the internal transactions between the members but also those with the environment, and hence the role of leadership and the appropriate sentience that has to be mobilized.

In practice, groups use all kinds of feelings and attitudes to maintain co-operation in task performance: love, affection, friendship, hatred, dislike and enmity as well as commitment to the group task. So far as a group is committed to its task, contrary sentience, including leadership's own, can be contained and controlled within the group; so far as commitment is tenuous, so far will the group find it impossible to control the contrary sentience. Under such circumstances, task leadership is castrated, the task redefined or irrelevant transactions with the environment have to be used to cope with the discordant feeling and attitudes.

Reference

Bion, W.R. 1961. *Experiences in Groups and Other Papers*. London: Tavistock Publications; New York: Basic Books.

New Paths in Family Studies

The family is the basic bio-social group in society. There was early evidence in the post-war period that it was seriously disturbed. The degree of disturbance has since become greatly magnified. Changes in the wider society negative to its well-being continue to take place. In engaging with this meta-problem the Institute has opened up a number of new paths which are reported under this Theme.

The Reduction of Group Tensions in the Family. The child guidance movement took the child out of the context of the family, to make him or her "the patient." The cardinal problem, therefore, was to get engaged with the family as a system rather than simply with an individual extruded from it. While the Clinic and Institute were still a joint organization, John Bowlby took a major step and had the fathers as well as the mothers of his child patients attend joint sessions. He has been acclaimed as the originator of family therapy.

His original paper reproduced here bespeaks the influence of the work on groups in the Tavistock at that time. The paper, presented at the World Congress of Mental Health in 1948, was the first to describe the therapeutic technique of seeing all members of a family together. In an account of the development of what became known as family therapy, Waldron-Skinner (1981) writes in the Introduction to her volume of historical papers:

> As is now well-known, this paper holds some claim to have initiated the whole family therapy movement, since it was on reading Bowlby's paper (and misunderstanding the extent to which Bowlby was engaging in conjoint therapeutic work) that John Elderkin Bell embarked on his own formative contributions in America (Bell, 1961).

She also notes "the enormously influential scene-setting work of R.D. Laing," also of the Tavistock, during the late 1950s and 1960s and selects his 1969 paper "Intervention in Social Situations" as representative:

> These two contributions by Bowlby and Laing are of particular interest. . . . They display both the simplicity and profundity of the change of approach required of all who embark on the treatment of the family group, whatever (their) original training.

Non-Medical Marital Therapy. Very little professional work with the family was going on in Britain in the decade after World War II. A large number of people were averse to coming to any treatment center under psychiatric auspices such as the marital unit in the Tavistock Clinic. The bulk of the work was carried out by such organizations as the Marriage Guidance Council which was entirely lay. The staff were without professional training and approached problems from a moral and religious rather than a psychological viewpoint.

The Institute secured the opportunity to enter the marital field through a crisis that developed in the London Family Welfare Association, as described in the Series Introduction. A comprehensive overview of the developments that have subsequently taken place is presented in the paper by Douglas Woodhouse. These have become so widespread that not all of them could be described within the limits of a single paper. They have led to the appearance of a new profession of psychologically trained non-medical marriage therapists. Major innovations in training methods were introduced to make this possible, such as the interpretation of caseworkers' counter-transferences in group case conferences conducted by a psychoanalyst (Balint, 1957). It was found, however, that case workers did not themselves necessarily have to undertake psychoanalytic training. Such a necessity would have prohibited any wide multiplier effect which was a principal aim of the program. This aim has been achieved. New theory has emerged concerning mutual projections between marriage partners.

Conjugal Roles and Social Networks. Little was known about how ordinary families functioned. Accordingly, research was undertaken to open up this area. It was found that conjugal roles varied in relation to the density of the kinship network of the families. Factors of social mobility and urbanization made the connections increasingly sparse. The conjugal relationship had to take a far higher level of stress. This is described in the contribution of Elizabeth Bott Spillius whose book, *Family and Social Network* (1957), rapidly attained the status of a classic and opened up the concept of an open network as distinct from a bounded group. A whole literature has been generated from this beginning.

Dual-Career Families: The Evolution of a Concept. A new field of study pioneered by the Institute is the work/family interface. This was opened up by Robert and Rhona Rapoport in their study of dual career families, a new phenomenon in the 1960s. They have since set up their own Institute and undertaken projects which have extended the scope of studies concerning the work/family interface. A number of new concepts have been introduced. Their contribution provides an overview of the field, emphasizing what needs to be done in the future.

These new paths all arose from what is recognizable as the distinctively Tavistock approach of domain-based research into field-determined generic problems. They show the interpretation of the clinical and non-clinical areas. The pathways they created are still being followed.

References

Balint, M. 1957. *The Doctor, His Patient and the Illness*. London: Pitman.
Bell, J.E. 1961. *Family Group Therapy*. Public Health Monograph 64. Washington, D.C.: U.S. Department of Health, Education and Welfare.
Bott, E. 1957. *Family and Social Network* (2nd edition, 1971). London: Tavistock Publications.
Waldron-Skinner, S. (Editor). 1981. *Developments in Family Therapy: Theories and Applications Since 1948*. London: Routledge and Kegan Paul.

John Bowlby

The Study and Reduction of Group Tensions in the Family*

Child guidance workers all over the world have come to recognize more and more clearly that the overt problem which is brought to the Clinic in the person of the child is not the real problem; the problem which as a rule we need to solve is the tension among all the different members of the family. Child guidance is thus concerned not with children but with the total family structure of the child who is brought for treatment. This outlook is especially helpful when we think of the family group as a structured group of a kind not dissimilar in its nature and dynamics from any other structured group, for instance a factory group. Many of the same principles of approach appear to apply. Those working in the field of industrial relations have often emphasized how much they have learned from those of us working in clinics. We on the child guidance side now feel it is our turn to be grateful, because in the last two years we have learned a great deal from the experience and methods of our industrially oriented colleagues.

In the case of both child guidance and industrial consultation, the problem which is brought, be it a child who bites his nails, or a difficulty in selecting foremen, is seen to be but a symptom of a more complex problem. In each case the problem is commonly found to involve many, even all, the people with whom the so-called patient comes into contact. With the child, the problem usually lies in the relationships between him or her and the members of the family. With the industrial worker, it lies in the relationships among all members of the factory, from management downwards. In each case our first task is to reorient those consulting us, in order to help them see the real problem, of which they themselves are probably a part, and to see the alleged problem in its true light as a symptom. Such reorientation is, of course, the traditional role of the physician who, consulted about headache or rash, is concerned to discover the disease process, in the knowledge that treatment of the symptom only is futile and perhaps dangerous.

It is notorious in child guidance work that one of our principal difficulties is

---

*A reproduction of the original—*Human Relations*, 2:123–28, 1949.

that of obtaining parental co-operation in resolving the adverse family relations. A similar difficulty arises, often less obviously but no less really, in industrial work, where management may be very loath to continue co-operation when it realizes that this may require extensive reconsideration of its relations with workers. Faced with a situation where the co-operation of key people is difficult to maintain, there is a temptation for the professional worker to solve the group problem by removing one or more of the individuals concerned. In industry, management may wish to sack the trouble-maker. A similar procedure in child guidance has been to take the child out of the home and put him or her elsewhere. Although occasionally unavoidable, this seems to me a policy of despair.

The procedure which we are using in the Tavistock—in child guidance, in adult patient groups and in industrial work—is different. In all these situations where there is tension in a group of people, it is our aim to help them to live together and to resolve their tensions. We do this in the belief that the experience of understanding and working through these tensions is itself valuable as giving all members of the group insight into the nature of their difficulties, and insight also into the techniques whereby similar problems can be overcome in future.

Procedures of this kind presuppose that members of the group have a need and a drive to live together in accord. One of the striking things which we meet with in child guidance work is the tremendously strong drive which exists in almost all parents and children to live together in greater harmony. We find that, though caught up in mutual jealousies and hostilities, none of them enjoys the situation, and all are desperately seeking for happier relations. Our task is thus one of promoting conditions in which the constructive forces latent in social groups can come into play. I liken it to the job of a surgeon: not to mend bones but to try to create conditions which permit bones to mend themselves. In group therapy, and in treating the tensions of groups, the aim should be to bring about those conditions which permit the group to heal itself.

Now, there are many ways of setting about this. The purpose of this paper is to indicate some of the methods which we are trying in the child guidance clinic at this time. I emphasize *trying,* as we certainly have not arrived at any clear conclusions. First, we do not nowadays undertake systematic, individual treatment of a case until we have made a contact with the father. To those of us who hitherto have not done this as a routine, the experience is a revelation. In the past many of us have tended to leave the father out until we have got into difficulties, and then have sought to bring him in. But by insisting that everyone relevant in the case should have an early opportunity of making his contribution, and of finding out whether he wants to collaborate with us, we find the way towards collaboration very much smoother. These first steps in a case are vital and repay very careful study, but I shall not say more about them here.

The clinical problems with which we are faced are, very often, those of families where there is a nagging mother, and a child who is rebelling; there is mutual irritation and jealousy and father is tending to take one side or the other, thereby making matters worse. In addition to individual interviewing, we have been attempting, experimentally, to deal with these tensions by bringing all parties together in a long session and examining the problems from the point of view of each.

An Illustrative Case

To illustrate this technique I will describe a case that I have been treating for a long time now. When originally referred 2½ years before the time of this writing, Henry was aged 13 and was attending a grammar school, for which he was well suited on grounds of intelligence. However, his work was poor and he had a bad reputation for being lazy, untidy and unco-operative. His mother, a very unhappy woman, was intensely bitter about him and poured forth complaints about his behavior at home. He was dirty, untidy, disobedient and cruel to his sister (five years younger than he), and forever meddling with the electricity or plumbing, so that either they had no electric light or the house was flooded. The history showed that there had been tension between this boy and his mother since his early years, that it had become exacerbated after his sister's birth and had festered on ever since.

The nature of the problem and its origins were fairly clear. The solution, however, was far from easy. The mother had no insight into the part she was playing, and blamed the boy. The boy was equally hostile and critical towards his mother, and had equally little insight into his own contribution. Each wanted to get the Clinic on his or her side against the other. Because of this intense mutual suspicion, and because I feared I would not get the boy's co-operation if his mother also came to the Clinic, I decided (probably mistakenly) to work alone with the boy, keeping in touch with the home and discussing the situation with the headmaster to see how far the boy could be helped at school. Progress was imperceptible. School reports remained very bad and the tension situation at home acute, as was shown by occasional interviews with father or mother. During therapeutic sessions Henry was evasive, although, as time went on, confidence in the therapist's good intentions increased. As might be expected there was a very strong negative transference, and opposition to analytic work was as pronounced as was his opposition to school work or helping in the home. (All these connections were, of course, interpreted.)

After two years of weekly treatment sessions, very many of which were missed, I decided to confront the main actors with the problem as I saw it. Thus, I planned a session in which I could see father, mother and boy together. This proved a very interesting and valuable session, and it is important to note that it lasted two hours, since it would have been very little use had it been limited to one.

Most of the first hour was spent in each member of the family complaining how very unpleasant and difficult the others were. A great deal of bitter feeling was expressed and, had we left off at that point, the session would have been most unconstructive. During this time I had spoken little, but during the second hour I began making interpretations. I made it clear to them that I thought each one of them was contributing to the problem, and described the techniques of hostility each used. I also traced out the history of the tension, starting, as I knew it had, in the boy's early years, and gave illustrations of the incidents which had occurred. I pointed out that the mother's treatment of the boy, especially her insistence on immediate obedience and her persistent nagging, had had a very adverse effect on Henry's behavior, but I also stated that I felt sure that her mistaken treatment of Henry was the result of her own childhood, which I had little doubt had been unhappy. For nearly half an hour thereafter she told us, through her tears, about her childhood and of her very unhappy relation with her parents—this, remember, in front of her husband, who may have known, and her 15-year-old son, who undoubtedly knew little of it.

After 90 minutes the atmosphere had changed very greatly and all three were beginning to have sympathy for the situation of the other. It was at this point that the desire of each one of them to live together happily with the others began to come into the open—it was of course present from the beginning, for without it the session would have had no chance of success. However, in the final half hour this need, which each one of them felt, to live more amicably with the others, manifested itself openly and each one of them realized that it was present in the others. A constructive discussion followed. We discussed Henry's irritating and self-frustrating behavior at home and at school from the point of view of how best he could be helped to change, which he obviously wanted to do, and how nagging made him worse. We discussed his mother's nagging from the point of view of her anxiety and its relation to her childhood; father remarked that the neighbors had for long criticized them both for nagging the boy too much. We discussed father's educational ambitions for Henry and the bitterness his son's failure had induced in him. In this final half hour all three found themselves co-operating in an honest endeavor to find new techniques for living together, each realizing that there was a common need to do so and that the ways they had set about it in the past had defeated their object. This proved the turning point in the case.

Relation of Joint Interview Technique to Other Therapeutic Techniques

This technique stems directly from techniques used by Bion (1948; Bion and Rickman, 1943) in adult group therapy and by members of the Tavistock Institute of Human Relations for dealing with tensions in social groups in industry (Jaques, 1948). It is a technique whereby the real tensions existing between individuals in the group are dealt with freely and openly in the group, much as, in an individual analysis, the tensions existing between different psychic systems within the individual are dealt with freely and openly with the analyst. At what point in handling a case the technique of joint interview is appropriate we do not yet know, though it appears that, before it can be used effectively, some private contact must be made with each member separately. Private interviews afterwards, to work through material raised, are also essential. My next interview in the case described was with the mother, to work through her childhood history and its reference to the present, and to work through also her relation to myself. Though she resented what she had felt to be my criticism of her treatment of her son, she also remarked what a good thing it would have been had her own parents had the benefits of clinical help. After a joint session of the kind described, private interviews are very different from what they are before. In the first place, the attempt of each party in the dispute to get the therapist on his side, and his fear that another party has probably already succeeded in this, are both much reduced. There has been a first hand demonstration of neutrality. Secondly, each has had a demonstration of the existence in the others of a desire to mend the relationship. The real situation, even if bad, is then found to be far less alarming and hopeless than the fantasy each had had of it.

I wish to emphasize that, so far as its use at the Tavistock Clinic is concerned, this technique is still in an experimental stage. Though we rarely employ it more than once or twice in a particular case, we are coming to use it almost as routine after the initial examination and before treatment is inaugurated. A joint interview at this time is valuable as being an opportunity for the workers to convey their opinion of the problem to parents and child together, extending help to all and blaming none. Though one such joint interview can never effect entirely the reorientation required—phantasies and misconceptions of many kinds will remain—experience suggests that it sets a process of reorientation in train, which can be developed later in private interviews. These private interviews are commonly carried on by two professional workers, psychiatrist or psychotherapist with the child, psychiatric social worker with the mother. When this is the plan, it is essential that both workers should participate in the joint interview, since strong emotional responses are evoked, which cannot be dealt with later by a worker who was not present. In particular it is essential for the psychiatric social worker to be present at such a joint interview, since it will usually be his or her task to continue work with the parents, helping them to understand their part in the problem and the nature and origin of any unfavorable attitudes they may have to the child.

When I first came to consider this technique, I felt not a little apprehensive of the scenes in which I might get involved. How much safer to keep the warring parties apart, to divide and conquer! But the recognition of the basic fact that people really do want to live happily together and that this drive is working for us gives confidence, much as a knowledge of the miraculous healing powers of the body gives confidence to the surgeon. Even so, one cannot help asking oneself whether it is a good thing for all these problems to be discussed in front of the child. But, once again, the answer is reassuring—in a fragmentary and recriminatory way they have already been discussed many times before. There is nothing new in the material discussed—but the atmosphere in which it is discussed is different and, one hopes better. I have come, in fact, no longer to be alarmed by the hideous scenes which may occasionally ensue in the use of this technique—the violent accusations, the cruel sarcasm, the vitriolic threats. The fact that these scenes occur in one's consulting room is most unpleasant, but we know that they have occurred before and that, if they occur in our consulting rooms, there is a chance that the parent may be helped towards a different view, and the child can observe that the therapist is, at least, not allying him- or herself with his accuser. By focussing our work on the tension existing between the child patient and the members of his family group, we are adding to the child guidance techniques already in use—psychotherapy along analytic lines, therapeutic interviews with parents, remedial teaching and so on—and developing techniques which permit of the direct study and therapy of the tension within the group.

Circular Reactions in Family and Other Social Groups

Moreover, it is not unimportant that the use of these techniques influences the social behavior of others besides the child. In the case I have described it was not only Henry who was helped in his social relations; his father and mother were helped also. And just as Henry's relations at school have been materially better during the past months, so, I believe, have his father's in the factory and his mother's in her office. Thus, child guidance work may be expected to contribute towards more co-operative *industrial* relations, in the same way that social psychologists working in the industrial field may be expected to contribute towards better *family* relations, through their influence on industrial personnel who are also parents. Margaret Mead (1948) has spoken of the vicious circle of insecure parents creating insecure children, who grow up to create an insecure society which in its turn creates more insecure parents. It is clear that there is much truth in this picture, yet it is only half the truth. The interconnections which Margaret Mead emphasizes can lead to beneficent circles as well as vicious. Though tension and friction in industry will lead to irritable workers taking it out on their spouses and children at home, happy and co-operative relations in the factory will lead to contented workers treating their spouses and children kindly. Moreover, employees in a factory are likely, to a degree far greater than they realize, to model their behavior towards their children on the pattern the management adopts towards them. Dictatorial and punishing management is likely to increase the dictatorial and punishing attitudes of the workers towards their children; equally, democratic and participatory behavior by management will encourage such parental attitudes in their employees. In a similar way changes brought about within the family group may lead to children growing up to be individually either more anxious and difficult and likely to increase tension and friction at their work and in their homes, or else friendly and co-operative, and thus able to adopt friendly give-and-take relations in their working and domestic lives. Such repercussions are obvious and will one day have to be taken into account quantitatively when we assess the value of our therapeutic techniques.

Techniques of changing key social relationships can thus have far reaching repercussions either for good or for evil, in the same way that man's agricultural methods can greatly improve soil fertility or finally destroy it. We see, furthermore, that to attain the end of a secure, contented and co-operative community in which parents can give love and security to their children, enabling them to grow up to be stable and contented people, able to sustain and further a just and friendly society, no one point in the circle is more vital than another. The vicious circle may be broken at any point, the virtuous circle may be promoted at any point. We may thus review our therapeutic resources— each designed for its particular task and each originating to some extent independently of the others—social therapy in industry, child guidance, marriage guidance, group therapy of adults, psychoanalysis of individuals, therapeutic transitional communities, and others—as specialized parts of one great therapeutic endeavor: that of reducing tensions and of fostering understanding co-operation within groups of human beings.

References

Bion, W.R. 1948. "Experiences in Groups." *Human Relations,* 1:314–20.
Bion, W.R. and J. Rickman. 1943. "Intra-Group Tensions in Therapy: Their Study as a Task of the Group." *Lancet,* 2:678–81.

Jaques, E. 1948. "Interpretive Group Discussion as a Method of Facilitating Social Change." *Human Relations*, 1:533–49.

Mead, M. 1948. "The Individual and Society." *Proceedings of the International Congress on Mental Health*, 4:121–27.

Douglas Woodhouse

Non-Medical Marital Therapy
The Growth of the Institute
of Marital Studies*

This paper deals with the evolution of a Tavistock-linked non-medical therapeutic unit concerned with marital problems and their implications for the work
of community services. Until 1968 it was called the Family Discussion Bureau, and thereafter, the Institute of Marital Studies.

The Evolution of the Unit and the Field

A Collaborative Pilot Experiment

Citizens Advice Bureaus (CABs) had been set up as part of the war effort. With
the peace, they became concerned with problems resulting from social dislocation and with the many questions raised by new social legislation. The director
of the Bureaux in London, Enid Eicholtz (later Enid Balint), recognized the
leading part played by marital problems and related family stress in the
ostensibly practical difficulties of the people served.

CABs in London had been administered by the Family Welfare Association
(FWA), founded in 1869 as the Charity Organisation Society, whose social
workers were increasingly presented with marital and related family problems
that defeated them. In 1948 Enid Eicholtz initiated the formation of a small
group of FWA staff to explore the possibility of offering more effective help.
Technical support had to be found outside the FWA and beyond contemporary
social casework. Help was sought from the Tavistock Institute of Human
Relations (TIHR) with its psychoanalytic and socio-dynamic orientation for
staff training and problems of organizational and strategic development. Particularly through Dr. A.T.M. Wilson (1949), the Tavistock had designated

*A requested overview.

marriage and marital stress as one of its central concerns. There was sufficient agreement on the part of the FWA group with the Tavistock approach for a joint steering committee to be set up to guide the new endeavor. Among the tenets agreed were:

- The need to link training and research with casework to close the gap between theory and practice and provide opportunity for the formulation and testing of working hypotheses.
- That marital problems could be studied at the necessary depth only by making use of therapeutic situations. That the advance of understanding required an opportunity for reflection combined with skill derived from practice.
- To endorse the casework principle that nothing effective can be done to or for people, only with them (Wilson, 1947a; 1947b; 1949).

Five years were allotted to a pilot experiment. Survey research was undertaken in two areas of London to discover needs and to develop acceptable approaches to marital and family problems. Group discussions with a wide range of people who had not openly sought help confirmed the need for a new service (Menzies, 1949). Severe problems existed within the healthy part of the community; the line between so-called normal families, who could cope, and those threatened by crisis proved difficult if not impossible to draw. At that time stigma was attached to marital difficulty. Few people were able to ask for help before difficulties became acute, but, with that point reached, help was acceptable if made available in a way that did not imply social failure. The majority of clients would be referred by workers in community services.

These open discussions led to the use of "Family Discussion" in place of "Marriage Welfare." Family discussion was neutral, applicable alike to preventive and therapeutic work, and suggested the joint, client/worker nature of the endeavor (Bannister et al., 1955).

The second task was to explore the possibility of using a psychoanalytic theory of personality in the development of casework. Those seeking help seldom regarded their problems as medical or themselves as psychiatric patients, but some of the special knowledge of the psychoanalytically trained psychiatrist was necessary for those wishing to give effective help to people with problems stemming from motives of which they were unaware. Making such knowledge available raised big issues for the analysts, but their doubts were met by the forceful argument that troubled marriages existed and, because the "dis-ease" was not medical, couples in difficulties were not getting the psychological help they needed.

The FDB group needed to gain such understanding of themselves as would keep them free from the emotional pressure exerted by clients and permit them to see the conflicting forces at work with sufficient detachment to get a clear picture of them (Sutherland, 1955). They had to learn to reflect on and evaluate their own subjective experience; "a limited though considerable change in personality was necessary for the new skill, though the amount of change necessary could only be judged as the work progressed" (Balint, quoted by Sutherland, 1955).

The focus that then developed was not so much on the psychodynamics of the individual as on the marital relationship—the process of interaction between the two individuals concerned. The marital relationship was conceived in system terms from the start, as was the family of which this relationship was the nucleus.

The container within which reflection was combined with the experience of clinical practice was the weekly case conference. Learning took place through the relationship developed between a consultant analyst and the group of caseworkers and also among the members themselves (Balint, M., 1954; Bannister et al., 1955).

The third separate, but complementary, component of these initial explorations was an investigation of patterns of living in ordinary urban families. A social anthropologist and a social psychologist collaborated with FDB consultants, case workers and psychologists from the Tavistock Clinic. This research developed new insights into conjugal roles and family networks (Bott, 1957; Vol. I, "Conjugal Roles and Social Networks"). The study was of marriage as much as of families and the interpretations and hypotheses developed enriched the texture of interdisciplinary collaboration in the group as a whole, adding to the concepts emerging from the casework.

THE MOVE TO THE TAVISTOCK AND ITS IMPLICATIONS

When the time allotted to the pilot project expired the question of continuing the unit on a permanent basis became pressing. Preoccupation with the development of professional competence in its specialized field and close involvement with the Tavistock militated against its integration into the professional life and culture of its parent organization. A solution was found when in 1956 the FDB became one of a growing number of Clinic-linked activities of the TIHR.

A marital unit had existed within the Clinic as part of the National Health Service since 1949 and was available to those referred through medical channels. With the addition of the FDB an alternative non-medical pathway became available.

A professional tension lay in the uncertain distinction between casework and psychotherapy. The staff were caseworkers, a professional identity preserved for many years until that of "marital therapist" was assumed in the mid-1980s. The tension is implicit in a contemporary paper by one of the Bureau's consultants:

> You will observe that personal analysis has been excluded from the training. In the Family Discussion Bureau we have deliberately held to a policy of not requiring it, and our experience has shown that good work can be done without it. Whether or not the work is better without it, it would be impossible to say. Certainly some of those caseworkers who have not been analysed previously do not wish to take this training now, as they feel they might then want to become more like the analyst. On the other hand, those who have had some personal analysis find that they can work easily at the same "levels" and in the same way as other caseworkers (Sutherland, 1956).

Operational tensions were related to changes in the patterns of referral and the network of community services with which the FDB was connected. When the transfer to the Tavistock took place the Bureau's clients were exclusively referred by CAB workers, social workers in various settings and probation officers. Thereafter, medical referrals, notably by general practitioners, progressively replaced them and still preponderate among referred cases. Latterly, self-referred cases have become the majority but there are often "hidden referrers" and many of these are doctors. Thus, operational connectedness shifted towards the medical network. While the unit's experience has been that the distinction between the "social" and "medical" in this field is unhelpful, some sociologists and social theorists remain critical of what has been called the "medicalization of marriage" (Morgan, 1985).

Institutional tensions were inherent in a situation in which working relationships with the National Health Service Clinic preponderated over those with the independent TIHR, which carried legal, administrative and financial responsibility for the unit. In this respect the FDB was in the same position as other Clinic-linked units. However, these had been generated within the organization whereas the Bureau had been introduced from outside. An important factor in the negotiations leading to its transfer from the FWA had been the judgement that, with support from central and local government, it would become self-financing. This was (and has continued to be) a difficult position to achieve. On numerous occasions survival was only secured through the willingness of TIHR to underwrite prospective deficits, thus affording a breathing space in which to reach solvency. For a time a small number of staff holding Clinic posts were seconded part-time for work in the FDB.

Government grants-in-aid are permissive, not mandatory, and subject to the ebb and flow of economic climate and political opinion. The community's concern about the social and mental health implications of marriage breakdown and stress is, in part, reflected through official funding. However, the paradoxical nature of marriage as a personal relationship and as a social institution makes for ambivalence at governmental, organizational and personal levels. Notwithstanding changed attitudes and increasing openness, support for intensive study and therapeutic intervention remains equivocal.

The Mix of Practice, Training and Research

The concept of the practice, training and research "mix" as a total function was articulated in the pilot experiment.

In the years immediately following the move to the Tavistock, energies were mainly devoted to staff development and to a fuller exposition of the Bureau's work than had hitherto been possible. *Marriage: Studies in Emotional Conflict and Growth* (Pincus, 1960) described practice with a range of troubled marriages. It took account of unconscious processes that influence an individual's choice of partner and discussed the nature of conflict in the interaction between couples. It emphasized the benign as well as the destructive aspects of conflict for personal development and maturation in marriage.

The four-person therapeutic technique developed out of the pilot experiment. Because the possibilities of creative change in the marital relationship had been found to be greater when both partners were involved, the Bureau had come to work exclusively with couples. However, the involvement of one caseworker with two clients so added to the complexities of transference and countertransference that two workers were deployed to avoid them. It had been realized that this technique had a potential for staff training, the less experienced learning from their more experienced colleagues (Bannister et al., 1955). It was later observed that the relationship developed between the caseworkers tended to reflect important aspects of the client-couple's interaction. That is, the therapeutic relationship system was influenced by that of the clients. Scrutiny of this unconsciously determined phenomenon advanced understanding of the couple's difficulties. Some characteristics of the weekly case-conference where such scrutiny took place have changed over time. The staff have become more sophisticated and those with and without analytic experience and training more evenly balanced, so that the role of the psychiatrist/psychoanalyst has become less prominent. The distinctive influence of the case-conference has been described as follows (Pincus, 1960):

> It is clear that in order to keep their vital self-awareness and to understand as far as possible the extent to which their own involvement may be distorting their understanding of their clients' difficulties, the caseworkers need a medium in which they, too, may develop and feel free to involve themselves in relationships. Without such freedom it would become very difficult for them to avoid

working in mental blinkers which would prevent them from seeing anything except the rational content of their clients' complaints and fears, and of their own anxieties. The group provides a setting in which these anxieties can be aired and tolerated. Caseworkers have an opportunity to discuss their cases in conference, but the constant gain in casework experience which this provides is seen as incidental to the vital atmosphere created by the group which can be internalized so that workers carry it with them to their clients. It is essential that the atmosphere should be predominantly accepting and supportive so that the workers can be spontaneous in their discussions, knowing as they do that these will reveal hidden aspects of their own personalities. But, in so far as the group avoids a destructively critical attitude, it must, nevertheless, make demands on its members, the chief being for a disciplined and discriminating attitude to their work.

THE TRAINING OF ALLIED PROFESSIONALS

The training of allied professionals began in 1956 as a result of a request for a training course for probation officers whose matrimonial casework service in Magistrates' courts was growing. The implications of stress in marital and family relationships for work with offenders became increasingly apparent. The courses sponsored by the Probation and Aftercare Department of the Home Office were held annually and continued without a break for thirty years. This longevity, though significant, was not their most important feature, which lay in their function as a laboratory in which to develop concepts, test patterns of training courses and apply learning gained in the working-group.

The term "working-group" has particular connotations. It is no accident that practitioners concerned with marital problems should find themselves paying attention to the group as a vehicle for containing and working through the emotional impact of working in this field. They could not be unaware, in themselves as in their clients, of resistance to personal change. Bion has documented processes by which members of a group can unconsciously co-operate to avoid the struggle with their real task (Bion, 1961). Couples can also unconsciously co-operate to maintain illusions about themselves. Alongside the impetus for change and development goes what Bion described as a hatred of learning about the self and of the experience of uncertainty which this invariably entails—until the individual gains some mastery and is able to assume that degree of personal autonomy which is required for reality-based co-operation with others. Bion's work had a profound influence within the Tavistock as a whole and stimulated what came to be known as group relations training (Trist and Sofer, 1959; Rice, 1965). FDB staff became progressively more involved with group relations conferences as part of their own in-house training and as conference staff.

The work with probation officers was precursor to a wide range of extra-mural courses and training events involving allied practitioners and their employing institutions in the statutory and voluntary services, such as marriage guidance councils, in addition to universities and training organizations in the United Kingdom and abroad.

The beginning of intra-mural training was also linked to work with the probation service following an approach to the Tavistock Clinic by the Home Office. In the year following the first extra-mural course, the first experienced probation officers were seconded for supervised marital casework in the unit. They, and the officers who followed, became in-service tutors to colleagues undertaking marital work in the courts.

The FDB received foundation support for the provision of fellowships for United Kingdom and overseas post-graduate students. These comprised practitioners and practitioner-teachers, principally from probation and social work and, increasingly, from the marriage guidance movement in the UK, as well as medical and social workers from abroad, who would return to key roles in their employing organizations. It became policy to "train the trainers" a corollary being the extension of supervisory skills outside the specialized setting of the FDB.

The growing volume of training stimulated collaboration with others in the Tavistock concerned with inter-disciplinary teaching, primarily the Clinic-linked School of Family Psychiatry and Community Mental Health. An important aspect of training is that it enables direct contact to be maintained with the preoccupations and working problems of those in the field and with developments abroad. Training is also an important source of recruitment when internal students or those invited onto the staff of training events apply and are selected to join the unit. Their experience in other settings enriches its knowledge base and, through them, links with community services are strengthened.

RESEARCH AND PUBLICATION

The appearance of *Marriage: Studies in Emotional Conflict and Growth* in 1960 stimulated research and publication. A national conference organized by the FDB was held for a multi-disciplinary group of trainers and social work teachers. This produced a widely read monograph (Institute of Marital Studies, 1962).

The study and comparison of cases showed the operation of phantasies shared by couples at different levels of personality development, the basis of unconscious collusion, and distinguished between different patterns of defense against anxiety. This led to better understanding of the four-person relationship, the variable use of conjoint (foursome) and individual sessions and the enhancement of the therapeutic process (Bannister and Pincus, 1965; Lyons, 1973). A parallel study was devoted to brief intensive work and its prerequisite: help for practitioners to withstand the pressures exerted by disturbed clients in crisis (Guthrie and Mattinson, 1971).

Wider applications of experience and theory included the submission of evidence to government and others regarding the personal and family services of local authorities, and reform of divorce laws. This was the basis for an outline strategy to promote comprehensive services for the family, preventive as well as remedial. It took account of the interdependence of the mental health aspects of marriage and divorce, the impact of social change and the requirements of professional training, practice and co-operation (Woodhouse, 1969).

An examination was made of the marital participation and interaction of couples previously resident in a hospital for the subnormal in an attempt to understand why many subjects considered handicapped when single had been able to use the commitment to their partners for their own personal development (Mattinson, 1970). Other work, arising from consultancy in a children's hospital, was based on treatment of couples having a child suffering from recalcitrant illness (encopresis and asthma). This led to efforts to develop an approach to understanding and helping such sick children through working with the marital interaction of their parents (Mainprice, 1974). A third area of exploration derived from long-term collaboration with university teachers of social work students and their fieldwork supervisors (Mattinson, 1975).

The FDB had now become an advanced center in its field and took the title of Institute of Marital Studies (IMS). This affirmed its identity among organizations with which it had growing links. It became one of the five autonomous units reporting to the Council in a reorganized Tavistock.

By the end of the 1960s therapeutic work and training were making important contributions to IMS budgets. So were the staff through considerable unpaid time and the making over to the unit of all income from writing. Research costs had been met out of general funds. A period of rapidly rising inflation now raised financial uncertainty to an insupportable level. Technical innovations were inextricably bound up with these pressures, the more so in a small working group organized to ensure collective responsibility for its affairs.

Negotiation of long-term training commitments which provided a continuing interface with the managers of community services became more prominent. Technical and financial considerations combined to promote research supported by trusts and foundations. The first such project was undertaken in a London Social Services Department. Over a period of three years four IMS staff were participant observers in the Department and worked with clients to whom the organization gave a high priority (Mattinson and Sinclair, 1979). The project began a process through which experience of negotiation with other institutions was widened and deepened. It established a pattern of collaborative action-research which was to be influential in the unit's development. It provided direct experience of the stressful working-world of colleagues in community services. Through the staff involved, task-related anxiety was brought back into the IMS. The new work had to be accommodated emotionally as well as organizationally by the total working group, including administrative staff. An equivalent of the case conference had to be found for such action-research projects. The search was broadened for relevant theory through which to explain the phenomena encountered. The project gave added emphasis to the need for expansion. A "critical mass" was needed sufficient to accommodate this kind of research, the development of therapeutic work and training, and to enable the IMS to respond to unpredictable events and opportunities.

Intensification of relationships between the IMS and other related organizations through training and field-based action-research had parallels in the area of policy. Regular *consultation* between the IMS and the other major organizations in receipt of government grants-in-aid for marital work was by now well established. Consideration of their different but complementary roles resulted in a joint approach to central government. This approach sought a national review of marital work and services in the light of knowledge and experience gained since the field had last been officially reviewed in 1947. As a result a multi-disciplinary working party was set up on which the IMS was represented. It published a report entitled *Marriage Matters* (Home Office, 1979).

The report confirmed the span of agencies and professional disciplines involved with marital difficulties in their various guises. These agencies and practitioners, while varied in terms of their primary tasks, had in common the need to understand the nature of marital interaction and its effect on their work. Problems of inter-professional collaboration were emphasized. A coordinating role was envisaged for government with a small central unit to promote the better use of existing local resources. The aim of *Marriage Matters* was to stimulate debate as a prelude to change within government and among the many professionals and agencies involved.

Following a change of government, however, the necessary central initiative to implement change was not forthcoming. The emerging social climate revealed increasingly stark contradictions. There had been growing recognition that collaboration, interdependence and the interplay of differences were prerequisites for the development of institutions as they were for individuals, couples and families. At the same time anxiety was increasingly voiced about the finite nature of resources in the face of escalating demands. This led to defensive, reactive strategies. The external boundaries of groups and organizations tended to become less permeable as preoccupation with survival and stress among practitioners increased. Lack of resources was invoked as an irrefutable reason for limiting the time-span of commitment. Tension between autonomy and dependency was increasingly dealt with by an aggressive emphasis on independence. Reliance on techniques in treatment and training, and the avoidance of sustained relationship grew; a premium came to be put on short-term remedies for the ills of a growing number and range of "casualties." Reductionist attitudes rather than those encouraging attention to process and the interplay of the inner and outer worlds of those in difficulty were reinforced. As Sutherland (1980) pointed out, "the pluralism in approaches thus reflects a situation not so much stimulating differences within a healthy enterprise as one with serious and dangerous contradictions."

Later Developments

The changing focus and practice of the major part of TIHR gradually became less congruent with those of the IMS and, in 1979, the unit transferred to the Tavistock Institute of Medical Psychology. This charitable foundation—the founding body first of the Clinic and then of TIHR—having retained a supportive role in relation to both organizations, assumed legal responsibility for the IMS. The new arrangement aimed to leave the unit free to maintain its working relationship with the Clinic and relevant activities of the Institute and to adopt a distinctive form of organization more suited to its future adaptive needs.

NEW PROJECTS AND THEMES

In its new context the unit engaged in a series of collaborative and substantially funded enterprises following on from the Social Services Department project. One—with groups of health visitors—concerned the development of a preventive model for enhancing a couple's capacity to contain the tension inherent in the advent of a child, particularly the first-born. It questioned the proposition of "crisis theorists" that pregnancy is a propitious time for prophylactic mental health intervention (Clulow, 1982). Other work involved participation in a program in the Probation Service aimed at effecting settlements between divorcing couples subject to welfare enquiries to protect the well-being of their children. The work cast doubt on legal and other procedures based on the premise of essentially rational conflict resolution. This leads to an underestimation of the primitive nature of the hostility between many couples who fail to act in the best interests of their children (Clulow and Vincent, 1987). Workshops for practitioners in a variety of settings were held in three diverse areas of the country to compare experiences of work with clients when one or both partners in a marriage had become unemployed and to study the psychological impact of the loss of the opportunity to work. Attention was drawn to the reluctance of relevant professionals to involve themselves and reasons for this were investigated (Daniel, 1985; Mattinson, 1988).

The issues raised by *Marriage Matters*—particularly the need to promote interdisciplinary training and collaboration—were a continuing concern. When it became clear that no central initiative would materialize, a three-year training-cum-research program was mounted involving 50 practitioners from front-line medical and non-medical services. It focussed on the impact of marital stress on the five participating agencies and on the task-related anxieties impeding inter-professional collaboration (Woodhouse and Pengelly, forthcoming).

Alongside collaborative action-research, there were successors to earlier endeavors in therapeutic practice and training. A study of a psychodynamic marital therapy again highlighted the perceptions and subjective experience of the two therapists as much as those of the couple, but paid further attention to the process of referral and to the assessment of the outcome (Clulow, 1985). Factors relevant to brief marital therapy and the problem of assessing outcome were also considered (Clulow et al., 1986; Balfour et al., 1986). The couples in both instances were actively engaged in assessing the work, re-emphasizing the original conception of the therapeutic encounter as a shared enterprise.

Extended experience of training groups for social work supervisors in an inner London local authority drew on earlier IMS work when exploring the nature of the tension engendered by the supervisory role and of the anxiety commonly associated with it (Dearnley, 1985). Two new courses were added: an internal one, the first of its kind in the UK, leading to a Diploma in Marital Psychotherapy, with an extra-mural foundation course linked to it.

Continuity was also evident in continuing collaboration with referring general practitioners. There was joint examination by a medical and an IMS practitioner of the way patients present marital stress to their family doctor (Cohen and Pugh, 1984). Meanwhile, therapeutic work prompted consideration of such contemporary issues as cross-cultural marriages (Cohen, 1982) and the effect of abortion on marriage (Mattinson, 1985). International work continued. An international summer school began in 1983. Links have been maintained with colleagues in Europe and beyond. The chairmanship of the Commission of Marriage and Inter-personal Relations of the International Union of Family Organisations passed to the IMS in 1986.

INTEGRITY AND UNCERTAINTY

As Clulow (1985) observed, the Greek word "therapy" is commonly assumed to mean *curing* or *healing*. Its first meaning is, however, *waiting on, serving, attending*. Marital therapy in the IMS is a process of attending to couples and their unconsciously motivated interaction. It calls for informed listening, is reflective, essentially responsive and is concerned with the mutual influence of couples and therapists.

An interventionist, entrepreneurial mode, however, had increasingly to be adopted alongside the responsive one with clients; the pursuit of financial viability had to go hand-in-hand with professional development. Pressure on limited resources increased; it was never possible to keep the contending claims of practice, training and research/publication in anything but uneasy equilibrium. The different work patterns required in these three areas were often in conflict. But the overall outcome of managing these stressful boundaries has been creative. The culture developed by members of the working group embodied an effective social system of defenses against the anxieties inherent in the unit's therapeutic and other work and in its boundary position within and beyond the Tavistock.

Recent social and political trends are testing the integrity of the IMS and the coherence of its tripartite role. Progressively reduced financial support from central government and restrictions on local government services signify changes in political philosophy and social theory—and therefore attitudes towards the relationship between welfare and personal development. Whether or not the changes in society are radical, or part of an oscillating process, only time will tell.

The unit perforce became less dependent on direct public funding. The balance between technical development and financial necessity moved sharply towards the latter. Reciprocal processes with the practice, training, research mix have been seriously affected, giving rise to concern, not least as regards effects on the unit's core activity—service to clients—demands for which have escalated.

Changes in the field of care have inevitably affected the pattern of the unit's relationship within its professional network. Probation and social workers have become increasingly concerned to apply treatment techniques in work with specific target groups. The trend has been away from casework with its emphasis on psychodynamic processes. The non-statutory marriage guidance movement has also been affected. There has been a proliferation of many diverse forms of counselling and other types of help for personal problems.

Training and consultation continue with members of all these groups. As would be expected, institutional change is uneven. Some members continue to seek help from a psychodynamic approach to their practice. Growing numbers of general practitioners are becoming more aware of the relational aspects of their primary task. One outcome has been the establishment of the Group for the Advancement of Psychodynamics and Psychotherapy in Social Work (GAPS) and, since 1983, the publication of its *Journal of Social Work Practice*.

The medical/social dichotomy, though still relevant to the IMS, is less of an issue than it was, but differences between psychodynamic approaches and those concerned with a "technology of behavior" (Barrett, 1979) have become more so. The areas of relevant uncertainty have widened considerably for the IMS no less than for other practitioners in the field of care. Uncertainty generates anxiety. The evolution of the IMS to date supports Menzies' proposition that "the success and viability of a social institution are intimately connected with the techniques it uses to contain anxiety" (Menzies, 1970). Much will turn on the efficacy of the unit's social defense system in enabling members to maintain the integrity of the IMS in the face of environmental changes different in kind and quality from those hitherto confronted.

Conceptual Developments

THERAPEUTIC PROCESSES

CONFLICT AND ANXIETY WITHIN THE PERSON AND IN MARRIAGE

The partners bring to their relationship all their previous experience. This includes their internal, unconscious relationship systems. There is the person with a visible, acknowledged identity together with aspects of his or her personality which have been split off and repressed in the early stages of his development. These processes take place as a means of dealing with—that is, defending against—anxiety aroused because the needs inherent in these "subselves" are experienced as incompatible and their expression impossible if reciprocal relationships with the environment are to be sustained.

This view of the person mainly derives from the work of the object relations school of psychoanalysis, though by no means exclusively so. It has been found relevant in working with the several thousands of couples seen in the unit and the many more considered with colleagues in other settings. An understanding of the legacies the marriage partners bring to the relationship, and their influence on its characteristics and vulnerabilities, is based on it. Some facets may obtrude more than others in any given instance, but the part played by unconscious anxiety arising from conflictful relationships within the person and between the self and others is central; the psychic strain and restrictive effects of maintaining defensive splits are all too obvious.

EMOTIONAL CONFLICT AND GROWTH

There can be no emotional growth without emotional conflict. Conflict does not invariably lead to growth but is an important ingredient of it. Change is feared when it threatens an identity evolved as a means of coping with unconscious anxiety. This is so even though the resulting partial experience of the self, perceptions of others and meanings ascribed to events give rise to unsatisfying or painful experience. Emotional growth, i.e., maturation, involves the reintegration of, and an altered relationship with, those aspects of the self which have been split off, repressed, denied. It therefore means a modification of the image, including the sexual image, the person has been impelled to assume and, through selective perception, has seen others as confirming—indeed has often coerced them into confirming. In some marriages conflict between the partners has the quality of a fight to the death, reflecting the violence with which the internal image of the self is liable to be defended when it is felt to be threatened.

Marriage is a transference relationship *par excellence*. The partners become a fundamental part of each other's environment; each is both subject and object and each is the object of the other's attachment. By its nature, the relationship is a primary one and the most direct heir to childhood experience in adult life. In it, emotive aspects of earlier actual and phantasy relationships are transferred by each onto the other; indeed, their interplay ensures that unconsciously, as well as consciously, experienced aspects of the past and the conflict and anxiety associated with them, are re-evoked—but in a new and present dimension. Thus, stress in marriage reflects conflict within the person, externalized and acted out in the partnership.

SHARED DEFENSES, INTERACTION AND THE POTENTIAL FOR DEVELOPMENT

This process makes the internal dilemmas of each partner accessible through their interaction. As well as biological imperatives and the basic human need for attachment, such interaction reveals the developmental as well as the defensive potential of the dynamic relationship system in which both partners become deeply involved emotionally, even if negatively. Such involvement is perhaps unremarkable in relationships of long-standing; together couples build up a psycho-biological system, one which becomes enmeshed in and supported by a complex of social roles and responsibilities. Therapeutic experience, however, leads to the conclusion that the original choice of each by the other in any continuing relationship is unconsciously purposeful in that complementarity is a dominant feature; each recognizes aspects of him- or herself, of which they are not consciously or willingly aware, in the person of the other. It shows that couples have deep-seated psychological preoccupations in common, notwithstanding differences in the way they may be articulated.

Developmental—and therefore therapeutic—potential lies in the fact that what is feared and rejected in the internal world, and is located in the person of the partner, is not lost but is "lived with." It is therefore available experientially and may be assimilated. Along with fear and rejection, there is evidence of a psychic need to reunite what Laing (1960) called the "divided self."

A basic role in marital interaction is ascribed to the mechanism of projective identification and the defense of projection (Klein, 1932). The less the projection, the greater the possibility that each partner may become more of a separate, autonomous person and less the receptacle of what the other rejects and denies. However, the process of withdrawing projections and of reintrojection is precarious and fitful. Both partners are collusively involved and each may confirm the worst fears of the other, especially when an emotionally significant life event disturbs the equilibrium or when change is attempted. Stress can become such that the containing function of the relationship (Jung, 1925) is threatened or overwhelmed. If help is sought, it is the task of therapy to afford a breathing space and a containing environment within which the implications of change for both partners may be tested.

Constellations within dyadic systems are infinitely variable as are patterns of attachment. At one end are those where mutual defenses support a shared unconscious purpose of the relationship which is anti-developmental—to avoid engagement with life. At the other, are couples where the mutual value of defenses lies in furthering the capacity to deal with internal conflict and external stress, supporting their containment and thus fostering growth (Morris, 1971). In terms of the defense of projection, developmental potential turns on how much of the personality is got rid of in this way; how violent is the mental act of projection; and the rigidity with which the defense is maintained.

INTERACTIVE PROCESSES IN THERAPEUTIC RELATIONSHIPS

A critical advance in marital work was to see that what the partners complained of in each other was an unwanted part of themselves (Sutherland, 1962). Caseworkers/therapists are also bound to become the object of their clients' projections, good and bad. With an emotionally significant relationship established, they too have transferred onto them feelings and attitudes arising from clients' internal needs which are not predominantly a reaction to the "real" workers; and the workers' responses are bound to be affected.

At the beginning of the unit's life, the emphasis was mainly on enabling staff to manage the sometimes disturbing experiences to which sustained relationships with clients can give rise and on safeguarding them from inappropriate responses—counter-transference in its original sense (Freud, 1910). Through supervision during training, and continuously in the work of the case conference, ways were found to help staff to become aware of these phenomena, to find an appropriate distance from clients and to distinguish between what in the work was a function of the client's and what of their own trans-ference; to understand the detail of the former in any given case and to accept professional responsibility for the latter. The use of the four-person therapeutic relationship was an added safeguard. As they are different people, the counter-transferences of the two caseworkers are also different. The interaction be-tween the therapeutic pair and their subjective experience of each other was gradually recognized as an added source of information about the dilemmas in their clients' relationship (Pincus, 1960). To give a simple example, it is common in four-person work for one of the therapeutic pair to feel that his or her colleague is colluding with one or other client to the detriment of the treatment. He or she may be. But how these differences are articulated and the difficulty of their resolution is frequently found to be an unconscious reaction to the clients. The workers' behavior has important similarities with the cou-ple's defense against anxiety in confronting specific differences. The process and its meaning may only become clear when the case is presented at con-ference which is a formal part of the therapeutic procedure.

Recognition that such reactions were not solely a product of the personal or technical deficiencies of workers was contemporary with what Mattin-son (1975) saw as the widening and enriching of the concept of counter-transference by those "who perceived the counter-transference as a function of the transference of the client. The reaction of the worker to the clients' transference need not be condemned, but could be noted and used for increas-ing the understanding of the clients' behavior."

Following Searles (1959), Mattinson summarized the IMS position on counter-transference in therapeutic interaction as

> an innate and inevitable ingredient which is sometimes a conscious reaction to the observed behaviour of the client, or which is sometimes an unconscious reaction to the felt and not consciously understood behaviour of the client, and which can be used for increasing understanding of the client. (In addition) . . . the resolution by the worker of the counter-transference (is) one of the main ingredients of casework which enables the client to resolve and relinquish the transference.

It is not that classical counter-transference, i.e., workers' transference, is disregarded as a factor militating against effective therapy. It is the change of emphasis that is important, one which points to the need for workers to be free to engage with clients in a human interaction within a structured, containing therapeutic environment. They have to discover what, for each of them, is the appropriate closeness to and distance from their clients in the knowledge that "you can exert no influence if you are not susceptible to influence" (Jung, 1931); that emotional involvement is the vehicle for change; that without it one is denied the opportunity to learn about critical aspects of clients' unconscious intra- and interpersonal conflicts which, being so, cannot be expressed in words.

INTERACTIVE PROCESSES IN TRAINING: THE REFLECTION PROCESS

The IMS was slow to recognize the full implications for training and trainers of what had come to be taken for granted in the unit's practice: explicit attempts to make use of the workers' unrecognized responses to clients' unconscious defenses against anxiety. This experience had indeed been taken into training aimed at helping practitioners develop understanding and skill in work with marital and related family stress relevant to their own setting and field of work. But so far as trainers were concerned, the emphasis had remained on helping them extend *their own* casework in the firm belief that what the teacher can offer trainees is bounded by his own practice experience.

In IMS courses, supervisors of social work students insisted that attention be paid to their supervisory problems as well as their own practice. Shared work on these issues enabled material to be assembled supporting the thesis, first put forward by Searles (1955) arising from his supervision of analytic work with psychiatric patients, to the effect that processes at work currently in the relationship between client and worker are often reflected in the relationship between worker and supervisor. Searles used the term "reflection process" to describe this mirroring phenomenon.

Simple of expression, the application of the concept can be more difficult in practice, the processes often being subtle in their manifestation. Included are

- the degree of involvement with the client that trainee workers or staff members are able to allow themselves
- the strength and flexibility of workers' psychological boundaries (a personal dimension)
- the capacity of the setting to facilitate and contain the work and its associated anxiety (an institutional dimension)
- the distinction between conscious and unconscious counter-transference (for example, negative counter-transference may be a response to the clients' projections, but it may also be a conscious reaction to objectively unpleasant or abhorrent aspects of their behavior which are not understood
- the extent to which the worker's responses are out of character and defensive, this being an indication of the degree of disturbance encountered

The full range of the reflection process is evidenced when a third-party (the supervisor in this instance) also reacts unconsciously. That is to say, when there is acting out in response to the trainee and his material which, while it may convey his consciously felt anxiety, is false and leads to an impasse between them. It was a supervisor's bewildered discomfort at her persistent and un-characteristically "waspish" treatment of an apparently impenetrable student, whose defensive lack of involvement in the supervision was seen to be similar to that of a mother with her delinquent son, that focussed attention on the process. It is one through which unconscious defenses against anxiety within one relationship system (the clients') can be carried over, via the "bridging" worker, into another adjacent one. When the meaning of this kind of interaction is unravelled, understanding of the client's defense is advanced and the trainee's work can change.

PROFESSIONAL AND INSTITUTIONAL PROCESSES

The institutional dimension is an important variable in the worker's response to clients and their relationships. Training work showed that marital problems were intimidating for subjective as much as technical reasons. Working with a focus on a couple's interaction could threaten the psychological distance social workers were generally enabled to maintain between themselves and clients when addressing the particular difficulties their agencies were established to treat—delinquency, mental illness, child neglect, etc. Marriage and marital problems, however, were often too near home for comfort. For the majority, their specialized institutional setting provided little or no support in managing this boundary and the anxiety engendered by work with the intimate relationship of marriage (Balint, E., 1959; Woodhouse, 1967).

By the mid-1970s, organizational boundaries in the personal social services had changed; many of the specialized services had been amalgamated; social workers, like their agencies, now had multiple roles and tasks. These changes and a better grasp of the functioning of open systems required a fresh assessment. Hence the importance, in the present context, of the local authority social services project and the relevance of the direct experience of IMS staff when practicing alongside social work colleagues.

The evidence suggested that a large proportion of the Social Service Department's time and resources were devoted to a core group of married clients with severe relationship problems, which it was ill adapted to treat. These clients evoked ambivalent responses from social workers who wished to help but feared being overwhelmed. Worker/client interaction was liable to reinforce the pattern of ambivalent attachments and the defenses of denial and splitting dominating the clients' lives. The culture and mode of functioning of the organization, itself under pressure from proliferating demand and increasingly restricted resources, abetted practitioners in avoiding or defending against the anxiety inherent in providing the kind of reliable, sustained though time-limited help appropriate to these deprived and demanding clients. Indeed, the institutional framework, in association with the clients, in itself stimulated anxiety. It diminished the ability to address their practical and emotional problems as interdependent and to do marital work.

Concerning the problem of engendering change in local authority social services, the setting in which the majority of social workers operate, Mattinson and Sinclair (1979) point out that

> If the workers are continually subjected to the splitting mechanisms of (these) clients, they too may become predisposed to this mode of behaviour, and as the individual worker can reflect his client's defence, so too may some of the organizational practices which the worker is expected to perform. The problem is that whereas the individual worker may eventually use his reflection constructively in understanding the client's emotional problem, it is much more difficult for the organization as a whole to do this once a particular practice has become institutionalized. Unfortunately, just as the resistance to change is believed to be greatest in clients exercising the most primitive psychic defences (and splitting is a very primitive defence), so group resistance to social change may be greatest in social systems also dominated by this mode.

Institutional resistance to change helps explain the constraints on the outcome of training. Trainees are potential change agents. Their attempts to introduce new perspectives on practice may be met by ambivalence if these are at variance with established social defenses. Reviewing a training course and their subsequent working experience, a group of well established probation officers reported feeling "like Christians in the catacombs" back in their agency.

Interaction Between Institutions

The Social Services Department project graphically confirmed that there is a strong tendency for the internal problems of individuals, couples and families to be externalized and to be mirrored by the relationship between practitioners to the detriment of collaboration. More recently other therapists have commented on the same processes (e.g., Reder, 1983; Will, 1983). Britton (1981) coined the phrase "complementary acting out" to describe their manifestations at the level of the service network.

However, it is clear that practitioners are not passive recipients of clients' projections. Not only do they have personal susceptibilities to anxiety and idiosyncratic ways of defending against it which they take into their work, they operate defenses which are embedded in their agency's culture and expressed in its rules, organizational procedures and ways of interpreting policy.

The common need for defenses against anxiety is an important factor in the cohesion of associations (Jaques, 1955). Staff whose psychological needs are sufficiently met by the prevailing social defense mechanisms will support and seek to preserve them. The alternative is to leave. Even a worker with mature ways of coping with personal anxiety will find it hard to resist a well developed professional or agency defense, particularly if, as is often the case, the nature of the work arouses strong and primitive anxieties (Hornby, 1983).

The program undertaken by Woodhouse and Pengelly (forthcoming) involved the study of work with more than a hundred cases that preoccupied experienced workers in one locality. It lasted three years and was mainly conducted in mixed-discipline workshops. The majority of the worrying cases brought into the program raised just such strong and primitive anxieties.

Anxieties of this kind and quality can threaten a practitioner's sense of professional adequacy and personal autonomy. The defenses discussed by Hornby (1983) were variously enacted by participating practitioners in their casework and in the program: denial to avoid experiencing envy of other workers' opportunities and skills; displacement of hostility; splitting off and projecting feelings of inadequacy and, especially in the few cases worked jointly, projective identification which could ensure that skill and competence was vested in one practitioner, uselessness and helplessness in another. The defensive use of boundaries—around the worker/client or doctor/patient relationship, or around agencies—was also prominent. The testing of mutual perceptions through working relationships was generally avoided and the tendency of practitioners to isolate themselves from one another was evidenced in case discussion and reports which showed workers behaving as if colleagues in other agencies relevant to the work did not exist or were unapproachable.

Collaboration involves the exploration of differences and the revelation of uncertainty. Such experience in itself can generate depressive and persecutory anxiety which takes time to modify. This was achieved to some extent among participants in the containing and enabling environment the program aimed to provide. It represented a "temporary institution," analogues of which are difficult to establish in local service networks, a fact recognized in *Marriage Matters* by the recommendation that local multi-disciplinary training and development groups be established.

All the processes described impede collaboration, but there is a further and more entrenched one. The socially structured defense mechanisms operating in agencies and professional groups, while they have features in common, are distinctive. They stem from the unconscious as well as the conscious anxiety inherent in the tasks practitioners are employed to perform. They are related to the work of doctors with the sick and dying; health visitors (community nurses) with mothers and babies and conflictual parent/child relationships; marriage counsellors with stress in intimate heterosexual relationship; probation officers with delinquents and tensions between conformity and individual liberty; and social workers with the disturbed and rejected and with parents who fail to care adequately for their children. However, such tasks afford practitioners their professional identity as well as the sentient group with which they identify and on which they depend for emotional support (Miller and Rice, 1967). Defenses against task-associated anxiety command deep emotional loyalty. They characterize their organizations but are seldom manifest in situations where they are accessible to the kind of work-related scrutiny that can facilitate modification and the mastery of the anxieties.

When workers share responsibility for clients or patients or engage in joint work, incompatibilities between agency defenses tend to emerge. These are accentuated when the clients involved employ primitive projective defenses, when their difficulties give rise to high levels of objective anxiety and, at the same time, stimulate powerful unconscious phantasies. The higher the level of anxiety, the greater the reliance on institutionalized defenses is likely to be and the more emotionally hazardous it becomes for practitioners to enter into each other's working-world for fear of losing hold of their own. Thus, in situations where collaboration is at a premium, as when children are at risk, it is often most difficult to achieve.

Other factors also influence inter-professional and inter-agency relationships. Some emanate from the personal characteristics of individuals; some are structural; others have to do with values, status and professional and wider politics. Dire consequences can follow failures in inter-professional and inter-agency collaboration. When they do, and public concern leads to official enquiry, refinement of practice guidelines and improved administrative and legal procedures are mainly looked to for remedy. Valuable as these are in themselves, such rational prescriptions commonly fail to embody recognition of what Will and Baird (1984) have called "real inter-professional vulnerabilities." Gross failures in collaboration between practitioners and agencies are invariably multi-faceted. Unless the inevitability of intense unconscious anxiety and conflict is acknowledged and their corollary in institutionalized as well as personal defenses against them accepted rather than denied or condemned, improved working relationships, especially under stressful conditions, are likely to remain elusive.

The meaning and purpose of stress and conflict in the relationship between couples point towards the need for an integrated approach to understanding them. This demands creative interaction within and between the discrete but interdependent open systems which, operating at different levels, constitute the caring services.

References

Balfour, F., C. Clulow and B. Dearnley. 1986. "The Outcome of Maritally Focussed Psychotherapy Offered as a Possible Model for Marital Psychotherapy Outcome Studies." *British Journal of Psychotherapy,* 3:133–43.

Balint, E. 1959. "Training Postgraduate Students in Social Casework." *British Journal of Medical Psychology,* 32:193–99.

Balint, M. 1954. "Method and Technique in the Teaching of Medical Psychology, II. Training General Practitioners in Psychotherapy." *British Journal of Medical Psychology,* 27:37–41.

Bannister, K., A. Lyons, L. Pincus, J. Robb, A. Shooter and J. Stephens. 1955. *Social Casework in Marital Problems.* London: Tavistock Publications.

Bannister, K. and L. Pincus. 1965. *Shared Phantasy in Marital Problems: Therapy in a Four-Person Relationship.* London: Institute of Marital Studies.

Barrett, W. 1979. *The Illusion of Technique.* London: William Kimber.

Bion, W.R. 1961. *Experiences in Groups and Other Papers.* London: Tavistock Publications; New York: Basic Books.

Bott, E. 1957. *Family and Social Network* (2nd edition, 1971). London: Tavistock Publications.

Britton, R. 1981. "Re-enactment as an Unwitting Professional Response to Family Dynamics." In *Psychotherapy with Families,* edited by S. Box, B. Copley, J. Magagna and E. Moustaki. London: Routledge and Kegan Paul.

Clulow, C.F. 1982. *To Have and to Hold: Marriage, the First Baby and Preparing Couples for Parenthood.* Aberdeen: Aberdeen University Press.

———. 1985. *Marital Therapy: An Inside View.* Aberdeen: Aberdeen University Press.

Clulow, C.F., B. Dearnley and F. Balfour. 1986. "Shared Phantasy and Therapeutic Structure in a Brief Marital Psychotherapy." *British Journal of Psychotherapy,* 3:124–32.

Clulow, C.F. and C. Vincent. 1987. *In the Child's Best Interests.* London: Tavistock, Sweet and Maxwell.

Cohen, N. 1982. "Same or Different? A Problem of Identity in Cross Cultural Marriages." *Journal of Family Therapy,* 4:177–99.

Cohen, N. and G. Pugh. 1984. "The Presentation of Marital Problems in General Practice." *The Practitioner,* 228:651–56.

Daniel, D. 1985. "Love and Work: Complementary Aspects of Personal Identity." *International Journal of Social Economics,* 12:48–55.

Dearnley, B. 1985. "A Plain Man's Guide to Supervision—Or New Clothes for the Emperor." *Journal of Social Work Practice,* 2:52–65.

Freud, S. 1910. *The Future Prospects of Psycho-Analytic Therapy,* Standard Edition, 11. London: Hogarth Press and the Institute of Psycho-Analysis.

———. 1926. *Inhibitions, Symptoms and Anxiety.* Standard Edition, 20. London: Hogarth Press and the Institute of Psycho-Analysis.

Guthrie, L. and J. Mattinson. 1971. *Brief Casework with a Marital Problem.* London: Institute of Marital Studies.

Home Office. 1979. *Marriage Matters.* London: Her Majesty's Stationery Office.

Hornby, S. 1983. "Collaboration in Social Work: A Major Practice Issue." *Journal of Social Work Practice,* 1:35–55.

Institute of Marital Studies. 1962. *The Marital Relationship as a Focus for Casework.* London: Institute of Marital Studies.

Jaques, E. 1955. "Social Systems as a Defence Against Persecutory and Depressive Anxiety." In *New Directions in Psycho-Analysis,* edited by M. Klein, P. Heimann and R. E. Money-Kyrle. London: Tavistock Publications; New York: Basic Books.

Jung, C. 1925. "Marriage as a Psychological Relationship in the Development of Personality." *Collected Works, Volume 17,* 1954. London: Routledge and Kegan Paul.

———. 1931. "Problems of Modern Psychotherapy." *Collected Works,* Volume 16, 1954. London: Routledge and Kegan Paul.

Klein, M. 1932. *The Psycho-Analysis of Children.* London: Hogarth Press.

Laing, R.D. 1960. *The Divided Self.* London: Tavistock Publications.

Lyons, A. 1973. "Therapeutic Intervention in Relation to the Institution of Marriage." In *Support, Innovation and Autonomy,* edited by R. Gosling. London: Tavistock Publications.

Mainprice, J. 1974. *Marital Interaction and Some Illnesses in Children.* London: Institute of Marital Studies.

Mattinson, J. 1970. *Marriage and Mental Handicap.* London: Duckworth; Pittsburgh: University of Pittsburgh Press.

———. 1975. *The Reflection Process in Casework Supervision.* London: Institute of Marital Studies.

———. 1985. "The Effects of Abortion on Marriage." In *CIBA Foundation Symposium 115, Abortion: Medical Progress and Social Implications.* London: Pitman.

———. 1988. *Work, Love and Marriage: The Impact of Unemployment.* London: Duckworth.

Menzies, I.E.P. 1949. "Factors Affecting Family Breakdown in Urban Communities." *Human Relations,* 2:363–73.

———. 1970. *The Functioning of Social Systems as a Defence Against Anxiety.* London: Tavistock Institute of Human Relations, Pamphlet No. 3.

Morgan, D.H.J. 1985. *The Family, Politics and Social Theory.* London: Routledge and Kegan Paul.

Morris, B. 1971. "An Educational Perspective on Mental Health." In *Towards Community Mental Health,* edited by J.D. Sutherland. London: Tavistock Publications.

Pincus, L. (Editor) 1973. *Marriage: Studies in Emotional Conflict and Growth.* London: Institute of Marital Studies. First edition 1960.

Reder, P. 1983. "Disorganised Families and the Helping Professions: 'Who's in Charge of What?' " *Journal of Family Therapy,* 1:23–36.

Rice, A.K. 1965. *Learning for Leadership: Interpersonal and Intergroup Relations.* London: Tavistock Publications.

Searles, H.F. 1955. "The Informational Value of the Supervisor's Emotional Experience." In *Collected Papers on Schizophrenia and Related Subjects,* 1965. London: Hogarth Press and the Institute for Marital Studies.

———. 1959. "Oedipal Love in the Counter Transference." In *Collected Papers on Schizophrenia and Related Subjects.* 1965. London: Hogarth Press and the Institute of Psycho-Analysis.

Sutherland, J.D. 1955. "Introduction." In *Social Casework in Marital Problems,* edited by K. Bannister, A. Lyons, L. Pincus, J. Robb, A. Shooter and J. Stephens. London: Tavistock Publications.

———. 1956. "Psychotherapy and Social Casework, 1." In *The Boundaries of Casework,* edited by E.M. Goldberg, E.E. Irvine, A.B. Lloyd Davies and K.F. McDougall. London: Association of Psychiatric Social Workers.

————. 1962. "Introduction." In *The Marital Relationship as a Focus for Casework*. London: Institute of Marital Studies.

————. 1980. *The Psychodynamic Image of Man: A Philosophy for the Caring Professions*. Aberdeen: Aberdeen University Press.

Trist, E.L. and C. Sofer. 1959. *Exploration in Group Relations*. Leicester: Leicester University Press.

Will, D. 1983. "Some Techniques for Working with Resistant Families of Adolescents." *Journal of Adolescence*, 6:13–26.

Will, D. and D. Baird. 1984. "An Integrated Approach to Dysfunction in Inter-Professional Systems." *Journal of Family Therapy*, 6:275–90.

Wilson, A.T.M. 1947a. "The Development of a Scientific Basis in Family Casework." *Social Work*, 4:62–69.

————. 1947b. "Some Implications of Medical Practice and Social Casework for Action Research." *Journal of Social Issues*, 3:11–28.

————. 1949. "Some Reflections and Suggestions on the Prevention and Treatment of Marital Problems." *Human Relations*, 2:233–51.

Wilson, A.T.M., I. Menzies and E. Eichholz. 1949. "Report of the Marriage Welfare Sub-Committee of the Family Welfare Association." *Social Work*, 6:258–62.

Woodhouse, D.L. 1967. "Short Residential Courses for Post-Graduate Social Workers." In *The Use of Small Groups in Training*, edited by R.H. Gosling et al. London: Tavistock Institute of Medical Psychology and Codicote Press.

————. 1969. "Marital Problems: A Strategy for Service and Research." In *The Future of Christian Marriage*, edited by J. Marshall. London: Chapman.

Woodhouse, D.L. and P.J.C. Pengelly. (Forthcoming). *Impediments to Collaboration: Implications of Stress in Couples and Families for the Network of Community Services*.

Elizabeth Bott Spillius

Conjugal Roles and Social Networks*

This paper will give an account of the sociological results of an intensive inter-disciplinary study of 20 London families. It will be confined to one problem: how to interpret the variations occurring in the way husbands and wives performed their conjugal roles.

A joint conjugal role-relationship is one in which husband and wife carry out many activities together, with a minimum of task differentiation and separation of interests. Husband and wife not only plan the affairs of the family together, but also exchange many household tasks and spend much of their leisure time together. A segregated conjugal role-relationship is one in which husband and wife have a clear differentiation of tasks and a considerable number of separate interests and activities; they have a division of labor into male tasks and female tasks; they expect to have different leisure pursuits; both have their own friends outside the home. Yet, these are only differences of degree. All families must have some division of labor between husband and wife; all families must have some joint activities.

Early in the research, it seemed likely that these differences of segregation roles were related to forces in the social environment and an effort was made to explain them in terms of social class. This attempt was not very successful. Most husbands in joint conjugal role-relationships were professionals, but there were several working-class families that had relatively little segregation and several professional families in which segregation was considerable. An attempt was also made to relate degree of segregation to the type of local area in which the family lived, since the families with most segregation lived in homogeneous areas of low population turnover, whereas those with predominantly joint role-relationships lived in heterogeneous areas of high population turnover. Once again, there were several exceptions. But there was a more important difficulty in these attempts to correlate segregation of conjugal roles with class position and type of local area. The research was not designed to produce valid statistical correlations. Our aim was to study the interrelation of various social and psychological factors within each family considered as a social system. Attempts at rudimentary statistical correlation did not make

*A shortened version of the original—*Human Relations*, 8:345–84, 1955.

clear how one factor affected another. Attempts to correlate segregation of conjugal roles with factors selected from the generalized social environment of the family did not yield a meaningful interpretation. I turned to look more closely at the immediate environment of the families, that is, at their external relationships with friends, neighbors, relatives, clubs, shops, places of work, etc. This approach proved to be more fruitful.

The external social relationships of all families appeared to assume the form of a network rather than of an organized group. In an organized group, the component individuals make up a larger social whole with common aims, interdependent roles and a distinctive sub-culture. In network formation some but not all of the component individuals have social relationships with one another. They do not form an organized group and the component external units do not make up a larger social whole; they are not surrounded by a common boundary.

Although all the research families belonged to networks rather than to groups, there was considerable variation in the connectedness of these networks. By connectedness I mean the extent to which the people known by a family know one another independently of the family. I use the term dispersed network to describe a network in which there are few relationships amongst the component units, and the term highly connected network to describe a network in which there are many such relationships.

A detailed examination of the research data reveals that the degree of segregation of conjugal roles is related to the degree of network connectedness. Those families with a high degree of segregation in role-relationships had a highly connected network; many of their friends, neighbors and relatives knew one another. Families with a relatively joint role-relationship between husband and wife had a dispersed network; few of their relatives, neighbors and friends knew one another. There were many degrees of variation between these two extremes. On the basis of our data, I should therefore like to put forward the following hypothesis: The degree of segregation in the role-relationship of husband and wife varies directly with the connectedness of the family's social network. The more connected the network, the more segregation between the roles of husband and wife. The more dispersed the network, the less segregation between the roles of husband and wife.

If one is to understand segregation of conjugal roles, one should examine the effect of the family's immediate social environment of friends, neighbors, relatives and institutions. The question remains, however, as to why some families should have highly connected networks whereas others have dispersed networks. In part, network connectedness depends on the family themselves. One family may choose to introduce their friends, neighbors and relatives to one another, whereas another may not. One family may move around a great deal so that its network becomes dispersed, whereas another family may stay put. But these choices are limited and shaped by a number of forces over which the family does not have direct control. At this point the total social environment becomes relevant. The economic and occupational system, the structure of formal institutions, the ecology of cities and many other factors affect the connectedness of networks, and limit and shape the decisions that families make. Factors associated with social class and neighborhood composition affect segregation of conjugal roles through direct action on the internal structure of the family, but indirectly through their effects on its network. Conceptually, the network stands between the family and the total social environment. The connectedness of a family's network depends, on the one hand, on certain forces in the total environment and, on the other, on the personalities of the members of the family and on the way they react to these forces.

*Methods of Collecting Data**

Although this paper will be devoted primarily to discussion of the effect of external social relationship on the role-relationship of husband and wife, the research as a whole was designed to investigate families not only sociologically but also psychologically. The research techniques accordingly consisted of a combination of the field-work method of the social anthropologist, in which the group under investigation is studied as a working whole in its natural habitat in so far as this is possible, and the case-study method in which individuals are studied by clinical interviews. No attempt was made to use statistical procedures.

The families studied were "ordinary," in the sense that they did not come to us for help with personal or familial problems, and they were usually able to cope themselves with such difficulties as they had. We sought them out, they did not come to us. In order to simplify the task for comparison, only families with young children were selected. In order further to restrict the number of variables, only English families of Protestant background were selected. All 20 families lived in London or Greater London, but they were scattered all over the area and did not form an organized group. Although the families resembled one another in phase of marriage and in national and religious background, they varied considerably in occupation and in socio-economic status; the net incomes of the husbands after tax ranged from £325 to £1,500 (at 1953 values).

Much difficulty was encountered in contacting suitable families, and the effort to find them taught us a good deal about the way families are related to other social groups. The 20 families were eventually contacted through the officials of various service institutions, such as doctors, hospitals, schools,

*For an account of field techniques see Robb (1953) and Bott (1957, Chapter 2).

local political parties and through friends of the family. Introductions were most successful when the contact person was well known and trusted by both husband and wife, and the most satisfactory channel of contact was through friends of the family.

After the contact person had told a prospective family about the research and had got their agreement to an explanatory interview by one of the research staff, one of the field workers visited the family at their home to describe what the research was about and what it would involve for the family. The field worker explained the background of the research, the content of the interviews, and the time they would take, and made it clear that the family could withdraw at any time, that the material would be treated with professional discretion and that if we wished to publish any confidential material that might reveal the couple's identity, we should consult them beforehand. The research staff also undertook to pay any expenses that the couple might incur as a result of the investigation. Although the provisional and explanatory nature of the first interview was always emphasized, we found that most of the couples who got that far had usually decided to take part in the research before they met the field worker, chiefly on the basis of what the contact person had told them. We have no systematic information about couples who were consulted but decided not to participate.

After a family had agreed to take part, the field worker paid several visits to them at home in the evening for joint interviews with the husband and wife. He or she also went at least once on the week-end to meet the children and observe the whole family together. There were thirteen home interviews on the average, the range being from eight to nineteen. Each home interview began with half an hour of casual chatting followed by more focussed discussions on particular topics during which notes were taken. The topics discussed were kinship, family background and personal history until marriage; the first phase of the family from marriage until the birth of the first child; an account of family life at the time of interviewing, including a daily, weekly and yearly diary; a description of external social relationships with service institutions such as schools, church, clinic, doctor, with voluntary associations and recreational institutions, and more informal relationships with friends, neighbors and relatives; an account of the division of labor between husband and wife in overall planning, in the economic support of the family, in domestic tasks and in child care; and finally, questions about values and ideology concerning family life, social class, money and financial management, and general political, social and religious matters. These topics were used as a general guide by the field worker; their order and the form of questioning were left to discretion. Usually he or she raised a topic, and the couple carried on the discussion themselves with occasional additional questions. The discussion frequently wandered away from the assigned topic, but little attempt was made to restrict such digressions, since all the behavior of husband and wife towards one another and towards the field worker was held to be significant data.

In addition to the interviews with the 20 families, discussions about families in general were held with various persons, particularly doctors, who had considerable knowledge of family life. Discussions were also held with various organized groups such as Community Centres and Townswomen's Guilds. These groups had no direct connection with the families we interviewed, and in most cases they were composed of considerably older people, usually women. These discussions were therefore not directly relevant to the analysis of the research families, but they provided useful information on the norms of family life. In a public, group situation, especially one which lasts for only one session, people seem much more willing to talk about norms than to discuss their actual behavior.

Classification of Families

If families are classified according to the extremes of the two dimensions of conjugal role-segregation and network connectedness, four patterns are logically possible: segregated conjugal role-relationship associated with a highly connected network; segregated conjugal role-relationship associated with a dispersed network; joint conjugal role-relationship associated with a highly connected network; and joint conjugal role-relationship associated with a dispersed network. Empirically, two of these patterns, the second and third, did not occur. There were no families in which a highly segregated conjugal role-relationship was associated with a dispersed network; there were no families in which a joint conjugal role-relationship was associated with a highly connected network.

Six of the research families were clustered in the first and fourth patterns. There was one family that conformed to the first pattern, a high degree of conjugal role-segregation combined with a highly connected network. There were five families that conformed to the fourth pattern, a joint conjugal role-relationship associated with a dispersed network. These six families represent the extremes of the research set. There were nine families that were intermediate in degree of conjugal role-segregation and similarly intermediate in degree of network connectedness. Finally there were five families that appeared to be in a state of transition both with respect to their network formation and with respect to their conjugal role-relationship.

Among the twenty families, there was thus some clustering at certain points along a possible continuum from a highly segregated to a very joint conjugal role-relationship, and along a second continuum from a highly connected to a dispersed network. The families did not fall into sharply separated types so that

TABLE 1   Relationship Among Conjugal Segregation, Type of Network and Type of Occupation*

Families in descending order of conjugal segregation	Type of network	Type of occupation
Newbolt	close-knit	semi-skilled manual
Mudge	medium-knit	semi-skilled manual
Dodgson (changing reluctantly from highly segregated to more joint)	transitional (move already made)	semi-skilled manual
Barkway	transitional (contemplating move)	clerical
Redfern	transitional (about to move)	semi-professional
Baldock	medium-knit	skilled manual
Apsley	medium-knit	professional
Wraith (becoming more joint)	transitional (several moves already made)	professional
Appleby	medium-knit	skilled manual clerical
Fawcett	medium-knit	clerical
Butler (changing eagerly from highly segregated to more joint)	transitional (move already made)	skilled manual
Thornton	medium-knit	semi-professional
Hartley	medium-knit	semi-professional
Salmon	medium-knit	semi-professional
Jarrold	medium-knit	skilled manual
Bruce	loose-knit	clerical
Denton	loose-knit	professional
Bullock	loose-knit	professional
Woodman	loose-knit	semi-professional
Daniels	loose-knit	semi-professional

*All names are fictitious

divisions are somewhat arbitrary, but for convenience of description, I shall divide the families into four groups (shown in Table 1): 1. highly segregated conjugal role-relationship associated with highly connected network; 2. joint conjugal role-relationship associated with dispersed network; 3. intermediate degrees of conjugal role-segregation and network connectedness, and 4. transitional families. No claim is made here that these are the only patterns that can occur; further research would probably reveal others. In the following discussion I shall be chiefly concerned not with these divisions, but rather with the fact that the order according to degree of conjugal role-segregation follows the order according to degree of network connectedness, and I shall attempt to show the mechanisms by which this relationship operates.

Highly Segregated Conjugal Role-Relationship Associated with Highly Connected Network

The research set contained only one family of this type—the Newbolts (Ns). They had been married four years when the interviewing began and had two small children. In the following discussion, I shall describe their actual behavior, indicating the points at which they depart from their norms.

EXTERNAL SOCIAL RELATIONSHIPS

Mr. N had a semi-skilled manual job at a factory in an East End area adjacent to the one in which they lived. He said that many other men in the local area had jobs at the same place, or were doing the same sort of work at similar factories and workshops nearby. Mrs. N did not work, but she felt that she was unusual in this respect. Most of the neighboring women and many of her female relatives had jobs; she did not think there was anything morally wrong with such work, but she said that she had never liked working and preferred to stay at home with the children. Mr. N said that he thought it was best for her and the children if she stayed at home, and added that he felt it was a bit of a reflection on a man if his wife had to go out to work.

The Ns used the services of a local hospital and a maternity and child welfare clinic. They expected to send their children to the local elementary school. They were also in touch with the local housing authority because they were trying to find a new flat. These various service institutions were not felt to have any particular relationship to one another, except in the sense that they were all felt to be foreign bodies, not really part of the local life. Mrs. N was a little bit afraid of them, particularly of the hospital and of doctors. On one occasion, while waiting with her baby and the field worker in an otherwise empty hospital room for a doctor to attend to the baby, she said in a whisper, "My husband says that we pay for it [the hospital services, through National Health subscriptions] and we should use it, but I don't like coming here. I don't like hospitals and doctors, do you?"

To the Ns, the local area was definitely a community in the social sense, a place with an identity of its own and a distinctive way of life. They spoke of it with great pride and contrasted it favorably with other areas. "It has a bad name, they say we are rough, but I think it's the best place there is. Everyone is friendly . . . there is no life in the West End compared with the East End. They drink champagne and we drink beer. When things are la-di-da you feel out of place." They took it for granted that the other inhabitants had similar feelings of local pride and loyalty. Both the Ns had grown up in the same area, as had most of their relatives and friends. Trips outside the area were like adventures into a foreign land, especially for Mrs. N, and very few informal social relationships were kept up with people outside the area. Physical distance was felt to be an almost insuperable barrier to social contact.

Physically, the area was far from ideal as a place to live. The houses were old-fashioned, inconvenient and crowded. The Ns were faced with a difficult choice of whether to move out of London to a modern flat on a new housing estate, or to stay put in cramped quarters, in the old familiar local area with their friends and relatives. They knew of several other young couples who were faced with a similar dilemma. Group discussions at a local community center and the research of the Institute of Community Studies indicated that many local residents feel this to be an important social and personal problem (Young, 1954).

The Ns felt that their neighbors were socially similar to themselves, meaning that they had the same sort of jobs, the same sort of background, the same sort of outlook on life. Because the Ns had grown up in the area, as had many of their relatives and neighbors, they knew a very considerable number of local people, and many of the people they knew were acquainted with one another. Their social network was highly connected. In fact there was considerable overlap of social roles; instead of there being people in three or four separate categories—friend, neighbor, relative and colleague—the same person frequently filled two, three or even four of these roles simultaneously.

The Ns took it for granted that Mr. N, like other husbands in their social circle, would have some form of recreation with men away from home. In his case it was football, although the most common form of recreation was felt to be drinking and visiting in the local pub, where many husbands spent an evening or two a week with their friends; quite frequently some of these men were friends of old standing, men who had belonged to the same childhood gang and others were work colleagues. Mr. N had kept in touch with one or two friends of his childhood; he also played football and went to matches with some of his colleagues; he mentioned that several of his friends knew one another. Mrs. N knew a bit about these men, but she did not expect to join in their activities with her husband. She had a nodding acquaintance with the wives of two or three of these men, and occasionally talked to them when she was out shopping.

Mrs. N also had her own separate relationships in which her husband did not expect to join. She knew many of her female neighbors, just as they knew one another; she took it for granted that a friendly relationship with a neighbor would be dropped if the woman moved away. Neighbors saw one another on the landings, in the street, in shops, occasionally over a cup of tea inside the flat or house. They talked over their own affairs and those of other neighbors. Neighbors frequently accused one another of something—of betraying a confidence, of taking the wrong side in a children's quarrel, of failing to return borrowed articles, of gossip. One has little privacy in such a situation. But if one wants to reap the rewards of companionship and receive small acts of mutual aid, one has to conform to local standards and one has to put up with being included in the gossip. Indeed, being gossiped about is as much a sign that one belongs to the neighborly network as being gossiped with. If one refuses to have anything to do with one's neighbors one is thought odd, but eventually one will be left alone; no gossip, no companionship.

With the exception of visiting relatives and an occasional Sunday outing with the children, the Ns spent very little of their leisure time in joint recreation; even though they could have got their relatives to mind the children for them, they rarely went out together. There was no joint entertaining of friends at home. From time to time Mr. N brought a friend home and Mrs. N made tea and talked a bit to the friend; female neighbors often dropped in during the evening to borrow something, but they did not stay long if Mr. N was there. There was no planned joint entertaining in which Mr. and Mrs. N asked another husband and wife to spend an evening with them. Such joint entertaining as existed was carried on with relatives, not with friends. Poverty does not explain the absence of joint entertaining, for the Ns considered themselves to be relatively well off. It did not seem to occur to them that they might spend their surplus money on entertainment of friends; they felt that such money should be spent on furniture, new things for the children or large gatherings of relatives at weddings, funerals and christenings.

There was much visiting and mutual aid between relatives, particularly by the women. The Ns had far more active social relationships with relatives than any other research family, and there was also a great deal of independent contact by their relatives with one another in addition to their contacts with the Ns themselves. The network of kin was highly connected, more so than those of neighbors or friends. The women were more active than the men in keeping up contacts with relatives, with the result that the networks of wives were more highly connected than the networks of their husbands. Although husbands were recognized to be less active in kinship affairs, Mr. N paid occasional visits to his mother, both by himself and with Mrs. N. There were some activities for which joint participation by husband and wife was felt to be desirable. At weddings, funerals and christenings, there were large assemblages of relatives, and it was felt to be important that both husband and wife should attend. Recent and prospective weddings, twenty-first birthday parties and christenings formed an important topic of discussion throughout the interviews with the Ns.

In a group discussion, a man living in the same local area as the Ns and having a similar sort of family life and kinship network summed up the situation by saying, "Men have friends. Women have relatives." For Mrs. N, there was no independent category of friend; friends were either neighbors or relatives. She had had a succession of girl friends in her adolescence, but she said that she did not see so much of them since they had all got married and had had children. She always described them as girl friends, not as friends. Both Mr. and Mrs. N used the term friend as if it applied only to men; the term neighbor, on the other hand, seemed to refer only to women. Mr. N looked rather shocked when I asked him if he saw much of the neighbors.

Later on in the group discussion, the same man observed, "Women don't have friends. They have Mum." In Mrs. N's case the relationship between herself and her mother was indeed very close. Her mother lived nearby and Mrs. N went to visit her nearly every day, taking her children along with her. She and her mother and her mother's sisters also went to visit Mrs. N's maternal grandmother. Together these women and their children formed an important group, helping one another in household tasks and child care, and providing aid for one another in crises. Within the network of relatives there was a nucleus composed of the grandmother, her daughters, and her daughters' daughters; the relationships of these women with one another were sufficiently intense and distinctive to warrant the term organized group in the sense defined above. Mrs. N's female relatives provided some of the domestic help and emotional support that, in other research families, a wife expected to get from her husband. Mrs. N felt tremendously attached to her mother emotionally. She felt that a bad relationship between mother and daughter was unnatural, a complete catastrophe. She would, I feel sure, have been deeply shocked by the seemingly cold and objective terms in which many of the women in the other research families analyzed their mothers' characters. The close tie with the mother is not only a source of help, however; it may also be a potential source of friction, for if her husband and her mother do not get along well together a young wife is likely to feel torn by conflicting loyalties. Mrs. N felt that she was particularly fortunate in that her husband and her mother liked each other.

There was considerable segregation between Mr. and Mrs. N in their external relationships. Mrs. N had her network and Mr. N had his. The number of joint external relationships was comparatively small. At the same time, there were many links between their networks: the husbands of some of Mrs. N's neighbors were men who were colleagues of Mr. N, some of Mrs. N's relatives also worked at the same place as Mr. N, and in a general way, his family was known to hers even before Mr. and Mrs. N got married. The connectedness of the combined networks of Mr. and Mrs. N was high compared to that of the families to be discussed below. But the Ns' total network was sharply divided into the husband's network and the wife's network. Furthermore, her network was more highly connected than his: many of the relatives and neighbors with whom she was in contact saw one another independently of her, whereas there were fewer independent links between Mr. N's colleagues, his football associates, and his friends from childhood.

Conjugal Role-Segregation

The previous description reveals considerable segregation between Mr. and Mrs. N in their external relationships. There was a similar segregation in the way they carried out their internal domestic tasks. They took it for granted that there should be a clear-cut division of labor between them, and that all husbands and wives in their social circle would organize their households in a similar way. One man said in a group discussion: "A lot of men wouldn't mind helping their wives if the curtains were drawn so people couldn't see." Although the Ns felt that major decisions should be made jointly, in the day-to-day running of the household he had his jobs and she had hers. He had control of the money and gave her a housekeeping allowance of £5 a week. Mrs. N did not know how much money he earned, and it did not seem to occur to her that a wife would want or need to know this. Although the Ns said that £5 was the amount most wives were given for housekeeping, Mrs. N had great difficulty in making it cover all the expenses of food, rent, utilities and five shillings' saving for Christmas. She told Mr. N whenever she ran short, and he left a pound or two under the clock when he went out the next morning. She said that he was very generous with his money and she felt that she was unusually fortunate in being spared financial quarrels.

Mrs. N was responsible for most of the housework and child care, although Mr. N did household repairs and helped to entertain the children on week-ends. Mrs. N expected that he would do some of the housework if she became ill, but this was usually unnecessary because her mother or her sister or one of her cousins would come to her aid. Indeed, these female relatives helped her a great deal even with the everyday tasks of housework and child care.

Attitudes Towards the Role-Relationship of Husband and Wife

Mr. and Mrs. N took it for granted that men had male interests and women had female interests and that there were few leisure activities that they would naturally share. In their view, a good husband was one who was generous with the housekeeping allowance, did not waste money on extravagant personal recreation, helped his wife with the housework if she got ill, and took an interest in the children. A good wife was a good manager and an affectionate mother, a woman who kept out of serious rows with neighbors and got along well with her own and her husband's relatives. A good marital relationship was one with a harmonious division of labor, but the Ns placed little stress on the importance of joint activities and shared interests. It is difficult to make any definite statement on the Ns' attitudes towards sexual relations, for they did not come to the Institute for clinical interviews. Judging from Mrs. N's references to such matters when Mr. N was absent, it seems likely that she felt that physical sexuality was an intrusion on a peaceful domestic relationship rather than an expression of such a relationship; it was as if sexuality were felt to be basically violent and disruptive. The findings of clinical workers and of other research workers suggest that among families like the Ns, there is little stress on the importance of physical sexuality for a happy marriage (Slater and Woodside, 1951).

Joint Conjugal Role-Relationships Associated with Dispersed Networks

There were five families of this type. All the husbands had professional or semi-professional occupations. Two of the husbands had been upwardly mobile in occupation relative to their fathers. All five families, however, had a well-established pattern of external relationships; they might make new relationships, but the basic pattern was likely to remain the same. Similarly, all had worked out a fairly stable division of labor in domestic tasks.

EXTERNAL SOCIAL RELATIONSHIPS

The husbands' occupations had little intrinsic connection with the local areas in which they lived. All five carried on their work at some distance from the area in which their homes were located, although two did some additional work at home. But in no case was there any feeling that the occupation was locally rooted.

Whether or not wives should work was considered to be a very controversial question by these families. Unless they were very well off financially—and none of these five families considered themselves to be so—both husband and wife welcomed the idea of a double income, even though much of the additional money had to be spent on caring for the children. But money was not the only consideration; women also wanted to work for the sake of the work itself. It was felt that if she desired it, a woman should have a career or some sort of special interest and skill comparable in seriousness to her husband's occupation; on the other hand, it was felt that young children needed their mother's care and that ideally she should drop her career at least until the youngest child was old enough to go to school. But most careers cannot easily be dropped and picked up again several years later. Two of the wives had solved the problem by continuing to work; they had made careful (and expensive) provision for the care of their children. One wife worked at home. One planned to take up her special interest again as soon as her youngest child went to nursery school, and the fifth wife was already doing so.

These husbands and wives maintained contact with schools, general practitioners, hospitals and in some cases local maternity and child welfare clinics. Most of them also used the services of a solicitor, an insurance agent and other similar professional people. Unlike the first type of family, they did not feel that service institutions were strange and alien; it did not bother them when they had to go out of their local area to find such services, and they were usually well informed about service institutions and could exploit them efficiently. They were not afraid of doctors. There was no strict division of labor between husband and wife in dealing with service institutions. The wife usually dealt with those institutions that catered for children, and the husband dealt with the legal and financial ones, but either could take over the other's duties if necessary.

These husbands and wives did not regard the neighborhood as a source of friends. In most cases husbands and wives had moved around a good deal both before and after marriage, and in no case were they living in the neighborhood in which they grew up. Four were living in areas of such a kind that only a few of the neighbors were felt to be socially similar to the family themselves. The fifth family was living in a suburb that the husband and wife felt to be composed of people socially similar to one another, but quite different from themselves. In all cases these husbands and wives were polite but somewhat distant to neighbors. In order to have become proper friends, the neighbors would have had not only to be socially similar to the family themselves, but also to share a large number of tastes and interests. Establishing such a relationship takes a long exploratory testing, and the feeling seems to have been that it was dangerous to make the test with neighbors since one ran the risk of being pestered by friendly attentions that one might not want to return. Since many of the neighbors probably had similar feelings, particularly when the neighborhood was socially heterogeneous, it is not surprising that intimate social relationships were not rapidly established. Since these families had so little social intercourse with their neighbors, they were very much less worried than the first type of family about gossip and conformity to local norms. Indeed, in the circumstances one can hardly say that there were any specifically local norms; certainly there was not the body of shared attitudes and values built up through personal interaction since childhood that was characteristic of the local area inhabited by the Ns.

The children were less discriminating than their parents. Unless restricted by their parents, they played with anyone in the street. This caused some of the parents a certain amount of anxiety, particularly when they felt that the area was very heterogeneous. Other parents adopted the view that mixing with children of other social classes was a good thing. In any case, all parents relied on their own influence and on the education of the children to erase any possibly bad effects of such contact.

It seemed very difficult for these families to find the sort of house and local area in which they wanted to live. They wanted to own a reasonably cheap house with a garden in central London, a house within easy reach of their friends, of plays, concerts, galleries and so forth. Ideally they wanted a cheap, reliable cleaning-woman-cum-baby-sitter to live nearby, possibly even with the family if they could afford it. Only one family had achieved something approaching this aim. The others were making do with various compromises, impeded by lack of money as well as by the scarcity of suitable houses.

For these families, friends were felt to provide the most important type of external relationship. Not all of each family's friends knew one another; it was not usual for a large number of a family's friends to be in intimate contact with one another independently of their contact with the family. The network of friends was typically dispersed (unconnected). Husband and wife had usually established friendships over a period of years in many different social contexts—at school, during the course of their professional training, in the Services, at various jobs and very occasionally even because of living in the same neighborhood. Their friends were scattered all over London, sometimes all over Britain. Because the network of friends was so dispersed, their social control over the family was dispersed and fragmented. The husband and wife were very sensitive to what their friends thought of them, but since the friends had so little contact with one another, they were not likely to present a unified body of public opinion. Amongst all the different bits of advice they might receive, husband and wife had to make up their own minds about what they should do. They were less persecuted by gossip than the first type of family, but they were also less sustained by it. Their friends did not form a solid body of helpers.

In marked contrast to the Ns, nearly all of the husband's and wife's friends were joint friends; it was felt to be important that both husband and wife should like a family friend, and if a friend was married, then it was hoped that all four partners to the relationship would like one another. Exceptions were tolerated, especially in the case of very old friends, but both husband and wife were uncomfortable if there was real disagreement between them over a friend. Friendship, like marriage, required shared interests and similar tastes, although there was some specialization of interests among different friends. For example, one couple might be golfing friends whereas others might be pub and drinking friends; still others were all-round friends, and it was these who were felt to be the most intimate.

Joint entertainment of friends was a major form of recreation. Even when poverty made invitations to dinner or parties impracticable, friends were still asked over jointly even if only for coffee or tea in the evening. It was considered provincial for husbands to cluster at one end of the room and wives at the other; everyone should be able to talk to everyone else. These husbands and wives usually had enough shared interests to make this possible. Many of them were highly educated, so that they had a common background of general topics, but even those who lacked such education usually make an attempt to talk about matters of general interest.

After these couples had had children, it had become increasingly difficult for them to visit their friends since they often lived at a considerable distance and most of them were also tied down by young children. Considerable expense and trouble were taken to make such visiting possible. It was obvious that friends were of primary importance to these families.

There were usually other forms of joint recreation besides visiting friends, such as eating in foreign restaurants, going to plays, the cinema and concerts. After children were born, there had been a marked drop in external joint recreation in preference for things that could be done at home. Going out had become a special occasion with all the paraphernalia of a baby-sitter and arrangements made in advance.

These five families had far less contact with their relatives than the Ns. Their relatives were not concentrated in the same local area as themselves, and in most cases were scattered all over the country and did not keep in close touch with one another. They formed a dispersed network. It was felt that friendly relations should be kept up with parents, and in several cases the birth of the children had led to a sort of reunion with parents. It seems likely that becoming a parent facilitates a resolution of some of the emotional tensions between adult children and their own parents, particularly between women and their mothers. It is possible that in some cases the arrival of children may exacerbate such tensions, but none of these five families had had such an experience. There are of course some obvious practical advantages in increased contact with parents; they are usually very fond of their grandchildren, so that they make affectionate and reliable baby-sitters. If they live close enough to take on this task their services are greatly appreciated.

Among the families with dispersed networks, there was not the tremendous stress on the mother-daughter relationship that was described for Mrs. N, although women were usually rather more active than men in keeping up kinship ties. There were also fewer conflicts of loyalty; it was felt that if conflicts arose between one's parents and one's spouse, one owed one's first loyalty to one's spouse. Unless special interests, particularly financial interests, were operating among relatives, there was no very strong obligation towards relatives outside the parental families of husband and wife. Even towards siblings there was often very little feeling of social obligation. These families were very much less subject to social control by their relatives than the

Ns, partly because they saw less of them, but also because the network of kin was dispersed so that its various members were less likely to share the same opinions and values.

In brief, the networks of these families were less highly connected than that of the Ns: many of their friends did not know one another, it was unusual for friends to know relatives, only a few relatives kept in touch with one another, and husband and wife had very little contact with neighbors. Furthermore, there was no sharp segregation between the wife's network and the husband's network. With the exception of a few old friends and some colleagues, husband and wife maintained joint external relationships.

CONJUGAL ROLE-SEGREGATION

As described above, these families had as little segregation as possible in their external relationships. There was a similar tendency towards joint organization in domestic tasks and child care. It was felt that efficient management demanded some division of labor, particularly after the children had been born; there had to be a basic differentiation between the husband's role as primary breadwinner and the wife's role as mother of young children. But in other respects such division of labor as existed was felt to be more a matter of convenience than of inherent differences between the sexes. The division of labor was flexible, and there was considerable helping and interchanging of tasks. Husbands were expected to take a very active part in child care. Financial affairs were managed jointly, and joint consultation was expected on all major decisions.

Husbands were expected to provide much of the help that Mrs. N was able to get from her female relatives. The wives of these families with dispersed networks were carrying a tremendous load of housework and child care, but they expected to carry if for a shorter time than Mrs. N. Relatives sometimes helped these wives, but only occasionally; they usually lived at some distance so that it was difficult for them to provide continuous assistance. Cleaning women were employed by four families and a children's nurse by one; all families would have hired more domestic help if they could have afforded it. In spite of their affection for their children, all five couples were looking forward to the time when their children were older and the burden of work would decrease. So far as they could see ahead they did not expect to provide continuous assistance to their married children.

In the case of Mrs. N and other wives with highly connected networks, the burden of housework and child care is more evenly distributed throughout the lifetime of the wife; when she is a girl she helps her mother with the younger children; when she herself has children, her mother and other female relatives help her; when she is a grandmother she helps her daughters.

Attitudes Towards the Role-Relationship of Husband and Wife

Among the families with dispersed networks, there were frequent discussions of whether there really were any psychological or temperamental differences between the sexes. These differences were not simply taken for granted as they were by the Ns. In some cases, so much stress was placed on shared interests and sexual equality (which was sometimes confused with identity, the notion of equality of complementary opposites being apparently a difficult idea to maintain consistently) that one sometimes felt that the possibility of the existence of social and temperamental differences between the sexes was being denied. In other cases, temperamental differences between the sexes were exaggerated to a point that belied the couple's actual joint activities and the whole pattern of shared interests that they felt to be so fundamental to their way of life. Quite frequently the same couple would minimize differences between the sexes on one occasion and exaggerate them on another. Sometimes these discussions about sexual differences were very serious; sometimes they were witty and facetious; but they were never neutral—they were felt to be an important problem. Such discussions may be interpreted as an attempt to air and to resolve the contradiction between the necessity for joint organization with its ethic of equality on the one hand, and the necessity for differentiation and recognition of sexual differences on the other. "After all," as one husband said, to conclude the discussion, "*vive la différence,* or where would we all be?"

It was felt that, in a good marriage, husband and wife should achieve a high degree of compatibility, based on their own particular combination of shared interests and complementary differences. Their relationship with each other should be more important than any separate relationship with outsiders. The conjugal relationship should be kept private, and revelations to outsiders, or letting down one's spouse in public, were felt to be serious offenses. A successful sexual relationship was felt by these couples to be very important for a happy marriage: it was as if successful sexual relations were felt to prove that all was well with the joint relationship, whereas unsatisfactory relations were indicative of a failure in the total relationship. In some cases one almost got the feeling that these husbands and wives felt a moral obligation to enjoy sexual relations, a feeling not expressed or suggested by the Ns.

The wives of these families seemed to feel that their position was rather difficult. They had certainly wanted children, and in all five cases they were getting a great deal of satisfaction from their maternal role. But at the same time, they felt tied down by their children and they did not like the inevitable drudgery associated with child care. Some were more affected than others, but most of them complained of isolation, boredom and fatigue. "You must excuse me if I sound half-witted. I've been talking to the children all day," was a not uncommon remark. These women wanted a career or some special interest that would make them feel that they were something more than children's nurses and housemaids. They wanted more joint entertainment with their husbands and more contact with friends. These complaints were not leveled specifically at their husbands—indeed in most cases they felt that their husbands were doing their best to make the situation easier—but against the social situation in which they found themselves and at the difficulty of satisfying contradictory desires at the same time. One wife summed it up by saying, "Society seems to be against married women. I don't know, it's all very difficult."

It may be felt that the problem could be solved if such a family moved to an area that was felt to be homogeneous and composed of people similar to themselves, for then the wife might be able to find friends among her neighbors and would feel less isolated and bored. It is difficult to imagine, however, that these families could feel that any local area, however homogeneous by objective criteria, could be full of potential friends, for their experience of moving about in the past and their varied social contacts make them very discriminating in their choice of friends. Further, their dislike of having their privacy broken into by neighbors is very deeply rooted; it diminishes after the children start playing with children in the neighborhood, but it never disappears entirely.

Intermediate Degrees of Conjugal Role-Segregation and Network Connectedness

There were nine families of this type in the research set. There was considerable variety of occupation amongst them. Four husbands had professional or semi-professional occupations very similar to the occupations of the second type of family described above. It was in recognition of the fact that these four families were similar in occupation but different in conjugal role-segregation from the second set of families that I concluded that conjugal role-segregation could not be attributed to occupational level alone. Of the five remaining husbands, one was a clerical worker, three had manual occupations similar in general level to that of Mr. N and one changed from a highly skilled manual job to an office job after the interviewing was completed.

There was considerable variation among these nine families in conjugal role-segregation. Some tended to have a fairly marked degree of segregation, approaching that of the Ns, whereas others were closer to the second set of families in having a relatively joint role-relationship. These variations in degree of segregation of conjugal roles within the nine intermediate families did not follow exactly the order according to occupational level. If the occupations of the husbands are arranged in order from the most joint to the most segregated conjugal role-relationship, the order is as follows: manual worker, professional, professional, clerical worker, professional, manual worker, professional, manual worker, manual worker. The variations in degree of segregation follow more closely the variations in degree of network connectedness. The families with the most dispersed networks had the most joint role-relationships, and the families with the most connected networks had the most conjugal role-segregation. The families with the most dispersed networks were those who had moved around a great deal so that they had established relationships with many people who did not know one another.

For brevity of description, I shall treat these nine intermediate families collectively, but it should be remembered that there were variations in degree amongst them, and that both network connectedness and conjugal role-segregation form continua so that it is somewhat arbitrary to divide families into separate types.

External Social Relationships

The data suggest two possible reasons for the intermediate degree in the connectedness of the networks of these families. First, most of them had been brought up in families whose networks had been less connected than that of the Ns, but more connected than that of the second set of families. With one exception these couples had moved around less than the second type of family both before and after marriage, so that more of their friends knew one another; several had had considerable continuity of relationships since childhood, and they had not developed the pattern of ignoring neighbors and relying chiefly on friends and colleagues that was described as typical of families with very dispersed networks.

Secondly, these families were living in areas where they felt that many of the neighbors were socially similar to themselves. In four cases these were suburban areas; in five cases they were mixed working-class areas in which the inhabitants were felt to be similar to one another in general occupational level although they worked at different jobs. Five families were living in or near the area where one or both of the partners had lived since childhood. In two of the remaining four cases, the area was similar to the one in which husband and wife had been brought up. In two cases, the present area differed considerably from the childhood area of one or other partner, but the couple had acclimatized themselves to the new situation.

If the husband and wife were living in the area in which they had been brought up, each was able to keep up some of the relationships that had been formed before marriage. This was also true of the Ns. The intermediate families differed from the Ns chiefly in that their jobs, and in some cases their education, had led them to make relationships with people who were not neighbors. Many neighbors were friends, but not all friends were neighbors. Even in the case of families in which one or both partners had moved to the area after marriage, each partner was able to form friendly relationships with at least some of the neighbors, who were in most cases felt to be socially similar to the couple themselves. Husband and wife were able to form independent, segregated relationships with neighbors. In particular, many of the wives spent a good deal of their leisure time during the day with neighboring women. Husband and wife also joined local clubs, most of these clubs being unisexual. (Voluntary associations appear to thrive best in areas where people are similar in social status but do not know one another well; the common activity gives people an opportunity to get to know one another better.)

In local areas inhabited by the intermediate families, many of the neighbors knew one another. There was not the very great familiarity built up over a long period of continuous residence as for the Ns, but there was not the standoffishness described as typical of the families with very dispersed networks. The intermediate families had networks of neighbors that were midway in degree of connectedness, and the husbands and wives were midway in sensitivity to the opinions of neighbors—more susceptible than the second set of families, but better able to maintain their privacy than the Ns.

Husbands and wives had some segregated relationships with neighbors, but they could also make joint relationships if all four partners liked one another. Some relationships were usually kept up with friends who had been made outside the area. Couples usually tried to arrange joint visits with these friends. These friends usually did not become intimate with the neighbors, however, so that the network remained fairly dispersed.

Relations with relatives were much like those described above for the second set of families. But if the relatives were living in the same local area as the family, there was considerable visiting and exchange of services, and if the relatives lived close to one another, the kinship network was fairly well connected.

The networks of these families were thus less highly connected than that of the Ns, but more highly connected than that of the second set of families. There was some overlapping of roles. Neighbors were sometimes friends; some relatives were both neighbors and friends. The overlapping was not as complete as it was with the Ns, but there was not the complete division into separate categories—friend, neighbor, relative—that was characteristic of the second set of families. The networks of husband and wife were less segregated than those of the Ns, but more segregated than those of the second set of families.

CONJUGAL ROLE-SEGREGATION

In external relationships, husband and wife had some joint relationships, particularly with relatives and with friends, and some segregated relationships, particularly with neighbors and local clubs.

In carrying out household tasks and child care, there was a fairly well-defined division of labor, a little more clearly marked than in the second type of family, more flexible than in the case of the Ns. Husbands helped, but there was a greater expectation of help from neighbors and relatives (if they lived close enough) than among the second set of families.

ATTITUDES TOWARDS THE ROLE-RELATIONSHIP OF HUSBAND AND WIFE

Although there were variations of degree, considerable stress was placed on the importance of shared interests and joint activities for a happy marriage. In general, the greater the stress that was placed on joint organization and shared interests, the greater was the importance attached to sexual relations. Like the families with dispersed networks, the intermediate families stressed the necessity for conjugal privacy and the precedence of the conjugal relationship over all external relationships, but there was a greater tolerance of social and temperamental differences between the sexes, and there was an easier acceptance of segregation in the activities of husband and wife. Wives often wanted some special interest of their own, other than housework and children, but they were able to find activities such as attending evening classes or local clubs that could be carried on without interfering with their housework and child care. And because, in most cases, they felt that at least some of the neighboring women were similar to themselves, they found it relatively easy to make friends among them, and they had people to talk to during the day. They complained less frequently of isolation and boredom than did the wives in families with very dispersed networks.

Transitional Families

There were five families in varying states of transition from one type of network to another. Two phases of transition can be distinguished: families who were in the process of deciding to move from one local area to another, a decision that was requiring considerable restructuring of their networks, and somewhat de-socialized families who had radically changed their pattern of external relationships and had not yet got used to their new situation. There were other families who had gone through the process of transition and had more or less settled down to the pattern typical of families with dispersed or intermediate networks.

FAMILIES IN THE PROCESS OF DECIDING TO MOVE

There were two such families. Both had relatively highly connected networks, and both had been socially mobile and were contemplating moving to suburban areas, which would be more compatible with their new social status. In both cases this meant cutting off old social ties with relatives and neighbors and building up new ones. One couple seemed to feel too bound to the old network to make the break; they also said they did not want to lower their current standard of living by spending a lot of money on a house. The second family moved after the interviewing was completed, and a brief return visit suggested that they would in time build up the intermediate type of network and conjugal role-segregation.

SOMEWHAT DE-SOCIALIZED FAMILIES

There were three families of this type. All three had been brought up in highly connected networks similar to the Ns, and all had moved away from their old areas and the people of their networks. For such a family, any move outside the area is a drastic step. This contrasts with the intermediate families who are not too upset by moving, provided that they move to an area of people who are felt to be socially similar to themselves.

One family had been very mobile occupationally, although they had moved primarily because of the requirements of the husband's occupation rather than to find a neighborhood compatible with their achieved status. They were living in relative isolation, with very few friends, almost no contacts with neighbors and very little contact with relatives, most of whom were living at a considerable distance. They seemed to be a bit stunned by the change in their immediate environment. They had some segregated interests, but they felt that joint organization and shared interests were the best basis of a conjugal relationship.

The other two families were working-class and had not been occupationally mobile. They were particularly important to the conceptual analysis of conjugal role-segregation for, although they were similar to the Ns in occupational level and in general cultural background, their conjugal role-relationship was more joint. It was their relatively dispersed networks that distinguished them from the Ns.

These two families had moved to a different local area because they could not find suitable accommodation in their old neighborhoods. They also wanted the amenities of a modern flat, and since their parents had died and many of their relatives had moved away, they felt that their main ties to the old local area were gone. Both seemed to feel that they were strangers in a land full of people who were all strangers to one another, and at first they did not know how to cope with the situation. They did not react to their new situation in exactly the same way. In both cases, husband and wife had turned to one another for help, especially at first, but for various personal reasons, one husband and wife were making a concerted effort to develop joint activities and shared interests, whereas the other couple did not take to the idea of a joint role-relationship with any enthusiasm.

In the first case, husband and wife tried to develop more joint relationships with friends, but this was difficult for them because they had had so little practice; they did not know the culture of a joint role-relationship, and their new acquaintances were in a similar predicament so that they got little external support for their efforts. The husband tried to get his wife to join in his club activities, but the structure of the club was such that her activities remained somewhat segregated from his. The husband helped his wife extensively with household tasks and child care, although he continued to plan the family finances. In the second case, the husband busied himself with his work and friends and spent a great deal of time on various committees with other men; his wife was becoming isolated and withdrawn into the home. They had more joint organization of domestic tasks than they had had before; she urged him to help her because her female relatives lived too far away to be of much assistance.

In both cases, however, nothing could really take the place of the old networks built up from childhood, and both couples felt a good deal of personal dissatisfaction. The husbands were perhaps less drastically affected, since they continued to work at their old jobs and their relationships with colleagues gave them considerable continuity. Both husband and wife often blamed their physical surroundings for their malaise, and they idealized their old local areas. They remembered only the friendliness and forgot the physical inconvenience and the unpleasant part of the gossip. On the whole, although one family had carried the process further than the other, both seemed to be developing a more joint division of labor than that which they had had before, and it seemed likely that they would eventually settle down in some intermediate form of network connectedness and conjugal role-segregation.

The research set did not contain any families who had moved in the other direction, that is, from a dispersed to a more connected network. But personal knowledge of families who had been accustomed to a dispersed network and were having to come to grips with a fairly highly connected one suggests that this type of change is also felt to be somewhat unpleasant. The privacy of husband and wife is encroached upon, and each is expected to take part in segregated activities, a state of affairs that they regard as provincial. These families could have refused to enter into the local network of social relationships, but in most cases they felt that the husband's career required it.

The Relationship Between Conjugal Role-Segregation and Network Connectedness

Connected networks are most likely to develop when husband and wife, together with their friends, neighbors and relatives, have all grown up in the same local area and have continued to live there after marriage. Husband and wife come to the marriage each with his or her own highly connected network. It is very likely that there will be some overlap of their networks; judging by the Ns' account of their genealogy, one of the common ways for husband and wife to meet each other is to be introduced by a person who is simultaneously a friend of one and a relative of the other.

Each partner makes a considerable emotional investment in relationships with the people in his network; each is engaged in reciprocal exchanges of material and emotional support with them; each is very sensitive to their opinions and values, not only because the relationships are intimate, but also because the people in the network know one another and share the same values so that they are able to apply consistent informal sanctions to one another.

The marriage is superimposed on these pre-existing relationships. As long as the couple continue to live in the same area, and as long as their friends, neighbors and relatives also continue to live within easy reach of the family and of one another, the segregated networks of husband and wife can be carried on after marriage. Some rearrangement is necessary; the husband is likely to stop seeing some of the friends of his youth, particularly those who work at a different place and go to different pubs and clubs; after children are born, the wife is likely to see less of her former girl friends and more of her mother and other female relatives. But apart from these readjustments, husband and wife can carry on their old external relationships, and they continue to be very sensitive to external social controls. In spite of the conjugal segregation in external relationships, the overlapping of the networks of husband and wife tends to ensure that each partner finds out about the other's activities. Although a wife may not know directly what a husband does with his friends away from home, one of the other men is likely to tell his wife or some other female relative who eventually passes the information on, either directly or through other women. Similarly any defection on the part of the wife is likely to be made known to her husband.

Because old relationships can be continued after marriage, both husband

and wife can satisfy some of their personal needs outside the marriage, so that their emotional investment in the conjugal relationship need not be as intense as in other types of family. Both husband and wife, but particularly the wife, can get outside help with domestic tasks and with child care. A rigid division of labor between husband and wife is therefore possible, since each can get outside help. The segregation in external relationships can be carried over to activities within the family.

Networks become dispersed when people move around from one place to another, or when they make new relationships that have no connection with their old ones. If both husband and wife have moved around a good deal before marriage, each will bring an already dispersed network to the marriage. After the marriage they will meet new people as well as some of the old ones, and these people will not necessarily know one another. Their external relationships are relatively discontinuous both in space and in time. Such continuity as they possess lies in their relationship with each other rather than in their external relationships. In facing the external world, they draw on each other, for their strongest emotional investment is made where there is continuity. Hence their high standards of conjugal compatibility, their stress on shared interests, on joint organization, on equality between husband and wife. They must get along well together, they must help one another as much as possible in carrying out familial tasks, for there is no sure external source of material and emotional help. Since their friends and relatives are physically scattered and few of them know one another, the husband and wife are not stringently controlled by a solid body of public opinion, but they are also unable to rely on consistent external support. Through their joint external relationships they present a united front to the world and they reaffirm their joint relationship with each other. No external person must seriously menace the conjugal relationship; joint relationships with friends give a source of emotional satisfaction outside the family without threatening their own relationship.

In between these two extremes are the intermediate and transitional families. In the intermediate type, husband and wife have moved around a certain amount so that they seek continuity with each other and make their strongest emotional investment in the conjugal relationship. At the same time, they are able to make some segregated relationships outside the family and they are able to rely on considerable casual help from the people outside the family, so that a fairly clearly defined division of labor into male tasks and female tasks can be made.

The transitional families illustrate some of the factors involved in changing from one type of network to another. Husbands and wives who change from a connected to a dispersed network find themselves suddenly thrust into a more joint relationship without the experience or the attitudes appropriate to it. The eventual outcome depends partly on the family and partly on the extent to which their new neighbors build up relationships with one another. An intermediate form of network connectedness seems to be the most likely outcome. Similarly, in the case of families who change from a dispersed to a more highly connected network, their first reaction is one of mild indignation at losing their privacy, but in time it seems likely that they will tend to develop an intermediate degree of network connectedness and conjugal role-segregation.

Factors Affecting the General Features of Urban Familial Networks

All the research families maintained relationships with external people and institutions—with a place of work, with service institutions such as schools, church, doctor, clinic, shops; with voluntary associations such as clubs, evening classes, and recreational institutions; they also maintained more informal relationships with colleagues, friends, neighbors and relatives. It is therefore incorrect to describe urban families as "isolated," indeed, no urban family could survive without its network of external relationships.

Urban families are not, however, contained within organized groups, for although they have many external relationships, the institutions and persons with which they are related are not linked up with one another to form an organized group. Furthermore, although individual members of a family frequently belong to groups, the family as a whole does not. There are marginal cases, such as the situation arising when all the members of the family belong to the same church or go to the same general practitioner, but in these cases the external institution or person controls only one aspect of the family's life and can hardly be said to "contain" the family in all its aspects.

In the literature on family sociology, there are frequent references to "the family in the community," with the implication that the community is an organized group within which the family is contained. Our data suggest that the usage is misleading. Of course every family must live in some sort of local area, but very few urban local areas can be called communities in the sense that they form cohesive social groups. The immediate social environment of urban families is best considered not as the local area in which they live, but rather as the network of actual social relationships they maintain, regardless of whether these are confined to the local area or run beyond its boundaries.

Small-scale, more isolated, relatively closed local groups provide a marked contrast. This type of community is frequently encountered in primitive societies, as well as in certain rural areas of industrialized societies. A family in such a local group knows no privacy; everyone knows everyone else. The situation of the urban family with a highly connected network is carried one step further in the relatively closed local group. The networks of the component families are so highly connected and the relationships within the local group are so clearly marked off from external relationships that the local population can properly be called an organized group. Families are encapsulated within this group; their activities are known to all, they cannot escape from the informal sanctions of gossip and public opinion, their external affairs are governed by the group to which they belong.

In many small-scale primitive societies, the elementary family is encapsulated not only within a local group but also within a corporate kin group. In such cases, the conjugal role-segregation between husband and wife becomes even more marked than that described above for urban families with highly connected networks. Marriage becomes a linking of kin groups rather than preponderantly a union between individuals acting on their own initiative.

These differences between the immediate social environment of families in urban industrialized societies and that of families in some small-scale primitive and rural communities exist, ultimately, because of differences in the total economic and social structure. The division of labor in a small-scale society is relatively simple; the division of labor in an industrial society is exceedingly complex. In a small-scale, relatively closed society, most of the services required by a family can be provided by the other families in the local group and in the kin group. In an urban industrialized society, such tasks and services are divided up and assigned to specialized institutions. Whereas a family in a small-scale, relatively closed society belongs to a small number of groups each with many functions, an urban family exists in a network of many separate, unconnected institutions each with a specialized function. In a small-scale, relatively closed society the local group and the kin group mediate between the family and the total society; in an urban industrialized society there is no single encapsulating group or institution that mediates between the family and the total society.

One of the results of this difference in the form of external relationships is that urban families have more freedom to govern their own affairs. In a small-scale, relatively closed society, the encapsulating groups have a great deal of control over the family. In an urban industrialized society, the doctor looks after the health of individual members of the family, the clinic looks after the health of the mother and child, the school educates children, the boss cares about the individual as an employee rather than as a husband, and even friends, neighbors and relatives may disagree among themselves as to how the affairs of the family should be conducted. Social control of the family is split up among so many agencies that no one of them has continuous, complete governing power. Within broad limits, a family can make its own decisions and regulate its own affairs.

The situation may be summed up by saying that urban families are more highly individuated than families in relatively closed communities. I feel that this term describes the situation of urban families more accurately than the more commonly used term "isolated." By "individuation" I mean that the elementary family is separated off, differentiated out as a distinct, and to some extent autonomous, social group. The individuation of urban families provides one source of variation in role performance. Because families are not encapsulated within governing and controlling groups, other than the nation as a whole, husband and wife are able, within broad limits, to perform their roles in accordance with their own personal needs. These broad limits are laid down by the ideal norms of the nation as a whole, many of which exist as laws and are enforced by the courts. But informal social control by relatives and neighbors is much less stringent and less consistent than in many small-scale societies, and much variation is possible.

The networks of urban families vary in degree of connectedness, namely in the extent to which the people with whom the family maintains relationships carry on relationships with one another. These variations are particularly evident in informal relationships between friends, neighbors and relatives. These differences are associated with differences in degree of conjugal role-segregation, which varies directly with the connectedness of the family's social network. Conceptually, the network stands between the family and the total social environment. Such variations are made possible by the complexity and variability of the economic, occupational, and other institutional systems that create a complex of forces affecting families in different ways and permitting selection and choice by the family. The connectedness of a family's network is a function, on the one hand, of a complex set of forces in the total environment and, on the other, of the family members themselves and their reaction to these forces.

References

Bott, E. 1957. *Family and Social Network* (2nd edition, 1971). London: Tavistock Publications.

Robb, J.H. 1953. "Clinical Studies in Marriage and the Family: A Symposium on Methods. IV: Experiences with Ordinary Families." *British Journal of Medical Psychology*, 26:215–21.

Slater, E. and M. Woodside. 1951. *Patterns of Marriage*. London: Cassell.

Wilson, A.T.M., E.L. Trist and A. Curle. 1952. "Transitional Communities and Social Reconnection. A Study of the Civil Resettlement of British Prisoners of War." In *Readings in Social Psychology* (2nd edition), edited by G.E. Swanson et al. New York: Holt.

Young, M. 1954. "The Planners and the Planned—The Family," *Journal of the Town Planning Institute*, 40:134–38.

Rhona Rapoport and Robert N. Rapoport

Dual-Career Families
The Evolution of a Concept*

Introduction

The concept of the "dual-career family" was introduced in our research on "Women in Top Jobs" (Rapoport and Rapoport, 1969). This paper presents the core findings of that study together with an overview of subsequent developments.

The original paper saw the dual-career family as a variant pattern on a single norm—the traditional family in which the husband was the sole breadwinner and pursued a career in the outside world, while the wife looked after the children and ran the home. The families described were strategically important as vanguards in a social change process. We did not suggest that they were representative of contemporary families, nor that they should provide the exclusive norm for the family of the future. Rather we thought that in the logic of things their numbers were likely to increase and that the experiences of pioneer families might help others evolve such patterns with less stress and strain.

In the twenty years that have since elapsed their increase has been such as to make the dual-career family a recognized structure among forms the family is now taking in relation to social change.

The original study was based on thirteen functioning dual-career families and three in which the dual-career aspect was given up by the wife breaking off her career. People may drop out for various reasons and for differing amounts of time at different points in their careers—men as well as women. In some situations special provisions are made for career interruptions by women which may obviate the need to drop out in the sense of resigning from a position in an organization. In other situations dropping out may simply mean a slackening of

*A requested overview.

the pace of activity. We use the term drop-out to refer to an indefinite cessation of activity whether in an organizational post or a less formal position.

The couples were chosen to represent a range of occupations for the women. They had to be intact families with at least one child still living at home. The sixteen families were interviewed by a pair of interviewers (one male, one female). There were ordinarily one or two joint interviews (husband and wife interviewed by both interviewers) and interviews with the husband and wife separately by individual interviewers. Each session lasted approximately three hours. Findings were checked in a follow-up interview.

Five foci of stress were identified: dilemmas of overload, personal norm, identity, social network and role cycling. In each area we shall discuss the sources of stress and the ways in which the couples have adapted to the ensuing strains.

Overload Dilemmas

The old folk expression "behind every successful man there is a woman" stands not only for a social psychological situation where the wife gives emotional support, advice, etc., but also for a whole culture complex of activities and relationships within which the wife is a helpmate. One of the couples began the interview by reversing this, stating that "behind every successful woman there is a man," meaning that the man encouraged his wife to cope with problems arising in her work, provided consultation on financial matters, etc. They did not mean that he gave the same sort of backing— shopping, mending, cooking, child-minding, etc.—that would be the obverse of the traditional picture.

In the dual-career families studied there were no reversals of the traditional roles (though they are by no means non-existent). The most usual situation was a rearrangement of the domestic side of their lives. Some household tasks were delegated to others, some reapportioned between husband, wife and children. The degree of overload experienced seemed to have been a function of at least four factors:

- *The degree to which having children and a family life (as distinct from simply being married) is salient*. With the exception of one couple, family life in general and children in particular were highly salient. The couples were very concerned with the possible effects on their children of their both pursuing careers. This implied a limitation in the degree to which the couples were willing to delegate child-care, even assuming the availability of satisfactory resources. There is an element of psychic strain involved in allowing two major areas of life, so different in their demands and characteristics, to be highly important. The overload, then, is not a simple arithmetical one of increased number of tasks to be accomplished, but one far more difficult to assess, which is related to the duality of emotional commitment and concern.

- *The degree to which the couple aspire to a high standard of domestic living.* Most of the couples aspired to a high standard—pleasant home and garden, cleanliness, good cooking. This made the management of the domestic side of their lives more complex, albeit by choice, than if they had kept to a lower standard. However, the notion of a lower material standard is almost a contradiction in terms to the notion of career success. The process tends to become circular in that once having acquired a taste for the high standards, the impetus to continue working and career development is increased.
- *The degree to which satisfactory arrangements for the re-apportionment of tasks is possible.* Here we found various combinations of conjugal role reorganizations and delegations of parts of the domestic work to children and helpers of various kinds.
- *The degree to which the sheer physical overload of tasks and their apportionment is adumbrated by a social-psychological overload.* This arises from struggling with the following conflicts: normative conflict, sex role identity maintenance, network management and role-cycling. Couples vary enormously in the degree to which these other sources of tension feed into the family system and the degree to which they can manage them.

For all the couples the overload issue was salient. They all emphasized the importance of physical health and energy as a prerequisite for making the dual-career family a possibility. They regarded it as important for their children to be healthy, too. Generally speaking, there was little room for illness in the systems that were evolved.

To deal with the overload issues much thought and effort was spent on arranging a system of domestic help. This had two sides: the availability of different kinds of domestic helpers and the couple's preferences as to which aspects of their domestic roles they wished to delegate. The delegation of the less desirable aspects of domestic labor was both the expected and the observed tendency. Given the low value placed on domestic work in our society, the dual-career couples have all had to devote considerable energy to improvising viable arrangements. A wide range is found: short term and long term; full-time and part-time; live-in and live-out; nannies, au pairs, dailies, students, secretaries-doubling-as-baby-sitters, couples with husband and wife dividing up the domestic part of the employing couple's household affairs, unmarried mothers and their babies taking over part of the premises, etc. Most of the couples used at least a duplex system; often they would shift from one type to another following a major transition like having a child, the youngest child entering school, etc. Sometimes the shift was associated with a difficult experience with the prior system; sometimes it was based on the couple's conception of a better arrangement for the particular stage, e.g., dropping a nannie and taking on an au pair as the infant reached school age. Simple as the tasks of household maintenance may be, the difficulties in obtaining reliable personnel to whom to delegate them is so great in contemporary British and American society as to call for all sorts of perquisites. Domestic helpers were not only offered the usual salary and private room arrangements (often with TV) but were sometimes given the use of one of the family cars and, in one case, a specially built apartment. Few of the couples used their parents in a major way, though many used them occasionally to look after children while they were away.

The area of childcare presents special problems. While most of our couples valued interaction with their children and felt that their children's welfare and development were of primary importance, they had to delegate at least part of the childcare in order to pursue their careers. Precisely because the children were so important, the issue of how to arrange this contributed heavily to the overload. Most of the families were aware of and concerned with modern conceptions of child development and the importance of parental involvement in it. As one couple put it: "We are all victims of our culture in the Spockean age" (i.e., this child-centered age). While compromises could be, and often were, made in the domestic care areas, none of the couples were willing to adopt a policy which would have meant possible harm to their children's physical or psychological development. It was not possible to assess the effects of the dual-career couples' child-rearing practices on their children. However, in detailed interviews it was striking how low the level of reported disturbance appeared to be. Although the couples were quite aware of potential negative effects, they also pointed to some of the positive affects of their pattern of life: fostering independence and responsibility, e.g., in getting children to help with household chores; fathers spending more time with their children; providing a student companion for the children. Most of the families interviewed had read or heard about the relevant research work and were concerned with the issue of potentially harmful "maternal deprivation."

The majority of the couples took precautions against placing complete reliance on any one helping figure and they tended to monitor carefully the interaction between children and domestic helpers. One mother describes the degree to which she had to rely on help and how distasteful it was to a strong and independent-minded person to feel dependent:

I had no one, so I had to go from hand to mouth. I never knew when I could make appointments ahead. It was such a strain that I got, not ill, but terribly upset— unable to cope, you know, and I put a high value on being able to cope . . .

The vulnerability of the woman, in particular, to malfunctioning in the domestic help area is expressed by Mrs. Y, who said that even when she is working or travelling, there is a "little corner of my mind somewhere that is thinking and worrying about the management of the children." Mr. Y, in contrast, reserves the comparable "little corner" in the back of his mind for forward planning of their work and the family's finances.

The general tendency was to place high value on having children and developing a close relationship with them. Even in the rare instances where children were sent to boarding school this was not, with one possible excep- tion, to unload the care of the children onto an institution but because of tradition (father and grandfather had gone to that school) or the child's own wishes.

Most of the couples thought that the main consequence of their both working was that there was "very little slack left in the system." Several indicated that they were both "whacked" by the time they got home and that they had very little energy left over for extra activities, particularly on week- nights.

While leisure activities tend to be sacrificed first under the impact of overload, the repercussions may spill over into the work lives of one or both of the partners and couples vary in the degree to which they protect this as a higher priority than other areas like activities with the children. Mr. S illustrates part of this pattern of spillover into work in discussing how he concerns himself with his wife's business problems:

one takes up time during the day thinking over these problems instead of perhaps dining with someone one ought to dine with for one's own business career . . . or, one comes home to commiserate, to work out a problem, or even to have a quiet evening and one can't because the wife is really worn out and exhausted and can't cope with it. . . .

Characteristic patterns of coping with these strains are:

- Deliberately to "work" at leisure—to discipline oneself to take vaca- tions, weekends in the country to unwind, etc. To conserve health and energy deliberately as a human resource.
- To delegate as much as possible of the less desired domestic chores and to provide adequate care for child-rearing—"suitable mothering" influ- ences and other relevant companionship needed by the growing child.

Strategies to provide the child with the best possible environments—home, school, etc.—consume major proportions of time.

- To modify one's work involvements in such a way as to be compatible with the other partner's and to diminish the strain of "overspill," e.g., from an excessively demanding work situation. Most of the couples avoided unnecessary travel and complex relationships at work so as to optimize participation in work and family spheres.

Dilemmas Arising from the Discrepancy Between Personal Norms and Social Norms

The women have found ways to continue their careers even after childbirth, stopping work only for a minimal period which did not interfere with their career development. In doing so they have had to deal with dilemmas arising from the clash between their personal norms—what they felt was right and proper behavior for themselves; and social norms—those they felt were held by the people around them.

These dilemmas arise because most women, even highly qualified ones, tend to drop their careers to fulfil traditional domestic roles even if this is accompanied by personal frustration. It is accepted as the right and proper thing to do by the majority of people in our society, and is supported from birth by a pervasive set of cultural symbols and manifestations: the importance attributed to mothering (assumed to be always the biological mother except in abnormal cases), the sanctity of the home and the housewife role, etc. The men and women in our study have deliberately adopted a variant pattern, extending the universalistic elements of their educational experience (where boys and girls were presumed to have similarly valuable potentials and were assumed equally to be able to realize them in work). For various reasons and under various circumstances they arrive at this pattern and the dilemma for them becomes resolved and dormant.

Under some circumstances, however, the dilemmas become reactivated. For example:

- at critical points in the family life cycle (particularly birth of the first child)
- at critical transition points in the career (or occupation) life cycle of either partner (role enlargement or contraction)
- at critical events in the life space of the children (illness, school problems, etc.)

A critical point in the family life cycle that reactivates these dilemmas is the birth of the first child. For example, when Mrs. O's baby was born, she had to overcome the feeling of distress when well meaning neighbors made such remarks as, "Oh, well, I suppose you won't mind when your baby doesn't recognize you as its mother." It took her some time to overcome the heightening of conflict aroused by such remarks before she assumed her preferred pattern of pursuing both career and family interests.

These remarks are manifestations of a larger set of cultural norms related to child-rearing practices. Most of the couples studied experienced pressure from these norms. All the dual-career families made similar resolutions but two of the three drop-outs resolved this dilemma in favor of the traditional norms at the point of the birth of the first baby. The third drop-out was occasioned by a crisis in the area of the children's life space (breakdown of care facilities accompanied by incipient signs of disturbance in the child).

Mrs. O, a civil servant with a social science degree, sums up how she resolved her dilemma:

> When I first went back to work there were the women who quoted [a noted child-psychiatrist] to me. I got so fed up with this man. I got all his books out before I went back permanently. Really it made me feel like a criminal . . . but I came to the conclusion that he was taking for his examples children who had been in institutions and comparing them with the kind of children who were in an ordinary mother's care . . . and it seemed to me to be such a long way off from what I was going to do . . . I think a lot of mothers have gripped onto him to justify staying at home. I went to see a number of friends of mine who have combined both and whose children are, in the main, older and who have turned out well-adjusted, independent, happy, thoroughly sort of normal children who seem to have a perfectly normal relationship with their parents, as far as one could judge. I was a bit unconvinced.

An example of how a critical transition in the occupational situation can reactivate this dilemma is seen with the Ss. Mrs. S, a clothing designer, discussed how she had been thrown into conflict (which immediately became a family conflict) when an offer was received to take over her firm and promote her products in a really big way. Mrs. S says that this conflict was exacerbated by its timing, coming at a period of her life (age about 40) when she was reviewing her personal norms and values. She felt that before she realized it, the children would have grown up and left home. In attempting to resolve this, Mr. and Mrs. S each played devil's advocate. Mr. S, arguing in favor of maximizing familial values, would say it was bad enough that the father could not spend more time with the children but to also have mother away so much was "terrible." Mrs. S would counter this with how a more senior position would enable her to be more flexible with her work hours, have more assistance and how they would have more and better vacations and be able to remove financial worries about the children's future. Then, when she took the position that she should stay at home, spend more time with the children, pursue mutual interests and so on, Mr. S would argue that it would be doing something to her which they would both regret later as she had so much invested in her career and derived so much satisfaction from it. They indicated that this was a period of "brinksmanship" in which each pushed the other over the brink until they had worked their way through the feelings of both of them about a new resolution to the dilemma. The resolution finally adopted was one in which she agreed to the take-over but with a number of provisions for more time with the family and contractual safeguards against her being drawn too deeply into the firm's business involvements.

There are several instances reported of events in the children's life space reactivating this dilemma. This may occur around a major focussed crisis, e.g., the child's disturbance or poor performance at school. More usually, it is aroused by small occurrences. Most of the working mothers cite the feelings aroused when they see other mothers wheeling their prams in the park, but they tend to put down these feelings relatively easily, saying that probably many of these mothers would rather be going to work. Occasionally, however, the dilemma is made more acute as when the child "uses" the fact that the mother works for "playing up" the mother's guilt by saying, for example, that she prefers her granny's house or the house of a non-working mum of a school friend. In continuing their work, most of these mothers emphasized the positive elements of the situation with which the children are reported by and large to have agreed. For example, having a happier and more interesting mum, having a mum who designs things—in one case the child's school uniform; having a mum who is on TV; etc.

Dilemmas of Identity

We are concerned here with dilemmas arising within the person about the very fundamental characteristics of the self—whether one is a "good" person, a "good" man or woman and so on. This is at a deeper level and more internally generated than the conflicts arising over specific behavioral patterns and stems from the socio-cultural definitions of work and family as intrinsically masculine and feminine. The quintessence of masculinity is still, in our culture, centered on work and competing successfully in the breadwinning roles. The quintessence of femininity is still centered on the domestic scene. While there are some occupations which have come to be defined as acceptable for women—such as nursing, primary school teaching and social work—these tend to be seen as temporary, part-time or for unmarried women. Conversely, where men enter these occupations it is probable that they encounter internal dilemmas of identity stemming from the same source of social stereotyping. In analyzing the dilemmas observed in this area it is important that we consider them to be a product of our contemporary socio-cultural situation.

Taking the specifically sexual component of the identity dilemmas, i.e., whether the individual feels "good" or a "real" man or woman, there seem to be at least three levels at which the issues are discussed in the literature—the physical, the psychological and the socio-cultural. Some observers assume that confusion arising at one level will necessarily be reflected in confusion at other levels. Thus we were told by one psychiatric colleague that men and women who cross sex lines socio-culturally (as have all the women in our study to some extent) would be characterized by a psychological confusion of sexual identity as well. The assumption, furthermore, was that women who wanted to enter the male world of competition would be highly motivated by competitiveness with men and, as a consequence, would emasculate their husbands and there would tend to ensue a sex life characterized by impotence and frigidity. This would be enhanced by their tendency to choose mates who fit into their needs in this regard.

While we did not focus on the sex lives of the couples in detail, the data seem to indicate that although these stereotyped conceptions may be present in some cases (doubtless the types of cases most seen in clinical practice), this is not by any means the universal picture. We find that, while competitiveness with men may be a prominent motive among some of the women, it is only one of many that seem important. Most are involved (to the extent that they are fighting battles in relation to this) in issues relating to financial security; the need to be creative (in ways that are difficult for them if focussed on the household); and the desire to be effective as an individual person. While autonomy—financial, psychological and otherwise—is a prominent part, it is coupled with, rather than exclusive of, the wish to be interdependent with their husbands. The occupational world is used by all the wives as the area in which they develop their separate personal identities. This makes it possible for husband and wife to relate as two individuals, each having a separate identity as a person. To the extent that each has a clear personal sexual identity associated with his physical make-up, physical relationships may even be enhanced. But it would take a more focussed and detailed study to investigate this.

What seems to happen is that they are able to go a certain way toward the establishment of ideal individual identities which are independent of socio-cultural definitions but indications of discomfort arise at a certain point. They seem to say, "this is as far as I go in experimenting with a new definition of sex roles without having it 'spill over' into my own psychological sense of self-esteem and possibly my physical capacity to carry on in this relationship." This point represents a limit to which an individual's psychological defenses are felt to be effective and in each of the couples one or more points seem to have evolved beyond which each knew it was dangerous to push the other. We have called these points identity tension lines.

In the O family, the matter of income is a crucial point. Mr. O encourages his wife to pursue her career and to be successful and effective in her work, but the amount of her income relative to his is a point of some tension between them. With the Xs the central issue is authority. Mr. X wanted his wife to follow her profession and to achieve the security that she wished in it. He even welcomed her earning more than himself and stabilizing the family income so that he could get on with what he valued more highly—creative designing work. However, he did not wish to have her in authority over jobs on which he himself was working.

Manifestations of the sex identity tension line are sometimes seen in subtle, often unrecognized, undercutting behavior by the husband toward the wife. This seems to be an indication of strain and a defensive manifestation rather than the preferred mode as it occurs in couples where the husbands make such statements as:

> My wife has at least as good an education as I have; she earns as much as I do. I don't see any reason why we shouldn't regard ourselves as equal partners, and that is what we do.

> We see our family as a collection of individuals, each with different skills and interests and as having evolved the capacity to live together.

> Our marriage is a form of partnership, and has to be understood in terms of the characteristics of partnerships.

Clearly, these are statements of fundamental ideals on which the dual-career family is based. In actually observed or reported interactions, when the tension point was approached the men tended to undercut their wives. Some cut across their wives in the interview situation, not allowing them to answer fully, as though to say, "I'm really better at this than you, dear." One actually prefaced his interruptions with statements of that type. Another, describing his wife's business practices, tended to make a bit of a joke of them, not expecting her to deal with her management role as "for real" as he did himself. He expressed surprise when a larger firm thought his wife's business worth a take-over bid but was reassured when they offered a ridiculously low sum. It must be emphasized, however, that these manifestations were subordinated to the more dominant aspect of their relationship, which was that the husband did in fact support, sponsor, encourage and otherwise facilitate his wife's career. It is to be expected that there would be some "backwash" of other feelings involved stemming from the sacrifices and threats that the pattern involved. These processes of *undercutting* and *supporting* are also present on the woman's side of the symbiotic relationship.

Where the dual-career situation persists, as it has in the couples studied, a balance is achieved which constitutes a resolution of the dilemma. In the families which are also a professional partnership (as with the Ys) these processes are accentuated. Where the working partnership is conducted at home there must be developed a way to soften the cut-and-thrust of critical competitive work modes lest it erode the husband/wife relationship. The Ys recognize that criticism is important for the maintenance of work standards and to stimulate creativity. Mr. Y says,

> It is important if one is to preserve this kind of relationship, to learn to criticize with love; and to accept criticism in work matters as different from attacks on the person.

The Ys themselves recognize that this is easier said than done and have learned to accept a good deal more overt conflict in their relationship than, for example, their parents were accustomed to.

Some of the wives developed a distinctive way of handling their dilemmas in relation to the sex-role identity issue. Where their occupational roles called for patterns of behavior sharply inconsistent with their conceptions of the wifely role, they more or less consciously segregated the two sets of roles. One wife said,

> When I'm at work I'm very authoritarian. I wear a white coat at work and I try to hang up my working personality with it when I leave the office.

To this was added her husband's view:

> I once visited my wife's company on business and by chance I saw her there. She was so different. I hardly recognized her. She seemed like someone else—some sort of tycoon—certainly not my wife.

Other wives presented their careers as a series of improvisations which allowed them to do something interesting rather than as a series of steps taken toward a career ambition or goal.

A given couple may have more than one tension line operating and the tension lines may shift through time. When either individual is pushed into a pattern too discrepant with his or her sense of personal (and sexual) identity defensive behavior begins to develop. The form this takes—attack, withdrawal of support, etc.—varies according to the couple's constellation.

Social Network Dilemmas

Each of the couples relates to its social environment through a network of relationships. The social network is variously composed of kin, friends, neighbors, work associates, service relationships, etc. The networks vary in size, multidimensionality and interconnectedness. Network composition is affected by personal preferences, convenience, obligations and pressures of various kinds. Family phase and occupation affiliation are of central importance in determining the composition and the quality of relationships. At different stages in the life cycle people may be added or dropped from the active network. For example, when a woman works, some of her work relationships may be important for the family in a way similar to those of her husband. When a couple have children they may enter into relationships with service personnel relating to children's care and activities and they may form relationships with families of their children's friends. As well as quantity of relationships, there is the matter of quality, some being kept rather superficial and others deeper; some relating only to one interest sector and others being more general.

The population with which we are concerned comprises very busy people committed to very demanding occupations. They have families whom they value highly. As these families are at the stage where there are growing children at home, this creates yet another very demanding situation. Because of the heavy demands in these immediate spheres, the couples tend to have a relatively smaller amount of active involvement with kin and friends than other professional middle class families. While some of the couples in our sample interacted frequently with relatives and some kin were drawn on to help with children occasionally, the more general pattern was for difficulties to appear in this area because of the divergence of the dual-career family from expected norms of kin behavior. This is one of the areas in which network dilemmas tended to arise. The second is that of friendship formation. Both areas involve difficulties as there is both a wish to sustain a relationship and a wish to protect oneself from it because of the criticism that is usually entailed in the reactions to a career wife and mother.

This kind of dilemma is illustrated in Mrs. O's experience. Because her husband was very close to his widowed mother, who lived with his spinster sister, she wished to be as nice to them as possible. On the other hand, they found it difficult to accept that she was not only a working wife but one with a very demanding schedule. Mrs. O described a characteristic incident:

> She (mother-in-law) will call up and ask if she can just drop around for a visit. I've got her pretty well trained now to realize that I cannot just have a chat with her or prepare things for her. . . . Early on, even my husband didn't realize what

a problem this was. When she telephoned once, I heard him say, "Yes, she'll be home on Thursday, drop in anytime in the afternoon." He didn't realize how precious that afternoon was for me . . . how many things I'd saved and planned to get done on that day. I couldn't spend it chatting with his mother. I've got her trained now to accept every third week-end.

Mrs. S describes similar difficulties with her husband's mother. Although Mr. S had four brothers, it was he who had always been close to her and in later years carried the burden. This was a recurrent source of conflict of loyalties in relation to his wife and family and a high level of tension developed when his mother developed a long terminal illness. Mrs. S says

> This was the first time I felt that my marriage might break up. He would return late at night and be so disturbed that we couldn't get any rest. This was when there were very heavy demands being made on me to keep my business going. Even when none of the others in the family would lift a finger and on doctors' advice he put her into a home, he felt so guilty that it disturbed our own relationship.

The dilemma over friendship is less a matter of obligations being modified in the light of the wife's career demands than of deviating from the usual choice patterns for friends. There seems to have been established, particularly among professionals and executives, a pattern of friendship based on the male's occupational associates. Typically, however, they are married to women who do not themselves pursue careers. The women in our study tended to report discomfort with social situations in which the other wives were not working or at least positively oriented towards the idea. Problems ranged from a lack of shared interests to awkward situations arising from expressions of criticism.

In dual-career families friendships are likely to be formed in ways different from those in mono-career families. Neighborhood is less important because casual visiting patterns are impossible. In only one family was the neighborhood a source of friends and in this case it was in a suburb with people of the same type. A striking feature of the dual-career families in this study is the tendency to form friendships on a couple basis. Because of the sharp difference in outlook and situation between career and non-career wives, most of our families associate primarily with other couples like themselves. This produces a situation in which it is the wife who has a determining role in the selection of friends though the end product is a couple-based relationship. There is a greater range of couples acceptable from the man's point of view so that the selection process can center on the wife's sense of comfort and acceptance. As the overload falls most heavily on the wife it is up to her to indicate whether she can handle friendships which are both gratifying and demanding.

Role Cycling Dilemmas

There is a good deal of literature on the life cycle and on cycles within specific spheres of life, e.g., the family life cycle. The family goes through phases which are named in the culture—engagement, marriage, honeymoon, parenthood. Each culture distinguishes different sub-phases, and not all possible phases are named and identified as separate. In ordinary usage in our own culture we do not have a designation for the cycle before having children or that in which children leave home. We call them all "parenthood," referring not to the whole family situation but only to roles of the marital partners. In other spheres there is a plethora of terms. For example, in the occupational sphere we have training, apprenticeship (internship, residency), establishment, etc., to retirement. Sociologists have evolved a more precise terminology. Alice Rossi (1968) indicates the utility of thinking in terms of role cycles. On marriage a young man enters the role of husband and has a cycle of experiences in the husband role. When he takes the additional role of father, he has another set of experiences which has its own cycle. In earlier work we outlined the critical importance of events at the transition points from one role to another, discussing the processes of unorganization, disorganization and restructuring that occur to accommodate the shifts in role. The life cycle of the larger units—families, careers, organizations—is seen as punctuated by these points of reorganization, which tend to be accompanied by a certain degree of turbulence and conflict. Put into a more general framework, the role cycle may be seen as having an *anticipatory* or preparatory phase; an *establishment* phase (called the "honeymoon" stage by Rossi) in which efforts are directed at stabilizing ways of managing the role, usually accompanied by heightened interest and involvement; a *plateau* (or steady-state) stage during which "the role is fully exercised"; followed eventually by a stage of *disengagement* when the role is given up voluntarily or under force of circumstances.

The couples in this study were mostly in the stage of familial roles that would be termed the plateau, in that they were married, had children and were functioning as parents in a family that was established, with children still at home. In three instances there were new first babies so that they had barely entered the plateau stage. In all the others it was well established. Our data indicate two basic types of role cycling conflicts: between the occupational roles of husband and wife and their family roles; and between the occupational role of the husband and that of the wife. Two potential conflicts will be discussed: the career-family cycling dilemmas and the dual-career cycling dilemmas.

In the former the parental role is one into which women are to some extent pushed by cultural expectations. The woman is particularly vulnerable as, even with modern methods of birth control, she may be catapulted into parenthood accidentally. The parental role is largely irrevocable and is one for which parents tend to be relatively poorly prepared. While none of our couples reported unplanned pregnancies, it is clear that the pressures to become parents were more keenly felt by the women. In several couples the decision to have the first child was pressed by the woman with the man acquiescing. The timing of this step in relation to the career role cycle was something that received considerable attention and two points of view were expressed.

Some stressed the importance of having been occupationally established before having children. They had a high income, a secure position with flexibility and perquisites of one kind or another, and could afford a great deal of domestic help. They were able to take time off to see that things worked out well. Their commitment to work was, by this time, so well established that dropping out seemed unthinkable.

One of the drop-out couples argued, in contrast, that as they had both reached the plateau stage of their careers, there was no need for the wife to work any longer. Her husband's earnings would be high and they had accumulated savings. They felt that for those in the establishment phase, struggling to make the grade, the pressure on women to continue working after becoming a mother was greater. As Mrs. K had previously established herself, they felt she could return whenever she wished. Had she become a parent earlier she might not have had sufficient status and contacts to make this possible.

None of the couples expressed strong feelings about the degree to which women had to curtail career involvements in favor of family demands as compared with men. This might have been more pronounced had we studied captive housewives. For the most part the women felt fortunate to have had as full a career as they had managed to achieve. They tended to accept as inevitable for the present that women would have to bear the main brunt of child care and domestic organization, so that there would naturally be more strain on the wife's career-family cycling problems than on the husband's. They were thankful for small mercies—having a husband who did not invite guests home to dinner at the last minute or who did not mind running a vacuum cleaner over the carpets. There were only a few who were very outspoken about their views that jointness and equality in the marital relationship should be equality in the degree to which each must curtail the demands of career in favor of joint familial commitments.

The second type of role cycling conflict—between demands of the two careers—was expressed by most couples. When Mrs. O wished to diminish the demands of her career so that she could spend more time with her growing children while continuing in a senior professional job, she considered taking a post in a remote part of the country. Mr. O, however, could not find a job in that area comparable to the one he held. So Mrs. O had to give up that opportunity.

When Mr. P was offered a promotion with his firm if he would move to the north of England, he turned it down because there was no possibility of a job for his wife comparable to the one she held in the London area.

In all these instances there was stress—both within the individual making the career sacrifice and to some extent between the pair. However, in all cases resolutions were made on the basis of recognition of joint interest in optimizing family-career decisions so as to keep the role systems functioning with minimal tension.

Subsequent Conceptual Developments

Our 1971 report was entitled *Dual-Career Families*. The pluralization indicated an appreciation of variations even among those representing this specialized type. The conceptual framework was in terms of the creativity involved in developing a new pattern. It was suggested that if this pattern were to become a realistic option for more people there would have to be a reorganization of domestic roles, improvements in child care facilities, and a more facilitative orientation on the part of planners and policy makers. Notwithstanding the critiques of a number of reviewers, the book did not call for a replacement of the conventional family norm by that of the dual-career family. On the contrary, the final paragraphs of the book read:

> For the much greater number of potential readers who are neither dual-career families, even prospectively, nor are planners, industrialists, educators or social scientists, but ordinary people interested in how other people in their society live and feel about the way they live, this book aims to secure a degree of tolerance and understanding of others that contributes to a more humane society. The particular type of integration of work and family life, independence and interdependence among family members will vary from one family to another. However, it is important to recognize the need for interdependence and the different balances in this as each couple and family work out what is best for them.
>
> Only in a society where such sympathetic insights are prevalent can a multiplicity of ways of achieving self-realization be achieved.

A second edition entitled *Dual-Career Families Re-Examined* appeared in 1976. By this time a considerable literature had emerged with detailed empirical studies adding to the data base. The sub-title of the second edition (Rapoport and Rapoport, 1976) was *New Integrations of Work and Family,* reflecting changes that were apparent in the interim. There was less emphasis on innovation and creativity. A dual-career family structure was no longer seen as so extraordinary a variant. More emphasis was placed on it as an option among a range of family types in which husbands and wives worked outside the home.

Research developments during the 1970s put the topic into the context of *social change*. There was a normalization of the idea of both parents working outside the home, and the larger category of dual-worker families was becoming a statistical as well as a value norm for advanced industrial societies. Other changes contributing to the breakdown in stereotyping between a single conception of the "normal" family and all other "deviants" included an increase in single-parent and reconstituted families.

A *conception of diversity and options* was beginning to emerge, together with a recognition that this involves stress, but that coping with stress is a process with which all families are faced. The tension lines for each type of family vary, but stress is always present, albeit in different degrees and forms.

A more relevant concept for the family relationship between men and women seemed to be equity rather than equality. The important point for family well-being was that the arrangements chosen were felt to be fair—rather than necessarily providing a specific resolution such as identical patterns for men and women (Rapoport and Rapoport, 1975).

The change process involved shifting bottlenecks. Initially, the principal bottleneck was assumed to be access to the workplace and to center on discriminatory stereotypes. With increasing qualifications of women to do the same kinds of jobs as men, and with their demonstrated competence, access to a wider range of jobs was achieved. It took some time before it became apparent that there was another workplace bottleneck—impeding advancement of women into senior positions. Then the bottlenecks in the home became more salient. Gross inequities were apparent in the domestic division of labor, making it impracticable for most women to pursue regular employment careers, even when they were competent and job opportunities were available.

In 1978 we edited a book reporting on twelve studies of working couples. This allowed for an expansion of the available data base encompassing different kinds of occupations and socio-cultural contexts and formulated conceptual advances. There was a further move toward an *appreciation of diversity* and its concomitants. There were different types of family structure which might be adaptable to the modern situation (rather than one adaptive type and a number of deviant types). What might be adaptive for a given family was likely to vary *at different stages of the family cycle*. We suggested the concept of the protean family:

> The kind of family that we envision as best suited to be a model for the future is not exclusively the dual-worker family. This is one option among many. Nor is the symmetrical family or any other family the model. Rather, we suggest as a guiding concept the protean family.
> The protean family is not a single type at all, but an idea of variation and change in family structure to suit, on the one hand, the makeup of the individuals

and, on the other, the situation they confront—in their internal life, in their occupational and community life, and in different phases of their life cycle (Rapoport and Rapoport, 1978).

The protean family was depicted as an enabling, problem-solving type of family competent to cope flexibly with specific stresses and to achieve optimal solutions for all its members.

There were two additional sets of edited papers seeking to integrate advances in this developing field: one edited by Pepitone-Rockwell (1980), the other by Joan Aldous (1982). For each we prepared integrative essays. In the 1980 volume, we called our paper "Three Generations of Dual-Career Family Research." We noted that two relevant shifts—statistical and normative— were apparent in the intervening decade. The statistical shift was in the proportion of households containing two earners (at the head-of-household level). In Britain this went from 30 percent in 1960 to 40 percent in 1970; in the United States from 25 percent in 1940 to 44 percent in 1980. Secondly, the pattern of married women working outside the home had become legitimated and many women indicated that they would work even if there were no financial need. They no longer felt like pioneers or deviants.

There was also a development of the research field. Originally research had focussed on women at work and had conceptualized family problems as "her" problems. When the concept of dual-career family was coined, family issues were conceptualized as jointly the concerns of husband and wife. Ultimately, in the third generation of studies the issues were conceptualized as interinstitutional—work-and-family.

Seventeen studies undertaken in the 1970s were analyzed and their degree of convergence was taken to be an indication of the robustness of the concept. In addition, it was noted that the concept had been fruitfully applied to counselling and to social policy, particularly in management. Gaps noted were in relation to the children of dual-career families, not only on how to provide for their care (a fairly well worked-over field) but on their personal development in this type of family structure as compared to others. Implications for social values and social planning were indicated.

In the Aldous volume we noted seven areas for further research. Some of the suggestions centered on elements not present when the early studies were done, e.g., the impact of new micro-technologies on family/work patterns, and some of the recent macro-economic developments. There was a further call for dynamic concepts to encompass life-cycle processes—rather than the more static notion that a family is of one type or another and stays that way. This links to the growing distinction between structure and process as family determinants of personal development. Also noted was a need to study social supports for dual-career families and how they might be enlarged and improved; and to learn more about how bottlenecks in the way of change toward greater gender-equity might be alleviated. We suggested that "we (should) focus explicitly on the linkages between work and family rather than focussing on first one set of bottlenecks and then on the other."

Other book-length studies expressing the work/family conceptualization and drawing on the field of work associated with the dual-career families concept were: Kanter's (1977) *Work and Family in the United States;* Hall and Hall's (1979) *The Two-Career Couple;* Piotrkowski's (1979) *Work and the Family System;* Rice's (1979) *Dual-Career Marriage;* Derr's (1980) *Work, Family and Career;* Moss and Fonda's (1980) *Work and the Family;* Voydanof's (1983) *Work and Family;* Hertz's (1986) *More Equal than Others;* and Sekaran's (1986) *Dual-Career Families.* The literature in professional journals has mushroomed (Piotrkowski, Rapoport and Rapoport, 1987).

Policy Concerns

Aside from conceptual domain, the work has contributed to several areas of policy concern. Sekaran (1986) notes that though to a certain extent dual-career couples bear a direct responsibility for their choice, they do better in achieving their cost-benefit balance if there is a work environment which adopts supportive policies. She calls this a "family friendly" type of organization. Researchers and practitioners have a role to play in creating family friendly policies and services which support the pattern.

The *work/family interface* has recently become a focus of attention of the Ford Foundation in its human rights program area and a conference on the topic was convened in 1988 by the Conference Board. A forthcoming Ford Foundation discussion paper put it thus:

> In shaping work and family policies for the future, it is necessary to address the fact that most families in the United States will have women as well as men supporting them and that most children now have and will continue to have, working mothers as well as working fathers. While families, out of necessity, have had to adapt in order to earn a living and care for their children, institutions in general, and employers in particular—both private sector and public sector—have not yet responded to these shifts in family patterns.

One recent development that may arguably have been affected by dual-career family research is the formulation that families—and children, in particular—require a secure base for healthy functioning and development. This supersedes the emphasis on a series of piecemeal specific measures such as child care services, maternal (later parental) leave, etc. The challenge is how to provide an array of services to facilitate the maintenance of stable bases in a diversity of families while ensuring reliable functioning in the workplace. This requires re-structuring of work organizations as well as families.

The term dual-career family has passed into the vernacular, being used in the press without customary academic acknowledgement. Articles in the *Wall Street Journal* and in various glossy magazines use the term in various ways— presenting vignettes expressing anxieties about how the new phenomenon would affect marital stability, sexual functioning, child mental health and so on. On the other hand, publications like *MS* have tended to use the term with more positive connotations—as an expression of gender equality. While many more pessimistic analyses, in both the professional and popular press, have derided the phenomenon as too stressful, too elitist, too greedy, there has been a trend toward seeing it as logically inevitable, and in some ways valuable. A new glossy magazine entitled *New Woman* aims to supersede the individualistic stance of *Vogue, Cosmopolitan* and other "women's" magazines and to present women in their three roles—as workers, wives and mothers.

The concept of dual-career families emerged in a social context of concern with the place of women as human resources in our society. It represented a social structural model of change rather than, as previously, regarding the issues as individual problems of women—as expressed in such publications as Myrdal and Klein's *Woman's Two Roles* (1956).

Initial responses to the concept were ambivalent: that it represented a temporary, even freakish phenomenon growing out of wartime needs; that it was an elitist concept not available to families unable to employ domestic help; that it was too stressful to be sustained and would lead to a variety of undesirable outcomes—from sexual impotence/frigidity to child disturbance and family dissolution.

Skolnick and Skolnick (1974), however, recognized it as a radical concept encompassing a fundamental change phenomenon rather than merely an account of an "alternative family pattern." Emery and Trist (1973) saw it as an adaptive manifestation of the transition from industrial to post-industrial society.

Many of the initially outlined dilemmas and bottlenecks have shifted. There is increased acknowledgement of the legitimacy—often the necessity—of sustaining dual-worker family structures. Emphasis has, therefore, moved to issues of how these may be supported. Such support is now often seen as the joint responsibility of families and other social institutions, rather than as a purely private matter.

In the work that lies ahead—both research and action—advances will come through an abandonment of earlier either/or approaches and a recognition of this interdependence. Men and women will need to learn more about the tension lines that emerge as they work at restructuring their interpersonal relationships; families will need to learn more about the management of expectable structural dilemmas; and work organizations and other social institutions will have to learn more about how to translate their expressed values of social responsibility from the level of platitudinous sentiments to viable policies and practices. These are all interdependent and need to be worked on simultaneously. In the past, attention has focussed on one bottleneck after another—the individual and his motivation; the organization and its discriminatory practices; the family and its iniquitous division of labor. When the original work on dual-career families was conceived the focal issue was how to combine family and work career so that women as well as men could contribute their trained skills to the economy. The dual-career family was identified as a new type of family that was accomplishing this objective. However, it was found (and subsequently replicated in other studies) that though such families existed and are increasingly prevalent, they do not necessarily practice in the domestic setting what they support in the workplace. That is to say, women and men seldom share equally in the tasks of housekeeping, child rearing and domestic organization. Focal attention is now beginning to be given to how more sharing in these areas could be achieved (Ehrensaft, 1987). What is needed is a new culture and set of values which will apply to personal, familial and occupational life—rather than the multiple standards that prevail today.

Massive collaborative-interactive cooperation between funders, researchers and those with the power to implement the implications of knowledge, is required to support those individuals who value gender equality in all spheres of life.

References

Aldous, J. (Editor) 1982. *Two Paychecks: Life in Dual Earner Families.* Beverly Hills, Ca.: Sage.

Derr, C.B. (Editor) 1980. *Work, Family and Career.* New York: Praeger.

Emery, F. and E.L. Trist. 1973. *Towards a Social Ecology.* London and New York: Plenum.

Ehrensaft, D. 1987. *Parenting Together.* New York: Free Press.

Hall, F. and D. Hall. 1979. *The Two-Career Couple.* Reading, Mass.: Addison-Wesley.

Hertz, R. 1986. *More Equal than Others: Women and Men in Dual-Career Marriage.* Berkeley: University of California Press.

Kanter, R. 1977. *Work and Family in the United States.* New York: Russell Sage.

Moss, P. and N. Fonda. (Editors) 1980. *Work and the Family.* London: Temple-Smith.

Myrdal, A. and V. Klein. 1956. *Woman's Two Roles; Home and Work.* London: Routledge and Kegan Paul.

Pepitone-Rockwell, F. (Editor) 1980. *Dual-Career Couples.* Beverly Hills, Ca.: Sage.

Piotrkowski, C. 1979. *Work and the Family System.* New York: Macmillan.

Piotrkowski, C., R.N. Rapoport and R. Rapoport. 1987. "Families and Work." In

Handbook of Marriage and the Family, edited by M. Sussman and S.K. Steinmetz, New York: Plenum.

Rapoport, R. and R.N. Rapoport. 1969. "The Dual-Career Family: A Variant Pattern and Social Change." *Human Relations,* 22:3–30.

———. 1971. *Dual-Career Families.* London and Baltimore: Penguin.

———. 1975. "Men, Women and Equity." *The Family Coordinator,* 24:421–32.

———. 1976. *Dual-Career Families Re-Examined: New Integrations of Work and Family.* London: Martin Robertson; New York: Harper & Row.

———. (Editors) 1978. *Working Couples.* New York and London: Harper & Row.

Rice, D. 1979. *Dual-Career Marriage.* Glencoe, Ill.: Free Press.

Rossi, A. 1968. "Transition to Parenthood." *Journal of Marriage and the Family,* 30:26–39.

Sekaran, U. 1986. *Dual-Career Families.* San Francisco: Jossey-Bass.

Skolnick, A. and J. Skolnick. 1974. *Intimacy, Family and Society.* Boston: Little, Brown.

Voydanof, P. (Editor) 1983. *Work and Family: Changing Roles of Men and Women in Dual-Career Marriages.* Palo Alto, Ca.: Mayfield.

The Dynamics of Organizational Change

One of the main objectives of the Institute was to advance understanding of the dynamics of organizational change. Carrying this out effectively necessitated building into organizations a new response-capability required more than ever by the changing society.

Bearing in mind the Lewinian principle that the best way to understand a system is to change it, opportunities were sought to work collaboratively with organizations in identifying changes that they needed to undertake. A new professional role had to be created, analogous to but different from the psycho-analytic role, that would enable the social scientist to facilitate the change process. This new role had to be acceptable to all stakeholders and permit intervention in situations of high conflict.

Working-Through Industrial Conflict. The project that became the proving ground for such endeavors was carried out during 1948–1951 in the London factories of a light engineering company (Glacier Metal). The project was led by Elliott Jaques. It is briefly described in the Series Introduction. The first contribution under this Theme is his analysis of the changes that took place in the Service Department of the Company, excerpted from his book, *The Changing Culture of a Factory* (1951). The Department was in severe conflict over an unresolved wages issue of long standing. This was worked through with Jaques' assistance and a Department Council (joint between management and labor) was formed after enormous distrust had been overcome.

The principles of taking the "independent role," conducting a "social analysis," and reporting only that which had been worked through and agreed for publication by all the stakeholders laid the foundations of an action-research model that had persisted until the present time. The extreme formality of Jaques' original role has been reduced and many variations have developed.

The Use of Unrecognized Cultural Mechanisms in an Expanding Machine Shop. The second contribution is A.K. Rice's account of changes taking place in the Line Shop of another department of the company. Conflicts between management and labor were contained in a negotiating committee sealed off from the rest of the department which needed to carry out, without a labor dispute, an expansion necessary for its economic survival. The latent function of the prolongation of the negotiations was to enable this to happen. When the expansion was completed the negotiations were rapidly concluded. The latent function was recognized by most members of the Shop when Rice interpreted it.

On the Dynamics of Social Structure. A new theory arising from the Glacier Project is presented in Jaques' paper under this title, which puts forward the view that the social structures and cultures of organizations can be used unconsciously as defenses against anxiety, especially of a persecutory and depressive nature. This means that the deep conflicts of the individual members are projected into these structures and cultures. Any change in the organization tends to disturb these projections which are important for the identity of the individual. This is one reason why change is resisted even when its apparent benefits are great.

Social Systems as a Defense Against Anxiety. The notion of the social structuring of psychological defenses did not gain immediate acceptance. Even now it is ignored by the majority of researchers in organizational behavior. The first detailed empirical study which gained credence for it is Isabel Menzies Lyth's first contribution to this Theme. A study of the training of nurses in a teaching hospital, it has become a classic that has opened up for many scholars the study of social systems as a defense against anxiety.

A Psychoanalytical Perspective on Social Institutions. Menzies' second paper further develops the theory that interventions have to pay attention to changes in structure and role as well as in psycho-social climate. She extends the psychoanalytical basis by making use of Bowlby's work on mother/child separation and then shows how that was accomplished by re-modelling a cot unit in a children's orthopedic hospital.

The Assumption of Ordinariness as a Denial Mechanism: Innovation and Conflict in a Coal Mine. The theme of social defenses is carried forward by Trist and his colleagues (1963) in an analysis of the social use of the mechanism of denial. A major organizational innovation had taken place in one seam of a colliery in north-east Britain. Management and labor agreed to apply it in a new seam that was just opening up and which was of critical importance for the economic future of the mine. The details of the innovation had never been made explicit by those originally involved (who were not too clear themselves) to those about to be involved, who assumed it was merely a new-fangled way of doing what they were already familiar with.

This attitude epitomizes a major problem in bringing about change. The threat of the genuinely novel is too often so great that the novelty is denied. Proper briefings about the new are not held, required training is not given, not enough time is allowed for unlearning the old and mourning its loss, or working through the anxieties surrounding the consequences of the new. The penalties for not doing so are severe.

Temporary Withdrawal from Work: The Formation of an Absence Culture.
During a time of full employment such as the 1950s there was substantial
concern in industry over the cost of the prevailing high levels of labor turnover,
absenteeism, accidents and sickness. Since little understanding of them had
been obtained by conventional methods, such as exit interviewing and social
surveys, the Tavistock Institute was asked by the British Iron and Steel Research Association to suggest a new approach. The method chosen was longi-
tudinal—to follow through, from records, a cohort of workers in particular
firms over a number of years. Three phases of organizational relationship were
found—induction crisis, differential transit and settled connection. As the
stayer role became more accepted disturbances in the individual's relationship
with the organization became internalized, illness being more frequent than
absenteeism or accidents.

The psycho-dynamics of this progression were explored in a series of
studies, the last of which, by Hill and Trist, is reported under this Theme. The
conclusion reached was that temporary withdrawal from work can act as a
psychological defense against the difficulties of maintaining a long-term relationship with an organization. This led to the idea of an "absence culture" and
what might be done to create an appropriate absence culture for a given
organization.

Freedom and Justice Within Walls. An opportunity to enter an entirely
different social system—the prison service—arose when the Prison Commissioners in Britain asked the Institute to undertake a systematic action-research
study to evaluate the effects of introducing the apparently successful "Norwich
Experiment" into Bristol local prison before making policy decisions to diffuse
this system to all local prisons. This project was carried out by Emery (1970).
In contrast to the regime in conventional local prisons, the Norwich system
allowed inmates to spend most of their waking hours "in association" outside
their cells.

The research plan was jointly negotiated with the Commission, the governor and his staff, and the local branch of the prison officers' association. The
results showed that great improvements were gained by the new freedom of
association, but the creation of officer pairs linked to a group of inmates was
not feasible.

When he returned to Australia Emery took part, jointly with the prison
authorities in Western Australia, in the design, on small group principles, of a
new maximum security prison. Regular relations between a group of officers
and a group of prisoners now seemed possible. Socio-technical principles were
used to design the work organization of the prison.

Shortly after the new prison was built, the Director of Corrections died and
his successor did not implement the program in the way planned. Thus a major

opportunity to test out a model of great relevance to the future of penal institutions was lost.

The organizational change studies reported under this Theme are of long duration. Change takes time and unfolds in unexpected ways. The researcher cannot follow through the changes unless he is prepared to give a long term commitment to what he undertakes. Unless very much larger social systems are actively implicated and sanction changes made at a more local level, these are not likely to persist if they differ too widely from prevailing norms, as is illustrated in the back-sliding in the Australian prison innovation.

References

Emery, F.E. 1970. *Freedom and Justice Within Walls: The Bristol Prison Experiment.* London: Tavistock Publications.

Jaques, E. 1951. *The Changing Culture of a Factory.* London: Tavistock Publications. Reissued 1987, New York: Garland.

Trist, E.L., G.W. Higgin, H. Murray and A.B. Pollock. 1963. *Organizational Choice: Capabilities of Groups at the Coal Face Under Changing Technologies.* London: Tavistock Publications. Reissued 1987, New York: Garland.

Elliott Jaques

Working-Through Industrial Conflict
The Service Department at the
Glacier Metal Company*

Whether people work more efficiently and with greater satisfaction when there is a direct financial incentive, such as that provided by piece-rate systems, can be considered an open question. Indeed, it is unlikely that such a question can be answered by itself, because the way people are paid is only one facet of a large number of interdependent sociological, technological, psychological, economic and cultural variables which interpenetrate to create social climate and community morale in industry. An opportunity to study this problem in some detail occurred, when in January, 1949, the research team received a request jointly from the management and the workers in the Service Department of the Glacier Metal Company, a light engineering company in London to assist them with discussions on whether or not they should switch over from piece-rates to hourly wage rates.

Organization and History of the Department

The Service Department is similar to a small company. It is a relatively independent unit engaged in the sale of replacement bearings and in repair work, with subsidiary manufacture of small runs or special orders. It has its own administrative staff, drawing office and sales organization, employing altogether some 100 people, 40 of whom were at this time on piece-rates.

It was first established as a separate department in 1931 as a result of an increased demand from customers for repair services. Until the war years the new shop felt itself to be separate from the rest of the factory. It had its own customers, with whom there was close personal contact, for much of the pricing of jobs was done by direct meeting between customers, supervision,

*A revision of Chapter 4 in *The Changing Culture of a Factory*. London: Tavistock Publications, 1951.

and operatives. This feeling of independence was fortified by the shop having its own gate and working different hours from other shops; its operatives were not asked to take part in the 1935 strike. During the depression years, its members felt more secure than other Glacier workers, because the shop was steadily growing and able to take on workers laid off in other parts of the factory.

During the war the work of the department had become so extensive that increasing systematization was introduced in costing, pricing and handling of stocks, and this brought an end to informal contact with customers. Also during this period there was some lessening in the amount of repair work carried out, customers preferring to obtain new rather than relined bearings. This change necessitated modifications in the department's activities, particularly with regard to their stores and commercial activities.

In 1943, a *Payment by Results on Time Basis Scheme* was introduced. This was a payment by results scheme with rates calculated in standard minutes, rather than a money contract for a given job which the operative could then complete as quickly as he wished. This new system was tried out for three months, at the end of which management was satisfied, but the workers were not so sure. Partly as a result of the attitude of their trade union officials, who pointed out that they seemed to be better off financially under the new system, the workers agreed to change over, on condition that they could change back if they wished. Although there is no indication that such a change was asked for, the *minute system,* as it became known, fell into disrepute, and the impression grew in the shop that it had been imposed by the management.

In 1947, the shop manager retired, and the present divisional manager and shop superintendent were brought in. They were most anxious, in line with the general policy of the firm, to establish good relations in the department, and to bring it into closer contact with the rest of the factory, but felt only partially successful. The workers' representatives, led by the convener of shop stewards of the Amalgamated Engineering Union, remained suspicious, not only of their own departmental management, but of the whole consultative set-up of the factory. They had withdrawn their Works Committee representatives in 1944 because they considered the Glacier model of joint consultation out of line with normal trade union practices, and had only consented as late as November, 1948, to elect representatives once again, for a trial period of one year, during which they intended to consider their position further.

Nature of the Problem

The proposal to change over to hourly rates was first mooted by the divisional manager in February, 1948, in a talk to the whole department, in which he reasoned that service work, which consisted of repair jobs, did not lend itself readily to payment by results, since no two jobs were alike and jobs differ each time they come through the department, because of distortions and varying conditions of the bearing shells. Piece-work prices as set on work of this sort could only be estimates, so that constant adjustments were necessary to ensure a fair rate. For a majority of jobs this meant a discussion to work out an adjustment on the existing rate, which not only used up time but involved complications in the costing and financial organization of the department. There had been continuous dissatisfaction with the piece-work system in use (the so-called *minute system*) ever since its introduction by the previous management in 1943; some jobs paid well, others not so well, with the result that it was possible for unskilled operatives to earn more than craftsmen. The chronic irritation produced by the system was believed by both management and workers to be costly in reduced output and in lowered morale.

The reaction of the operatives remained reasonably favorable to the proposed changeover at intermittent discussions held during the year, and the management agreed to get out proposals for an average hourly rate for piece-rate operatives, based on the average level of piece-rate earnings for the shop. On 31 December, 1948, the divisional manager called a meeting of all operatives and offered an average flat hourly wage of 2s. 8¾d, not including the national bonus, to the piece-workers. This figure included a deduction of about a penny an hour per operative to allow for a possible slight decrease in productivity under a flat-rate scheme. Since this was an average some would earn less, and others more. The exact method for determining each individual's rate had been left to be agreed between management and the workers' representatives.

During this meeting one question was raised which was to recur frequently, "How would output be maintained when piece-work incentives were withdrawn?" The divisional manager's opinion was that this was essentially up to the workers themselves, but he was confident that people would behave responsibly and that output would suffer little, if at all. Checks on the level of productivity would have to be made, he thought, but this could be done in broad terms and need not be related to individuals.

A *Wages Committee,* composed of the Shop Committee, the divisional manager, the shop superintendent and the shop accountant was set up to consider the matter in more detail. It held its first meeting on 2 January, 1949, when the workers' representatives reported mixed feelings in the shop, with some in favor and some suspicious of the proposed changeover, the latter attitude expressing itself in such comments as "What are the management up to now?" and "What are they going to get out of this?" In view of the suspicions complete facilities were given to the Shop Committee chairman to make whatever checks he liked. This included the provision of detailed department figures from which he could make independent calculations in consultation with his own trade union officials. It was also decided to enlist the co-operation of the research team both "to obtain advice on how to avoid likely pitfalls," and with the hope that the presence of outsiders might in some way alleviate some of their difficulties. In reply to this request, the research team project officer met the divisional manager on 5 January, and on behalf of the research team, agreed to provide consultant services.

Negotiations About Payment

The Shop Committee chairman spent much of January and February reviewing the wages figures and consulting with his district officials. This review completed, the second formal meeting of the Wages Committee was called.

Wages Committee: 23 February. As this was the first meeting the consultant had attended, he took the opportunity at the outset to explain his role as laid down in the terms of reference of the project. The management then explained that although the piece-workers, because of the penny an hour deductions, would lose 2s.–4s. per week per person, this would be offset by their greater security. The workers would not accept this, because there were certain operatives who would lose materially. One person in the shop, who (it was admitted) was earning anomalously high rates, would suddenly be deprived of about £1 10s. a week; and another group of six or seven would lose between 6s. and 12s. In spite of these difficulties, however, the Shop Committee did consider that the proposed new set-up would be better for the shop as a whole; and therefore, provided that a satisfactory formula could be found to ensure that no one would suffer too much, it did not seem unfair that some should lose a little in order to achieve a better balanced wage structure for all.

During this meeting the consultant suggested that there might be value in finding out in more detail what the Shop felt about the new proposals, in order to take into account the operatives' feelings, not only about the wages question, but also about the morale issues which would inevitably be bound up with it. This suggestion was not discussed; instead a small sub-committee composed of the two Works Committee representatives, one Shop Committee member, the divisional manager, and the departmental superintendent was set up to work out a fair method of calculating individual wages, so that no one would lose too heavily.

Wages Sub-Committee: 25 February. The divisional manager opened the meeting, saying that its purpose was, first, to consider how the research team could help to organize group discussions to enquire into attitudes towards the proposed change-over and, second, to discuss proposals for calculating individual wages under a flat-rate scheme. The Shop Committee chairman immediately disagreed. They were there only to talk about wages proposals. The Shop Committee itself was the sole body which could take decisions on finding out what the workers on the shop floor were thinking. The consultant referred here to the Shop Committee's suspicion of himself and his role, and emphasized that he and other members of the research team would act only in concert with the Wages Committee as a whole. But this suspicion of him must surely in part indicate suspicion amongst themselves, and the fear that one party would be able to use him against the other.

This reference to existing attitudes in the group seemed to reassure them, and they went on to a discussion of various wages proposals. But, during the next hour and a half, not more than fifteen minutes were spent on the proposals themselves; the rest went on a wide variety of general morale issues such as: How much will the change-over alter the existing relationship among workers, between workers and management, and particularly between workers and supervisors? What happens if wages are fixed and production goes up? What techniques can be used to get general agreement in the shop? How will the supervisors behave under such a scheme? Can a supervisor be guaranteed that no worker on his section will earn more than he does?

When the consultant commented that their talk was demonstrating how inextricably the wages proposals were tied up with other morale issues in the shop, the divisional manager suggested that each supervisor might be asked to enquire into the feelings of his section. The Shop Committee chairman opposed this "investigation of workers' attitudes, since all supervisors were on management's side."

The divisional manager complained, "You're suggesting there are two sides to the table. I feel that we're all in this together."

"There *are* two sides to the table, and I don't want the supervisors poking their noses into the Shop Committee's business."

"I don't think we can go on if you're going to use language like that."

"I don't care whether you object to my language or not. I'm going to be blunt; this is the way I feel about the matter."

The atmosphere was charged. There had recurred in a slightly different form what had earlier appeared as suspicion that the research team would usurp the Shop Committee function, and possibly act on behalf of management alone. The consultant therefore interpreted this to them as a displacement on to supervision of suspicion towards himself and the research team, representing once again their own suspicion of each other at the moment. This, however, was vigorously denied. But, quite unexpectedly, it was suddenly recognized that there was no representative of supervision on the Wages Committee, and they decided to remedy this shortcoming before the next meeting.

Shop Committee: 2 March. A few days later, the consultant was invited by the superintendent to attend a meeting in his office. Agreeing, the consultant found himself at a private meeting of the Shop Committee; the Shop Committee chairman having arranged this with the superintendent. The consultant having raised the issue of the suspicion in the Committee of the research team, the suspicion itself appeared to be diminished somewhat. But what, he asked them, was to be his role at such a meeting; did they wish his advice on how better to handle management; and what would they say if they saw him or any other member of the research team meeting privately with management, or with supervision? Surely, he said, if he would help them against management, they would have every reason to suspect that he might equally help management against them.

This last point struck home, and made it possible to settle two important questions before the consultant agreed to remain with them. First, he would comment only on their own relations with one another, and on their work as a Committee; that is, he would not put forward views on any persons or groups other than those immediately present. Secondly, they should raise at the beginning of the next meeting of the Wages Committee the question whether or not the research team might meet independently in this way with any section of the department—management, supervision or workers.

During this meeting, the Shop Committee members expressed far more anxiety than they had dared reveal openly in the Wages Committee. The management, they feared, was trying to put something over on them, and if output went down, would scrap the whole scheme and put them back on piece-rates. They were uncertain what to do, because the people on the shop floor whom they represented were deeply suspicious of the proposals. Because, from their discussion, there was little indication that they had a rounded picture of the attitudes of their constituents, the consultant suggested they might find their job a lot easier if they would undertake serious discussions throughout the shop before proceeding further. This would not only acquaint them with shop attitudes, but would give the shop an opportunity for more active participation, and would make it easier for themselves to report back developments as they occurred. Although some continued to maintain that the shop was interested in nothing but the size of the pay packet, the Committee as a whole accepted the suggestion and asked for the assistance of the research team.

In a short special meeting the next day, the Wages Committee adopted the principle of the research team co-operating with sub-groups in the department, and the consultant found himself in a position he had not previously experienced—a relationship with a group composed of management, supervisors and workers, and at the same time carrying on independent relations with the component parts. Role conflicts that might arise—as, for example, when meeting separately with the workers, he had already learned of attitudes towards management which had not been expressed in the Wages Committee meetings—he hoped to avoid by relying more than ever on the general method of confining his remarks to what was happening in the here-and-now of each group. Although it was impossible for him not to be affected in his observations of the total group by what he knew from contact with the parts, he anticipated that he could avoid confusion on this score by the ordinary procedure of always having tangible evidence in the here-and-now, under whatever condition, for the interpretation made.

Attitudes at Shop Floor Level

Group Discussions: 8 March. The forty piece-workers were divided into five groups of eight, with one Shop Committee member delegated to each. To obtain a comprehensive picture it was decided to have one of the two Works Committee representatives and two members of the research team present at every group, one of these latter to take part in the discussion, and the other to record. A short meeting had been arranged between the research team members and the two Works Committee representatives half an hour before the first discussion to make sure that everything was set. Unexpectedly, however, the divisional manager turned up, explaining that, although he was not expected, he felt compelled to express his fear that the two Works Committee men might so orient the discussions as to have nothing talked about but the size of the pay packet. He hoped that this would not be so, and that they would also discuss in general how to improve the atmosphere in the shop, adding that he was surprised that so little mistrust of management had been reported so far in the Wages Committee.

The Works Committee representatives replied that they had no desire to lead the discussions in any particular way, but wished only to present the facts and to find out what the shop floor was thinking. Accepting this assurance, the divisional manager withdrew, leaving the two trade unionists looking at each other. One commented "He certainly seems anxious about our discussions." The other nodded in acquiescence.

CONTENT OF GROUP DISCUSSIONS

The groups ran smoothly. Each session lasted its full hour, and most had to be broken off to allow the next to come in. To meet the suspicion present in every group that research team members would report secretly to management, the workers' representatives explained that we were there at the request of the Shop Committee. But in no case did this seem noticeably to diminish the suspicion, and this, the consultant suggested, meant that the workers were suspicious that their own Shop Committee was in league with management. This interpretation brought into the open such comments as "the Shop Committee are management stooges and buffers," and allowed partial resolution at least of some of the workers' strong concealed doubts regarding the integrity of their committee.

The wide variety of matters raised during the discussions is summarized below, categorized under the rough headings used by the Shop Committee chairman.

MATTERS RELATING TO THE PAY PACKET

Since most people were frustrated by the existing piece-rate system, the Shop Committee received definite instructions to negotiate with management a change-over to an hourly wage, to be calculated on each individual's existing basic rate plus 65 percent. This figure of 65 percent was alleged to have been read from a productivity chart posted in the department, which recorded the average weekly piece-rate bonus earned over the past year. Since the institution of an hourly wage would bring considerable savings on overheads by eliminating the complex administrative set-up required under a piece-rate system, the Shop Committee was asked to secure a proper distribution of the savings throughout the department.

Next came a demand for a slight increase in pay, which grew out of strong expectation that under the new set-up the workers would be able to increase their productivity. Under piece-rates, every man was out for himself; there was no time to help others out of a jam. People tried to put aside jobs unlikely to pay well, and these so-called "bad jobs" often led to bottle-necks. An hourly rate with a secure pay packet would overcome these difficulties, since it would no longer matter if a job was "good" or "bad," and there would be no barriers against co-operative work. And what was more, the workers' wives would also be happier, knowing for sure what money to expect each week.

But what would happen if productivity increased? Would management institute an effective and agreed method of recognizing satisfactory efforts? It was proposed that the practice should be introduced of having a continuous measure of the productivity of the shop.

SAFEGUARDS AND GUARANTEES

The number of safeguards and guarantees asked for in most groups provided one indication of the morale problems in the shop. The management might wish to change back to piece-rates at a lower level if the new scheme did not work, and the Shop Committee was asked to secure some kind of guarantee that any agreed rate would be upheld. If another department changed over to hourly wages at a higher rate than that which they obtained, would they be able to re-open negotiations to increase their own rate? Or if they settled for too low a rate, this could be used by management to drive hard bargains with other piece-rate departments making a change-over.

Under a flat hourly system supervision might begin to "push them around and tie them to their benches." A trial run of the new system for a period of three months was demanded, with the provision that there would be a minimum of interference from supervision; otherwise the workers would never be allowed sufficient time to get used to the new system and show what they could do when they had settled down. The sick, the elderly and other categories unable to work quickly might find themselves penalized, and how, it was asked, could they ensure that a man would be given satisfactory opportunities to increase his skill and, hence, his basic rate. Appropriate protection against such eventualities had somehow to be obtained.

GENERAL MORALE QUESTIONS

The department was not thought to be as happy a place as it could be. There were mixed feelings toward the supervisors, who were felt to drive the operatives too hard, but mainly because they themselves were being driven by shop management, which "must have something up its sleeve; they must be getting something out of it or they wouldn't have proposed the scheme in the first place." After all, had management not originally put forward the proposal that the operatives should drop a penny an hour on their existing rates, on the grounds that there was likely to be some drop in production if the piece-rate system with its incentives was discontinued? Surely here was proof that management had no confidence whatsoever in them as workers.

A second factor was the memory the workers had of how the original piece-rate system had been introduced by the previous management four years before, when they had been promised that if they did not like the new system, they could discontinue it. In spite of much criticism at the time, nothing had been done about changing it, and the shop was left feeling that the scheme had been forced upon it. As a result, they were fearful that the present management would impose the scheme they were now considering, even if they did not agree to it.

Interdependence of Morale and Methods of Payment

Shop Committee: 9 March. The following day the Shop Committee met to consider the results of their discussions with the rest of the workers, and decided to press for basic rates plus 65 percent, though they would be prepared to come down to 60 percent if necessary, with the proviso that before accepting any scheme they must first check the new earnings of each individual so that no outstanding injustices would be done. Although the consultant pointed out to them the strong taboo which was operating against the management and the workers talking to each other about their behavior, they determined that morale issues, particularly those dealing with the behavior of supervision and management, were to be held in abeyance for fear that raising them too directly might "get them all thrown out of the office by management."

Wages Committee: 10 March. A meeting of the full Wages Committee took place the next afternoon at 3 o'clock, at which the Shop Committee put forward their proposal for a 65 percent increment. The management, taken aback, explained that the average bonus was 57 percent, the operatives having made the error of taking the highest figure to be the average. The Shop Committee men were not inclined to recognize their error, and confusion as to where the figure of 65 percent had come from led to a stalemate. Apart from one moment when the management expressed appreciation of the Shop Committee chairman's statement that with a fair wage the operatives would certainly keep up and possibly even increase production, an interminable, if rather polite, wrangling over percentages was all that ensued until the overtly calm and friendly atmosphere turned into silence. This seemed to the consultant an appropriate moment to take up certain aspects of their relationship.

He first pointed out that whatever arrangement they came to they would still be faced with the need to resolve the emotional stresses between the people in the room. These stresses had been demonstrated in the operatives' unwillingness to recognize their error in the discussion of the 65 percent, and they could be seen again when the divisional manager had asked what would happen if productivity went down. The Shop Committee had snapped back that management did not have faith in the workers; and this in turn management vigorously denied.

The consultant then suggested that, if one also took into account what was known from previous meetings—e.g., the divisional manager's anxiety on the morning of the group discussions, and management's fears in general that workers could not be trusted to keep production up; the Shop Committee's oft implied suspicion of management; and the first hot-tempered argument between them all, management, supervisors and workers alike—it was obvious that much more was going on under the surface than would appear from the placid atmosphere in the Committee.

In short, there was evidence from both the present and the past of strained relationships. How could they hope to arrive at a mutually agreed and satisfactory wage level for the shop so long as their fears and suspicions of each other were preventing them from conducting their negotiations with proper effectiveness?

Reactions to these remarks were immediate. The divisional manager said that they would be better off if they would take some of these attitudes into account, the supervisor, that it was about time such problems, which everyone knew existed, were discussed openly, and the Shop Committee chairman, that they all deserved the "kick in the pants" which had been given them. The consultant observed that it was not a matter of "kicking people in the pants" but that there were issues which affected their discussions and prevented them from reaching agreed solutions.

The atmosphere became easier, and they managed to reach conclusion on the point that small adjustments should be made in the case of those individuals who stood to lose too much. With this as a kind of successful test-out, one of the Shop Committee members revealed that the shop floor suspicion that management was trying to "fiddle" had arisen from the proposal that a penny an hour should be taken off their wages because of possible loss of production. With such frankness as the keynote, the divisional manager replied that he was now satisfied that the shop would maintain production, and was prepared to drop the proposal about the penny deduction.

This constructive atmosphere soon evaporated. Too many other problems were plaguing them. What would happen to individuals who lost money? Could productivity be maintained with the new types of work coming in? Complaints were made about current rate fixing, and there were problems about individuals whose present basic pay was too low. All these questions, though aired, remained unresolved. Everyone was worn out, so that when the divisional manager and the superintendent suggested that they should find some way or other of calculating a reasonable percentage figure and report back, this proposal was jumped at all around.

Two notable features characterized this meeting. One concerned the fact that, hard as they were still trying to confine themselves to the financial aspects of the change-over, they spent between 50 and 75 percent of the time, directly or indirectly, on the related morale issues. As a result there was an openly expressed dissatisfaction in each meeting that everyone "kept bringing up side issues." The other notable feature was the greater security of the Shop Committee, who now spoke more as representatives and less as individuals, the group discussions having increased their confidence.

Shop Committee: 16 March. Certain morale issues were now becoming pressing in spite of the attempts to keep them back. The Foundry had opened negotiations to change over from a group bonus to an hourly rate, and the service department workers' leaders were unsure how their own position would be affected if the Foundry changed over before them to either a higher or a lower equivalent rate. There were also divergent opinions among them regarding the shop's ability to maintain the existing level of productivity—the chairman arguing that the Committee itself should be able to guarantee a good production rate, while others were afraid that this meant taking too much on themselves, particularly in view of their fear that supervision would adopt a "nose to the grindstone" attitude.

The consultant referred to their difficulty in confining themselves to the wages question, to their lack of agreement with each other, and their anxiety about having too much responsibility, and queried whether some of their suspicion of management did not represent an outlet for their uncertainties about their own position *vis-à-vis* both their own constituents and workers' representatives from other departments.

A heated discussion followed, out of which emerged a general line that was maintained in all their dealings with management during the next few weeks: first they would try to negotiate a satisfactory hourly rate; this having been done, they would then take up morale questions before finally agreeing to the change-over.

Supervisors and Shop Committee: 30 March. At this stage another event of considerable importance in the life of the department occurred. The superintendent and the Shop Committee chairman arranged a joint meeting of all Supervisors and Shop Committee members to go into the differences which existed between them. The consultant was asked to attend. Discussion centered on tooling problems, which were used indirectly as a means of talking about their relations with each other. The consultant interpreted the undertone as an argument in which supervisors accused workers of not putting their backs into it, and workers accused supervisors of not properly carrying out their responsibilities. One supervisor thought workers raised these tooling problems just to be awkward. Shop Committee members—and they said this went for the rest of the shop too—believed it was no use bringing these matters up because you got no change out of supervision.

The meeting then got on to the difficulty of timing and assessing piece-rates on some of the jobs coming through. Stating that it was departmental policy to compensate a worker on a poorly timed job by giving him an appropriate *Additional Wages Issue,* the superintendent looked at the supervisors and said, "That is what you do, isn't it?" As a "yes" came from one of the supervisors, some of the workers' representatives broke in with, "Why don't you ask the chaps in your section what they think about it?"

The net effect of these exchanges was an arrangement for workers' representatives to be brought more into consultation when prices were being fixed. As a member of the Shop Committee put it, "You don't tell us anything, and expect us to work with you—where is the co-operation round here, anyhow?"

Feeling that the occasion had been profitable, they arranged a further meeting in two weeks' time, and asked the consultant to continue in attendance, as they found it valuable to have "general comments about things which seemed to be going on at the sides of the discussion."

Bargaining Versus Working-Through

Wages Committee: 7 April. Whether each side should stick to traditional bargaining techniques, or whether both together should try to work out an agreed rate derived from all the available facts, created the dilemma which dominated the next meeting of the Wages Committee. The divisional manager announced that the average percentage bonus of the shop was 57 percent, equivalent to an average hourly rate of 2s. 11¼d. Then the trouble started. The management referred to the 57 percent as the "maximum rate," and the Shop Committee referred to it as the "minimum." The meeting, scheduled to last "five or ten minutes—just time to allow the announcement of the calculated rate"—went on for two and a half hours.

Pointing to the continuing lack of confidence between management and workers, the consultant said that in all their discussions a central issue was the kind of relations they wanted to have in the department. Did they want one power group pitted against another, or did they want to work together? That they were striving to work out something together was clear: but it was also noticeable that from time to time they reverted to bargaining methods; as in the present maximum-minimum argument. Bargaining, as traditionally employed, led to the setting up of rates which were the resultant of the relative power of management and workers. In departing from this principle, which in one sense described what they were trying to do, they were facing the problem of what could be considered a reasonable wage for operatives in a factory of this kind at this time. This meant facing, sooner or later, the complex morale problems in the department, including the relation between the wages of all groups—management, supervisors, operatives and office workers.

Without resolving much, they finally arrived at the compromise solution of agreeing to discuss the 57 percent with the shop, in order to determine whether the workers wished them to go ahead with further discussions about the conditions under which such a wage could be implemented; that is to say, no commitment was undertaken on either side in taking this figure to the shop floor, and it was realized that they would have to face the possibility of fairly long and serious discussion afterwards.

The First Ballot: 13 May. By the next week the divisional manager, the superintendent and the Shop Committee chairman had prepared a document to be circulated to each person in the department. After a summary of the early developments, the document ran as follows:

> Management started off by considering that the Shop would be ready to accept a slightly lower wage-earning on average because of the advantage of working on a stabilized basis not subject to the hazards of piece-work, and because it was considered that production might suffer to some slight extent when the direct piece-work incentive was withdrawn. Your representatives, however, objected to this view, suggesting that we ought to pay the same amount of wages in the Shop on the new system as on the old, and that it would be up to the Shop itself to give as high an output on the new basis as on the old. Management consider this an extremely responsible attitude to take and accept the principle put forward by your representatives as a basis for discussion.
>
> The principle of payment proposed is that each worker should receive a new flat rate made up of his present basic rate, plus a 57 per cent. increment, which is equal to the average bonus earnings of the Shop. This would mean that there would be some levelling out of wages, with less spread between the top and bottom, although an adjustment might be made in the case of a few people where it is considered that injustice would be done by adopting such a basis. . . .
>
> The position at the moment is that you are being asked to come to a decision as to whether you would regard the basis outlined above as being satisfactory in principle. There are still important matters to be solved and discussions are continuing on these. They are mainly, the need to preserve a correct relationship between rates earned in the Service Shop and by other Departments, such as Tool Room and Millwrights, and we are proposing to ask representatives of these shops to discuss this issue with us. Furthermore, we have to consider to what extent, if at all, there should be any adjustment in rates established on a new basis in accordance with falling outputs, or alternatively, increased output, whether this arises from greater or lesser productivity on the one hand, or greater or lesser volume of work on the other hand. Subject, however, to final decision on these issues, we should like to know if you think the general basis proposed would be satisfactory. On this proposed new basis your own new rate would be as shown on the bottom of this note. (The actual rate for each individual was appended.)
>
> Signed, Divisional Manager
> Chairman of Shop Committee.

Following the circulation of this document the superintendent and the Shop Committee chairman together met each person in the department, offering an individual explanation of the document and inviting anyone with difficulties to see either one of them separately or both of them together. Six people, worried because they were likely to take a considerable drop in earnings, came to see the Shop Committee chairman, who brought in the superintendent, and between them certain increases were agreed in individual cases where real hardship seemed to be occurring.

Taking up Underlying Morale Problems

On the afternoon of 13 May, at a closed meeting of the workers and their elected representatives, the shop received a comprehensive report on developments thus far, and voted unanimously to have their representatives carry on with negotiations for a flat rate. Accordingly, a series of meetings was arranged between the personnel manager, the works manager, the superintendents and elected workers' representatives of the Millwrights Department and of the Tool Room, representatives of the Grade III Staff Committee, and the management and workers' representatives of the Service Department. The relationship between the rates of the Service Department operatives and those of the Tool Makers, the Millwrights and junior supervision was thought satisfactory. Certain anomalies in individual cases in the Tool Room and the Millwrights Department were, however, thrown up. These were taken up by management and workers together, and the rates of certain individuals in these two departments were increased.

It was interesting to note that because the Service Department negotiations were not treated in a sectional way either by the management or workers, they provided the opportunity for straightening out certain wages problems—and, hence, morale difficulties—in other departments, although this process was not taken as far as it might have been at the time in relation to yet other departments.

Wages Committee: 31 May. With the wage relationship to Tool Room, Millwrights and Supervision cleared, the Service Department was now in a position to finalize arrangements, and the Wages Committee began to tackle the more general morale questions which they had found so distracting. The main points raised by the operatives during the group discussions in March were summarized on a sheet which the Shop Committee Chairman had kept, and which he took out at this meeting, saying that he and the Shop Committee had a number of points to raise. The sheet ran somewhat as follows:

1. Pay packet issues
   (a) Negotiate on a 65 percent basis
   (b) Take up who gets the savings on overheads
   (c) The rates and adjustment on rates if production goes up
2. Safeguards and Guarantees
   (a) Make sure the pay packet agreed will be protected
   (b) Get a guarantee of no change back to piece-work at a lower rate
   (c) See that Service Department rates will not set a precedent for other departments, and that, if any other departments negotiate a higher rate, Service Department negotiations can be re-opened

(d) Make sure of satisfactory conditions of work with a minimum of interference from supervision

(e) Get security for special individuals such as sick, or older people, or slower workers

(f) Arrange proper facilities for workers to increase their skill

3. General Morale Issues

(a) Get out the causes of the present disharmony in the department

(b) Cannot the shop be more independent from the rest of the works, as it used to be?

(c) Find out why the section supervisors seem to be more driven and less cordial

(d) Take up why the management does not trust the shop to keep up production

(e) Find out if management has anything up its sleeve

(f) If the workers do not want the scheme, will it be forced upon them?

(g) If the scheme is accepted before the summer holidays, will members taking holidays before the scheme is implemented be reimbursed?*

They went through the above summary point by point, first agreeing 57 percent as the new basis on which they were negotiating, subject to final confirmation by the district trade union officials, who had been kept informed of all developments. As regards the eventual disposal of the benefits from savings on overheads, and whether there would be any merit increase if the Shop managed to increase productivity, the divisional manager issued the reminder that although Service Department profits were apparently high, this was largely due to the low cost at which replacement bearings were supplied from the main works; and increased profits, therefore, should go to the company as a whole, in whose prosperity the department would share. The Shop Committee chairman did not argue, but put down "no agreement" beside these points on his sheet.

The atmosphere up to this point had been friendly, but with conditions of work under the new scheme as the topic the conversation became more heated.

---

*All these points except 3(g) arose during the group discussion in March. This last point arose during May, and some explanation is necessary. The workers get two weeks paid holiday each year; the amount of pay being calculated by taking the average of a man's basic rate on 1 July of the preceding year and 30 June of the holiday year. Thus, if the Service Department had changed to a higher rate of basic pay before 30 June, this would have meant a higher rate of pay during the holiday. The practice was for the whole factory to shut down during the two weeks holiday period, with some few individuals taking their holidays earlier and remaining as a kind of skeleton staff during the holiday break. If, however, such individuals in the Service Department took their holidays before the new wage rate came into effect, they would lose any benefits accruing. The above point, 3(g), was meant to cover this particular difficulty. As will be seen shortly the matter of holiday pay became an issue of considerable importance and nearly wrecked the whole scheme.

The workers complained that other departments always seemed to get the best machines, equipment and everything else, leaving the Service Department as the poor relation; and the divisional manager's explanation that the different nature of the work in other departments necessitated new equipment far more frequently was of no avail.

Referring to the increasing heat of the discussion, the consultant interpreted what again seemed to him to be an implicit statement of the workers' lack of confidence in their own management. He commented that the Shop Committee felt that a management "who got talked out of their profits" were stooges to the rest of management in the company. In view of the rational explanations that had been given, he went on to say that many of these feelings represented attitudes towards past managements, which were being projected into the present situation. This point was not taken up, and the meeting turned to consider the course to be adopted if other departments went on to an hourly rate at a higher level than theirs. The divisional manager could give no guarantee as to the outcome, and once again the Shop Committee became worried and the chairman wrote "no agreement" beside this point on his sheet. Asked by the divisional manager what he meant by "no agreement," the Shop Committee chairman replied that these were matters of such importance that the negotiations could not proceed unless some agreement could be assured regarding them. A deadlock ensued.

The consultant asked whether they could agree on any of these points, most of which were matters for the future, without setting up some mechanism for discussing general department policy. Without some mechanism in which management, supervision and workers alike had confidence, a deadlock such as that existing at present was always likely to occur. The supervisors' representative expressed agreement, but it was too late to take up so large an issue.

In closing the meeting, the divisional manager said he would like time to consider in detail the list of points raised by the shop, and the Shop Committee chairman gave him the list to be typed and circulated to everyone. The circulation of this list represented a striking change. The morale problems of the shop were now out in the open. Thus, in order to arrive at a wages agreement, the Wages Committee was committed to the task of attempting the satisfactory resolution of these problems.

Supervisors and Shop Committee: 18 May and 1 June. In the meantime, the supervisors and Shop Committee had been getting on with their meetings, and working through a wide range of difficulties. At their meeting on 18 May, following an interpretation of strained relations in the group, one of the workers' representatives took the plunge and brought out the general feeling in the shop that the supervisors were looking more glum and wearing longer faces than they should. This comment was taken in good faith by the supervisors and led to a serious discussion about the difficulties which supervision and shop management were feeling because of the increasingly competitive economic situation.

Then, at the next meeting on 1 June, an event of some significance occurred, when the superintendent, conscientiously trying to provide information on all matters of importance, reported on certain rebuilding plans that were being put under way in the shop. This information, instead of being gratefully received, led to sharp criticism of this expenditure from both supervisors and workers. Apparently there had been a long history, about which the superintendent knew nothing, of hostility towards the previous departmental management for having engaged repeatedly in expensive rebuilding without consultation either with supervision or workers. The whole of the unresolved bad feelings about these past events flowed out into criticism of the present rebuilding plans.

The consultant observed how their discussion illustrated the inadequacy of merely reporting to people what you had already planned to do. To be serious about consultation meant taking people and their attitudes and feelings into account before final plans were laid; hence, in order to have employed consultation in this case, it would have been necessary to have reported the rebuilding proposals at a much earlier stage, and to have obtained general agreement before going ahead with plans. This interpretation led on to a more general discussion of the principles of consultation and their application to the day-to-day running of the department, a discussion which was continued at subsequent meetings of this group.

Establishing the Shop Council

Wages Committee: 2 June: 10:00 a.m. The Wages Committee met again in the morning of 2 June, just two days after their previous meeting. The atmosphere was tense, everyone sensing that a critical point had been reached, and this attitude became reflected in what turned into a full day of intensely serious work.

The divisional manager opened the meeting by stating they had three main points to consider:

1. A guarantee from the shop that production would not suffer.
2. A guarantee from management to the shop concerning benefits from increasing productivity.
3. The establishment of some mechanism for making possible increased participation of the total shop in the making of departmental policy.

The first two points had arisen frequently in their previous discussions, but the third expressed a new attitude on the part of departmental management. In explaining the origin of this attitude he referred to his realization at the last meeting that the workers felt that departmental management were prone to give way to the demands of other departments. He also referred to a report he had received about the furor caused in the meeting between the Supervisors and the Shop Committee by the plans for rebuilding in the shop. He had not expected that those plans would create so much ho ility and resentment, since they had been fully discussed with the people in the stores, who, after all were mainly concerned. He and his colleagues therefore considered that, if they were seriously to go ahead with joint consultation, it would be necessary for them to take supervision and workers more fully into consultation on shop policy.

With these comments from the divisional manager, the meeting moved on to a discussion of the list of points which had been circulated, about which, now that they were out in the open, they could speak frankly. The workers asked management point-blank whether or not they had anything up their sleeve— whether they were hiding anything. Management denied this, and made a declaration that they had been quite open throughout the negotiations.

A number of points were quickly dealt with. Special individuals would be taken care of, and opportunities to increase skill arranged for those seeking up-grading; if workers did not want the new scheme, it would not be forced on them; and if the scheme was introduced before the summer holidays, shop employees who took their holidays beforehand would be reimbursed. The more general morale issues, they saw, would take some time to clear up, but now that a start had been made on them, they would go on until solutions were obtained.

Nevertheless a number of awkward questions still remained. Who got the savings on overheads? What happened if productivity went up or down? What happened if any other department got a higher rate? What guarantees were there that the agreed flat rate would be secure, and that there would be no change back to piece-work at a lower level? It was management's view that a policy-making group for the department should be established and these issues referred to it. The divisional manager used the words "shop council" to describe such a body, and declared his willingness to vest authority for policy-making in a shop council of this kind, if supervisors and workers would agree to co-operate.

This proposal served once again to bring to the surface the workers' feelings of suspicion and mistrust: They found it difficult, they said, to have confidence in such a plan because of previous experience with management and super-visors. They again referred to the way they considered the "minutes system" had been imposed four years before and to the existing discontent about rate-fixing. The consultant indicated how suspicion and mistrust, arising out of past as well as present experience, had turned into a barrier between workers and that greater stake in the running of the department they had so frequently claimed. The Shop Committee members looked at each other, and their chairman, trying apparently to gauge the feeling of his co-workers, said they would be willing to look further into the question of what a shop council might do.

The superintendent suggested that the Shop Committee should meet by itself, talk over their attitude towards the setting up of a shop council, and, if they so wished, bring back specific suggestions on how they thought such a body might be established. This idea was accepted, and arrangements were made for the Shop Committee to meet later that afternoon, while the Shop Committee chairman, at his request, would meet with the consultant meanwhile, in order to clarify plans to bring before his committee.

Shop Committee chairman, 2 June: 1:00 p.m. The Shop Committee chairman was in a dilemma. He had been a staunch trade unionist for thirty years, and carried with him a burning suspicion of management built up through a variety of experience in some of the most severely distressed industrial areas in England and Scotland. Mixed with this suspicion was his wish to realize what he expressed as "his dream to see the workers participate in management," not just for himself, but for the younger workers who were now growing up. "My industrial life has been hell, and I don't want to see my children go through the same thing. But it's difficult to take an opportunity like this when you see it, when you've had the kind of experience in industry that I've had in the past."

The consultant talked with him for nearly three hours, during lunch and after, about his conflicting feelings, and gradually he began to clarify his thought and spontaneously outlined a variety of possible ways in which a shop council could be set up, and what it could do. These he crystallized into a proposal that a Council of some twelve members should be established, representative of all sections of the department, and composed of shop management, the full Shop Committee, and representatives of stores, of the clerical staff and of supervision.

Shop Committee, 2 June: 4:00 p.m. Following this discussion, the chairman called together his committee, and put forward his plans. But some of his fellow workers were just as mistrustful of management as he was. As one member put it, "I don't intend to put the next four years of my life into something that can't possibly work out." The consultant stressed that he could not advise them whether or not to co-operate in a shop council with management. That decision they must make for themselves. But it did seem to him that, as a group of workers, they had arrived at a cross-roads, and he felt constrained, therefore, to point out how their own anxieties and suspicions were effectively inhibiting them from arriving at any decision whatever.

They realized that their conflicts were not easily to be resolved. With some hesitation, therefore, they adopted the line that they had nothing much to lose in going ahead. They could give management a trial and, if things did not work out, at least they would be no worse off than they were, and would know better where they stood.

Wages Committee: 2 June: 4:45 p.m. Accordingly they brought together the other members of the Wages Committee and informed them that they were willing to go ahead with the setting up of the shop council, to which they would refer all outstanding issues that had arisen during the wages negotiations. The Wages Committee was thus placed in a position to take up with the Shop whether they would finally agree to the change-over on a 57 percent basis. But before this was done, final agreement to the wages change-over and to the proposal to establish a Shop Council had to be obtained from the trade union officials and from the managing director. The Shop Committee chairman was delegated to see the former, and the divisional manager, accompanied by the consultant, was to see the latter. The agreement of the trade union officials was readily obtained, since they had been kept in touch all along with what was going on. The discussion with the managing director was, however, a bit more difficult, since he was anxious lest the Service Department might be trying to set up its own show separated from the rest of the factory.

The service divisional manager, however, put a forceful case to show that the proposed developments in the department were a natural and integral part of the company's policy of joint consultation. Although he was not sure where it would lead, he was most anxious to get ahead and see if consultation carried forward in this way at shop floor level would lead to improved relations. He himself felt it was the correct thing to do, and might have important results.

This provided an opportunity to clarify the role of the Shop Council. It would be responsible for matters which affected the Service Department alone; on questions which affected other sections of the company, however, it would clearly be necessary for management and workers in the Department to consult with the Works Council. This point having been straightened out, the managing director agreed the scheme and gave the Service Department full scope to make whatever arrangements were necessary.

Wages Committee: 13 June. The decision to refer to Works Council a matter which affected policy outside the Service Department compelled the workers' representatives to consider their attitude towards the rest of the factory and their doubts as to whether they could operate effectively in the social structure outside their own department. These questions arose when the divisional manager reported his conversation with the managing director, and was attacked by the Shop Committee, who criticized the Works Council and the firm's consultative set-up, maintaining that top management could get whatever it wanted by talking the workers' representatives out of their demands or their arguments.

This clearly expressed fear of management reminded the consultant that it

400 The Dynamics of Organizational Change

had been at the Shop Committee's suggestion that he had accompanied the divisional manager to see the managing director the previous week. It would seem, therefore, he said, that the workers now perceived him as someone who could somehow magically protect them against the rest of the works, and particularly the management. If, he argued, this was the case, did it not indicate some insecurity and a fear that they were not strong enough to cope by themselves with their present situation?

This was denied by one of the workers' representatives, who said that the workers did not expect the consultant to solve problems for them, but that they did find an outside interpreter useful. The point was not completely denied, however, for the Shop Committee members had a short discussion among themselves, in which they came to the conclusion that they had to get on and try to solve their problems on their own.

The consultant then went on to say how much both the management and the workers were carrying on tradition inside themselves, in spite of the development which had taken place in the firm. From time to time members of the management had shown anxiety over entrusting authority to their subordinates, and the workers were bound down by their own mistrust and suspicion, and what seemed to be a fear of losing the present situation in which they could criticize management action and yet feel little or no burden of responsibility.

The same worker who had spoken a few moments before said in a rather critical way "What you mean is, we should trust each other and let it go at that!"

The consultant, commenting on how much suspicion was implicit in this remark, referred back to his earlier interpretation. Such feelings of suspicion seemed to be maintained to avoid facing lack of confidence, and from fear of an inability to operate the social structure of the company so as to meet their own needs and the needs of others. He emphasized that the task of finding correct and satisfactory relations among themselves, and with other sections of the company, was clearly one which was still on their agenda. This topic was then dropped, and they decided to go ahead with a final ballot.

Implementing the Wages Change-Over

The Second Ballot, 16 June. The ballot was held on 16 June. Immediately preceding it, the Superintendent and the Shop Committee chairman addressed the Department to make sure that all were quite clear about the issue upon which they were voting. The ballot paper read as follows:

> Do you wish to change the method of calculating your wages from the present piece-rates to a flat hourly rate?

If you agree to this change, you must leave to the findings of a Shop Council (to be set up as representative of all London Service Station personnel) further discussion as to what is to be done if production rises or falls as a result of the change. The Council, when constituted, will discuss and decide on all problems arising out of this issue. Such decisions may, of course, need agreeing with the Managing Director and/or Works Council, where Main Works interests are involved.

YES, I do wish to change.

NO, I do not wish to change.

In all, forty piece-rate workers in the department voted. Twenty-eight were in favor of the change-over, and twelve were opposed.

Wages Committee: 17 June. The day after the ballot the Wages Committee considered whether or not this 70 percent majority was sufficient to warrant a change-over. In order to assist the discussion, the Superintendent provided the following figures. Under the new scheme, seven people in the department would lose from 2d. to 9½d. while thirteen would gain from 2d. to 7d. per hour. Total pay lost per hour would be 5s. 2d., and the total gained 6s. 5d. per hour. In other words, the earnings of the department as a whole would increase slightly under the new arrangement.

The Shop Committee decided that they would be acting in the best interests of the shop by accepting the majority view, but were worried about what management might do if the people who were not in favor of the scheme should for a period of time remain unco-operative. In reply, the divisional manager expressed the opinion that if the situation which they feared became such as to require drastic action, he would refer it to the Shop Council.

The Shop Committee became angry, their chairman protesting "You can't make us responsible for disciplining people. Put your cards on the table. What do you intend to do? Suppose all twelve worked in a half-hearted way, would you sack them instantaneously?"

The divisional manager protested he was not "holding any cards," but was being quite straightforward.

The consultant asked whether it was not true that whatever management replied, they would be wrong—for the workers' representatives were once more testing them out at a crucial point in their negotiations. He exaggerated the example, and asked whether the management would dismiss those who had voted against the change-over if they downed tools. Management immediately replied in unison "of course not," and the Shop Committee, somewhat reassured, concurred that it would be a drastic situation and would require discussion jointly between management and workers. This led to some clarification of the potential functions of the Shop Council and of its members. The Council would establish general policy, and full responsibility and authority would be delegated to management to carry out this policy, subject always to checking and criticism by the other members of the Council.

The Wages Committee then adjourned for ten minutes, while the Shop Committee held an independent meeting before coming to a final decision. Immediately the others had gone, the Shop Committee members unleashed the anger which they had held bottled up, for, in their estimation, management had been rather reticent over what they would do about workers who were not fully co-operative under the new scheme. In order to test this assessment, they would attempt to get a written agreement from management not to fire anyone whose work was affected because they were opposed to the change-over.

With this test-out to serve as guarantee, they reaffirmed their decision that it would be for the welfare of the shop as a whole to put the new system into effect since, unless they changed over, those unskilled workers now earning anomalously high wages would be holding up the others. Better relationships could be established with a flat-rate system, in which wage levels were determined more by skill and ability than by the quirks of individual piece-rates.

The rest of the Wages Committee then returned, and the Shop Committee reported their readiness to implement the change-over, if they could arrive at a final agreement on the question of dismissal. Management had no objection whatsoever to their proposal, and a short note to the effect that there would be no arbitrary dismissals was written into the minute book and signed. Largely through the patience of management, the suspicions of the workers had been dealt with and another test-out situation successfully passed through.

A Report to the Shop: 21 June. At this stage the consultant became concerned whether the Shop had been sufficiently informed of the reason why their Committee had taken the decision to change over. He therefore got in touch with the Shop Committee chairman and asked him whether it would not be wise to meet all the operatives in the department and give them a detailed explanation of the way the negotiations had been carried on. This the chairman thought was a useful idea, and having made the necessary arrangements through the superintendent, spoke to the workers at a closed meeting on 21 June. His report contained a number of points which indicate how far changes had occurred.

He explained that the Shop Committee had decided there was a sufficient majority for the new scheme on the following grounds: it would allow more equitable payment on the basis of skill; it would overcome the present difficulties in assessing proper piece-rates, and remove many pay anomalies in the department; and it would provide a fair wage for the great majority of the department, and hence would lead to increasing harmony. There was also the value of greater security to the individual, in having a fixed and known pay packet. He then reviewed in detail the way the negotiations had been carried on, and showed the manner in which they had taken up with management the various points raised in the group discussions in the shop. Finally, he stated that the Shop Committee had tested management very severely, making many criticisms and creating a great many difficulties, partly at least in order to see how management would react. On the whole, he felt that management's attitude had been fair throughout and he himself now thought that there was a reasonable hope of obtaining co-operative working relations between the management and the workers. Following the explanation, the Shop supported its Committee's decision and agreed to give the new scheme a fair trial.

The Holiday Incident

The troubles, however, were not yet over. Having decided on the change-over, the workers requested that it be implemented before the holidays, in order to get the advantage in that year of the increased holiday pay which they would receive. This the management readily agreed to do but, on checking with the Finance Office on 25 June, they were chagrined to discover that, unless the change was implemented before 30 June, they would not benefit, since that was the day on which the holiday rates of pay were calculated. And even if they changed before 30 June, they would not get the full benefit of the increase, since their coming holiday pay would be the average of the new rate and the rate in force on 1 July of the previous year. An emergency meeting of the Wages Committee was called and the management explained the position.

The attitude of the Shop Committee was "Ah-ha! so this is what you've had up your sleeves all the time." The management, however, was firm, and pointed out, as was indeed the case, that the workers were just as responsible as anyone else for knowing about holiday wages regulations. There then followed some heated discussion, during which the consultant had an opportunity to indicate how once again the workers were testing management sincerity. Their increased capacity to speak frankly to each other allowed these suspicions to be resolved, and the workers to recognize and admit that they were just as much in the wrong as management. They decided to send the divisional manager to find out from the managing director whether any special arrangement could be made.

The difficulty was complex. The Foundry had changed over from a group bonus to flat-rates earlier that week, and the works director had said they would get their holiday pay on the new rates. He too, realizing his error, had gone back to the Foundry, and the same trouble had arisen there. Hearing about this the Service Department decided to sit tight until it saw what the Foundry would do.

The two departments were told by the managing director that they could have the full new rates for the holiday if they felt this was fair. The Foundry decided to take it. The Service Department Shop Committee vacillated. The superintendent took the Shop Committee chairman to task for his vacillation, because every hour that went by meant that it was becoming increasingly difficult to get the accounts out by 30 June if they should decide to take the new rates. Pushed into a decision, the Shop Committee followed the Foundry and took the full rate, because everyone in the Shop had expected it and they wanted to give the new method the best possible start. By a considerable effort the superintendent, the shop accountant and the office staff were able to get the accounts out just in time.

There was general satisfaction in the Shop over management's special efforts, and what seemed at first a nasty situation was handled in such a way that it contributed to better departmental morale and management-worker relations. On 28 June the new method of payment was implemented.

Conclusion

What had begun as an issue to do with wages and methods of payment soon led into the complex ramifications of inter-group stresses so frequently tied up with wage questions. These were summed up on the sheet of paper which outlined the pay-packet issues, the safeguards and guarantees, and the general morale problems which were raised in the group discussions with the shop. The seriousness of the managers and of the workers' representatives in their desire to arrive at a constructive solution of their problems allowed them to face and explore this wide range of questions and attitudes which kept cropping up and obtruding in such a way as to hold up their discussions. Their constructive purpose being strong enough to withstand the strain of working-through differences which occasionally reached the point of violent discussion, it became possible for the department to move up to an entirely new plane of discussion, and to accomplish the change-over to a new system of payment by means of the creation of an entirely new institution, a Shop Council, which gave promise of being a mechanism through which members could take part in setting policy for the department.

The process of working-through the wages problem by recognizing and doing justice to the wholeness of the pattern of attitudes, group relations, administrative practices and technological changes of which the wages question forms an integral part, made it possible for the shop to achieve a double result: they introduced a new method of payment which provided a generally accepted and favored solution to the immediate problem; but more than this, they have set in motion a process and an institution which will ensure for them that, however the new methods work out, it is likely that they will be able to deal more readily with similar problems in the future by being able to recognize them earlier, and by being better equipped to cope with them as they arise.

A.K. Rice

The Use of Unrecognized Cultural Mechanisms in an Expanding Machine Shop

With a Contribution to the Theory of Leadership*

Cultural techniques include the mechanisms for handling relationships between persons and between groups. Such mechanisms are largely unrecognized and difficult to identify. Hence it is seldom easy to demonstrate how groups use them to bring about observable social change. An opportunity to illustrate their use arose during work on the Glacier Project (Jaques, 1951; Vol. I, "Working-Through Industrial Conflict"), when, in November 1949, the workers' committee of the factory's mass production unit, the Line Shop, asked the research team of the Tavistock Institute of Human Relations to cooperate in an investigation of the reasons for the apparent apathy of the workers of the shop towards joint consultation.

The Line Shop had been faced with the need to expand to meet an urgent demand for its products. The process of expansion aroused acute feelings of anxiety in the workers. It will be shown how the unrecognized techniques for allaying these anxieties led to the emergence of other problems and affected the character of the joint consultative procedures which were used to solve them. It will also be shown that although the attempts to deal with the emergent problems were apparently unsuccessful, the workers' committee accurately represented its constituents and contributed positively to the successful accomplishment of the task of expansion.

The paper is presented in three parts: first, a description of the economic position, organization and social climate of the shop; second, an analysis of the use by the shop of unrecognized cultural mechanisms; and finally, a brief discussion of the leadership roles taken in the shop. In accordance with project policy, the author drafted the paper and submitted it to the Subcommittee of the

*A shortened and rewritten version of the original—*Human Relations*, 4:143–60, 1951.

Shop Council, who in discussion modified and revised it. The author acknowl-
edges their active help and collaboration.*

Economic and Social Background

The Line Shop is a machine shop which produces finished light bearings and
bushes for the motor industry in a highly competitive market. It uses mass-
production methods, organized in lines of from three to twenty-four interdependent machine operations. The bearings are precision products which have
to be machined to tolerances of the order of ± 100,000th inch, but jobs are so
broken down that high degrees of engineering skill are not demanded. Many
machine operations, however, although repetitive, require considerable dex-
terity and experience. Runs vary from a few days to weeks, and a change of job
nearly always requires a change in the number and kind of manufacturing
operations included in a line. Job changes, absenteeism and labor turnover
make frequent transfers from line to line necessary.

The Line Shop is managed by a superintendent, who was appointed in June
1949. He is responsible to the works manager and has responsible to him a
foreman in charge of production. Each line is controlled by a supervisor who is
also responsible for setting up his machines. A Production Engineering Department advises the superintendent on production methods and ratefixing. The
shop draws on common factory services for tools, maintenance and general
stores.

The joint consultative bodies are:

- The Shop Committee representing workers, composed of 10 members of
  recognized trade unions.
- The Shop Council composed of superintendent, foreman, two assistant
  foremen, all supervisors and members of the Shop Committee.
- Subcommittee of the Shop Council, composed of superintendent, foreman, one representative of the supervisors, three members of the Shop
  Committee and the officers of the Council.

The establishment of the Line Shop, in 1934, was regarded with fear and
distrust by other workers who saw in the new production techniques a threat to
their security and status. Women and juveniles were employed at low rates of
pay, and working speeds were very high. The shop soon became known as the

---

*Members of the research team engaged on this sub-project: Elliott Jaques, Director of the
Project; K.W. Bamforth, J.M.M. Hill, and I. Leff, Research Fellows; and G. Ladhams, part-time
consultant.

"sweat shop." In April 1935 a strike was called. It did not have union support and ended in failure. There was a longer term effect, however, and at the end of World War II management tried to halt the trend towards the de-skilling of jobs and the use of cheap labor by introducing into the Line Shop demobilized servicemen in place of many of the war-time female employees.

Expansion during World War II increased the numbers employed to a peak of 300 in 1944. At the end of the war night-shifts stopped, and by the end of 1947 there were 180 workers. In the early months of 1949, there was a trade recession and many employees were dismissed. The Line Shop suffered most severely. Over a period of four months the number of workers was reduced from 180 to 80. In the summer of 1949, a recovery of the trade position, completed by devaluation in the autumn, led to the second expansion.

Severe competition has demanded a constant technical struggle to develop faster production methods while retaining high standards of accuracy. But the motor industry is an unstable market and causes a varying work-load in the shop. Plenty of work imposes pressure to meet delivery schedules—unless advantage is taken of the demand, customers will be lost. Too little work arouses anxiety that workers will be dismissed and that supervisors will either have to leave or to accept a reduction in rank. The crisis of 1949 is fresh in memory, and the recent expansion with its scramble to meet tight delivery times is an uncomfortable reminder of much that has happened in the past. A dilemma must be faced: on the one hand, cutting costs and increasing speeds earns the shop the reputation for "sweating," and demands toleration for the reduction of the number of workers required for the production of particular bearings; on the other, resisting the constant reorganization aggravates fears of future redundancy.

Many other factors reinforce the climate of insecurity. Frequent changes in shop management and the constant transferring of supervisors from line to line are indications of the severe strain under which those in authority have worked. Daily events—changes in work group membership, shifting of machine tools, fluctuating bonuses, variations in the quality of raw materials, and the need to introduce and to train newcomers without reducing output—prevent the line work-groups from settling down to a steady and reassuring rhythm of work. When members of the shop compare themselves with other workers in the factory, their skills seem more easily acquired than the skills required in other departments. They feel that they are judged by quantity rather than quality and that, in the determination of their worth, the exercise of ingenuity, initiative and improvisation are discounted.

The above account is the background to a series of events which occurred between October 1949 and October 1950. In the first phase the Shop Committee resigned, resumed power, and four of its members resigned again; and the research team undertook the first investigation and reported its results to the shop. In the second phase the Shop Committee increasingly involved the management in its dealings with the problems of its constituents; and the research team undertook a second investigation. The third phase was characterized by a wage negotiation in which only three members of the Shop Committee took part, and from which the other members of the Committee and the workers were, by general consent, excluded.

The Use of Unrecognized Cultural Mechanisms

The First Phase, October 1949 to January 1950:
The Fight/Flight Group Culture

RESIGNATION OF THE SHOP COMMITTEE

To analyze the meaning of these events, the concepts developed by Bion (1948–51; Sutherland, Vol. I, "Bion Revisited") in his work on group behavior will be used. In October 1949 the Shop Committee resigned, having decided that it was not representative because of the number of new workers in the shop. Thirty-two nominations for a new committee were received. But 23 of the nominees withdrew before the election, and the remainder included some who were said to have been nominated as a joke. The members of the Shop Committee thereupon postponed the election, temporarily resumed office, and sought help from the research team. The Shop Council confirmed the request for help and agreed that "all aspects of the work and relationships within the Line Shop should be investigated." Members of the research team held discussions with each working group and reported the results to the whole shop.

The investigation showed that the Shop Committee was not considered to be effective in handling shop problems and its meetings were resented as a waste of time. The workers recognized, and accepted the necessity of fulfilling, the increased demand for bearings to keep the shop from losing ground to its competitors. They liked working on fast moving, smoothly running lines and they resented everything—meetings, the disturbance of established working teams, and the introduction of inexperienced newcomers—which dislocated production. But they disliked having to accept constant reorganization and were uncomfortable at the prospect of being classed as "sweats."

Using the concepts outlined in the previous section, this situation may be described as follows: The sophisticated group, that is the group producing bearings in a competitive market, was suffused with the emotions associated with the fight/flight basic assumption. The fight, led by management, was against competitors who threatened the security of the shop. The fight/flight culture, however, demanded that the members of the group accept reorganization and tolerate feelings of guilt about sweating. These demands were difficult to concede, and there was a conflict between the basic group and each individual in it.

SCAPEGOATING OF THE RATEFIXER

This conflict led the workers to ask themselves what they got for their hard work and high speed. They turned their attention to earnings and complained about fluctuations in the bonus rates; such complaints, however, brought them face to face with a problem. Management was responsible for the situation in which the fluctuations occurred. But management also provided the leadership necessary to keep the shop full of work. Some other target for their complaints had to be found. The ratefixer was readily available. He timed operations and drew up the layouts which set job times. And so, disregarding explicit company policy that the authority of the ratefixer was only advisory, the workers placed on him responsibility for earnings, and sought relief from their discomfort by denouncing him. They granted his skill in determining operational times, but they sharply questioned his judgment in assessing average workers and average speeds. The group was still using a fight/flight culture; but the target was now an immediate and known person, instead of a distant and impersonal competitor.

INTERACTION OF THE SHOP COMMITTEE AND ITS CONSTITUENTS

At the end of December, the members of the Shop Committee formally withdrew their resignations, and received a vote of confidence from the shop.

In January, at a meeting of the Shop Council called to discuss the report of the investigation, the committee produced four proposals for dealing with shop problems:

(a) To raise the base rates with a corresponding reduction in the proportion of total wage represented by bonus;

(b) To maintain present rates, but to revise the rating standards used in ratefixing.

(c) To change to a flat, hourly-wage payment;

(d) To transfer authority from ratefixer to management for deciding extra payments for allowances, and to pay all other work at time and a half instead of time and a third.

These proposals were referred back to the Shop Committee and management. Within a few days of the meeting, four members of the committee resigned again and were not replaced.

The recall of the Shop Committee arose out of the difficulty in which the workers found themselves when they sought leaders to deal with the ratefixer. They could not pick shop management to provide this leadership since shop management and the ratefixer were both part of company management. Other leaders had to be found, but they had to be unusual leaders. For although at the manifest level the workers were opposing the ratefixer, they were intuitively aware that they were also opposing their own shop management. To be too successful would be to jeopardize their security by making the shop less competitive. They therefore sought to get leadership which would not too seriously embarrass management by recalling the Shop Committee which they had recently condemned.

The Shop Committee, still smarting under the apparent apathy and ingratitude of its constituents, accepted office again, but realized that it could command little support. When management, even though prepared to re-examine the methods of payment and of ratefixing, was nevertheless not prepared to be stampeded into hurried concessions, the committee lost heart. In using the report of the investigation as the prop for its proposals, it foreshadowed the subsequent flight. It also foreshadowed a change in the group culture of the shop. The four who resigned again became the leaders of the fight/flight group—leading it in flight from the consequences of its attack upon the ratefixer.

It may now also be suggested—in view of the findings of the investigation in November and of the subsequent events in the shop—that when, in October, the total Shop Committee had resigned, they had been using one of the techniques of the fight/flight culture and had run away from the problems of representation. That they had correctly interpreted the mood of their constituents was shown when the shop followed their lead by not providing sufficient candidates for a new committee.

The Second Phase, February to March 1950: The Dependent Culture

CONFLICT ABOUT INTERLINE MOBILITY AND THE INTRODUCTION OF NEWCOMERS

The second investigation by the research team at the beginning of February showed that bonus earning was still an urgent problem but that the emphasis had changed. Complaints about fluctuation had become complaints about low

TABLE I   Line Shop Labor Turnover Data, October 1949–October 1950

Month	Entrants	Leavers and transfers to other shops	Total at end of month
1949			
October			125
November	21	3	143
December	11	2	152
1950			
January	13	5	160
February	16	4	172
March	23	5	190
April	13	8	195
May	16	6	205
June	9	8	206
July	4	3	207
August	11	5	213
September	25	14	224
October	16	30	210

earnings on difficult and complex jobs. In addition, two problems—interline mobility and the introduction of newcomers—previously discussed only in relation to their effects on bonus fluctuations emerged as problems in their own right.

The workers said that job layouts were being used as excuses to transfer those who were not wanted. There were two kinds of worker: core members of lines, who were never transferred, and the others, who were continually pushed around. A test check of interline movement for the first thirteen weeks in 1950 showed, however, that no distinction could be made between core members and the others, only three workers had stayed on the same line during normal working hours.

The workers resented newcomers because experienced operatives had to stop work to help them. The introduction of newcomers also aggravated fears of possible redundancy, particularly as the total number approached the number employed before the 1949 crisis. The numbers employed together with entrants and leavers are shown in Table I.

Although the complaints voiced during the second investigation were about the same things as during the first, a change had taken place in their tone and context. By the beginning of February, explanations about the reasons for transfers within the shop could not eradicate feelings of rejection among those transferred, and information about the shop load could not reassure workers that their jobs would not soon be in jeopardy. The workers could no longer get a sense of security from challenging their competitors or criticizing the ratefixer. Their disquiet was great, and they behaved as though they wished the management to look after and protect them. In Bion's terms the change may be stated thus: the tension caused by the sophisticated group using the fight/flight basic assumption (*ba*) to suppress the emotions associated with dependence had increased until the dependent *ba* could no longer be contained at the proto-mental level. By early February the group composed of the workers in the Line Shop was behaving as if it had made, and was acting upon, the dependent *ba* and there was a conflict between the sophisticated and the basic groups.

Because the workers were now leaning upon management, they badly needed management to be infallible. But to maintain a belief in such perfect reliability, they had to cope with their knowledge of management's responsibility for the expansion and the transfers, and with their own observation of the kind of mistakes which are inevitable in any industrial organization. They suppressed their knowledge and observations by turning once again upon the ratefixer—who could be held responsible for the layouts which made transfers necessary—and again making him the scapegoat upon whom they might displace any perceptions of management fallibility, however slight. To the extent that this mechanism of displacements did not succeed, they became depressed.

But even when the workers managed to maintain a perfectionistic belief in the reliability of management, they then had to construct the complementary belief that they fully deserved management's care and attention. In addition, therefore, to finding a scapegoat for management, they sought a scapegoat for their own mistakes and bouts of irresponsibility. Already resenting the newcomers as potential rivals for jobs, they now heaped upon them criticisms for being greedy for attention and ungrateful for what was done for them.

REQUEST FOR A FLAT RATE

On 8 February, after a preliminary meeting between the Subcommittee of the Shop Council and the Company Management, the members of the Shop Committee who had not resigned decided to negotiate for a flat rate method of payment. They then turned to consider whether to start negotiations at once, or to seek ratification of their decisions from the shop. Strong opinions were expressed in favor of each course, the final decision being that they should go back to the shop for sanction. Having taken this decision, they then went even further and entrusted the conduct of the shop meetings to management; only one member of the Shop Committee taking an active part in them.

One way of describing this behavior of the members of the Shop Committee is to consider their position both as members of the dependent group and as its potential leaders in the consultative system. One of the characteristics of a dependent group is its concern for the welfare of each of its members. It values them all. The request for a flat rate—a method of payment which asserts the value of the individual to the group whatever his output—may therefore be interpreted as a direct manifestation of the group culture of the shop, expressed by the members of the Shop Committee as representatives of the workers. In addition, the members of the Committee were aware, however unconsciously, that the group they were leading in the consultative system was a dependent group. They recognized that a dependent group demands omnipotent leadership and neither expects nor wishes to be consulted by leaders to whom omnipotence has been attributed. The members of the Committee wanted to lead but they felt oppressed by the demands made upon them. In this conflict they themselves turned to management for help and reassurance.

During this phase the Sub-committee of the Shop Council, by refusing to consider other methods of payment, to accept suggestions for experimental approaches to shop problems, or to permit further investigation, protected the shop from what Bion called "the hatred of learning by experience." That both the Shop Committee and the Sub-committee of the Council had accurately assessed the feelings of the workers was shown when, on 15 March, the day-shift meeting gave a vote of 120 against three in favor of the negotiations for a flat rate.

The Third Phase, The End of March 1950 Onwards: The Return of a Fight/Flight Culture

BEGINNING OF CHANGE IN THE GROUP CULTURE

By the middle of March management was beginning to experience difficulty in obtaining sufficient new workers and the shop was becoming increasingly heavily loaded with orders. This was well known to the workers and they were becoming reassured by it. On 17 March, two days after the day-shift meeting, a meeting was held with the night-shift. It differed markedly from that with the day-shift. At the day-shift meeting there were few questions and an almost unanimous vote in favor of negotiating for a flat rate. In the night-shift meeting there were pointed questions, discussion was lively; workers said they did not know the members of the Shop Committee or what they were doing. The voting was inconclusive; 12 voted for and 12 against negotiating, while 20 abstained and asked for more information. Some of this difference may have been due to the different sizes of the meetings and to the times at which they were held; the day-shift meeting being held in the last hour of the working day, and the night-shift meeting, which lasted longer, being held in the middle of the shift. But the differences are not altogether accounted for by size and time. An additional factor was that a change from a dependent to a fight/flight culture had taken place in the shop during the few days between the two meetings.

The change in culture was also reflected in the meeting of the Sub-committee of the Shop Council on 23 March. The workers' representatives strongly opposed further discussions at shop floor level. In their previous experience of a fight/flight culture, it will be recalled, they had been rejected, and had then found themselves involved in an abortive attack upon management; in the dependent culture, they had been oppressed by the impossible demands of their constituents that they should be omnipotent. They wanted to avoid either possibility. A new course, however, was now open to them: to take up the offensive on behalf of their group, but to protect the group from the consequences. This new course had been made possible by the reassurance given to the shop by the combination of the increasing load of work and the shortage of labor. The need for a new course had been indicated to the committee by the attacks made upon it by its constituents at the night-shift meeting.

Prolongation of the Wage Negotiation

The negotiating group consisted of the works director, personnel director, works manager, cost accountant, production engineer, ratefixer, superintendent, shop foreman, one supervisors' representative and three leading members of the Shop Committee. At its first meeting in May, the three leading members of the Shop Committee said that their constituents would be unlikely to accept current basic rates plus average shop bonus. At this and succeeding meetings members struggled against the condition, previously accepted, that the total wage bill should remain the same, and, while negotiating for a flat rate, they bargained for higher rates of pay. They also subscribed to the idea of introducing a grading and merit rating scheme which would widen the range of pay between the experienced and inexperienced. They were once more prepared to accept the principle by which those who worked hardest should be best rewarded, in contrast to their attitude a month before when they wanted everyone treated the same. The negotiations were prolonged and both management and members of the Shop Committee were reluctant to release information about their deliberations to the shop or even to other members of the Committee. The fight/flight culture was once more in operation, but the resulting conflict between workers and management was now encapsulated in the negotiating group. To understand the implications of this return to the fight/flight culture, albeit in a different form, it must be seen in the setting of the whole movement through the three phases as outlined in the following section.

The Three Phases—Recapitulation

The three phases which have been described in the previous sections occurred during a period in which there was a continuous process of expansion in the numbers employed in the shop. Seen as a whole, the pattern of behavior in the Line Shop from October 1949 to October 1950 may be described as one in which the workers were making constant attempts to find adaptive cultural mechanisms with which to allay the feelings of insecurity aroused by expansion. During what has been described as the first phase the shop used a fight/flight culture. The phase ended with the shop in flight for the second time; the problems which had emerged—bonus and ratefixing—had produced too great a conflict between management and Shop Committee leadership, with the result that there was a partial return to the unstable situation with which the period had started. The failure of the fight/flight culture as an adaptive mechanism was followed by a change in the group culture, and the shop then behaved as if it had made, and was acting upon, the dependent basic assumption. During this period the Shop Committee made a dependent relationship with management, in which leadership in the consultative system devolved upon the three leading members of the Committee. When the dependent culture no longer sufficed to allay feelings of insecurity, because of the inability of those in the shop to continue denying the fallibility of management, the fight/flight culture was again adopted.

The experiences gained during the operation of the dependent culture, however, allowed the techniques of the fight/flight culture to be used in a way which differed from that in which it had been used in the first phase. Although the dependent culture could not provide long-term stability, it did provide a transitional period during which those in the shop, and members of the Shop Committee in particular, could recover from their previous failure and learn new ways of behaving. The experience, under the protection of management, of meeting their constituents face to face, of successfully disentangling the consultative and investigation processes, and of receiving an overwhelming vote to continue negotiations, reassured the leading members of the committee to the extent that they became able to carry within their own group much of the conflict in the shop resulting from the attempts of its members to adapt themselves to the expansion. When, in the third phase, the shop returned to a fight/flight culture, it was able to use the culture in a new and more stable manner. During the first phase, a conflict between the basic group and the needs of its individual members had led to flight and had preceded a change in group culture. But now the fight on behalf of individual needs could be encapsulated within the negotiating group. By this mechanism, consistent with the fight/flight culture, the total shop group was freed to use its culture in performing its sophisticated task—the production of bearings in a competitive market.

Leadership at Manifest and at Unconscious Levels of Behavior

The analysis of the use by the Line Shop of unrecognized cultural mechanisms may serve to throw some light on certain aspects of relations between leaders and followers. During the period which is covered by this paper, the consultative system of the Line Shop operated mainly at the level of the basic assumptions and formed, not a system of communication at the manifest level, but a part of the mechanism of unrecognized communication whereby the group culture was expressed and maintained. At the manifest level, the task of the Committee was to determine the opinions of its constituents about current events and future policy and, in the light of those opinions, to take such action on behalf of the workers as it judged appropriate. The sanction for this task was based upon the belief that it would be in harmony with the sophisticated task of the shop, that is, with the production of bearings in the face of severe competition. In each of the situations described, however, the sanction for the behavior of the Shop Committee has been shown to have derived, not so much from the sophisticated group as from the unconscious group culture, that is from the group operating upon either a fight/flight or a dependent *ba*. It is not surprising, therefore, that the members of the Shop Committee found it difficult to take part, as elected leaders of the workers, in discussions of current problems and future policy, since, at the sophisticated level of bearing production, the leadership roles in the shop belonged exclusively to management. The Shop Committee was expected, and allowed, to lead only when there was conflict between the sophisticated group and the basic group or between the basic group and the individuals who composed it, and when management's leadership of the basic group was felt by the group to be inadequate.

When the members of the shop felt persecuted by the basic assumption of the fight/flight group they looked for leadership in handling the disagreeable emotions associated with it. Because of the conventions surrounding representation, the members of the Shop Committee were, in the eyes of their constituents, protected from retaliation. They could, therefore, be abandoned without compunction. Abandonment did not, however, necessarily mean that the committee was no longer taking a leadership role, but that the level at which leadership was being exercised had changed from the manifest to the unconscious.

These phenomena may be stated more generally. At the manifest level leadership can be considered as requiring, for its successful exercise, followership in the same direction as that taken by the leader. But at the unconscious level, leaders may fill required leadership roles, and yet move in a direction which, at the manifest level, appears to differ from that taken by their followers. Where there is conflict between the sophisticated group and the basic group, or between the basic group and its members as individuals, different kinds of leadership may therefore be required simultaneously. If the kinds of leadership demanded cannot all be provided by the leader of the sophisticated group, the leader may be rendered impotent by the conflicting demands made upon him. In some circumstances other leaders may take some of the conflicting roles, and the group may demand of these leaders that they accept what may manifestly appear as apathy and ingratitude. If, instead of accepting the role they have been given, they try to operate at a sophisticated level, they are likely to be rejected. Thus the failure to provide sufficient candidates for a new committee in October 1949 was not only a following of the flight lead given by the Shop Committee; it was also a rejection of the committee for failing to protect its constituents from the feelings which they had tried to escape.

In field theory terms, locomotion induced by the leader of a group at reality level may be followed, not only by a restructuring of the social field at this level, but also by a restructuring at the irreality level, demanding leadership and locomotion in different directions. In this situation it is possible for the regions of high potential within the manifest and unconscious fields of the same group to be in different positions. The important point is that a restructuring of a social field at the reality level may only be possible if the restructuring at the irreality level is in different directions and has different leaders. In a situation such as that of the Line Shop, in which two kinds of leadership are provided by the social structure—management and representative—it can be seen how they may be used by the group at different levels simultaneously. The diagram in Figure 1 represents different kinds of leadership in the reality-irreality dimension.

Whichever way the workers in the Line Shop turned in their attempts to find solutions to their current problems, they were brought face to face with their basic insecurity and with their inability to extricate themselves from the consequent dilemma in which they found themselves. They wanted the problems solved, but they also wanted them to remain unsolved so that they might feel justified in their choice of scapegoats and have readily available means of expressing feelings which caused them so much discomfort. By first taking up and keeping alive the problems which emerged as symptoms of the growing

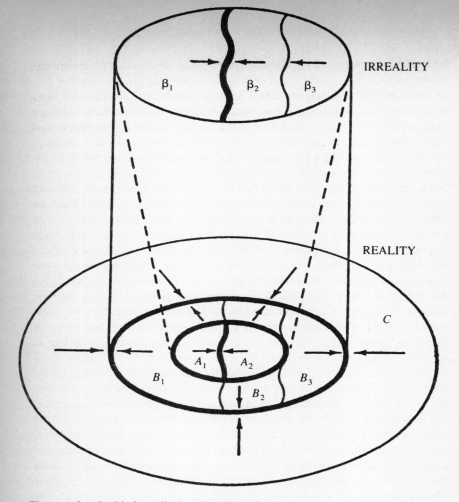

Figure 1. Leadership in reality-irreality dimension.

The diagram represents in simplified form the group structure of the Line Shop during the third phase, at a time when the negotiating group was in session.

Key: Reality level: A: region of negotiating group (A_1, management; A_2, leading members of Shop Committee); B: region of the Line Shop (B_1, management; B_2, Shop Committee; B_3, workers); C: region of competitors.

   Irreality level: β: region of the Line Shop ($β_1$, management; $β_2$, Shop Committee; $β_3$, workers).

At the reality level, the boundary zone CB is a barrier with a centripetal force field, BA a barrier with a centrifugal force field, and A_1A_2 a barrier with a centripetal force field. At the irreality level the boundary zone $β_1β_2$ is a barrier with a centripetal force field. The maintenance of the centripetal force at the barrier CB is made possible by the enclosure of the centripetal force field at A_1A_2 in the region A. This enclosure is in turn made possible by the existence at the irreality level of the centripetal force field in the region β. It will be noted that at the reality end the vectors in the regions A_2 and B_3 are in opposite directions, but that at the irreality level in the corresponding regions $β_2$ and $β_3$ they are in the same direction.

insecurity, and then by encapsulating the struggle with these problems within the negotiating group, management and Shop Committee simultaneously provided leadership of the sophisticated group and of the basic groups and made possible the sophisticated task on which the group was engaged. The Shop Committee thus made a positive contribution to the successful accomplishment of the task of expansion.

References

Bion, W.R. 1948–1951. "Experiences in Groups." *Human Relations,* 1:314–20, 487–96; 2:13–22, 295–303; 3:3–14, 395–402; 4:221–27.
Jaques, E. 1951. *The Changing Culture of a Factory.* London: Tavistock Publications. Reissued 1987, New York: Garland.

Elliott Jaques

On the Dynamics of Social Structure

A Contribution to the Psychoanalytical Study of Social Phenomena Deriving from the Views of Melanie Klein*

Many observers have noted that there is a strikingly close correspondence between certain group phenomena and those processes in the individual that represent what Melanie Klein has called the psychotic level of human development. Schmideberg (1931), for instance, has pointed to the psychotic-like content of primitive rites and ceremonies; and Bion (1955) has suggested that the emotional life of the group is only understandable in terms of processes at this very primitive level. My own recent experience (Jaques, 1951) has impressed upon me how much institutions are used by their individual members to reinforce mechanisms of defense against anxiety, and in particular against recurrence of the early paranoid and depressive anxieties first described by Melanie Klein (1932; 1948a; 1952a). It is as though the members of groups unconsciously place part of the contents of their deep inner lives outside themselves and pool these parts in the emotional life of the group. May not sufficiently deep analysis of the individual take us into the group?

Answers to these last questions may be forthcoming in the light of recent advances in the understanding of psychotic processes as a normal part of personality development. It is the purpose of this paper to examine to what extent these developments in psychoanalysis provide a bridge linking individual and group behavior: and to what extent an understanding of them in the individual contributes to the comprehension of the dynamics of group behavior. In connecting social behavior with mechanisms pertaining to this very deep stratum, I in no way wish to suggest that social relationships are totally determined by unconscious factors, or indeed that they are purely defensive in character. I do propose, however, to limit my present considerations to these particular connections. The specific hypothesis I shall consider is that one of the primary cohesive elements binding individuals into institutionalized human

*A reproduction of the original—*Human Relations*, 6:3–24, 1953.

association is that of defense against anxiety emanating from the psychotic developmental level (and conversely, although I shall not deal with the hypothesis here, that psychotic-like desocialization occurs in those who have not developed the ability to use the mechanism of association in social groups to avoid psychotic anxiety).

Social institutions, as I shall here use the term, are either social structures or cultural mechanisms. Social structures are systems of roles, or positions, which may be taken up and occupied by persons. Cultural mechanisms are conventions, customs, taboos which are used in regulating the relations among members of a society. For purposes of analysis institutions can be defined independently of the particular individuals who occupy roles within them. But in real life the workings of institutions take place through real people using cultural mechanisms within a social structure; and the unconscious or implicit functions of an institution are specifically determined by the particular individuals who are associated as members of the institution, occupying roles within it and operating the culture. Changes may occur in the unconscious functions of an institution through change in personnel, without there necessarily being any apparent change in manifest structure or functions. And conversely, as is so often noted, the imposition of a change in manifest structure or culture to resolve a problem may often leave the problem unsolved because the unconscious relationships remain unchanged.

Some Recent Developments in Psychoanalysis

The extensions to psychoanalytical theory made by Melanie Klein concern the early infantile or pre-oedipal phases of development. She has described two early developmental phases which correspond to two predominant types of anxiety—paranoid and depressive. The period when paranoid anxiety predominates normally extends over the first three to four months of development. Depressive anxiety normally predominates for the subsequent months to the end of the first year. The terms paranoid-schizoid (or simply, paranoid) position and depressive position are used to connote the predominance of the particular pattern of impulses, anxieties and defenses which characterizes each of these phases in development.

The infant projects its libidinal and aggressive, or good and bad, impulses onto external objects. The earliest of such objects are the mother's breasts, and these are experienced as good or bad depending on whether good or bad impulses are projected into them. The good and bad breasts are introjected and constitute the primitive good and bad internal objects which lay the foundation of the ego and super-ego. The strength of the libidinal and aggressive impulses will determine the degree of goodness and badness of the internalized objects;

and will determine the degree to which the infant will be disturbed by phantasies of persecution by bad objects, that is to say, disturbed by paranoid anxiety.

The conception of phantasy requires separate comment. It is here used in the sense, elaborated by Susan Isaacs (1948), of completely *unconscious* autistic activity. The early infantile processes being described have, however, a physical or object-like content rather than an autistic mental content. To the infant, projection and introjection are physical acts—acts of regurgitating and excreting, of eating and incorporating. And the objects which are incorporated are unconsciously real inside, in the sense of constituting an inner world, or an internal society, the functioning of which has real effects on conscious perceptions and behavior. Thus, phantasy persecution, for example, refers to intrapsychic activity in which the infant feels under actual attack by its internal obj cts and through unconscious projection of the inner situation may perceive and behave towards persons in the outside world as though they are hostile and threatening.

In the paranoid position, the characteristic defense against anxiety is that of splitting all internal objects into good and bad, the idealization of the good and the projection of the bad. The more intense the aggressive impulses, the more intense are the phantasies of persecution; and correspondingly, the more profound and complete the splitting, the more intense the idealization, and the greater the projection. Given a balance between libidinal and aggressive impulses, and given loving parental support, the internal world is felt as sufficiently replete with good objects to ward off persecution by the bad, and paranoid anxiety is kept within tolerable limits.

After the first three or four months of life, aggressive impulses and persecutory anxiety diminish if external parental support is sufficiently consistent. Concurrently, the infant begins to recognize mother, father and others as real persons; relationships undergo a fundamental change. He or she now sees whole objects, compact of both good and bad, instead of dealing with parts— for example breasts—split into either wholly good or wholly bad objects. The perception of both good and bad in a whole object, however, creates a new type of anxiety: that of losing the good loved objects by virtue of sadistic attacks on its bad aspect. To the extent that greed and sadistic impulses are strong and uncontrolled, the infant's loved objects are destroyed and torn into pieces. This destruction goes on in both the external and the internal world. In consequence the infant suffers persecution at the hands of the internally attacked object, and depression as a result of pining for the lost good object, also guilt for the attack upon it. The depressive anxieties, comprising persecution and guilt, may be dealt with by mourning, in which the underlying feelings of loss, guilt and love are experienced and tolerated because of successful restoration and reparation of the lost bad object. Successful mourning of this kind depends upon the experience of real, good loved objects in the outside world incorporated in the paranoid position and reinforced in the depressive phase.

To the extent that mourning is unsuccessful, good objects outside and inside are felt to be irreparably damaged and lost. Despair and depression are experienced, and mechanisms of defense are brought into play. These defense mechanisms, characteristic of the depressive position, are known as the manic defenses. The essential feature of the manic defenses is a denial of psychic reality, including a denial of the loss of the loved object. This denial is accompanied by an omnipotent control over, and contempt for, the damaged object as a means of avoiding persecution by the damaged bits. Omnipotence is accompanied by splitting, and a reification and idealization of the good part of the original whole object, and projective identification with it. Finally, the manic defense system may be bolstered by a regression to the paranoid position and its defenses. This regression, however, strengthens the fear of persecution and may lead to an intensification of omnipotence.

The paranoid and depressive anxieties here described color the character of the relations with parents during the oedipal phase of development. These anxieties are incorporated, but not necessarily resolved, in the oedipal relationships; and they continue in greater or lesser degree into childhood and adulthood. Analysis of patients reveals the early infantile object relations as forming the unconscious core of conscious relationships and activities in adult life. And the attendant defenses against paranoid and depressive anxieties are found at the core of the pattern of adult defense mechanisms against anxiety and guilt. After infancy, the child or adult, in making whole object relationships, turns largely to the use of the mechanisms of projective and introjective identification. Projective identification, unconsciously puts internal objects, good or bad, or good or bad impulses, into persons (or things) in the external world. Introjective identification takes persons and things in the outside world into the self, so that what one does comes not so much from oneself but from the internalized other influencing one's behavior. Much of the rest of this paper will be devoted to illustrating these mechanisms.

Projection, Introjection and Identification in Social Relationships

In *Group Psychology and the Analysis of the Ego* Freud (1922) takes as his starting point in group psychology the relationship between the group and its leader. The essence of this relationship he sees in the mechanism of identification—of the members of the group with the leader and with each other. He gives a definition of a primary group as a number of individuals who have substituted one and the same object for their ego ideal and have consequently identified themselves with one another in their ego. Group processes in this sense can be linked to earlier forms of behavior and in particular to oedipal relationships, since "identification is known to psychoanalysis as the earliest expression of an emotional tie with another person." But Freud did not explicitly develop the concept of identification beyond that of identification by introjection, a conception deriving from his work on the retention of lost objects through introjection. In his analysis of group life he does, however, differentiate between identification of the ego with an object (or identification by introjection) and what he terms replacement of the ego-ideal by an object. Thus, in the two cases he describes, the Army and the Church, soldiers replace their ego-ideal by the leader, whereas Christians take Christ into themselves and identify with him.

Like Freud, Melanie Klein sees introjection as one of the primary processes whereby the infant makes emotional relationships with its objects. But she considers that introjection interacts with the process of projection in the making of these relationships. She expressed the view that "object relations exist from the beginning of life, that the relation to the first object implies its introjection and projection and that from the beginning object relations are molded by an interaction between introjection and projection, between internal and external objects and situations" (Klein, 1952a). Such a formulation seems to me to be consistent with, although not explicit in, the view of Freud expressed above. That is to say, identification of the ego with an object is identification by introjection; this is explicit in Freud. But replacement of the ego-ideal by an object seems to me to be one case of identification by projection. Thus, the soldiers who take their leader for their ego-ideal are in effect projectively identifying with him, or putting part of themselves into him. It is this common or shared projective identification which enables the soldiers to identify with each other. In the extreme form of projective identification of this kind the followers become totally dependent on the leader, because each has given up a part of him- or herself to the leader. Melanie Klein wrote that "the projection of good feelings and good parts of the self into the mother is essential for the infant's ability to develop good object-relations and to integrate his ego. However, if this projective process is carried out excessively, good parts of the personality are felt to be lost, and in this way the mother becomes the ego-ideal; this process too results in weakening and impoverishing the ego. Very soon such processes extend to other people, and the result may be an overstrong dependence on these external representatives of one's own good parts." Indeed, it is just such an extreme of projective identification which might explain the case of panic described by Freud, where the Assyrians take to flight on learning that Holofernes, their leader, has had his head cut off by Judith. For not only has the commonly shared external object (the figurehead) binding them all together been lost but, the leader having lost his head, every soldier has lost his head by projective identification.

I shall take as the basis of my analysis of group processes the conception of identification in group formation as described by Freud, but with particular reference to the processes of introjective and projective identification as elaborated by Melanie Klein. Such a form of analysis has been suggested in another context by Paula Heimann (1952a)—"Such taking in and expelling consists of an active interplay between the organism and the outer world; on this primordial pattern rests all intercourse between subject and object, no matter how complex and sophisticated such intercourse appears. (I believe that in the last analysis we may find it at the bottom of all our complicated dealings with one another.) The patterns Nature uses seem to be few, but she is inexhaustible in their variation." I shall try to show how individuals make unconscious use of institutions by associating in these institutions and unconsciously co-operating to reinforce internal defenses against anxiety and guilt. These social defenses bear a reciprocal relationship with the internal defense mechanisms. For instance, the schizoid and manic defenses against anxiety and guilt both involve splitting and projection mechanisms, and, through projection, a link with the outside world. When external objects are shared with others and used in common for purposes of projection, phantasy social relationships may be established through projective identification with the common object. These phantasy relationships are further elaborated by introjection; and the two-way character of social relationships is mediated by virtue of the two-way play of projective and introjective identification.

I shall employ the phrase *phantasy social form and content of an institution* to refer to the form and content of social relationships at the level of the common individual phantasies which the members of an institution share by projective and introjective identification. Phantasy is used in the sense of completely unconscious intra-psychic activity as defined above. From this point of view the character of institutions is determined and colored not only by their explicit or consciously agreed and accepted functions, but also by their manifold unrecognized functions at the phantasy level.

Illustrations of Socially Structured Defense Mechanisms

It is not my intention in this paper to explore either systematically or comprehensively the manner in which social defense mechanisms operate. I shall first examine certain paranoid anxieties and defenses, and then depressive anxieties and defenses, keeping them to some extent separate for purposes of explication, and giving illustrations from everyday experience. Then I shall present case material from a social study in industry in which I may make some of the theoretical considerations more clear by showing the interaction of paranoid and depressive phenomena.

DEFENSES AGAINST PARANOID ANXIETY

One example of social mechanisms of defense against paranoid anxieties is that of putting bad internal objects and impulses into particular members of an institution, who, whatever their explicit function in a society, are unconsciously selected, or themselves choose to introject bad objects and impulses and either to *absorb* them or to *deflect* them.

The process of absorption may be seen, for example, in the case of a First Officer in a ship, whose duty it is to take responsibility for everything that goes wrong. Everyone's bad objects and impulses may be deposited within the First Officer, who is regarded by common consent as the source of trouble. By this mechanism the members of the crew can find relief from their own internal persecution. And the ship's captain can be thereby more readily idealized and identified with as a good protective figure. Ships' officers in the normal course of promotion are expected to accept this masochistic role, and the norm is to accept it without demur.

The process of deflection may be seen in certain aspects of the complex situation of nations at war. The manifest social structure is that of two opposing armies, each backed and supported by its community. At the phantasy level, however, we may consider the following possibility. The members of each community put their bad objects and sadistic impulses into the commonly shared and accepted external enemy. They rid themselves of their hostile destructive impulses by projecting them into their armies for deflection against the enemy. Paranoid anxiety in the total community, army and civilian alike, may be alleviated, or at least transmuted into fear of known and identifiable external enemies, since the bad impulses and objects projected into the enemy return, not in the form of introjected phantastic persecutors, but in the form of actual physical attack which can be experienced in reality. Under appropriate conditions, objective fear may be more readily coped with than phantasy persecution. The enemy is fought against not in the solitary isolation of the unconscious inner world, but in co-operation with comrades-in-arms in real life. Not only individuals rid themselves of phantastic persecution in this way; the members of the army are temporarily freed from depressive anxiety because their own sadistic impulses can be denied by attributing their aggressiveness to the performance of their duty, that is, expressing the aggressive impulses collected and introjected from all the community. And members of the community may also avoid guilt by getting social sanction for hatred of the enemy. Social sanction means that denial of unconscious hatred and destructive impulses against internal objects can be reinforced by turning these impulses against a commonly shared and publicly hated real external enemy.

Social co-operation at the reality level may thus allow for a redistribution of bad objects and impulses in the phantasy relations obtaining among the members of a society. This process may be compared with Freud's (1922) definition of the redistribution of libido in the group. In conjunction with such a redistribution, introjective identification makes it possible for individuals to take in social sanction and support. The primitive aim of the absorption and deflection mechanism is to achieve a non-return at the phantasy level of the projected phantasy bad objects and impulses.

But even where absorption and deflection are not entirely successful (and mechanisms at the phantasy level can never be completely controlled), the social defense mechanisms provide some gain. Paula Heimann (1952b) has described the introjection of projected bad objects and their related impulses into the ego, where they are maintained in a split-off state, subjected to intra-psychic projection and kept under attack. In the cases described above, the ego receives support from the social sanctions which are introjected, and which legitimize the intra-psychic projection and aggression. The First Officer, for example, may be introjected, and the impulses projected into him introjected as well. But in the phantasy social situation other members of the crew who also attack the First Officer are identified with by introjection, partly into the ego, and partly into the super-ego. Hence the ego is reinforced by possession of the internalized members of the crew, all of whom take part in the attack on the segregated bad objects within the ego. And there is an alleviation of the harshness of the super-ego by adding to it objects which socially sanction and legitimize the attack.

These illustrations are obviously not completely elaborated. Nor are they intended to be so. They are abstractions from real life situations in which a fuller analysis would show defenses against persecutory and depressive anxiety interacting with each other and with other more explicit functions of the group. But perhaps they suffice to indicate how the use of the concepts of introjective and projective identification regarded as interacting mechanisms may serve to add further dimensions to Freud's analysis of the Army and the Church. We may also note that the social mechanisms described contain, in their most primitive aspects, features which may be related to the earliest attempts of the infant, described by Melanie Klein (1948b; 1952b), to deal with persecutory anxiety in relation to part objects by means of splitting and projection and introjection of both the good and bad objects and impulses. If we now turn to the question of social defenses against depressive anxieties, we shall be able to illustrate further some of the general points.

DEFENSES AGAINST DEPRESSIVE ANXIETY

Let us consider now certain aspects of the problem of the scapegoating of a minority group. As seen from the viewpoint of the community at large, the community is split into a good majority group and a bad minority—a split consistent with the splitting of internal objects into good and bad, and the creation of a good and bad internal world. The persecuting group's belief in its own good is preserved by heaping contempt upon and attacking the scapegoated group. The internal splitting mechanisms and preservation of the internal good objects of individuals, and the attack upon and contempt for internal bad persecutory objects, are reinforced by introjective identification of individuals with other members taking part in the group-sanctioned attack upon the scapegoat.

If we now turn to the minority groups, we may ask why only some minorities are selected for persecution while others are not. Here a feature often overlooked in considerations of minority problems may be of help. The members of the persecuted minority commonly entertain a precise and defined hatred and contempt for their persecutors which matches in intensity the contempt and aggression to which they themselves are subjected. That this should be so is perhaps not surprising. But in view of the selective factor in choice of persecuted minorities, must we not consider the possibility that one of the operative factors in this selection is the consensus in the minority group, at the phantasy level, to seek contempt and suffering. That is to say, there is an unconscious co-operation (or collusion) at the phantasy level between persecutor and persecuted. For the members of the minority group, such a collusion carries its own gains—such as social justification for feelings of contempt and hatred for an external persecutor, with consequent alleviation of guilt and reinforcement of denial in the protection of internal good objects.

Another way in which depressive anxiety may be alleviated by social mechanisms is through manic denial of destructive impulses and destroyed good objects, and the reinforcement of good impulses and good objects, by participation in group idealization. These social mechanisms are the reflection in the group of denial and idealization, shown by Melanie Klein (1948a) to be important defenses against depressive anxiety.

The operation of these social mechanisms may be seen in mourning ceremonies. The bereaved are joined by others in a common display of grief, and in public reiteration of the good qualities of the deceased. Bad objects and impulses are got rid of by projection into the corpse, disguised by the decoration of the corpse, and safely put out of the way through projective identification with the dead during the burial ceremony; failure of the mechanism increases the prospect of persecution by demonic figures. At the same time good objects and impulses are also projected into the dead person. Public and socially sanctioned idealization of the deceased then reinforces the sense that the good object has after all not been destroyed, for the person's "good works" are held to live on in the memory of the community as well as the surviving family, a memory which is reified in the tombstone. Failure of the mechanism increases the prospect of haunting by guilt-provoking ghosts.

Hence, through mourning as a social process, the community and the bereaved are provided with the opportunity of splitting the destroyed part of the loved object from the loved part, of burying the destroyed bad objects and impulses, and of protecting the good loved part as an eternal memory. And even where the mechanisms fail, there is a partial gain in facing demons and ghosts in company with others, rather than whistling past the graveyard alone.

One general feature of each of the instances cited is that the phantasy social systems established have survival value for the group as well as affording protection against anxiety in the individual. Thus, for example, in the case of the mourning ceremony the social idealizing and manic denial make it possible for a bereaved person to reduce the internal chaos and weather the immediate and intense impact of death, and to undertake the process of mature internal mourning at his own time and his own pace. Melanie Klein (1948a) states that "many mourners can only make slow steps in reestablishing the bonds with the external world because they are struggling against the chaos inside." But there is a general social gain as well, in that all those associated in the mourning ceremony can further their internal mourning and continue the life-long process of working-through the unresolved conflicts of the infantile depressive position. As Melanie Klein has described the process, "It seems that every advance in the process of mourning results in a deepening in the individual's relation to his inner objects, in the happiness of regaining them after they were felt to be lost (Paradise Lost and Regained), in an increased trust in them and love for them because they proved to be good and helpful after all." Hence through the mourning ceremony the toleration of ambivalence is increased and friendship ties in the community can be strengthened. Or again, in the case of the first officer, the ship's crew, in a situation made difficult by close confinement and isolation from other groups, is enabled to co-operate with the captain in carrying out the required and consciously planned tasks by isolating and concentrating their bad objects and impulses within an available human receptacle.

Case Study

I shall now turn to a more detailed and precise discussion of phantasy social systems as defense mechanisms for the individual, and also as mechanisms allowing the group to proceed with the sophisticated or survival tasks, in examining a case study from industry. It may be noted that the conception of sophisticated tasks derives from Bion's (1948–51) conception of the sophisticated task of the work or W group. I am refraining from using Bion's more elaborate conceptual scheme defining what he terms the "basic assumptions" of groups, since the relationship between the operation of basic assumptions and that of depressive and persecutory phenomena remains to be worked out.

The case to be presented is one part of a larger study carried out in a light engineering factory, the Glacier Metal Company, between June 1948 and September 1951. The relationship with the firm was a therapeutic one in the sense that work was done only on request from groups or individuals within the firm for assistance in working through intra-group stresses or in dealing with organizational problems. The relationship between the social consultant (or therapist) and the people with whom he worked was a confidential one; and the only reports published are those which have been worked through with the people concerned and agreed by them for publication. Within these terms of reference a detailed report on the first three years of the project has been published (Jaques, 1951).

The illustration I shall use is taken from work done with one department in the factory; a department employing roughly 60 people.* It was organized with a departmental manager as head. Under him was a superintendent, who in turn was responsible for four foremen, each of whom had a working group of 10 to 16 operatives. The operatives had elected five representatives, two of whom were shop stewards, to negotiate with the departmental manager on matters affecting the department. One such matter had to do with a change in methods of wages payment. The shop had been on piece rates (i.e., the operatives were paid a basic wage plus a bonus dependent on their output). This method of payment had, for a number of years, been felt to be unsatisfactory. From the workers' point of view it mean uncertainty about what their weekly wage would be, and for the management it meant complicated rate-fixing and administrative arrangements. For all concerned the quite frequent wrangling about rates which took place was felt as unnecessarily disturbing. The possibility of changing over to a flat-rate method of payment had been discussed for over a year before the project began, but in spite of the fact that the change was commonly desired they had not been able to come to a decision.

A PERIOD OF NEGOTIATION

Work with the department began in January 1949, by attendance at the discussions of a subcommittee composed of the departmental manager, the superintendent, and three of the workers' representatives. The general tone of the

---

*This case material is a condensation of earlier published material (Jaques, 1950; Jaques et al., 1951).

discussions was friendly. The committee members laid stress upon the fact that good relations existed in the department and that they all wanted to strive for further improvement. From time to time, however, there was sharp disagreement over specific points. These disagreements led the workers' representatives to state that there were many matters on which they felt they could not trust the management. These statements of suspicion were answered by the management members, who emphasized that they, for their part, had great trust in the workers' sense of responsibility.

The workers' suspicion of management also revealed itself in discussions which were held at shop floor level between the elected representatives and their worker constituents. The purpose of these discussions was to elicit in a detailed and concrete manner the views of the workers about the proposed change-over. The workers were on the whole in favor of the change-over, but there was some doubt as to whether they could trust the management to implement and administer it fairly. What guarantees did they have, they asked, that management had nothing up its sleeve? At the same time, the workers showed an ambivalent attitude towards their own representatives. They urged and, indeed, empowered them to carry on negotiations with management, but at the same time suspected that the representatives were management "stooges" and did not take the workers' views sufficiently into account. This latter negative attitude towards their representatives came out more clearly in interviews with individual workers, in which opinions were expressed that although the elected representatives were known as militant trade unionists, nevertheless they were seen as being outwitted by the management and not carrying their representative role as effectively as they might.

The day-to-day working relationships between supervisors and workers were quite different from those to be expected from the views stated above. Work in the shop was carried out with good morale, and the supervisors were felt to be doing their best for the workers. A high proportion of those in the shop had been employed in the company for five years or more, and genuinely good personal relationships had been established.

The discussions in the committee composed of the managers and elected representatives went on for seven months, between January and July 1949. The participants had a great deal of difficulty in working towards a decision, becoming embroiled in arguments which were sometimes quite heated and which had no obvious cause—other than the workers' suspicion of the management, counterbalanced by the management's idealization of the workers. Much of both the suspicion and the idealization, however, was autistic in the sense that although consciously experienced it was not expressed openly as between managers and workers. These attitudes came out much more sharply when the elected representatives and the managers were meeting separately. The workers expressed deep suspicion and mistrust, while the managers expressed some of their anxieties about how responsible the workers could be—anxieties which lay behind their rather strong sense of the workers' responsibility and of their complete faith in them.

ANALYSIS OF THE NEGOTIATION PHASE

I now wish to apply certain of our theoretical formulations to the above data. This is in no sense intended to be a complete analysis of the material. Many important factors, such as changes in the executive organization of the shop, personal attitudes and changes in personnel, and variations in the economic and production situations, all played a part in determining the changes which occurred. What I do wish to do, however, is to demonstrate how we may be able, if we assume the operation of defenses against paranoid and depressive anxiety at the phantasy social level, to explain some of the very great difficulties encountered by the members of the department. And I would emphasize here that these difficulties were encountered in spite of the high morale implied in the willingness of those concerned to face and to work-through in a serious manner the group stresses they experienced in trying to arrive at a commonly desired goal.

The degree of inhibition of the autistic suspicion and idealization becomes understandable, I believe, if we make the following assumptions about unconscious attitudes at the phantasy level. The workers in the shop had split the managers into good and bad, the good managers being those with whom they worked, and the bad being the same managers, but in the negotiation situation. They had unconsciously projected their hostile, destructive impulses into their elected representatives so that the representatives could deflect or redirect these impulses against the bad "management" with whom negotiations were carried on, while the good objects and impulses could be put into individual real managers in the day-to-day work situation. This splitting of the management into good and bad, and the projective identification with the elected representatives against the bad management, served two purposes. At the reality level it allowed the good relations necessary to the work task of the department to be maintained; at the phantasy level it provided a system of social relationships reinforcing individual defenses against paranoid and depressive anxiety.

Putting their good impulses into the managers in the work situation allowed the workers to reintroject the good relations with management and hence to preserve an undamaged good object and alleviate depressive anxiety. This depressive anxiety was further avoided by reversion to the paranoid position in the negotiating situation. As Melanie Klein has frequently pointed out, paranoid fears and suspicions are often used as a defense against the depressive position. During the negotiations, the workers partially avoided paranoid anxiety by putting their bad impulses into their elected representatives who, though consciously the negotiating representatives of the workers, became unconsciously the representatives of their bad impulses. These split-off bad impulses were partially dealt with and avoided because they were directed against the bad objects put into management in the negotiation situation by the workers and their representatives.

The other mechanism for dealing with the workers' own projected bad objects and impulses was to reintroject them into the ego in the form of a reintrojection of the workers' representatives as bad objects maintained as a segregated part of the ego. Intra-psychic projection and aggression against these internal bad objects were supported by introjective identification with the other workers who had taken part in electing the representatives, and who also held that the representatives were not doing their job properly. That is to say, the other members of the department were introjected to reinforce the intra-psychic projection, and as a protection against the internal bad representatives attacking back. In addition to defense against internal persecution, the introjection of the other workers provided social sanction for considering the internalized representatives as bad, offsetting the harshness of super-ego recrimination for attacking objects which contained a good as well as a persecuting component.

From the point of view of the elected representatives, anxiety about bad impulses was diminished by the unconscious acceptance of the bad impulses and objects of all the workers they represented. They could feel that their own hostile and aggressive impulses did not belong to them but to the people on whose behalf they were acting. They were thus able to derive external social sanction for their aggression and hostile suspicion. But the mechanism did not operate with complete success, for there was still their own unconscious suspicion and hostility to be dealt with, and the reality of what they considered to be the good external management. Hence there was some anxiety and guilt about damaging the good managers. The primary defense mechanism against the onset of depressive anxiety was that of retreat to the paranoid position. This came out as a rigid clinging to attitudes of suspicion and hostility even in situations where there was a conscious feeling that some of this suspicion was not justified by the situation actually being experienced by the representatives.

From the management side, the suspicions expressed by the elected representatives were countered by the reiteration of the view that the workers could be trusted to do their part. This positive attitude unconsciously contained both idealization of the workers and placation of the hostile representatives. The idealization can be understood as an unconscious mechanism for diminishing guilt which was stimulated by fears of injuring or destroying workers in the day-to-day situation through the exercise of managerial authority—an authority which there is good reason to believe is, at least to some extent, unconsciously felt to be uncontrolled and omnipotent. To the extent that managers unconsciously felt their authority to be bad, they feared retaliation by the operatives. This in turn led to a reinforcement of the idealization of the elected representatives as a means of placating the hostility of the workers, and hence of placating internal persecuting objects in the management themselves. These idealizing and placatory mechanisms were employed in the meetings with the elected representatives, so that reality mechanisms could operate in the relationships with workers in the work situation, less encumbered with the content of uncontrolled phantasy.

It can thus be seen that the unconscious use of paranoid attitudes by the workers and idealizing and placatory attitudes by the management were complementary and reinforced each other. A circular process was set in motion. The more the workers' representatives attacked the managers, the more the managers idealized them in order to placate them. The greater the concessions given by management to the workers, the greater was the guilt and fear of depressive anxiety in the workers, and hence the greater the retreat to paranoid attitudes as a means of avoiding depressive anxiety. The situation was partly resolved by interpretations made to the negotiating group of managers and representatives about their suppression of autistic suspicion and idealization. The open interpretation of this suppression, based on evidence perceived in the actual course of discussion, allowed for some increase in mutual confidence. Then, in June, six months after the discussions began, these attitudes, rather than the wages problem, were for a time taken as the main focus of consideration. A partial resolution occurred, and the workers decided, after a ballot in the whole department, to try out a flat-rate method of payment. The condition for the change-over, however, was the setting up of a Council, composed of managers and elected representatives, which would have the authority to determine departmental policy—a procedure for which the principles had already been established in the company. The prime principle was that of unanimous agreement on all decisions, and the agreement to work-through all obstacles to unanimous decision by discovering sources of disagreement so that they could be resolved.

ANALYSIS OF THE POST-NEGOTIATION PHASE

It appeared as though the open discussion of autistic attitudes facilitated a restructuring of the phantasy social relations in the department—a restructuring which brought with it a greater degree of conscious or ego control over their relationships. However, the fact that there was only a partial restructuring of social relations at the phantasy level showed itself in the subsequent history of the Shop Council. For, following the change-over to a flat-rate method of payment, the Council came up against the major question of re-assessing the times in which given jobs ought to be done.

Under piece rates an assessment of times was necessary both for calculation of the bonus to operatives and for giving estimated prices to customers. On flat rates it was required only for providing estimates for customers; but the times thus set inevitably constituted targets for the workers. Under piece rates, if a worker did not achieve the target it meant that he lost his bonus; in other words, he himself paid for any drop in effort. Under flat rates, however, a drop below the target meant that the worker was getting paid for work that he was not doing. A detailed exploration of workers' attitudes showed that the change-over from piece rates to flat rates had in no way altered their personal targets and personal rate of work. They felt guilty whenever they fell below their estimated targets, because they were no longer paying for the difference. In order to avoid this guilt, the workers applied strong pressure to keep the estimated times on jobs as high as possible , as well as pressure to get the so-called "tight times" (job times that were difficult to achieve) re-assessed. There were strong resistances to any changes in job assessment methods which the workers suspected might set difficult targets for them.

On the management side, the change-over to flat rates inevitably stirred whatever unconscious anxieties there might have been about authority. For, under piece rates, the bonus payment itself acted as an impersonal and independent disciplinarian, ensuring that workers put in the necessary effort. Under flat rates it was up to managers to see that a reasonable rate of work was maintained. This forced upon them more direct responsibility for the supervision of their subordinates and brought them more directly face to face with the authority they held.

The newly constituted Council with its managers and elected representatives had great difficulty in coping with the more manifest depressive anxiety in both the managers and the workers. This was evident in managers' views that the Council might possibly turn out to be a bad thing because it slowed down administrative developments in the department. Similar opinions that the Council would not work and might not prove worthwhile played some part in the decision of five out of six of the elected representatives not to stand for re-election in the shop elections which occurred sixteen months following the setting up of the Council. These five were replaced by five newly elected representatives, who in turn brought with them a considerable amount of suspicion. That is, there was again a retreat to the paranoid position while the managers' depressive anxiety continued to show to some extent in the form of depressive feelings that the Council would not work. It was only slowly, over a period of two years, that the Council became able to operate in the new situation as a constitutional mechanism for getting agreement on policy, and at the same time for intuitively containing the phantasy social relationships. These changes led to wider changes in the company which became permanent.

This case study, then, illustrates the development of an explicit social institution, that of meetings between management and elected representatives, which allowed for the establishment of unconscious mechanisms at the phantasy level for dealing with paranoid and depressive anxieties. The main mechanisms were those of management idealizing the hostile workers, and the workers maintaining an attitude of suspicion towards the idealizing management. To the extent that splitting and projective identification operated successfully, these unconscious mechanisms helped individuals to deal with anxiety, by getting their anxieties into the phantasy social relations structured in the management-elected representative group. In this way the anxieties were eliminated from the day-to-day work situation, allowing for the efficient operation of the sophisticated work task and the achievement of good working relationships.

However, it will also be noted that the elected representative-management group was charged with a sophisticated work task—that of negotiating new methods of wage payment. They found it difficult to get on with the sophisticated task itself. In terms of the theory here propounded, these difficulties have been explained as arising from the manner in which the predominant unconscious phantasy relations in the negotiating group ran counter to the requirements of the sophisticated task. In other words, an essentially constitutional procedure, that of elected representatives meeting with an executive body, was difficult to operate because it was being used in an unrecognized fashion at the phantasy level to help deal with the depressive and paranoid anxieties of the members of the department as a whole.

Some Observations on Social Change

In the above case study, it might be said that social change was sought when the structure and culture no longer met the requirements of the individual members of the department, and in particular of the managers and the elected representatives. Manifest changes were brought about, and in turn appeared to lead to a considerable restructuring of the phantasy social form and content of the institution. Change having taken place, however, the individual members found themselves in the grip of new relationships to which they had to conform because they were self-made. But they had brought about more than they had bargained for, in the sense that the new relationships under flat rates and the policy-making Council had to be experienced before their implications could be fully appreciated.

The effects of the change on individuals were different according to the roles they occupied. The elected representatives were able to change roles by the simple expedient of not standing for re-election. And this expedient, it will be noted, was resorted to by five of the six representatives. The managers, however, were in a very different position. They could not relinquish or change their roles without, in a major sense, changing their position, and possibly status, in the organization as a whole. They had, therefore, individually to bear considerable personal stress in adjusting themselves to the new situation.

It is unlikely that members of an institution can ever bring about social changes which perfectly suit the needs of each individual. Once change is undertaken it is more than likely that individuals will have to adjust and change personally in order to catch up with the changes they have produced. And until the readjustment is made at the phantasy level, the individual's social defenses against psychotic anxiety are likely to be weakened. It may well be because of the effects on the unconscious defense systems of individuals against psychotic anxiety that social change—and, in particular, imposed social change—is resisted. For it is one thing to readjust to changes which the individual has himself helped to bring about. It is quite another to be required to adjust one's internal defense system in order to conform to changes brought about by some outside agency. The intractability of many social problems—economic and political—which is often laid at the door of human ignorance, stupidity, selfishness or power seeking, may become more understandable if seen in the context of groups of people clinging to the institutions they have, through unconscious fear that changes in social relationships will disturb social defenses against psychotic anxiety.

Finally, the conception of social change itself may be reconsidered. Changes may occur in the unconscious functions of an institution, for example, through change in personnel, without there being necessarily any apparent change in manifest structure or functions. And conversely, as is so often noted, the imposition of a change in manifest structure or culture for the purpose of resolving a problem may often leave the problem unsolved because the unconscious relationships remain unchanged. It is necessary, I think, to differentiate between manifest change and change at the phantasy level; a differentiation the value of which is well and clearly illustrated by Rice (1951) in his description of the use of unrecognized cultural mechanisms in an expanding machine-shop.

In differentiating between social change at the manifest and at the phantasy level, I am making a differentiation between what is familiar in the psychological field as the difference between symptomatic change and personality change. To facilitate personality change, analysis of unconscious motivation is required. To facilitate social change at the phantasy level requires nothing less, in my estimation, than analysis of the dynamics of the phantasy content of social relationships. This does not mean an analysis of each individual. It means an analysis of the common individual anxieties and the structuring and operation of social defenses against them. In practice this would call for an analysis of the unconscious collusive relations among members of a group or groups seeking change—whether between the members of majority groups and the members of scape-goated minorities; or between management and labor; or between political parties; or between husbands and wives seeking to patch up an unsuccessful marriage. What I have sought to demonstrate is that social stress is unconsciously motivated and has a purpose in the emotional economy of the individual and the group. Thus to a certain extent social stress is adaptive; that is to say, it represents the best form of adaptation which members of a group or of a society have been able to achieve in the face of environmental stress and pressure of unevenly distributed anxiety. Effective social change must show the way towards better adaptation, taking into account the needs of individuals to deal with paranoid and depressive anxiety.

References

Bion, W.R. 1948–1951. "Experiences in Groups." *Human Relations*, 1:314–20, 487–96; 2:13–22, 295–303; 3:3–14, 395–402; 4:221–27.
———. 1955. "Group Dynamics: A Re-view." *International Journal of Psycho-Analysis*, 33:235–47.
Freud, S. 1922. *Group Psychology and the Analysis of the Ego*. London: Hogarth Press.
———. 1940. "Mourning and Melancholia." In *Collected Papers, Volume 4*. London: Hogarth Press.
Heimann, P. 1952a. "Functions of Introjection and Projection." In *Developments in Psycho-Analysis*, edited by J. Riviere. London: Hogarth Press.
———. 1952b. "Preliminary Notes on Some Defence Mechanisms in Paranoid States." *International Journal of Psycho-Analysis*. 33:208–13.
Isaacs, S. 1948. "The Nature and Function of Phantasy." *International Journal of Psycho-Analysis*. 29:98–115.
Jaques, E. 1950. "Collaborative Group Methods in a Wage Negotiation Situation." *Human Relations*, 3:223–49.
———. 1951. *The Changing Culture of a Factory*. London: Tavistock Publications. Reissued 1987, New York: Garland
Jaques, E., A.K. Rice and J.M.M. Hill. 1951. "The Social and Psychological Impact of a Change in Method of Wage Payment." *Human Relations*, 4:315–40.
Klein, M. 1932. *The Psycho-Analysis of Children*. London: Hogarth Press.
———. 1948a. "Mourning and Its Relation to Manic-Depressive States." In *Contributions to Psycho-Analysis 1921–1945*. London: Hogarth Press.
———. 1948b. "The Oedipus Complex in the Light of Early Anxieties." In *Contributions to Psycho-Analysis 1921–1945*. London: Hogarth Press.
———. 1952a. "The Emotional Life of the Infant." In *Developments in Psycho-Analysis*, edited by J. Riviere. London: Hogarth Press.
———. 1952b. "Notes on Some Schizoid Mechanisms." In *Developments in Psycho-Analysis*, edited by J. Riviere. London: Hogarth Press.
Rice, A.K. 1951. "The Use of Unrecognized Cultural Mechanisms in an Expanding Machine-Shop." *Human Relations*, 4:143–60.
Schmideberg, M.R. 1931. "The Role of Psychotic Mechanisms in Cultural Development." *International Journal of Psycho-Analysis*, 12:331–67.

Isabel Menzies Lyth

Social Systems as a Defense Against Anxiety

An Empirical Study of the Nursing Service of a General Hospital*

Introduction

This study was initiated by the nursing service of a general teaching hospital in London which sought help in planning the training of student nurses of whom there were 500 in the hospital. Trained nursing staff numbered 150. The student nurses spent all but six months of their three years of undergraduate training working full-time in wards and departments as "staff" while learning and practicing nursing skills. They carried out most of the actual nursing. The task with which the nursing service was struggling was effectively to reconcile two needs: for wards and departments to have adequate numbers of appropriate student nurses as staff; for student nurses, as students, to have the practical experience required for their training. Senior nurses feared the system was at the point of breakdown with serious consequences for student nurse training since patient care naturally tended to take priority whenever there was conflict. The study was carried out within a sociotherapeutic relationship the outcome of which, it was hoped, would be institutional change. The early part was devoted to an exploration of the nature of the problem and its impact on the people involved. While doing this "diagnostic" exploration we became aware of the high level of tension, distress and anxiety in the nursing service. How could nurses tolerate so much anxiety? We found much evidence that they could not. Withdrawal from duty was common. One-third did not complete their training; the majority of these left at their own request. Senior staff changed their jobs appreciably more frequently than workers at similar levels in other professions. Sickness rates were high, especially for minor illnesses requiring only a few days' absence from duty.

*A shortened version of the original—*Human Relations*, 13:95–121, 1960.

The relief of this anxiety seemed to us an important therapeutic task in itself and, moreover, proved to have a close connection with the development of more effective techniques of student-nurse allocation. In this paper I attempt to elucidate the nature and effect of the anxiety level in the hospital.

Nature of the Anxiety

The primary task of a hospital is to care for ill people who cannot be cared for in their own homes. The major responsibility for this task lies with the nursing service, which provides continuous care, day and night, all year around. The nursing service bears the full, immediate and concentrated impact of stress arising from patient-care.

The situations likely to evoke stress in nurses are familiar. Nurses are in constant contact with people who are physically ill or injured, often seriously. The recovery of patients is not certain and may not be complete. Nursing patients with incurable diseases is one of the nurse's most distressing tasks. Nurses face the reality of suffering and death as few lay people do. Their work involves carrying out tasks which, by ordinary standards, are distasteful, disgusting and frightening. Intimate physical contact with patients arouses libidinal and erotic wishes that may be difficult to control. The work arouses strong and conflicting feelings: pity, compassion and love; guilt and anxiety; hatred and resentment of the patients who arouse these feelings; envy of the care they receive.

The objective situation confronting the nurse bears a striking resemblance to the phantasy* situations that exist in every individual in the deepest and most primitive levels of the mind. The intensity and complexity of the nurse's anxieties are to be attributed primarily to the peculiar capacity of the objective features of the work to stimulate afresh these early situations and their accompanying emotions.

The elements of these phantasies may be traced back to earliest infancy.† The infant experiences two opposing sets of feelings and impulses, libidinal and aggressive. These stem from instinctual sources and are described by the constructs of the life-instinct and the death-instinct. Feeling omnipotent and attributing dynamic reality to these feelings and impulses, the infant believes that the libidinal impulses are literally life-giving and the aggressive impulses death-dealing; similar feelings, impulses and powers are attributed to other people and to important parts of people. The objects and the instruments of the

---

*Throughout this paper I follow the convention of using fantasy to mean conscious fantasy and phantasy to mean unconscious phantasy.

†In my description of infantile psychic life I follow the work of Freud, particularly as developed and elaborated by Melanie Klein (1952b; 1959).

libidinal and aggressive impulses are phantasized as the infant's own and other people's bodies and bodily products. Physical and psychic experiences are intimately interwoven. The infant's psychic experience of objective reality is greatly influenced by its own feelings and phantasies, moods and wishes.

Through their psychic experience infants build up an inner world peopled by themselves and the objects of their feelings and impulses. In the inner world, these exist in a form and condition largely determined by phantasies. Because of the operation of aggressive forces, the inner world contains many damaged, injured or dead objects. The atmosphere is charged with death and destruction. This gives rise to great anxiety. Infants thus fear for the effect of aggressive forces on the people they love and on themselves, grieving and mourning over others' suffering and experiencing depression and despair about their own inadequate ability to right their wrongs. They fear the demands that will be made on them for reparation and the punishment and the revenge that may result, and that libidinal impulses (their own and those of other people) cannot control the aggressive impulses sufficiently to prevent chaos and destruction. The poignancy of the situation is increased because love and longing themselves are felt to be so close to aggression. Greed, frustration and envy so easily replace a loving relationship. This phantasy world is characterized by a violence and intensity of feeling quite foreign to the emotional life of the normal adult.

In the hospital situation the direct impact on the nurse of physical illness was intensified by having to meet and deal with psychological stress in other people, including colleagues. Quite short conversations with patients or relatives showed that their conscious concept of illness and treatment was a rich intermixture of objective knowledge, logical deduction and fantasy. The degree of stress was heavily conditioned by the fantasy, which was in turn, conditioned, as in nurses, by the early phantasy-situations. Unconsciously, the nurse associated the patients' and relatives' distress with that experienced by the people in the nurse's own phantasy-world, which increased personal anxiety and difficulty in handling it.

Patients and relatives had complicated feelings towards the hospital, which were expressed particularly and most directly to nurses, and often puzzled and distressed them. Patients and relatives showed appreciation, gratitude, affection, respect; a touching relief that the hospital coped; helpfulness and concern for the nurses. But patients often resented their dependence; accepted grudgingly the discipline imposed by treatment and hospital routine; envied nurses their health and skills; were demanding, possessive and jealous. Patients, like nurses, found strong libidinal and erotic feelings stimulated by nursing care, and sometimes behaved in ways that increased the nurses' difficulties, for example by unnecessary physical exposure. Relatives could also be demanding and critical, the more so because they resented the feeling that hospitalization implied inadequacies in themselves. They envied nurses their skill and jealously resented the nurse's intimate contact with "their" patient.

In a more subtle way, both patients and relatives made psychological demands on nurses that increased their experience of stress. The hospital was expected to do more than accept the ill patients, care for their physical needs, and help realistically with their psychological stress. Implicitly it was expected to accept and, by so doing, free patients and relatives from, certain aspects of the emotional problems aroused by the patient and the illness. The hospital, particularly the nurses, had projected into them feelings such as depression and anxiety, fear of the patient and the illness, disgust at the illness and necessary nursing tasks. Patients and relatives treated the staff in such a way as to ensure that the nurses experienced these feelings instead of, or partly instead of, themselves, for example by refusing or trying to refuse to participate in important decisions about the patient and so forcing responsibility and anxiety back on the hospital. Thus, to the nurses' own deep and intense anxieties were psychically added those of other people. We were struck by the number of patients whose physical condition alone did not warrant hospitalization. In some cases, it seemed clear that they had been hospitalized because they and their relatives could not tolerate the stress of their being ill at home.

The nurses projected infantile phantasy-situations into current work-situations and experienced the objective situations as a mixture of objective reality and phantasy. They then re-experienced painfully and vividly in relation to current objective reality many of the feelings appropriate to the phantasies. In thus projecting phantasy-situations into objective reality, the nurses were using an important and universal technique for mastering anxiety and modifying the phantasy-situations. The objective situations symbolize the phantasy-situations and successful mastery of the objective situations gives reassurance about the mastery of the phantasy-situations. To be effective, such symbolization requires that the symbol *represents* the phantasy object, but *is not equated* with it. The symbol's own distinctive, objective characteristics must also be recognized and used. If, for any reason, the symbol and the phantasy object become almost or completely equated, the anxieties aroused by the phantasy object are aroused in full intensity by the symbolic object. The symbol then ceases to perform its function in containing and modifying anxiety (Segal, 1957). The close resemblance of the phantasy and objective situations in nursing constitutes a threat that symbolic representation will degenerate into symbolic equation and that nurses will consequently experience the full force of their primitive infantile anxieties in consciousness. Modified instances of this phenomenon were not uncommon in this hospital. For example, a nurse whose mother had had several gynecological operations broke down and had to give up nursing shortly after beginning her tour of duty on the gynecological ward.

To understand the sources of the anxiety was one thing: to understand why overt anxiety remained chronically at so high a level was another. Therefore our attention was directed to the adaptive and defensive techniques within the nursing service.

Defensive Techniques in the Nursing Service

In developing a structure, culture and mode of functioning, a social organization is influenced by a number of interacting factors, crucial among which is its primary task, i.e., the task it was created to perform (Rice, 1958) and the technology that this requires. The influences of the primary task and technology can easily be exaggerated. Indeed, I would prefer to regard them as limiting factors. The need to ensure viability through efficient enough performance of the primary task and the types of technology available to do this set limits to possible organization. Within these limits, the culture, structure and mode of functioning are determined by the psychological needs of the members (Trist and Bamforth, 1951).

The need of the members of the organization to use it in the struggle against anxiety leads to the development of socially structured defense mechanisms, which appear as elements in the structure, culture and mode of functioning of the organization (Jaques, 1955). An important aspect of such socially structured defense mechanisms is an attempt by individuals to externalize and give substance in objective reality to their characteristic psychic defense mechanisms. A social defense system develops over time through collusive interaction and agreement, often unconscious, between members of the organization as to what form it shall take. The socially structured defense mechanisms then tend to become an aspect of external reality with which old and new members of the institution must come to terms.

It is impossible here to describe the social defense system fully, so I shall illustrate only a few of its striking and typical features. I shall confine myself mainly to defense used within the nursing service and refer minimally to ways in which the nursing service made use of and was used by other people, notably patients and doctors. For convenience of exposition, I shall list the defense as if they were separate, although, in operation, they functioned simultaneously and interacted with each other.

SPLITTING UP THE NURSE/PATIENT RELATIONSHIP

The focus of anxiety for the nurse lay in the relation with the patient. The closer and more concentrated this relationship, the more the nurse was likely to experience the impact of anxiety. The nursing service attempted to protect the individual nurse from anxiety by splitting up contact with patients. It is hardly too much to say that the nurse did not nurse patients. The total work-load of a ward or department was broken down into lists of tasks, each of which was allocated to a particular student nurse, who performed patient-centered tasks for a large number of patients, perhaps as many as all the patients in a ward. As a corollary, the student performed only a few tasks for, and had restricted contact with, any one patient, and was thus prevented from contact with the totality of any one patient and his or her illness.

Depersonalization, Categorization and Denial of the Significance of the Individual

The protection afforded by the task-list system was reinforced by a number of other devices that inhibited the development of a full person-to-person relationship between nurse and patient. The implicit aim of such devices, which operated both structurally and culturally, may be described as depersonalization or elimination of individual distinctiveness in both nurse and patient. For example, nurses often talked about patients not by name but by bed number or by disease or diseased organ: "the liver in bed 10" or "the pneumonia in bed 15." Nurses themselves deprecated this practice, but it persisted. There was an almost explicit "ethic" that any patient must be the same as any other patient. It must not matter to the nurses whom they nursed or what illness. Nurses found it difficult to express preferences even for types of patients or for men or women patients. Conversely, it should not matter to the patient which nurse attended or, indeed, how many different nurses did. By implication it was the duty, as well as the need and privilege, of the patient to be nursed and of the nurse to nurse, regardless of the fact that a patient might need to "nurse" a distressed nurse and nurses might sometimes need to be "nursed." Outside the specific requirements of physical illness and treatment, the way patients were nursed was determined largely by their membership in the category patient and minimally by idiosyncratic wants and needs. For example, there was only one way of bed-making except when the physical illness required another, only one time to wash all patients—in the morning.

The nurses' uniforms were a symbol of an expected inner and behavioral uniformity; a nurse became a kind of agglomeration of nursing skills, without individuality; each was thus interchangeable with another of the same seniority. Socially permitted differences between nurses tended to be restricted to a few major categories, outwardly differentiated by minor differences in insignia on the same basic uniform. This attempted to create an operational identity between all nurses in the same category. To an extent indicating clearly the need for "blanket" decisions, duties and privileges were allotted to categories of people and not to individuals according to their personal capacities and needs. Something of the same reduction of individual distinctiveness existed between operational sub-units. Attempts were made to standardize all equipment and layout to the limits allowed by the different nursing tasks, but disregarding the idiosyncratic social and psychological resources and needs of each unit.

DETACHMENT AND DENIAL OF FEELINGS

The entrant into any profession that works with people needs to develop adequate professional detachment. He or she must learn to control feelings, refrain from excessive involvement, avoid disturbing identifications and maintain professional independence against manipulation and demands for unprofessional behavior. The reduction of individual distinctiveness aided detachment by minimizing the mutual interaction of personalities, which might lead to "attachment." It was reinforced by an implicit operational policy of "detachment." "A good nurse doesn't mind moving." A good nurse is willing and able without disturbance to move from ward to ward or hospital to hospital at a moment's notice. The implicit rationale appeared to be that a student nurse would learn to be detached psychologically if given sufficient experience of being detached literally and physically. This approach comes dangerously close to concrete thinking. Most senior nurses did not subscribe personally to this implicit rationale. They were aware of the personal distress as well as the operational disturbance caused by over-frequent moves. However, in their formal roles they continued to initiate frequent moves and made little other training provision for developing genuine professional detachment. The pain and distress of breaking relationships and the importance of stable and continuing relationships were implicitly denied by the system, although they were often stressed personally by people in the system.

This denial was reinforced by denial of the disturbing feelings that arose within relationships. Interpersonal repressive techniques were culturally required and typically used to deal with emotional stress. Both student nurses and staff showed panic about emotional outbursts. Brisk, reassuring behavior and advice of the "stiff upper lip," "pull yourself together" variety were characteristic. Student nurses suffered severely from emotional strain and habitually complained that the senior staff did not understand and made no effort to help them. Indeed, when the emotional stress arose from nurses' having made a mistake, they were usually reprimanded instead of being helped. A student nurse told me that she had made a mistake that hastened the death of a dying patient. She was reprimanded separately by four senior nurses, and not comforted. However, student nurses were wrong when they said that senior nurses did not understand or feel for their distress. In personal conversation with us, seniors showed considerable understanding and sympathy and often remembered surprisingly vividly some of the agonies of their own training. But they lacked confidence in their ability to handle emotional stress in any way other than by repressive techniques, and often said, "In any case, the students won't come and talk to us."

THE ATTEMPT TO ELIMINATE DECISIONS BY RITUAL TASK-PERFORMANCE

Making a decision implies making a choice between different possible courses of action and committing oneself to one of them, the choice being made in the absence of full factual information about the effects of the choice. All decisions are thus attended by uncertainty about their outcome and consequently by some conflict and anxiety. The anxiety consequent on decision-making is likely to be acute if a decision affects the treatment and welfare of patients. To spare staff this anxiety, the nursing service attempted to minimize the number and variety of decisions. For example, the student nurse was instructed to perform the task-list in a way reminiscent of performing a ritual. Precise instructions were given about the way each task must be performed, the order of the tasks and the time for their performance, although such precise instructions were not objectively necessary, or even wholly desirable.

Much time and effort were expended in standardizing nursing procedures in cases where there were a number of effective alternatives. Both teachers and practical-work supervisors impressed on the student nurse the importance of carrying out the ritual, reinforcing this by fostering an attitude to work that regarded every task as almost a matter of life and death, to be treated with appropriate seriousness. This attitude applied even to those tasks that could be effectively performed by an unskilled lay person. As a corollary, student nurses were actively discouraged from using their own discretion and initiative to plan their work realistically in relation to the objective situation, for example, at times of crisis to discriminate between tasks on the grounds of urgency or relative importance and act accordingly. Student nurses are the staff most affected by "rituals," since ritualization is easy to apply to their roles and tasks, but attempts were also made to ritualize the task-structure of the more complex senior staff roles and to standardize task-performance.

REDUCING THE WEIGHT OF RESPONSIBILITY IN DECISION-MAKING BY CHECKS AND COUNTERCHECKS

The psychological burden of anxiety arising from a final, committing decision by a single person was dissipated in a number of ways, so that its impact was reduced. The final act of commitment was postponed by checking and re-checking decisions for validity and postponing action as long as possible. Executive action following decisions was also checked and re-checked at intervening stages. Individuals spent much time in private rumination over decisions and actions. Whenever possible, they involved other nurses in decision-making and in reviewing actions. Nursing procedures prescribed considerable checking between individuals, but it was also a strongly developed habit among nurses outside areas of prescribed behavior. The practice of checking and counter-checking was applied not only to situations where mistakes might have serious consequences, such as in giving dangerous drugs, but also to many situations where the implications of a decision were of only the slightest consequence. Nurses consulted not only their immediate seniors but also their juniors and nurses or other staff with whom they had no functional relationship but who happened to be available.

Collusive Social Redistribution of Responsibility and Irresponsibility

Each nurse had to face and, in some way, resolve a painful conflict over accepting the responsibility of the role. Nursing tends to evoke a strong sense of responsibility, and nurses often discharged their duties at considerable personal cost. On the other hand, the heavy burden of responsibility was difficult to bear consistently, and nurses were tempted to abandon it. Each nurse had wishes and impulses that would lead to irresponsible action, to skipping boring, repetitive tasks or to becoming libidinally or emotionally attached to patients. The balance of opposing forces in the conflict varied between individuals; some are naturally "more responsible" than others, but the conflict was always present. To experience this conflict fully and intrapsychically would be extremely stressful. The intrapsychic conflict was alleviated by a technique that partly converted it into an interpersonal conflict. People in certain roles tended to be described by themselves and others as responsible, while people in other roles were described as irresponsible. Nurses habitually complained that other nurses were irresponsible, behaved carelessly and impulsively, and in consequence needed to be ceaselessly supervised and disciplined. The complaints commonly referred not to individuals or to specific incidents but to whole categories of nurses, usually a category junior to the speaker. The implication was that the juniors were not only less responsible now than the speaker, but also less responsible than she was when she was in the same junior position. Few nurses recognized or admitted such tendencies in themselves. Many people complained that their seniors, as a category, imposed unnecessarily strict and repressive discipline, and treated them as though they had no sense of responsibility. Few senior staff seemed able to recognize such features in their own behavior to subordinates. These juniors and seniors were, with few exceptions, the same people viewed from above or below, as the case might be.

We came to realize that the complaints stemmed from a collusive system of denial, splitting and projection that was culturally acceptable to, indeed culturally required of, nurses. Each nurse tended to split off aspects of herself from her conscious personality and to project them into other nurses. Her irresponsible impulses, which she feared she could not control, were attributed to her juniors. Her painfully severe attitude to these impulses and burdensome sense of responsibility were attributed to her seniors. Consequently, she identified juniors with her irresponsible self and treated them with the severity that self was felt to deserve. Similarly, she identified seniors with her own harsh disciplinary attitude to her irresponsible self and expected harsh discipline. There was psychic truth in the assertion that juniors were irresponsible and seniors harsh disciplinarians. These were the roles assigned to them. There was also objective truth, since people acted objectively on the psychic roles assigned to them. Discipline was often harsh and sometimes unfair, since the multiple projection also led the senior to identify all juniors with her irresponsible self and so with each other. Thus, she failed to discriminate between them sufficiently. Nurses complained about being reprimanded for other people's mistakes while no serious effort was made to find the real culprit. A staff nurse* said, " If a mistake has been made, you must reprimand someone, even if you don't know who really did it." Irresponsible behavior was also quite common, mainly in tasks remote from direct patient-care. The interpersonal conflict was painful but was less so than experiencing the conflict fully intrapsychically, and it could more easily be evaded. The disciplining eye of seniors could not follow juniors all the time, nor did the junior confront her senior with irresponsibility all the time.

Purposeful Obscurity in the Formal Distribution of Responsibility

Additional protection from the impact of responsibility for specific tasks was given by the fact that the formal structure and role system failed to define fully enough who was responsible for what and to whom. This matched and objectified the obscurity about the location of psychic responsibility that inevitably arose from the massive system of projection described above. The content and boundaries of roles were obscure, especially at senior levels. The respon-

*In the nursing service, a sister is the head nurse in a ward and a staff nurse is a fully qualified nurse who is her deputy.

sibilities were more onerous at this level so that protection was felt as very necessary. Also the more complex roles and role-relationships made it easier to evade definition. The content of the role of the student nurse was rigidly prescribed by her task-list. However, in practice, she was unlikely to have the same task-list for any length of time. She might, and frequently did, have two completely different task-lists in a single day. There was therefore a lack of stable person/role constellations, and it became very difficult to assign responsibility finally to a person, a role or a person/role constellation.

Responsibility and authority on wards were generalized in a way that made them non-specific and prevented them from falling firmly on one person, even the sister. Each nurse was held to be responsible for the work of every nurse junior to her. Junior, in this context, implied no hierarchical relationship, and was determined only by the length of time a student nurse had been in training, and all students were "junior" to trained staff. Every nurse was expected to initiate disciplinary action in relation to any failure by any junior nurse. Such diffused responsibility meant, of course, that responsibility was not generally experienced specifically or seriously. This was a policy for inactivity.

THE REDUCTION OF THE IMPACT OF RESPONSIBILITY BY DELEGATION TO SUPERIORS

Delegation in the hospital seemed to move in a direction opposite to the usual one. Tasks were frequently forced upwards in the hierarchy so that all responsibility for their performance could be disclaimed. Insofar as this happened, the heavy burden of responsibility on the individual was reduced.

The results of years of this practice were visible in the nursing service at the time of the study. We were struck by the low level of tasks carried out by nursing staff and students in relation to their personal ability, skill and position in the hierarchy. Formally and informally, tasks were assigned to staff at a level well above that at which one found comparable tasks in other institutions. The task of allocating student nurses to practical duties was a case in point. This work was carried out by the first and second assistant matrons* and took up a considerable proportion of their working-time. The task was such that, if policy were clearly defined and the task appropriately organized, it could be efficiently performed by a competent clerk part-time under the supervision of a senior nurse. We saw this delegation upward in operation a number of times as new tasks developed for nurses out of changes resulting from our study. The senior staff decided to change the practical training for post-graduate students so that they might have better training in administration and supervision. The

---

*The nurses third and fourth in seniority in administration.

students were now to spend six months continuously in one operational unit during which time they would act as understudy-cum-shadow to the sister or staff nurse. Personal compatibility was felt to be important, and it was suggested that, with training, the sisters should take part in the selection of the fourth-year students for their own wards, a task within their competence. At first there was enthusiasm for the proposal, but as definite plans were made and the ward sisters began to feel that they had no developed skill for selection, they requested that, after all, senior staff should continue to select for them as they had always done. The senior staff, although already overburdened, accepted the task.

The repeated occurrence of such incidents by mutual collusive agreement between superiors and subordinates is hardly surprising considering the mutual projection system described above. Nurses as subordinates tended to feel very dependent on their superiors in whom they had psychically vested, by projection, some of the best and most competent parts of themselves. They felt that their projections gave them the right to expect their superiors to undertake their tasks and make decisions for them. On the other hand, nurses as superiors did not feel they could fully trust their subordinates in whom they had psychically vested the irresponsible and incompetent parts of themselves. Their acceptance of their subordinates' projections also conveyed a sense of duty to accept their subordinates' responsibilities.

IDEALIZATION AND UNDERESTIMATION OF PERSONAL DEVELOPMENTAL POSSIBILITIES

In order to reduce anxiety about the continuous efficient performance of nursing tasks, nurses sought assurance that the nursing service was staffed with responsible, competent people. To a considerable extent, the hospital dealt with this problem by attempting to recruit and select staff, that is student nurses, who were already mature and responsible people. This was reflected in phrases like "nurses are born not made" or "nursing is a vocation." This was a kind of idealization of the potential nursing recruit, and implied a belief that responsibility and personal maturity cannot be taught or developed. As a corollary, the training system was mainly oriented to the communication of essential facts and techniques, and paid minimal attention to teaching events oriented to personal maturation within the professional setting. The nursing service faced the dilemma that, while a strong sense of responsibility and discipline were necessary for the welfare of patients, a considerable proportion of actual nursing tasks were extremely simple. This hospital, in common with most similar British hospitals, attempted to solve this dilemma by the recruitment of large numbers of high-level student nurses who, it was hoped, would be prepared to accept the temporary lowering of their operational level because they were in training. This was no real solution. It contributed to the 30–50 percent wastage of student nurses during training: students who were too "high-level" for the job they were doing, felt degraded and diminished by it and could not tolerate the situation until they were qualified. It also contributed to great suffering among students and staff.

Avoidance of Change

Change is an excursion into the unknown. It implies a commitment to future events that are not entirely predictable and to their consequences, and inevitably provokes doubt and anxiety. Any significant change within a social system implies changes in existing social relationships and in social structure, which implies in turn a change in the operation of the social system as a defense system. While this change is proceeding, anxiety is likely to be more open and intense. This is a familiar experience while the individual's defenses are being restructured in the course of psychoanalytic therapy. Jaques (1955) has stressed that resistance to social change can be better understood if it is seen as the resistance of groups of people unconsciously clinging to existing institutions because changes threaten existing social defenses against deep and intense anxieties.

It is understandable that the nursing service, whose tasks stimulated such primitive and intense anxieties, should anticipate change with unusually severe anxiety. In order to avoid this anxiety, the service tried to avoid change wherever possible and to cling to the familiar, even when the familiar had obviously ceased to be appropriate or relevant. Changes tended to be initiated only at the point of crisis. The presenting problem was a good example of the difficulty in initiating and carrying through change. Staff and student nurses had long felt that the methods in operation were unsatisfactory and had wanted to change them. They had, however, been unable to do so. The problem was approaching the point of breakdown and the limits of the capacities of the people concerned when we were called in. Other examples of this clinging to the inappropriate familiar could be observed. Changes in medical practice and the initiation of the National Health Service had led to more rapid patient turnover, an increase in the proportion of acutely ill patients, a wider range of illness to be nursed in each ward and greater variation in the work-load of a ward from day to day. These changes pointed to the need for increasing flexibility in the work organization in wards. In fact, no such increase had taken place. Indeed, the difficulty inherent in trying to deal with a fluctuating work-load by the rather rigid system described above tended to be handled by increased prescription and rigidity and by reiteration of the familiar. The greater the anxiety the greater the need for reassurance in rather compulsive repetition.

Commentary on the Social Defense System

The characteristic feature of the social defense system was its orientation to helping the individual to avoid the conscious experience of anxiety, guilt, doubt and uncertainty. This was done by eliminating situations, events, tasks, activities and relationships that caused anxiety or, more correctly, evoked anxieties connected with primitive psychological remnants in the personality. Little attempt was made positively to help the individual confront the anxiety-evoking experiences and, by so doing, to develop her capacity to tolerate and deal more effectively with them. Basically, the potential anxieties in the nursing situation were felt to be too deep and dangerous for full confrontation. They threatened personal disruption and social chaos. In fact, of course, the attempt to avoid such confrontation could never be completely successful. A compromise was inevitable between the implicit aims of the social defense system and the demands of reality as expressed in the need to pursue the primary task.

It followed that the psychic defense mechanisms that had, over time, been built into the socially structured defense system of the nursing service were, in the main, those which by evasion give protection from the full experience of anxiety. These were derived from the most primitive psychic defense mechanisms typical of the young infant's attempts to deal, mainly by evasion, with the severe anxieties aroused by the interplay of instincts. Individuals vary in the extent to which they are able, as they grow older, to modify or abandon their early defense mechanisms and develop other methods of dealing with their anxieties. Notably, these other methods include the ability to confront the anxiety-situations in their original or symbolic forms and to work them over; to approach and tolerate psychic and objective reality; to differentiate between them and to perform constructive and objectively successful activities in relation to them. Every individual is at risk that objective or psychic events stimulating acute anxiety will lead to partial or complete abandonment of the more mature methods of dealing with anxiety and to regression to more primitive methods of defense. The intense anxiety evoked by the nursing task had precipitated just such individual regression to primitive types of defense. These had been projected and given objective existence in the social structure and culture of the nursing service, with the result that anxiety was to some extent contained, but that true mastery of anxiety by deep working-through and modification was seriously inhibited. Thus, it was to be expected that nurses would persistently experience a higher degree of anxiety than was justified by the objective situation.

Consideration in more detail of how the socially structured defense system failed to support the individual in the struggle towards more effective mastery of anxiety may be approached from two different but related points of view. First, I will consider how far the current functioning of the nursing service gave rise to experiences that reassured nurses or aroused anxiety. As a direct consequence of the social organization, many situations and incidents arose that aroused anxiety. On the other hand, the social system frequently deprived nurses of necessary reassurance and satisfaction. In other words, the social defense system itself aroused a good deal of secondary anxiety as well as failing to alleviate primary anxiety.

THREAT OF CRISIS AND OPERATIONAL BREAKDOWN

From the operational point of view, the nursing service was cumbersome and inflexible. It could not easily adapt to short- or long-term changes in conditions. The task-list system and minutely prescribed task-performance made it difficult to adjust work-loads when necessary by postponing or omitting less urgent or important tasks. The total demands on a ward varied considerably and at short notice according to factors such as types and numbers of patients and days on which operations took place. The numbers and categories of student nurses also varied considerably and at short notice. Recurrent shortages of second-year or third-year nurses occurred while they spent six weeks in school; sickness or leave frequently reduced numbers. The work/staff ratio, therefore, varied considerably and often suddenly. Since work could not easily be reduced, this generated considerable pressure, tension and uncertainty among staff and students. Even when the work/staff ratio was satisfactory, the threat of a sudden increase was always present. The nurses seemed to have a constant sense of impending crisis. They were haunted by fear of failing to carry out their duties adequately as pressure of work increased. Conversely, they rarely experienced the satisfaction and lessening of anxiety that came from knowing they had the ability to carry out their work realistically and efficiently.

The nursing service was organized in a way that made it difficult for one person, or even a close group of people, to make a rapid and effective decision. Diffusion of responsibility prevented adequate and specific concentration of authority for making and implementing decisions. The organization of working groups made it difficult to achieve adequate concentration of knowledge. In a ward, only the sister and the staff nurse were in a position to collect and co-ordinate knowledge. However, they had to do this for a unit of such size and complexity that it was impossible to do it effectively. They were, inevitably, badly briefed. We came across many cases where the sister did not remember how many nurses were on duty or what each was supposed to do, and had to have recourse to a written list. Such instances cannot be attributed primarily to individual inadequacy. Decisions tended to be made, therefore, by people who felt that they lacked adequate knowledge of relevant and ascertainable facts. This led to both anxiety and anger. To this anxiety was added the anxiety that decisions would not be taken in time, since decision-making was made so slow and cumbersome by the system of checking and counter-checking and by the obscurity surrounding the location of responsibility.

Excessive Movement of Student Nurses

The fact that a rise in work/staff ratios could be met only within very narrow limits by a reduction in the work-load meant that it was often necessary to have staff reinforcements, usually, to move student nurses. The defense of rigid work organization thus appeared as a factor contributory to the presenting problem of student-allocation, and the consequent distress and anxiety. Denial of the importance of relationships and feelings did not adequately protect the nurses, especially since the moves most directly affected student nurses, who had not yet fully developed these defenses. Nurses grieved and mourned over broken relationships with patients and other nurses; they felt they were failing their patients. They felt strange in new surroundings. They had to learn new duties and make relationships with new patients and staff, and probably had to nurse types of illness they had never nursed before. Until they got to know more about the new situation they suffered anxiety, uncertainties and doubts. Senior staff estimated that it took a student two weeks to settle down in a new ward. We regarded this as an underestimate. The suddenness of many moves increased the difficulty. It did not allow adequate time for preparing for parting and made the parting more traumatic. Patients could not be handed over properly to other nurses. Sudden transfers to a different ward allowed little opportunity for psychological preparation for what was to come. Nurses tended to feel acutely deprived by this lack of preparation. As one young woman said, "If only I had known a bit sooner that I was going to the diabetic ward, I would have read up about diabetics and that would have helped a lot." Janis (1958) has described how the effects of anticipated traumatic events can be alleviated if an advance opportunity is provided to work over the anxieties—an opportunity denied to the nurses.

This situation did indeed help to produce a defensive psychological detachment. Students protected themselves against the pain and anxiety of transfers, or the threat of transfers, by limiting their psychological involvement in any situation, with patients or other staff. This reduced their interest and sense of responsibility and fostered a "don't care" attitude of which nurses and patients complained bitterly. Nurses felt anxious and guilty when they detected such feelings in themselves, and angry, hurt and disappointed when they found them in others. The resulting detachment also reduced the possibility of satisfaction from work well done in a job one deeply cared about.

UNDER-EMPLOYMENT OF STUDENT NURSES

Understandably, since work-loads were so variable and it was difficult to adjust tasks, the nursing service tried to plan its establishment to meet peak rather than average loads. As a result, student nurses quite often had too little work. They hardly ever complained of overwork but rather a number complained of not having enough work, although they still complained of stress. We observed obvious under-employment in spite of the fact that student nurses were apt to make themselves look busy doing something and talked of having to look busy to avoid censure from the sister. Senior staff often seemed to feel it necessary to explain why their students were not busier, and would say they were "having a slack day" or they had "an extra nurse today."

Student nurses were also under-employed in terms of level of work. A number of elements in the defense system contributed to this. Consider, for example, the assignment of duties to whole categories of student nurses. Since nurses found it so difficult to tolerate inefficiency and mistakes, the level of duties for each category was pitched low, near to the expected level of the least competent nurse in the category. In addition, the policy that made student nurses the effective nursing staff of the hospital condemned them to the repetitive performance of simple tasks to an extent far beyond that necessary for their training. The performance of simple tasks need not of itself imply that the student nurse's role was at a low level. The level depends also on how much opportunity was given for the use of discretion and judgment in the organization of the tasks—which, when and how. In fact, the social defense system specifically minimized the exercise of discretion and judgment in the student nurse's organization of tasks, for example, through the task-list system. This ultimately determined the under-employment of many student nurses who were capable of exercising a good deal of judgment and could quickly have been trained to use it effectively. Similar under-employment was obvious in senior staff connected, for example, with the practice of delegating upwards.

Under-employment of this kind stimulates anxiety and guilt, which are particularly acute when under-employment implies failing to use one's capacities fully in the service of other people in need. Nurses found the limitations on their performance very frustrating. They often experienced a painful sense of failure when they had faithfully performed their prescribed tasks, and expressed guilt and concern about incidents in which they had carried out instructions to the letter, but, in so doing, had practiced what they considered to be bad nursing. For example, a nurse had been told to give a patient who had been sleeping badly a sleeping draught at a certain time. In the interval he had fallen into a deep natural sleep. Obeying her orders, she woke him up to give him the medicine. Her common sense and judgment told her to leave him asleep and she felt very guilty that she had disturbed him. The nurses felt they were being forced to abandon common-sense principles of good nursing, and they resented it.

Jaques (1956) discussed the use of discretion and came to the conclusion that the level of responsibility experienced in a job was related solely to the exercise of discretion and not to carrying out the prescribed elements. We may say that the level of responsibility in the nurse's job is minimized by the attempt to eliminate the use of discretion. Nurses felt insulted, indeed almost assaulted, by being deprived of the opportunity to be more responsible. They felt, and were, devalued by the social system. They were intuitively aware that the further development of their capacity for responsibility was being inhibited by the work and training situation and they greatly resented this. The bitterness of the experience was intensified because they were constantly being exhorted to behave responsibly, which, in the ordinary usage of the word in a work-situation, they were prevented from doing. We came to the conclusion that senior staff tended to use the word "responsible" differently from ordinary usage. For them, a responsible nurse was one who carried out prescriptions to the letter. There was an essential conflict between staff and students that greatly added to stress and bitterness on both sides. Jaques (1956) stated that workers in industry cannot rest content until they have reached a level of work that deploys to the full their capacity for discretionary responsibility. Student nurses, who were, in effect, workers in the hospital for most of their time, were certainly not content.

DEPRIVATION OF PERSONAL SATISFACTIONS

The nursing service seemed to provide unusually little in the way of direct satisfaction for staff and students. Although the dictum "nursing should be a vocation" implied that nurses should not expect ordinary job satisfaction, its absence added to stress. Mention has already been made of a number of ways in which nurses were deprived of positive satisfactions potentially existent in the profession. Satisfaction was also reduced by the attempt to evade anxiety by splitting up the nurse-patient relationship and converting patients who need nursing into tasks that must be performed. Although the nursing *service* had considerable success in nursing patients, the individual nurse had little direct experience of success. Success and satisfaction were dissipated in much the same way as anxiety. Nurses missed the reassurance of seeing patients get better in a way they could easily connect with their own efforts. The nurses' longing for this kind of experience was shown in the excitement and pleasure felt by a nurse who was chosen to "special" a patient, that is give special, individual care to a very ill patient in a crisis. The gratitude of patients, an important reward for nurses, was also dissipated. Patients were grateful to the hospital or to the nurses for their treatment and recovery, but they could not easily express gratitude in any direct way to individual nurses. There were too many and they were too mobile. Ward sisters, too, were deprived of potential satisfaction in their roles. Many of them would have liked closer contact with patients, and more opportunity to use their nursing skills directly. Much of their time was spent in initiating and training student nurses who came to their wards. The excessive movement of students meant that sisters were frequently deprived of the return on that training time and the reward of seeing the nurse develop under their supervision. The reward of their work, like the nurse's, was dissipated and impersonal.

The nursing service inhibited in a number of ways the realization of satisfactions in relationships with colleagues. The traditional relationship between staff and students was such that students were singled out by staff almost solely for reprimand or criticism. Good work was taken for granted and little praise given. Students complained that no one noticed when they worked well, when they stayed late on duty, or when they did some extra task for a patient's comfort. Work-teams were notably impermanent. Even three-monthly moves of student nurses made it difficult to weld together a strong, cohesive work-team. The more frequent moves, and the threat of moves, made it almost impossible. In such circumstances, it was difficult to build a team that functioned effectively on the basis of real knowledge of the strengths and weaknesses of each member, her needs as well as her contribution, and adapted to the way of working and type of relationship each person preferred. Nurses felt hurt and resentful about the lack of importance attached to their personal contribution to the work, and the work itself was less satisfying when it had to be done not only in accordance with the task-list system, but also within an informal, but rigid, organization. Nurses missed the satisfaction of investing their own personality thoroughly in their work and making a highly personal contribution.

Support for the individual was notably lacking throughout the whole nursing service within working relationships. Compensation was sought in intense relationships with other nurses off duty. Working-groups were characterized by isolation of their members. Nurses frequently did not know what other members of their team were doing or even what their formal duties were; indeed, they often did not know whether other members of their team were on duty or not. They pursued their own tasks with minimal regard to those of their colleagues. This practice led to frequent difficulties between nurses. One nurse, carrying out her own tasks correctly by the prescription, might undo work done by another nurse also carrying out her tasks correctly by the prescription, because they did not plan their work together and co-ordinate it. Bad feeling usually followed. One nurse might be extremely busy while another had not enough to do. Sharing work was rare. Nurses complained bitterly about this. They said "there is no team spirit, no one helps you, no one cares." They felt guilty about not helping and angry about not being helped. They felt deprived by the lack of close, responsible, friendly relations with colleagues.

The lack of personal support and help was particularly painful for the student nurses as they watched the care and attention given to patients. It was our impression that a significant number of nurses entered the profession under some confusion about their future roles and functions. They perceived the hospital as a kind and supportive organization particularly well-equipped to deal with dependency needs, and they expected to have the privilege of being dependent themselves. However, because of the categorization they were denied the privilege except on very rare occasions, notably when they became sick themselves and were nursed in the hospital.

I go on now to consider the second general approach to the failure of the social defense to alleviate anxiety. This arose from the direct impact of the social defense system on the individual, regardless of specific experiences, that is, from the more directly psychological interaction between the social defense system and the individual nurse.

Although I have used the term "socially structured defense system" as a construct to describe certain features of the nursing service as a continuing social institution, I wish to make it clear that I do not imply that the nursing service *as an institution* operates the defenses. Defenses are, and can be, operated only by individuals. Their behavior is the link between their psychic defenses and the institution. Membership necessitates an adequate degree of matching between individual and social defense systems. I will not attempt to define the degree of matching, but state simply that if the discrepancy between social and individual defense systems is too great, some breakdown in the individual's relation with the institution is inevitable. The form of breakdown varies, but it commonly takes the form of a temporary or permanent break in the individual's membership. For example continuing to use one's own defenses and to follow one's own idiosyncratic behavior patterns may make an individual intolerable to other members of the institution who are more adapted to the social defense system. They may then respond with rejection. Trying to behave in a way consistent with the social defense system rather than individual defenses, will increase anxieties and make it impossible for the individual to continue membership. Theoretically, matching between social and individual defenses can be achieved by a re-structuring of the social defense system to match the individual, by a re-structuring of the individual defense system to match the social, or by a combination of the two. The processes by which an adequate degree of matching is achieved are too complicated to describe here in detail. It must suffice to say that they depend heavily on repeated projection of the psychic defense system into the social defense system and repeated introjection of the social defense system into the psychic defense system. This allows continuous testing of match and fit as the individual experiences his or her own and other people's reactions (Heimann, 1952).

The social defense system of the nursing service has been described as an historical development through collusive interaction between individuals to project and reify relevant elements of their psychic defense systems. However, from the point of view of new entrants to the nursing service, the social defense system at the time of entry is a datum, an aspect of external reality to which they must react and adapt. Fenichel (1946) makes a similar point. He states that social institutions arise through the efforts of human beings to satisfy their needs, but that social institutions then become external realities comparatively independent of individuals which affect the structure of the individual. The student nurses were faced with a particularly difficult task in adapting to the nursing service and developing an adequate match between the social defense system and their psychic defense systems. It will be clear that the nursing service was very resistant to change, especially change in the functioning of its defense system. For the student nurses, this meant that the social defense system was to an unusual extent immutable. In the process of matching between the psychic and social defense systems, the emphasis was heavily on the modification of the individual's psychic defenses. This meant in practice that the social defense system had to be incorporated and used more or less as it was found, and psychic defenses re-structured as necessary to match it.

An earlier section of this paper described how the social defense system of the hospital was built on primitive psychic defenses, those characteristic of the earliest phases of infancy. The fact that the student nurses had to incorporate and use this defense system has certain intrapsychic consequences. These defenses are oriented to the violent, terrifying situations of infancy, and rely heavily on violent splitting which dissipates the anxiety. They avoid the experience of anxiety and effectively prevent the individual from confronting it. Thus, the individual cannot bring the content of the phantasy anxiety situations into effective contact with reality. Unrealistic or pathological anxiety cannot be differentiated from realistic anxiety arising from real dangers. Therefore, anxiety tends to remain permanently at a level determined more by the phantasies than by the reality. The forced introjection of the hospital defense system, therefore, perpetuates in the individual a considerable degree of pathological anxiety.

The enforced use of this defense system inhibited maturation in many ways and even led to regression. It interfered with the capacity for symbol formation; it inhibited the capacity for abstract thought and conceptualization; it prevented full development of the individual's knowledge, understanding and skills. The social defense system inhibited the psychic integration on which the development of such capacities depends. Individuals were prevented from realizing to the full their capacity for concern, compassion and sympathy, and for action based on these feelings which would strengthen their belief in their own good aspects and capacity to use them. The defense system struck directly, therefore, at the roots of sublimatory activities in which infantile anxieties could be re-worked in symbolic form and modified.

In general, one may say that forced introjection of the defense system prevented the personal defensive maturation that alone would allow for the modification of the remnants of infantile anxiety and diminish the extent to which early anxieties may be re-evoked and projected into current real situations. Indeed, in many cases, it forced the individual to regress to a maturational level below that achieved before entering the hospital. In this, the nursing service failed its individual members desperately. It seemed clear that a major motivational factor in the choice of nursing as a career was the wish to have the opportunity to develop the capacity for sublimatory activities in the nursing of the sick, and through that to achieve better mastery of infantile anxiety situations, modification of pathological anxiety, and personal maturation.

Conclusion

Attention has been concentrated mainly on the way in which the social defense system in the nursing service was ineffective in containing anxiety in its members. It did not help them work it through. Incidentally, however, mention was made from time to time of the effect of the social defense system on diminishing the efficiency of task-performance. The inefficiencies were not so great as to prevent task-performance from continuing, although at a less than optimum level and accompanied by fears that it might be in jeopardy.

Inefficiencies noted include high staff/patient ratios, bad nursing practice, excessive staff turnover, failure to train students effectively for their future roles. Further, the high level of anxiety in nurses added to the stress of illness and hospitalization for patients and had adverse effects on such factors as recovery rates. A later investigation (Revans, 1959) connected recovery rates of patients quite directly with the morale of the nursing staff. Thus the social structure of the nursing service is defective not only as a means of handling anxiety, but also as a method of organizing its tasks. These two aspects of the situation cannot be regarded as separate. The inefficiency is an inevitable consequence of the chosen defense system.

The success and viability of a social institution are intimately connected with the techniques it uses to contain anxiety. Analogous hypotheses about the individual have long been widely accepted. Freud (1948) put forward such ideas as his work developed. The work of Melanie Klein and her colleagues has given a central position to anxiety and the defenses in personality development and ego-functioning (Klein, 1948). Similarly, an understanding of this aspect of the functioning of a social institution is an important diagnostic and therapeutic tool in facilitating social change. Bion (1955) and Jaques (1955) stress the importance of understanding these phenomena and relate difficulties in achieving social change to difficulty in tolerating the anxieties that are released as social defenses are re-structured. The many failures experienced by social scientists and others in attempts to change social institutions would seem to be connected with their not taking sufficient account of the need to analyze anxieties and defenses.

The nursing service illustrated the problem of achieving social change to a marked degree. Efforts to initiate serious change were often met with acute anxiety and hostility. The people concerned felt very threatened, the threat being of nothing less than social chaos and individual breakdown. To give up known ways of behavior and embark on the unknown were felt to be intolerable. In general, it may be postulated that resistance to social change is likely to be greatest in institutions whose social defense systems are dominated by primitive psychic defense mechanisms, those which have been collectively described by Melanie Klein as the paranoid-schizoid defenses (Klein, 1952a; 1959). One may compare this socio-therapeutic experience with the common experience in psychoanalytical therapy, that the most difficult work is with patients whose defenses are mainly of this kind, or in phases of the analysis when such defenses predominate.

Some therapeutic results were achieved in the hospital, notably in relation to the presenting symptom. For example, a planned set of courses was prepared for student nurses, which jointly ensured that the student nurse had adequate training and that the hospital was adequately staffed, and took more realistic account of the real discrepancies between training and staffing needs. To prevent emergencies from interfering with the implementation of the planned courses, a reserve pool of mobile nurses was created. The common feature of the changes, however, was that they involved minimal disturbance of the existing defense system. Indeed, it might be more correct to say that they involved reinforcing and strengthening the existing type of defense. Proposals were made for more far-reaching change, involving a re-structuring of the social defense system. For example, one suggestion was that a limited experiment be done in ward organization, eliminating the task-list system and substituting some form of patient assignment. However, although the senior staff discussed such proposals with courage and seriousness, they did not feel able to proceed with the plans. This happened in spite of our clearly expressed view that, unless there were some fairly radical changes in the system, the problems of the nursing service might well become extremely serious. The decision seemed to us quite comprehensible, however, in view of the anxiety and the defense system. These would have made the therapeutic task of accomplishing change very difficult for both the nursing service and the therapist.

References

Bion, W.R. 1955. "Group Dynamics: A Review." In *New Directions in Psycho-Analysis,* edited by M. Klein, P. Heimann and R.E. Money-Kyrle. London: Tavistock Publications; New York: Basic Books.

Fenichel, O. 1946. *The Psycho-Analytic Theory of the Neuroses.* New York: Norton.

Freud, S. 1948. *Inhibitions, Symptoms and Anxiety.* London: Hogarth Press and Institute of Psycho-Analysis.

Heimann, P. 1952. "Certain Functions of Introjection and Projection in Earliest Infancy." In *Developments in Psycho-Analysis,* edited by J. Riviere. London: Hogarth Press and Institute of Psycho-Analysis.

Jaques, E. 1955. "Social Systems as a Defence against Persecutory and Depressive Anxiety." In *New Directions in Psycho-Analysis,* edited by M. Klein, P. Heimann and R.E. Money-Kyrle. London: Tavistock Publications; New York: Basic Books.

———. 1956. *Measurement of Responsibility: A Study of Work, Payment, and Individual Capacity.* London: Tavistock Publications; Cambridge, Mass.: Harvard University Press.

Janis, I.L. 1958. *Psychological Stress: Psycho-Analytic and Behavioural Studies of Surgical Patients.* London: Chapman and Hall.

Klein, M. 1948. "The Importance of Symbol Formation in the Development of the Ego." In *Contributions to Psycho-Analysis 1921–1945.* London: Hogarth Press and Institute of Psycho-Analysis.

———. 1952a. "Notes on Some Schizoid Mechanisms." In *Developments in Psycho-Analysis,* edited by J. Riviere. London: Hogarth Press and Institute of Psycho-Analysis.

———. 1952b. "Some Theoretical Conclusions Regarding the Emotional Life of the Infant." In *Developments in Psycho-Analysis,* edited by J. Riviere. London: Hogarth Press and Institute of Psycho-Analysis.

———. 1959. "Our Adult World and Its Roots in Infancy." *Human Relations,* 12:291–303.

Revans, R.W. 1959. "The Hospital as an Organism: A Study in Communications and Morale." *Proceedings of 6th Annual International Meeting of the Institute of Management Sciences.* London and New York: Pergamon Press.

Rice, A.K. 1958. *Productivity and Social Organization: The Ahmedabad Experiment.* London: Tavistock Publications. Reissued 1987, New York: Garland.

Segal, H. 1957. "Notes on Symbol Formation." *International Journal of Psycho-Analysis,* 38:391–97.

Trist, E.L. and K.W. Bamforth. 1951. "Some Social and Psychological Consequences of the Longwall Method of Coal Getting. *Human Relations,* 4:3–38.

Isabel Menzies Lyth

A Psychoanalytical Perspective on Social Institutions*

Psychoanalysis has made many contributions to our understanding of social institutions. It has done so through extending the understanding derived from exploration of the one-to-one relationship in clinical psychoanalysis to the larger and more complex relationships in groups and institutions. This is widely recognized. Less well recognized is psychoanalysis' other contribution, the derivatives from the psychoanalytic method in work with institutions and how this illuminates understanding of their content and dynamics. Wallace's view, quoted by Almansi (1986), that Freud's most valuable gift to anthropology was the clinical method of psychoanalysis and the unequalled insights it provides, is equally applicable to work with social institutions.

This paper is concerned with the second type of psychoanalytic contribution to institutional practice. Central to this approach is a deep conviction about the existence of the unconscious such as most easily comes through having an analysis oneself. This was how it came to Freud as he pursued the difficult course of his self-analysis. A useful alternative experience is membership of a group where the work is based on psychoanalytic principles as applied to group phenomena and directed towards increasing insight into group process (Bion, 1961). There is no harm in having both. They are different and complementary, the latter leading more directly into work with institutions. Such experience develops the capacity to recognize and understand the unconscious mind, both content and dynamics, and its manifestations in the conscious thoughts, feelings, speech and behavior of the people one is working with—and in ourselves. One also learns to recognize its presence in the institution itself—its structure, sub-systems and culture.

In institutional practice psychoanalytic understanding is extremely useful in orientating oneself to the nature of the situation, even if it is unlikely that one would interpret deep unconscious content directly to the client, as a psychoanalyst might to a patient. Perhaps more important than content are the dynamic psycho-social processes that go on in institutions at both conscious and

*A new paper.

unconscious levels. Of particular significance are the defenses developed to deal with anxiety-provoking content and with the difficulties in collaborating to accomplish a common task. These defenses appear in the structure of the institution itself and permeate its whole way of functioning.

People do not say what they really mean even when they honestly and sincerely say what they consciously think, let alone when they do not. Neither patients nor clients are likely to be absolutely sincere and honest, although they become increasingly so if work is going well and trust in the analyst or consultant is growing. In the institutional setting it is not only the unconscious thoughts and feelings one needs to understand, but also the implicit; what is not being said. Thoughts conscious in some people, or even shared in two's and three's, are not openly shared with everyone in a work situation where they could be realistically and constructively used. The ability to see behind what is being said or done to what is unconscious or implicit, to understand it, to open it up and explore it with the client is a focal skill for the institutional consultant. This implies recognizing the defenses that are holding the content unconscious or implicit and helping the client to give them up or modify them. Such an approach is familiar to the psychoanalyst and the methods he uses to accomplish this task are in many ways directly transferable to institutional practice.

The approach of the consultant to the client institution that facilitates the elucidation of such situations strikingly resembles Freud's recommendations about the way the psychoanalyst may best gain access to his patient's mind (Freud, 1911–15). Freud recommends "evenly suspended attention," not directing one's attention to anything in particular, not making a premature selection or pre-judgment about what is significant, which might distract one's attention from whatever might turn out to be significant. If one can hold to this attitude something will—hopefully—evolve that begins to clarify the meaning of what the patient is showing the analyst. Bion developed this point further (Bion, 1970). He recommends eschewing memory and desire, not consciously summoning up memories about the patient or what has previously happened; previous understanding about the patient; desires for him or for the progress of the analysis, or for that matter for oneself.

Bain (1982) stresses the value to the institutional consultant of ignorance and adds that, even if one is not ignorant, a "cultivated ignorance" is essential to the role of the social consultant. In a paper on work done in the Royal National Orthopaedic Hospital (RNOH) in London, I talk of the need to take a fresh look at the situation, to set aside habitual ways of looking at things, to blind oneself to the obvious, to think again (Menzies Lyth, 1982). It is beneficial if the client too can foster these attitudes so that consultant and client together can work towards the emergence of new meanings and appropriate action. In other words, the consultant may—indeed should—encourage the members of the client institution to speak as freely and widely as they can about their work situation, relationships and experiences, something akin to psycho-analytic free association. In the initial exploratory survey of the nursing situation in a general teaching hospital I invited nurses to talk about the presenting problem—difficulties in the deployment of student nurses in practical training—but also invited them to talk about anything at all that seemed to them significant in their experience of nursing (Menzies, 1960; Vol. I, "Social Systems as a Defense Against Anxiety"). This invitation evoked much of the material that led to our deeper understanding of the work and training situation, particularly the anxiety patterns and the socially structured defenses developed to cope with them.

The strain of this way of working is considerable for the consultant, as it is for the analyst. One does not have many props since one has at least temporarily pushed to the back of one's mind such conventionally useful things as memory, consciously set objectives and theory; they are not to be directly used for guidance in the field. One exists most of the time in a state of partially self-imposed ignorance which may feel profound, frightening and painful. One needs faith that there is light at the end of the tunnel even when one does not have much hope.

If one can hold on to ignorance and evenly suspended attention, meaning will probably emerge and one will experience the reward of at least one mystery or part of a mystery solved, uncertainty and doubt dispersed. But this will not last, especially if one communicates one's understanding to the client who accepts one's interpretation and is prepared and able to proceed again into the unknown. One is thrown back on ignorance, uncertainty and doubt and must experience the process all over again. One may need to give a good deal of support to the client to go along with the process, especially a client who is accustomed to using the "expert" and expects him to produce a definitive answer quickly. If one resists this pressure, one may be bitterly attacked as though one is delinquently withholding goodies to which the client is entitled. Failing that, the client clutches at straws and magical unrealistic answers.

I have often had the experience while consulting with a group that I was the only person in the room who did not know what was going on. The group members "knew," that is, had abandoned ignorance. Fortunately, clients can identify with the model presented by the consultant and learn to work this way so that collaboration in the process becomes progressively easier and more rewarding to both parties. Patients are similar. A new patient may ask an analyst to tell him or her what to do about a problem or how to use an interpretation; experienced patients know, even if they may not like it, that they must take responsibility and work out what to do for themselves.

This introduces another way that psychoanalytically oriented consultancy runs in parallel with psychoanalysis—the initiative for taking appropriate action as insights and meaning evolve lies with the client. Just as patients make their own life decisions without advice or suggestion, so clients make their own decisions about change and are responsible for implementing them. Ultimately they must take the responsibility and face the consequences. The analyst's or consultant's responsibility lies in helping insights develop, freeing thinking about problems, helping the client to get away from unhelpful methods of thinking and behaving, facilitating the evolution of ideas for change, and helping the client to bear the anxiety and uncertainty of the change process. This latter feature is notable in psychoanalytically orientated consultants and others whose work has been influenced by them. They stay around. Other consultants without that orientation are more likely to do their investigations and send their report to their clients—a blue-print of what they should do about their problems and leave the clients to do what they can on their own. This seems to happen surprisingly often, as for example, in the repetitive attempts to re-organize the British Health and Social Services. It is unlikely to be effective: clients are left on their own with what may well be the most difficult part of the task—the implementation of change. It would be unthinkable to give patients a detailed report on their psycho-pathology, instruct them as to what to do about it and send them away to do it.

I find it as unthinkable to leave a client institution in a similar situation. Serious change in a social institution inevitably involves re-structuring the social defense system, and this implies freeing underlying anxieties until new defenses or, better, adaptations and sublimations are developed (Jaques, 1955; Vol. I, "On the Dynamics of Social Structure"). There is a sense in which all change is felt as catastrophic even when it is rationally recognized as for the better, since it threatens the established and familiar order and requires new attitudes and behavior, changes in relationships and a move into a comparatively unknown future (Bion, 1970). Some of the changes that institutions make actually bring their members into more direct and overt contact with difficult tasks and stressful situations than before. This is a potentially maturational experience for the members who "learn" to confront reality and deal with it more effectively. But while the change is taking place the problem of containment is central: the presence of someone who can give strength and support, help manage the anxiety, continue the process of developing insight and help define the exact nature of desirable changes.

I am indebted to Bain for helping me formulate my ideas on the function of the consultant who follows a dynamic approach to institutional practice (Bain, 1982). He states that the institutional consultant must concern himself with three kinds of analysis: role analysis, structure analysis and work culture analysis.

Of these work culture analysis appears the most closely related to psychoanalysis. It considers such things as attitudes and beliefs, patterns of relationships, traditions, the psycho-social context in which work is done and how people collaborate in doing it. A second look, however, may show that both roles and structure are infiltrated and partially determined by dynamics familiar to psychoanalysis. For example, the content of roles is partially determined by projection systems which contribute to the view taken by themselves and others of the incumbents of the different roles and of the roles themselves. Anxieties about one's capacity to do one's job may be projected downwards into subordinates and their roles. This is linked with a tendency to arrogate their capacities so that the subordinates' capacities are underestimated and their roles diminished. Projection of one's capacities upwards also takes place along with an expectation that one's superiors will take over one's responsibilities, so that anxiety about one's capacity to do one's job properly is relieved. Anxieties about whether one's subordinates are capable and trustworthy—partly arising from one's own projections—may lead to unduly narrow and rigid prescription of their roles and to unnecessarily close supervision. The effects of such attributions can be seen in roles at all levels in a structure as was found in the nursing service of the general teaching hospital the author studied (Menzies, 1960; Vol. I, "Social Systems as a Defense Against Anxiety"). But they are probably most obvious in the lowest rung of the hierarchy where the role content may be well below the capacity of the workers. Bain found this strikingly in his work in Baric, a computer processing company, as I did among student nurses in the general teaching hospital. Similar factors influence structure: diminution of the content of roles may lead to too many levels in the hierarchy with people doing jobs that people below them could easily do, and to too many supervisors.

This three-pronged analysis may seem very different from what goes on in psychoanalysis, which may appear to be more analogous to work culture analysis. I do not think this is so, however. Psychoanalysis is directly concerned with the patient's internal world as he or she shows it to the analyst. This internal world consists of images and phantasies—conscious and unconscious—of other people, the self and inter-personal relationships, of roles and role relationships, all of which exist within a structure. It is a social system, an imaginary institution. Psychoanalytic exploration of this internal world changes it, that is, the patient's personality. The internal changes are reflected in changed relationships with the external world. For example, analysis of internal role systems leads to changes in the roles the patient operates and how he or she operates them. Fenichel (1946) writes that social institutions arise through the efforts of human beings to satisfy their needs, but social institutions then become external realities comparatively independent of individuals that affect the structure of the individuals themselves. Participation in a psychoanalysis, like participation in other social institutions, changes the structure of the personality.

There are also differences between psychoanalytic practice and institutional practice which limit the full and direct transfer of method from the one to the other and require variations and modifications. For example, patients take action in the external world themselves, and cope with the way they and the changes within them affect and are affected by real people and situations that facilitate or inhibit these efforts. If and when an institution uses a consultant to facilitate institutional change, individuals or even small groups with whom the consultant is working cannot usually take decisions or initiate action on their own. Other people and groups need to be involved if understanding and insights are to grow and relevant action take place. The work must usually range fairly widely throughout the institution. Significant changes in the designated problem area require counter-balancing changes in surrounding areas if they are to be effective and lasting.

Bain found in Baric that the level of the operators' role could only be raised if the structure and other roles were also changed, with less supervision, fewer supervisory roles and so on (Bain, 1982). Similarly in the RNOH a significant change in the nursery nurses' role had to be balanced by change in the roles of the staff nurse and ward sister. They delegated more patient and family care to the nursery nurses and themselves became more involved in management, technical nursing, support and training. The nursery nurses took over certain aspects of the social worker's role in family care, while the latter did less work directly with families and trained and supported the nurses. Work was done with other wards and departments both to help develop attitudes consistent with those in the Cot Unit itself and to assist in desirable role and structure modification.

Role analysis, structure analysis and work culture analysis need to be explicit and related to one another at all stages of the work if real and lasting progress is to be made. Too often in my experience in institutional consultancy one or two types of analysis are neglected and the consultant concentrates on the others. Psychoanalytically orientated workers may, and often do, concentrate exclusively on some form of work culture analysis oriented to achieving significant attitude change. They go into an institution to conduct sensitivity or support groups, usually for "carers" like nurses or social workers. Their aim is to increase the sensitivity of the carers to their clients and themselves and to help them bear the stress of their work. It is not difficult to achieve such changes within the group itself. The carers want to be sensitive and less stressed. The problem is that the carers often return to a work situation where roles, structure and work culture are changed minimally, if at all, and this may make it impossible for them to deploy their changed attitudes in changed behavior. The danger is that people become disappointed, frustrated and disillusioned. Attitudes change back in defense against these feelings, and in line with the demands of the institutional system. Or people can no longer tolerate the system and leave. The consultants and what they stand for may be discredited.

The author's role in two therapeutic communities caring for delinquent and deprived children illustrates this point. I was a management consultant. My task was continuously to explore with the staff the therapeutic impact of the roles and structure in the institution and help modify them so that the institution as a whole would become more therapeutic. Therapy was understood by the staff and by me as the impact on the children of the whole institution and not only activities more usually regarded as therapeutic or developmental, such as counselling or education; staff sensitivity was not enough. Work culture analysis was not neglected but was carried out mainly by another consultant, who particularly handled staff attitudes and relations to children, their own feelings and distress. The division was not rigid and, perhaps strangely, it worked. Too many therapeutic communities appear to lack sufficient awareness of role and structural factors; their therapeutic impact, therefore, is diminished because these are inadequate (Menzies Lyth, 1985).

By contrast, consultants who lack a psychoanalytic orientation may well confine themselves to role and structure without sufficient understanding of the contribution to them of unconscious content and dynamics. They may suggest changes in role and structure without the backing of the requisite changes in work culture. Indeed, attention to work culture might not support these ideas about role and structure. Consequently nothing effective may happen. For example, there seems to be an urgent need for more work-culture analysis if real improvement is to be effected in the British Health and Social Services.

Psychoanalytic practice and consultancy differ in ways that mean the consultant may not be able to follow Freud's precepts fully. The psychoanalyst refrains as far as possible from contact with the patient outside the analysis and with his or her relatives and friends. The analyst is to be as much as possible a mirror that reflects the patient back to him- or herself and shows nothing about the analyst. This practice is recommended for the protection of both patients and the analysis, to give freedom for fantasy and to help the patients follow their own directions. Desirable as this is in institutional consultancy, it is possible to a much more limited extent. One usually has to function in the client's territory so that one shares activities and places in a perfectly ordinary way: coffee, drinks, meals, canteen, lavatories and so forth. It is inevitably more sociable and it may be difficult to fend off ordinary human curiosity about oneself without seeming, or even being, offensive. One can hardly avoid contact with spouses or relatives especially in residential institutions. But, one has to try to keep one's distance, not to get too drawn in, and, of course, not to let one's own or one's clients' social feelings interfere with the work. Holding the balance of one's social and work relationships is often a problem. One may be perceived as being too much in the pockets of certain people. Who does one eat with in the canteen, and why? Does one mix enough socially with the lowest level workers? It is conventional for higher managers to entertain outside consultants—dinner in the Matron's flat, not the student nurses' canteen. One has to wend one's way carefully through these intricacies, noting that they are likely to have an effect on the transference and counter-transference and on one's own transference to the client. It is important to understand what that effect is.

Transference is still an important concept, even if it gets a bit cluttered by the greater real presentation of oneself to one's clients and the wider view one has of clients than of patients. To further the work, it may be essential to draw such transference phenomena into work culture analysis, especially if they lead to suspicion of bias. This will not necessarily be easy or welcome. Careful attention to the counter-transference is also necessary, one's own bias may make careful observation and deduction more difficult.

Here another difference between psychoanalysis and consultancy is helpful. One need not work alone. An institutional consultancy may, in any case, be too big an undertaking for one person. The advantages of having at least one colleague are inestimable. It is not really advisable to work alone. It is an old Tavistock Institute principle that it takes a group to study a group. At least, a person working alone needs his or her own consultant "to come home to." As regards transference and counter-transference, two people can be very useful in helping each other sort them out, check and re-check them and disentangle each other from relationships that interfere with work or from attitudes inconsistent with consultancy. Several times after I had done a long continuous spell of work in the RNOH I would become too possessive of the children and too identified with the hospital. I would begin to talk about "our children." My colleague, Tim Dartington, said, "They are not our children, you know." That was all that was necessary to remind me of my place. Two or more people give added richness to interpretation of the data. Their perspectives are different, their field experiences are different since they do not always work alongside each other. Their relationships with different members of the client institution are different. Two people are much more than twice one in my experience. I have done a great deal of useful work in cars, buses and trains going to and from the field with colleagues, and am grateful to them for the insights they have helped to develop.

Note-taking and keeping of records are another example of differences. Freud discouraged the analyst from making notes during sessions since it would involve selection of data and would interfere with evenly suspended attention. Having a colleague in the field allows other possibilities. One can split the roles, one person conducting the discussion with evenly suspended attention while the other takes notes, inevitably selectively. But selective notes may be useful afterwards in conjunction with memory from evenly suspended attention in recording significant aspects of what went on and keeping track of the vast amount of data one collects in the field.

Then there is the question of reports. I have already criticized the practice of sending the blue-print type of report to clients. However, reports are useful in certain forms and in certain settings. A written report may be a useful mnemonic. It would never by choice, however, be my first report. Its contents would initially be reported verbally in a face-to-face situation where one could work with the effect of the conclusions on the client, tackle resistance to their acceptance as a means to further understanding, stand corrected and amend them if one was wrong. The final document would probably be a distillation of joint work between the client and oneself. This was done regularly in one of the children's communities, the Cotswold Community. I worked there on two consecutive days a month and sent a "field-note" outlining where I thought we had got to and giving them something to work on by themselves until my next visit. I had trust and respect for that particular client and felt this was a safe and profitable way of working.

A complication is that one may be obliged to write reports, for example, if one is being financed by a research grant. In the RNOH we had to submit annual and final reports to the Department of Health and Social Security who financed the study. The same principle applied. The reports crystallized discussions with the Project Steering Committee and other people in the hospital and were approved by them before being sent. The question of confidentiality is implicit in this and also affects wider publication. As a rule one cannot effectively disguise an institution. One's clients are literate and interested in themselves and entitled to be told where the work will be published. Results can only be professionally and ethnically published when contents have been agreed and consent given for publication. Sometimes one cannot publish.

The end of a consultancy is rather like the end of an analysis. One needs to work through termination to ensure that the patient or client will be able to manage alone. For patients this means more than simply sustaining the gains that have been made or solving the problem originally brought. It means that they can continue to make progress on their own, through having "learned" a method of tackling problems which will survive the departure of the analyst or consultant and facilitate creative developments in the future. In the RNOH after we left the ward sister* and her staff re-organized the care of latency children in a unit separate from the Cot Unit where we had worked together. The exciting thing was that this was not a slavish copy of the model we had developed together but a different model realistically related to the needs of latency children and taking into account the differences in resources, notably

*The head nurse in a ward.

that while all Cot Unit staff were permanent the latency unit was mainly staffed by transitory student nurses.

The institutional consultant like the psychoanalyst evolves principles—or theories—about healthy functioning. Principles for the individual and the institution have much in common: avoidance of the use of regressed defenses, more adaptation and sublimation, full deployment of the individual's capacities and creativity. Such principles act as a useful guideline when one is diagnosing the nature of the problem in an institution. They give some indication of the direction beneficial change might take. Objectives to work towards are joint exploration of the current situation, sharing the results of the exploration, helping the client accept the reality of his situation, working through resistance and helping the client move towards appropriate action.

An example of consultancy which used such background principles for diagnosis and objective setting and which resulted in successful moves towards change in the directions indicated by the principles concerns the care of children up to 4 years old in the Cot Unit of the RNOH (Menzies Lyth, 1982). The problem was to develop care methods which would sustain and develop in a healthy way the child patients' capacity for making attachments and satisfying relationships. The principles used derived from the work of Bowlby (1969). Briefly, the capacity to develop lasting and meaningful relationships develops in accordance with the opportunity the child, particularly the very young child, has to form secure attachments.

The good ordinary family provides an excellent opportunity where the young child is likely to form a focal intense attachment, usually, but not always, with his or her mother. Additional usually less intense attachments are formed with others including father, siblings, grandparents, other relatives and friends, the attachment circle expanding as the child gets older. Moreover, the people in the circle of attachment are attached to each other, and so provide models of attachment with which to identify. A child not only loves his or her mother as she is experienced but identifies with father loving mother, and extends the concept of the male loving the female. Fortunately for our joint work, these principles were also accepted by most of the hospital staff, especially those with whom we worked most closely, and who were most directly concerned with the care of the children—nurses, teachers, social workers, the pediatrician and the surgeons. They showed a degree of concern and understanding of children's needs which in our experience was quite unusual in children's institutions.

We defined a mutually acceptable objective for change in the Cot Unit as being to establish a care-situation as close as possible to that provided by a good ordinary home. There was, of course, an "easier said than done" aspect to that and it took a long time to work out in precise detail what could practicably be done in the hospital setting. Attention had to be given to a great deal of hostility and resistance to the changes especially from people outside the Cot Unit but affected by it.

The unit was as near to the size of an ordinary family as possible. The Cot Unit was already as small as practicable in staffing terms: twelve cots of which occupancy on average was about 7–8. The fairly low cot occupancy was due partly to the policy of one surgeon who quite rightly believed, before any objective developed with us, that the best place to nurse a child was at home whenever the physical condition permitted it, and that was for a good part of the treatment. The resident staff on the Cot Unit consisted of only one staff nurse, three nursery nurses, a nursery teacher and a social worker. As hospital wards go, this one was excellent. Ward furniture could also be moved around at the discretion of the staff and families to create semi-enclosed still smaller units.

The major sub-objective was to sustain the basic attachment to the mother as far as possible by helping the mother to optimize her presence with the child. We set the objective as "optimize" because in the long-stay situation and often very far away from home, it was not possible for the mother to be present 24 hours of every day as is usually possible in a short-stay setting. Hospital staff came to accept as part of their duties the need to work out with each mother, child and family what was best for them. The hospital was open to all family members, relatives and friends, and this helped to sustain other important attachments. Very importantly, the mother could bring other children to the hospital with her which certainly increased her presence, and could bring other adults who helped while away the often dreary hours in the hospital. Her presence was also sustained through the careful exploration of the mother's role with her child in the hospital, keeping her as much in her normal role as possible, the child's main caretaker, protector, authority, playmate, comforter. This was quite hard for the nursery nurses who had gone into their profession to look after children and who now devoted a great part of their time to sustaining and supporting mothers who were looking after their children themselves. But it was not too difficult to work with their resistance and to teach and support them while they developed a new, more demanding and more rewarding, role as the main support for the family's own care of its hospitalized child.

However, all that could be and was done to sustain maternal and family presence was not enough completely to avoid times when no close member of the family was present. At worst, there were some children from overseas whose mothers were never present and other family members rarely if at all. For all children, but especially for those children, it was important to provide an alternative attachment figure from the hospital staff. A case-assignment system was developed whereby each patient and family were assigned their own nursery nurse who worked with the family to care for the child when they were there and took over the sole care of the child when they were not there, or in parts of the hospital where family were not allowed to be present such as in operating theaters just prior to operations or in the early stages of care in the post-operative recovery ward. Careful plans were made for re-assignment when the assigned nurse was off-duty or absent on escort duty. The secondary assigned nurses were part of the close attachment system of the unit and were already well known to the child and family. Care-taking never became indiscriminate, a care method only too common in children's institutions and fatal to the development and maintenance of the capacity for attachment and making healthy relationships.

One last point on attachment. The small size of the Unit and the permanence of its staff set up a situation rather like that of the good ordinary family; staff developed strong attachments among themselves which not only provided good models of attachment for the children but facilitated their becoming secondary attachment figures when necessary. It was quite like the ordinary family circle where father, grandmother, aunts and friends provide good secondary attachment figures and care-takers in the absence of the mother.

Boundary control is another matter of great importance in children's institutions which too often seem totally unaware of its significance. The good ordinary family usually guards its physical and psychological boundaries quite carefully, regulating both entry and exit and particularly protecting its children from unwarranted intrusion and from excessive freedom to go out. A system of boundary control was gradually developed whereby no-one came into the Unit who did not have business there. This move by the ward sister provoked perhaps more hostility and resistance than any other single move; people took as a personal criticism or even an insult the general view that too many visitors, often strangers, were not good for the children, however kindly they were. Careful boundary crossing procedures were also developed for those staff from outside the Unit who did have business with the children. For example, when a doctor visits a child in an ordinary home, the mother or another family adult accompanies the doctor to the child and stays with them; so in the hospital anyone coming in to do something for a child made contact through his mother, another family care-taker, the assigned nurse or all of them.

The objective of this paper has been to show that it is possible to help institutions to develop ways of working that embody some of the principles of healthy institutional functioning, and that this can be done by consultancy that embodies both psychoanalytical principles and an understanding of institutional functioning. This possibility gives cause for some optimism that institutions can be helped to better ways of functioning that make them more healthy and rewarding environments for their members and also contribute to their personal maturation and development.

References

Almansi, R.J. 1986. Review of "Freud and Anthropology," Psychological Issues Monograph 55, by E.R. Wallace. *Journal of the American Psychoanalytic Association*, 34:725–28.

Bain, A. 1982. *The Baric Experiment*. London: Tavistock Institute Occasional Paper No.4.

Bion, W.R. 1961. *Experiences in Groups and Other Papers*. London: Tavistock Publications; New York: Basic Books.

———.1970. *Attention and Interpretation*. London: Tavistock Publications.

Bowlby, J. 1969. *Attachment and Loss*. London: Hogarth Press.

Fenichel, O. 1946. *The Psycho-Analytic Theory of Neurosis*. London: Routledge and Kegan Paul.

Freud, S. 1911–15. *Papers on Technique*. Standard Edition Vol.12.

Jaques, E. 1955. "Social Systems as a Defence Against Persecutory and Depressive Anxiety." In *New Directions in Psycho-Analysis*, edited by M. Klein, P. Heimann and R.E. Money-Kyrle. London: Tavistock Publications; New York: Basic Books.

Menzies, I.E.P. 1960. "A Case-Study in the Functioning of Social Systems as a Defence Against Anxiety: A Report on a Study of the Nursing Service of a General Hospital." *Human Relations*, 13:95–121.

———. 1970. *The Functioning of Social Systems as a Defence Against Anxiety*. London: Tavistock Institute of Human Relations, Pamphlet No.3.

Menzies Lyth, I. 1982. *The Psychological Welfare of Children Making Long Stays in Hospital*. London: Tavistock Institute Occasional Paper No.3.

———. 1985. "The Development of the Self in Children in Institutions." *Journal of Child Psychotherapy*, 11:49–64.

*Eric Trist, Gurth Higgin, Hugh Murray
and Alexander Pollock*

The Assumption of Ordinariness as a Denial Mechanism

Innovation and Conflict in a Coal Mine*

This paper describes and analyzes an episode in an action-research project undertaken by the Tavistock Institute of Human Relations in the British coal-mining industry that continued, with interruptions, for eight years during the 1950s. It shows how what Bion (1961) called the "hatred of learning through experience" all but defeated an innovative collaborative endeavor by occasioning conflicts in which management and labor regressed to traditional adversarial positions.

The innovation in question introduced a new form of work organization, known as "composite working." This occurred spontaneously in three different coalfields and heralded what Emery (1978) has called a "new paradigm of work." It offers an alternative to technocratic bureaucracy in which self-regulating, multi-skilled work groups become building blocks for a more democratic and efficient organizational form. In so doing it rejects the technological imperative and seeks to find the best match between, or, in systems language, the joint optimization of, the social and technical system. It has therefore become known as the "socio-technical" approach. Under suitable conditions it leads to higher productivity and higher job satisfaction than conventional work systems.

The socio-technical approach has now made some headway in all western industrialized countries, but against enormous resistance. This fact is not surprising, as it runs counter to long-held beliefs about how work should be organized (Trist et al., 1963) and disturbs the socially structured psychological defenses (Jaques, 1953) that managers and workers alike have built up to adapt

*A shortened and rewritten version of chapters 19–22 in Trist et al., *Organizational Choice*. London: Tavistock Publications, 1963.

to conventional organizational forms. These constitute key elements in their identity (Holland, 1985).

The colliery was a village pit on which the community was totally dependent. The National Coal Board had already threatened to close it, but closure had been averted by a major organizational innovation in one of the seams—the Manley—which for the first time introduced composite working into semi-mechanized longwalls, then the prevailing form of mining.

The success of the Manley innovation was phenomenal—in productivity, quality of output and operating costs. It was no less so as regards earnings and work satisfaction, and in relationships among teams and between labor and management. There was virtually no voluntary absenteeism and accidents and sickness were halved. A major factor in this success was that component groups, which were self-selected, had previously worked together on "shortwalls"—a pre-longwall technology in which composite working was traditional.

Narrative

THE CHARACTER OF THE DRIFT

The episode now to be described reports the course of events in the opening up of a new production unit in an old colliery. In its early life the geological conditions were difficult in the extreme and in the team, which was a new group put together for extraneous reasons, the majority had no previous experience of the technology or the method of working. Geological and socio-psychological circumstances aggravated each other.

The unit or panel comprised the first two faces of a new drift—a tunnel sloping down from the surface to the coal area. Work began, therefore, near the outcrop, a major factor in creating difficult mining conditions, which improved when the faces got farther in and cover became more substantial. Coal height was 28", above which were 4" of ramble (loose stone). The panel consisted of two 80-yard longwall faces, east and west of a main roadway. Face conveyor belts fed onto a main conveyor which discharged into a hopper from which tubs were filled. Face supports were wooden props and steel straps, with collapsible steel chocks which reinforced the roof support system. This was the customary set-up before faces became completely mechanized. The coal was won by pneumatic picks rather than undercut by electrical coal cutters as it was on the Manley. This put a premium on hewing experience and skill which varied widely among faceworkers.

The drift was separate from the other workings of the colliery and the double unit was a new enterprise expected to produce coal equal to 25 percent of the previous output of the whole mine, whose life it would considerably extend. The venture was based on the very imperfect understandings of the Manley innovation, a main cause of the nearly complete failure which occurred.

A complement of 51 faceworkers was planned with six spare men to provide substitutes in case of absences. The hewing task, carried out over one or two shifts, embraces breaking coal from the face with pneumatic picks, filling it onto the face conveyor and setting roof supports as the face is cleared. The "hewers" are followed on the next shift by the "pullers" who advance the face conveyors and the steel chocks. At the same time the "stonemen" enlarge and advance the three roadways (tunnels) between and at the end of the faces on the panel.

In composite working all team members are multi-skilled (in this case in hewing, pulling and stonework); they can thus exchange shifts and practice task continuity (deploying themselves as necessary to carry on with succeeding tasks); they share equally in a common pay note. Teams are self-regulating and practice what we called "responsible autonomy" (Trist and Bamforth, 1951).

Both management and men expected "teething troubles," but it was hoped that the advantages of composite working would begin to be realized within a few weeks. No-one expected the teething troubles to last seven months, or that eleven months would elapse before the planned level of output was regularly maintained.

One of the conditions of the composite agreement was that the men should make themselves up into sets of the required number. In the present case this condition was waived by both management and lodge (trade union local branch). The colliery was in process of reorganization and a number of under-ground workers were becoming redundant. Management and lodge agreed to draft these men into the new team, together with those who had been engaged on the development of the drift.

A meeting of the team was held by the lodge a few days before the start to acquaint the men with the agreement, to allocate them provisionally to tasks and shifts, and to appoint team captains for different task groups. Eight men volunteered for pulling and ten for stonework, the remaining 33 being allo-cated to hewing. Three team captains were elected. Several men expressed anxiety lest they were condemning themselves to permanent nightshift and received assurance that after a week or two it would be possible to start rotating shifts.

Representatives of the lodge, together with the three team captains, then met with management to agree on final details. Although there had been a vague expectation that three shifts would be worked, it was decided to have only two, concentrating coal-getting on the dayshift (9 a.m.–4:30 p.m.) and doing pulling and stonework on the nightshift (4:30 p.m.–midnight). The 33 men on the hewing shift were to be deployed 16 to each face, with one man in the main roadway, while on the nightshift there were to be four pullers to each face, six stonemen in the main roadway and two in each of the face-end roadways. There were three deputies (supervisors) all of whom came from machine-cut rather than hewing faces. In charge was an undermanager recently appointed to the pit.

THE FIRST WEEK: INITIAL FAILURE

Before going in on the first morning, the 33 men on the hewing shift allocated themselves to places by cavilling. Cavilling is a time-honored practice for the allocation of men and groups to work places within a seam on a chance basis— one was more likely to receive justice at the hands of chance than of management. More than two-thirds of these men had little or no recent experience with either longwall working or the use of pneumatic picks. The lack of hewing experience soon began to show, and it became obvious that the target advance of 4 feet 6 inches was not going to be achieved.

The manager visited the face and outlined the immediate requirements for stabilizing the situation. From this point on he retained direct control and ordered the concentration of effort on one face per shift. But managerial attention was no substitute for experience in a team confronted by bad conditions. In the early morning of Saturday, 20 yards closed completely and it was decided to abandon both faces and win them out afresh. This took a fortnight.

A SECOND ATTEMPT GETS INTO DIFFICULTIES

The manager now held a meeting with twelve of the men, at which several decisions were made. A token foreshift of hewers was arranged for the breaking-in task; supervisory reinforcements were granted; and the production target was reduced. The manager also decided not to hold the team to the wages agreement but to pay a day-wage.

The pattern of advance in the seven subsequent weeks until the next crisis was one of concentration on alternate faces each day. During this period conditions remained bad.

According to the deputies, the differences in effectiveness among the men on the hewing shift were too great to continue much longer. The men expressed similar feelings and there was some belief that not all the men were pulling their weight. This applied not only to the quantity of coal hewn but also to the quality of timbering. These problems gave rise to tension between as well as within shifts. The additional supervisors allocated to the hewing shift officially had the sole task of instruction, but they were subjected to pressure to reinforce the hewing so that little progress was made in training men in the use of pneumatic picks.

THE ISSUE OF RECONSTITUTING THE TEAM

It was with some knowledge of this background that the manager met the team captains on the Saturday of week 4. He asked them to dissolve the existing team so that the men could choose a new one from among all those working in the drift. Would they meet him again on Monday after discussing his proposal at the lodge meeting? To agree would have meant to accept a modification of the sacrosanct cavilling rules. Conveniently, the agenda for the lodge meeting was full and no time was found to discuss such a critical issue. A message was sent to the manager, who had heard of the intention to cavil for shifts. In reply he insisted on experienced pullers staying for the time being with their task. If cavils were drawn for shifts and inexperienced men allocated to pulling, he would stop the face and disband the team. The lodge decided that two committee men should attend a meeting on Wednesday between the manager and the team captains.

At that meeting no agreement was reached. The manager repeated his view that dissension was hampering progress, adding that he knew that some men wanted to leave the team and that there were others whom the team would like to drop. Would they settle this? For his part, he was willing to provide two extra hewers on dayshift and two extra pullers and one stoneman on nightshift, to be paid for by him and not out of the common note. Union officers visited the face for a "pep talk" with the team, but decisions were left to the lodge meeting the following Sunday.

At this meeting the chairman outlined the events of the previous two weeks, and gave the manager's view. The manager, he said, seemed reasonable; the men for their part, had a responsibility too—"we have to put our own house in order." The formal purpose of the meeting was to consider the manager's suggestion that the team reform itself, but this topic, with its implication of discarding members, was put aside. The chairman first presented the situation in its wider setting as seen by the lodge committee, there being three considerations: the nature of the agreement, the importance of the drift to the life of the pit and the present position as a test of the new type of agreement.

The chairman then moved to the question of team changes and stressed the need to avoid hasty judgments about people's worth. In the case of men who wished to come off the team of their own accord, there was nothing the union could do to stop them, but those who left the team would have to take what jobs could be found for them elsewhere in the pit, which might not be particularly well paid.

On the question of dropping men, some of those present who came from other parts of the pit expressed surprise that inequality of contribution should be regarded as something to worry about and cited their own teams as examples. It was pointed out that in those teams the men had chosen each other and had therefore accepted these differences in advance, whereas on this team the men had been placed together.

Five older men left the team and were transferred. The management expressed the view that they had left because the younger men had been reproaching them with failing to keep up. This was unlikely but is an instance of management's perception of the nature and causes of the dissension. At the same time two of the younger men from the dayshift left the pit and the industry and another went off sick, returning only to light work. The team was thus reduced by eight, six of whom were replaced by the six spare men in the drift, who were not replaced. Though volunteers were called for, none was forthcoming.

CRISIS AND RESOLUTION

THE MANAGER ENFORCES THE AGREEMENT

For the three weeks following the lodge meeting in week 6 things remained quiet, mainly because of the Christmas and New Year holidays, though two more men left the industry and informal shift exchanges began. A man wanting to change his shift had to find someone on the other shift with whom to change. Some of the hewers were accused of monopolizing the dayshift and capitalizing on their lack of experience to stay on it.

Though within the hewing shift the feeling remained that certain men were not doing their share, this feeling was never directed at specific individuals.

The first full week after the holiday period (week 9) began quite well and on the Monday the hewing shift, with two men short, cleared off the coal with the exception of 20 yards; they were not able to keep up this pace.

The manager had a talk with the team captains: things were not going well; he had done all he could; from now (week 9) on he intended to pay strictly in accordance with the agreement. Disappointed that none of his efforts had had much effect, he believed there was still dissension in the team over differences in qualifications, ability and night-shift, which the men would not admit and which was the main cause of lack of progress. Following this announcement of his intention to pay in accordance with the agreement, he visited the face, criticizing the timbering, which was bad in places, and putting his foot down on finding experienced pullers on the hewing shift. His insistence that three of these men return to nightshift caused particular dismay.

Towards the end of this week, and more so in the next, conversation centered on the level of pay to be expected under a strictly interpreted agreement. There were rumors about people leaving, though no-one could ever say who, and only one man gave notice. The others, as the Thursday of week 10 drew nearer, contented themselves with speculating about other jobs. The present level of earnings was little enough, in their view, for the work involved under such bad conditions and anything less would not be worth it. There was also some doubt about whether the agreement was enforceable, given the nature of the conditions. They changed their attitude to management: the manager was now regarded as obstinate in his general attitude and rigid in his insistence on adhering to the original plan; as to the undermanager, "things have got beyond him."

Meanwhile, conditions were once again deteriorating, particularly on the West face. On the Wednesday nightshift (week 10) the manager inspected the West face and decided that conditions were so bad that he would withdraw the men and shorten the face. By allowing the western half to close, he could concentrate on rectifying the support of the eastern half—the 40 yards nearest to the maingate.

The deputies expected things to come to a head on the Thursday when the men found how much their pay had dropped. When they received their pay they were in a state of considerable shock and they went in a body to the office and asked the manager to see four representatives—one from each face and shift. The manager agreed to see three. He refused to discuss paying more and insisted on sticking to the agreement. The shortening of the face meant a reduction in manpower and he asked them to make up a set of 42 from all the men available in the drift. He wanted only experienced pullers on the nightshift for at least the next fortnight, after which they could think about rotating inexperienced men to learn the job. He asked the three men to see him again the next afternoon, hoping that the shortened face would provide the opportunity to get the nine worst men off the team.

To the men, picking a team of 42 or choosing nine to be dropped was the same and could not be allowed. There was a procedure in the cavilling rules for handling such circumstances. The only way open to the manager to achieve his aim within the rules would have been to take the whole set off the face and then to ask for volunteers, of which none would have been forthcoming. As to his view that less work was being done than could be expected, they believed he had misinterpreted the circumstances and had failed to allow for the conditions. Despite his visits to the panel and his action in shortening the West face, they felt he was unaware of how bad conditions had become, especially for the nightshift.

Before the three-man delegation met him again on the Friday one man was replaced as he was thought too prone to agree with the manager; the latter was now told that none of his requests was acceptable and that the whole situation would have to be discussed at the lodge.

THE LODGE ATTITUDE

At the lodge meeting on the Sunday (beginning week 11) the secretary said that the manager had informed him that the West face had been shortened and that it had therefore become necessary to reduce the size of the team. The chairman said that the men in this pit had always been opposed to anything which savored of "survival of the fittest" or anything which could lead to one man being preferred over another "because someone liked the color of his eyes or the way his hair was parted." The cavilling rules had been built up to deal with this and to cover situations of the kind which had arisen. They had to be followed, despite the manager's opinion that the cavilling rules should be "thrown out of the window." He was getting tough and putting the blame on the men. Although 10 percent of the responsibility lay with the men, the manager had been told about conditions but had refused to take notice. If he continued to ignore the facts, the lodge would seek a meeting with higher management. If he refused to arrange this, they would declare a dispute and such a meeting would follow automatically. A fortnight ago the manager had been delighted with the Monday achievement of removing all but 20 yards, but had refused to listen when the difficulties of pulling were described. There was nothing in the agreement which compelled the team to attempt an advance of 4 feet 6 inches; if they felt 3 feet was more within their scope and would give more time for pulling then that was what the team captains should decide. Also, work such as digging chocks out and digging to get them in again fell outside the scope of the agreement. Some of the men raised similar points; these were noted as material with which to approach the manager.

It was then moved and seconded that cavils should be drawn to decide who should leave the team. The chairman thought that the manager had rushed them and proposed the actual procedure be carried over until the next meeting. This was agreed. One of the men remarked that the manager seemed to know a good deal about what went on in the team and that, although he heard things officially from the deputies, some of the men also must have let things slip. The chairman observed that no reasonable man would mistake things said in the heat of the moment for considered opinions, but the manager was not a reasonable man. It was agreed that no-one should see the manager unless a member of the lodge committee was present.

In the following week (week 11) the lodge committee met the manager without reaching agreement. Nevertheless, the manager felt that at least each side had stated its case and had disagreed without "getting at each other's throats." During this week the Area Labour Relations Officer made an unofficial visit to the pit and looked around the drift. There was a further meeting in week 12 between the lodge committee and the manager when the question of pay was again raised and again refused, but the manager and members of the committee agreed to visit the drift together to see both hewing and pulling. A lodge meeting was held to report progress, the committee announcing that if they were "unable to get any sense out of the manager" they would be prepared to withdraw labor from the drift, "even if this meant jeopardizing the output of the colliery."

During the three weeks of negotiation output was low. In week 12 some of the pullers decided that they had had enough of continuous nightshift and unsuccessful canvassing and "put the cavils in" for a change of shifts. That the manager had insisted on leaving experienced pullers on nightshift was discounted; he was not paying enough; they were being imposed upon and had therefore no obligation to stay on nightshift. More resentment was expressed than ever before that some men on dayshift had never been off it and never would be unless a formal procedure prevented evasions. Some dayshift men queried the validity of the cavils but were challenged to bring their queries to the lodge meeting. The deputy agreed to enforce the cavilling allocations by sending home anyone who turned up on the wrong shift.

In the first week of the crisis the feeling about the level of earnings had been one of resentment, mixed with surprise that the manager had chosen to enforce the agreement in the week during which output had been the highest. It was, they said, ironic that the highest output should have produced the lowest pay. The second week's pay was lower still. When this became known the mood changed from resentment to dismay. In the third week, despite earnings which were even lower, the atmosphere became more cheerful. The change, remarked on by both men and deputies, was attributed to the fact that negotiations, however difficult, were still proceeding. This was taken as a sign that a settlement was likely to be reached.

THE NEW AGREEMENT

In week 13 the proposed visits by the manager and members of the lodge committee were made to both shifts and another meeting was held at which the Area Labour Relations Officer was present. Agreement was reached on the following points:

- The rate of payment for output above the basic was increased to an acceptable figure and the manager agreed to make up the wages for weeks 12 and 13 to the level before he enforced the strict agreement.

- The target was reduced by 11 percent to enable the men to accept the task as within their compass.
- The manager made a list of the men he wanted on each shift and it was agreed to follow this for two or three weeks.
- Although the manager had withdrawn the extra men when he enforced the agreement, he now agreed to put two extra men, paid by himself and not off the team's earnings, into the face-end roadways where the work was falling behind.
- Four men were cavilled off the team (which had already lost five because of sickness or transfer to other industries). Contrary to the manager's original intention these four stayed in the drift as "spare men."

This agreement was endorsed by the lodge meeting on the Sunday and work on the Monday of week 14 went noticeably better.

THE EFFECTS OF THE SETTLEMENT

On the first shift under the new arrangements all the coal was taken off and the air-pipes and conveyors moved over into their new positions. Though this was not repeated for both faces for several weeks, the rate of output improved until in week 17 it reached the level planned for the shortened face. In week 22 a start was made on opening out the West face and 10 weeks later this was completed, output just exceeding the planned target. The scheduled target, however, was not consistently maintained until after week 44.

For the first week under the new agreement (week 14) pay just exceeded that for the two previous weeks when it had been made up. Some of the men thought such a difference too small for so marked an increase in output, but the team generally did not accept this as a valid point. Before the actual earnings became known there was a good deal of speculation about what they would be, expressed in the form, "I wonder what he will give us," as if somehow the figure depended upon the goodwill of the manager.

In week 16 some of the men began to exchange shifts on an individual basis, but there was no system of shift rotation over the team as a whole. On the Monday of week 17, 25 men appeared on dayshift instead of the scheduled 19 and there were 6 men short on nightshift. The undermanager and the deputies regarded this as proof that the team could not manage its own shift changes and took over the function themselves, designating the men they wished to see on nightshift and again announcing that anyone coming on the wrong shift would be sent home. In the following week a blackboard was put up at the meeting-place, on which men entered their names for the next week's shifts. The deputies, with the undermanager, rearranged such men as they thought necessary, on the principle that regular nightshift men should be given a spell on dayshift and that less able dayshift men should be brought into the nightshift. In addition, dayshift men with no pulling experience were brought into nightshift every other week to complete the statutory period of training. At this time it was a simple enough matter to allow everyone to alternate night and day.

After the extension of the West face, new men were fed into the team. This complicated attempts at equitable shift rotation and management retained control on an ad hoc basis. Once the face had been extended to its normal length and the team built up to full strength, the rotation of shifts became more systematized. Eighteen men, in three groups of six, rotated weekly over all three shifts, while the remainder alternated two weeks' dayshift with one week's nightshift. Within this broad pattern there was room for private arrangements among individuals. By this time the drift had settled down to regular production.

Things remained at this level for six more months. There was then a drop in coal height of 7 percent and a consequent reduction of output. There was also pressure from the men for a change in rates of pay. Following a precedent from elsewhere in the pit where better rates had been obtained for single units, the manager offered to treat the panel as two separate faces. He still felt that there was some dissension among the men and that such a change might help. The offer was accepted. The team split into two by mutual selection and work on the new basis began, 73 weeks after the opening of the drift.

Analysis

THE ASSUMPTION OF ORDINARINESS

This account has been a chronicle of how things went wrong. Management, lodge and members of the team all assumed that the drift would be an ordinary unit, to be run in the ordinary way and unlikely to experience more than ordinary difficulties. The untenability of this assumption, yet the persistence of behavior based on it, suggest that, in a way they were unable to recognize, those concerned were using the idea of ordinariness as a means of psychological defense against elements in the situation they were unwilling to confront. The principal effect was that the panel was treated throughout as a production unit under difficulties, rather than perceived for what it was—a training and development project working under the stress of a demand for full production. Though the need for support was conceded, the time allowed (8 weeks) was no more than a token period and the underlying assumption manifested itself in a number of ways, especially in the emphasis on coal production as the primary task. Though, in words, the need for training and acquiring experience was acknowledged, preoccupation with output carried the real message of action.

The degree of unreality in assuming ordinariness may be measured by the fact that an inexperienced management and an inexperienced work team were brought together in a novel task under conditions likely to be difficult—especially in the beginning. The undermanager was new to the pit. It was, moreover, his first appointment as an undermanager. The deputies were new to each other and to the men, and the majority of the men were new to any form of longwall working. Though no-one knew the problems likely to arise in developing a hewing panel on composite principles, there was ample precedent for anticipating trouble if the scatter of hewing abilities was too wide. Moreover, plenty of experience was available in the neighborhood to suggest that the roof was likely to be awkward until the faces were farther in from the outcrop—which meant that pulling experience would be at a premium.

All this was known by management and lodge when they entered negotiations. It was known also by the men. Yet it was all disregarded. The pit was under severe pressure to become economic—as soon as possible—and there was a great deal of anxiety about this; hence the preoccupation with production. The Manley composite panels had been successful—beyond expectation and without trouble. The real effort, however, in the Manley negotiations had been on the terms of the agreement. Problems of work organization had been left to take care of themselves. This they had done, in a very remarkable way, but no analysis had been made of the reasons. It was simply taken for granted that such problems would take care of themselves again. Meanwhile, reorganization elsewhere in the colliery had made redundant a considerable number of faceworkers. The lodge sought conditions for their redeployment without the relegation of any from facework status. Moreover, the one piece of "hard news" which had circulated about the Manley was that earnings were high—higher than earnings had ever been in the pit. It was an attractive prospect, therefore, to workers finishing odd jobs in older workings and wondering what might happen to them, to join a new drift and get in on the advantages of the new type of agreement.

This situation led to a feature which was not ordinary about the drift: the team was drafted, not self-selected, with the result that there was no commitment to accepting the differences in skill and experience which were later discovered. Even the safeguard inherent in the traditional procedure for forming teams was dispensed with. One may infer that the pretense that special measures were unnecessary and that unusual risks were justified covered a pervasive fear that the drift would not succeed, with the serious repercussions this would have for the future of the colliery—its death. This is the underneath anxiety, intense in the change situation, which brought about the collusive denial of reality which in turn led to the initial assumption of ordinariness.

TABLE I   Developments in the Drift

Week	Events	M	R	L	T
1	Difficulties too great for unorganized and inexperienced team. Face closes under extremely bad conditions.	—			<20
2	Rewinning.	—			0
3	Rewinning. Manager meets 12 of team: reinforcements granted; production target reduced—alternate face concentration; token third shift of 8 hewers to break in; make up of wages on a day basis.	1			0
4	Poor production progress—conditions still bad. No internal team organization; no permanent team captains; differences in hewing ability cause trouble; face supervisors pressed into working rather than instructing. Manager meets team captains: wants team dissolved and new team picked, eliminating poorest workers.	1	5		<50
5	Manager meets 2 representatives of lodge committee and team captains; no agreement over dropping poorer workers. Manager offers further reinforcements.	2	10		<50
6	Lodge meeting reviews situation, chairman supports manager, holds men back on premature demands for shift changes, warns against hasty judgements over dropping men. 5 volunteers come off (older men).	1	10	5	<50
7	Three younger men leave. 6 spare men make up team, are not themselves replaced. Volunteers called for, none come forward.	—	10	8	<50
8	Christmas holidays. 2 more men leave.	—	10	10	<50
9	Manager loses patience with poor production and inability of the men to sort themselves out. Enforces agreement. Withdraws extra labor. 2 more leavers.	1	0	12	<40
10	Manager shortens West face by half in view of persistent bad conditions. Only 42 men now required. He asks for new team, dropping 9 poorest. Delegation of men refuse to make such judgements; want cavils. Pay under strict agreement drops. Shock and resentment. Manager refuses to pay outside the agreement.	2	0		<30
11	Lodge insists on cavils over the 9 surplus men. Previous support of manager replaced by opposition. Proposal to seek meeting with higher management. If refused by manager, lodge would declare dispute—such a meeting then automatic. Manager and lodge committee meet—no agreement. Area Labour Relations Officer visits pit.	3	0		<30

TABLE 1   *Continued*

Week	Events	M	R	L	T
12	Manager/lodge committee meeting: manager refuses to do anything about pay but agrees to visit day and night shift with representatives of lodge. At subsequent lodge meeting, committee announces intention of withdrawing labor from the drift if manager won't come to terms.	2	0		<30
13	A new agreement is reached between management and lodge with the help of the Area Labour Relations Officer. Wages improved, target reduced, redundant men cavilled off (only 4 left out of 9). Special men to remain in key roles on each shift until difficulties overcome. Two men granted as reinforcements.	2	0		<30
14–17	Face management steps in and creates rotation system. Planned production reached, proportional to shortened face, within three weeks of the settlement.	—	2		<70
18–21	Consolidation of team.	—	2		<70
22–33	West face opened out. Planned target reached for first time in week 33.	—	2		<90
34–43	Fluctuation about planned target.	—	2		<100
44–72	Steady state production.	1	0		=100
73–	The two faces go on separate notes as better prices for single units had been obtained elsewhere in the pit.	—	0		=100

M = Meetings (management/lodge, lodge); R = Reinforcements (cumulative); L = Leavers (cumulative); T = percent production target

THE REACTIONS TO FAILURE

The reactions to what transpired after work began may best be followed from Table 1, which relates the events previously described to the amount of activity induced in wider managerial and negotiating systems and to the levels of reinforcement, leaving, and productivity which characterized different phases in the socio-technical history of the drift.

One might have supposed that the closure of the face at the end of the first week would have given a big enough shock to cause a radical re-appraisal of the whole undertaking. Confrontation of what had happened, however, at a higher level of reality would have meant giving up the assumption of ordinariness. Instead, during weeks 4, 5 and 6 its role as the "chosen" defense was bolstered by a series of measures that attempted to make it work in defiance of

the facts. This is the latent meaning of the generous reinforcements offered by
the manager (equal to one-fifth of the team's strength) and of the extent of his
support by the lodge.

Nevertheless, a split in attitudes and relations was already detectable. At the
same time as giving reinforcement, the manager asked the team to reorganize
itself in a way which brought it into direct collision with the revered cavilling
rules that regulated the relations between management and workers. The men,
perceiving this as an attack, started to go into opposition. This is the negative
side of the collusive process, just as much lacking in task orientation as the
positive side. It led to a type of impasse, familiar in industrial relations, in
which no learning takes place from what is being experienced.

As the illusion wore thin and the impasse became more apparent the men
began to despair (by week 9 a quarter of the team had left), while the manager,
desperate over costs and production and interpreting the men's lack of response
as an act of hostility, enforced the agreement as regards both pay and manpower. This sudden regression to coercive control—punishment-centered bureaucracy in Gouldner's terms (1954:207)—produced the corresponding stereotype of militancy in the men's reaction, and manager and lodge found
themselves in head-on conflict, with a threat of a dispute.

In the terms introduced by Bion (1961) for the description of unconscious
group processes, basic assumption fight/flight (*baF*) had been mobilized and
suffused the behavior of the group. Management and workers fought each other
in common flight from the problems that had to be solved in the real task
situation. In week 12 the mood on both sides changed after the visit of the Area
Labour Relations Officer. In Bion's terms, basic assumption fight/flight had
now been replaced in the emotional life of the group by basic assumption
dependence (*baD*), and in this modality a settlement was reached with the help
of a "wise and benevolent" figure representing the higher authority of the Area
General Manager—an extremely "good object" to everyone in the pit. Within
three weeks there was a dramatic improvement in productive performance with
the target reached in proportion to the shortened face.

The new agreement recognized more of the realities of the situation than had
the original and represents a partial undoing of the assumption of ordinariness, some learning through experience having taken place. On the other hand,
the working group continued in a management-dependent phase for several
months, with the deputies stepping in and making all arrangements for face
deployment and task-shift rotation. This had a reality component in that new
skills and relationships could not be consolidated until the face was opened out
again and the team built up to full strength. Some outside help on matters of
organization was beneficial while task learning proceeded and new members
were being absorbed. Nevertheless, it was 11 months before the production
target was regularly reached. Even after 18 months, when the panel split into

two teams on separate pay notes, there was still doubt in the mind of the manager (and the observations of the research team confirmed this) as to whether the drift teams had attained the cohesive independence of the Manley panels. The original collusive denial of reality and the subsequent pattern of interactions between management, lodge and the working group had impaired, at least for a time, the capacity to develop responsible autonomy.

CORRECTIVE MEASURES

With the situation structured as it was and the process started on the path taken, the subsequent course of events was to a large extent already determined. The available resources were used, the actors in all roles behaving very much according to expectation. As soon as the working group and immediate face management showed themselves unable to contain the situation, representatives of the next largest system (the colliery) stepped in, with the manager taking direct control and the lodge becoming officially involved. When the situation still remained out of hand, the even larger Area system became implicated. Though a settlement was now reached, matters were only put right in the 13th week after much expenditure of emotion and time, serious losses in production and the incurrence of substantial additional costs in rewinning faces, making up wages and remunerating reinforcements. The working group was inhibited from developing responsible autonomy and the whole episode may serve as an illustration that no amount of management from the outside—whether supportive or coercive—can replace effective self-regulation by the primary group.

One may ask what measures not immediately available in the surrounding work culture—since those available were used—might have prevented the situation from developing in such a troublesome manner. To answer this question, one must ask how an assumption of ordinariness might have been prevented in the first place, which is equivalent to asking what might have permitted the negotiating group to provide leadership in the reality rather than the irreality dimension (cf. Lewin, 1935). The view is put forward that members of the negotiating group would have been able to master more of their own anxieties, which represented those of the colliery at large, and so been able to work out a more realistic scheme if they had had a fuller understanding of the reasons for the success of the Manley panels. They would then have known something of the conditions required for effective team work in composite longwall working and would have recognized the serious implications of their absence in the drift. At the same time such a fuller understanding would have demonstrated that it was not impossible to make a plan which would have brought the required conditions into existence. An effective plan, however, would have entailed complete abandonment of the assumption of ordinariness—with its implications that full production was realizable after a brief period of settling in. The drift could then have been set up as a special training and development unit with the prior task of becoming a balanced and cohesive work force as a condition for attempting target production.

Such a step, however, would not have been easy within the norms of the prevailing work culture. These permitted the crisis to be resolved without a dispute and, in the end, a level of production to be reached better than that likely to have been achieved under conventional arrangements. What the prevailing norms did not provide was any precedent, or "tool kit," for analyzing factors in the socio-psychological system in a way which would have broken down the assumption of ordinariness in the starting situation, and avoided the consequent tensions and loss of production.

The negotiations which led to the wages and manning agreement which had been so successful in launching the Manley panels had taken a year to complete, during which the many difficulties encountered had been successfully worked through. Matters of work organization, however, had scarcely been discussed. They were left "in the hands of the tradition" which was trusted to take care of them; that is, it was supposed that organizational matters would remain on familiar ground. In the Manley undertaking they did, as the men in various sub-groups had previously worked together, often on composite short walls, and were in any case self-selected sets. None of this was the case in the drift. New ground, unfamiliar to all, had to be broken.

With the results of both the Manley and the drift to hand, the next job of the research team was to make an explicit formulation of the psychological and sociological aspects of composite longwall working. These yielded a new set of principles which could be used for converting other panels from conventional to composite longwall working.

The Institute had begun its studies of group dynamics in industrial settings by feeding in appropriately timed interventions as the work proceeded. This followed the psychoanalytic tradition and had been successful in projects such as the Glacier Project (Jaques, 1951). This, however, had not been concerned with an order of change that constituted a paradigm shift, as did the change from conventional to composite working in longwall coal-mining.

In such cases the research team has not only to develop an explicit model of the emergent system but to offer it to those concerned who have a cognitive as well as an emotional problem in making the shift. For there is a discontinuity and to encounter the novel casts doubt on familiar maps as well as on deeply held beliefs. The double difficulty that ensues creates confusion which clears up when they can clearly envisage the alternative as an articulated systematic whole and find that it is suitable for them. In the meanwhile, they tend to be trapped in their hatred of learning through experience and usually need intellectual as well as emotional assistance in order to get out of the trap. Otherwise they remain in the grip of such primitive defenses as denial.

The present project points to one set of conditions under which the psychoanalytic model of intervention has to be transcended in action research in organizational settings.

References

Bion, W.R. 1961. *Experiences in Groups.* London: Tavistock Publications; New York: Basic Books.

Emery, Fred. 1978. *The Emergence of a New Paradigm of Work.* Canberra: Centre for Continuing Education, the Australian National University.

Gouldner, A.W. 1954. *Patterns of Industrial Bureaucracy.* Glencoe Ill.: Free Press.

Holland, N. 1985. *The "I."* New Haven and London: Yale University Press.

Jaques, E. 1951. *The Changing Culture of a Factory.* London: Tavistock Publications. Reissued 1987, New York: Garland.

———. 1953. "On the Dynamics of Social Structure." *Human Relations,* 6:3–24.

Klein, M. 1959. "Our Adult World and Its Roots in Infancy." *Human Relations,* 12:291–303.

Lewin, K. 1935. *A Dynamic Theory of Personality.* New York: McGraw-Hill.

Pines, M. (Editor) 1985. *Bion and Group Psychotherapy.* London and Boston: Routledge and Kegan Paul.

Sutherland, J.D. 1985. "Bion Revisited." In *Bion and Group Psychotherapy,* edited by M. Pines. London and Boston: Routledge and Kegan Paul.

Trist, E.L. and K.W. Bamforth. 1951. "Some Social and Psychological Consequences of the Longwall Method of Coal Getting." *Human Relations,* 4:3–38.

Trist, E.L., G.W. Higgin, H. Murray and A.B. Pollock. 1963. *Organizational Choice: Capabilities of Groups at the Coal Face Under Changing Technologies.* London: Tavistock Publications. Reissued 1987, New York: Garland.

John Hill and Eric Trist

Temporary Withdrawal from Work Under Full Employment
The Formation of an Absence Culture*

Introduction

In the decades of full employment following World War II, industry in several western countries became concerned over the high levels of labor turnover and absence. Sample surveys and exit interviews threw little light on how these high levels came about.

A firm in the steel industry, the Park Gate Iron and Steel Company in Sheffield, asked the Institute to find a new way that would help them to reduce their problem with labor turnover and absence. Our response was to try out a process approach—to follow through a cohort of entrants over a four-year period. The company kept meticulous records so that the fact-gathering part of the inquiry did not present much difficulty. The results, however, showed that there were systematic problems to which there were no easy solutions (Hill and Trist, 1953).

The quantitative aspects of the results generated widespread interest and quite a large academic literature, especially in Scandinavia. The qualitative aspects, however, which involved a number of key psychoanalytic concepts, were totally disregarded. They need attention today as much as then.

Following through entrants from the time of joining to the time of leaving yielded what we called "survival curves"—the proportion at any given time who had not left. Though the slope of these curves varied greatly between different firms, they had a general shape. Over the first few weeks or months there was an explosion of leaving which we called the *induction crisis*. The slope of the curve was very steep. Over the next six months to two years the slope became more gentle; this was called the period of *differential transit* when there was an increase in absenteeism. After this the rate of leaving

*A shortened and rewritten version of the original—*Human Relations*, 8:121–52, 1955.

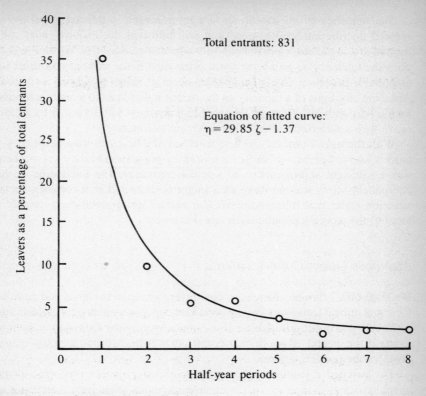

Figure I. Survival curve (Park Gate)

leveled off in what we called the period of *settled connection* when sickness increased. The survival curve for Park Gate is given in Figure I.

As contrasted with labor turnover, absences are a "stayer" phenomenon. One of the uses of absence is to provide a means of temporary withdrawal from the stress of continuing in, as distinct from breaking, a work relationship.

The group examined were all subject to the same broad socio-economic conditions during the four years' service studied. Detailed records made it possible to examine the forms of absence for each of the 289 individuals in the stayer group. These forms were classified as absences due to accidents; certified sickness; uncertified sickness; other reasonable explanation; and no reasonable explanation. The data showed the familiar pattern of monthly fluctuations not significantly different from random, superimposed upon seasonal variations which could be allowed for.

The tendency to go absent, by whatever means, produced a positively skewed distribution whose mode and tail indicated the majority who conformed to a social norm and the minority who deviated from it. We then asked: does the tendency to go absent more often than is the custom constitute an unalterable pattern or do certain changes occur as length of service increases? Are there any signs of a capacity on the part of individuals to learn to maintain themselves with less frequent recourse to temporary withdrawal, i.e., to improve their relationship with their employing institution?

With the overall annual absence level varying no more than between 5.5 percent and 6.5 percent of shifts for a working population of over 3,500, there was a sufficient approximation to a broad constancy. The fluctuation in the component forms was no more than might be expected in a complex social situation under real life conditions. Our entrant group comprised roughly a tenth of the working population at any one time.

Absences Other Than Accidents

We shall now examine changes in our stayers group in the level and form of their withdrawal from work during these first four years of service, divided into eight half-yearly periods. Table 1 shows that absences rise from 637 in the first to 775 in the second, from which they fall to 626 in the fifth and then stay at that level for the remaining three.

The survival distribution of entrants to the steel works conforms to the characteristic J-shaped curve. In comparison with other published cases it combines a fairly sharp induction crisis with a comparatively short period of differential transit—the curve tends to flatten out after a period of about two-and-a-half years.

Joining and leaving a firm is a publicly and legally institutionalized process regulated by contract. Knowledge of how to join a firm must exist outside the firm itself otherwise it would normally get no entrants. In going through the process of joining it the entrant acquires knowledge and experience of the means of leaving it. A desire to break the contract can be put into effect simply, and the terms of the contract provide the amount of notice (a week in most cases) that must be given. No barrier of any strength exists, therefore, to prevent painful feelings arising during the entrant's first encounter with the firm from being acted out immediately—by leaving. The characteristically high starting point of the survival curve in the present case bears witness to the extent to which this occurs.

Very different is the picture of temporary withdrawal from work. Absences are not publicly institutionalized acts. They tend to be regulated by internal cultural characteristics of individual firms—by what may be called an *absence*

TABLE I   Total Numbers of Absences Sustained per Half-Yearly Period of Service

Half-yearly period of service	1st	2nd	3rd	4th	5th	6th	7th	8th	Total
Number of absences	637	775	719	667	626	630	618	630	5,302

culture. This in the majority of cases is expressed in the pattern of *taking a day off* which accounts for 75 percent of industrial absences. The possibilities of withdrawal by absence are not known by the entrant; they are cultural mechanisms ignorance of which marks out the newcomer. Absorption of these cultural mechanisms is a process taking some time.

Involved is learning to remain a member of an organization while being away from it. One of the reasons for the high rate of leaving in the early period of service is the comparative lack of other means of withdrawal at the entrant's disposal through which to express the intense conflicts that may be experienced (during the induction crisis)—without leading to a breach of the relationship.

MEETING THE STRESSES OF "STAYING"

Concern is with the resort to absences by stayers, who, having survived their induction crisis, are prepared to endure—in ways tolerable both to themselves and to the firm—the tensions consequent on continuing with, rather than breaking, their work relationship. One result appears to be the considerably increased level of absence which characterizes the stayers' group during their second and third half years of service. Such stayers have had time to learn the prevailing absence culture to the point where they can operate it more freely. Their need to do so is also greater; for it is just when the role of stayer is fully taken and the person begins genuinely to identify him- or herself with being an employee that the role of leaver becomes less available as a means of alleviating stress. A person starts, therefore, to make more use of the role of absentee which, correspondingly, has become more available. He or she increases the rate of temporary withdrawal—but within limits which are not likely to lead to termination of employment. The firm and the employee have become more valuable to each other. There is a greater investment on both sides in containing stress arising between them within the on-going relationship that has become established.

One would not, however, expect the employee to increase the rate of absence beyond a point. As the relationship between the individual and the employing organization goes on, it needs to "work through" to a position of relatively stable mutual acceptance. After the wave of leaving associated with induction and the wave of absence associated with differential transit, one would expect a diminution of both as the relationship becomes one of settled connection. The extent to which this was the case at Park Gate may be seen from Table 1. Not only does some kind of equilibrium appear to be reached after two and a half years, but this levelling out of the absence curve coincides with the levelling out of the survival curve as the latter approaches conditions defined in labor turnover terms as those of settled connection.

Overall, the 289 stayers incurred 2,798 absences in their first two years as against 2,504 in their next two years. During the period of differential transit they incurred 1,494 as against 1,248 during the final year of settled connection.

The best available indicator of the degree of disturbance that had to be contained is the difference between the absences (637, 775) for the first and second periods. Similarly, the best indicator of the extent to which the difficulties of continuing with the relationship have later been worked through, is the comparison of the combined absences (1,494) for the first two periods of differential transit with those (1,248) of the last two of settled connection. The first of these changes points to the degree of stress involved in taking the stayer, as distinct from the leaver, role; the second to the degree of success in maintaining it.

CHANGES IN THE PREFERRED MODE OF WITHDRAWAL

Within this culture absences may be grouped according to their position on two parallel scales, one sociological and the other psychological. The first is in terms of the degree of sanction received from the employing authority; the second in terms of the degree to which the individual himself accepts responsibility for his actions. Sanctioned absences may be subdivided into those few (able-bodied) absences which are sanctioned prior to the event and the very much larger number of retrospectively sanctioned absences, comprising both certified and uncertified sickness and those able-bodied absences where an acceptable reason is given on return to work. Unsanctioned absences, where either no excuse is given or the excuse is unacceptable, comprise the large group of "no reason" absences. A property of such a scheme is that high or low degrees of sanction and acceptance of responsibility go together.

The expectation arises that an improved relation with the firm would be exhibited by the progressive substitution of more for less sanctioned forms of absence. This would mean that the norms of acceptable conduct were becoming progressively internalized by the entrant. The relative incommunicability of the sanctioning criteria, except through direct experience over a period of time, and the need for such a period to absorb the absence culture, make it

TABLE 2   Numbers of Other Absences Sustained per Half-Yearly Period of Service

Category	Half-yearly period of service								Total
	1st	2nd	3rd	4th	5th	6th	7th	8th	
No reason (unsanctioned)	371	473	431	363	335	298	275	274	2,820
Certified sickness (sanctioned)	56	77	91	85	75	82	87	105	658
Uncertified sickness (sanctioned)	62	70	72	84	91	116	129	122	746
Permission (sanctioned)	7	30	5	11	13	21	13	19	119
Sufficient reason (sanctioned)	121	106	99	109	96	102	105	97	835
Total sanctioned absences	246	283	267	289	275	321	334	343	2,358

likely that entrants would engage in an active process of trial and error as well as the more passive process of observing others in order to discover the precise nature and limits of the sanctioning criteria. The persistence in specific acts of condemned behavior becomes progressively more condemned as time goes on. While the old hand may acquire certain privileges, some acts that are sanctioned for the newcomer may be condemned for those with longer service. The question arises not only of different levels, but of different forms of absence being variously tolerated according to the phase of a man's relationship with his firm.

In order to test the hypothesis that over the course of time sanctioned absences would be progressively substituted for unsanctioned, the numbers of absences falling within these two broad categories were separated and their incidence in half-yearly periods calculated. The results (Table 2) are in accordance with expectation. Over the course of service unsanctioned forms of absence declined while sanctioned forms rose.

Broadly speaking, the overall increase in sanctioned absence is attributable to a higher rate of sickness in the later periods of service—especially the marked and continuous rise in uncertified sickness.

Sources of absence may be located in other regions of the life-space than that comprised by the person/work relationship. In the main, able-bodied absences of both the prospectively and retrospectively sanctioned types are occasioned by happenings in people's life elsewhere than at work, which can legitimately keep them away from it. These events are interference phenomena deriving from the fact that people have other social roles. There is no reason to suppose that such absences would either increase or decrease as a person's service progressed; rather that they would balance out. The data support this.

By contrast, the incidence of temporary sickness is closely connected with the person/work relationship. The outstanding fact is the continued rise of uncertified sickness. If the most disturbed periods of differential transit are compared with the least disturbed periods of settled connection, uncertified sickness increases by 77 percent. Even certified sickness increases by 14 percent. At the same time voluntary unsanctioned absenteeism decreases by 35 percent.

The problem of the substitution of sanctioned for unsanctioned absences becomes, therefore, very largely that of understanding how uncertified sickness comes to take the place of no-reason able-bodied absences—how a way of illness becomes preferred to a way of delinquency. If both the illnesses and the delinquencies are of a minor order, they are nevertheless frequent and common indications of everyday stress.

The rise in uncertified sickness could be due to an increase in conscious malingering. A number of circumstances, however, support the view that this was not the case. Considerable efforts were made by the firm to assure themselves of the validity of reasons for absence and an elaborate and clearly defined absence culture had come into existence, the possibility of which rested upon effective investigation and categorization of absences.

THE PROGRESSIVE INTERNALIZATION OF STRESS

The fact that uncertified sickness comes to be substituted for no-reason able-bodied absence means that a form of illness has taken over from a form of conduct. This suggests that a psychological component is active in the illnesses in question. No intervening institution or third party, such as a doctor, is involved in their appraisal. Uncertified sickness and no-reason absences belong to the same order in that both are dealt with directly in the relationship between the individual and the firm. They are equivalent in that both belong to the same time scale—that of the "day off"—so that the same amount of withdrawal is obtainable through either form.

Despite their common adherence to the day-off pattern, no-reason absences and uncertified sickness belong, in feeling, to different psychological worlds. In the first a day is taken, while in the second it is lost. In passing from one of these worlds to the other, employees pass from taking it out directly on the firm to taking it out in some measure on themselves, thus exchanging the role of an offender for that of a casualty—however minor in both cases. What was once projected now becomes introjected. A stronger prohibition is at work preventing the open expression of hostility against the firm. The need not to injure the object has been strengthened. This would only come about, however, so far as the firm had itself come to be perceived as relatively good by the individual.

It may be suggested that tensions in the person/work relationship previously dealt with predominantly by paranoid means and expressed in a mild "conduct disorder," taking the form of voluntary absenteeism, later give rise to reactions rather more depressive in coloring, with the associated symptom formations of minor illness. (The psychoanalytic concepts introduced at this and certain other points in the paper derive from the views of Melanie Klein on the paranoid and depressive positions [Klein, 1948].) The tensions are not completely resolved by this change. Were they so, there would be no need for the minor illnesses. A more complete resolution would depend on an individual facing his own bad feelings to a greater extent than he appears to do. Incompletely accepted by him, but not so easily expressed openly towards the firm, these feelings tend to be denied and split off often in a process of somatic conversion—hence the minor illnesses, which carry, in a covert form, hostilities formerly overt in the relationship.

In effecting this compromise the absence culture must undoubtedly play a part, as much as the personal tendencies of the individual. At Park Gate it was the physical causes of absence that were accepted with least question and the psychological and behavioral that were subject to most scrutiny. No convention existed by which a man, too angry with his foreman to contain himself, might ask to go off shift in order to get command of himself and deal with the situation. Yet his absence next day with a pain or a cold would be sanctioned. A rise in uncertified sickness with length of service is a collusive process taking place between person and firm. There is a tacit understanding that the easiest way of keeping certain awkward feelings out of work relationships is to keep them in an unrecognized (somatized) form. Forces in the firm, therefore, tend to combine with forces in the individual employee to produce the norms governing absence behavior.

The first main step by which the stress of the person/work relationship becomes progressively more internalized is taken as part of the change from an orientation based primarily on the leaver role to one based primarily on the stayer role. That this first change should take place at all implies that paranoid attitudes with their attendant fears, suspicions and hostilities, aroused during the induction crisis, are at least partially modifiable. For the employed individual to begin safely to adopt the stayer role he or she must perceive the employing firm as an object sufficiently good to permit, within certain limits, the projection of bad feelings onto it and the acting out of certain internal bad object-relations in external behavior towards it—without breaking the actual work relationship. Drifters, or floaters, with a history of chronic job change seem incapable of taking this first crucial step—no matter what the objective characteristics of the firm may be. Undoubtedly, in many cases the intensity of the persecutory anxieties and hostilities in the personality is too great for assumptions of sufficient goodness to be made, even provisionally, either about the firm or about oneself, so that the pain and the risk of testing out the real object cannot be endured within the bounds of a continuing relationship.

However, a firm which tolerates an increased rate of absence on the part of the individual during the period of settling in, even if at that point the employee has recourse largely to unsanctioned means, shows, however implicitly, a true understanding of the real needs and difficulties arising from attempting to make an enduring employee relationship. It shows itself as non-rejecting, as serious and sincere in inducting the employee into a more permanent relationship; as competent, moreover, in the means adopted to bring this about. To the continuing demonstration of such an attitude most individuals tend to respond in kind. People will find it increasingly difficult to maintain as a predominantly bad object an employing authority that treats them with implicit understanding. As this authority comes to be accepted as predominantly good it becomes difficult to go on treating it deliberately and overtly in a hostile, predatory, neglectful, selfish, contemptuous, defiant or irresponsible way (i.e., in terms of the manic defense)—without being arrested by one's own guilt. Therefore, the role of unsanctioned absentee becomes progressively less available just as the role of leaver had done previously. In this way the second main step comes about.

No relationship can become problem-free. Though perceived after a time as better rather than worse, no employing authority can appear to its employees as wholly (ideally) good, nor they to it. As the role of unsanctioned absentee, in addition to that of leaver, becomes relatively unavailable, the stress, bad feeling and hostility inevitably involved in continuing with the work relationship must somehow be dealt with either realistically or neurotically. The exceptionally well-adjusted individual may be able to cope with this situation without recourse to any means of temporary withdrawal. The present study suggests that such individuals are relatively rare. For the more ordinary majority a certain level of absence seems to persist as a needed and permanent feature of a continuing work-relationship.

With the barriers strengthened against both leaving and unsanctioned absence, the field of sanctioned absences represents the only remaining direction in which locomotions expressing the need for temporary withdrawal may legitimately take place. Only sickness, therefore, remains. The suggestion is that recourse is had to some kind of sickness when the individual, no longer able, in virtue of the improved relationship, to project (still persisting) bad feelings onto the firm as freely as was once possible, is nevertheless unable adequately to contend with them at a psychological level internally.

In the stayers' group in our study, the type of sickness increasing as a result of this process is for the most part of the very minor character included in the uncertified category. This increase, though considerable (75 percent), is not of

TABLE 3   Number of Accidents Sustained per Half-Yearly Period of Service

Category	Half-yearly period of service								Total
	1st	2nd	3rd	4th	5th	6th	7th	8th	
Number of accidents	20	19	21	15	16	11	9	13	124

so high an order as to prevent a fall (16 percent) in the overall level of absence. This suggests that the degree of stress in this group was not particularly great and that the process of coming to terms was well advanced. It cannot be assumed that this would be the case in all circumstances, and even in the data at Park Gate there is a hint that certified sickness (belonging to the longer time scale of a week or more) was on the increase towards the end of the four years under study.

Just as there is a dynamic connectedness between leaving and the phase of induction crisis, and between unsanctioned absence and the phase of differential transit, so would there appear to be a dynamic connectedness between sanctioned absence (in the form of sickness) and the phase of settled connection.

Accidents

ACCIDENTS IN THE ABSENCE FRAME OF REFERENCE

Accidents, when regarded in terms of sanctioning and responsibility, combine a high degree of sanctioning—so far as the absence is concerned—with a low degree of acceptance of responsibility. For an accident is precisely an event for which the individual does not usually accept responsibility, while absence arising from an accident is probably the most highly sanctioned of all forms of absence from work.

The substitution of sanctioned for unsanctioned absences arose from an improved relation of the entrant with the firm and indicated both a progressive acceptance of responsibility and a progressive internalization of the firm as a good employing authority. This being so, accidents are likely to fall during the course of service despite the highly sanctioned character of the absences to which they give rise. The incidence of accidents during the course of service is consistent with such a postulate (Table 3). In the last four periods there were only 49 accidents as compared with 75 in the first.

For the eight half-yearly periods the correlations between the accident series and the other absence series are shown in Table 4. They confirm the analysis made in terms of the progressive internalization of the stresses. Of the two

TABLE 4   Correlations Between Accident Series and Other Absences Series

Category of other absences	Correlation coefficient	Significance
No reason	+.850	Significant ($p<.01$)
Sufficient reason	+.286	Not significant
Permission	−.248	Not significant
Certified sickness	−.420	Not significant
Uncertified sickness	−.944	Significant ($p<.001$)

significant coefficients the positive association is with no-reason absences—providing further evidence that the occurrence of accidents is connected with a bad relationship with the employing authority. The negative association is with uncertified sickness—suggesting that the tendency to have accidents is not unrelated to difficulties over internalization.

ACCIDENT-FREE AND ACCIDENT-SUSTAINING GROUPS

The expectation arises of a differing degree of change occurring among the accident-free and the accident-sustaining groups with regard to other forms of withdrawal, especially those that are unsanctioned. The accident-free group, comprising a larger proportion of conformants to the social norm, sustain a consistently lower level of absences than the accident-sustainers (Figure 2). They have a relatively less severe induction crisis and fewer absences in the second period, and reach a stable level of absences more quickly. Conversely, the accident-sustaining group experience a more severe induction crisis, more absences during the second period and take longer to reach a stable level. Indeed, the curve of absences for these accident-sustainers had not leveled out even after four years' service.

PART OF BODY INJURED

As regards the parts of the body subject to work-related injury, the human body may be regarded as comprising three regions: the parts directly in contact with the work performed—hand, foot, head or eye; a connecting region comprising parts once removed from actual contact—wrist, arm, ankle or leg; a central region comprising back, chest, shoulder and abdomen.

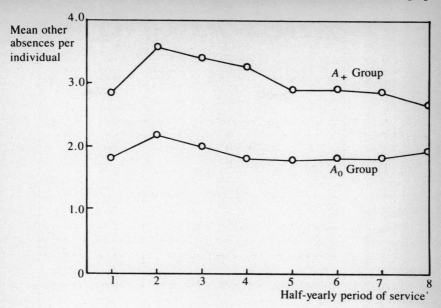

Figure 2. Mean other absences per individual among accident free (A_0) and accident-sustaining (A_+) groups

Opportunities for injury at work may be expected to occur with greatest frequency in the contact region and it would be mainly in this region that modifications of behavior resulting from an improvement in the person/work relationship should show themselves. Results, reported in Table 5, are in accordance with expectation. Altogether 69 of the accidents resulted in injury to some part of the contact region, 47 in the first two years' service and 22 in the second. The connecting region accounted for 34 accidents equally distributed between the first and second two years, while the central region accounted for only 16—9 in the first two years and 7 in the second.

TYPES OF MISHAP

Accidents occurring in the steel works were classified according to common industrial categorization into ten different types of mishap. Four of these accounted for 76 percent of the accidents: handling objects; being hit by falling objects; falls of employees; and stepping on and striking objects. The numbers of accidents in each of the four major classes occurring to the stayers' group in each of the eight half-yearly periods are given in Table 6.

TABLE 5   Part of the Body Injured per Half-Yearly Period of Service

Type of body region	Detail of components	Half-yearly period of service								Period 1–4	Total Period 5–8	Period 1–8
		1st	2nd	3rd	4th	5th	6th	7th	8th			
Contact	Hand	8	3	6	3	2	3	2	2	20	9	29
	Foot	3	6	4	1	3	—	—	1	14	4	18
	Head	3	—	3	2	2	—	1	2	8	5	13
	Eye	1	1	1	2	2	—	2	—	5	4	9
	Total	15	10	14	8	9	3	5	5	47	22	69
Connecting	Wrist	—	1	1	—	3	1	—	—	2	4	6
	Arm	—	—	1	1	1	1	2	1	2	5	7
	Ankle	1	2	2	3	—	3	—	1	8	4	12
	Leg	2	1	1	1	—	1	1	2	5	4	9
	Totals	3	4	5	5	4	6	3	4	17	17	34
Central	Back	—	—	—	1	1	—	—	2	1	3	4
	Shoulder	1	2	—	—	—	—	—	1	3	1	4
	Chest	1	2	—	—	—	—	—	—	3	—	3
	Abdomen	—	—	—	—	—	1	—	—	—	1	1
	Misc.	—	1	1	1	1	1	1	—	2	2	4
	Totals	2	5	1	1	2	1	1	3	9	7	16
Multiple injuries		—	—	1	1	1	1	—	1	2	3	5
Grand total		20	19	21	15	16	11	9	13	75	49	124

TABLE 6 Types of Mishap per Half-Yearly Period of Service

Class	*1st*	*2nd*	*3rd*	*4th*	*5th*	*6th*	*7th*	*8th*	*Period 1–4*	*Total Period 5–8*	*Period 1–8*
	Half-yearly period of service										
Handling objects	4	1	3	1	5	6	2	5	9	18	27
Hit by falling objects	6	6	9	2	2	—	—	—	23	2	25
Falls of employees	3	7	1	3	4	2	1	3	14	10	24
Stepping on or striking objects	3	3	3	5	1	3	1	3	14	8	22
Other	4	2	5	4	4	—	5	2	15	11	26
Total	20	19	21	15	16	11	9	13	75	49	124

Both for the works as a whole and for the 289 four-year survivors, accidents arising from handling objects were the largest group. In comparison with other types they represent those accidents which are most under the control of the person who has them. The employee has an accident from dealing with material that is literally in his own hands.

In contrast to other classes of accidents which show a decline with length of service, accidents due to handling objects not only do not decline but rise. The number occurring in the second two years is double that for the first two years. Concealed within the general decline is a rise in those accidents most under the control of the worker who sustains them. Furthermore, the period in which most accidents due to handling objects occur coincides with the almost complete disappearance of accidents due to being hit by falling objects. The blocking of opportunities in one region may result in more opportunities being taken in another.

The very process of blocking opportunities for accidents occurs not only through such methods as guarding and fool-proofing, in which physical barriers are introduced, but also in regulation and prohibition in which organizational barriers are set up. The effectiveness of such organizational barriers depends on their acceptance by individual employees, which varies with the extent to which the firm is internalized and authority itself accepted. It varies with the extent to which empirical specification of safety regulations can be made. For example, stacking methods may be routinized and laid down explicitly but it may be more difficult to specify how objects should be handled when this depends on skill (i.e., the non-specifiable routines carried inside a person).

Furthermore, the data of Table 6 may be related to the data of Table 5. Apart from handling objects, the accidents represented are essentially *accidents of contact*—with the environment in which the person has come to work. By contrast, accidents arising from handling objects are *accidents of activity*—of the person himself in his environment.

It is consistent with the earlier result that contact accidents exhibit a decrease in the later period. The view is submitted that contact accidents belong psychologically to the world of persecutory phenomena. What, one might ask, could be more persecutory than an environment in which one is hit by falling objects, is made to fall down, or is liable to step on or strike harmful things? In each of these cases the something that happens to the individual comes from outside. The noxious agency is experienced as a force entirely beyond the person's own control, and therefore such accidents cannot possibly be seen as his or her own fault. Blame must lie entirely with the environment, which, of course, is that to which the person has been exposed by the employing authority. The physical environment, however, will not be found so apt, as it were, to "attack" in such ways as the relationship with employing authority improves.

The psychological belongingness of activity accidents, on the other hand, would seem to be with a more depressive mode of feeling. It is not, of course, suggested in relation to accidents, any more than in relation to other absences, that the giving up of the paranoid for the depressive position is complete. They continue to co-exist but a change of emphasis seems to occur as service proceeds. For in these cases some of the badness at least must be regarded by the individual as his or her own, since his or her own faulty activity has certainly contributed to, even if it may not entirely have caused, the accident. The increase in activity accidents that goes along with the decrease in contact accidents is a suggestive parallel to the increase in sanctioned absences that goes along with the decrease in unsanctioned absences. The likelihood is that the one as much as the other reflects some of the difficulties of maintaining the greater degree of internalization demanded by an improved state of the person/work relationship.

Conclusions

The present study has revealed, as regards absence phenomena in general, both a characteristic intractability and certain possibilities of change. The relations people make with their fellows reflect unconsciously the relationships subsisting within their own personalities. Certain characteristics begin to emerge of the individual who has many absences, including perhaps one or more accidents. Such people would seem to lack the ordinary capacity to internalize a good object; to be rather prone to paranoid hostility and apt to disown responsibility for what they do and to remain ignorant of their real motivation. A bad relationship with one's own super-ego may easily be acted out in a bad relation with the employing authority, without insight on the individual's part. One way of acting out such a bad relation is through a more or less violent break in the employment contract, either by leaving or by getting oneself dismissed.

The reactions we have studied have occurred among a quasi-permanent remainder. By contrast with leavers, stayers appear to need permanent relations of rather a bad kind to be tolerated by their objects, in this case represented externally by their firm, and tend to hold on in a dependent way to a particular work relationship that tolerates them in this role. It is precisely this dependence and the consequent need for tolerance that accounts for the fact that some change occurs. For the firm is not unreservedly and permanently tolerant, and to remain securely a member of it involves for such individuals a modification of behavior. The peculiar painfulness of their predicament arises from just this. For, denied by their dependence access to the more obvious means of withdrawal implied in labor turnover, they do not join the ranks of the chronic unemployables, passing through a variety of jobs and accumulating in each sufficient tension to make the act of leaving an aggressive temporary relief. On the contrary, they make a more or less permanent relationship with their employing authority which is tolerable to them through resort to unsanctioned means of withdrawal and accidents. They may thus tend to become members of an accident- and absence-addicted minority. When the choice of conformity or ejection is forced upon them, they choose slowly and painfully to conform by substituting sanctioned sickness for those means which become less tenable as their service proceeds.

Especially in times of full employment, it is necessary for industrial organizations to take and absorb entrants according to the personality distribution within the surrounding community. Comparatively little can be done by a firm to change the basic personality characteristics of its employees but more might be done to help the adjustment of entrants. Indeed, it is along these lines that a reduction of labor turnover itself might be achieved by the improvement of induction procedures (Hill, 1968). Furthermore, we have no evidence that the absence-addicted deviates among the population examined were also the least productive workers. One of the results that emerges is that progressive improvement can occur even among those whose initial adjustment is most difficult. At the same time, within the writers' experience, one of the striking facts about the Park Gate is the recognition and toleration of a level of unsanctioned absences.

Understanding, recognition and tolerance of absence phenomena in their different forms are necessary for their effective control. This paper provides a new theoretical framework and new empirical findings on the basis of which conscious design of appropriate absence cultures may be undertaken.

Research proceeding in the mining industry in parallel with this study (Trist and Bamforth, 1951; Trist et al., 1963) showed that the restructuring of jobs in ways that enhanced the quality of the work experience reduced no-reason absences from 4.3 to 0.4 percent, while cutting sickness and accidents in half in a stayers group followed for two years. The most effective intervention strategies are likely to involve job and organizational re-design of a basic kind. These affect the whole shape of the survival curve in a positive direction and alter the basic character of the organization.

References

Hill, J.M.M. 1968. *A Study of Labour Turnover (E.D.C. for Food Manufacturing)*. London: National Economic Development Office.

Hill, J.M.M. and E.L. Trist. 1953. "A Consideration of Industrial Accidents as a Means of Withdrawal from the Work Situation." *Human Relations*, 6:357–80.

Klein, M. 1948. "Mourning and Its Relation to Manic-Depressive States." In *Contributions to Psycho-Analysis 1921–1945*. London: Hogarth Press.

Trist, E.L. and K.W. Bamforth. 1951. "Some Social and Psychological Consequences of the Longwall Method of Coal Getting." *Human Relations*, 4:3–38.

Trist, E.L., G.W. Higgin, H. Murray and A.B. Pollock. 1963. *Organizational Choice*. London: Tavistock Publications.

Fred Emery

Freedom and Justice Within Walls
The Bristol Prison Experiment
and an Australian Sequel*

Bristol Local Prison

This experiment was carried out in the Bristol Local Prison in the period 1958–1960. The inmates were given greater opportunities to associate with each other in their leisure hours and an attempt was made to measure the effects of this change on the social atmosphere of the prison.

The Prison Commissioners invited the Tavistock Institute to participate in an experiment to test the applicability of the "Norwich scheme" to medium-sized local prisons. This invitation was accepted on the mutual understanding that the interests of both staff and inmates would be considered and that it would probably be impossible to measure the effects of the experiment on the reform or rehabilitation of the inmates.

The Norwich system involved two changes from the normal pattern of local prisons: a daily routine allowing inmates to spend most of their waking hours outside their cells in association with each other and a change in the officers' responsibilities for inmates.

In its completed form, the study is very much like an iceberg: the part exposed to the light of day is only a fraction of the total, and is deceptively clear and pristine. The data presented could not have been interpreted and ordered but for the multitude of informal observations and conversations with staff and inmates. Methodologically, the key part in the study was played by the small randomly selected samples of officers and inmates. Long initial interviews with those men provided the orientation to, and entry into, the daily life of the

*This is a very abridged version of the book published by Tavistock Publications in 1970 under this title. It excludes the detailed discussion of the contradictions in the inmate/officer roles and summarizes the findings. Added to this is an extract from *Hope Within Walls*, a design study for a maximum security prison which explicitly sought to spell out the implications of the Bristol Experiment, and a note on what subsequently happened.

prison. Repeated interviews with the same men not only gave evidence of the psychological significance of what was going on, but also served to preserve the openness of the author's relation to the prison community. Thus, despite the considerable turnover in inmate population, it was possible to feel after a period of absence that one was returning home. Similarly, this set of relations provided the base from which one was able to explore what had, in fact, happened in disciplinary and other incidents of importance.

The sample of officers and inmates was selected with some care so that, although small, they provide a reasonably unbiased representation of what were judged to be the key groups for the purposes of this study. Amongst the uniformed staff, these are the basic grade officers who are still in the prime of their careers and, amongst the inmates, the ordinary prisoners other than those who tend to be in and out on very short sentences for such crimes as vagrancy.

In a sense these core samples are called upon to serve the various functions of a microscope, trace element and reagent. At the same time, an effort has been made to avoid basing any significant part of the argument on these data alone.

Although no conscious attempt has been made to avoid theoretical issues, this report has been overwhelmingly concerned with practical matters. It was created under the constant awareness that statements made in it might become the basis of decisions affecting real people in the here-and-now. This is not in itself unusual in the work of the Tavistock Institute. However, in this instance, I was more than ordinarily impressed with the fact that the issues involved suffering for the inmates and danger to life and limb for the staff—they were not simply those of more or less optimum conditions of welfare, profit or happiness. Of still greater import was the fact that prisons, of all present-day institutions, were felt to be notoriously lacking in those higher guiding purposes and conditions of day-to-day cooperation that normally allow a body of people to test and correct false counsel.

Insofar as the report might influence decisions made for a wide class of prisons, it has been necessary to omit those details that alone would depict Bristol Prison as a flesh-and-blood affair and to concentrate on the bare bones of oft-repeated behaviors that might tell a general story.

The study could not have been carried out unless we had been given a clear, unambiguous guarantee that neither praise nor blame would be attributed to identifiable individuals, whether staff or inmates.

Socio-Psychological Aspects of Prisons

In examining social systems, I have elsewhere (Emery, 1959) found it useful to inquire into what I have termed their "boundary conditions"—those aspects of the institutionalized complex of men and material things that mediate between the social system and the wider setting. The key and distinctive boundary condition of a productive enterprise is its technological system. Through the technological system, the enterprise achieves those productive ends that relate it to society; through this arises the major set of independent limitations and requirements of the social system. Hence the appropriateness of the term "socio-technical system" for productive enterprises. The material apparatus of a prison clearly plays no such dominant role. Unlike a factory, the typical prison problem is not that of adapting the social system to technological modifications but of trying to adapt old material means to newly modified social systems.

The key to the difference would seem to be in the obvious and indisputable fact that one is primarily concerned with things, the other with human beings. The prison achieves its institutional ends only by doing certain things with and to its inmates. It must therefore give primary consideration to the psychological properties of the inmates, because these make some measures effective and others non-effective. These common psychological properties constitute the key boundary conditions of the prison—they are an essential part of the prison and yet they must, in large measure, be treated as a given, i.e., as existing and obeyed laws and influences that are independent of the wishes of prison administrations. The material means (cells, walls, workshops, etc.), the type of staff and the system of staff roles are devised, more or less appropriately, to achieve the institutional ends with the kind of inmates that are thrust upon them. Basically, the prison is one of the class of socio-psychological, as distinct from socio-technical, institutions. It differs, however, from hospitals—medical and mental—and from religious, educational and political institutions in that it is based on the premise of doing something against the wishes of its inmates, and usually against their interests.

If this interpretation is correct, then the key to an understanding of prisons should be the analysis of the psychological characteristics of the inmates and of the ways in which these are coped with by the staff.

The basic psychological fact about the inmates of a prison is that they are, with few exceptions, confined against their will in conditions of life not of their making and seen by them as depriving and degrading relative to the life they would be leading if free. The generality of this state of affairs arises from the social fact that the inmates (the "objects" handled by the institution) are defined by the State, not by any subordinate part of the society, as a morally inferior class of persons who constitute a cost to the society.

In all prison-like institutions there is, therefore, a body of officials concerned with confining, against their will, a much larger body of men. The staff are also impelled to maintain a detailed regulation of the internal life of the prison in order to prevent escape and carry out other institutional purposes such as maintaining health of inmates, good order, production and rehabilitation. Even in the exceptional case where the goal of rehabilitation is a real factor in determining the ordering of internal life, one must still expect that the great majority of the inmates will be impelled by their own needs and beliefs to seek to create a different form of life. In this persisting conflict of wills over detention and the regulation of daily life, the staff can only maintain the superiority of their own wills through their possession of greater material force. Unlike moral persuasion, the influence of physical force only extends as far as the eyes and ears of its wielders and their allies, and is only as effective as the willingness of its wielders to use it. Without exception, all classes of man-made institutions for the detention of men have been unable to achieve complete power (Polanski, 1942). Except where solitary confinement is the norm, an inmate society with its own ends and culture has emerged within the interstices of the official order. In the common characteristics and interaction of these two ways of life, official and inmate, it has been possible to detect social and psychological processes of conflict and accommodation that are common to all these institutions (Abel, 1951; Adler, 1958; Foreman, 1959). The differences arise from differences in the strength of the conflicting wills and in the resources, personal and otherwise, that are available to the contending parties. In all cases, however, these institutions continue only so long as the official order of life predominates.

The study of the common psychological characteristics of prison inmates is thus, in the first instance, a study of those forces impelling the inmates towards greater control over their own affairs at the expense of staff control. While any listing of these forces must be incomplete, the following appear to be the major ones, commonly recognized in scientific studies of prisons.

By their usual standards of reference, the inmates perceive prison as relatively depriving. They see themselves as deprived of their normal freedom of access to pleasurable and interesting pursuits and to those things (alcohol, tobacco, gambling and sex) that play an important role in their culture in handling intra-personal tensions.

They are relatively deprived of the customary supports and behavioral settings for their usual living habits. In particular, they tend to find themselves with a circumscribed and impoverished "home territory" and a lack of personal possessions.

They find themselves deprived of the usual supports for their self-image. Materially, the clothes they wear are not their own and are not of their choice (although younger inmates continually seek to restyle them); they lack the supply of razor blades, brushes, cleaning materials, etc., to maintain a reasonable level of personal appearance.

Of at least equal significance, they are deprived of their usual freedom of association. Their prison associates are less likely to be acceptable as either a private or a public definition of themselves than the men and, of course, women that they would normally seek out.

The inmates perceive the status they are accorded in prison as relatively degrading. Most are accustomed to social inferiority, but find that in prison they are treated as morally inferior to officers who are socio-economically their equals and are treated as morally no better than the other inmates (who will normally cover a wide range of criminality and depravity). The reception process for new inmates is basically conducted as a "degradation ceremony" (Garfinkel, 1955–56). If this initial lesson does not sink home, the staff can usually be counted upon to contrive further informal degradation rites until the inmate accepts, at least publicly, his inferior status. In the day-to-day life of the prison, the inmate finds himself ordered about, reprimanded and punished for the slightest misdemeanor, to a degree which is reserved in ordinary life for children and household animals.

These deprivations and degradations will tend to generate in the inmate a state of emotional tension. They will tend to see the deprivations and degradations as unjust and unwarranted. The deprivations experienced in prison are rather more complex and varied than could be legally pronounced as punishment and, hence, easily seen as more than "just desserts" for a crime committed; the degradations are not easily reconciled with the inmates' notion of the human dignity that the law is believed to protect. These tendencies will operate in the specific instance even when, as is usual, the inmate accepts that imprisonment and some deprivation are deserved. Whatever it is that characterizes the imprisoned criminals, it is not an absence of a sense of justice, not the absence of moral standards, despite the fact that in civil life they may readily commit an injustice or forget their morals. Like others, in the presence of what they consider to be injustice, the inmates will tend to experience "that sympathetic reaction of outrage, horror shock, resentment and anger" (Cahn, 1949).

While many of the deprivations and degradations of prison are not necessarily great in themselves (nor in themselves arouse strong or lasting feelings of injustice), they become significant because they occur so frequently, and in so many parts of prison life. The whole *prison milieu* assumes this character (Lewin, 1936). Even customs that are required for the inmates' own benefit acquire the connotation of alien imposed restrictions. The more these deprivations and degradations touch upon the inmate's self-image, the more the whole situation will take on this character. Where the prison milieu as a whole seems to be like this, the inmate will tend to feel tense (Sykes, 1958).

There is constant awareness that the deprivations and degradations are being imposed by men with whom they are in close daily contact. It is this sense of personally inflicted punishment that gives to the prison the character of strife and creates its pervading atmosphere of hatred. These two features in themselves induce in the inmates many of the behaviors that they customarily show in prisons. On the one hand, "the exercise of every form of cheating and deceit occurs more readily in proportion as the situation acquires the character of strife. In such a strife, the individual may use, without hesitation, methods he would probably not employ in any but a hostile atmosphere" (Lewin, 1936). On the other hand, the hatred of officers, insofar as it emerges as a common feeling, provides a common denominator for joint inmate action that is otherwise lacking (Hoffer, 1952).

In hatred, the individual is drawn away from himself, "his weal and future." What would be inconsistencies with respect to his own self-system may become consistent when cognition is centered upon the hated object or person. "Recentering" of the cognitive structure appears to be more effective, the more unified, unambiguous, vivid and tangible the "devil," and is more likely to take place when there already exist tendencies to hate and reject oneself. Self-rejection may in the case of the inmates derive from social rejection. Moreover, such rejection is likely to lead the object of hatred to be seen as malevolent *vis-à-vis* the person, and the existence of a malevolent and powerful human agent will lead to efforts at alliance with others. The existence of hatred creates the psychological schism between inmates and staff that is a necessary prerequisite to the emergence and maintenance of a secret inmate world within the prison.

The above paragraphs point only to the *kinds* of pressure that may be expected to arise from the inmates of a closed prison. The *level* of inmate pressure against the staff appears to be largely influenced by the perceived gap between life "inside" and "outside" (relative deprivations and degradations).

The Prison

Bristol Prison is a Local Prison with an average population, during 1957–60, of approximately 360 men and juveniles. The only striking difference between it and other medium-sized Locals is its higher incidence of reported inmate offenses. In fact, for the four years prior to 1958, it had a rate of offenses higher than any other Local irrespective of size. This difference suggests a persistently higher level of tension between staff and inmates, but the difference is not so great as to warrant any *a priori* assumption of qualitative difference.

Overcrowding is for the inmates a primary characteristic of the Local Prison. They must expect to be more or less continuously exposed to, and forced to rub shoulders with, strangers, many of them violent and treacherous. They will find it very difficult to achieve any degree of privacy or to associate selectively with inmates of their own choosing. Persons come into Bristol Prison for all kinds of crimes—the majority for theft, burglary and similar crimes against property, but there is always a substantial minority who have been imprisoned for fraud, violence or sexual offenses.

Regardless of crime committed, the Local Prisons hold all ordinary prisoners with sentences of less than five years, and they act as clearing-houses or temporary holding-places for all other classes of prisoner. Ordinary prisoners with sentences of more than five years spend up to the first 20 months in a Local.

At any time about half the population is serving sentences of eight months or less. Over a period of six months, about 40 percent of the original population can be expected to leave and their beds and work-places occupied by new inmates. This turnover inhibits the growth of an inmate society, but it does so rather less than would be expected of, say, a military unit with similar turnover. The Local Prison draws most of its inmates from the surrounding localities and, invariably, draws very heavily on one or two not-so-select suburbs of the major city in its catchment area. Hence, many come from the same area and know each other or have common acquaintances. Repeated and overlapping periods of imprisonment also help to maintain a core of stable inmate relations. Of at least equal importance to these personal networks is the continuity of inmate culture. The ease with which this is transmitted over time is, for the most part, due to its basic values being derived, even if in a distorted way, from the values prevalent in the working classes of the society. This culture is primarily oriented to coping with, and exploiting, the weakness of the individual staff, the more stable system of staff roles and rules, and the familiar environmental features of the prison. Unlike most cultures, the inmate culture does not arise from evaluations of men who are freely engaged in common endeavors, and consequently it does not define the characteristics and potentialities of the inmate group beyond a crude typing of inmate and staff roles and a cultural definition of inmate suffering and its conditions (i.e., ways of "doing bird"). It is a culture without heroes or villains because there are no "common causes." The features to which the inmate culture refer are fairly similar in all Local Prisons, and hence one can understand why "ordinaries," having had previous experience in another prison, are able so quickly to assimilate the local variations and relate themselves in a meaningful way to the pattern of inmate life.

"A" Hall* is largely populated by physically fit men, about 60 percent being between 25 and 40 years of age, but there are two constant minorities: one of

---

*"A" Hall is where the adult prisoners are kept. The adolescents are physically isolated in "D" Hall. The experiment also covered them but they are not the focus of the following analysis. It is enough to note that they experienced no transitional problems and that the general rate of incidents fell to 70 percent less than would have been expected under the old regime.

about 15 percent, of men over 50, chronically ill or physically handicapped; and the other, of similar proportion, of young men under 25. The over-forties are a very settled group with a rate of inmate offenses equal to only about one-fourth of the average, but among them are many who confront the staff with the sort of problems to be found in old men's homes. The under-twenty-fives form a marked contrast, with their sensitivity to any suggestion of being pushed around and their concern with proving their manliness. This minority tended to offend at twice the average rate for A Hall.

Thus, while relatively homogeneous with respect to classification, A Hall shows major differences according to age. It is believed that the age differential is the most significant of the ecological variables affecting the life of the inmates and staff control. Previous crime shows no major relation, and differences in prison experience tend to be related to age.

The Experiment

The aim was simple: to introduce periods of free association where no such periods had existed. The experimental aspect was how to do this without endangering security and good order.

The prison officers were overwhelmingly of the view that the prisoners would abuse any such reduction in close personal supervision. Detailed analysis of the records for the 60 weeks before the start of the experiment supported their views. Over that period there was a strong correlation between the frequency of incidents of indiscipline and looseness of supervision. Amongst inmates the majority view was that the association periods would increase their exposure to predatory and violent inmates and to arbitrary acts of spite by the officers.

The prison had been designed for living in the cells, not for association or communal eating. The lack of space meant that association could be provided for only half the inmates at a time, on alternate days. Nevertheless, the changes constituted a substantial increase in the space of free movement for the great majority of inmates. They were as follows:

- The narrow confines of the cells ceased to be the dominant feature of every day (assuming a 6:30 am to 9:30 pm day), 60 percent of an ordinary week would be spent in the cells. On association days under the new scheme the time spent in cells was reduced from 60 to 25 percent.
- Almost four hours were available every second day in which to mix with other inmates, with complete freedom of conversation and opportunities for engaging in leisure pursuits.
- The conditions also enabled men to form a wider range of friendships and

to sustain them with frequent open contact and joint participation in games.

- The environment itself changes its appearance for inmates, not simply representing an increase of something already offered. Association emerges as a farther area inside the prison, alongside the cell, the exercise yard and the work-places. Hence the psychological environment is more varied and less boring. With association, the range of behavioral settings in the prison more closely corresponds to that existing outside and hence should tend to reduce initial suffering.

The change also affected the inmate-officer relation. To a much greater extent those relations are open to the public view of other officers and inmates, and to a lesser degree private relationships handled at the cell door. During association the officer's role is reduced to that of a policeman assuring good order and the inmate does not have to be continually looking over his shoulder, as he would on exercise or in the workshop, to see that he is not "going too slow or too fast, idling, talking out of turn," etc. Although association is carried out under the eyes of the officers, there are fewer official requirements to trip up the incautious or indiscreet inmate and less possibility of an officer unjustly charging an inmate.

Results

The process of settling down took eight weeks after the introduction of the new system. A lot of organizational snags had to be ironed out, particularly with respect to communal eating arrangements and the different patterns of movement around the prison. The incident rate went up quite alarmingly. As one officer observed, "everything that was not nailed down was changing hands illegally." The senior staff were patient because there was a striking absence of serious incidents, i.e., those involving a challenge to the authority of an officer.

For purposes of analysis comparison was confined to the 64 weeks prior to the transitional period and the 64 weeks after. Before the change only 40 percent of inmates thought it was a good idea. After the change only 15 percent chose to remain in their cells. As one old recidivist said of that minority, "some queer ones and some real old jailbirds do their time behind locked doors because they don't know any other way. They have had too much of the old system." The association periods were periods of social activity. On average, about two-thirds of the inmates engaged in games they organized for darts, table tennis, dominoes and chess at both the noon and evening association. The older men tended to watch the games, read papers or listen to radio (there was no TV). Idle brooding or gossiping was minimal.

TABLE I   Approximation to Poisson distribution of incidents/week

	Before (64 weeks)	After (64 weeks)
Domestic sector	$\chi^2 = 14.25, p < .02$	$\chi^2 = 2.62$ n.s.
Work sector	$\chi^2 = 6.49, p < .05$	$\chi^2 = 1.29$ n.s.

The changes in staff attitudes were even more striking. Before the change none of the officers thought that the other officers wanted association introduced. After the change only five percent thought that the others wanted to go back to the old system. (This was despite the fact that privately some 30 percent preferred the old system.)

Before the change only 30 percent of the officers thought that association would be good for the inmates (regardless of whether the inmates liked it or not). After the change there were no officers who thought that association was bad for the inmates. Before the change half of the officers thought that association would, as in the big American prisons, increase the power of "barons" and "toughs." After the change only five percent thought this had happened.

The most significant change was in the reduction of serious incidents in the domestic sector of prison life. Before the change one in three of all incidents could be expected to flare into a challenge to the authority of the officer involved (or be seen as such). After the change only one in seven did so. In the

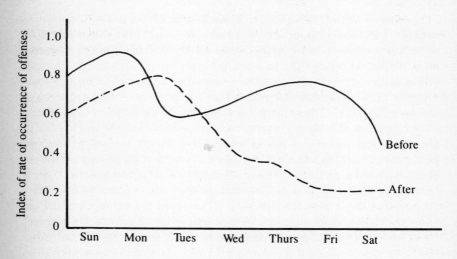

Figure 1. Weekly pattern of offenses—domestic sector. For both periods, a statistical comparison of the first and last half showed no significant difference.

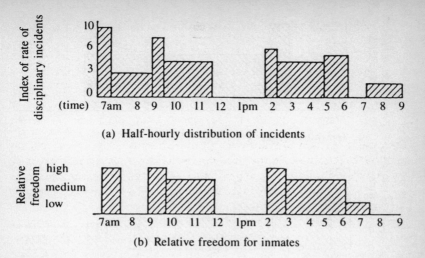

(a) Half-hourly distribution of incidents

(b) Relative freedom for inmates

Figure 2. Half-hourly distribution of incidents and opportunities for inmate interaction before change, averaged for all weekdays in the "before" period. The pattern did not differ significantly between the first and last half of the "before" period, or among the days of the week for the entire period.

other part of prison life, the workshops, there was no change in what, in any case, was a relatively low rate of incidents (Table 1).

For incidents of all kinds, petty as well as serious, for the prison as a whole, work plus domestic sector, the rate declined (Figure 1). It was calculated that if incidents had occurred at the same rate as before there would have been 44 percent more than actually occurred.

These outcomes were welcome but would not, in themselves, have led to the change in the attitudes of the officers and inmates toward extended association. They could have been interpreted as a relaxation of standards. As mentioned previously, officers had opposed the introduction of association because their experience was that "if you give the inmates an inch, they will take a mile." Comparison of graphs (a) and (b) in Figure 2 shows that before the change the evidence supported the officers' view. The level of incidents closely followed the occurrence of opportunities—the more freedom for inmate interaction, the higher the rate of incidents.

Our contention was that this connection was due to the level of tension in the prison, not to innate inmate propensities (nor, as some inmates alleged, innate officer propensities). As shown in Figure 3, the introduction of association eventually broke the nexus between "opportunities" and incidents.

After the transition period the rate of occurrence of disciplinary incidents

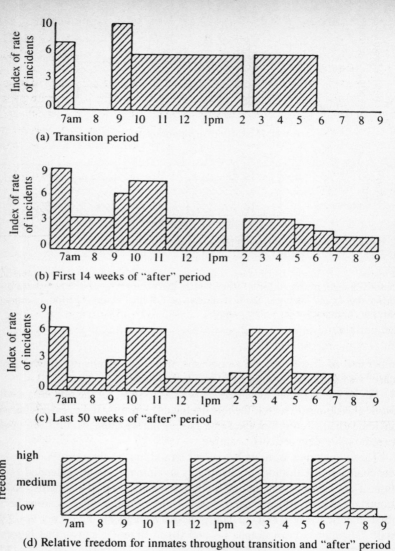

(a) Transition period

(b) First 14 weeks of "after" period

(c) Last 50 weeks of "after" period

(d) Relative freedom for inmates throughout transition and "after" period

Figure 3. Half-hourly distribution of disciplinary incidents and opportunities for inmate interaction after the changeover, averaged for all weekdays in each period. Only the 50-week period was long enough to permit a statistical test of the stability of the pattern. No significant difference was found between the first and last half of this period, nor between weekdays for the entire period.

ceased to correspond to the degree of freedom for the inmates (graphs [b] and [c] compared with [d]). Association was marked by a low level of incidents, exercise ceased to be a focal point and, apart from the early morning "slopping out," most incidents occurred during work.

Supporting the evidence presented in the graphs is the absence of pilfering and vandalism of association materials. Up to January 1960, there were no signs of deliberate destruction or damage to tables, chairs, etc., and the games material was still completely intact. The only noticeable wear was no more than could be expected with continual, normal use. Similarly, there were no noticed cases of premeditated violence between prisoners.

One further finding needs reporting. At the time of the changeover, Bristol was the most tightly "screwed down" Local Prison in England. It had been so ever since it was called upon to hold the overflow from the big military prison to the south of it in 1945. This tradition was carried by a core of the officers. As a result, the patterns of officer reporting rates and of particular officers reporting particular inmates deviated markedly from the "poissonian distribution" one would expect if it was just a matter of chance which officer was on duty at the time and place of an offense. After the change, the patterns were not significantly different from a poissonian distribution: the game, known to inmates and staff alike as "chasey," was over. Despite its name, that game was neither playful nor trivial. It was a potent and rather frightening process of enforcing informal sanctions.

The experiment was judged successful in increasing the space of free movement for inmates, despite the level of over-crowding that then prevailed. It was also successful in reducing the injustices to which inmates were exposed, and it significantly reduced the danger and stress in the working life of the officers. Bristol lost the dubious honor of being the tightest Local in England, and even ten years later could only make fifth or sixth place.

An Australian Design for a Maximum Security Prison: Hope Within Walls

(with Merrelyn Emery and Cy de Jago)

When the Western Australian government decided that a new maximum security prison was needed the Director of the Corrective Services Department and the architect did a world tour of modern maximum security prisons. This revealed several disquieting facts:

- With the use of modern technologies in construction, surveillance and remote control, extremely high degrees of secure confinement could be achieved but the costs of construction and maintenance were extremely high.
- The costs to the inmates were very much higher than the simple deprivation of freedom to mix in society stipulated in the court sentences. It seemed that many of the inmates would be less fitted to mix in society *after* serving sentences than they were before commitment.
- The level of tension and strife in these prisons made them unsuitable places of employment for the staff.
- The desperate state of some of the inmates produced a high level of deliberate destructiveness and hence an even higher cost of maintenance.
- The more desperate inmates gravitated to so-called *intractable blocks*. Their hostility was so implacable that it was inconceivable that they would ever, wittingly, be returned to society (but, of course, their sentences would eventually run out).

The Design

There was a clear understanding that the design of the new prison had to break new ground. A broadly based planning committee was established to ensure a better marriage of architectural, operational and social science considerations. As is fairly typical of committees, each "wild" thought was quickly encapsulated in the concrete practicalities of the others. *Inexorably the planning process was grinding on to produce yet another "modern" maximum security prison.*

To break with this built-in assumption it was decided that planning should be moved into a different mode of a "search conference" (M. and E. Emery, 1977). That is, that the committee members, plus two of the authors with experience of these settings, be locked away together and freed from external interference until they could come up with an acceptable design for a new strategy.

The product of that week's conference was a report entitled "The Structure and Function of Life in a Long Term Maximum Security Prison," summarized in what follows. The new prison was to be built by 1974 at Canningvale on the edge of suburban Perth, Western Australia. By the time of the search conference set up by the Western Australia Department of Corrections there was available a set of working drawings for the building. Present at the conference (26–30 March, 1970) were the Director of the Corrective Services Department (Colin Campbell), his deputies, three superintendents from local prisons, a trade officer, a recreation expert, the union president, an adviser from the

University of Western Australia, the architect and his assistant, and the two authors from the Australian National University. The group worked intensively during the period of residence at the Wooroolloo prison.

Before examining the details of the design, it was necessary to define the institutional ends that this prison should serve. These ends were to be achieved by choosing as an integrated set those material ends and staff roles most appropriate to the criteria defining human outcomes.

OUTCOMES FOR THE INMATES

A long-term maximum security sentence may be up to 10 years. An inmate should, at the end of his 10 years, be able to return outside and resume an adequate civil life. He should be:

- physically fit
- unbroken in spirit
- able and willing to enter into normal social relations
- able and willing to enter into work in at least a semi-skilled capacity

This list of criteria does not imply any goal with respect to reformation of character, and there will be, therefore, no necessary separation of first offenders and recidivists. Most inmates will be recidivists and to some degree institutionalized but it is postulated that the structure of this prison will go a long way towards ensuring the formation of new behavior patterns.

To achieve this outcome means sustaining a quality of life on:

- a day-to-day level where there are present the six necessary and sufficient conditions for satisfaction through the areas of work, domesticity and leisure. These criteria for a satisfying life also form the basis for designing staff systems and are spelt out in greater detail in the section on Outcomes for Staff
- a structured time perspective of the day, week, month, season, year, etc.
- a social dimension which includes contacts with and opportunities for some contact with (for Australian conditions) beer, gambling and women

To achieve this outcome entails avoidance of the institutionalization of inmates or the "old lag" syndrome. Therefore, there must be also on the part of inmates

- an interest in the prison itself, maintained by the sharing of responsibility for domestic work and leisure objectives
- a maintenance of interpersonal skills by designing structural arrange-

ments, for both inmates and staff, built around a small group as the basic
unit, rather than the individual
- a maintenance of contact with the outside world and its rapid complex of
  changes which will preclude the possibility of Rip Van Winkle effects
  such as those noted in returned prisoners of war. This implies conversa-
  tional contacts with staff and access to radio, daily press and television

Monitoring for the above criteria should proceed at regular intervals, e.g.,
weekly, by each staff manning group, using rating scales devised in terms of the
above indicators. Other tension and climate indices to be monitored include
inmate fights; sick bay calls; productivity in terms of damage to machines and
wastage of materials; voluntary participation in recreation. Staff reports on
inmates must feed into the central control superintendent and chief officer, and
back from them on a short time loop. Constant touch is, therefore maintained
with both the small group and community levels of quality of functioning.

It may seem strange that these are put forward as achievable outcomes for a
maximum security prison when one of the authors reached quite pessimistic
conclusions after his work on the Bristol Prison Experiment. We shall take each
of his three conclusions in turn:

> Given the requirement of medium or maximum security, the prison regime
> cannot be expected to be a reformative agent.

We would not wish to change this formulation. The job of a prison as an
institution is to keep a person out of trouble, and reduce trouble for the
community. This does not, however, preclude a prison regime from being more
supportive of individual officers who can aspire to ideals that are higher than
those that are practicable for the institution and less supportive of those whose
behaviors would degrade the purposes of the institution.

> Given the requirement of security, a level of internal freedom cannot be found
> that will automatically secure good order. Supervision and coercion will be
> necessary.

This proposition we now flatly disagree with. By shifting the basic imprisoned
unit from the individual (or three per cell) to the small group (the wing) and the
small collection of three groups (the block) we think a large measure of internal
freedom can be achieved with improved changes of "good order." Organization of work life around small semi-autonomous work groups offers a further
reinforcement of "freedom with good order." The size of the small wing
groups (4–10) has been deliberately kept below the limit where contagious
group emotions are likely. Allowing this degree of free interaction does, of

course, increase inmate capability for breaching security, but we are convinced that technical improvements put the staff much further in front than they were in Bristol when Emery studied them in the late fifties. Supervision will, of course, still be there but at the key points and not as something that adds up for the inmate to a stiffling "big brother" atmosphere. Coercion will still be there but not as something available to some staff as an active policy tool.

> Given the requirements of security and good order, the role of the ordinary officer cannot be defined as that of also being the prisoner's friend and counsellor.

We think that this proposition needs to be reconsidered. For technical reasons the individual officer does not, and will not, be so encumbered with concern for security as in the past. We will be able to avoid even the past hysteria over temporarily lost keys with all of its accompanying cloud of suspicion about individual officers. The "staff teams" that we propose in the next section should circumvent the suspicion, in the Bristol-type prison, that close inmate/staff contacts are potentially collusive and corruptive, and hence to be avoided. In this context we believe it will be possible for staff members, so motivated, to act as a very positive influence on some inmates. This influence may be enhanced if such staff have access to members of the helping professions (e.g., psychologists, psychiatrists). This same influence is likely to be seriously attenuated if these officers have to compete with members of the helping professions in offering their help to inmates. Even where people, including prison officers, have a will to help this can be seriously hindered by their own lack of self-awareness. Their potentiality in this new prison setting could be materially enhanced by *voluntary* participation in T-grouping.

Outcomes for the Staff

Outcomes for the staff are primarily:

* Job satisfaction where the criteria are optimal variety of tasks within a shift or roster period; opportunities for learning on the job; areas for decision-making; social support and respect; meaningfulness of the job; a desirable future.
* Adequate pay and material conditions for the job—this is strictly a matter for the industry but affects quality of staff function.

These criteria are the same as those worked out for industrial groups (Emery and Thorsrud, 1977).

To obtain the proposed and agreed-to outcomes, it is necessary to organize life for the inmates and for the staff on the basis of small semi-autonomous groups. To ensure that the inmates have an area of semi-autonomy it is necessary to design staff teams that provide adequate flexibility to handle security-endangering incidents, whilst avoiding any over-manning.

For the staff, this means that at any given moment decisions as to division and allocation of tasks within the team on duty will be made by that staff group itself. Manning is determined by the contingencies of the job itself.

For the inmates, this means that there will be left free some areas, such as evening recreation pursuits and some domestic functions, about which the small domestic group make their own decisions.

CONSTRAINTS

The many different aspects of security fall into two main classes: physical or external controls; maintenance of good order. Implicit in the use and maintenance of security features is an inter-dependence of the two types, i.e., when the level of good order is high there is little necessity to resort to reliance on security.

It is necessary for the psychological well-being of inmates that the possibility of escape exist. As a corollary of this criterion, no two escapes should happen in the same way. (NB: It will not be known until the prison is in operation what escape hatches are, in fact, built into the design—inmates are more imaginative and ingenious than prison designers and staff.) It is possible to stress security at the risk of good order. Therefore, it becomes necessary to design security in such a way as to leave room within the secure perimeters for a satisfying and human life.

GOOD ORDER

The basis for this is designed in by means of the small cohesive group structures of both staff and inmates. Domestic and work groups of between four and 10 members will maximize stability through the operation of group forces towards staff-inmate cooperation (see Sykes [1958] for description of inmate motives with respect to smooth group functioning and "stirrers").

There are three basic and interdependent elements in the structure which are productive of good order:

- Small domestically based groups of inmates housed in their own physically separate wings and blocks.
- Small shift-based groups of staff where the responsibility for decision-

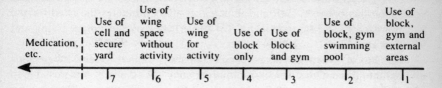

Figure 4. Scale of good order

making about operations of two blocks is that of a *group* of officers. The senior officer of the group will participate in the work of the group. Group function will guard against maladaptive relations growing between inmates and staff, e.g., corruption based on permanence and the individual nature of staff/inmate proximity.

• It is essential that the blocks not be overwhelmed by staff. Apart from the operation of group forces which will militate against the event, realistic manning removes the possibility of staff "getting at" inmates because of boredom, etc.

Good order can be objectively measured on the scale shown in Figure 4. Good order is being maintained when 90 percent of the time is spent at point one on the scale of privileges. Block or wing positions on this scale will be monitored at frequent regular intervals.

Entry to maximum security is via assessment or remand and exit is by transfer to other institutions, i.e., there is normally no final discharge from this prison. This increases the potential for good order by means of staff preparedness for new inmates and the exit procedure is another factor in providing a desirable future for inmates.

SECURITY

Security features are designed within a concept of active security. By active security we mean that the staff will try to keep at least one step ahead of trouble by analyzing trends in inmate morale, inmate group formation and effectiveness of staff teams, and by constantly probing and reviewing the existing security arrangements.

The need for excessive reliance on passive security (by high walls and electronic surveillance) has been reduced by organizing things so that at any one time life is going on in small separate "social islands." These are physically secure and surveillance and control of movements between the islands is unified by a central control. This arrangement eliminates the chance of mass confrontations between staff and inmates. It also eliminates the need for the psychologically stifling practice of TV surveillance over ordinary living and working areas.

Each block, when at 100 percent occupancy, cannot exceed 28 persons divided into three wings of maximum occupancy 10, 10 and 8. It is possible to close off wings, as well as individual cells. All courtyards, etc., will be secure. Four of them will be netted over. There is little possibility of escape over the roof because of the guard towers. Size limitations on groups will apply to workshops and leisure. With recreational activities in the gym, and outside sporting events, the total number involved may rise to 56, but players will be separated from spectators and the latter separated by blocks. Judgments as to whether this number should be allowed at any given time will be based on tension indicators, as discussed above.

Both security and good order will be at risk if occupancy rate is allowed to rise above 85–90 percent. The question of the temporarily violent or intractable inmate and his control or support is resolved by removing responsibility for the final decisions as to his future from disciplinary staff to the Director of the Department. In the event of an extreme situation, where ratings on the security scale move beyond point 6, there will be the opportunity for treatment, either by group therapy or medication, on site, i.e., in the home wing or sick bay. The inmate, or inmates, will then pass from staff to medical responsibility. (This was a conscious, and much debated, decision not to follow the tradition of having a "prison within the prison" for so-called intractables.)

PATTERNS OF LIFE

Within the criteria for a satisfying life bounded by maximum security and translated into architectural reality, there are three interdependent patterns of daily living and a community structure of weekly and fortnightly routines.

WORK

Work serves positive functions for the inmate as well as for the institution. It is necessary to design the work so that it is intrinsically interesting, allows for the development of marketable skills and develops as an integral and congruent part of the total life of the institution. It is necessary that work is a satisfying activity, and that the appropriate structure of work groups is present to promote this satisfaction. Although the choice of work is not the basic problem, it may be as well to search out alternatives to the traditional prison "shops." Secure workshops within a secure perimeter will make easier the formation of semi-autonomous work groups.

Implementation Setback

The driving force behind the design process had been Colin Campbell, the Director of the Corrective Services Department of West Australia. He had concluded that Fremantle Prison, the existing maximum security prison, was archaic (it was over 100 years old) and a source of great stress for inmates and staff. A tour of new developments in the western world had convinced him that the craze for air-conditioned concrete tombs with constant electronic surveillance had no future in a society that valued human life to the point where it banned capital punishment.

Campbell introduced a crash program so that enough officers would be trained for "group management" before the actual prison was ready to receive its first batch of inmates. As the design was for a single-storied structure not much more complicated, except for its electronics, than a motel, it did not seem impossible that the training program could be met.

Statistical projections emerging at this time suggested that by 1990 West Australia would have too few long-term prisoners to warrant the maintenance of Canningvale. (The architect, who was fully involved in all of the socio-technical design phases, had allowed for this by designing the facility so that it could be sold off as a conference center.) In any case, the government of the day wavered on the plea of costs and public unconcern about conditions at the Fremantle prison. Campbell died, prematurely, in 1977. Succeeding governments prevaricated but the statistical projections were revised, upwards, and the public was alarmed by a series of highly publicized murders. At last, in March 1983, Canningvale received its first batch of inmates—but only as medium security risks. It had become an overflow facility so that more cells would be freed up in the old Fremantle Prison for long-term prisoners who would be held under the old conditions.

As a final irony, the Canningvale medium security prison moved, in January 1988, to a form of group management that they call "unit management"—while one officer is secure in the central observation cabin, another is outside making contacts with the inmates. Two people do not make a group. The idea has a comforting ring because it was derived from Eric Anderson's description of the Danish prison at Ringge. It does nothing, however, qualitatively to change the interface between inmates and officers, which is what the Campbell/Emery design was about.

It is not as if just the thrust of the idea was lost. In December of 1988 none of the current bureaucrats could recall having seen the report or knew where a copy might be found within the Department.

References

Abel, T. 1951. "The Sociology of Concentration Camps." *Social Forces,* 30:150–54.
Adler, A.G. 1958. "Ideas Toward a Sociology of the Concentration Camps." *American Journal of Sociology,* 68:513–22.
Cahn, E.N. 1949. *The Sense of Injustice.* New York: New York University Press.
Emery, F.E. 1959. *Some Characteristics of Socio-Technical Systems.* London: Tavistock Institute Document No.258.
———. 1970. *Freedom and Justice Within Walls: The Bristol Prison Experiment.* London: Tavistock Publications.
Emery, F. and E. Thorsrud. 1977. *Democracy at Work.* Leiden: Martinus Nijhoff.
Emery, M. and F. Emery. 1978. "Searching: For New Directions, In New Ways . . . For New Times." In *Management Handbook for Public Administrators,* edited by J.W. Sutherland. New York and London: Van Nostrand.
Foreman, P.B. 1959. "Buchenwald and Modern P.O.W. Detention Policy." *Social Forces,* 37:289–98.
Garfinkel, H. 1955–56. "Conditions of Successful Degradation Ceremonies." *American Journal of Sociology,* 61:421–22.
Hoffer, E. 1952. *The True Believer.* London: Secker and Warburg.
Lewin, K. 1936. *Dynamic Theory of Personality.* New York: McGraw-Hill.
Polanski, N.A. 1942. "The Prison as an Autocracy." *Journal of Criminal Law and Criminology,* 33:16–22.
Sykes, G. 1958. *The Society of Captives.* Princeton, N.J.: Princeton University Press.

The Unconscious in Culture and Society

Studies at the macro-social level needed to be made in the socio-psychological perspective as much as at the micro and intermediate levels. Experience of Nazism and Stalinism, or more recently that of a country such as Iran, has brought a realization of what can happen when unconscious forces gain control in a society. Both Freud and Jung issued warnings about what would happen should such possibilities become actual.

A number of Institute members, some doubly trained in psychoanalysis and social anthropology or working in teams containing this combination, have advanced understanding of the role of unconscious forces in the formation of culture and the larger structure of society. As with the projects concerned with smaller social units, these "macro projects" were brought to its attention by organizations having special responsibilities in the areas concerned. Because they represent responses to felt needs they are in as widely different areas as are the projects on organizational change. The underlying unity is not that of a formal research program but is provided by the continuing readiness to respond to generic themes that are field determined. They provide a set of opportunities for domain-based research at the macro level which complement those at the meso and micro levels.

Culture as a Psycho-Social Process. In an attempt to relate sociological and psychological frames of reference for the purpose of action research, Trist introduced a concept of culture as a psycho-social process. The concept derives from the personality-culture approach originally put forward by Edward Sapir (1927) but incorporates recent psychoanalytic and social theory. Cultural patterns are distinguished from cultural objects. One set of patterns is outwardly directed and the other inwardly directed. The latter contains unconscious as well as conscious elements. The psycho-social concept of culture, which enables a very wide range of phenomena to be treated in the same frame of reference, lies between the purely psycho-biological and purely sociological frames of reference, which can now be related to each other. This is necessary in action-research projects where different aspects of the phenomena under investigation have to be considered together in real time.

Thoughts on the Meaning of the Word Democracy. There have been many studies, both psychological and sociological, of various aspects of democracy. The one made by Donald Winnicott in 1947, is unique. A child psychiatrist and analyst, he applies his well-known ideas concerning the "ordinary devoted mother and her baby" to society. So long as this relationship is "good enough" (it can scarcely be ideal in a workaday world) the infant is set on a trail that enables him or her to cope, as a reasonably responsible and tolerant adult, with a good deal of contradiction and uncertainty. This is necessary for people to be able to "live with democracy" inside themselves. Unless there is a critical mass of such individuals in a society it will not be able to sustain a democratic order. Factors that disturb the security of the mother/child relationship, such as the economic necessity of large numbers of women going out to work while their children are still too young to handle language, may have negative consequences for future capacity for democracy.

Notes on the Russian National Character. Dicks' contribution on the Russian national character is a shortened version of his monograph on this topic (Dicks, 1952). He was tri-lingual in Russian, German and English and spent a good deal of his youth in Russia and Germany. During World War II he undertook a study of Nazi ideology and the German national character from a psychoanalytic point of view in collaboration with the American sociologist, Edward Shils (Dicks, 1950). He and Shils reached similar conclusions to the authors of *The Authoritarian Personality* (Adorno et al., 1950) which strengthened confidence in this type of approach. Dicks now went on to make what he called *Observations on Contemporary Russian Behavior* (1960) at the Harvard Center for Russian Studies. The dynamics shown are substantially different from the German case, especially regarding the presence of an underlying "good mother figure" who coexisted with an authoritarian persecutory father. These studies point to a link between psychopathology and social pathology. Dicks shows that the basic social character of the large majority of Russians in the 1960s stemmed from that of the traditional peasant family. Further studies are needed to discover how far this may still be true after another 30 years.

Latent Content of Television Viewing. That the media in all their forms may have an unconscious as well as a conscious content is now widely accepted. This was not so in the late 1950s when Emery made a comprehensive analysis of the viewing situation. On the basis of this, he conducted a novel experimental study of the psychological effects on pre-adolescent boys of seeing a Western film on television. The results show that effective communication takes place between the latent content of the film and the latent preoccupations of the viewers. This, the second part of his study, is presented under this Theme.

Asylum and Society. Physical treatments, especially by drugs, have shortened the periods spent in hospital by psychotic patients but have created the "re-admissions problem." It would seem that the full benefits of these treatments cannot be realized while the attitude to mental illness in the larger society remains basically unchanged. The paper by Elizabeth Bott Spillius shows that the surrounding culture still demands that "madness" be contained in the mental hospital so that society can maintain an image of itself as "sane." For deep unconscious reasons the split has to be preserved. This creates conflict inside hospitals between a duty to protect society and a wish to help the patient. This conflict is not fully recognized and creates dis-ease among medical staff, which impairs performance. In the long run contact with a supporting family is the most important factor in determining whether or not a patient becomes permanently hospitalized, not his "psychosis." When he loses this support he has no social place outside the hospital, which becomes his asylum.

This paper is unusual in the literature on mental hospitals in that it gives an anthropological picture of the hospital as an open system in its society, together with an analysis of its dynamic in terms of psychoanalytic concepts.

References

Adorno, T.W., E. Frenkel-Brunswik, D.J. Levinson and N. Sanford (Editors). 1950. *The Authoritarian Personality.* New York: Harper and Row.

Dicks, H.V. 1950. "Personality Traits and National Socialist Ideology: A War-Time Study of German Prisoners of War." *Human Relations,* 3:111–54. Reprinted in *Propaganda in War and Crisis,* edited by D. Lerner. New York: Stewart, 1951.

———. 1952. "Observations on Contemporary Russian Behaviour." *Human Relations,* 5:111–75.

———. 1960. "Some Notes on Russian National Character." In *The Transformation of Russian Society; Aspects of Social Change since 1861,* edited by C.E. Black. Cambridge, Mass.: Harvard University Press.

Sapir, E. 1927. "The Impact of Culture on Personality." In *Selected Writings,* edited by D.G. Mandelbaum. Berkeley: University of California Press.

Eric Trist

Culture as a Psycho-Social Process*

Social psychology is the intervening discipline between general psychology and general sociology. Its function is to enable the social and psychological fields to become related to each other. For this purpose it requires a concept of culture as a psycho-social process.

The psychologist begins with people whether as individuals or as members of particular groups. Since, however, individuals and groups exist in a society, he or she is obliged to follow them through into the institutional systems in which they take roles and make relationships. On the sociological side, the anthropologist in particular follows the opposite course, being concerned first with social structure, as otherwise there would be no institutional framework in which to place the people to be described. This determines the methods used, apart altogether from decisions subsequently made regarding the sociological or psychological emphasis of interests.

At the time that the original version of this paper was prepared I was engaged in the first phase of an action-research program focussing on methods of work organization at the coal face (Trist and Bamforth, 1951). This experience forced me to combine a psychological with a sociological approach. Elliott Jaques had to do the same in the Glacier project, which he was carrying out in parallel and which involved learning about group processes at all levels of the organization as they were occurring (Jaques, 1951). It is my contention that action research, which expresses the social engagement of social science, compels the research worker to make interdisciplinary combinations in order to understand the many-sided real-life situations being dealt with. These processes operate dynamically through time. To proceed with field projects I needed a concept such as culture as a psycho-social process to act as the medium through which I could bring together the sociological and psychological phenomena I was encountering. They can be separated only by abstracting them from their event contexts when they become static categories.

*Based on a paper contributed to the Symposium on the Concept of Culture arranged by the Anthropological Section of the British Association for the Advancement of Science (1950). Apart from a synopsis in the *Proceedings*, it has not been previously published. A few later references have been added and a few minor changes made in the text which was lost for many years and only came to light when the present volume was being prepared.

The two projects mentioned drew attention to the way in which psychological forces, unconscious as well as conscious, at the level of the group and of the individual, interacted with structural forces to bring into existence a concrete "field" with a dynamic pattern which is specific for a given social situation, even though it may have wider implications. The aim of action research is to understand such dynamic patterns. To gain such an understanding is impossible with either psychological or sociological concepts alone. The social scientist is forced by the nature of such data to search for concepts that will enable psychological and sociological constructs to be brought into effective communication.

For a considerable number of years the concept of culture had been moving into a position where it could function as the middle and intervening term. It was well set on this course in the inter-war period when Edward Sapir's (1927) interest in the impact of culture on personality exercised a major influence. The even earlier work of Thomas and Znaniecki (1918/1920) on *The Polish Peasant in Europe and America* exercised a strong effect in the same direction. The concept of attitudes as task-set, which had grown up in general psychology, was re-inforced by the sociological insights of these workers. A concept of social attitudes emerged which gave defined psychological content to social norms. The usefulness of the concept of social attitudes, however, was limited by its segmental character. It was unable, externally, to make comprehensive reference to the structure of social systems or, internally, to reach down to emotional phenomena at the deeper levels of personality. The concept of culture has no such disadvantage and may be used in relation to all phenomena of a type to be referred to as psycho-social processes.

Historically, there have been two major conceptual schemes in the human sciences: that of the psycho-physical system, or organism, and that of social structure, or the institutional system. The first of these is non-social and is concerned with the relationship of psychological processes, externally to the stimulus-field of the physical environment and, internally to the physiological environment of the organism. Examples of psycho-physical constructs are those of configuration in gestalt psychology, with such corollaries as the law of prägnanz and the principle of closure; retroactive inhibition in learning; and libido theory in psychoanalysis. The second frame of reference is non-psychological and is concerned with social process for its own sake. Externally, social systems may be related to the physical environment in the ecological sense, but internally to real people only in terms of the institutional roles taken by persons and groups in social structures.

The concept of the psycho-social organism or, more generally, of psycho-social systems, is proposed as a third frame of reference to focus research on processes whose distinctive character is that of being psychological and social at the same time. It is to this frame of reference that the concept of culture will be ordered. The function of culture as a psycho-social process is to permit the psycho-physical organism to operate socially and the institutional structure to operate psychologically. Some of the properties and varieties of cultural phenomena will now be outlined.

Empirically, it may be shown that the process character of cultural phenomena as psycho-social is genuinely distinctive in that more is in question than a mere admixture of psychological and social factors. A number of such processes have been investigated. The work of the late Sir Frederic Bartlett (1932) on the social fashioning of memory schemata may be regarded as having provided the first experimental demonstration. In field theory terms, psycho-social processes are resultant compounds in which the psychological component attains social existence while the social component attains psychological existence.

As regards function, cultural phenomena may be viewed as having the status of techniques in the dimension of means/ends relations. In this perspective culture may be seen as the instrumental aspect of social life as distinct from the structural. An example would be ritual. But means frequently become ends as substitutive goals become established; and ends, once immediate, often become incidental to the pursuit of remoter goals. With such phenomena learning theory has long made us familiar. The practice of culture tends to enlarge the scope, increase the differentiation and change the direction of social objectives, and in so doing modifies in some measure the social structure in which it operates.

To be included under techniques are not only skills in the manual or cognitive sense but customs, attitudes and systems of strategy and tactics of an emotional order, used wittingly and unwittingly in making inter-personal and inter-group relations. They deal with social objects of all types—good, bad and mixed—with varying degrees of success. Many such phenomena appear as defense mechanisms against anxiety. But anxiety is a psycho-physical rather than a psycho-social concept. Recent developments in psychoanalysis have shown how defense mechanisms may also be seen in a psycho-social perspective as techniques of "object-relations" (A. Freud, 1946; Klein, 1948; Fairbairn, 1952). Certain of these techniques may pervade groups in given environmental situations—as in the hospitals described by Menzies (1960; Vol. I, "Social Systems as a Defense Against Anxiety").

With regard to content, a distinction may be made between cultural objects and cultural patterns. Cultural objects are artifacts of all kinds, whether technological, utilitarian, sacred or aesthetic. They are behavioral products determined by cultural patterns. They are external to the individual and are experienced as non-psychological. They include written language and documents; all representational and recording systems; and all technologies when ordered to the psycho-social organism. They correspond to the quasi-conceptual, quasi-social and quasi-physical facts of Lewin's life-space (Lewin, 1935; 1936). They constitute the material on which the archaeologist and culture historian are accustomed to work. They encompass the simple tools of pre-literate peoples and the complex systems of the modern engineer or computer expert.

As regards cultural patterns, one large class may be defined to include all cultural patterns with primary external reference. These include all forms of knowledge and skill, spoken language, beliefs, codes of morals and manners, values, prejudices and social attitudes, as these are carried by the individual. All cultural patterns are internal in the sense of being located in the person. Those listed, however, refer directly to external social objects and are regarded by the individual as his psychological possessions rather than as himself. By this is meant that they exist within him as material which he can use, of which he is partly aware, and which he is able to make available to himself by the normal processes of recall. Awareness tends to be of content rather than of structure; the "grammars" remain intuitive and are left for the social scientist to "write."

But there are also cultural patterns with primary internal reference. These patterns refer to unconscious internal objects in the psychoanalytic sense and compose the basic social character of the individual. He regards them as part of himself and they are usually so regarded by others. Beyond a certain point of perception their social configuration becomes lost. They appear merely as personal idiosyncrasies or as universal qualities. They act as an internal source of influence on the patterns at a more conscious level and reach into society through them. They may also be directly, though still unconsciously, projected onto various types of external social objects which themselves are then partly fashioned by these investments. Topics of this kind have been investigated in many studies. Notable are those of H.V. Dicks (1950; Vol. I, "Notes on the Russian National Character") on the relationship between Nazi ideology and character traits. The corroboration of his findings by the authors of *The Authoritarian Personality* (Adorno et al., 1950) has suggested that the concepts of social and, indeed, national character are not the fictions they had been supposed to be.

From the psycho-physical point of view cultural patterns can be said to exist at all levels of consciousness. But while consciousness (or unconsciousness) is a property of the psycho-physical organism, the phantasy activity of the internal world is a psycho-social process (Isaacs, 1952). Cultural patterns related to the deeper character level derive from the phantasy activity of unconscious systems of internal object-relations. This phantasy activity is the basic process of "culture" within the individual, founded as one is on the activities of the living "internal society" composed by these object-relations. Beyond studies which draw on psychoanalysis are those which emanate from Jung (1934–1954) which postulate that the individual carries a collective unconscious containing archetypes of a psycho-social character. These have been used by such writers as Joseph Campbell (1959–1968) to explain the structure and function of myths in both Eastern and Western societies.

Socialization may be taken up from the point of view of the degree of universality in the distribution of given cultural patterns in groups of various sizes, as these are organized in terms of institutional systems. The wider the distribution, the more forcibly do structural factors come into play—and produce standardization (norms). In field theory terms, this would be regarded as the induction of group standards through the power-field of the institutionalized group. From the standpoint of developmental psychology the early phases of socialization are seen as involving the internalization of social norms and values. They are part of the frustrating necessity of having to grow up in a particular family, which exemplifies in its own way the kinship system of a given society. It has to learn to manage this situation in terms of the culture of this society—as this has come to exist in them as one group of interacting individuals.

But it must be remembered that, on the Rorschach for example, an "original" response is one pole of the same continuum of which a "popular" response is the opposite. Some degree of variation always remains from the fact of the internal location of culture, which means that it is continually being re-vamped in personality terms. Always, the actual existence of culture is in personal versions (Sapir, 1927), however close such versions may be to each other. It is this personal quality that allows culture to impart vitality to a society and the culture-carrying individual to function as an agent of social change.

Cultural patterns operate socially only in concrete situations where inter-personal and inter-group relations are actually taking place. Here, we may distinguish autistic behavior as an exclusively intra-personal function, from social behavior involving inter-personal and inter-group relations.

There is evidence from work on groups that new and different forces begin to operate when the two-person situation is changed to that of the small face-to-face group. The work of Bion (1961), with his theory of "basic assumptions" has pioneered this area. The different approach of S.H. Foulkes (1964) similarly attests to the existence of a level of group behavior over and above that of the component individuals. Lewin's (1951) work on group decision-making during World War II showed still another way of attesting to the reality of the group level.

As group studies develop with larger social units it is likely that still other forces will come into focus. Political processes arise at the level of inter-group relations (Higgin and Bridger, 1964; Vol. I, "The Psycho-Dynamics of an Inter-Group Experience"). Dangerous processes of regression appear in the large face-to-face group (Turquet, 1975; Main, 1975). There is grave fallacy in proceeding in one jump from personality to society. Psychologically, it is in the area between small social units and the larger society that our knowledge is least developed (Crozier, 1974; Trist, 1977).

Beyond the large face-to-face group a wide range of communications media influence personal attitudes and social behavior. They may act as variety attenuators (Beer, 1979), and agents of distortion as well as extending the range of information available to the individual. One may begin to think of an order of social magnitude: the person; the pair; the triad; the double pair; the singular group; the multiple group; the singular organization; the multiple organization; the singular community; the multiple community; the total society; transnational social orders. It seems likely that at each step there will be changes in quality as well as quantity in the processes which occur though there will be many continuants.

Perhaps enough has been said to illustrate the usefulness of a concept of culture which regards cultural phenomena as consisting of a variety of psychosocial patterns which persons and groups actively operate in order to take roles and make relationships in the institutionalized social systems of their society. These societal systems have an objective, impersonal reality which is independent of the individual himself. From the point of view of sociology they are non-psychological. The social environment also contains the various sets of behavioral products which have been called cultural objects. These include all the technologies of material culture; they, like institutions, are experienced as non-psychological. But, without psycho-social patterns which individuals themselves carry, they would be quite unable to operate socially the psychophysical systems on which they are founded as biological organisms, while the institutions of society and its heritage of "products" would exercise no effect on behavior.

References

Adorno, T.W., E. Frenkel-Brunswik, D.J. Levinson and N. Sanford (Editors). 1950. *The Authoritarian Personality.* New York: Harper and Row.
Bartlett, Sir F. 1932. *Remembering.* Cambridge: Cambridge University Press.
Beer, S. 1979. *The Heart of Enterprise.* New York: Wiley.
Bion, W.R. 1961. *Experiences in Groups and Other Papers.* London: Tavistock Publications; New York: Basic Books.
Campbell, J. 1959–1968. *The Masks of God.* New York: Viking Press.
Crozier, M. 1974. "The Relationship Between Micro- and Macrosociology." *Human Relations,* 25:239–52.
Dicks, H.V. 1950. "Personality Traits and National Socialist Ideology: A War-Time Study of German Prisoners of War." *Human Relations,* 3:111–54. Reprinted in *Propaganda in War and Crisis,* edited by D. Lerner. New York: Stewart, 1951.
———. 1972. *Licensed Mass Murder.* New York: Basic Books.
Fairbairn, W.R.D. 1952. *Psycho-Analytic Studies of the Personality.* London: Tavistock Publications.

Foulkes, S.H. 1964. *Therapeutic Group Analysis*. London: Allen and Unwin.

Freud, A. 1946. *The Ego and the Mechanisms of Defence*. New York: International Universities Press.

Higgin, G.W. and H. Bridger. 1964. "The Psycho-Dynamics of an Inter-Group Experience." *Human Relations*, 17:391–444.

Isaacs, S. 1952. "On the Nature and Function of Phantasy." In *Developments in Psycho-Analysis*, edited by S. Isaacs, M. Klein and J. Riviere. London: Hogarth Press.

Jaques, E. 1951. *The Changing Culture of a Factory*. London: Tavistock Publications. Reissued 1987, New York: Garland.

———. 1953. "On the Dynamics of Social Structure." *Human Relations*, 6:3–24.

Jung, C.G. 1934–1945. "Archetypes of the Collective Unconscious." In *Collected Works, 9.1*. London: Routledge and Kegan Paul.

Klein, M. 1948. *Contributions to Psycho-Analysis 1921–1945*. London: Hogarth Press.

Lewin, K. 1935. *A Dynamic Theory of Personality*. New York: Macmillan.

———. 1936. *Principles of Topological Psychology*. New York: McGraw-Hill.

———. 1951. "Frontiers in Group Dynamics." *Human Relations*, 1:5–41 and 143–53.

Main, T.F. 1975. "Some Psychodynamics of Large Groups." In *The Large Group: Therapy and Dynamics*, edited by L. Kreeger. London: Constable.

Menzies, I.E.P. 1960. "A Case-Study in the Functioning of Social Systems as a Defence Against Anxiety: A Report on a Study of the Nursing Service of a General Hospital." *Human Relations*, 13:95–121.

Sapir, E. 1927. "The Impact of Culture on Personality." In *Selected Writings*, edited by D.G. Mandelbaum. Berkeley: University of California Press.

Thomas, W.I. and F. Znaniecki. 1918/1920. *The Polish Peasant in Europe and America*, Volumes I and II. Reprinted 1958, New York: Dover.

Trist, E.L. 1977. "A Concept of Organizational Ecology." *Australian Journal of Management*, 2:161–75.

Trist, E.L. and K.W. Bamforth. 1951. "Some Social and Psychological Consequences of the Longwall Method of Coal Getting." *Human Relations*, 4:3–38.

Turquet, P. 1975. "Threats to Identity in the Large Group." In *The Large Group: Therapy and Dynamics*, edited by L. Kreeger. London: Constable.

D.W. Winnicott

Thoughts on the Meaning of the Word Democracy*

In submitting this article (April 1949) I realize that I am offering comments on a subject that is outside my own specialty. Sociologists and political scientists may at first resent this impertinence. Yet it seems to me to be valuable for workers to cross the boundaries from time to time, provided that they realize (as I do indeed) that their remarks must inevitably appear näive to those who know the relevant literature and who are accustomed to a professional language of which the intruder is ignorant.

This word *democracy* has great importance at the present time. It is used in all sorts of different senses; here are a few:

- A social system in which the people rule.
- A social system in which the people choose the leader.
- A social system in which people choose the government.
- A social system in which the government allows the people freedom of thought and expression of opinion and freedom of enterprise.
- A social system which, being on a run of good fortune, can afford to allow individuals freedom of action.

One can study:

- The etymology of the word.
- The history of social institutions: Greek, Roman, etc.
- The use made of the word by various countries and cultures at the present time: Great Britain, U.S.A., Russia, etc.
- The abuse of the word by dictators and others: hoodwinking the people, etc.

In any discussion on a term, such as democracy, it is obviously of first importance that a definition should be reached, suitable for the particular type of discussion.

*A reproduction of the original—*Human Relations*, 4:171–85, 1950.

Psychology of the Use of the Term

Is it possible to study the use of this term psychologically? We accept and are accustomed to psychological studies of other difficult terms such as "normal mind," "healthy personality," "individual well-adjusted to society," and we expect such studies to prove valuable insofar as they give unconscious emotional factors their full import. One of the tasks of psychology is to study and present the latent ideas that exist in the use of such concepts, not confining attention to obvious or conscious meaning. An attempt is made in this article to initiate a psychological study.

Working Definition of the Term

It does seem that an important latent meaning of this term can be found, namely, that a democratic society is "mature," that is to say that it has a quality that is allied to the quality of individual maturity which characterizes its healthy members. Democracy is here defined, therefore, as "society well-adjusted to its *healthy* individual members." This definition is in accord with the view expressed recently by R.E. Money-Kyrle (1948).

It is the way people use this term that is important to the psychologist. A psychological study is justified if there is implied in the term the element of *maturity*. The suggestion is that in all uses of the term there can be found to be implied the idea of maturity or relative maturity, though it is difficult, as all will admit, to define these terms adequately.

In psychiatric terms, the normal or healthy individual can be said to be one who is mature; according to his or her chronological age and social setting, there is an appropriate degree of emotional development. (In this argument physical maturity is assumed.)

Psychiatric health is therefore a term without fixed meaning. In the same way the term "democratic" need not have a fixed meaning. Used by a community it may mean *the more rather than less mature in society structure*. In this way one would expect the frozen meaning of the word to be different in Britain, the U.S. and the U.S.S.R., and yet to find that the term retains value because of its implying the recognition of maturity as health.

How can one study the emotional development of society? Such a study must be closely related to the study of the individual. The two studies must take place simultaneously.

An attempt must be made to state the accepted qualities of democratic machinery. The machinery must exist for the *election* of leaders by free vote, true secret ballot. The machinery must exist for the people *to get rid of* leaders by secret ballot. The machinery must exist for the illogical election and removal of leaders. The essence of democratic machinery is the free vote (secret ballot). The point of this is that it ensures the freedom of the people to express deep feelings, *apart from conscious thoughts.*

In the exercise of the secret vote, the whole responsibility for action is taken by individuals, if they are healthy enough to take it. The vote expresses the outcome of the struggle within oneself, the external scene having been internalized and so brought into association with the interplay of forces in one's own personal inner world. That is to say, the decision as to which way to vote is the expression of a solution of a struggle within oneself. The process seems to be somewhat as follows. The external scene, with its many social and political aspects, is made personal in the sense that one gradually identifies oneself with all the parties to the struggle. This means that the external scene is perceived in terms of one's own internal struggle, and one temporarily allows the internal struggle to be waged in terms of the external political scene. This to-and-fro process involves work and takes time, and it is part of democratic machinery to arrange for a period of preparation. A sudden election would produce an acute sense of frustration in the electorate. Each voter's inner world has to be turned into a political arena over a limited period.

It would be possible to take a community and to impose on it the machinery that belongs to democracy, but this would not be to create a democracy. Someone would be needed to continue to maintain the machinery (for secret ballot, etc.), and also to force the people to accept the results.

Innate Democratic Tendency

A democracy is an achievement, at a point of time, of a limited society, i.e., of a society that has some natural boundary. Of a true democracy (as the term is used today) one can say, "*In this society at this time there is sufficient maturity in the emotional development of a sufficient proportion of the individuals that comprise it for there to exist an innate tendency towards the creation and recreation and maintenance of the democratic machinery.*" By innate I intend to convey the following: the natural tendencies in human nature (hereditary) bud and flower into the democratic way of life (social maturity), but this only happens through the healthy emotional development of individuals; only a proportion of individuals in a social group will have had the luck to develop to maturity and therefore it is only through them that the innate (inherited) tendency of the group towards social maturity can be implemented.

It would be important to know what proportion of mature individuals is necessary if there is to be an innate democratic tendency. In another way of expressing this, what proportion of anti-social individuals can a society contain without submergence of innate democratic tendency?

If the war, and the evacuation scheme in particular, increased the proportion of anti-social children in Great Britain from X percent to (say) $5X$ percent, this could easily affect the education system, so that the educational orientation must be towards the $5X$ percent anti-socials, crying out for dictatorship methods and away from the $100 - 5X$ percent children who are not anti-social. A decade later this problem would be stated in this way, that, whereas society can cope with X percent criminals by segregation of them in prisons, $5X$ percent of them tends to produce a general reorientation towards criminals.

Immature Identification with Society

In a society at any one time, if there are X individuals who show their lack of sense of society by developing an anti-social tendency, there are Z individuals reacting to inner insecurity by the alternative tendency—identification with authority. This is unhealthy and immature, because it is not an identification with authority that rises out of self-discovery. It is a sense of frame without a sense of picture, a sense of form without retention of spontaneity. This is a pro-society tendency that is anti-individual. People who develop in this way can be called "hidden anti-socials."

Hidden anti-socials are not "whole persons" any more than are manifest anti-socials, since each needs to find and to control the conflicting force in the external world outside the self. By contrast, the healthy person, who is capable of becoming depressed, is able to find the whole conflict within the self as well as being able to see the whole conflict outside the self, in external (shared) reality. When healthy persons come together they each contribute a whole world, because each brings a whole person.

Hidden anti-socials provide material for a type of leadership which is sociologically immature. Moreover this element in a society greatly strengthens the danger from its frank anti-social elements, especially as ordinary people so easily let those with an urge to lead get into key positions. Once in such positions, these immature leaders immediately gather to themselves the obvious anti-socials, who welcome them (the immature anti-individual leaders) as their natural masters (false resolution of splitting).

The Indeterminates

It is never as simple as this, because, if there are $(X + Z)$ percent anti-social individuals in a community, it is not true to say that $100 - (X + Z)$ percent are "social." There are those in an indeterminate position. One could put it as shown in Table 1. The whole democratic burden falls on the $100 - (X + Y + Z)$

TABLE I   Individuals and Society

Anti-socials	$X\%$
Indeterminates	$Y\%$
Pro-society but anti-individual	$Z\%$
Healthy individuals capable of social contribution	$100 - (X + Y + Z)\%$
Total	100%

percent of individuals who are maturing as individuals, and who are gradually becoming able to add a social sense to their well-grounded personal development.

What percentage does $100 - (X + Y + Z)$ percent represent, for instance, in Great Britain today? Possibly it is quite small, say 30 percent. Perhaps, if there are 30 percent mature persons, as many as 20 percent of the indeterminates will be sufficiently influenced to be counted as mature, thus bringing the total to 50 percent. If, however, the mature percentage should drop to 20, it must be expected that there will be a bigger fall in the percentage of indeterminates able to act in a mature way.

If 30 percent maturity in a community collects 20 percent of the indeterminates while 20 percent maturity collects only 10 percent of the indeterminates, the totals will be 50 percent and 30 percent respectively of people who can be counted on to act in a mature way. Whereas 50 percent total might indicate sufficient innate democratic tendency for practical purposes, 30 percent could not be counted as sufficient to avoid submergence by the sum of the anti-socials (hidden and manifest) and the indeterminates who would be drawn by weakness or fear into association with them.

There follows an anti-democratic tendency, a tendency towards dictatorship, characterized at first by a feverish bolstering up of the democratic façade (hoodwinking function of the term). One sign of this tendency is the corrective institution, the localized dictatorship, the practicing ground for the personally-immature leaders who are reversed anti-socials (pro-social but anti-individual). This, the corrective institution, has both the prison and the mental hospital of a healthy society perilously near to it, and for this reason the doctors of criminals and of the insane have to be constantly on guard lest they find themselves being used, without at first knowing it, as agents of the anti-democratic tendency. There must, in fact, always be a borderline in which there is no clear distinction between corrective treatment of the political or ideational opponent and the therapy of the insane person. (Here lies the social danger of physical methods of therapy of the mental patient, as compared with true psychotherapy, or even the acceptance of a state of insanity. In psychotherapy the patient is a person on equal terms with the doctor, with a right to be ill, and also a right to claim health and full responsibility for personal political or ideational views.)

Creation of an Innate Democratic Factor

If democracy is maturity, and maturity is health, and health is desirable, then we wish to see whether anything can be done to foster it. Certainly it will not help to impose democratic machinery on a country. We must turn to the $100 - (X + Y + Z)$ group of individuals. All depends on them. Members of this group can instigate research.

We find that at any one time we can do nothing to increase the quantity of this innate democratic factor comparable in importance to what has already been done (or not done) by the parents and homes of these individuals when they were infants and children and adolescents. We can, however, try to avoid compromising the future. We can try to avoid interfering with the homes that can cope, and are actually coping, with their own individual children and adolescents. These *ordinary good homes* provide the only setting in which the innate democratic factor can be created. The ordinary good home is something that defies statistical investigation. It has no news value, is not spectacular and does not produce the men and women whose names are publicly known. My assumption, based on 20,000 case histories, taken personally over a period of 25 years, is that in the community in which I work the ordinary good home is common, even usual. This is indeed a modest statement of positive contribution, but there is a surprising amount of complexity in its application.

Factors Adverse to the Functioning of the Ordinary Good Home

It is very difficult for people to recognize that the essential of a democracy really does lie with the ordinary man and woman and the ordinary, commonplace home. Even if a wise government policy gives parents freedom to run their homes in their own way, it is not certain that officials putting official policies into practice will respect the parents' position.

Ordinary good parents do need help. They need all that science can offer in respect of physical health and the prevention and treatment of physical disease; also they want instruction in child care and help when their children have psychological illnesses or present behavior problems. But, if they seek such assistance, can they be sure they will not have their responsibilities lifted from them? If this happens they cease to be creators of the innate democratic factor.

Many parents are not ordinarily good parents. They are psychiatric cases, or they are immature, or they are anti-social in a wide sense, and socialized only in a restricted sense; or they are unmarried, or in an unstable relationship, or bickering, or separated from each other, and so on. These parents get attention from society because of their defects. The thing is, can society see that the orientation towards these pathological features must not be allowed to affect society's orientation towards the ordinary healthy homes?

In any case, the parents' attempt to provide a home for their children, in which the children can grow as individuals, and each *gradually add* a capacity to identify with the parents and then with wider groupings, starts at the beginning, when the mother comes to terms with her infant. Here the father is the protecting agent which frees the mother to devote herself to her baby. The place of the home has long been recognized, and in recent years a great deal has been found out by psychologists as to the ways in which a stable home enables children not only to find themselves and to find each other, but also makes them begin to qualify for membership of society in a wider sense.

This matter of interference with the early infant/mother relationship, however, needs some special consideration. In our society there is increasing interference at this point, and there is extra danger from the fact that some psychologists actually claim that at the beginning it is only physical care that counts. This can only mean that in the unconscious fantasy of people in general the most awful ideas cluster round the infant/mother relationship. Anxiety in the unconscious is represented in practice by:

- Over-emphasis by physicians and even by psychologists on *physical* processes and health.
- Various theories that breast-feeding is bad, that the baby must be trained as soon as born, that babies should not be handled by their mothers, etc. . . . and (in the negative) that breast-feeding *must* be established, that no training whatever should be given, that babies should never be allowed to cry, etc.
- Interference with the mother's access to her baby in the first days, and with her first presentation of external reality to the infant. This, after all, is the basis of the new individual's capacity eventually to become related to ever-widening external reality, and if the mother's tremendous contribution, *through her being devoted,* is spoiled or prevented, there is no hope that the individual will pass eventually into the $100 - (X + Y + Z)$ group that alone generates the innate democratic factor.

Development of Subsidiary Themes: Election of Persons

Another essential part of the democratic machinery is that it is a *person* who is elected. There is all the difference in the world between the vote for a person, the vote for a party with a set tendency, and the support of a clear-cut principle by ballot.

The election of a person implies that the electors believe in themselves as persons, and therefore believe in the person they nominate or vote for. The person elected has the opportunity to act as a person. As a whole (healthy) person one has the total conflict within, which enables one to get a view, albeit a personal one, of total external situations. One may of course belong to a party and be known to have a certain tendency. Nevertheless one can adapt in a delicate way to changing conditions; if one actually changes one's main tendency one can put oneself up for re-election.

The election of a party or a group tendency is relatively less mature. It does not require of the electors a trust in a human being. For immature persons, nevertheless, it is the only logical procedure, precisely because an immature person cannot conceive of, or believe in, a truly mature individual. The result of the vote for a party or tendency, a thing and not a person, is the establishment of a rigid outlook, ill-adapted for delicate reactions. This *thing* that is elected cannot be loved or hated, and it is suitable for individuals who have a poorly developed sense of self. It could be said that in a system of voting it is less democratic, because less mature (in terms of emotional development of the individual), when the accent is on the vote for the principle or party and not on the vote for the person.

Much further removed from anything associated with the word democracy is the ballot on a specific point. There is little of maturity about a referendum (although this can be made to fit in with a mature system on exceptional occasions). As an example of the way in which a referendum is un-useful can be cited the peace ballot, between the wars, in Great Britain. People were asked to answer a specific question ("Are you in favor of peace or war?"). A large number of people abstained from voting because they knew that the question was an unfair one. Of those who voted a big proportion put their crosses by the word peace, although in actual fact, when circumstances rearranged themselves, they were in favor of the war when it came, and took part in the fighting. The point is that in this type of questioning there is only room for the expression of the *conscious* wish. There is no relation between putting one's tick against the word "peace" in such a ballot and voting for a person who is known to be eager for peace provided the failure to fight does not mean a lazy abandonment of aspirations and responsibilities and the betrayal of friends.

The same objection applies to much of Gallup Poll and other questionnaires, even although a great deal of trouble is taken to avoid exactly this pitfall. In any case, a vote on a specific point is a very poor substitute indeed for the vote in favor of a person who, once elected, has a space of time in which he can use his own judgment. The referendum has nothing to do with democracy.

Support of Democratic Tendency

The most valuable support is given in a negative way by organized non-interference with the ordinary good mother/infant relationship, and with the ordinary good home. For more intelligent support, even of this negative kind, much research is needed on the emotional development of the infant and the child of all ages, and also on the psychology of the nursing mother and of the father's function at various stages. The existence of some such studies shows a belief in the value of education, which of course can only be given insofar as there is understanding, and which can only be usefully given to the emotionally mature or healthy individuals. Another important negative contribution would be the avoidance of attempts to implant democratic machinery on total communities. (From a distance it seems that some such attempt has been made in Japan.) The result can only be failure, and a setback to true democratic growth. The alternative and valuable action is to support the emotionally mature individuals, however few they may be, and to let time do the rest.

Parent/Child Relationship

The democratic set-up includes the provision of a certain degree of stability for the elected rulers; as long as they can manage their job without alienating the support of their electors, they carry on. In this way the people arrange for a certain amount of stability which they could not maintain through direct voting on every point even if that were possible. The psychological consideration here is that there is in the history of every individual the fact of the parent/child relationship. Although in the mature democratic way of political life the electors are presumably mature human beings, it cannot be assumed that there is no place for a residue of the parent/child relationship, with its obvious advantages. To some extent, in the democratic election mature people elect temporary parents, which means that they also acknowledge the fact that to some extent the electors remain children. Even the elected temporary parents, the rulers of the democratic political system, are children themselves outside their professional political work. If in driving their cars they exceed the speed limit they come under ordinary judicial censure because driving a car is not part of their job of ruling. As political leaders, and only as such, they are temporarily parents, and after being deposed at an election they revert to being children. It is as if it is convenient to play a game of parents and children because things work out better that way. In other words, because there are advantages in the parent/child relationship, some of this is retained; but, for this to be possible, a sufficient proportion of individuals need to be grown-up enough not to mind playing at being children.

In the same way it is thought to be bad for these people who are playing at parents to have no parents themselves. In the game it is generally thought that there should be another house of representatives to which the rulers who are directly elected by the people should be responsible. In Britain this function belongs to the House of Lords, which is to some extent composed of those who have a hereditary title, and to some extent by those who have won a position there by eminence in various branches of public work. Once again the "parents" of the parents are persons, and capable of making positive contributions as human beings. And it makes sense to love or to hate or to respect or to despise persons. There can be no substitute in a society for the human beings or being at the top, insofar as that society is to be rated according to its quality of emotional maturity.

And further, in a study of the social setting in Great Britain, we can see that the Lords are children, relative to the Crown. Here in each case we come again to a person, who holds his position by heredity, and also by maintaining the love of his people by his personality and actions. It is certainly helpful when the reigning monarch quite easily and sincerely carries the matter a stage further and proclaims a belief in God. Thus the problems that now cluster around the idea of isolationism could be postponed.

Geographical Boundary of a Democracy

For the development of a democracy, in the sense of a mature society structure, it seems that it is necessary that there should be some natural geographical boundary for that society. Obviously, until recently and even now, the fact that Great Britain is sea-bound (except for its relation to Eire) has been very much responsible for the maturity of our society structure. Switzerland has (less satisfactorily) mountain limits. The United States until recently had the advantage of a west which offered unlimited exploitation; this meant that the United States, while being united by positive ties, did not until recently need to start to feel to the full the internal struggles of a closed community, united in spite of hate as well as because of love.

A state that has no natural frontier cannot relax an active adaptation to neighbors. In one sense, fear *simplifies* the emotional situation, for many of the indeterminate Y and some of the less severe of the anti-social X become able to identify with the state on the basis of a cohesive reaction to an external persecution threat. This simplification is detrimental, however, to the development towards maturity, which is a difficult thing, involving full acknowledgement of essential conflict, and the non-employment of any way out or way round (defenses).

In any case, the basis for a society is the whole human personality, and the personality has a limit. The diagram of a healthy person is a circle (sphere) so that whatever is not-self can be described as either inside or outside that person. It is not possible for persons to get further in society-building than they can get with their own personal development. For these reasons we regard with suspicion the use of terms like "world-citizenship." Perhaps only a few really great and fairly aged men and women ever get as far in their own development as to be justified in thinking in such wide terms.

If the whole world were our society, then it would need to be at times in a depressed mood (as a person at times inevitably has to be), and it would have to be able fully to acknowledge essential conflict within itself. The concept of a global society brings with it the idea of the world's suicide, as well as the idea of the world's happiness. For this reason we expect the militant protagonists of the world state to be individuals who are in a manic swing of a manic-depressive psychosis.

Education in Democratic Lore

Such democratic tendency as exists can be strengthened by a study of the psychology of social as well as of individual maturity. The results of such study must be given in understandable language to the existing democracies and to healthy individuals everywhere so that they may become *intelligently self-conscious*. Unless they are self-conscious they cannot know what to attack and what to defend, nor can they recognize threats to democracy when these arise. "The price of freedom is eternal vigilance"—vigilance by whom?—by two or three of the $100 - (X + Y + Z)$ percent mature individuals. The others are busy just being ordinary good parents, handing on the job of growing up, and of being grown-up, to their children.

Democracy at War

The question must be asked, is there such a thing as democracy at war? The answer is certainly not a plain yes. In fact, there are some reasons why, in war-time, there should be an announcement of temporary suspension of democracy because of war. It is clear that mature healthy individuals, collectively forming a democracy, should be able to go to war to defend what is valued, already possessed, etc.; and to fight anti-democratic tendencies insofar as there are people to support such tendencies by fighting. Nevertheless, it must be but seldom that things have worked out that way.

According to the description given above, a community is never composed of 100 percent of healthy, mature individuals. As soon as war approaches, there is a re-arrangement of groups, so that by the time war is being fought it is not the healthy who are doing all the fighting. Taking our four groups

- Many of the anti-socials, along with mild paranoids, feel better because of actual war, and they welcome the real persecution threat. They find a pro-social tendency by active fighting.

- Of the indeterminates, many step over into what is the thing to do, perhaps using the grim reality of war to grow up as they would not otherwise have done.
- Of the hidden anti-socials, probably some find opportunity for the urge to dominate in the various key positions which war creates.
- The mature, healthy individuals do not necessarily show up as well as the others. They are not so certain as the others are that the enemy is bad. They have doubts. Also they have a bigger positive stake in the world's culture, and in beauty and in friendship, and they cannot easily believe war is necessary. Compared with the near-paranoids they are slow in getting the gun in hand and in pulling the trigger. In fact they miss the bus to the front line, even if when they get there they are the reliable factor and the ones best able to adapt to adversity.

Moreover, some of the healthy of peace-time become anti-social in war (conscientious objectors) not from cowardice but from a genuine personal doubt, just as the peace-time anti-socials tend to find themselves in brave action in war. For these and other reasons, when a democratic society is fighting, it is the whole group that fights, and it would be difficult to find an instance of a war conducted by just those of a community who provide the innate democratic factor in peace. It may be that, when a war has disturbed a democracy, it is best to say that at that moment democracy is at an end, and those who like that way of life will have to start again and fight inside the group for the re-establishment of democratic machinery, after the end of the external conflict. This is a large subject, and it deserves the attention of large-minded people.

Reference

Money-Kyrle, R.E. 1948. *Psycho-Analysis and Politics*. Westport, Conn.: Greenwood Press. Reprinted 1973.

Henry Dicks

Notes on the Russian National Character*

This chapter is a condensed restatement of some conclusions arrived at by the writer on the strength of intensive interviews with Soviet defectors (Dicks, 1952) revised in the light of later work by others and of reading some relevant Russian authors of the period under review. Since there has to be some pruning in such a large theme, this essay is almost entirely about the peasantry. Bearers of power in the Soviet Union are largely the children of Great Russian peasants, or the urban working class, many of whom have retained a close connection with their peasant background.

It may be desirable first to summarize the general conceptual framework within which I approached the interviews with Russian defectors. Some familiarity of the reader with psychoanalytic terms will be assumed.

Personal data and literary products can be used by a skilled psychiatric observer and interviewer working with psychoanalytic concepts for making inferences about deeper attitudes and motivations. For present purposes the analyst has only to vary his focus from what is idiosyncratic for individuals to what is *recurrent* in material from his sources.

By such means there can be defined a *modal character* which is shared by representatives of a given national cultural group over and above subgroup differences. It is this modal configuration of traits of behavior which I mean when speaking of "national character." Within the context of this volume's theme of transformation, I shall be interested in exploring what variation this basic configuration has undergone, and where it shows itself as still a live factor in my interpretation of the contemporary Russian scene.

So far the psychiatrist is in his own field—the motivations of individual behavior. Some extrapolations will also be made from personality study into the sphere of sociopolitical behavior, and these rest on more debatable conceptual ground. The writer is aware that the description of the functioning of a

*A reproduction of the original in C.E. Black (Editor), *The Transformation of Russian Society; Aspects of Social Change Since 1861*. Cambridge, Mass.: Harvard University Press, 1960.

society demands not only insight into the personalities of an adequate sample of members of that society, but also needs to consider historical, economic and similar factors. To this extent this paper is only *one* strand in a canvas woven by several disciplines, and it should not be assigned more status than its modest title of "some notes." There is, however, one crucial aspect of personality psychology inseparable from the interpretation of social behavior. This is the area of attitude to authority.

It is here assumed that the kind of experience a child has in authority relations within the primary family group will be internalized to form the basis of his later expectations as to how the role of power-bearer and of subordinate, of leader and of led, will be played in the wider social group. I assume further that a given culture rests on an internalized and more or less unconscious system of mental images or models for the regulation and channeling of psychological needs of individuals and for signaling what is sanctioned and approved, or forbidden and punished. The way authority roles are exercised within a society sharing such an internalized unconscious system will be conditioned by the qualities of this system—including its rigidities and irrationalities based on the culture "myth" concerning human nature. The main mental mechanisms involved in transferring the internal system of the members to the interpretation of their external world are those of displacement and substitution, and of projection and identification. It is precisely this shared regulation of biopsychological need systems and authority relations which imparts to a culture its distinctive modal characteristics.

Though some of my earlier conclusions have changed while thinking about the question at hand, my main concepts about the source of the authority problem in Russians do not seem controverted by any subsequent observations or reading.

The procedure will be followed of describing first some of the more fundamental characteristics of Russian behavior and relating them to the primary family group. This is the psychiatrist's proper sphere. Next there will be included some interpretations about the motivations of wider social behavior by reference to primary object relations. It is hoped that by stressing the nature of the primary processes we may be able to form estimates as to the depth and degree of irrationality behind some of the secondary social processes.

In 1952 my account of the modal Russian personality stressed ambivalence as the outstanding trait. Ambivalence as such is a universal characteristic of human beings. It is the manner in which this ambivalence is manifested and countered or disposed of which provides a key to the interpretation of Russian character. It is seen to oscillate in large swings of mood in relation to self, to primary love objects, and to out-groups. The quality of these swings is most readily understood in terms of oral need satisfactions or deprivations. At one end there is the "omnivorousness," the lusty greed and zest for life, the tendency to rush at things and "swallow them whole"; the need for quick and full gratification; the spells of manic omnipotence feeling and optimistic belief in unlimited achievement; the overflowing vitality, spontaneity and anarchic demand for abolition of all bounds and limitations to giving and receiving.

At the other end of the spectrum there is melancholy, dreary apathy; frugality; meanness and suspicion of universal hostility; anxious and sullen submissiveness; self-depreciation and moral masochism, together with a grudging admission of the necessity for a depriving and arbitrary authority, thought of as the only safeguard against the excesses of Russian nature. In this mood we find a diffuse guilt feeling, a capacity for subtle empathy, and a ruminative self-doubt and self-torment. Outward servility and secret obstinacy coexist, as if one could bend the knee to Caesar in outward conformity and yet inwardly remain wholly on the side of God before whom all men are equally small and fallible. Nothing is so persistent in the Russian as a sense of moral outrage (*izdevatel'stvo*)—that ubiquitous feeling of guilt and shame at injustice and a sensitiveness about whom to trust not to hurt one. The Russian can vary between feeling that he or she is no good or superior to all the rest of mankind. One can concede another's social status and at the same time be consumed with envy of superior wealth.

Whether in Bacchanalian mood or in depression, Russians always need direct, spontaneous, heart-to-heart contact and communication, a sense of being loved and belonging, and they respect that need in others. They love the fun of teamwork which goes with a swing and a song, and a total investment of strength and feeling. They understand commands and obedience. But they are distressed by distant hauteur, formalism and bureaucratic protocol and hierarchy, preferring direct informal leadership and spontaneous improvization to methodical procedure in tackling difficulties. Elaborate hierarchy troubles them, as does any kind of rigidly and uniformly controlled activity.

A word should be added about what is connoted by unconscious oral needs and phantasies which to the writer appear to play such a large part in the Russian character. It is at primitive oral levels of human development (at the stage of the baby up to a year or so in age) that objects can be only partly distinguished in terms of self and not-self, and ego is not yet clearly demarcated. The contrast between objects felt to be "good" and "bad" is extreme, according to whether they gratify or deprive. At the oral level also there is an almost total separation between the attribution of loving and destructive powers to the self and to the external objects on whom this primitive dichotomy is projected. This concept helps us to understand the deeply embedded feeling that there are inscrutable remote and uncontrollable powers who can do what they like, which is part of the tacit assumption of Russians about the world. To this type of feeling we give the name paranoid because of its domination of the mind in mental disorders of that category. This ties in with Margaret Mead's statement that "friends could behave like enemies" and then like friends again (see below). As examples of the break-in of oral level phantasy from my interviews, the following may suffice: grandmothers threaten children that they must keep their mouths shut because the devil who is ever lurking near will get in through the mouth, or smash the child's teeth and gain possession; "blood-sucker," "man-eater," hyena and such are standard epithets for capitalist enemies as well as Soviet oppressors. Here the bad objects are *outside* the self.

We also begin to understand the frequent appearance in Russian myth and self-appraisal of feelings of omnipotence, of a giantlike strength—even of infants—against which strong measures of constraint and control have to be taken. As Gorer and Rickman (1949) pointed out, Russian women swaddle their children because they believe that, left unconstrained with their uncon-trolled strength, they will injure themselves. The peasant Khor's personality moved Turgenev to write about Peter the Great that he was a typical Russian, "so confident in his strength and power that he is not averse to breaking himself." The Russian word for "break" is *lomat'* and this carries the meaning of extreme exertion, as in the English "breaking one's neck" (to achieve a goal). Here the dangerous powers are located *inside*. This is the other side of paranoid feeling, more often experienced as a sense of anxiety or guilt.

About the same time as my study Margaret Mead (1951) wrote:

> In this traditional [Russian] character, thought and action were so interchange-able, that there was a tendency for all effort to dissipate itself in talk or in symbolic behavior. While there was a strong emphasis on the need for certain kinds of control . . . this control was seen as imposed from without; lacking it, the individual would revert to an original impulsive and uncontrolled state. Those forms of behavior which involved self-control rather than endurance, measurement rather than unstinted giving or taking, and calculation rather than immediate response to a situation, were extremely undeveloped. The distinctions between the individual and the group and between the self and others were also less emphasized than in the West, while the organization of the *mir*, the large, extended families and religious and social rituals stressed confession and com-plete revelation of self to others and the merging of the individual in the group. . . .
>
> Traditional Russian character assumed the co-existence of both good and evil in all individuals, and, in attitudes towards individuals, an expectation that friends could behave like enemies was combined with an expectation that this behavior could also be reversed—by confession, repentance and restoration of the former state. . . . Little distinction was made between thought and deed, between the desire to murder and the murder itself. All men were held to be

guilty, in some degree, of all human crimes. Against this lack of distinction between thought and deed there was a strong emphasis upon distinction among persons, on a purely social basis, an intolerance of any ambiguity between superiors and subordinates. This rigidity in matters of deference and precedence, however, was relieved by a strong countertendency to establish complete equality among all human souls and to wipe out all social distinctions.

While this may be said to outline one end of the spectrum of the Russian modal personality as it is revealed both in literature and by my interviews, the behavioral characteristics here described are in great contrast to the other end of the scale—the expected role behavior of the elite. Although this is particularly true of the Communist Party elite, it may also be said to have been the role of pre-Communist authorities since Peter I, at least, to educate and force this modal-character structure toward a higher level of mastery over primitive impulses, to catch up with the West. The Communist revolution is sometimes compared to Russia's passing through the puritan phase of development, and there are grounds for making this comparison. The germs of puritan attitudes were discernible in Russia despite all that was stated above. Religious asceticism existed in Russia for centuries, for example, among the Old Believers. There was also a rather uncritical swallowing of Western scientific rationalism once it penetrated to the intelligentsia—typical of the Russians' immoderation in what they do. The "New Man" in Soviet psychology is he who overcomes his anarchic spontaneity in favor of leaderlike abstinence from immediate impulse gratification; he who suppresses sentiment and private feeling through systematic thought and planned purposeful activity in wholehearted pursuit of the party line. Virtue and charisma are attached by the culture to those who show this rational mastery over impulse and greed as against mere passive capacity to endure deprivation. This contrast between the modal mass character and the puritan prescription for elite behavior has been one of the abiding tensions in Russian society, part of that sense of the alien and remote character of elites which forms at once their claim to veneration and their incurring of highly ambivalent resentment. Dudintsev, in *Not by Bread Alone,* has a cynical party bureaucrat, Drozdov, say this to his wife: "Touch me where you like, you will always find a living, tender, sensitive spot. That's why I need armour like a snail . . . my strong will . . . not a bad thing for a man . . . holds him in check."

This is the sacrifice of modal Russian character which a man who climbs the party ladder to success has to make. This, indeed, is what I have called in psychoanalytic terms the oral-anal conflict in the Russian character. It need not be assumed from my emphasis on this polarization that there are not, or will not be, intermediate positions; nor that the educational efforts and the economic changes in the Soviet Union will not produce an approximation to personalities more typical of an industrial society. The conflict, however, goes on both within the culture and within individuals who share in it. Such a conflict is much less settled than in Western European society.

It is in the context of these basic traits, including beliefs about the deeper nature of the child and about what is hidden in mankind, that we should look at the relationships in the primary social and economic unit of rural Russia—the peasant family as it existed on countless small holdings and, from available evidence, as it still exists today. It is typically a patriarchal family of grandfather and grandmother with their sons, wives and children, as well as any unmarried daughters and sons, living incredibly close together, farming the holding by joint labor. There is little privacy and the children participate in all that goes on in this living space. At the head of the household the child perceives a composite authority figure, a blend of both grandparents, of which one is the almost wholly awe-inspiring and arbitrary father-figure, shouting commands from his seat of power on the stove or at the head of the table. The other is an equally unpredictable, on the whole indulgent but also nagging and dominant, mother-figure, who inculcates prayer and demonology. Both claim divine sanction for their right to rule and chastise all their dependents, adults and children alike, and they are also the prescribed objects of love and pious duty. (One cannot help making the analogies: tsar and church, state and party.)

The typical prevailing feeling of terrified reverence for authority is best denoted by the Russian word *strakh*. In the family setting its presence leads to the phenomenon of marked duplicity in behavior. On the one hand, there is an astonishing degree of priggish, dutiful lip service and subjection to the grandfather; on the other hand, in his absence, something not far short of conspiracy of the adult sons against their father. This ambivalence is well described by Gladkov (1949) speaking of his father's relation during his childhood to the grandfather: "He nourished in himself a constant resentment against grandfather. . . . He bore himself with contempt toward grandfather in his absence, but to his face he expressed devotion and unconditional subordination."

Periodically there occur violent outbursts against the authority of the grandfather by the grown-up sons in fits of sudden desperation, more often than not terminated by remorseful and self-humiliating contrition (such as prostration at his feet) and begging for forgiveness. The motive ascribed to these revolts is the sons' wish for freedom to leave home because the old man will not make over to them their independent plot of land, their inheritance. But it is also moral outrage and hurt dignity as a result of his tyranny. It is no accident that parricide forms such a prominent theme in Russian literature. The child's own image of immediate adults is of people subject to higher authority and filled with ambivalent resentment and submissive love for the authority figure. A little later he learns that even grandfather is but a serf and can be bullied and humiliated by his *barin* (landowner, lord) or the police. There is indeed a series of infinite regress, leading via grandfather to the barin and so to the tsar and to God.

A correlate of this situation is the frequency with which the sons identify themselves with grandfather's arbitrary power and play their own role in due course in a like manner. Aggression passes down the echelon of the family structure: the grandmother, herself under her husband's heel, coerces and torments her daughters-in-law; the adult sons assert their status and dignity by beating or bullying their wives, children or younger brothers. Lowest in rank order is the daughter-in-law, as a "stranger." At all levels of this group, obedience is exacted by beating, threats of expulsion from the homestead and invocation of terrible sanctions based on a near-medieval religious and demon-ological system of beliefs, followed by contrition, tears and forgiveness. Emotion of every kind flows fully and unrestrainedly in comparison to, say, a nineteenth-century English family.

In sum, the typical childhood of a Russian peasant, including many a prominent Russian now in his prime, was spent in helpless participation in scenes of his elders' crude emotional oscillations between tenderness and brutality. He received an ambivalent perception of his own father as strong and good as well as cowardly and weak, his mother (grandparents' daughter-in-law) as lovable but despised, and himself as powerless and dependent. A rich if chaotic inner world of emotional potentials is thus created. The experience also develops a capacity to tolerate silently the most contradictory and powerful emotions. The nature of the identifications made is highly paradoxical. The little boy will tend to idealize and to identify himself in part with the victim position—with the tender, persecuted, suffering mother. There is evidence that this theme is later elaborated into the hero fantasy of rescuing the oppressed, suffering mother-figure. For example, the fairy tale of the prince who delivers the maiden from the evil sorcerer, Koshchei "The Immortal" (cf. "Firebird"). Such motivations are also one source of fervent love of the mother-country. It was remarkable how often my interviewees expressed the postwar state of Russia in terms of their "starving, neglected mother." But it makes for a kind of despair about weak, tender emotions which can never lead to happy endings. These are covered only by a defensive identification with the power and cruelty of the male line, by repression of the inner "mother's boy" in favor of rugged, swaggering "masculine" behavior. The mother-figure is treated with sadistic contempt in fantasy—for instance, the unprintable standard oath of Russian men—and also revered, pitied and idealized. Girls will harbor much hostility toward men and rebellion against the marital role as a fate not much worse than death. Love is always tragic in Russia. The strong, independent woman is admired.

The young child receives a good deal of spoiling, praise and love from the *babushka,* from aunts and neighboring women, and a special kind of intimate, almost forbidden, love from his own mother who scarcely dares show she is human. All these female figures, except perhaps the tragic mother, convey a sense of support and shield the child from the excess of paternal wrath. The boy's emotional reward comes when he feels he is considered strong, a good little helper, an eager student, and above all obedient and quiet. From this source we may visualize arising some typical attitudes toward good citizenship behavior in present Russian society.

Lastly there is also a strongly marked motive to escape from the tyranny and oppression toward a distant beckoning land of freedom, equality and opportunity, where one can be one's own master and lead one's own life. This may have its sources in the oedipal feelings about the mother. The tight control of the kinship group by the patriarch, no less than the experience of swaddling in infancy, may be more reasons for the need for more space, more elbowroom (*prostor*), by which the Russians are driven despite the size of their territory. Qualities which may be expected to persist, and are indeed seen to be modal, are a high degree of *strakh,* a duplicity of behavior which combines a certain priggish eager-beaver subordination with a capacity for impassive absorption of humiliation and indignity, together with a smoldering sensitiveness and vindictive revolt in quick sympathy with the underdog against the authority that perpetuates these insults. This *strakh* has nothing to do with cowardice in external danger, but with a kind of awe given to authority-bearers. An example is the poor fellow Suchok, in Turgenev, who was more afraid of the barin than of drowning when his boat sank.

The economic situation of most peasants ensured that the Russian learned to live on very little. But this itself, together with the fitful indulgences by the mother-figures of childhood, may partly account for the undoubted longing for softness and tenderness and fat living as a basic motif. This is very directly expressed at the most typical end of the scale, and is strongly counteracted in the authoritarian leader sort of person. Periods of joy and happiness occur when the child sees his elders in merry harmonious teamwork at harvest time for the common purpose; and at festival times when, relaxed and all status forgotten, they feast and dance together, full of warmth and generosity. At the peasant level, it is this nature-imposed rhythm and economic necessity which exacts the discipline, not any principle or consistent handling by humans, which modally is fitful and arbitrary as well as contradictory.

The March 1917 revolution was made by the heirs of the epoch just sketched against authorities essentially unchanged for centuries. It was a revolt against intolerable conditions as were all the desperate anarchic spontaneous mass risings which ineffectively preceded it. There followed a brief honeymoon *à la Russe*—a spate of egalitarian sentiment and talking in town and village meetings, and of possession of land taken from the murdered father-figures. The authorities whom the Russians had thrown off had been weak and ineffective, men, though remote in status, too much like themselves: unorganized, lazy, greedy. Into the power vacuum stepped Lenin and his coterie of exiles, with an appeal which was thoroughly culture-congenial: a father speaking in angry peasant tones yet in the terms of Western science, promising bread and land and revenge on oppressors, a severe order and a material plenty. It would be interesting to attempt, however imperfectly, an analysis of the psychological vicissitudes of authority relations with this peasant character, of their mutual interaction, during the last eighty or ninety years.

During Turgenev's time the established order was a unity and could be taken for granted by both him and his characters. As a barin himself, he could naively describe his wonderment at the human qualities he discovers among his peasants: how wise and shrewd the old men; how tender the muzhik in his friendship and how like the barins in his veneration of order. In brief, during the Victorian era there is no difficulty in transposing our concepts from the family to the social scene, except for that tiny top crust—the French-speaking upper aristocracy, almost entirely alien to their own lower orders. The peasants viewed the "infinite regress of authorities," to which allusion was made above, much as sons viewed fathers and grandfathers, with *strakh* and duplicity, but with an understanding of their authoritarian ferocities and a use of the same methods of propitiation and self-abasement toward them that they expected to receive from their own dependents. These traits were so ingrained that they persisted into the writer's own recollection of peasant behavior in the early 1900s. Serfdom seemed like a safe order, a knowing where one stood. The barin, the village mayor (*starosta*) and the county police were near to their "children." Their impact was personal and their *izdevatel'stvo* was often linked with tenderness and paternalism. The bad object that deprived could be projected into a blurred distant "They," but was also attributed to one's own sinfulness.

As serfdom is abolished there always comes a loosening of the bonds of pious tradition, felt by the older peasants as a dangerous loss of security. For what happened to the barin begins to happen to the elder's own authority over his sons. The predicament is touchingly presented by Gladkov (1949) whose grandfather's family were Old Believers and anticlerical. In a scene in which the eldest son tells his father that times have changed and he feels free to leave home where there is no land. The old man, in an effort to preserve his hold over his son, bursts out:

We are the servants of God. We are *krest'iane* [peasants; *krest* means cross]. From olden times we bear the labor of the cross; but never the slaves of Anti-

Christ and his angels, of priests or of German [the Russian is *nemetskii,* meaning "foreigner" in general and German in particular] authority, of heretics who smoke tobacco, of shaven men with their tinsel and badges. You young have no freedom nor sense but what comes from the elders. In them alone is order and firmness of life.

This quotation illuminates the complex feelings of the peasant in the 1890s. There is his own identification with due authority and fear of anarchy of the young. At the same time, there is total hostility to what are felt to be *alien,* bureaucratic, newfangled secular authorities and their hirelings—the clergy. Gladkov's book might have been satirizing the incursion of the Communists into the life of the village. Equally, that plea could have belonged to the era of Peter the Great. Long suffering and hard fate are transfigured by the sanction of the Cross which gives the dignity of moral principle both to humility and to obstinacy.

After the reforms of the 1860s, secularization evolved along with industrialization and social mobility. The almost mythical freedom and opportunity of factory work lures the emancipated landless sons to the cities. They take with them their ambivalent expectations of oppression and of boundless hope. They already have a conviction that the urban dweller (*fabrichnyi chelovek*) is a smarter fellow than they. They find nothing reassuring in labor conditions which exploit and deprive, without the compensation of paternal affection. Gorky was the finest painter of these conditions. Crafty townsmen and kulaks multiply in the countryside and batten on the average peasant no less than on his barin. They are hated as "man-eaters" and "fat men." We still read of religious resignation, in Gladkov, for instance, as a valued form of defense against mounting despair and envious resentment. Peasant-saints, ambivalently preaching love and self-surrender but also calling for the repentance of the oppressors, seem ubiquitous and revered by the population just as the people of India revere their holy men.

Another attitude is so typical that it requires mention. Gladkov describes the scene of arrival of the police inspector in his native village for the supervision of rent and debt collection. When his carriage appears, the whole population berates its children, pushes the wives around and flogs its horses—even the chickens scatter. This behavior means: "Look, we are calling our dependents to order to show due reverence." But it also means: "Scatter, for the Antichrist is riding among us. *We,* the heads of families, show *strakh,* but see how we can control all this undisciplined rabble." In miniature, here is the quintessence of modal Russian authority feelings as felt by the underlings: hate of the policemen who come to support and protect the exploiters—the barin and his bailiff; eagerness to show one's siding with authority by displacing the resentment down to "stupid, unruly women and children," who must be made to toe the line and punished. Scenes with similar meaning were reported to me by the defectors I interviewed, and I have also witnessed such things personally. The police or the mayor could not be seen instrumentally—only as total enemies. Some of this is, doubtless, more of a feudal than a specific Russian trait.

Closely related is the culturally prevalent mechanism of self-undoing. Caught in hopeless impotent revolt against the all-powerful creditor or oppressor, resignation and passivity fail, and smoldering hate turns against the self and its good objects. This well-documented behavior pattern of Russian life, widespread in all classes, usually takes the form of depressive apathy, neglect or desertion of work and family, wife and child beating, bouts of desperate, reckless drinking. Both observer and subject usually have insight that this is a symbolic attack on the authorities. In my more recent interview material there were many examples of this "throwing in the sponge," of "making of one's own ruin a stick to beat the authorities with." It is like Dostoevsky's Raskolnikov, who makes a total mad protest by murder, equivalent to suicide, accusing and expiating at one and the same time the guilt of the evil dominating persecutor with whom he also feels at one.

Scenes like those reported during the collectivization of farms under Stalin, when peasants destroyed crops and livestock rather than hand them over, knowing they would be shot or deported, occurred often during prerevolutionary days at impoundings of property for debt. Behavior under MVD interrogation as described by my interviewees followed the same pattern: "Do what you like—I am through." "All right—kill me then," and so on.

The Soviet masters of Russia with Lenin at their head have given convincing evidence of both their Russian-ness and their hate of Russian-ness in the above sense. Psychologically we may think of them as a conspiratorial band of determined parricides who were able to catalyze the release of endless paranoid hate of Russians for the bad inner authority figure; to sanction cathartic revenge against ever-present scapegoats, and so to free also the lusty, constructive omnipotence feelings. It was a psycho-catharsis on the grand scale. But how to ride this storm of anarchic, savage hate that accompanied the constructive energy? The Bolsheviks' Russian-ness was demonstrated by their wholesale, uncompromising acceptance of Western patterns of socialism but with their paranoid lack of discrimination of finer shades between black and white, by their belief that nothing was impossible, by their magical faith in the entirely scientific rational nature of their system, supplanting the sense of mission of orthodox Russian Christianity, ever watchful of the least error which would enable "the devil to get in." It was thus consonant with the deepest modal phantasies that before long they re-established the persistent authority model inherent in the Russian mind: an absolute power which is the sole repository of Truth and which cannot be questioned or deviated from. This restoration was well on its way by 1928 and completed during the purges and by the reintroduction of officer status with tsarist-like accoutrements and ranks during World War II. People's commissars became ministers. It is true that they still called one "comrade," a relic of the days of equality, and that some Bolsheviks were friendly fatherly persons who pitied one.

The new elite bases its goal values on the doctrine of the will—the doctrine that man can master his own nature as well as the environment. This is culture-congenial where it stresses maximum effort, achievement and surpassing the foreigners. It is resented when it means the exercise of authority in that impersonally implacable, *nemetskii,* alien way which has been the most hated feature of Communist rule. Not only was increasing instrumentalism and decreasing expressiveness bound to come because of the growing complexity of industrialization and bureaucratization. It came also because of the internal conflict of the rapidly promoted men who implemented the plan. Though they came, except in the earliest days, chiefly from the people, these men had made the closest identifications with the Western-thinking Leninist group, with its proclaimed goals of mastering the backward muzhik and turning him into a disciplined Communist paragon—the ideal industrial man. This has meant incessant war by the party against the Russian peasant character in themselves and in the masses.

For Bolshevik phantasies, greed, hate and apathy no less than unpolitical, human relations were a threat to the efforts to build, change and control. This cursed anarchic human material was the only obstacle to a wonderful scheme. Hence, people must not be allowed to have doubts, guilt, ambivalence or personal wishes. The mechanisms of displacement and projection which are by nature designed to buffer the personality against excessive guilt feelings are massively mobilized at all levels by the party elite to a degree which constitutes a qualitative change from prerevolutionary patterns. The compulsive, inhuman tempo to industrialize and build up an invulnerable military-technological empire is due, I suspect, to this paranoid dynamic. Sadistic dominance needs are projected to foreign out-groups, creating an "encirclement" situation and a siege mentality. This externalizes the "enemy" and deflects hate, with its attendant guilt, from the in-group authority to the "blood-sucking" imperial-ists, symbols of themselves, who enact the role of everyone's oppressive father-image but also of one's own anarchic greed and hate. Internal deviation can also be projected in this way as the work of agents of the external enemy. Leites and Bernaut (1954), in a notably subtle analysis of Bolshevik mentality, have shown the phantasy-thought process by which the inner split of total submission—total hostility can create this recurring public myth of the party leader turned enemy. A succession of these figures can then be unmasked as scapegoats drawing upon themselves the wrath and execration of the group and thus purging collective guilt feelings in the people for having felt traitorous toward the government as a whole.

This mechanism is still to some extent in line with modal behavior: it demonstrates the power of supreme authority, the all-seeing eye, to level even the strong. It increases *strakh* with its bracing and reassuring aspects. What is uncertain is the degree to which the rulers consciously use such mechanisms, and to what extent they are impelled by unconscious forces to rely on such myths and ritual expiations. We now know that the top Nazi leaders were as much the victims as the cold-blooded exploiters of their own paranoid fantasies, not unlike some of the more fanciful Soviet ideological propaganda themes. This behavior makes the most sense when we interpret it as the secondary elaboration of that early oral conflict in the Russian, that war in the mind against the bogy of anarchic strength and destructive power which has to be counteracted by all the forces available to a primitive ego.

Another, more readily understandable, mechanism of defense against typical conflicts is that of *manic denial,* observed also in tense managerial personalities of the West. This is akin to the compulsive drive, seeking escape from doubt and guilt feelings by the restless urge for achievement and organizing activity. Here we find motivations for coercing the "backward masses" (symbols of the subject's id) to higher tempo and norms; for the need of more and more technical mastery over nature and machines in an effort to convince oneself that everything is under control. The practice as well as the terminology of Bolshevism are replete with this pseudo-objective technological scientism. The all-pervading secret police, for example, are dignified by the term "apparatus."

The effect of this war by paranoid pseudo-rationality against the depressive, insightful, sensitive side of the Russian character is clearly discernible. We do not know how deep this effect is, for the Russian is adept at lip-service conformity and dissimulation. We know something of the attitudes of men who deserted during and after World War II—and of those who refused to be repatriated from German captivity. In the case of my own sample most of them were peasants or rural intelligentsia and under age thirty-five. They felt ethically betrayed by the falsity of their masters' descriptions of Western conditions. They also had put into practice what the dispossessed sons had always done—to walk away when possible as a gesture of defiance. The chief recurring reason given was the revolt against the party's *izdevatel'stvo* against the people—their own poor hungry mothers symbolizing their motherland and people. These men—and they could not all have been atypical—felt morally insulted because after a war in which they felt they had saved the country they were again mistrusted, coerced and terrified into total compliance. Theirs was the groan of Russians through the ages. That part of them which sought love and nurturance from their own government felt enraged—not with what had been done but by the manner. It has been typically Russian for this situation to recur from generation to generation.

The chief changes after 1917 were: (1) the regression in thinking and feeling toward the least mature and most psychotic layer of Russian phantasy—from the humane, broad tolerance of good and evil toward an acceptance of black and white mythology, a need to betray and become a turncoat, to deny friends and one's real feelings; (2) impoverishment of free communication, and suspicion of one's neighbor as a possible informer; (3) limitation of privacy; (4) lack of security from terror; and (5) the conscious awareness of disappointed expectations that the government would speed a higher standard of living and of the amenities of life.

Defectors in the younger age group showed a significantly greater acceptance than the older ones of "Soviet reality," and their defection was motivated less by principle than by their chance exposure to the West and by material dissatisfactions (R.A. Bauer, A. Inkeles and C. Kluckhohn, 1956). They seemed to demand more from their regime. This in itself is perhaps a significant achievement of the Soviets—the truly downtrodden do not aspire to rising standards.

For a time after Stalin's death, Khrushchev not only permitted execration of the archtyrant as the supreme scapegoat, but himself wept before his comrades when he reported being forced by Stalin to dance the gopak. Turgenev recounts the story of the peasant Ovsianikov whose barin made him dance (just as Stalin did Khrushchev) as part of his sense of possession of the serf, and then praised the humiliated man. He thus not only expressed his identification with the insulted and oppressed, but on this and other occasions staked his claim as heir to idealized Little Father Lenin and displayed his own need to deny guilt as one of Stalin's leading henchmen. Since then, as we know, he showed more tyrannical features, tempered with the gruff, jovial, oral behavior he typified. His standing in the popular mind appears not to have been improved by the latter: it has been reported that he was "not respected because he was too close to the people." This *panebratstvo* (hail-fellow-well-met) is not the modern Soviet-conditioned people's idea of a top leader any more than it would have been respected by the generations that preceded them. Such is the Russian ambivalence. Now, as ever, the Russians value sincerity and real warmth, and are quick at spotting false cordiality in a calculating confidence-trickster. A leader ought to be distant and dignified, and severe like an angry father. It remains to be seen which Khrushchev is.

In trying to strike a balance between change and persistence of the old, we must try to look at the available phenomena from the Russian point of view.

The Communist leaders have known how to use to the breaking point, but always stopping short of it, that contradiction in Russians which wants omnipotently to possess and achieve everything preferably by spurts of group effort, but which also counts abstinence and postponement of gratification a virtue. Within limits, they have given immense opportunities for able people to traverse the whole gamut of social mobility and economic success. They have created a literate population whose education has made them aware not only of their own history but of economic standards, of the fun of machine-mindedness into which so much dominance need has been channeled. They have used xenophobia and envy of the rich neighbor to divert hate from themselves to the West, weaving healthy Russian love of country into this parricidal and near-demonological theme, and thereby adding a persecutory paranoid urgency to their people's effort.

The leadership has also played the role of authority according to the modal stereotype. Utter devotion is demanded but really not expected—that is, there is reliance on external sanctions and controls on the tacit Russian assumption that there is a totally hostile traitor in every man. This leads one to ask: can a society be said to be maturing if it continues to treat *all* its citizens as potential traitors and saboteurs, not fit to have mental freedom? This deep "fault" in Russian unconscious imagery has fostered the rise to power mainly of the most sado-masochistic, authority-identified and insecure among the citizens, who have for lack of other inner models aped the hate-invested, rigid and status-conscious authority models of Russian culture, minus their easygoing toler-ance and laxity. These soulless party men have made a hollow mockery of the longing for spiritual freedom, justice and equality. Perhaps they have killed the revolution. We have seen that the young generation, especially in the cities, have so far accepted and adapted to the cruelty and unprincipledness of this production machine. With them lies the future. Will they, who know no other system and whose chief value seems to be, according to reliable studies, the expectancy of bigger and better careers and rewards from it, be content with this hedging in of their freedom, especially in the sphere of contact with the West, and of criticism and discussion of men and policies and priorities?

There has been a great concretization of thought and action as the result of technical education. Can the strengthening of realistic thinking in the technical sphere for long be kept out of the political sphere which is still dominated by poorly disguised modal fantasies and myths? Again, we do not know what millions of fathers and mothers and babushkas are transmitting to their children in private. My guess is that it is not very different from Gorky's or Gladkov's nursery experiences. A young simple cowherd from Viatka oblast said this to me: "In the USSR May 1 and November 7 are great feast days. But we in our village have a holiday called Easter . . . have you heard of it?"

It is thus not easy to guess how and in what direction this great society will develop its values and guiding goal aspirations. Perhaps with the lessening of their ancient sense of underprivilegedness through technical achievement, together with the enduring religious values still transmitted by Russian mothers—with the passing in a few years of the last remnants of the original Leninists and Stalinists and the emergence of a solid, educated middle layer of professional and managerial personalities—one can hope for a reduction in the primitive defensive, paranoid features of Soviet attitudes. They are, with us, heirs of the same deep currents of civilization and ideas. But they have yet to show that they can tolerate doubt and uncertainty of feeling and thought without excessive anxiety, which is revealed in the aggressive dogmatism of their recent behavior toward all those not in complete agreement with their notion of truth.

References

Bauer, R.A., A. Inkeles and C. Kluckhon. 1956. *How the Soviet System Works.* Cambridge, Mass.: Harvard University Press.

Dicks, H.V. 1952. "Observations on Contemporary Russian Behaviour." *Human Relations,* 5:111–76.

Gladkov, F. 1949. *Povest' o detstve.* Moscow.

Gorer, G. and J. Rickman. 1949. *The People of Great Russia.* London: Cresset Press.

Leites, N.C. and E. Bernaut. 1954. *Ritual of Liquidation.* Glencoe, Ill.: Free Press.

Mead, M. 1951. *Soviet Attitudes Toward Authority.* New York: McGraw-Hill.

Fred Emery

Latent Content of Television Viewing

This is the second of two papers by Fred Emery on this topic. The first contains a critical overview of the relevant literature from which a broad theory is developed. From this are derived the hypotheses which are tested empirically in the second paper.

To explore the latent meaning of television viewing and test the hypotheses of the theoretical study (Emery, 1959) a Western-type film was selected for showing to pre-adolescent boys on the grounds that it would be likely to create a high degree of attention and interest and thus magnify whatever effects there might be. Before selecting the particular film an analysis was made of the themes, characters and major actions of some hundred recent Western films as revealed in published synopses. This analysis showed two major types of Western: those in which action centered on the simple conflict of a good man and a bad man and those centered on a trio consisting of two men, one more socially powerful than the other, and a woman. The latter type of film, which might well be described as "Oedipal," constituted two-thirds of the sample. It was expected that the effect of a Western film would be related to the basic pattern it followed and the manner in which this pattern was worked out.

With these considerations in mind, *The Lone Hand* was selected. This film is not a typical Western. It differs significantly in that:

- it displays both of the typical patterns—the good-bad centered on the adult hero and the Oedipal centered on the child hero
- both patterns are worked out in an atypical fashion. The good-bad conflict has the formal successful outcome but the outcome follows more or less accidentally after the prolonged victory of evil. Throughout the body of the film the adult hero has renounced good and there exists no positive adult hero. The triadic conflict in this film has the quite common unsuccessful outcome (unsuccessful in that the hero renounces his Oedipal strivings) but is worked out with more than the usual amount of violence towards the hero. The qualities of a nightmare are involved in one

*A shortened and rewritten version of the second of two original papers—*Human Relations*, 12:215–32, 1959.

particular sequence on a cliff face in which the child hero is attempting to escape being killed by a shadowy figure who he thinks is his father.

These differences were considered important to our study. The first made it possible to study what personality factors lead a child to experience the film as one of the patterns rather than the other. The preponderance of "evil forces" (although there was not a single censorable act of sadism or lust) made it more likely that the audience would show some changes. The presence of the boy as the story-teller and as a central character added to the likelihood of the audience becoming involved and also provided an alternative hero for identification.

A large number of techniques were considered for measuring psychological changes in the audience. The final selection was dictated by the hypotheses underlying the study. It was held that within the normal range of personality differences to be found in four school classes of boys (43 boys in all), even though of similar age (10 to 13 years) and from homes of similar socio-economic status (lower-middle and working class), *there would be no consistent shift in the direction or degree of aggression*. This hypothesis was contrary to that put forward in the experimental studies of Siegel (1956), Maccoby (1956), and Albert (1957). Each of these had predicted, in line with Fesbach's (1955) "Hypothesis of equivalence of forms" that there would be a reduction in expression of aggression and anxiety about aggression due to watching films of violence. Their own studies had failed consistently to show such effects and it seemed most unlikely, on psychological grounds, that such a prediction could be made without specifying certain personality factors. It did seem feasible to predict that viewing the film *would increase (at least temporarily) the child's feelings of being confronted by a dominating and hostile environment*. This prediction was based on the assumption that the child in identifying himself with either hero in the film (or with both at different times) will vicariously experience the anxieties, frustrations, temptations, etc., of the hero and will also experience the environment in much the same way as it confronts the hero. Thus, if the hero experiences a harsh, depriving environment then so to some extent will the person identifying with him. If the hero adopts a defiant, aggressive stance toward this environment so, to some extent, will the person identifying with him. However, when one considers how the film experience might carry over into the person's ordinary life, the immediate problem is the lack of congruence between this life and the manifest world of the film. In the film world one may in identifying with the hero strongly wish to draw a gun on and kill the villain, but in the real world there is no such villain, no gun, and an absence of the concerns impelling the film hero to violence. It is in the latent content of the film that one finds a certain congruence and hence the greatest chance of carrying over into real life. Although the actions and concrete circumstances of the Western film are markedly different from those of everyday life they still involve basic features such as the general relations of men to their own actions and desires, to other men, and to the social environment at large. It is very likely that it is because of the manifest differences that the film can work out these basic problems and yet retain and entertain its audiences.

On these grounds more specific hypotheses were set up about the psychological changes likely to be produced by *The Lone Hand*.

"Heroes" and Themes

The Lone Hand contains the two themes:

- good versus evil (a dyadic pattern basically composed of super-ego versus id type forces),
- young male competing for female with older male (what will be called the "triadic pattern" or Oedipal theme).

The basic psychological problems of boys from 10 to 13 in the Australian culture (as in American, British and most such societies) are those of controlling their own asocial tendencies and directing their interests and energies into socially approved activities (Piaget, 1932; Havighurst, 1952). This problem is persistent and significant because, at this period, children are being coerced into work relations at school; they are being forced to order their lives and control their own desires in terms of the "performance principle" of a work-centered repressive society (cf. Marcuse, 1956). Internally, this problem will be reflected in a conflict of super-ego, ego and id type forces (cf. Chein's definitions, 1944).

On the other hand, the Oedipal problem will not be characteristic of boys at this age. Generally speaking, this type of problem will have been resolved at or about the school-starting age and will not be relevant again until adolescence.

It was predicted that viewers would tend to prefer those themes that are most similar to their own basic problems. In this instance the specific prediction was that *the boys would interpret the film in terms of the good-bad theme, not the triadic theme*.

To test this hypothesis the boys were asked, on the morning immediately following the televised viewing (it was not possible to fit this test into the afternoon's experimental session owing to the length of the film) and again a month later, to write down the story of the film as they would tell it to a friend who had not seen it. They were further instructed to keep the story to about a page in length and to mention only those things that they thought important.

These instructions were adopted because previous experience had shown

TABLE I   Attributed Themes (First Recall)

Theme	No. mentioning theme (N = 42)
Good vs. bad only	18
Both	8
Triadic only	2
None	14

that many children of this age could recall almost every incident after twenty-four hours. The notion of "what they would tell a friend" may have introduced a bias toward conformity.

These selective recalls were analyzed for evidence of the two themes. The first theme was regarded as present in a recall if the points were made that "Zachary turned outlaw, and then caught the outlaws": the second theme of creating and maintaining the family circle received very few adequate mentions so it was decided to regard this theme as present in a recall if Sarah received any mention in an active role. Even though this scoring procedure tended to overestimate the second theme, the hypothesis was upheld. It might be asked whether the method of first recall (basically selection not recall) affects subsequent recall in that without this, the other matters might well have persisted better in memory (in fact, a slight reverse tendency was observed).

In keeping with this is the fact that by the second recall only five boys mentioned any one of the four incidents that were central to the working out of the Oedipal theme:

- Zachary's outburst of rage against his son
- The pursuit of Joshua on the cliff face by a man he believed to be his father
- The boys releasing the pigeons into the church with the threatened consequence of breaking up the Zachary-Sarah relation
- Sarah leaving the home

There can be little question but that these had a strong impact at the moment of viewing. The first two incidents and the last involved strong dramatic tensions and the third was the main item of comic relief (this impact is reflected in the photographs taken of the children at the critical point of each incident). The reason for ignoring these incidents in the recall seems, therefore, to be not simply failure to notice but subsequent rejection of them as not fitting in with the first theme.

It was predicted that a boy who is having difficulty in maintaining an adequate balance among his id, ego and super-ego forces will be primarily concerned, at the phantasy level of film-viewing, with identifying with Zachary and vicariously experiencing the satisfaction of achieving such a balance rather than with submitting to the induced forces of the film, toward identification with Joshua, and experiencing additional challenges to his adequacy: i.e., *the more unbalanced boys will tend to identify with Zachary.*

Evidence of "unbalance," in the sense used above, was sought in the extreme scores (top and bottom quartiles) of extrapunitiveness and ego-defensiveness and low scores in the Group Conformity Rating (GCR) as measured by the Picture-Frustration Test. (Note that there are some serious doubts about the consistency of the GCR measure, see Lindzey and Goldwyn, 1953/1954.)

As predicted, extreme scores on extrapunitiveness were significantly related to selection of Zachary as primary identificant ($p<.01$; $p<.05$, with age held constant as age correlated with choice of hero and the older boys' tendency to have extreme scores on extrapunitiveness). Low GCR scores were related to selecting Zachary ($p<.05$, age unrelated to GCR score). Ego-defensiveness showed no such relation.

Despite the evidence for this hypothesis there may well be other explanations. One possible alternative is that Zachary is selected not because of the latent problems of the viewers but because of the appeals of the manifest level of the successful Western man of action—shooting, riding and fighting (cf. Elkin, 1950). These features are in fact what the boys said they liked about Western films in general but no particular value can be placed on such "reasons." In line with this hypothesis, of "interest in action" *per se,* one might expect that those who are most extraverted would tend to identify with Zachary. Taking regularity of contact with peers and engaging in active pursuits (as against reading, viewing and other passive pursuits) as evidence of extraversion there is no evidence in this sample that it is related to selection of "hero."

The evidence so far considered suggests that personality factors will affect choice both of heroes and of themes. In this respect also it suggests some of the ways in which individuals may protect themselves from film content that would otherwise be psychologically disturbing.

Psychological Changes

Three main hypotheses were postulated:

1. that viewing *The Lone Hand* would produce no consistent shift in the sample of the direction or degree of their aggressive tendencies (as measured by the Rosenzweig Picture-Frustration Test);
2. that viewing *The Lone Hand* would, at least temporarily,
   (a) create the feeling of being threatened by a powerful and hostile environment, and

(b) encourage the viewer to take an "active posture" toward these "dangers";

3. that the memories of *The Lone Hand* would tend to be assimilated to a stereotype of the Western action film.

The first hypothesis was not a central proposition in the theory held by the author as most likely to account for psychological changes in the viewing situation. It was given major importance because it has been *the* hypothesis that has guided recent experimental work in this field (Maccoby, 1956; Siegel, 1956; Albert, 1957). Despite the theoretical guise that this hypothesis has been given, it appears to have come from the "common-sense" belief that films displaying violence have somehow or another contributed to or modified the display of aggression by children in modern societies. Two formulations have been current and are reflected in the experimental studies: (a) that viewing films of violence vicariously satisfies aggressive tendencies and thus serves as a "safety valve" (Siegel and Maccoby); (b) that such viewing arouses aggressive tendencies (Albert). It is sufficient at the moment to note that the related experimental studies failed to show any such consistent relation between viewing films of violence and aggressive tendencies. Theoretically it is difficult to see how one could predict any such consistent relationship without specifying those personality factors of the viewer which mediate between viewing and subsequent psychological changes, a point that Maccoby makes in considering the contradictory results of her two experiments. It may well be that these personality factors are so distributed in samples such as those used as to cancel out the different individual responses.

The Picture-Frustration Test (Child Form) (P-F) was administered to each group one week before viewing and again within ten minutes after viewing. Scoring was according to Rosenzweig's categories. To minimize effects of bias no scoring was done until all records, both "before" and "after" tests, were to hand. Each of the twenty-four test items was then scored right through all records—this minimized the effect of scoring bias on the "between-test" and "between individual" difference. The order of analysis of the twenty-four items was randomized so as to avoid a systematic bias between the earlier and later items in the test (the type of item differs between the first and second half of the test). Although cumbersome and rather time-consuming, these procedures were deemed necessary in the absence of another person to do a lengthy check analysis. It seems reasonable to assume that errors arising from the scorer's idiosyncrasies and from temporal shifts in his judgments were so distributed as not to affect the significance of the differences reported below.

Comparison of the "before-after" scores on the P-F revealed a small but significant increase in extrapunitiveness (mean "before" score $=13.4$; mean "after" score $=14.5$; $t=3.06$ [Edwards, 1950:286]; for df$=43$, $p<.01$). However, this difference is not significantly larger than would be expected if no viewing had occurred. Repeated administrations of the Picture-Frustration Test have consistently shown an increase in amount of extrapunitiveness of this order (Zuk, 1956; French, 1950; Franklin and Brozek, 1949). The same has been shown in related tests such as Albert's adaptation of the P-F test and in doll play. As Siegel and Zuk have experimentally demonstrated, this phenomenon arises from the testee experiencing the test situation as being increasingly permissive of aggressive expression. Siegel states that "the young child becomes accustomed to looking to adults for cues as to what behaviour is appropriate or acceptable, particularly in a situation which is unfamiliar to him. From a permissive adult's behaviour, the child may legitimately conclude that aggression *is* acceptable in a play session, and, therefore, he will give increasing expression to his own aggressive motivation." Evidence of this process was observed in this study. In each of the "before viewing" administrations several boys asked whether the instructions meant that they could really write down anything or whether the teachers would see what they had written. In the second and freer entertainment situation only one boy of the three groups asked a similar question and the language used in the test was noticeably "freer."

Thus *there are no grounds for rejecting the first hypothesis.*

As this finding is in line with those of Siegel, Maccoby and Albert it seems unnecessary to center any further studies on the aggression hypothesis in this crude form: it may be possible to resurrect it when something more is known of the psychological processes involved in viewing particular themes.

The second hypothesis is based on the argument that a boy who identifies with either the boy or the adult hero in this film will tend to experience a shift in what has elsewhere been described as his silent framework. It is suggested that as "self-cum-hero" the viewer is unconsciously living out his problem of controlling his asocial tendencies in a social environment that threatens to punish lack of control and rewards successful control (the other theme in this picture, the Oedipal one, is not considered because it apparently did not exist for the sample). In this film the problem is depicted in such a way that the asocial forces appear to be of unmanageable proportions; even Zachary, the adult hero, explicitly renounces the "performance principle" and spends the greater part of the film in active alliance with the asocial forces. The "successful" moral outcome to the film is depicted as a chance occurrence and hence, while it gives further force to the repeated suggestion that this "alliance with evil" is an unsatisfactory solution to the problem, it does little to modify the impression of the great strength of the asocial forces. Thus the direction of shift in the silent framework of these boys was expected to be in the direction of *increasing (at least temporarily) their feelings of being threatened by a powerful and hostile environment.* As measured by responses to a Thematic Apper-

TABLE 2   Effect on Circumstances Depicted in TAT Story

"After" story judged as:	No. of cases	
	Judge A	Judge B
Worse	34	31
About the same	5	8
Better	5	5

ception Test picture, it was predicted that *the stories given immediately after viewing would differ from those given immediately before viewing in depicting the story hero as subjected to a more powerful actively hostile environment.* At the level of consciousness it was predicted that the underlying shift would be reflected in the increased expression of a negative mood in the "after" stories (i.e., increased pessimism).

These predictions were in line with the effects that Crandall (1951) experimentally demonstrated in his study on "Induced Frustration and Punishment-Reward Expectancy in Thematic Apperception Stories." The TAT was selected after consideration of a number of alternatives on the grounds that any shift was likely to be at the unconscious level and hence would be detected only by a projective test. This test provides evidence of how an individual unconsciously relates himself to others and it also provides an indication of the prevailing consciously felt mood (this latter being one of the conscious reflections of the psychological changes induced by viewing). As this study was concerned only with exploring the hypothesis only one TAT card was used, 13B, showing a little boy sitting on the doorstep of a log cabin. Further cards could not have been used without discarding the P-F test needed for testing the first hypothesis.

Several levels of analysis of the "before" and "after" stories given by the boys supported the hypothesis. At the simplest level, each pair of stories was compared by two psychologists (working independently, without knowledge of which was before and which after, and with the order of presentation randomized). The comparison was based on "Which of the two stories depicts the boy in the worse circumstances?"—judgments of equality were allowed. This shift can be taken as some evidence of a change in the unconscious attitude of an individual: it being assumed that the TAT story is a projection of the individual's own "silent framework" (Table 2).

The nature of the shift is partly elaborated by the classification of the stories shown in Table 3.

This clearly supports the prediction that viewing would create, at least temporarily, the feelings of being faced with a more powerful and hostile

TABLE 3   Responsibility for Outcome in TAT Stories

	As willed by hero	As willed by others	
		For hero	Against hero
"Before" story	17	6	18
"After" story	5	5	31

3 stories unclassifiable. For $a \times b$, $\chi^2 = 7.45$; $p < .01$

environment. Significantly more frequently the fate of the hero of the story is seen as determined by outside forces, regardless of what he does.

It is difficult to get from these same stories an independent measure of mood, since the same features partly contribute to the first judgment. The following table should therefore be judged in this light. This gives some evidence of a shift in mood that supports the earlier prediction of increased pessimism.

It should be noted that no significant difference in effects existed between those identifying with Zachary and those identifying with Joshua. This may simply be due to the levelling-out effect of the more unbalanced boys, who might be expected to be more influenced, identifying with Zachary and hence avoiding the potentially stronger impact of the film. This might be tested in a study of a film having only one hero. Alternatively, Albert (1957) has suggested, regarding his own failure to observe any relation between identification and aggressiveness (changes in extrapunitiveness), that the relation exists at an unconscious level and acts too slowly to be observed in a single film. It is doubtful whether Albert's measured differences in aggressiveness are psychologically meaningful or his questions on identification direct enough.

As suggested by Hypothesis 2(b), the film was not expected to have an entirely one-sided effect. In heightening the awareness of, and concern for, the dangers inherent in man's relation to himself and his fellows the film also depicts a solution—a posture that the individual can take vis-à-vis his hostile environment. This posture of action is reiterated throughout, and as "self-cum-

TABLE 4   Number of Stories Mentioning at Least One Unit of Positive Behavior (Gratification, Succorance, Etc.)

	Mentioning	Not mentioning
"Before" stories	20	24
"After" stories	7	37

($\chi^2 = 7.7$, $p < .01$)

hero" the viewer vicariously experiences the need for and the ego-defensive value of the posture.

Unfortunately no *systematic* evidence was collected regarding this hypothesis. It was not even clear what psychological tools would be of use.

Some incidental evidence appears in the TAT stories. Although there was a general change toward perceiving the environment as hostile and dominant, *the hero was depicted as more active*. In 10 of the "before" stories and in 22 "after" stories the boy was depicted as actively trying to change or defend his situation. Consistent with the first hypothesis, the increased activity was not that of uninstigated aggression (aggression against an adult figure occurred in 15 of the "before" stories and 18 of the "after" stories).

The Lone Hand is probably different in emphasis from the stereotyped Western in that it gives rather more emphasis to the hostile environment and less emphasis to the posture of action. It has in common with all Westerns this stereotyped pattern of endlessly and repetitiously saying "Beware" and offering always the same answer, not "take care" but "take action." *This similarity should lead to the memory traces of* The Lone Hand *being readily assimilated to the existing stereotype* (Hypothesis 3). Comparison of recall one day after and a month later gives some support for this hypothesis. At the final recall the story had been boiled down to "a man who joined the outlaws then caught them." As already noted, only five boys mentioned any one of the four incidents that were central to the Oedipal theme and to that extent not typical of the stereotyped, good versus evil Western. An analysis of the number of times each incident was mentioned in conjunction with the older incidents (using McQuitty's [1957] method of simple linkage analysis) revealed that the core pattern of recalled incidents was the ambush of the wheat wagon and the ambush of the mule train, with the latter as the connecting link to recall of other incidents. This stereotyping can be expected to lessen the effects due to peculiarities of the particular film. Where, as in this case, there is a rather heavier emphasis upon environmental threats, the anxiety that might thus be temporarily generated would tend to be offset by these memory changes (just as in the viewing situation the more unbalanced boys protected themselves, to some extent, by identifying with Zachary).

On the other hand, the similarity of these films should enable each to contribute to those cumulative psychological effects associated with the stereotype. Thus it may be that the problem of "cumulative effects" is primarily a question of the establishment of unconscious assumptions about one's relation to the world and of adopting postures of the sort implicit in the stereotyped themes. The present study was not primarily designed to throw light on the nature and effect of these stereotypes, but some data were collected on attitudes to the various themes and media. It was predicted that those boys most "addicted" to the Western theme (as expressed in preferences for films, comics and television) would be more ready to adopt the posture of the hero. This prediction was upheld in that these boys showed significantly more increase in ego-defensiveness (as measured by the P-F) after viewing than did the other boys ($p<.01$). It is not clear what "readiness to adopt" means in this context: among the alternatives it may be that the addicts identify more thoroughly or that the same degree of identification sets off stronger existing internal psychological processes. There is some evidence for the former hypothesis in that these "addicts" were significantly less inclined to see their outside world as more hostile and dominating after viewing (as measured by the TAT story: $p=.06$). That is, it would seem that the stronger pre-existing stereotype enabled them more readily to offset the environmental threats by making with the hero the appropriate postural changes toward greater ego-defensiveness. This ego-defensiveness is not aggressiveness but the tendency to take defensive action. As Ichheiser (1950) has made clear, this behavior is frequently interpreted by others, from their own standpoint, as aggressiveness. While the heightened ego-defensiveness may not persist for long after viewing it does seem likely that the potency of this posture (habit-strength) would tend to become slightly stronger relative to other alternative postures. Further work on this problem would probably entail a close study of the reactions of specially selected samples of addicts to their favorite theme and some more adequate conceptualization and measurement of the notions of silent framework, stereotype and posture.

Summary

The following may be regarded as the main findings of this study:

- That the psychological significance of Western films is due primarily to *latent* themes of an Oedipal or good versus bad (super-ego versus id) type and not to the manifest themes.
- That pre-adolescent boys will be attracted by the good versus bad pattern.
- That viewing a film involves some selective processes (of identification and of interpretation) whereby the viewer defends himself from anxiety-arousing aspects of the film.
- That certain temporary changes may be brought about in the way in which an individual sees himself in relation to his social environment.
- That these changes do not appear to involve systematic changes in aggressive drives.
- That in line with changes in his self-perceptions the individual will tend correspondingly to adopt the posture or pose of the hero.

These findings cannot be regarded as firmly established, but the evidence justifies their adoption as working hypotheses for further studies.

References

Albert, R.S. 1957. "The Role of Mass Media and the Effect of Aggressive Film Content upon Children's Aggressive Responses and Identification Choices." *Genetic Psychology Monographs,* 55:221–85.

Chein, L. 1944. "Awareness of Self and Structure of the Ego." *Psychological Review,* 51:303–14.

Crandall, V.J. 1951. "Induced Frustration and Punishment-Reward Expectancy in Thematic Apperception Stories." *Journal of Consulting Psychology,* 15:400–04.

Edwards, A.L. 1950. *Experimental Design in Psychological Research.* New York: Rienhard.

Elkin, F. 1950. "The Psychological Appeal of the Hollywood Western." *Journal of Educational Sociology,* 24:72–85.

Emery, F. 1959. "Psychological Effects of the Western Film: A Study in Television Viewing." *Human Relations,* 12:215–32.

Fesbach, S. 1955. "The Drive-Reducing Function of Fantasy Behavior." *Journal of Abnormal and Social Psychology,* 50:3–11.

Franklin, J.C. and J. Brozek. 1949. "The Rosenzweig Picture-Frustration Test as a Measure of Frustration Response in Semi-Starvation." *Journal of Consulting Psychology,* 13:293–301.

French, R.L. 1950. "Changes in Performance on the Rosenzweig Picture-Frustration Study following Experimentally Induced Frustration." *Journal of Consulting Psychology,* 14:111–15.

Havighurst, R.J. 1952. 2nd edition. *Developmental Tasks and Education.* New York: Longmans.

Ichheiser, G. 1950. "Frustration and Aggression or Frustration and Defense: A Counter Hypothesis." *Journal of Genetic Psychology,* 43:125–40.

Lindzey, G. and R.M. Goldwyn. 1953/54. "Validity of the Rosenzweig Picture-Frustration Study." *Journal of Personality,* 22:519–47.

Maccoby, E.E., H. Levin and B.M. Selya. 1956. "The Effects of Emotional Arousal on the Retention of Film Content: A Failure to Replicate." *Journal of Abnormal and Social Psychology,* 53:373–74.

Marcuse, H. 1956. *Eros and Civilization.* London: Routledge and Kegan Paul.

McQuitty, L.L. 1957. "Elementary Linkage Analysis." *Educational and Psychological Measurement,* 17:207–09.

Piaget, J. 1932. *The Moral Judgement of the Child.* New York: Harcourt Brace.

Zuk, G.H. 1956. "The Influence of Social Context on Impulse and Control Tendencies in Pre-Adolescents." *Genetic Psychology Monographs.* 54:117–66.

Elizabeth Bott Spillius

Asylum and Society*

Introduction

Since first publishing this paper (Bott, 1976) I have changed my view of what its central theme should be. The original research was a study of a typical large British mental hospital carried out between 1957 and 1972. It had two main themes: the persistence of chronic hospitalization and the presence of endemic conflict in the hospital. I devoted a great deal of discussion to the first theme because it was assumed in the 1960s that the number of long-stay "chronic" patients was rapidly declining. The big old hospitals in the country were to be closed down and replaced by psychiatric wards in general hospitals for short-stay "acute" patients. The remaining chronics would be housed in a reduced number of the old country hospitals or, better, in some sort of facility provided by local government authorities. "Community care" was a fashionable idea, though little real effort was made either by the National Health Service or local government authorities to make concrete plans for it.

Now, 30 years after the study began and 12 years after its first publication, it is generally accepted that long-stay patients, including young long-stay patients, are still accumulating and that providing care for them will be a continuing social problem. Interest in mental health circles is no longer focused on whether services for the chronically mentally ill will be needed but on what form these services should take, specifically on whether and how chronically ill patients can be cared for in the community near to their homes (Wing and Furlong, 1986; Clifford, 1988; Griffiths, 1988).

In keeping with this new attitude, my own focus of interest has shifted to the second theme—the presence of an inherent conflict in the hospital. This theme is important because it is likely to occur in any institution, whatever its form, that provides services for the mentally ill. The basic conflict occurs between the mental patient and his or her society. This means immediate relatives along with neighbors, the police and courts; beyond them, it means the structure of the health services and of the wider society itself. The hospital provides

*A new paper based on "Hospital and Society"—*British Journal of Medical Psychology*, 49:97–140, 1976.

services in the form of treatment and care intended to benefit but also to "manage" the individual patient—i.e., to control the patient on behalf of society. The chief reason for admission to a mental hospital is that relatives and society cannot manage the patient, so that the hospital is expected to carry out this task on their behalf.

Since patient and society are in conflict and the hospital serves both, the hospital has an intrinsic conflict within itself. In the hospital I studied this conflict was not explicitly recognized; it was often evaded or obscured by social defenses. It is intrinsic in all institutions that treat and care for mental patients; it can be handled well or handled badly, but it cannot be eliminated.

By British standards the hospital was large, its mean annual size between 1905 and 1972 having been 1840 patients. It was situated on the outskirts of a village, which it dominated, and near an industrial town where many of its patients worked, though neither the village nor the town belonged to its catchment area, which was some 20 miles away in north London. The catchment area had varied in size from a population of 427,000 to 1,076,000. It included two local government authorities, which added to the difficulty of joint planning by community and hospital.

The hospital was divided into two main buildings, one composed of 24 long-stay wards for patients of all ages, including admission wards for patients over 65 years of age, and a second of 8 short- and medium-stay active treatment wards for patients under 65 years of age. At the beginning of the study about three-quarters of the patients were long stay; later this proportion decreased to about two-thirds. The grounds were particularly beautiful, a strange contrast to the grim Edwardian buildings. There were 18 medical staff members: 4 consultants, one of whom also acted as medical superintendent, 4 other relatively senior doctors and 10 junior staff members in various stages of training. In 1957 there were 174 trained nursing staff (of whom 100 were men) and 173 unqualified nursing assistants (of whom only 42 were men). There was a high turnover among the nurses, particularly among unqualified nurses. There were a handful of psychologists and social workers and 20–30 occupational and industrial therapists. In the 1960s the number of clerical and administrative staff varied between 250 and 350.

A general practitioner and/or a community social worker were usually involved in securing a patient's admission to the hospital. The duty doctor of the hospital made the decision of whether to admit the patient or not, often with very little knowledge of family circumstances. In 1972 80 percent of patients were admitted "informally," meaning that legally they could leave the hospital whenever they liked. Of those admitted compulsorily, half were reclassified as informal within a few days of admission.

As early as 1930 the hospital had a reputation for being unusually humane and kindly. In this respect it presented a considerable contrast to accounts of state hospitals in the United States (Belknap, 1956; Dunham and Weinberg, 1960; Salisbury, 1962; Goffman, 1961; Bucher and Schatzman, 1962). Various forms of physical treatment were introduced in the 1940s. Since the early 1950s the medical superintendent and senior medical staff had been widely recognized as having a "psychodynamic" as distinct from an exclusively "organic" orientation and the hospital was considered in psychiatric circles to be favorably disposed towards psychoanalysis and the psychoanalytic training of its staff. In the 1950s and 1960s various forms of social therapy were adopted. In 1972 the hospital was "regionalized," meaning that it was rearranged so that each medical unit, which consisted of a number of wards responsible to a particular consultant, would take all the patients from a particular geographical sector of the catchment area, the objective being to improve continuity of care and allow the development of an effective domiciliary service. This change was the end result of a long and painful process begun by the consultant whose wards I was studying.

My initial study was based on interviews, group discussions and observations of the wards of Dr. Dennis Scott, one of the four consultants. For various reasons I had to abandon the study periodically, and whenever I returned the hospital had somewhat changed. In the process of trying to understand why certain changes had occurred but others had not, I examined the adoption of various new methods of physical and social treatment and related them to trends of change in admission and discharge rates. The lack of fit that soon became apparent led me to conclude that I had been paying too much attention to what was going on inside the hospital and too little to the hospital's connections with its environment.

The changes that occurred in the hospital and the use made of it by its public were a function of changes in the environment as well as in policies and treatment methods inside the hospital. Between 1934 and 1955 an increasing number of people started to use the hospital for short stays, the increase being especially marked among older people. Changes in family structure and social network formation (Bott, 1951; 1971) during and after the war made families more willing to seek professional help for personal difficulties and perhaps less able to care for disturbed relatives at home. Such receptiveness was met by the provision of new physical and social treatments that aroused hope that mental illness would become as treatable—and therefore as ordinary—as physical illness.

Yet the hospital continued to provide long-term custodial care. Among older people the demand for such care increased, as one would expect from the increased number of older people in the general population. Among people under 65 there was only a slight trend of decline in the rate of chronic hospitalization from 1934 until the late 1960s. Although the decline was statistically significant, it was not so marked as one would have expected from the usual assumption in psychiatric circles at the time that long-stay patients were no longer being created in sizable numbers.

The finding that chronic hospitalization among patients under 65 had decreased less than expected is of special importance. It indicates a comparatively stable aspect of the relationship between the hospital and its environment, a relationship that had not been much affected by changes of psychiatric fashion, redefinition of madness as illness, or by such environmental changes as alterations in family and network structure. It may indicate an unchanging core of mental illness, but it is more likely that chronic hospitalization is not a reliable indicator of such illness, but a result of the pattern of relationships between the patient, his or her significant others and the hospital. Whether a patient eventually ends up inside or outside the hospital depends on which offers a more viable social place.

The Admission Process

It is now common to speak of the use society makes of mental hospitals and of the function such hospitals perform for society. Admission is the crucial transaction in which the nature of this use becomes manifest. There are two types of admission, temporary and permanent, though no-one knows when a patient is admitted for the first time which sort he or she will turn out to be.

I did not study either process directly. My discussion is therefore based on the work of others, particularly that of Dennis Scott and his colleagues (Scott, 1973, 1974; Scott and Ashworth, 1965, 1967, 1969; Scott et al., 1967, 1970). All his papers deal with the process of admission and the part it plays in the relation between the patient and his or her significant others. I have also been much influenced by Erving Goffman's (1969) paper "The Insanity of Place," which describes with painful acuteness the destruction of one's sense of self by the madness in another whom one cares about. His paper is unique in describing the process before hospitalization—a corrective to retrospective accounts from inside hospitals, but a corrective also to facile assertions that the typical situation is one in which an innocent deviant is victimized by persecutory relatives and over-conventional society.

Although in 1972 90 percent of patients at the hospital had informal legal status, they did not come in of their own accord; typically patients are admitted in a crisis in which someone—usually a relative—decides that their behavior is abnormal. It is a rare patient indeed who comes to the hospital explicitly seeking treatment for self-acknowledged difficulties. People who want treatment go elsewhere, for all the treatments that are offered at a mental hospital are available outside it (Tonnesmann, 1968). Patients come to a mental hospital because someone thinks they cannot be held responsible for their behavior and need to be controlled and removed from their customary social place.

The behavior called mental illness is a form of social deviance. Like other forms of deviance—genius, crime, rebellion—it arouses strong reactions, usually negative, because implicitly it attacks the norms people live by. It differs from other forms of deviance in that it is not supposed to be the patient's fault. In this respect attitudes towards mental and physical illness are similar, for in neither is the patient blamed or held responsible for the state. But in physical illness the disability is restricted to the body, whereas mental illness affects the person's sense of self. Further, as Goffman so poignantly describes in the paper mentioned earlier, the person behaves in a way that destroys the sense of self of the people close by. As well as feeling guilt and a terrible sense of failure, they begin to feel that something absolutely crucial in themselves is being attacked. It is for this reason that the relatives of the disturbed person get so wildly distressed, sometimes over things that seem trivial to an outsider. The interactional framework that has defined the relative's sense of self is being destroyed. Scott puts it in slightly different language: "Physical illness is a role but mental illness is an identity." One *has* a physical illness; one *is* a mental illness. And between the person who will become a patient and the relatives there is what he calls "identity warfare"—a battle for psychic survival (Scott, 1974).

Usually it is a relative who makes the first crucial decision in which the patient's behavior is redefined as "ill." Such redefinition, distressing though it is, takes some of the pain out of patients' behavior, for it makes it unintended; they do not mean it; they are not responsible for themselves. But it is this very redefinition that makes it terrible. It annihilates a person's identity as a responsible adult and, for the relatives, is fraught with often unacknowledged anxiety and fear of revenge. The fault is defined as residing in the illness, not the person. The person is "not oneself." This is the process that Scott describes as "closure" (Scott and Ashworth, 1967). So long as the closure is maintained, what used to be a relationship is dismembered into illness in the patient and health in the relative, a process to which a patient may obligingly and even cunningly contribute.

Calling madness "mental illness" is a comparatively recent phenomenon, part of a humane attempt by the medical profession and mental health propagandists to take away its stigma and accord it the same dignity and respectability as physical illness. The definition assumes that the illness is a concrete disease inside an individual which is, or one day will be, treatable and curable in the same way as many physical illnesses are. Sociologists and many psychiatrists have been critical of this definition of madness as a concrete disease entity inside the individual. (See especially Goffman, 1961, 1969; Szasz, 1961; Laing and Esterson, 1964; Cooper, 1967; and Scott's various papers, especially Scott and Ashworth, 1967, 1969; Scott, 1973, 1974). Their criticism is based on the fact that behavior that is labelled mentally ill is crucially involved in and defined by interaction with other people. On the matter of causes as distinct from effects of the disturbed behavior, the various authors disagree. Laing and Cooper regard mental illness as a form of social deviance created by families and society. My view (which is also Scott's and Goffman's) is that, whatever the cause, the view that madness is only deviance from conventional norms fails to appreciate the destruction the mad person, or, more accurately, the mad part of the person, wreaks not only on conventional society but on *any* form of society. The view that the patient is an innocent victim ignores the extent to which he or she controls and manipulates both associates and self to destroy the basis of thinking and gratification for both.

Whatever the cause of the behavior that is defined as mentally ill, once a patient has been removed to a mental hospital the distinctive feature of his situation is that, rightly or wrongly, someone thinks that control of his interpersonal behavior is required. This fact puts the disturbance in interpersonal and social behavior into the center of the picture, whatever the state of affairs inside the patient may be.

When relatives seek hospital admission for their potential patient, they are not merely seeking relief from an excruciatingly painful conflict. They are rarely satisfied if a doctor promises to admit the patient because the behavior in question is intolerable. Typically they want a clear statement that the patient is *ill,* and that it is because of this illness that the patient is being admitted. Only then can they feel at least partially absolved of responsibility. If need be they can tell the patient (and themselves) that they did not want to get rid of the patient; it was the doctor's decision; it was "because of the illness." They can assure themselves that the madness is in the patient, not in themselves, for relatives are tacitly pronounced "well" by the same act that pronounces the patient "ill." Henceforth responsibility for the care, control and treatment of the patient is placed squarely on the shoulders of the doctor and the hospital for as long as the patient remains in hospital. It has become a medical not an interpersonal problem.

Thus relatives say and usually also feel that they want help for their patient, but act as if the help had to take the form of removal, control and care. They will accept treatment easily only if it does not threaten their own status as "sane" and if it avoids making explicit the hatred of and dependence on the patient that the relatives have secured his admission to get relief from.

Having an illness absolves the patients of responsibility and entitles them to care. But the stigma is enormous, and admission to the hospital, especially for the first time, is a catastrophe. It alters one's sense of self irrevocably, a fact that people who work constantly in mental hospitals tend to become almost unaware of. Accepting the labelling of oneself as ill, even as a person with difficulties or disturbance is usually impossible; patients are unwilling to say how the hospital might help or that they need help in any case, or even why and how they come to be in the hospital. But they usually do not leave the hospital. Thus they act as if they find it a relief to be away from their relatives: they use the hospital as a refuge but cannot say so.

However, refusal to accept the ill status does not mean that one fails to perceive in oneself, or to see that others perceive in one, the sort of attributes that are generally considered to indicate mental illness. Scott and Ashworth (1965) developed a test, which they call the Family Relationship Test, in which patients and their relatives are asked to ascribe various adjectives to themselves and to each other; the patient is also asked to predict how the relatives would see him or her. Virtually all patients who took this test used ill adjectives to describe themselves; they also thought that their relatives would see them as ill. Accepting ill attributes and acknowledging a socially perceived and defined ill status are thus entirely different things.

In spite of its degradation, the status of mental patient gives one considerable power. Every act, however mad, that challenges the former *status quo* in one's relation with relatives still lacerates their sense of identity, even when the patient is in the hospital. The patient can continue to use supposed mindlessness to attack not only relatives' sanity but also his or her own. And every self-damaging act hurts the relatives yet again. The patient has an advantage in the identity warfare. A growing body of work in the United States in the 1960s established that mental patients, including chronic patients, are able to modify their behavior to secure the ends they desire (Braginsky et al., 1966); Fontana et al., 1968; Ludwig and Farrelly, 1966; Towbin, 1966). Patients who want to stay in the hospital know how to behave as if they were more ill, and patients who want to leave know how to behave so as to seem less ill.

In his relations with nursing and medical staff, the patient has a similar advantage. One of the important elements of what Talcott Parsons (1951) has described as the "sick role" is that patients, though not held responsible for being ill, *are* held responsible for cooperating with the doctors who are trying to help them get better. In the case of patients in mental hospitals these two expectations lead to a built-in contradiction: the patient is expected to cooperate with doctors and nurses, but, cannot be expected to cooperate since the ill state involves the whole identity. One is assumed not to have enough mind to cooperate with. (Erikson, 1957 makes the same point in a slightly different form.) Certain patients make the fullest use of the opportunities for evasion and confusion that these contradictory expectations allow.

To the ordinary citizen, the propaganda attempt to make mental illness respectable has not had much effect. Anything that involves destruction of predictable behavior and capacity to think is not regarded as similar to physical illness. Studies of public attitudes to mental illness show that people in general, like relatives, are reluctant to label people as mentally ill and will tolerate behavior deviations as "eccentricities" for some considerable time, but once the label of "mental illness" has been assigned the impulse to reject the person so labelled becomes intense (Sarbin and Mancuso, 1970). The term mental illness has thus suffered the fate of most euphemisms; it has come to mean the same thing as the term "madness" it was intended to replace. Stigma still attaches to mental illness and to the hospitals and people that deal with it. Public attitudes towards mental hospitals fluctuate between a wish not to know they exist and sudden concern over the welfare of their inmates, with occasional bouts of fear that dangerous madmen are being irresponsibly released into the community.

For the doctor and the hospital, the basis on which admission is conducted is crucial to the definition of the setting in which the work of the hospital goes on. Before a patient can be put into the hospital someone, usually a relative with the support of a general practitioner or social worker, has to get a hospital doctor to agree to the admission. What general practitioners and hospital doctors are asked to do is give the sanction of expert medical opinion to a lay decision by relatives, a decision that has already been made. By agreeing to admission, they confirm the relatives' view that the patient is incapable of accepting responsibility for behavior and that the hospital doctor and staff should accept responsibility for care and control. Further, the admitting doctor tacitly confirms the relatives' belief and hope that the trouble is a medical matter, that it consists of a concrete disease entity inside the patient as an individual. An admitting doctor also undertakes, tacitly or explicitly, to provide treatment and to try to cure the patient. For the doctor and the hospital, all these aspects combine to form a fateful decision which leads inevitably to conflict within the hospital, a conflict which is often as unacknowledged as the conflict between relatives and patient or within the patient's own self.

The admission situation would be much more straightforward if the relatives could make it clear to the patient that it was they themselves who wanted the patient sent to the hospital because they found the patient's behavior temporarily impossible, perhaps also with acknowledgement that the patient also found the situation intolerable. But such direct acknowledgement of conflict and hatred contravenes the implicit rules of social interaction, as well as being especially intolerable to people who are frightened of madness in themselves and each other. If a doctor refuses to grant admission except on the basis of such acknowledgement of need for mutual respite, the relatives are likely to feel very persecuted, especially if there is no other hospital they can send their patient to.

There is thus a dishonest element in the work expected of doctors and mental hospitals, though hospitals and their doctors usually comply without protest, even without realizing the contradictoriness of what they are being expected to do, which is to treat the patient's illness in order to help the patient but also to control the patient on behalf of the people with whom the patient has an untenable relationship.

There is a consistent thread of feeling running through all the social and personal attitudes towards mental illness, mental patients and mental hospitals. All concerned act as if they agreed, without having to reflect on it, that madness cannot be contained and accommodated as part of ordinary personal and social life. It is beyond the pale. If it is kept inside it will destroy: destroy the individual, the family, the fabric of society. At all costs it must be separated off and sent somewhere else, and the main task of the mental hospital is to be that "somewhere else."

Lack of Social Place: Chronic Hospitalization

Most patients come into the hospital in crisis, calm down, and go home—"on the conveyor belt," as one doctor put it. But some get stuck in the hospital. Dennis Scott has been particularly concerned, both clinically and in research, to find out what sorts of patient get stuck in the hospital and why (Scott et al., 1967; Scott, 1973). His studies indicate that in spite of the early discharge policy and the increasing frequency of readmissions, mental hospital patients can still be divided into two distinct sets, which he calls "community centered" and "hospital centered." Community centered patients are those who, regardless of the number of times they go in and out of the hospital, eventually end up spending most of their time outside. Hospital centered patients, regardless of number of discharges and readmissions, eventually spend most of their time (defined as over 80 percent of the two-year period after first admission) in the hospital. Among first-admitted patients of all diagnoses in 1964, 15 percent became hospital centered. Among first admitted schizophrenics in 1964 20 percent became hospital centered.

Scott and a psychologist (Casson) carried out a statistical examination of first admitted patients who became community centered and of first admitted patients who became hospital centered (Scott et al., 1970). Scott then revised the clinical approach of his team to detect and concentrate therapeutic effort on patients likely to get stuck in hospital (Scott, 1973, 1974). He expanded the plan to include a domiciliary service to give help outside the hospital and to prevent unnecessary hospitalization. The development of this service in the catchment area made essential the regionalization of Scott's clinical unit.

According to Scott, patients who become chronically hospitalized have no viable place in society. There are two main causes of such lack of social place: violent, permanent discordance with close relatives, especially parents; and social isolation, often following the withdrawal or death of parents. All patients admitted to a mental hospital are in a state of discordance and distress in their personal world; such discordance is the crucial feature of admission. But in most cases it is temporary, whereas the distinctive feature of patients who get stuck is that it is permanent.

Scott identified several types of patient likely to get stuck in the hospital, but the type he studied most were young adults, usually diagnosed as schizophrenic, in what he calls "untenable" situations with their parents, the nature of the untenability being that the patients do not support their parents' view of themselves (the parents) as healthy and well. The parents think they themselves are well, meaning sane; the parents think the patient thinks they are well; the patient does not confirm this expectation, but thinks the parents are ill, too (Scott et al., 1970; Scott, 1973, 1974). None of these discordant expectations is openly recognized or discussible by parents or patients; the feelings of hatred and dependence are so painful that they are wrapped in confusion and assertions of illness and helplessness. When such patients are discharged they are soon readmitted in crisis. Such relatives and patients manage to agree tacitly on two issues: that there shall be no clarification of the state of relationship between parents and patient, and that the doctor and the hospital staff should accept all responsibility for dealing with the patient's state. This set of patients alerted Scott and his team to what he calls the "treatment barrier," that is, the unwillingness of both patient and relative to be helped in any fashion that threatens the status quo. The relatives are opposed to any shift that threatens the safe location of madness in the patient and of the patient in the hospital. In Scott's experience such relatives do not sever physical contact with their patient; typically they make conscientious visitors. The parents are painfully dependent on the patient to confirm their identity, their sense of self; once disaster has struck, the patient's being in the hospital fulfills the function of making him or her the identifiable vessel of what the relatives often feel, with varying degrees of awareness, to be a family taint (Scott and Ashworth, 1969).

Sometimes such patients are very skillful in enlisting the doctor's aid in the identity war. The doctor is almost sure to be more sympathetic to the patient than to the relatives, for the doctor sees the patient more often, and is likely to think that the patient is more obviously in need of help, less able to cope with life, more victimized. And the patient is usually young, which is appealing and makes the state of mind seem particularly tragic. Hence the temptation for the doctor to see the patient as a helpless victim of family and social pathology. It is easy to overlook the fact that victims so readily use their capacity to control the feelings of relatives so as to collude with the victimization, to attack their own sanity by getting others to do it for them. But this process, although deliberate, is not necessarily conscious; and even when it is, or is partially so, patients are adept at confusing themselves and others so that the destructiveness of their attack on their own sanity and on that of others becomes difficult to perceive.

Relatives are likely to get wild with rage and distress if they feel that the doctor is too sympathetic to the patient and is therefore accusing the relatives of making the patient ill; the doctor, the relative feels, is threatening the location of sanity and madness in their rightful places, and, like the patient, the doctor is threatening the relative's identity.

The doctor, not surprisingly, is likely to feel attacked from all quarters. In such circumstances thinking straight is more than usually difficult, and the solution of keeping the patient in the hospital seems not unreasonable. But even this decision is usually not taken very deliberately. Patients get transferred to a long-stay ward after failing to improve for some time, and the doctor loses sight of them.

Socially isolated patients also tend to become long-stay hospital residents. There are several types of isolation. Patients who have been incapacitated but kept and supported at home by parents are likely to become hospital centered when the parents die. Middle-aged women whose children have left home and who are not emotionally attached to their husbands or to meaningful work run considerable risk of becoming chronically hospitalized, depression being the typical complaint. Elderly patients without relatives willing or able to care for them are another well-defined set, some degree of senile dementia being the typical complaint. The size of this set of chronically hospitalized patients has increased considerably since the 1930s, which is not the case among the other types of isolated patient. Patients suffering from psychoses of organic or toxic origin were also present among the chronically hospitalized group, but here too the crucial factor was the patient/relative relationship rather than the degree of disability in itself.

Although neither Scott nor I made a systematic comparison according to psychiatric criteria of the severity of symptoms among hospital and community centered patients, it was clear from ordinary clinical practice, both inside the hospital and in out-patient clinics, that some patients who got stuck in the hospital were not especially severely disturbed, whereas some of those who went home to their families were too incapacitated to work and lead independent lives. It is difficult to know how prevalent such disability is since ordinary clinical practice does not provide accurate information about what happens to patients once they go home (cf. Brown et al., 1966). I believe that whether patients end up inside or outside the hospital does not depend primarily on the severity of the psychiatric disorder. It depends on the type and severity of discordance between patient and society, and thus on whether home or hospital offers the patient a more viable social place.

Organically oriented psychiatrists consider that chronic hospitalization occurs because the disease process involved in madness incapacitates patients and prevents them from occupying their social places outside hospital. In the 1950s and 1960s the popular psychiatric view was that mental hospitals "institutionalized" patients and thus incapacitated them for life outside hospital. Scott's work and to some extent that of Goffman, Szasz, Laing and others suggests that the crucial factor in chronic hospitalization is the nature of the relationship between the patient and society, especially the relatives. If the patient and relatives are in a violently discordant but mutually dependent relationship, the patient is likely to end up permanently in the hospital. For the patient the hospital is an asylum; for the relatives it acts as a place that contains and controls the madness and its destruction of their own sense of their identity as sane. In cases in which a patient is socially isolated, particularly if the relatives die or withdraw themselves from contact, the patient may use the hospital as a substitute for a world in which he or she feels they cannot make a place. In brief, chronic hospitalization occurs when a hospital place is accessible and appears to the patient to offer a more viable social place than could be found outside.

It seems extremely unlikely that society or its health services can eliminate either the mad aspects of familial relationships or madness in individuals. But finding the best place to contain and care for it poses considerable problems.

Control, Care and Treatment

My thesis is that the admission process, combined with the way the hospital is connected to its environment, leads to the development inside the hospital of conflicts ultimately deriving from the basic conflict between madness and sanity, between patient and society. When my study began there was no open controversy or awareness of conflict over this issue, only an occasional voicing of an ill-defined feeling that something confusing was going on that made staff, especially doctors, uneasy and dissatisfied without knowing why. "This is a marvellous place to work because of the permissive atmosphere, but there is something odd about it. I don't know how to describe it," said a young doctor who had recently come from a much more authoritarian hospital. "The hospital is like schizophrenia itself," said another, "split up in bits, projections all over the place, parts not communicating with other parts. Things are always getting lost in this place—people, ideas, decisions. There is an overpowering sense of inertia." Or another, in 1961: "Do you want a chunk of my private paranoia? Trying to change anything here is like falling into an animal trap. Once you get outside your own ward everything is chaos. Each misunderstanding is understandable, but there are just too many. It couldn't be chance. But I stay here, don't I?" More recent studies indicate that these feelings of discomfort, even demoralization, have not altered much in the past thirty years (Hinshelwood, 1979, 1986; Donati, in press).

Being wise after the event, it is now my view that what was making these doctors uncomfortable was an unarticulated sense that something the hospital was doing was not straightforward. There is a sort of dishonesty in unknowingly allowing the hospital to be used to treat and house individuals who are acting as the receptacles of the madness that their relatives cannot bear to face as part of their family or as part of themselves. Malaise was aggravated by certain organizational features peculiar to the research hospital, but the basic dilemma is built into the organization of all mental hospitals that use the traditional definitions of why and how patients are admitted, because these definitions land the hospital in a situation of trying to help an individual on behalf of a society which does not recognize its wish to get rid of the individual as well as to help him.

In the formal medical-nursing model the functions of control, care and treatment are supposed to act simultaneously in the interests of patient and society. Yet it is usually thought that control and care operate in the interests of society and that only treatment operates in the interests of the patient. It is, however, widely recognized that patients, relatives and staff sometimes regard treatment as punishment meted out by the hospital on behalf of society—hardly surprising in view of the ferocity of the early physical treatments—whereas custodial care is sometimes regarded as a refuge from society. Further, many doctors have come to regard ward regimes and nursing care as a major component of treatment—the only treatment in some programs.

The *control* component of hospital activities consists of a set of regulations and restrictions designed to prevent patients escaping or hurting themselves or causing offenses to others. The regulations and rules are usually thought to be carried out for the benefit of society rather than to help the patient, except in the sense that preventing suicide can be considered helpful to the patient.

The general public has different views of the need for control from the views of people who are closely acquainted with mental patients in mental hospitals. The cultural stereotype still is that mental patients are dangerous and would all try to escape if they were not locked up, whereas to patients, relatives and hospital staff it is inertia rather than violence that is the typical problem. The difficult issue is to get patients to leave the hospital, not to keep them in.

Doctors carry overall responsibility for the control function, but it is the nursing staff who immediately exercise it and, unless the doctor is particularly active in defining the way he or she wants the nursing staff to exercise control, they regard themselves as being responsible for the control function to the senior nursing staff and the medical superintendent; ultimately, though more tacitly, they regard themselves as responsible to the external society. Generally speaking, nurses accept the control function as their rightful task whereas doctors would like to get rid of it.

Standards of control used to be much more stringent than they were even in 1957 when my study began. Preventing suicides and escapes was no longer a major preoccupation of the nursing staff, and standards of cleanliness and order were less exacting than they were during the 1930s. But even at that time nursing staff regarded themselves as—and felt they were regarded by others as—responsible for maintaining something close to the usual standards of control and care. Sometimes nurses made the social basis of their anxiety about patients' freedom very clear, as when a former nursing officer complained that the medical staff were allowing certain wards to run riot with permissiveness; he was worried that it would end with the nursing staff in court if there was a suicide. Another nurse complained about a medical program of doing nothing for patients, saying he knew it was designed to make the patients take responsibility for themselves but thought it damaging to the ward nursing staff to see the ward and the patients get into a filthy, disorderly state. Again, adherence to the control function showed itself in the content of the rumors that usually circulated when a ward was starting a new program. The typical content of such rumors was that patients were being allowed to indulge themselves sexually or to be violent—the two instinctual urges that it is traditionally the task of society to keep under control.

Although hospital doctors are ultimately responsible for the control function, most of them do not like it. Many try to avoid it because they feel it interferes with treatment. But, in the hospital situation, control and authority were always a crucial part of the treatment setting: it is a doctor who decides whether a patient can come into the hospital; a doctor decides, or is at least in charge of the team who decide, on a patient's general ward program, work regime and treatment; it was a doctor who used to determine a patient's "privileges" and "passes"; and it is a doctor, or a team headed by a doctor, who usually decides when a patient leaves the hospital. In law, in the eyes of the general public, in the opinion of relatives and of patients, the doctor is the ultimate authority, and holds this authority on behalf of society. Control is an integral part of the job.

If a hospital doctor denies this social and administrative authority or avoids its implications, he or she is sure to run into trouble. Some doctors at the research hospital tried to get their nursing staff not only to exercise the control function but also to take responsibility for it in the eyes of the patients, so that the doctor could be devoted entirely to psychotherapy; this procedure led to conflict between nurses and doctors. In some hospitals the responsibility for the control function may be assigned to administrative doctors and the treatment function to clinical doctors, which leads to conflicts between the two, as at Chestnut Lodge (Stanton and Schwartz, 1954). In group or community therapy a doctor may allow the group to exercise control, which leads to experiments by patients to discover what sort of violence they need to perpetrate in order to force doctors to show their hand (Rapoport and Rapoport, 1957; Rapoport, 1960). A doctor may collude with patients in idealizing the therapeutic endeavor of his or her own unit while locating the control function in the parent hospital or the parent society (Cooper, 1967). Doctors may differ in how they express their responsibility for the control function, but they cannot get rid of it.

The hospital provides *care* as well as control—shelter, food, work, recreation, a social round of sorts—the framework of a life that would normally be provided by patients themselves or by their relatives and society. It is the nursing staff who provide the care, though other staff and patients may help. Everyone agrees that care is provided in the interests of the patients though opinions differ sharply on what their interests are. Although nursing staff are expected to provide the care in the interests of the patient, they are kept very much aware by frequent contacts with relatives that it is the relatives and society to whom they are responsible for providing the care. If the desires of patients and the desires of relatives differ, the nursing staff are caught in the middle. There is likely to be a marked element of competitiveness in the relationship between relatives and nurses because the nurses carry out functions that relatives would be executing if the patient were at home. Relatives often feel guilty about not looking after their patient, though without admitting it to themselves; hence they sometimes accuse the nursing staff of the neglect and other faults in providing care of which they themselves feel guilty. Sometimes, of course, nurses are neglectful.

To chronic patients the hospital becomes home. They resist being banished from it. This is the "institutionalization" so much criticized in the 1950s. In the research hospital many nursing staff on chronic wards thought it would be cruel to send patients outside. They felt that the young doctors who were trying to clear out the chronic wards were only trying to enhance their own reputations and to save the Health Service money, not to help the patients. The young doctors thought the nursing staff were trying to hold on to their ward workers. Most relatives wanted their chronic patients to stay in the hospital; a few were willing to try having them at home; some had lost contact. Patients wanted things to stay as they were, with the provision of more recreational facilities. One patient who had lived in the hospital for many years caused much amusement by saying, "There are so many changes and upsets here now that I might as well go home."

Treatment is usually thought of as the special province of the doctor though nurses, psychologists, social workers, occupational therapists and industrial therapists may help. In theory treatment is supposed to benefit the patient, relatives and society. Often it pleases none. It depends on the situation and the type of treatment. No conflict arises if the doctor sticks to forms of physical treatment and ward management that require only a minimum of cooperation from patients and relatives, though even in the case of the gentlest physical treatment patients may avoid treatment by not taking it, as in the case of pills.

If the rift between patient and relatives is not deep, a traditional program of admission ward activities combined with drugs will usually repair the damaged relationship sufficiently for the patient to return home. Even before the use of physical treatments, "cures" were frequently achieved merely by the refuge and cooling off provided by the process of admission. "Patients come in raving," said an admission ward doctor in 1958, "and then get better, I really don't know why. I feel that all I'm doing is superintending a process of spontaneous remission. Anyway I haven't time to do anything else."

When the relationship between patient and relatives is untenable the doctor is caught in conflicts of loyalty to the patient and to society, and treatment in hospital becomes virtually impossible. "We know you have your methods," is a not uncommon remark by a relative, meaning that he thinks the doctor ought to use treatment to punish the patient and make him conform. It is not surprising that patients do not want such treatment, or that many sociologists, adopting the patient's point of view, hold that doctors delude patients into thinking they are ill instead of only socially nonconforming. If, on the other hand, a doctor provides a form of treatment that the patient accepts but the relative does not, the relative may attack the doctor and appeal to higher authority to try to obstruct the process. A doctor who uses a form of treatment that requires the cooperation of both patient and relative, when the relative and the patient have a deeply untenable relationship, will be opposed by both. Whatever their differences with each other, neither relatives nor patient want to face the painful issues they are trying to use hospitalization to avoid. One might think it reasonable that such relatives and patients should agree to lead separate and independent lives but this, too, is often unthinkable to them, for their mutual dependence is as intense as their unacknowledged hatred. Thus, in cases of acute discordance between patient and relatives, no method of treatment that ignores the discordance can have much effect, but treatments that take the discordance into account are likely to arouse strong resistance, certainly from relatives and usually from patients as well.

Organizational Arrangements

At the time of my research the senior medical staff found it convenient to have a division of labor between themselves and the medical superintendent in which they were freed of what they regarded as tiresome administration, because they wanted to get on with therapeutic work on their admission wards. The hospital was divided into four medical units on the basis of age, sex and diagnosis, not on the basis of where the patients lived. The hospital staff provided out-patient clinics at certain general hospitals in the catchment area but there was no assurance that the doctor who initially saw a patient there would be on the team that saw the patient in hospital; and there was no likelihood that the doctor who treated a patient on the admission ward would be the doctor who followed him up in the community after he had left the hospital. Although in 1964 the Ministry of Health suggested regionalization (Ministry of Health, 1964), meaning the division of the hospital into sub-units each taking patients from one geographical subdivision of the catchment area, this policy was not put into effect at the research hospital until 1972. At first none of the senior staff wanted such a change.

The wards of the hospital were grouped into three types of unit: nursing units, each headed by a pair of assistant matrons or assistant chief male nurses; medical units, each headed by a consultant; and buildings. These three types of unit did not coincide. The Admissions Building, for example, contained two nursing units and parts of three medical units, but each medical unit also had wards in other nursing units and buildings. The chronic building contained four nursing units, involving one whole medical unit and bits of three others. The three types of unit thus overlapped in a complex fashion such that a ward was not contained within a unit larger than the ward but smaller than the hospital as a whole. The opportunities for confusion and misunderstanding were impressive. It was particularly difficult to initiate a therapeutic change. Since the wards of one medical team did not coincide with nursing units and therefore had little autonomy, it was impossible to confine the effects of a ward change to one medical team. A change reverberated through the hospital, causing the maximum amount of upheaval. To be successful a ward change had to be planned at the top, involving not only the ward doctor, the consultant, and the senior nursing staff, but also the medical superintendent. Sometimes the senior administrative staff had to be brought into the consultations as well, and, if the change involved other central services such as those provided by the psychologists, occupational therapists, and social workers, both the immediate workers involved *and* the heads of their departments also had to be brought into the planning, often over a considerable period of time. This arrangement had developed more or less by accident in the 1940s and 1950s. Everyone agreed that it impeded change, but no one was keen to alter it. They could not see how such change would benefit individual patients, and during the 1950s and 1960s the treatment and care of patients as individuals were the primary interests of the senior medical staff.

These were times of therapeutic innovation and ferment. Several new methods of treatment were being introduced and doctors were very much involved in their success. The hospital was generally thought of as psychodynamic in orientation, and its medical superintendent and senior medical staff had a reputation for allowing junior medical staff to develop their own ideas and therapeutic experiments. Senior staff also allowed and encouraged junior medical staff to train in individual psychoanalysis, although this training was not specifically or immediately usable in the hospital setting. Some psychotherapy was practiced with selected patients from 1950 onwards and some group therapy was also practiced in the early 1950s, but this psychodynamic orientation did not preclude physical treatments. Electroconvulsion therapy had been adopted in 1944, insulin therapy in 1947, transorbital lobotomies from 1947 to 1950 and tranquilizers in 1956/57. Insulin therapy was discontinued in 1958; no surgery had been carried out for several years when I arrived; and by the 1970s ECT was rarely though occasionally used. From 1956 onwards various forms of social therapy were introduced, especially group nursing and an integrated program of occupational therapy and industrial rehabilitation on chronic wards, and ward community therapy on two admission wards (Jones, 1952; Rapoport and Rapoport, 1957; Rapoport, 1960). The occupational therapy and industrial rehabilitation program was also used for patients on admission wards. In the mid-1960s Scott began his method of family therapy, ward management and community psychiatry. By the late 1960s he had evolved a method of ward, team and community practice quite different from the traditional hospital matrix in which it had evolved.

Several of these experiments led doctors and ward staff to establish new types of contact with relatives, community social workers, hostels, etc., but they were hampered in the development of a community-based approach by the fact that the hospital was not regionalized. Usually the attempt at social therapy was eventually given up before it had led to a redefinition of the unit of treatment as the patient in his environment instead of the patient as an individual.

Living with Madness

The Chronic Hospital was the most peaceful part of the system and remained so even though many changes were introduced into it. It was mainly located in a very large old building containing twenty-four wards of long-stay geriatric patients, including their admission wards. This building also contained the offices of the medical superintendent and all the other senior staff except the other three consultants. It was ten minutes' walk to the Admissions Hospital, but socially and emotionally the Chronic Hospital was in another world— peaceful, orderly and dominated by the ethos of the nursing staff.

The medical superintendent and an experienced senior hospital medical officer were in charge of the geriatric wards for women. The doctors of the other wards in the Chronic Building were mainly junior, temporary and psychiatrically inexperienced, though each ward doctor was responsible to one of the three consultants. But the sisters and charge nurses* thought of the junior

*The head nurse and her deputy in a ward.

doctors mainly as general practitioners who were dealing with their patients' physical ailments. The nursing staff looked to the senior nursing staff as the people they were responsible to. In this respect the socio-medical organization of the Chronic Hospital was similar to the organization of the whole hospital during the custodial period, when the nursing staff managed the wards under the leadership of the senior nursing staff and the medical superintendent, with the doctors acting as visitors to individual patients but taking no part in ward management.

Only the doctors, especially the young ward doctors, and occasionally a social worker, felt vexed by the inertia of the chronic wards; they thought relatives and patients were virtually malingering and that many patients should have been having a go at life outside. Nurses did not like being accused of institutionalizing patients, but the young doctors soon left to do their stint in the admission wards. In spite of the general atmosphere of changelessness and tranquility, many changes were adopted on the chronic wards in the 1950s and 1960s: nearly all ward doors were unlocked; patients were accordingly re-grouped; group nursing was started; patients were given individualized clothing; tranquilizers were introduced; more recreation was provided; and an extensive program of occupational and industrial therapy was developed. New programs were readily absorbed into the even tenor of chronic ward life. The new activities made life more pleasant, but they did not lead to a vastly increased number of discharges of chronic patients.

Over the years the chronic part of a mental hospital develops a chronic culture, a set of customary methods of living with madness and disablement. Compared to the American mental hospitals described in the sociological literature, the chronic culture of the hospital I studied was kindly and humane, though slow moving and sometimes tranquil to the point of unreality. (For studies of chronic culture see especially Belknap, 1956; Dunham and Weinberg, 1960; Salisbury, 1962; Goffman, 1961; Bucher and Schatzman, 1962.)

Nurses usually adhere to the cultural definitions of madness as something to be shunned and, even though they know that many of their patients do not typically behave in a mad way, the fact that patients have been medically defined as ill means that it is legitimate to regard all of them as mad. Since nurses cannot get away from the madness physically, they get away from it emotionally; they develop some form of relationship that locates madness in the patient and sanity in themselves, with a barrier to prevent contamination. (See also Hinshelwood, 1986.) Such an arrangement allows the nurses to stay in the situation without feeling that their minds are being damaged. It justifies the use of control by the nurses, entitles patients to care and refuge, and is a virtual guarantee that they will continue to be thought ill and therefore will not be sent outside.

The basic method by which nursing staff stay physically in contact with patients while leaving emotionally consists of some form of routinization—a concentration on activities rather than on the people who do them. (Cf. Cohler and Shapiro, 1964; Tudor Will, 1952, 1957; Moss and Hunter, 1963; Coser, 1963; Hinshelwood, 1979, 1986; Donati, in press.) All these authors discuss in various ways the anxieties and defenses involved in nursing psychotics and/or chronically ill patients.

The simple realities of life on an understaffed large chronic ward provide ample opportunity for concentration on routine, which is simultaneously used to avoid contact with patients and to get the work done. One of the characteristic expressions of concentration on routine was the attitude towards talking to patients. If there were two nurses on a shift, they talked to each other, not to the patients. Several students who worked temporarily on chronic wards reported that if they talked too much to patients the sister or the nurse would say, "You're supposed to talk to me!" Talking to patients is dangerous because it threatens to puncture the barrier that keeps sanity and madness in their proper places.

There were two main forms of routinization, one involving an *authoritarian regime* based on strict rules, the other based on *a form of unconscious collusion* between patient and nurse.

The *authoritarian regime* was most common on male wards, especially on those where the patients were young or middle aged. On such wards there was an undercurrent of tension and fear; the atmosphere was often military, sometimes quite explicitly so; frequently the charge nurses had been in the army. The role of army sergeant was one of the few acceptable models for a male charge nurse, one that countered the public stereotype of nursing as a female occupation. Many of the male nurses I talked to were very contemptuous of what they called the "Florence Nightingale" approach of the female nurses, and made it clear that they themselves had more realistic as well as more conservative attitudes towards the whole situation of mental hospitals and patients. Many authors have described similar attitudes as characteristic of male nurses in other hospitals. (See especially Jones and Sidebotham, 1962; Martin, 1962; Cumming, Clancy and Cumming, 1956; Scheff, 1962; Belknap, 1956; Bucher and Schatzman, 1962.)

The other form of routinization, the *collusive* type, was more common on female than on male wards. It involved a curiously peaceful but unreal atmosphere in which the nurses were thoughtful, even tender to patients, and patients seemed passive and dependent on the nurses, especially the sister. When she passed by their faces lit up; when she was not there they lapsed into apathetic withdrawal. It seemed probable that this sort of relationship was based on unconscious collusion between patient and nurse. The nurse acted as if she were the psychological recipient of the patient's capacity to think, whereas the patient acted as though she were the recipient of the nurse's unwanted feelings. By this means patients were felt to be as different from the nurse as possible. Madness was safely lodged in the patient, and the fear of the patient contaminating the nurse with it was reduced by the sense that the patient was helpless and dependent because the nurse had absorbed all the available willpower and capacity to think.

Many sisters and a few charge nurses expressed considerable emotional satisfaction from having this sort of relationship with patients, though they were not aware of their use of projection or of the collusive element in their adaptation. The closest anyone came to expressing it directly occurred in the case of a sister who said she liked looking after psychotic patients because they were helpless and needed care, and that many of her personal problems had disappeared or become less troublesome since she had taken up psychiatric nursing. Sometimes patients pointed out a sister's or nurse's use of projection. One such patient on a disturbed ward had a fit of temper and broke a lot of dishes. The assistant matron looked at her angrily and said, "*Now* look what you've done!" to which the patient replied, "That's not my bad temper. That's sister's bad temper and I'm letting it out for her." The junior staff and several patients exploded with laughter because everyone knew that that particular sister had trouble controlling her temper.

The chronic wards I observed gave an impression of being bare of an indigenous patient culture and informal social structure, a state of affairs that Somner and Osmond (1962) aptly describe as the "schizophrenic no-society," though one might equally well describe it as the "chronic ward no-society." There appeared to be none of the inventiveness and zest that one finds among normal people even in prisons and other conditions of deprivation. Shared perceptions and shared interpretations of them, which form the basis for the growth of culture and social structure, did not appear to be present in their usual forms. Insofar as a patient culture operated, it seemed to be mediated through the staff. In terms of my hypothesis, this occurred because patients lodged much of their capacity to think in the staff.

In Britain there are sometimes reports of individual instances of cruelty to patients. It seems inevitable that the structure of the nursing situation should lead to occasional outbursts of violence from both nurses and patients. In the authoritarian form of routinization, violence is always just below the surface. In the collusive form, the helplessness of certain patients is likely to stir such feelings of guilt in the nurse that she or he may lash out in rage at the offensively submissive object. Sometimes patients, safe in their cloak of illness, may provoke the staff knowing that staff are not supposed to retaliate and may be punished for it.

Some of the problems of living with madness and disability will arise in any form of socio-medical organization—in hostels, in foster families, perhaps even in group homes. The definition of personal disablement as a medical problem has a debilitating effect, which could perhaps be mitigated in a different form of organization. In the present system patients have to act as if they were more ill than they really are to retain their social refuge; nurses have to engage in considerable self-deception because the care they provide for social reasons is regarded by society, including relatives, as a medical rather than a social necessity.

Conflict, Defense and Change: The Admissions Hospital

The Admissions Hospital was situated near the entrance gates, expressive of its close contact with the outside world. It contained four wards for women and four for men, in each case consisting of a psychotic admission ward, a neurotic admission ward and two medium-stay wards. The task of the Admission Hospital was to treat patients and send them home if possible. Patients who became long stay eventually got sent to the chronic wards.

The three consultants (excluding the medical superintendent) spent most of their time in the Admissions Hospital though each was also responsible for a number of chronic wards. Each consultant was the leader of a "firm" (team) of four or five doctors who were in immediate charge of the wards. Compared to the Chronic Hospital the Admissions Hospital was lavishly staffed with nurses, psychologists, social workers and occupational therapists, as well as doctors.

In the socio-medical organization of the Admissions Hospital the consultant was the leader of his team of doctors and there were frequent meetings both of this group and of a larger set of staff including nurses, occupational therapists, psychologists and social workers, depending on the plans of the particular therapeutic program. The ward doctor and/or consultant was the leader of the ward and the sister or charge nurse was immediately responsible to the doctor rather than, or as well as, to the senior nursing staff. It was universally agreed in the Admissions Hospital that a major aspect of any treatment program was the way the ward was run—its organization as a group, its activities, its rules, its personal relationships. In some programs it was the *only* form of treatment. The doctor was no longer only a visitor of patients as individuals; he defined his job as manager of a group enterprise whose purpose was therapeutic. Thus by the late 1950s it was clear that a major change had already taken place in the definition of treatment as a social enterprise and in the role relationship of doctor and nurse.

Because of the doctors' interventions in ward management, the executive management function of the most senior nursing staff on treatment wards had declined and their job, so far as the Admissions Hospital was concerned, came to consist of staffing the wards with nurses, whom they also recruited and trained. The senior nursing staff thus provided a central service for the several medical teams of the hospital. They played no executive role in forming the therapeutic policies of the various medical teams and conflict therefore easily arose. The medical teams were likely to think that the nurses essential to their therapeutic policies were being arbitrarily shifted about in order to obstruct the therapeutic goals of their team. The senior nursing staff were likely to think that the consultants were willfully ignorant of the demands of the other teams, of nurse training, of the nursing profession, and of the standards and expectations of external bodies. To "improve communication" in matters of this sort involved everyone in endless meetings. Because they wanted to get on with their clinical work, the consultants were content to let the medical superintendent "bring the matron round."

Several new methods of physical and social treatment were adopted during the period of my study. All these innovations aroused considerable enthusiasm but none were spectacularly successful in the research hospital or elsewhere—nothing comparable, say, to streptomycin as a cure for tuberculosis. Drugs and other physical treatments relieved symptoms. Psychotherapy was not practicable or effective in a mental hospital setting because it conflicted acutely with the control function and in any case could not be used on a wide scale. Industrial therapy, at least at the research hospital, made an enormous difference to the quality of life of both patients and staff, though it did not increase the outflow of chronic patients. Ward community therapy aroused immense enthusiasm for a time but the results were not of such obvious efficacy as to be adopted by the unconverted; it was extremely arduous for the staff without giving any clear evidence that the effort inside the hospital had improved patients' ability to cope with life outside.

My impression was that several customary features of hospital practice were acting not only as methods of getting the work done but also as defenses against the anxieties inherent in the mental hospital situation, especially anxieties concerning the use made of the hospital by society and anxiety that existing treatments were not as successful as people wanted them to be. (See Jaques' [1955; Vol. I, "On the Dynamics of Social Structure"] and Menzies' [1960; Vol. I, "Social Systems as a Defense Against Anxiety"] work on institutions as defenses against anxiety.)

Throughout the hospital at various times it seemed that there was a defense of "not knowing"—a disinclination to find things out, especially anything that might threaten the prevailing *modus vivendi*. No systematic attempt was being made, for example, to evaluate various treatment methods. The nature of therapeutic work with patients is such that meaningful measures of effectiveness are exceedingly difficult to devise. In the research hospital it was striking that even simple crucial facts were not known. Records, for example, were kept in such a way that no one knew how many patients were becoming long stay or whether the various therapeutic programs were having an effect on chronic hospitalization. Until my investigation no one knew that the first-admission rate had stopped increasing in 1955, before the introduction of tranquilizers and the more radical forms of social therapy. It was difficult to get figures on the hospital population according to age and length of stay in spite of the fullest cooperation from all the staff concerned.

Because society's expectations of mental hospitals are equivocal, and because indications of the success or failure of treatments are so difficult to get, treatments and methods of care may be adopted or abandoned for reasons that have little to do with their stated aims—because they fit in with the doctors' value system or wish to cure; because they offer hope in the face of uncertainty; or because they give some protection against a half-felt sense by doctors that their skills are being misused. Psychiatrists and mental hospitals are therefore notoriously susceptible to ideological controversy and to bouts of optimism and despair.

Idealization and denigration appeared to be commonly used defenses. When a particular ward started a new therapeutic program, the ward staff usually became utterly dedicated to the new venture, which became almost sacrosanct; their hostility and uncertainty were projected on to outsiders in other wards, who were felt to be hostile and interfering, which indeed they often were. Envy of inventiveness and jealousy of the special attention paid to other parts of the hospital are endemic in the hospital situation. Finding an external enemy appears to be a very common development in almost all types of therapeutic innovation; if it is not the parent hospital, it is the parent society, or people who adhere to other points of view.

It seems likely that seemingly inefficient arrangements may be retained precisely because they make communication difficult, for peaceful coexistence in an institution is often preferred to confrontation. Indeed, when confrontation and change did come, they were thoroughly unpleasant. Although several of the hospital's experiments in social therapy had established new links with the community, it was not until Scott and other senior doctors pressed on to a more radical redefinition of the unit of treatment as the patient in his environment that change inside the hospital became extensive, leading to regionalization and the breakdown of the amicable *modus vivendi*. Regionalization was a painful process, with sharp differences of view on what the relationship of the hospital to society was and should be, and with acute conflict over the extent to which the regionalized units should be administratively autonomous.

So long as people in the external society have feelings of horror and dread of madness, mental hospitals will be pressed into accommodating madness in a way that will relieve society of responsibility and allow its members to regard themselves as sane. If, like the research hospital at the beginning of my study, a psychiatric institution accepts patients for treatment as individuals on medical grounds and also provides a home for those who fail to improve, it will have divided loyalties to the patient and to society, and the stage will be set for a debilitating form of conflict inside the institution. If a hospital provides medical treatment for patients as individuals but refuses to provide long-term care, it is likely that many patients will eventually end up drifting from one hospital to another in search of a resting place. This state of affairs appears to be occurring in the case of the psychiatric clinics in general hospitals. If the institution refuses to allow its treatment facilities to be used to treat patients as isolated individuals, there will be protests from relatives and the other social bodies to whom they complain. Finally, if an institution frankly accepts its task as providing a home for social rejects, it will be stigmatized as a hopeless chronic institution, inappropriate for medical service, however much the social refuge may be needed by certain patients and by society.

None of these institutional forms is entirely desirable from anyone's point of view. All involve either constant conflict or shutting one's eyes to what one does not want to see. Perhaps a first step in planning might be to accept madness and the dread of it as social and personal facts. Then one would at least be in a better position to work at devising institutional forms that would make madness, in both patient and society, bearable rather than curable or beyond understanding.

References

Belknap, I. 1956. *Human Problems of a State Mental Hospital*. New York: McGraw-Hill.

Bott, E. 1957. *Family and Social Network* (2nd edition, 1971). London: Tavistock Publications.

———. 1976. "Hospital and Society." *British Journal of Medical Psychology*, 49:97–140.

Braginsky, B.M., M. Grosse and K. Ring. 1966. "Controlling Outcomes Through Impression Management: An Experimental Study of the Manipulative Tactics of Mental Patients." *Journal of Consulting and Clinical Psychology*, 30:295–300.

Brown, G.W., M. Bone, B. Dalinson, and J.K. Wing. 1966. *Schizophrenia and Social Care: A Comparative Follow-Up Study of 339 Schizophrenic Patients*. Maudsley Monograph No.17. London: Oxford University Press.

Bucher, R. and L. Schatzman. 1962. "The Logic of the State Mental Hospital." *Social Problems*, 9:337–49.

Clifford, P. 1988. "Out of the Cuckoo's Nest: The Move of T2 Ward from Bexley Hospital to 215 Sydenham Road." In *Community Care in Practice*, edited by T. Lavender and F. Holloway. London: Wiley.

Cohler, J. and L. Shapiro. 1964. "Avoidance Patterns in Staff-Patient Interaction on a Chronic Schizophrenic Ward." *Psychiatry*, 27:377–88.

Cooper, D. 1967. *Psychiatry and Anti-Psychiatry*. London: Tavistock Publications.

Coser, R.L. 1963. "Alienation and the Social Structure." In *The Hospital in Modern Society*, edited by E. Freidson. New York: The Free Press.

Cumming, E., I.L.W. Clancy and J. Cumming. 1956. "Improving Patient Care Through Organizational Changes in the Mental Hospital." *Psychiatry*, 19:249–61.

Donati, F. In press. "Madness and Morale: Psycho-Analytic Observations of the Life of a Long-Stay Psychiatric Ward." *British Journal of Psychotherapy.*

Dunham, H.W. and S.K. Weinberg. 1960. *The Culture of the State Mental Hospital.* Detroit: Wayne State University Press.

Erikson, K.T. 1957. "Patient Role and Social Uncertainty: A Dilemma of the Mentally Ill." *Psychiatry,* 20:263–74.

Fontana, A.F., E.B. Klein, E. Lewis and L. Levine. 1968. "Presentation of Self in Mental Illness." *Journal of Consulting and Clinical Psychology,* 32:110–19.

Goffman, E. 1961. *Asylums.* New York: Doubleday.

———. 1969. "The Insanity of Place." *Psychiatry,* 32:357–87.

Griffiths, Sir Roy. 1988. *Community Care: Agenda for Action. A Report to the Secretary of State for Social Services.* London: Her Majesty's Stationery Office.

Hinshelwood, R.D. 1979. "Demoralization and the Hospital Community." *Group Analysis,* 12:84–95.

———. 1986. "The Psychotherapist's Role in a Large Psychiatric Institution." *Psycho-Analytic Psychotherapy,* 2:207–15.

Jaques, E. 1955. "Social Systems as a Defence Against Persecutory and Depressive Anxiety." In *New Directions in Psycho-Analysis,* edited by M. Klein, P. Heimann and R.E. Money-Kyrle. London: Tavistock Publications; New York: Basic Books.

Jones, K. and R. Sidebotham. 1962. *Mental Hospitals at Work.* London: Routledge and Kegan Paul.

Jones, M. 1952. *The Therapeutic Community.* New York: Basic Books.

Laing, R.D. and A. Esterson. 1964. *Sanity, Madness and the Family.* London: Tavistock Publications.

Ludwig, A.M. and F. Farrelly. 1966. "The Code of Chronicity." *Archives of General Psychiatry,* 15:562–68.

Martin, D.V. 1962. *Adventure in Psychiatry.* Oxford: Bruno Cassier.

Menzies, I.E.P. 1960. "A Case-Study in the Functioning of Social Systems as a Defence Against Anxiety: A Report on a Study of the Nursing Service of a General Hospital." *Human Relations,* 13:95–121.

Ministry of Health. 1964. *Improving the Effectiveness of Hospitals for the Mentally Ill.* Ministry of Health Circular, HM(64), 45. London: Her Majesty's Stationery Office.

Moss, M.C. and P. Hunter. 1963. "Community Methods of Treatment." *British Journal of Medical Psychology,* 36:85–91.

Parsons, T. 1951. "Illness and the Role of the Physician: A Sociological Perspective." *American Journal of Orthopsychiatry,* 21:452–60.

Rapoport, R.N. and R. Rapoport. 1957. " 'Democratization' and Authority in a Therapeutic Community." *Behavioral Science,* 2:128–33.

Rapoport, R.N. with R. Rapoport and I. Rosow. 1960. *Community as Doctor.* London: Tavistock Publications.

Salisbury, R.F. 1982. *Structures of Custodial Care.* Berkeley: University of California Press.

Sarbin, T.R. and J.C. Mancuso. 1970. "Failure of a Moral Enterprise: Attitudes of the Public toward Mental Illness." *Journal of Consulting and Clinical Psychology,* 35:159–73.

Scheff, T.J. 1962. "Differential Displacement of Treatment Goals in a Mental Hospital." *Administrative Sciences Quarterly,* 7:208–17.

Scott, R.D. 1973. "The Treatment Barrier." *British Journal of Medical Psychology,* 46:45–67.

———. 1974. "Cultural Frontiers in the Mental Hospital Service." *Schizophrenia*

Bulletin, 10:58–73.

Scott, R.D. and P.L. Ashworth. 1965. "The 'Axis Value' and the Transfer of Psychosis." *British Journal of Medical Psychology,* 38:97–116.

———. 1967. " 'Closure' at the First Schizophrenic Breakdown: A Family Study." *British Journal of Medical Psychology,* 40:109–45.

———. 1969. "The Shadow of the Ancestor: A Historical Factor in the Transmission of Schizophrenia." *British Journal of Medical Psychology,* 42:13–32.

Scott, R.D., P.L. Ashworth and P.D. Casson. 1970. "Violation of Parental Role Structure and Outcome in Schizophrenia." *Social Science and Medicine,* 4:41–64.

Scott, R.D., P.D. Casson and P.L. Ashworth. 1967. "A New Method and Concept for Presenting and Analyzing Hospitalization Data for Psychiatric Admissions." Unpublished paper.

Somner, R. and H. Osmond. 1962. "The Schizophrenic No-Society." *Psychiatry,* 25:244–55.

Stanton, A. and M. Schwartz. 1954. *The Mental Hospital.* New York: Basic Books.

Szasz, T.S. 1961. *The Myth of Mental Illness.* New York: Hoeber.

Tonnesmann, M. 1968. "Consideration of Some of the Problems Met by the Psycho-Analyst in the Medical Officer's Role in a Medical Hospital." Paper to the Section on Application of Psycho-Analysis, British Psycho-Analytical Society, 18 September, 1968.

Towbin, A.P. 1966. "Understanding the Mentally Deranged." *Journal of Existentialism,* 7:63–83.

Tudor Will, G.E. 1952. "A Sociopsychiatric Nursing Approach to Intervention in a Problem of Mutual Withdrawal on a Mental Hospital Ward." *Psychiatry,* 15:193–217.

———. 1957. "Psychiatric Nursing Administration and Its Implications for Patient Care." In *The Patient and the Mental Hospital,* edited by M. Greenblatt, D.J. Levinson and R.H. Williams. Glencoe, Ill.: The Free Press.

Wing, J.K. and R. Furlong. 1986. "A Haven for the Severely Disabled within the Context of a Comprehensive Psychiatric Community Service." *British Journal of Psychiatry,* 149:449–57.

Contributors

Elizabeth Bott Spillius, Ph.D. Fellow, Royal Anthropological Institute; Member, British Psycho-Analytical Society (Training Analyst). Formerly, Research Staff, Tavistock Institute; Lecturer in Anthropology, London School of Economics.

John Bowlby, C.B.E., M.D. (retired). Fellow, Royal Society of Medicine; Fellow, Royal College of Psychiatry; Member, Medical Research Council; Member, British Psycho-Analytic Society. Formerly, Head, Department of Children and Parents, Tavistock Clinic.

Harold Bridger, T.D., B.Sc., President, International Committee on Occupational Mental Health; Bowie Medalist, British Institute of Management; Member, British Psycho-Analytical Society; Head, Career Development and Institutional Change Unit, Tavistock Institute; Founder and Chairman, Institute of Transitional Dynamics, Luzerne.

Adam Curle, D.Phil. (retired). Fellow, Royal Anthropological Institute; Emeritus Professor of Peace Studies, Bradford University. Formerly, Professor of Education, Harvard University; Lecturer in Social Psychology, Oxford; Research Staff, Tavistock Institute.

Henry Dicks, M.D., F.R.C.P. (deceased). Past President and Fellow, Royal College of Psychiatry; Head, Marital Unit, Tavistock Clinic. Formerly, Professor of Psychiatry, Leeds University.

Fred Emery, Ph.D. (retired). Fellow, British Psychological Society; Elton Mayo Award, Australian Psychological Society. Formerly, Senior Fellow, Center for Continuing Education and Research School for the Social Sciences, Australian National University; Chairman, Human Resources Centre, Tavistock Institute; Lecturer in Psychology, Melbourne University.

Merrelyn Emery, Ph.D. Lecturer, Centre for Continuing Education, Australian National University.

Eléanore Herbert, M.A. (deceased). Lecturer in Educational Psychology, Manchester University.

Gurth Higgin, Ph.D. (deceased). Professor Emeritus in Continuing Management Education, University of Loughborough. Formerly Chairman, Human Resources Centre, Tavistock Institute.

John Hill, M.A. Fellow, Royal Statistical Society; Member, British Psycho-Analytical Society. In psychoanalytic consulting practice. Formerly, Research Staff, Tavistock Institute.

Gunnar Hjelholt, Ph.D. Fellow, formerly Secretary-general, European Institute for Trans-National Studies of Group and Organizational Development (EIT). Independent consultant.

Elliott Jaques, M.D., Ph.D. Fellow, International Academy of Management; Emeritus Professor and Chairman, Social Sciences Department, Brunel University; Member, British Psycho-Analytical Society; Fellow, Royal College of Psychiatry. Formerly, Member, Management Committee, Tavistock Institute.

Isabel Menzies Lyth, M.A. Member, British Psycho-Analytical Society (Training Analyst); in psychoanalytic consulting practice. Formerly, Senior Staff, Tavistock Institute; Lecturer in Economics, University of St. Andrews.

Eric J. Miller, Ph.D. Fellow, Royal Anthropological Institute; Director, Group Relations Training Program; Senior Staff, Tavistock Institute.

Hugh Murray, Ph.D. Fellow, British Psychological Society; Senior Staff, Tavistock Institute. Formerly, Clinical Psychologist, Monyhull Hospital.

Alexander Pollock, M.A. Member, British Psycho-Analytical Society; Associate Fellow, British Psychological Society. In psychoanalytic consulting practice. Formerly, Senior Staff, Tavistock Institute.

Rhona Rapoport, Ph.D. Fellow, Royal Anthropological Institute; Member, British Psycho-Analytical Society. Co-founder and Director, Institute of Family and Environmental Research, London, England. Formerly, Research Staff, Tavistock Institute.

Robert N. Rapoport, Ph.D. Fellow, American Anthropological Society. Co-founder and Director, Institute of Family and Environmental Research, London, England. Formerly, Research Staff, Tavistock Institute.

A. K. Rice, Sc.D. (deceased). Chairman, Centre for Applied Social Research, Tavistock Institute. Co-founder A.K. Rice Institute, Washington, D.C. Formerly, Deputy Chairman, Industrial Welfare Society, London.

J. D. Sutherland, C.B.E., Ph.D. (retired). Fellow, Royal College of Physicians (Edinburgh); Fellow, Royal College of Psychiatry; Member, British Psycho-Analytical Society (Training Analyst); Visiting Fellow, Menninger Foundation. Founder, Scottish Institute of Human Relations. Formerly, Director, Tavistock Clinic; Sometime Editor, *International Journal of Psycho-Analysis*.

Eric Trist, O.B.E., Ph.D., LL.D. (Hon.) (retired). Fellow, International Academy of Management. Formerly, Member, Psychological Committee, British Social Science Research Council; Professor Emeritus of Organizational Behavior and Social Ecology, Wharton School, University of Pennsylvania; Professor under the same title at York University, Toronto, and UCLA; Founder Member and Chairman (1958–1962), Tavistock Institute.

A.T.M. Wilson, M.D. (deceased). Fellow, Royal College of Psychiatry; Member, British Psycho-Analytical Society; Secretary, Royal Society of Medicine; Professor of Management, London Graduate School of Business Studies; Adviser in the Social Sciences, Unilever Ltd.; Founder Member and Chairman (1948–1958), Tavistock Institute.

D. W. Winnicott, M.D., F.R.C.P. (deceased). Fellow, Royal College of Psychiatry; Fellow, Royal College of Pediatrics; Member, British Psycho-Analytical Society (Training Analyst); Member, Tavistock Association.

Douglas Woodhouse A.A.P.S.W. (retired). Formerly, Chairman, Institute of Marital Studies, Tavistock Institute.

Subject Index

Name Index